CITY OF FLIGHT

CITY OF FLIGHT

The History of Aviation
in St. Louis

James J. Horgan

The Patrice Press
St. Louis, Missouri

**Library of Congress
Cataloging In Publication Data**

Horgan, James J., 1940-
    City of Flight.

    Bibliography: p.
    Includes index.
    1. Aeronautics—Missouri—Saint Louis—
        History.
I. Title.
TL522.M8H67   1984   629.13′009778   84-25449
ISBN: 0-935284-79-6

Printed in the United States of America

Published by
The Patrice Press
1701 S. Eighth Street
St. Louis MO 63104

For my father,
William S. Horgan,
who gave me
the interest in aviation.

Contents

Part III. Air Industries

Acknowledgments

THIS BOOK was my doctoral dissertation at Saint Louis University, where I received a Ph.D. in history in 1965. The department stored a copy in its archives and sent another on to the university library, where it sat like so many others and (one hopes) was examined from time to time.

But Gregory M. Franzwa came upon it some years ago and determined to make it available to the general public. He is a historian of the West himself and — what is of more immediate enhancement to historians like me — the owner/publisher of The Patrice Press and a believer in the value of local history. For his support of the profession, and for his confidence in this volume, I am grateful. And I am pleased that his friend John T. Tucker has provided generous financial support for the undertaking.

In the course of my research, I had help from a great many people. I want to thank Dr. Jasper Cross, my dissertation adviser, as well as the other members of my committee: Rev. John Francis Bannon, S.J., Dr. Thomas P. Neill, Dr. Paul G. Steinbicker, and Rev. Edward R. Vollmar, S.J. Mrs. Fred C. Harrington, Mrs. Arthur W. Felt, Mrs. Ernst A. Stadler, and Mrs. John C. Dotzman of the Missouri Historical Society uncovered invaluable source material from their files for me. Lloyd F. Engelhardt of St. Louis opened his vast store of aeronautical periodicals collected over the years. George A. Page Jr. of Reynoldsburg, Ohio, formerly chief design engineer at Curtiss-Wright, aided my research on that company and led me to Mr. Engelhardt's basement bonanza. Pearl I. Young of Lancaster, Pennsylvania, generously provided me with information on the activities of John Wise, as well as the aerial occurrences at the Louisiana Purchase Exposition. Dr. Russell Parkinson unselfishly drove one hundred miles from Columbia, Missouri, to deliver Miss Young's documents to me. Roland C. Marquart, transportation commissioner of the St. Louis Chamber of

Commerce, gave me valuable advice on the investigation of this topic. William T. Larkins, vice president of the American Aviation Historical Society, and AAHS members Arnold Swanberg of Great Falls, Montana, E.T. Smallwood of Oakland, California, and R.D. Woodcock of Haverford, Pennsylvania, provided me with significant information. L.J. Sutorius of St. Louis allowed me to use his aviation scrapbook. Charles Zoller, librarian of McDonnell Aircraft, rendered many services to me as I gathered details on that company. My father, William S. Horgan, supplied me with helpful information on McDonnell, where he was an aeronautical engineer until his retirement. Mitchell E. Giblo, executive director of the National Aeronautic Association, answered my many questions on aviation records. David E. Leigh, manager of Lambert-St. Louis Municipal Airport, gave me detailed information on the operations of that airfield. Wanda D. Odom of the NAA provided information on more recent records, as did Debra Spaeth, operations chairman of the Balloon Federation of America, who also led me to Nikki Caplan, St. Louis' foremost balloonist today. Ms. Caplan was very helpful on current developments in the field. William Gellhausen of St. Louis took the time to draw an excellent map of the air facilities in the St. Louis area, the basis for the map on page 4 of this book. The generous assistance of all these people has made my task much easier.

James J. Horgan
San Antonio, Florida
June 1984

Portions of this dissertation have appeared in such scholarly periodicals as the *Bulletin of the Missouri Historical Society; The Bulletin of The Wingfoot Lighter-Than-Air Society;* and the *Journal of the American Aviation Historical Society.*

Introduction

ST. LOUIS HAS LONG BEEN a significant center of aviation. From balloon exhibitions in the 1830s to space explorations in the 1960s, the city has participated in all phases of aeronautics. It is the purpose of this study to narrate the story of this facet of the city's image.

There are three principal factors responsible for the extraordinary aeronautic distinction of St. Louis. The first is its central geographic location, which was undoubtedly the primary reason for its success in ballooning. Long flights could be made in any direction with little hindrance from mountains or water. This, in turn, also contributed to the establishment of large aviation industries in the city, since the area offered ease of access from any part of the nation, water and rail market transportation, and a degree of military safety. The second major factor was the energetic leadership of its aeronautic enthusiasts (particularly Albert Bond Lambert), who devoted themselves to making St. Louis the leading center of aviation in the country. Finally, the honor is due to the spirit of its citizens in support of aeronautics. This is shown by such actions as the 300,000-strong crowd which witnessed Glenn Curtiss in 1909 and the five-to-one majorities which voted extra taxes upon themselves in 1928 and 1942 for the development of a fine municipal airport. These reasons, at least in part, explain the city's rise to prominence in aeronautics.

In order to provide a logical understanding of the scope of the subject, the topic is organized in three parts: Air Facilities, Air Activities, and Air Industries. Each in itself is a separate story. St. Louis became an outstanding air center primarily because it was the scene of numerous air spectacles, balloon races, and air meets. It could not, however, have entertained such events unless its leaders and citizens had provided the city with suitable facilities, nor could its aeronautic reputation have endured unless the city had played a significant role in commercial aviation and air industry. Because St. Louis excelled in each area, it earned the title, "City of Flight."

While complete material is available for the sundry air activities which St. Louis witnessed, for they were compact units and are relatively easy to detail, only a comparatively minute amount of sources is readily accessible for the air facilities and air industries, since they functioned over a period of years and are more difficult to document. The treatment of these latter aspects, therefore, must of necessity be somewhat cursory. Because a comprehensive history such as that of aviation in St. Louis can never completely cover all aspects of the subject, this study will confine itself to the more important events and more significant occurrences. No attempt will be made to treat in depth such topics as Scott Field or Parks Air College in nearby Illinois, such eminent St. Louisans as James Doolittle or Edward O'Hare, or such minor events as the 1947 Air Fair or the 1963 Air Show. Each was a part of the general picture of the air history of St. Louis, but will not be treated with detailed coverage here.

This study sweeps through a century and a half, but there is a special feeling in the period from the 1904 World's Fair to the spectacular flight of Charles A. Lindbergh in 1927. What a wide-eyed age it was! Hundreds of thousands came out to gawk at the latest aeronautical technology, to marvel at attempts to harness the air, and to take inspiration from the heroic achievements of the aeronautical pioneers. That was Saint Louis at its most engaging. This book is a celebration of that spirit.

CITY OF FLIGHT

Part One:
Air Facilities

I
Airports, Airfields, &
Ascension Grounds

ONE OF THE PRIMARY FACTORS which contributed to St.
Louis' success as a leading air center has been the superior
caliber of its aeronautic facilities. Public parks grew into well
equipped ascension grounds; open farmland developed into well
furnished airfields and airports. As the city's aeronautic activities
increased, its citizens kept pace by providing the necessary facilities.

During the nineteenth century, pioneer balloonists found few adequate furnishings in any section of the country. They made their
ascensions from whatever square, park, or field was available.
These aeronauts generally erected a high fence around the site and
charged a nominal admission fee to defray the cost of the gas used
for inflation. Most spectators, however, preferred to view the action from outside the enclosure and thus watch the ascension for
free, although they were unable to witness the details preliminary
to the flight.

St. Louis and its residents were no different from the rest of the
nation. Richard Clayton used an empty lot at Fourth and Market
streets to make one of the earliest recorded balloon ascensions in
the city on May 17, 1836. He, too, had difficulty in persuading the
crowd to cooperate financially.[1] Another field near the center of
the city was utilized in 1841, when a Mr. S. Hobart made two

ascensions, using gas he had manufactured himself with vitriol and a number of other chemicals.[2] Washington Square at Clark Avenue and Twelfth Street was the scene of the start of John Wise's record-breaking flight of July 1-2, 1859.[3] Unlike Hobart's vehicle, however, his balloon was inflated with hydrogen provided by the St. Louis Gaslight Company.[4] Lindell Park was also used for ballooning during the century,[5] as was Van Der Ahe baseball stadium.[6] When ballooning and other aeronautic endeavors in the city began to increase in the early 1900s, however, more suitable facilities were provided.

For the aerial tournament of 1907, an ascension site and race course were laid out at the eastern end of Forest Park, the location of the headquarters of the newly-formed Aero Club of St. Louis. Grandstands were erected to accommodate 13,000 spectators,[7] and Laclede Gas Light Company, which had been formed in 1889 by the merger of four small corporations within the city,[8] supplied an extremely light coal gas for the balloons and dirigibles from its huge 4,000,000-cubic-foot gasometer.[9] The superior quality of the Laclede gas and the efficiency of its operation had been one of the primary reasons for the Aero Club of America's selection of St. Louis as the site for the tournament,[10] and that company would be in part responsible for making St. Louis the foremost national center of free balloon racing.

In later years, the Laclede plant at Second and Rutger streets was a frequent starting point for balloon ascensions, for the convenient location had all the necessary equipment on hand for the balloonists. Among the more notable flights begun from that factory were Captain Charles Chandler's successful Lahm Cup attempt in the *United States No. 10* in 1907,[11] Albert Bond Lambert's 450-mile trip to Tiger, Georgia, in the *Yankee* in 1908,[12] and A. Holland Forbes' record-breaking Lahm Cup trial in the *New York* in 1909.[3] No formal races were conducted at that site, however, for the area was limited in size and was unable to accommodate more than one or two balloons at a single time.

For the balloon contests during Centennial Week in 1909, the Aero Club of St. Louis utilized its newly-developed ascension grounds at Chouteau and Newstead avenues. Laclede again provided for the simultaneous inflation of all the bags with hydrogen from its huge gas retort at the field.[14] These grounds were also the starting point of the International Balloon Race in the following year. The site was doubled in size when the Aero Club leased additional adjacent property and erected 2,000 seats for the spectators.[15] Laclede manufactured the lightest coal gas ever developed

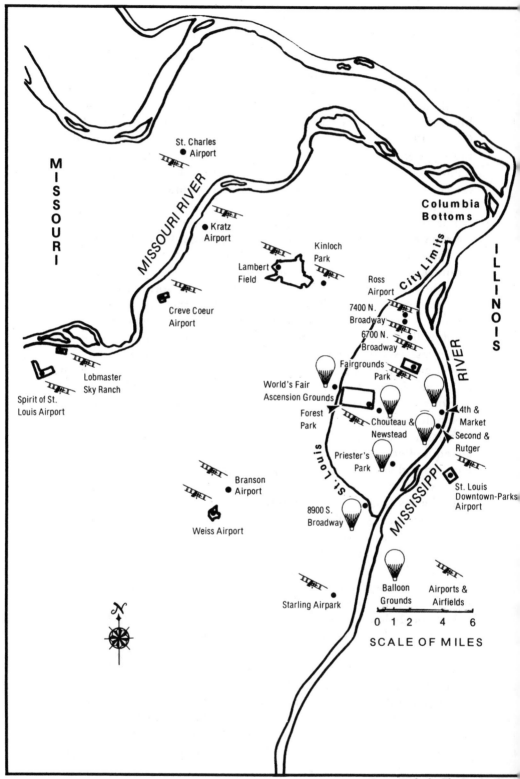

MISSOURI

MISSOURI RIVER

St. Charles
Airport

Columbia
Bottoms

City Limits

ILLINOIS

Kratz
Airport

Kinloch
Park

Lambert
Field

Ross
Airport

RIVER

Creve Coeur
Airport

7400 N.
Broadway

6700 N.
Broadway

Lobmaster
Sky Ranch

Fairgrounds
Park

Spirit of St.
Louis Airport

World's Fair
Ascension Grounds

4th &
Market

Forest
Park

Chouteau &
Newstead

Second &
Rutger

Priester's
Park

St. Louis

Branson
Airport

St. Louis
Downtown-Parks
Airport

Weiss Airport

8900 S.
Broadway

MISSISSIPPI

Starling Airpark

Balloon
Grounds

Airports &
Airfields

0 1 2   4   6

SCALE OF MILES

Cartography by The Patrice Press

for ballooning and piped it to the field from its Rutger Street plant.[16]

In 1914, St. Louis was host to its first National Balloon Race. By that time, the Aero Club was making use of the facilities at Priester's Park at Grand Avenue and Meramec Street. There an 8,000-seat amphitheater had been erected, and underneath the circular ascension site, 420 feet in diameter, a network of gas mains had been laid,[17] connecting the balloons to a Laclede gasometer which pumped at the rate of 160,000 cubic feet per hour.[18] This same location, then known as Meramec Park, saw service during 1917 as a training ground for balloon pilots. Lieutenant Albert Bond Lambert conducted the school under the auspices of the Missouri Aeronautical Society and qualified hundreds of officers for wartime service.[19] The society used its facilities at the park for two contests in 1919, the Army-Navy[20] and National Balloon Races,[21] with Laclede again supplying the gas.

A decade later, a field at 8900 South Broadway was utilized for the International Balloon Race, for it was sufficiently spacious and was in close proximity to Laclede Gas Light's main plant at 523 Catalan Street, from which the gas was pumped.[22] This was the city's last major balloon race. From Fourth and Market to Chouteau and Newstead to Priester's Park — the facilities St. Louis prepared for lighter-than-air craft, coupled with its unique geographical position and the driving spirit of its aeronautic leaders, earned for the city an international reputation in the realm of ballooning. This aspect of flight placed St. Louis on the world's air map, but the city was not lax in its preparations for the advent of machines of the heavier-than-air variety.

Residents of St. Louis witnessed their first sustained airplane flights during Centennial Week in 1909. A course had been laid out near Art Hill in Forest Park, but the abundance of trees in the heavily-wooded area proved exceedingly hazardous and greatly cramped the flying operations. Because of their need for a suitable field, the officials of the Aero Club of St. Louis immediately appropriated $20,000 to develop such a site and visited several possible locations on October 10, 1909.[23] Their choice was Kinloch Park. While not strictly an airport, this was the city's first permanent airfield.

Situated twelve miles from downtown St. Louis, this former racetrack was rolled smooth in August 1910 and hangars and grandstands were erected in preparation for one of the Aero Club's greatest undertakings, the International Aeronautic Tournament of that year.[24] Kinloch Park, known for a time as Lambert Field, in honor of the man who had been so influential in its development,[25] was the center of widespread activity for the following three years. The increasingly energetic Aero Club maintained its headquarters at the field; it was the scene of two major air meets (1910 and 1911) and numerous minor ones; and Tom Benoist, the city's earliest great aviation industrialist, conducted a flying school and testing ground there.[26] Despite the excellence of its equipment, Kinloch Park, which measured approximately 3,000 feet in both length and width,[27] was abandoned in 1913 when the Aero Club's lease expired and activity shifted to a somewhat larger airfield at 7400 North Broadway, a tract of land within the confines of the city itself.[28]

Tom Benoist operated from this location during that year, and the hangars on the field housed the vehicles of a number of resident airmen.[29] A nearby airfield at 6700 North Broadway, adjacent to Bellefontaine Cemetery, was also in extensive use during the pre-war years.[30] Developed in 1910, this tract of land, 3,500 feet long and 500 feet wide, was the scene of Captain Thomas Scott Baldwin's celebrated river flight and impromptu air show in his *Red Devil* that year.[31] In 1911, an air meet was conducted at Fairgrounds Park, a 128-acre former racetrack,[32] but unlike at Kinloch and the Broadway airfields, no further flying activity took place at that location.

Although these early sites were the scene of extensive aerial operations, St. Louis' first "airport" in the commercial sense of the term did not come into active existence until 1920. In March of 1918, the city's postmaster, Colin M. Selph, who was eager to obtain airmail service between St. Louis and Chicago, consulted departmental officials in Washington to urge them to establish such a route.[33] During his visit, Congress passed a bill appropriating $850,000 for airmail service throughout the United States. The cities of St. Louis and Chicago were specifically included in the act.[34]

Upon his return to the city, Postmaster Selph consulted with Mayor Henry W. Kiel, Major Albert Bond Lambert and James W. Bemis of the Missouri Aeronautical Society, John Ring of the Advertising Club, Park Commissioner Nelson Cunliff, and Thomas H. Lovelace and W.B. Weisenburger of the Chamber of Commerce.[35] With the cooperation of these civic leaders, a 100-acre airmail field was established in the southeast section of Forest Park.[36] In April 1919, an Army hangar 200 feet long and 66 feet wide was shipped from Middletown, Pennsylvania, and erected on the field.[37] The St. Louis Board of Aldermen and the Chamber of Commerce each appropriated $12,500 to cover the cost of the steel hangar and the preparation of the airfield. Major Lambert, in the name of the Missouri Aeronautical Society, agreed to furnish $3,000 for further expenses.[38]

Negotiations between St. Louis leaders and Washington officials continued for more than a year until, with the help of Congressman L.C. Dyer, a contract was signed on July 7, 1920,

> by and between the City of St. Louis and the United States of America, for the use of Forest Park as a landing place for aeroplanes of the United States Aerial Mail Service and for hangar uses.[39]

After formal ceremonies of inauguration, the first plane, a Curtiss JN-4H "Jenny" piloted by E. Hamilton Lee, left for Chicago via Chanute Field, Rantoul, Illinois, at 9:11 a.m. August 16, 1920, with 150 pounds of mail in six pouches. A southbound plane had departed from Maywood Field, Chicago, at 8:35 a.m. and arrived at Forest Park at 12:25 p.m., thirty-five minutes ahead of schedule, with 230 pounds of mail. While the fastest railroad time between the two cities was 7 hours and 40 minutes, the average flying time for the mail planes cut three hours from that pace.[40]

At an initial rate of 2¢ per ounce, the mail service offered one round-trip flight each day, except Sundays and holidays. The schedule called for the St. Louis plane to depart at 9:00 a.m., arriving at 1:30 p.m., while the Chicago plane would leave at 8:30 a.m., arriving at 1:00 p.m.[41] During the first month of operation, a total of 10,690 pounds of mail was carried between the two cities, and the four-man crew — Earl Bashley and Russell Jones from St. Louis and H.C. Brown and Ralph A. Reed from Chicago — earned an efficiency rating of Class C, the highest award on the government scale. Computed on the basis of trips made without damage to mail or plane, speed, and punctuality, the efficiency rating was categorized in three classes: "C" for 90 percent, "B" for 85 percent, and "A" for all lower scores. The St. Louis-Chicago pilots earned a rating of 94 percent, thereby gaining an automatic 10 percent bonus in pay for their outstanding performance.[42]

The route continued in operation until June 30, 1921, when it was canceled in the economy drive of the new Harding Congress, both as a reaction to the wartime spending spree and because this and other short runs were of little timesaving value.[43] The Forest Park airfield, which had hosted private local fliers as well as government mail pilots,[44] soon passed into disuse. Even before it had come into formal existence, however, another less ephemeral airfield had been

E. Hamilton Lee made the first Chicago-to-St. Louis airmail flight on August 16, 1920. Lee and his Curtiss "Jenny" are shown in Forest Park shortly after his arrival.

established.

On June 18, 1920, the Missouri Aeronautical Society, represented by Major Albert Bond Lambert, William and Frank Robertson (two pioneers in the rising aviation industry), and Randall Foster, presi-

George J. Herwig Collection

The first hangar at "St. Louis Flying Field" was built on the west edge of the present Lambert Field, about 1920.

George J. Herwig Collection

The 1920 hangar faced east and stood about where the 1933 terminal building was built. The line of cars in the distance is parked along Long Road. Denny Road (later Lindbergh Boulevard) parallels Long still further to the west.

dent of the Flying Club of St. Louis, took control of a 160-acre [45] cornfield on Natural Bridge Road in Bridgeton, six miles west of the city limits and eleven miles northwest of downtown St. Louis. The selection was made with a view to passenger service between St. Louis and other cities, inasmuch as the Forest Park mail field was "too small and too closely hemmed in by buildings and wires . . . to be a desirable place for landing with a large plane."[46] Major Lambert assumed a five-year lease on the tract from its owner, Mrs. Mary Jane Weldon, for $2,000 per year, with an option to purchase the land for $400 per acre. At his own expense, he proceeded to develop the field by clearing, grading, and draining the land, improving the adjacent roads, and erecting hangars. After suitable facilities had been installed, Lambert offered free use of the St. Louis Flying Field, as it was then termed, to anyone desiring to engage in aerial activity of any kind. [47]

Wholesale improvements on the airfield were completed in 1923 in preparation for the epic International Air Races of that year.[48] Major Lambert placed the Flying Field at the disposal of the St. Louis Aeronautic Corporation, the unit organized to conduct the tournament. The corporation took control of the Bridgeton field, which then consisted of 183 acres, and then leased additional tracts of 316 acres to provide the space necessary for the meet.[49] A total of $172,756.29 was spent in bringing the airfield into unequaled excellence,[50] and on October 4, 1923, the tract of polished earth was dedicated the "Lambert-St. Louis Flying Field" in honor of the man who had so unselfishly devoted himself to its development.[51] The airfield, soon to become the city's municipal airport, would never lose that identification.

At the close of the meet, the field was reduced to its original size of approximately 170 acres, and in February 1925, upon the expiration of his lease, Albert Bond Lambert purchased the airfield under the 1920 option price of $400 per acre. He paid Mrs. Weldon $68,352 for her property.[52] The sole proprietor of his own airfield, the St. Louis "dean of aviation"[53] encouraged and welcomed the use of the Flying Field by aviators of every kind.

On June 23, 1923, the 35th Division, Aviation Section, Missouri National Guard, was formally organized under Major William B. Robertson and thereafter trained at the airfield in Curtiss "Jennies."[54] The commanding officer himself was already making use of Lambert Field as a base for his passenger and freight service through the facilities of the Robertson Aircraft Corporation, which he operated with his brother Frank.[55] By July 1928, the bustling air center had been dubbed "the new Union Station of St. Louis." McIntyre Air Lines was then offering semi-regular service to Tulsa by trimotor several times per week; Robertson Aircraft Corporation operated a regular run for mail and passengers (for $30 one way and $50 round trip) to Chicago; the Von Hoffmann Aircraft Company, Bridgeton Aircraft Corporation, and Parks Air Lines each maintained a flying school and charter service at the field; and several airlines and industries were making plans to establish headquarters there.[56] The *St. Louis Globe-Democrat* commented:

> . . . this airport has become more than a place where men and women of daring might go for brief, sight-seeing excursions into the ether. It has outgrown being just a location for some hangars convenient to house a few privately-owned ships. From having been a plaything for a few wealthy and a few other daring men several years ago, it has grown into a business enterprise necessary for the accommodation of the city's business travel . . .[57]

Major Lambert's greatest desire, however, had yet to be realized. He wanted the City of St. Louis to take possession of his Flying Field as a municipal airport. Mayor Victor Miller and the city administration agreed to his proposal in November 1927, whereupon the pharmaceutical philanthropist offered the airfield to the officials for $68,352, the price he had paid for the tract alone in 1925, despite the fact that the land and its improvements had a current market value of $250,000. The city accepted the generous offer contingent upon the passage of an airport bond issue in 1928, but without any obligation on its part whether the referendum were passed or not. Lambert agreed to the conditions and on February 7, 1928, he leased the 170-acre tract to the city for a period of fifteen months for the sum of $1.00.[58]

Based on a survey conducted by the engineering firm of B. Russell Shaw and Company in the autumn of 1927, civic officials recommended that a total of 608 acres be acquired for the airport.[59] In January 1928, the Board of Aldermen passed a measure appropriating $50,000 for the development of the field.[60] While $40,000 of the sum was to be used for grading the land and erecting the necessary buildings and facilities,[61] the remaining $10,000 was put to immediate use in partial payment for 76 acres of land known as the Harrington Tract, adjacent to the main airfield. Lambert himself paid the remaining $66,000 for the land, as well as an additional $108,075 for further tracts. His action was necessary because the Bridgeton and Anglum landowners refused to extend options to the city based on the contingency of the bond issue passage. On his own volition, therefore, Major Lambert acquired as much land as possible on a cash basis, holding it for the city at cost, but again with no obligation on the latter's part to buy it from him in any event.[62]

The Lambert Field control tower, weather bureau, and airport offices were housed in this building in 1929.

Such magnanimity was unprecedented.

His faith, however, was well rewarded. Under the chairmanship of Edwin B. Meissner, the Municipal Airport Bond Issue Committee conducted a spirited campaign on behalf of the $2,000,000 proposal. Virtually every civic leader, organization, and newspaper in the city stood firmly behind the measure. As a reminder for the voters as they went to the polls in the primary election on August 7, 1928, three dirigibles from Scott Field, Belleville, Illinois, circled overhead, accompanied by a massive Ford trimotor from the Robertson Aircraft Corporation, as well as a glimmering Curtiss "Robin," the first one produced at the growing Curtiss-Robertson Airplane Manufacturing Company at Lambert Field.[63] St. Louisans that day exhibited the spirit which had traditionally characterized them as among the most air-minded in the nation. By a thundering margin of five to one, the $2,000,000 bond issue was approved. The actual vote was 116,135 to 20,656.[64]

With the help of Major Lambert, Director of Public Welfare Harry

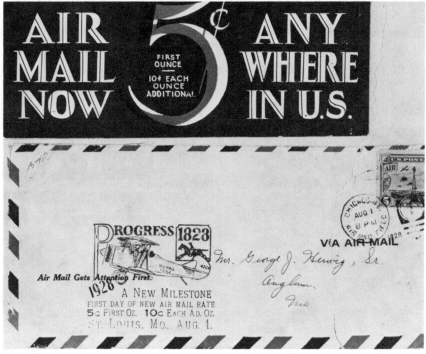

AIR MAIL NOW 5¢ ANY WHERE IN U.S.
FIRST OUNCE
10¢ EACH OUNCE ADDITIONAL

PROGRESS 1823
Air Mail Gets Attention First
1928 A NEW MILESTONE
FIRST DAY OF NEW AIR MAIL RATE
5¢ FIRST OZ. 10¢ EACH AD. OZ.
ST. LOUIS, MO., AUG. 1.

VIA AIR MAIL

Mr. George J. Herwig, Sr.
Anglum.
Mo.

George J. Herwig Collection

A "First Day" cover for the new 5¢ airmail, addressed to George J. Herwig Sr. at Anglum, Missouri, on August 1, 1928.

L. Salisbury, who had general charge of the project, outlined a tentative budget for the bond issue funds. In all, 693 acres of land would be acquired (Lambert's 246, plus additional tracts of 162, 85, and 200 acres) for $485,000. The city planned to spend $438,000 on the necessary buildings, $20,000 for rolling stock, including automobiles, field cars, and tractors, $90,000 for the improvement of adjoining roads, $15,000 for water facilities, $10,000 for the lighting system, $3,000 for surveying, and $835,000 for drainage and grading of the field and the construction of proper runways. With a planned outlay of $1,896,000 budgeted, officials held the remaining $104,000 in reserve for emergency expenses.[65]

Lambert himself turned everything over to the city at cost. Because of his foresight and generosity in securing the necessary options on the required tracts, St. Louis would pay a mere $650 per acre for the land, while San Diego, for instance, had to expend $6,000 and Chicago $12,000 per acre for their municipal airports.[66] The superb magnanimity of the man who had maintained the airfield for eight years at his own expense, except for the improve-

Dedication ceremonies for Lambert Field took place on July 12, 1930. The address was delivered by Rear Admiral Richard E. Byrd, who had flown over the North Pole in 1926 and the South Pole in 1929.

ments added by the St. Louis Aeronautic Corporation in 1923, resulted in the city's first true airport, and one of which its citizens could be justifiably proud.

Despite the fact that money, men, and material stood ready for the full development of the site, there were some of the opinion that an unwarranted lethargy was clogging the wheels of progress. On January 28, 1929, in a somewhat surprising action, Major Lambert resigned from the Airport Technical Committee because he felt that Welfare Director Salisbury was moving too slowly and was unjustified in his refusal to engage an airport engineer to supervise comprehensive budget plans. From that date, Lambert served only as an unofficial adviser to the project. [67]

Development continued, however, and on July 12, 1930, the field was officially dedicated the "Lambert-St. Louis Municipal Airport" by Rear Admiral Richard E. Byrd. [68] No title more fitting could have been chosen. By that date, the airport comprised 546 acres with

Photo by Gregory M. Franzwa

The present Mounted Police Station is a relic from the days when Forest Park was the principal St. Louis airport. The Planetarium is in the background. The foreground is "Aviation Field," still called that by the athletic teams that play there.

numerous hangars and six runways, the longest of which was a concrete strip 3,000 feet long.[69] Prospects were bright for the airport's continued growth and prosperity.

With the rapid expansion of the aviation industry and air travel in the late 1920s and early 1930s, Lambert Field came to be a significant center of air activity of every description. Transcontinental Air Transport ("The Lindbergh Line") set up its national headquarters in St. Louis in 1928[70] and inaugurated coast-to-coast air-rail service through St. Louis in cooperation with the Pennsylvania and Santa Fe Railroads in June 1929.[71] By 1930, several other airlines had included St. Louis in their routes: Universal Division of American Airways, Interstate Division of American Airways, Transcontinental and Western Air (formed by the merger of TAT with Western Air Express in 1930),[72] Robertson Air Lines, and Rapid Air

George J. Herwig Collection

The small brick building sandwiched between two hangars was the passenger terminal for Universal Air Lines. This photo was made in 1929. A Fokker mail plane is in the foreground.

Transit. At that time, five service companies were in operation at the field: Von Hoffman Aircraft Company, Detroit Aircraft Company, Robertson Airplane Service Company, Ryan Service Station, and Universal Aviation Company. Von Hoffmann and Universal also operated major flying schools, and Curtiss-Wright Airplane Manufacturing Company was producing a wide line of private aircraft. The National Guard and Naval Reserve continued to maintain bases at the field, and the Lambert Flying Club, Pelican Club, and Fresh Air Airplane Company were among the independent flying organizations using the facilities at the airport.[73] After a decade of existence and only two years of intensive development, Lambert Field was one of the busiest municipal airports in the nation.

The last of the $2,000,000 bond issue appropriation dissipated on July 13, 1932, when the cornerstone of the $150,000 terminal building was dedicated in formal ceremonies by Myrtle Lambert, the daughter of St. Louis' celebrated aviation enthusiast.[74] During the fiscal year 1932, 322,265 pounds of mail was handed at the airport, an increase of 495 percent over the 1927 amount. In that same year, 24,113 people arrived or departed by the airlines, which made 37 daily landings and takeoffs from the field. A total of 82 planes and 175 pilots made the airport their headquarters, and some 750,000 people visited it during the year.[75]

By 1938, activity at the field had increased considerably. Approxi-

George J. Herwig Collection

This crowd has gathered in front of the terminal building for a 1932 function. The field light is at left.

mately 40,000 passengers arrived or departed during the year, more than 170,000 landings and takeoffs of all types of aircraft were made, and the post office branch at the field handled 528,112 pounds of mail (258,374 received and 269,738 dispatched).[76] By the following year, there were established at the airport: three major airlines (American, Chicago and Southern, and Transcontinental and Western), three flying schools (led by Robertson Aviation School), three aviation service companies (St. Louis, Brayton, and Robertson), three aircraft manufacturers (Monocoupe, McDonnell, and Curtiss-Wright), two military flying units (the Missouri National Guard and the Naval Reserve), and numerous minor groups and individual plane owners.

Located in the administration building were offices of the Civil Aeronautics Authority Communications System and a branch of the United States Weather Bureau, as well as a unit of the Department of Agriculture. An extensive lighting system blanketed the airfield, together with a network of radio beams, for night flying. Lambert Field then consisted of six runways, the longest of which ran 5,500 feet. In spite of the high cost of maintaining the municipal airfield, Airport Manager Ralph Page reported that income in 1939

Construction on a new terminal building for Lambert Field was begun in 1932.

The new terminal had just opened when this 1933 photo was taken.

This is a mid-1950s view of the hangars on the west edge of Lambert Field. The old terminal building is out of the picture at right.

Lambert Field looked like this in April 1937. The vertical road coming in from the top is Lindbergh Boulevard. The road across the bottom is Natural Bridge; to the right is Brown Road.

from office, restaurant, and concession rentals, together with landing fees, approximated operating expenses. Public interest in airports, airplanes, and aviation was so keen during that period that a

George J. Herwig Collection

These are pilots, students and mechanics of Robertson Aircraft Corp. in 1926 (above) and 1927 (below).

George J. Herwig Collection

pleasant Sunday afternoon would bring 10,000 visitors to the field.[77]

In order that St. Louis might keep pace with the necessary facilities in the rapidly maturing air age, a number of surveys were conducted to determine the city's specific air needs. In 1939, George M. Parker of the Air Board of the Chamber of Commerce appointed

George J. Herwig Collection

Aircraft, including a new Ryan "Brougham" similar to Lindbergh's Spirit of St. Louis, *at Lambert Field in 1927.*

a special committee under St. Louis celebrated son, Colonel (later General) James H. Doolittle, along with Colonel Philip R. Love and George B. Logan, to investigate the status of the local air facilities. The Doolittle Committee reported:

> Full advantage of Lambert-St. Louis Airport should be taken before any new airport is undertaken in view of the investment which the city has already made at that field, and which would obviously be affected by any new airport.[78]

Impressed with the need for further airport expansion, Mayor Bernard F. Dickmann set up in April 1940 another committee, again headed by Jimmy Doolittle, together with G.J. Brandewiede, George B. Logan, and Albert Bond Lambert, to study the improvements required at Lambert Field and to ascertain the most suitable site for a secondary airport, if one were deemed necessary. While it was unable to settle on a favorable location for another airfield, the committee recommended that full use be made of Lambert Field, and that if the time came when the development of a second site were necessary, air transport should remain at the municipal airport, with all other traffic being handled at the secondary field.[79]

A third study was undertaken in May 1941 by J. Gates Williams to survey all possible sites for a secondary airport in the greater St. Louis area. His committee made four recommendations to the Air

Board of the Chamber of Commerce: 1) the immediate adoption of a long range airport program for the St. Louis area; 2) the bringing to fruition of a number of detailed specifics for the further development of Lambert Field; 3) the scheduling of a bond issue for the funds necessary for airport expansion; and 4) the acquisition of Columbia Bottoms as a secondary airport, and if possible, a third site elsewhere.[80] The estimated cost of the projects was: $500,000 for the purchase of additional land adjacent to Lambert Field; $1,500,000 for new runways and added improvements at the municipal airport; and $2,500,000 for the development of one or two secondary airfields.[81]

In August of 1941, still another investigation of secondary airport sites, prompted by Mayor William Dee Becker, was conducted by Charles B. Donaldson and T.E. Flaherty of the Civil Aeronautics Authority, along with Charles H. Ellaby and Max Doyne of the St. Louis Airport Commission.[82] Their report, aired before the full commission on September 4, 1941,[83] covered twenty-two possible secondary sites in the St. Louis area on the Missouri side of the Mississippi River. The CAA excluded all twenty-two from consideration, even the two most favored locations: Gravois Creek was deemed unsuitable because of irregular terrain, and Columbia Bottoms, fronting on both the Mississippi and Missouri Rivers, because of its distance from the city and the high cost of the necessary flood protection.[84]

The St. Louis Airport Commission then engaged, for a fee of $4,500, the consulting engineering firm of Horner and Shifrin to make specific recommendations for the improvement of Lambert Field. Submitted in February 1942, their report, containing five or six designs for possible development, was so well received that the Airport Commission hired the team to undertake a further study of secondary airport sites. In August 1942, Horner and Shifrin recommended Columbia Bottoms, whereupon both St. Louis and St. Louis County settled on it as the only feasible location for a second major airport on the Missouri side of the river.[85]

With a reasonably definite program in mind, the civic leaders, as in 1928, took the issue to the voters. The Citizens' Airport Bond Issue Committee, chaired by the aging but active Albert Bond Lambert, along with Mayor William Dee Becker, J. Gates Williams, and Charles M. Polk, put forth a vigorous campaign in support of the measure:

> The purpose of the proposed bond issue amounting to $4,500,000
> is to provide funds which, with financial assistance from the Fed-

eral Government, will permit the expansion and development of the Lambert St. Louis Municipal Airport, the acquisition of a second airport and the setting up of a long-range program for additional airport developments. . . . The airport bond issue of 1928 won by a ratio of five to one. Where would St. Louis be today, had the results been the other way?[86]

The voters expressed their will on August 4, 1942, with a ratio identical to that of 1928. They passed the bond issue by a vote of 80,064 to 16,693.[87] Again, the spirit of its citizens made possible St. Louis' aeronautic progress.

While work proceeded on the expansion of Lambert Field, which then consisted of 536 acres,[88] a storm of controversy arose over the development of Columbia Bottoms as a secondary airport. On July 14, 1943, the five airlines serving St. Louis (American, Eastern, Transcontinental and Western, Mid-Continent, and Chicago and Southern)[89] submitted a report at a joint meeting of the City Airport Commission, the County Planning Commission, and the Air Board of the Chamber of Commerce. The airline officials recommended the Gravois Creek or Tesson Ferry locations to the exclusion of all twenty previously-discussed other possibilities, and they were particularly adamant in their objections to the Columbia Bottoms tract, condemning it for its flood danger and its distance from the center of the city.[90]

As a quasi-solution to the problem, Mayor Aloys P. Kaufmann announced on October 3, 1943, that the city would abandon its plans for an additional airport for the duration of the war and would concentrate on the development of Lambert Field. In spite of heavy criticism from J. Gates Williams of the Air Board of the Chamber of Commerce,[91] the proposal was carried out, with Horner and Shifrin leading the way by means of detailed studies throughout 1944.[92]

By 1945, Lambert-St. Louis Municipal Airport consisted of 1,060 acres with four runways, the largest of which was 6,300 feet long and fully paved with concrete. Eleven hangars and an administration building sprouted from the airfield, as well as the enormous Curtiss-Wright complex and the burgeoning McDonnell plant. The CAA rated the airport Class IV, the highest then attainable. At that time, the city's program for air development, in accordance with earlier plans, was threefold:

(1) Expansion of Lambert Field to its ultimate area of 1,400 acres. (2) Acquisition and development of a second major air field (Columbia Bottoms). (3) Development of numerous minor and small private fields both within and without the city limits to serve all sections of the metropolitan area.[93]

This view of Lambert Field is to the north, over the construction site for the 1955 terminal building.

The airlines continued their protest to the Columbia Bottoms site,[94] a vast, 4,354-acre water-surrounded tract held by 70 different landowners,[95] but St. Louis was bent on developing it into a secondary municipal airport. By the spring of 1945, the city had purchased 600 acres of the district, with condemnation proceedings advancing for the acquisition of the remainder.[96]

To assist its airport expansion program, the city applied to the Civil Aeronautics Authority on November 28, 1946, for $15,209,358 in federal funds: $6,152,575 for Lambert Field, $7,229,023 for Columbia Bottoms, $537,440 for a small airfield at Morganford Road and River Des Peres, $600,939 for one at Hampton and Columbia Avenues, and $689,381 for the enlargement of the recently-established Ross Airport on North Broadway.[97] Two of these proposals soon saw their demise. On January 15, 1947, the Aldermanic Public Utilities Committee killed the suggested Morganford airport because of its undue cost and the heavy opposition of the local residents.[98] On July 18, 1947, the CAA snuffed out the incipient Hampton-Columbia airport as unsuitable on account of irregular terrain and uncertain foundation rock.[99] The three other proposals, in part, came to fruition.

On March 21, 1946, the Aldermanic Board of Estimate and Apportionment approved a five-year lease on a forty-acre, city-owned tract of land east of Broadway between Thatcher and Humboldt avenues to the Ross Aviation Corporation for the establishment within the city limits of a small airport for privately-owned light planes. To encourage the development of such enterprises, the city levied the nominal rental fee of $1.00 for the entire period. Walter W. Ross, the ex-Navy pilot who was president of the corporation, planned to lease an additional privately-owned 32 acres, on which he would construct three runways and facilities for storing and servicing small aircraft.[100] Ross Airport, at 7700 North Broadway, was formally opened on June 30, 1946, with a brief air show and parachute exhibition. The facilities at the airport consisted of a hangar with space for ten light planes, along with an oiled runway 3,000 feet in length and a sod runway 2,850 feet long.[101] Two years later, the airport held the same equipment and Ross himself was busily engaged in making improvements and promoting the use of his waterfront airfield.[102]

The controversial Columbia Bottoms site was approved by the CAA on July 18, 1947, even though that body had earlier opposed it.[103] By 1950, the city had taken possession of the entire 4,354 acres in question, but the project of developing it into an airport was abandoned indefinitely at that time in favor of pursuing the pressing needs at Lambert Field.[104]

The municipal airport was an overburdened center of widespread activity. During fiscal 1946, 233,078 passengers arrived at or departed from the field (as opposed to 128,925 in fiscal 1945 and 86,188 in fiscal 1941); 4,399,228 pounds of mail was handled (as opposed to 3,718,850 pounds in fiscal 1945 and 1,072,919 in fiscal 1941); 1,751,157 pounds of express was received and dispatched (as opposed to 1,362,234 pounds in fiscal 1945 and 267,489 pounds in fiscal 1941); and there were 34,265 airline movements (as opposed to 19,797 in fiscal 1945 and 14,709 in fiscal 1943 [sic].[105] During the single month of August 1946, the total traffic of civil, commercial, and military planes amounted to 24,005 aircraft.[106] Thousands of spectators visited the airport, especially to view the massive Douglas DC-4s and Lockheed Constellations, each sporting four powerful engines. Twenty-one of such multi-engined flights per day took place at Lambert Field in August 1946: American scheduled ten, Chicago and Southern eight, TWA two, and Eastern one.[107] The airport was a busy place, but badly overcrowded.

Between January 1, 1945, and August 26, 1946, a total of $3,322,800 had been spent on the expansion and improvement of

George J. Herwig Collection

Major Albert Bond Lambert in later years.

Lambert Field, as compared with $3,000,000 during the previous twenty-five years. Among the principal expenses at the municipal airport were: $672,000 for land acquisition, $706,500 for enclosing Cold Water Creek (a project then 82 percent complete), $158,500 for runway improvement, and $46,900 for remodeling the administration building (a project then 60 percent complete).[108]

In spite of the vast outlay of funds, Major Albert Bond Lambert, a member of the St. Louis Airport Commission, was vigorous in his criticism, just as he had been in 1929, of the laggard airport expansion, and made a statement to that effect on September 30, 1946. By his own reckoning, the city's aging air leader (who would die of heart disease twelve days later)[109] determined that the drainage of newly-acquired 867 acres would be completed in June 1947; the grading of the field in June 1948; runways in May 1949; the new terminal building in August 1950; and the field lighting system in

February 1951.[110] Such a slow rate of progress he felt, was grossly unwarranted, especially since funds had been available since 1942. Editorially, the *St. Louis Post-Dispatch* was in full agreement:

> Where aviation is concerned, St. Louis is sprawling on its river like a placid catfish. . . . Airline pilots know where we stand. Some of them say they wouldn't stop here for a whistle if they had any choice. They complain of "skimpy" landing strips and a crowded field, crowded hangars, crowded terminal building. . . . Figures also tell the story. Since 1941, airline flights into Lambert Field have nearly tripled; passengers have tripled; air cargo has increased five times. But Lambert remains a relic facing a non-distant future of 160-ton planes.[111]

With a $1,000,000 grant from the CAA on September 8, 1947,[112] together with promises of more to come, Chairman Milton M. Kinsey of the City Airport Commission moved to complete the necessary expansion as soon as possible. A striking new terminal building, designed by Hellmuth, Yamasaki, and Leinweber, was begun in 1953 and dedicated in formal ceremonies on March 10, 1956, by Mayor Raymond R. Tucker upon its completion.[113] As high as a four-story building and 412 feet long, the contemporary structure consisted of three sets of intersection barrel vaults expressed in thin shell concrete, with sides of glass and no interior pillars or piers.[114] The unique edifice and its related facilities were built at a cost of $7,728,000, with the federal government supplying funds above the $7,200,000 which the city had raised through additional bond issues and the sale of property to McDonnell Aircraft Corporation. Buildings and utilities were estimated to have cost $5,880,000; roads and parking areas $725,000; furnishings, fixtures, and equipment $150,000; and the aircraft parking apron $973,000. The entire 85-acre complex approximated $24.50 per square foot in cost.[115]

In 1956, Lambert-St. Louis Municipal Airport comprised 1,282 acres and had a total value (field and facilities) of $23,000,000. Its main runway, 10,020 feet long and 200 feet wide, was matched only by Boston, Billings, and Denver, and it had two 6,000-foot fully paved concrete runways, one of which was programmed for instrument landings.[116]

In 1961, the airport was served by eight major airlines (American, Braniff, Central, Continental, Delta, Eastern, Ozark, and TWA),[117] and its facilities were continuing to expand. By the same date, there were four small private airports in operation in St. Louis County (Ross Airport and the Columbia Bottoms site having been abandoned). Starling Airpark, rated Class 1 by the Federal Aviation Agency (based on the length of the longest runway — 1,800 to

Courtesy George F. Hellmuth

In 1956, three graceful, thinshell concrete domes replaced the old 1933 terminal building. The new terminal, designed by the St. Louis architectural firm of Hellmuth, Yamasaki and Leinweber to be expanded to six domes, now is considered to be complete with four.

2,699 feet), was located thirteen miles south of the city and was equipped with two unpaved landing strips, offering storage service, gasoline, and minor repairs to light aircraft. Creve Coeur Airport, situated seventeen miles west-southwest of the city, was rated a Class 2 airfield (according to its runway length of 2,700 to 3,699 feet) and offered the same facilities as Starling. Weiss Airport, a Class 2 airfield eleven miles southwest of the city, was equipped with a paved runway, as well as a dirt strip, and featured night lights, storage space, gasoline, and repair facilities. Lobmaster Sky Ranch, another Class 2 field three miles northwest of Chesterfield and eighteen miles west of St. Louis, was outfitted with facilities much the same as those at Weiss.[118]

This last airfield became involved in a heated controversy three years later. During the summer of 1964, Paul D. Haglin and William Honey were making preparations to open their Spirit of St. Louis Airport, situated on the south side of U.S. Highway 40 in the Gumbo Bottoms area of Chesterfield, a short distance from the Missouri River. Their location, however, was one-half mile away and directly across U.S. Highway 40 from Lobmaster Field, which had opened there in 1959.[119] Harold V. Baker, operator of the Sky Ranch, raised a vigorous protest, citing the obvious hazards involved, particularly in view of the fact that the Federal Aviation Agency reported that there were 217 near misses between airplanes throughout the nation from January 1 to August 8, 1964.[120] The Spirit of St.

Courtesy Gene Taylor, Weiss Airport

This is Weiss Airport in 1955. The principal runway and taxi strip are crushed rock. A parallel runway to the west is sod, as is one which crosses the picture from left to right. The diagonal road is Rudder Road, named for Sam Rudder, a nearby farmer. The three-lane highway in the foreground is old U.S. 66, now Interstate 44.

Louis owners, however, proposed that a control tower be built at their expense to supervise the traffic at both fields and insure safety. On July 15, they broached their plan at an FAA hearing of the dispute at Lambert Field.[121]

While the offer was still pending, Harold Baker, together with Lewis Enterprises, Inc., which owned Lobmaster Sky Ranch, brought suit in St. Louis County Circuit Court to enjoin the new airport from opening August 15, as scheduled, on the grounds that its operation would create a safety hazard. Haglin and Honey, in turn, pressed their own action against Samuel D. Lobmaster, the founder of the airport, alleging a breach of contract under an earlier arrangement for joint operation,[122] and they instituted a second suit to enjoin airplanes from the Sky Ranch from using their airspace.[123] For a time, Arthur Lewis of Lewis Enterprises considered selling his 280-acre field at $3,250 per acre, for $910,000, but he withdrew his offer

Courtesy Richard E. Hrabko, Airport Director

This photo of Spirit of St. Louis Airport was taken just after it opened in 1965. The main hangar is at the far end of the field, and the tower is at left. The road in the lower right corner is Highway 40. The view is to the southwest.

on August 20, shortly after he had made it![124] Although Circuit Judge Drew W. Luten Jr. granted a temporary restraining order against the Spirit of St. Louis owners,[125] Haglin and Honey dropped their court proceedings against Lobmaster Field on September 15 in the hopes that tempers would cool and a favorable settlement might be reached.[126]

The issue came to a head on November 5, 1964, when Circuit Judge Noah Weinstein, satisfied that joint air traffic control from a single tower would insure maximum safety, a plan approved by the FAA, decreed that the Spirit of St. Louis Airport was free to open as soon as Paul D. Haglin paid a damage settlement of $22,575 to Lewis Enterprises ($15,291) and Harold V. Baker ($7,284) on the grounds that he had "intentionally and knowingly deprived the plaintiffs [Lobmaster] of certain property rights" by developing an adjacent airfield.[127] The defendants made payment immediately, and the Spirit of St. Louis Airport opened on November 7. "One of the largest privately owned airports in the country," as a result of its substantial size and its 5,100-foot asphalt runway "capable of serving jets,"[128] the new field handled more than 100 takeoffs and landings from the controversial control tower during the day.[129] The Gumbo battlefield was quiet.

In spite of the fact that a number of small airports had blossomed

George J. Herwig Collection

The old Parks Airport is the predecessor to what is now St. Louis Downtown-Parks Airport. The current field is on the site of the old Curtiss-Steinberg Field, a short distance from the old site.

in the greater St. Louis area, Lambert Field was still overburdened with a surfeit of traffic. In 1962, the airport was the sixth busiest in the nation, with 1,448,900 passengers originating or terminating flights there,[130] and by 1964, when it was rapidly outgrowing its facilities,[131] there was even talk of barring light planes from the field.[132] A secondary airport was needed to relieve the pressure on the municipal airfield. Attention focused on the dormant Parks Metropolitan Airport in Cahokia, Illinois.

Begun in 1928 by a St. Louis syndicate,[133] the field was soon taken over by the Curtiss-Wright Corporation, which named it the Curtiss-Steinberg Airport and initiated flying operations on February 26, 1930.[134] During World War II, the field was leased by Oliver Parks, president of Parks Air College and Parks Aircraft Sales and Service Corporation, for the training of Army Air Force cadets.[135] When Curtiss-Wright withdrew from St. Louis as a result of the postwar government cutbacks in the aircraft industry, Oliver Parks purchased the 568-acre airfield, which was then equipped with three concrete runways and four brick and steel hangars, from the corporation in December 1945 for $435,000, and renamed it Parks Metropolitan Airport.[136]

He continued to operate it himself, and for a time in 1949 the City of St. Louis was even considering leasing the field from him as a secondary municipal airport.[137] This plan was abandoned, however, and Parks soon found that his enterprise was too big and too expensive for private operation. In 1959, he was forced to close the airport.[138] Despite an impulse to cash in on the housing boom and use his valuable acreage for subdivision development, he came to realize the invaluable asset an airport provided for a community. He kept his airfield idle but intact thereafter, although at a cost of $110,000 in taxes and interest alone.[139] A group of East St. Louis businessmen, known as the Southwest Civic Memorial Airport Association, was soon organized to gain options on the airfield and adjacent tracts so that they might operate Parks Field if and when it again became feasible.[140]

Faced with the necessity of a secondary municipal airport, the joint City-County Airport Commission hired the consulting engineering firm of Landrum and Brown for $30,000 to study the situation in detail. In March of 1964, the concern made its report, but gave no specific recommendations in regard to Parks Airport, only that the cost of developing it during the next decade would approximate $7,095,700. Landrum and Brown, however, did strongly urge the acquisition of another site — Weiss Airport. For the expansion of this 109-acre tract to 700 fully-equipped acres, the consultants estimated that the cost would total $14,551,000, with the necessary finances being provided by city and county bond issues and matching federal funds.[141]

Shocked at the survey findings, the *St. Louis Globe-Democrat* threw its support behind the development of the East Side airfield, particularly because of the lower cost (less than half as much) and its ease of access to downtown St. Louis (6.5 miles or 15 minutes as opposed to 15.3 miles or 45 minutes). The newspaper editorialized:

> There have been years of dawdling over the decision for a new metropolitan port facility. Charges of special interest have been batted around. And many individuals have sincere convictions as to location.
>
> The public — and the Globe-Democrat — have no concern save to get the job done.
>
> Parks is the most convenient, the most suitable for development, the most practical and least costly site for the vast majority of people in this 2,000,000 metropolitan complex.[142]

Mayor Raymond R. Tucker, together with a number of civic leaders, took a stand in favor of acquiring both airfields as secondary municipal airports.[143] To that end, the Bi-State Development Agency expressed an interest in financing the reopening of Parks Airport, while the City-County Airport Commission prepared to take control of Weiss Field.

On November 14, 1964, the St. Louis Board of Aldermen unanimously passed a bill authorizing the city to lend Bi-State $500,000 over a period of seven years to assist in its renovation of Parks Metropolitan Airport.[144] The money, to be repaid at 3.87 percent interest beginning in 1972, would supplement the $1,700,000 in revenue bonds the company planned to issue, along with $275,000 from the Illinois Department of Aeronautics[145] and $1,037,475 from the Federal Aviation Agency.[146] The last impediment to the purchase was removed on December 28, 1964, when the Interstate Commerce Commission, which had jurisdiction over the matter since Bi-State also controlled the transit system in the greater St. Louis area, formally approved the issuance of the revenue bonds,[147] $1,100,000 of which were Class A bearing 4.5 percent interest and $600,000 Class B with 5 percent interest.[148] The entire stock was purchased by Indiana National Homes, Inc., a concern which owned the bulk of the 525-acre Illinois airfield.[149] Bi-State then bought the airport from its major creditor for $2,068,826 and made arrangements for the Southwest Civic Memorial Airport Association to operate the airport when it began to function again.[150] With development proceeding at a rapid pace, the much-needed airfield was tentatively scheduled to reopen on April 1, 1965.[151]

Negotiations for Weiss Airport were not nearly so smooth. To stimulate the conversion of the private airfield into a municipal airport, the Federal Aviation Agency allocated on October 17, 1964, the sum of $347,830 for the project, on the condition that before July 1, 1965, the amount would be matched by local authorities (approximately $200,000 each by both St. Louis and St. Louis County if both planned to share in the expansion of the airfield.)[152] For a time, St. Louis County Supervisor Lawrence K. Roos was cool to the idea of involving the county in the endeavor because of the great expense,[153] but he finally agreed to the proposal of joint development on November 18, 1964, with a strong reservation. Said Roos:

> I want to make it public right now that this airport will be operated as is for at least ten years, and there are no plans for expansion involving a bond issue or any other type of further financial commitment.[154]

The economy-minded supervisor's reticence was somewhat understandable, for it was widely felt that the requisite bond issues, estimated at $3,240,000 for both city and county, would have had little chance of passage at that time in any event.[155] Civic leaders were of the opinion that the best procedure, as with Parks Airport, called for the Bi-State Development Agency to take control of the $800,000 airfield and renovate it systematically for the next decade, when further funds might be made available through bond issues.[156]

While strategy was being formulated for the acquisition of the airport, Chairman John Fabick of the joint City-County Airport Commission became the cynosure of widespread controversy. Fabick's tractor firm had recently purchased 82 acres of land adjacent to Weiss Airport, and as a result, charges of conflict of interest were raised against him.[157] Although the chairman had voluntarily abstained from any part in the airport negotiations, had offered the land at cost to the city if needed for a secondary airport, and had been absolved of any malpractice by his fellow commissioners,[158] his position was untenable. Under heavy criticism, particulary from County Supervisor Roos,[159] Fabick resigned on December 4, 1964, and was replaced by F. William Human Jr.[160]

The only remaining roadblock to the acquisition of Weiss Airport was the Board of Aldermen of Fenton, Missouri, the municipality within which the airport lay. They refused to change the zoning ordinances of the tracts of land necessary for the full expansion of the airfield into a secondary municipal airport. The adamant aldermen remained firm in their opposition to the establishment of such a facility in Fenton (essentially in the hope that taxable light industry might occupy the area) and held fast in their determination to keep the area zoned for one-acre farms.[161] Despite the fact that the assistant attorney general of Missouri, Thomas E. Eichhorst, expressed the opinion that state law gave cities broad condemnation authority in planning for airports, even over adverse zoning regulations,[162] the Fenton opposition was formidable. On February 2, 1965, the aldermen of neighboring Sunset Hills joined the protest by passing a resolution against the proposed airport on the grounds that it would be a detriment to their city, depress property values, and "create a potential nuisance" to Sunset Hills residents.[163]

While the debate over Weiss Field continued, Walter T. Malloy, St. Louis' director of public utilities, urged that two other sites be developed: one in north St. Louis County, near the St. Louis Training School, and another in the central county area, near Ladue and Ballas Roads.[164] With these and the two projects under discussion, the city would be encompassed by a ring of much-needed public airports. As it was, however, St. Louis was at least confident of one secondary airport to relieve its overburdened municipal airfield.

In 1964, there were 275,000 takeoffs and landings at Lambert Field.[165] On October 27 of that year, single-plane service to Europe was inaugurated by TWA,[166] giving the airport a quasi-international status, and by December, there were 43 pure jet airplanes arriving daily at the field from all parts of the nation.[167] At that time, Lambert-St. Louis Municipal Airport had a total area of 1,786 acres, which embraced a contemporary terminal building, numerous hangars, and four primary runways with lengths of 10,018 by 200 feet, 7,600 by 200 feet, 6,000 by 150 feet, and 4,600 by 150 feet. FAA-rated Class 9, the highest attainable, the field was then served by seven major airlines (American, Braniff, Central, Delta, Eastern, Ozark, and TWA). The object of an investment of approximately $24,200,000 ($5,700,000 of which was in federal grants) during the previous twenty-two years, Lambert Field in 1964, with all its accessories and equipment, had a total worth of between $50,000,000 and $100,000,000.[168] During that year, the airport grossed $2,284,000 in revenue, with a pure net profit of only $6,575, along with $642,000 which the Airport Commission was able to set aside for the purchase of additional land and the financing of new improvements.[169] As in the past, Lambert Field was in a continuous state of expansion for the needs of the future.

The fact that St. Louis was able to provide itself with adequate air facilities contributed immeasurably to its aeronautic greatness. The Chouteau-Newstead ascension site brought major balloon races to the city; Kinloch Park became a home to fledgling aviators; Lambert Field enabled St. Louis to lend itself fully to commercial aviation. Little of any aeronautical merit could have occurred in the city had it not been equipped with such superior airports, airfields, and ascension grounds.

Part Two:
Air Activities

II
John Wise and the Era
of Balloons, 1830-1900

ST. LOUIS OWES ITS REPUTATION as an air center to the sundry air activities it has hosted throughout its history. By far the greater number of them concerned the field of ballooning, for it was in this phase of flight that the city first gained aeronautical eminence.

Curiously enough, while men and women have been interested in flight almost from the beginning of their existence, it was not until the end of the eighteenth century that this dream was fulfilled. The invention of the first real balloon by Joseph and Etienne Montgolfier in 1782 marked the beginning of the human adventure in the sky.[1] The two brothers, who were papermakers in the French village of Annonay, noticed scraps of burnt paper being carried up the chimney by the smoke from their hearth fire. They came to the conclusion that if such a force could be harnessed, then people might fly.

After experimenting with 700-cubic-foot smoke-filled silk bags in 1782, they decided to hold a public demonstration. The Montgolfiers constructed an ornately-decorated paper-lined linen bag of 23,000-cubic-foot capacity and thirty-five feet in diameter.[2] In the presence of thousands of people at Annonay on June 5, 1783, they built a fire beneath it. The unmanned balloon gradually rose to a height of

Premiere ascension du ballon à l'aire chaude des frères Montgolfier à Paris. 1783

Photocopy by Gregory M. Franzwa

This early French lithograph depicts man's first ascent — in a Montgolfier balloon in 1783.

6,000 feet and drifted for more than a mile before the hot, smoky air cooled and it sank back to the earth.[3] The incident caused a sensation throughout France and the world.

> Thus the first balloon invented was one that could have been invented at any time since the birth of weaving. For thirty centuries people could have built hot air balloons — they had the materials; all they needed was the idea.[4]

The first air-borne passengers were a sheep, a rooster, and a duck, sent aloft in a cage by the Montgolfier brothers at Versailles in the presence of King Louis XVI, Marie Antoinette, and their court, on September 19, 1783.[5] This success was soon followed by the first human ascension. In a Montgolfier balloon, Jean François Pilâtre de Rozier and the Marquis d'Arlandes made history's first free flight from Paris on November 21, 1783.[6] Carrying bundles of straw for fuel and pails of water to extinguish possible fires in the bag itself, they stood in the fire-bearing wicker basket for twenty minutes as the flimsy linen-and-paper balloon traveled five and one-half miles over the French countryside.[7]

While the Montgolfier brothers were experimenting with hot air balloons, a French physicist, Jacques A.C. Charles, developed the hydrogen balloon, making use of the gas Henry Cavendish had discovered in 1766. It was only one-fourteenth the weight of normal air.[8] On August 27, 1783, Charles sent aloft from the Champ de Mars the first hydrogen-filled balloon, a rubberized cloth bag, and on December 1, 1783, he and a M. Robert made the first free ascension in a balloon of that type.[9] "Soon hot air balloons were to be called *montgolfières,* to distinguish them from the hydrogen-filled *charlières.*"[10]

Ironically, the first recorded man to fly was also the first recorded aviation fatality. Jean François Pilâtre de Rozier reasoned that if a hot air balloon were good and a hydrogen balloon better, than a combination of the two would provide the best lifting force of all. He secured a hydrogen-filled balloon, built a fire in the wicker basket, and began an attempt to cross the English Channel on June 15, 1785. Amazingly, he and a M. Romain, his passenger, reached a height of several thousand feet before the inflammable gas exploded and the balloon crashed to the earth engulfed in flames.[11]

With both the hot air and the hydrogen varieties in use, the era of ballooning was forcefully inaugurated and the science advanced with bold strides. The latter soon replaced the former in popularity, however, for although they were much more expensive, gas balloons were relatively safer and much more efficient than paper "montgolfiers.''

The bags were usually made of silk, with three coats of special varnish. They were encased in a net of ropes which came down around the bag and fastened to a wooden ring. The basket was suspended from this. One-man balloons were as small as twenty feet in diameter. Giants for proposed ocean flights were as large as one hundred feet in diameter.

The bag had a wooden valve at the top with a cord running down to the basket. A pull on the cord would discharge gas. The bottom of the bag was a wide, open tube. A hydrogen balloon usually left the ground about half filled with gas in a long pear-shape. As it rose into thinner atmosphere, the gas expanded it to apple shape. If the gas continued to expand after the bag was fully distended, the excess gas floated out the open tube at the bottom — otherwise, the bag would burst, and surprisingly, this was not too dangerous. The fabric of the balloon usually gathered in the top of the net and acted like a parachute to float the basket to earth.

The balloon was raised by dumping out sand ballast. It was lowered by letting out gas through the valve at the top. When it was in still air it could be controlled by tossing out a handful rather than a bagful of sand. One balloonist reported that his bag jumped up twenty feet when he threw out a chicken bone.[12]

On January 7, 1785, John Jeffries, an American doctor, and Jean Pierre Blanchard made the first air crossing of the English Channel, from Dover to Calais.[13] Eight years later, ballooning came to the United States when Blanchard made an ascent from Philadelphia in the presence of George Washington, on January 9, 1793.[14] He made a forty-five minute flight to New Jersey and carried a ''passport'' from the president asking American citizens to give the balloonist whatever aid he needed.[15]

Throughout the early years of the nineteenth century many men took to the air, but the art of ballooning saw relatively slow development because it was looked upon as ''too dangerous and presumptuous.'' Only in the mid-1850s did it become widespread and popular.[16] Developments still occurred, nonetheless, and St. Louis made its voice heard.

The earliest evidence of aviation activity in the city was recorded on May 31, 1830. On that date, St. Louis County Court Justice Mary Philip Leduc certified and filed the ''Description of an invention for propelling balloons and boats'' which Dr. Claude George Brun had presented to him. The device was a simple motor, presumably operated by muscle power:

This machine is nothing but an endless screw placed fore and aft of the balloon, connected by a through running axis, resting on two diametrically overlapping collars, in the width, and revolving by means of a pulley and a belt communicating with the basket. The same machine may also propel a boat, either by a screw thread of large dimension, revolving in the atmosphere, or, by a smaller one, if it is submerged in the water, and put in motion by any force.[17]

Dr. Brun was undoubtedly an avid scientist and tinkerer, for the same document contains descriptions of five other inventions of his: a bread mill, a "Flying Ferry" (a bridge of wire cables), a wood plane, an iron for pressing clothes, and a pivot for vertical machine shafts.

Aeronautical development continued throughout the century and St. Louis maintained its participation. On May 17, 1836, Richard Clayton, a prominent American balloonist who had made a record trip of 350 miles the previous year, made the ninth ascension of his career from an enclosure at Fourth and Market streets in St. Louis. This was one of the first recorded balloon flights to start from the city.

In order to defray his expenses, Clayton levied an admission charge of $1.00 for adults and 50¢ for children.[18] In spite of a morning rain, he ascended at 6:30 p.m., drifted off to the south at a height of 1½ miles, and landed thirty minutes later in a field six miles away. Because of the meagerness of the receipts, it was felt that Clayton might avoid St. Louis in further flights. The *Missouri Republican* editorialized: "Our citizens cannot expect to have such splendid scenes presented to them unless those who undertake them are well compensated."[19]

The situation did not improve, however, for a Mr. S. Hobart, who made two ascensions from the city in 1841. He used a balloon of "mammoth dimensions," for it was constructed of 1,100 yards of silk and had a gas capacity of 20,000 cubic feet, "being much the largest in the United States.[20] With this he made an eight-mile flight on August 14[21] and a ten-mile trip on October 9, taking with him on the latter occasion a Miss Day, a fourteen-year-old St. Louis girl.[22] The admission price to view the first ascension from within the enclosure had been the same as Clayton had charged, but Hobart reduced it by one-half and added his special attraction for the second trip. On both occasions, however, his receipts were "hundreds of dollars less than expenses," and on his last flight he even lost his balloon when the wind blew it into a forest after he had landed.[23] It is no wonder that there is no record of further flights by Hobart from St. Louis.

In the ensuing years, the city was host to several other pioneer aeronauts. In 1855, the noted French balloonist Eugène Godard performed in St. Louis.[24] Three years later, Silas M. Brooks, manager of the St. Louis Museum, made several exhibitions of his aeronautical prowess in the city and throughout the Midwest for the Ericsson Hydrogen Balloon Company of St. Louis.[25] In 1859, there occurred the single most significant aerial voyage ever begun from St. Louis — the flight of John Wise in the *Atlantic*.

Born in Lancaster, Pennsylvania, on February 24, 1808, John Wise soon developed an interest in the field which was to occupy his life.

> I would spend hours in the night lying upon a straw-heap looking at the stars and the moon, and the arrival of a comet gave me rapturous joy. It was this kind of natural bent that first led me to indulge in aerial projects.[26]

His first experiments were with kites, and with them he sent many of his pet kittens into the clouds.[27] Turning next to tissue-paper parachutes, he successfully dropped many of his hapless pets from rooftops and gable windows. At the age of 14, he read an account of a balloon voyage in Italy and began experimenting with hot air "montgolfiers." One of his first paper balloons, carrying a fire in its basket, ascended several hundred feet, but it came down on a thatched roof and set it afire.[28] After that, the townspeople of Lancaster were hardly enthusiastic over the efforts of the young scientist.

After Wise had tried theology as a vocation, he was apprenticed to a cabinetmaker for four and one-half years. He then became a pianoforte maker until 1835, when he left the occupation to become a professional ballonist.[29] His accomplishments in that field made him the greatest American ballonist of the nineteenth century.[30]

> When I first conceived the idea of making a balloon, I had never seen an ascension with one, nor had I any practical knowledge of its construction. . . . I intended merely to gratify my desire of sailing aloft to enjoy a prospect that I had ever considered must be grand and sublime . . .[31]

After studying the atmosphere, pneumatics, and hydrostatics, and after consulting with several Philadelphia scientists, Wise constructed a balloon of domestic muslin and coated it with a varnish of bird lime and linseed oil to make it airtight. It was a hydrogen balloon 28 feet in diameter, to which was attached a basket two and one-half feet in diameter at the bottom and three feet eight inches deep. The balloon and rigging weighed 186 pounds and had a lifting power of 375 pounds.[32]

He advertised a public ascension from Ninth and Green streets in Philadelphia for April 30, 1835, but when the day came it was stormy, so the demonstration was rescheduled for May 2.[33] At 4:30 p.m. that afternoon the balloon ascended, bounced off a chimney, and descended into a vacant lot 400 yards away. To quiet the milling crowd which soon surrounded his balloon, Wise shouted, ''For heaven's sake, gentlemen, will you give me a chance to make the ascension?''[34] He then took off his coat and boots, and also discarded his instruments and sand ballast. With the balloon thus eighteen pounds lighter, he then arose and after an hour and fifteen minutes landed nine miles away at Haddonfield.[35]

> I had now visited the shrine of intellectual grandeur, and its attractions were seductive. I had dreamed a magnificent dream, which I felt convinced could be realized. Such were my reflections, when recurring to this event. Although many of my friends desired me, in the most persuasive manner, to give up the idea of repeating the experiment, looking upon it as an extremely dangerous business, I resolved in my own mind to pursue it as long as it afforded me the same enjoyment which I experienced in my first essay.[36]

For the rest of his life John Wise devoted himself to aeronautics, and he did experience the dangers about which his friends had been concerned. On August 11, 1838, after ascending from Easton, Pennsylvania, his balloon burst at an altitude of 13,000 feet because of the expansion of the hydrogen. The ruptured envelope, however, gathered at the top of the net rigging and the whole apparatus acted as a parachute. Wise landed hard, but unhurt.[37] Amazed at his discovery, he decided to attempt it deliberately. On October 1, 1838, he ascended from Philadelphia, collapsed the bag by pulling a rope which opened a seam, and descended successfully.[38]

These incidents led him to the development of ''his greatest contribution'' to the science of ballooning — the ''rip panel,'' which allowed balloonists to deflate their gasbags instantly on landing and thus not be dragged all over the countryside on windy days.[39] This was one of the two major developments (exclusive of the motor for dirigibility) in the technique of ballooning in the nineteenth century. The other was the ''drag rope,'' a line up to several thousand feet in length, which trailed along the ground and kept the balloon at a fixed altitude. If the balloon rose, more of the rope was lifted into the basket, causing the bag to descend because of the increased airborne weight; if the balloon sank too close to the ground, more of the rope was payed out, causing the bag to rise again.[40] This device, often utilized by balloonists appearing in St. Louis, was first used by Charles Green, Wise's counterpart in England and the greatest European balloonist of the century. [41]

The highest ambition of John Wise was to cross the Atlantic Ocean by balloon, utilizing a west-east current which he had discovered in the atmosphere. [42] In a Lancaster newspaper in June 1843, he advertised his findings and his intention:

> Having from long experience in aeronautics, been convinced that a constant and regular current of air is blowing at all times from west to east, with a velocity of from twenty to forty, or even sixty miles per hour, according to its height from the earth; and having discovered a composition which renders silk or muslin impervious to hydrogen gas, so that a balloon may be kept aloft for many weeks, I feel confident, with these advantages, that a trip across the Atlantic will not be attended with as much real danger as by the common mode of transition. [43]

Wise's primary concern was financial. He consulted a number of Philadelphia businessmen during the winter of 1842-1843, but all refused him aid because they felt the undertaking was too impractical and dangerous. The aeronaut, however, was determined to carry it through, and in the spring of 1843, he decided to petition Congress at its next session. [44]

On December 20, 1843, Wise drew up a petition for an appropriation of $15,000 to enable him to construct a balloon of 100 feet in diameter, with a lifting force of 25,000 pounds, in which he and a crew could cross the ocean. The request was received by both the Senate and the House of Representatives and sent to the respective committees on Naval Affairs, but it was never reported on the floor. [45]

This was not the last time that John Wise communicated with the United States government. When the Mexican War broke out, he devised a plan for capturing the Castle of San Juan de Ulloa in Vera Cruz. On October 22, 1846, he sent his scheme to the War Department. Wise proposed to drop 18,000 pounds of bombs on the fortress from a height of one mile, out of gun range, from a balloon 100 feet in diameter, with a lifting force of 30,000 pounds, attached by a five-mile cable to a ship in the harbor. He later wrote: [46]

> The War Department, however, was not sufficiently advanced in its ideas to give the propositon the consideration it deserved, and like many other good suggestions it came to nothing. [47]

Since the transatlantic voyage had been his obsession since 1842, Wise decided to appeal to Congress a second time. Senator Stephen A. Douglas introduced his petition to the Senate on December 30,

1850. Wise requested an appropriation of $20,000, with which he would construct a balloon 100 feet in diameter, with a lifting power of sixteen tons. In this vehicle, he intended: 1) to demonstrate aerial bombing over Washington; 2) to travel to St. Louis and sail his balloon to the Atlantic coast in order to verify his previous observations as to the west-east aerial current; and 3) to ascend from New York and make a flight across the ocean to the continent of Europe. After some discussion as to which committee should have jurisdiction over the petition (that on Territories, Public Lands, Canals and Roads, or Foreign Relations), it was referred to the Committee on Naval Affairs.[48] Just as in 1843, the committee never made a report on it, and the aeronaut "very speedily gave up all hope of obtaining assistance from Congress."[49]

Seven years later, John Wise did secure the financial help he sought. In 1858, O.A. Gager, a man of substantial means from Bennington, Vermont, made an ascension with John La Mountain[50] in a balloon Wise had built, It was Gager's first aerial excursion and he became so enthusiastic that he agreed to finance Wise in building a large balloon and making some experimental voyages from the interior of the United States, with a view to inaugurating transatlantic service for passengers and mail.[51] Wise suggested that they make a flight from St. Louis to New York City, and on that proposition the Trans-Atlantic Balloon Company was organized. It consisted of five members, each owning an equal share of the whole concern: John Wise, John La Mountain, O.A. Gager, a Mr. Johnson, and a Mr. Gilbert.[52]

Their balloon, christened the *Atlantic,* was built at Wise's direction by John La Mountain on the fairgrounds at Lansingburg, New York, out of 2,250 yards of oiled Chinese silk.[53] Work was begun in September 1858, under La Mountain's supervision, using women to sew the "breadths of the silk together," the *Atlantic* was completed in six months.[54]

> The balloon was a spheroid of fifty feet transversely, and nearly sixty feet perpendicularly. It was rigged with a strong hempen network, and underneath it was suspended a wicker car, and beneath this again a boat of very light but very good workmanship, capable of carrying in the water a thousand pounds. This boat was cased in a heavy canvas jacket, by which it was attached with ropes pending from the concentrating hoop underneath the neck of the balloon. To this hoop was also fastened, by ropes of nine feet length, the wicker car. The ropes holding the boat passed down from the hoop along the outside of the wicker car, and the boat hung fifteen feet below the car.[55]

It was truly a "monster balloon,"[56] for up to that time, it was the largest ever built.[57]

Of the five members of the Trans-Atlantic Balloon Company, it was decided that three should make the flight from St. Louis to New York City.

> For navigating the balloon "Atlantic," the company was arranged in the following manner: Director-in-Chief, John Wise; Aeronaut, John Lamountane; Scientific Observer, O.A. Gager.[58]

Gager and Wise proceeded to St. Louis early in June 1859, and La Mountain arrived on June 28 with the *Atlantic,* which was inspected and put on public display in Verandah Hall.[59] The City Board Council gave the aeronauts free use of Washington Square at Clark Avenue and Twelfth Street, and they announced that they would make the ascension from the field on Friday afternoon, July 1.[60]

People began gathering at the square at 1:00 p.m. Some paid an admission fee and got within the wooden enclosure the aeronauts had erected, but most spectators preferred to stand outside and view the ascension for free.[61] The St. Louis Gaslight Company made the inflation with hydrogen from an eight-inch pipe.[62] Although the *Atlantic* was capable of holding 120,000 cubic feet of gas, it was decided to put in only 65,000 cubic feet, at a cost of $195, in order to leave room for expansion in the upper atmosphere.[63]

As the balloon was being inflated, a reporter from the *Daily Missouri Republican,* William Hyde, asked Director-in-Chief Wise for permission to accompany the three voyagers. Perhaps conscious of the favorable publicity which might result, Wise granted his request, but only on the condition that Hyde agree to be landed if it were necessary to lighten the ship.[64]

The boat and basket were then stocked with provisions and equipment for the trip.

> The cargo consisted of nine hundred pounds of sand in bags, a large quantity of cold chickens, tongue, potted meat, sandwiches, etc.; numerous dark colored, long-necked vessels, containing champagne, sherry, sparkling catawba, claret, madeira, brandy and porter; a plentiful supply of overcoats, shawls, blankets and fur gloves, a couple or three carpet bags, chock full of what is expressed in that convertible phrase, 'a change,' a pail of iced lemonade and a bucket of water; a compass, barometer, thermometer and chart; bundles of the principal St. Louis newspapers; an express package directed to New York city; cards of candidates for clerkships in several of the Courts, tumblers, cups and knives, and perhaps other articles which have escaped me.[65]

The most interesting item was the express pouch, which was

specifically labeled:

> T.B. Marsh, Agent United States Express Company, No. 82
> Broadway, New York. This bag is sent from St. Louis, by the aerial
> ship *Atlantic,* July 1st. Please forward to destination from landing
> of balloon by Express, as above directed. C.W. Ford, Agent
> St. Louis. [66]

Although there is evidence that Richard Clayton carried some letters
by balloon from Cincinnati, July 4, 1835,[67] this express package may
have been the first mail ever carried by air.[68]

When all was in readiness, La Mountain, Gager, and Hyde took
their stations in the lifeboat, and Wise, as director of the flight,
climbed into the wicker basket, into which descended the valve rope
for controlling the gas.[69] At 6:40 p.m. July 1, 1859, the restraining
lines were cast off and the *Atlantic* rose and sailed off to the north-
northwest. Wise described the spirit of the liftoff:[70]

> The cheers of the audience, inside and outside the arena, were of
> the heartiest kind. We responded with a parting farewell and a
> lingering look upon the thousands of upturned faces that cheered
> us onward.[71]

Silas M. Brooks, a local balloonist, ascended a few minutes before
the *Atlantic* in the *Comet,* a small pilot balloon. He escorted the
voyagers for a time, and kept them company through the night.[72]

The object of the journey was "a landing in close proximity to one
of the Eastern cities," preferably New York, and since the *Atlantic*
had sufficient lifting power to stay aloft for twenty hours, success
was expected, for "the average speed of balloons is fifty miles per
hour."[73]

The *Atlantic* sailed along smoothly, and all through the night it
emitted a phosphorescent glow caused by the heat of the afternoon
sun on the hydrogen gas.[74] Of the four occupants, John Wise was
the only veteran balloonist, having made 239 ascensions;[75] this
was William Hyde's first trip. O.A. Gager had made one previous
ascension, and John La Mountain was a novice with a half-dozen
aerial voyages to his credit.[76] The veteran, however, made a foolish
mistake. About midnight, Wise decided to take a nap. He bade his
companions below goodnight and was soon fast asleep. Shortly
thereafter, John La Mountain noticed that, because of the great altitude, the hydrogen had expanded to the full limits of the balloon,
which was in danger of bursting. He could hear the gas rushing
noisily through the neck of the balloon, and he called to Wise to
open the valve at the top of the bag to relieve the pressure. When he
got no answer, La Mountain asked Gager to climb up into the basket
and see what was the matter. Gager found Wise breathing spasmo-

The Atlantic *at night is depicted inaccurately in this old magazine lithograph. A rowboat was suspended beneath the basket during most of the flight.*

dically, for the neck of the bag was expelling hydrogen full in his face. The amateur balloonist vigorously shook the nearly asphyxiated veteran pilot and barely revived him.[77]

As the *Atlantic* sailed serenely on its course, reports on its progress filtered back to St. Louis. In all, seven messages were received by the *Daily Missouri Republican*. At 1:00 a.m. July 2, a train on the St. Louis, Alton and Terre Haute Railroad sighted the *Atlantic* over Pana, Illinois, with Brooks' *Comet* not far off. At 4:00 a.m. Wise was seen over Fort Wayne, Indiana, with Brooks a considerable distance to the south. At 7:00 a.m., the balloon was heading due east over Fremont, Ohio, with no sign of the *Comet*. At 7:30 a.m., it was over Sandusky, Ohio, and the name *Atlantic* on its side was clearly visible to the local residents; the balloonists tossed papers overboard, but they fell into Lake Erie. At 9:30 a.m., the balloon was over Fairport, Ohio. At 11:30 a.m., it was near Dunville, Canada. At 12:35 p.m., it was over Niagara Falls, the last reported sighting before the voyage ended.[78]

Counter-currents probably slowed their progress in the early stages of the flight, for it took the balloonists over six hours to reach

This old lithograph also is inaccurate — the crew had jettisoned the lifeboat before landing in a strong gale in upstate New York.

Pana, Illinois, only 93 miles from St. Louis.[79] In the next six and one-half hours, their pace increased considerably as they traveled the 300 miles to Sandusky, Ohio.[80] Continuing at a rapid clip, the *Atlantic* crossed Lake Erie lengthwise, 250 miles in three hours.[81] John Wise found this part "the most monotonous of the whole voyage," but at times they descended close to the water and hailed several boats, just as they had greeted townsmen on land.[82]

New York City was their intended destination, but by the time they were over Lake Erie, they realized that they had been blown too far to the north. Gager suggested that they land near Rochester and that he and Hyde get off and take the mail to New York, while Wise and La Mountain flew on in an attempt to reach Boston or Portland.[83]

When they tried to land, however, they were caught up in a violent gale and swept out over Lake Ontario. In a frantic effort to gain altitude, the four men began tossing their equipment overboard:

blankets, coats, food, navigating instruments, papers, the express pouch,[84] and everything else expendable. John Wise suggested that they swamp the balloon and take the chance of being rescued by a passing ship.[85] The other three, however, preferred to remain in the air, so all four took positions in the wicker basket and they jettisoned the lifeboat.[86]

After sweeping over the lake for fifty miles at a speed in excess of one hundred miles per hour,[87] they were carried ashore by the wind and into a forest. The balloonists tossed out their grappling hook, but because of the high velocity of the *Atlantic,* its three tines were broken off one by one as the anchor bounced against the trees. The balloon went crashing through the woods for more than a mile before its netting was completely torn off and the bag itself punctured, leaving the four men suspended in the wicker basket twenty feet above the ground. Miraculously, no one was seriously hurt, and only La Mountain suffered slight bruises.[88] "Thus ended the greatest balloon voyage that was ever made," John Wise later exulted.[89]

The flight of the *Atlantic* was terminated on the estate of Truman O. Whitney, near Sackett's Harbor in the township of Henderson, Jefferson County, New York, at 2:20 p.m., by John La Mountain's watch, July 2, 1859.[90] The duration of the voyage was 19 hours and 40 minutes.[91] The distance, however, is variously cited as 804,[92] 822,[93] 870,[94] 900-1,200,[95] 1,000,[96] 1,120,[97] 1,150,[98] and 1,200 miles.[99] These differences are caused in part by the confusion between distance in a straight airline and distance along the actual twisting course of flight. The lower figures undoubtedly refer to the airline, while the higher ones refer to the course as actually traveled. The official length of a balloon voyage is always reckoned as the shortest distance betwen the starting and landing points — the airline distance.[100] Hence, perhaps the most accurate figures on the distance of John Wise's flight are: 826 miles in an airline and 1,150 miles in all.[101]

In any event, the flight of the *Atlantic* set a new world's record. The longest previous distance was 480 miles, a mark set by England's Charles Green, with Robert Holland and Monck Mason, in a flight from London to Weilburg, Germany, in 18 hours, November 7-8, 1836.[102] John Wise's record of 826 miles stood for 41 years until it was broken by Count Henry de la Vaulx in a flight from Paris to Korostycheff, Russia, 1,193 miles in 35 hours and 45 minutes, October 8-10, 1900.[103]

The purpose of the St. Louis-Henderson voyage was to demonstrate what Wise already knew, "that in our latitude, and over the breadth of the temperate zone, there exists an airstream from west to east.''[104] He considered the flight an eminent success, marred only by imperfections in machinery, rather than in scientific calculations.[105]

The *Daily Missouri Republican* glowed in its praise for Wise, La Mountain, Gager, and Hyde:

> They have done a deed which will render their names immortal in the annals of science, even if they intended to stop here; but when it is considered that this is only the first of a series of more startling adventures — such as crossing from the Pacific to the Atlantic seaboard — then sailing over the Atlantic Ocean, and lastly, a voyage around the world, the affair begins to assume an unparalleled grandeur.[106]

Although none of these predictions ever materialized, John Wise never abandoned his dream of crossing the Atlantic by balloon.

On July 30, 1859, Wise returned to St. Louis with his son Charles. They made a balloon ascension at 11:00 a.m. that day, took measurements with their barometer and thermometer, and landed thirty miles northeast of St. Louis at 1:20 p.m., when a rain squall forced them down. As were almost all of John Wise's flights, it was for scientific purposes, rather than for pure pleasure.[107]

During the Civil War, John Wise served in Thaddeus Sobieski Constantine Lowe's Balloon Corps of the Army of the Potomac. Secretary of War Simon Cameron had invited him to join the unit, and the Pennsylvania aeronaut made many reconnaissance observations for the infantry and artillery, notably at Bull Run.[108]

After the war, Wise continued in his profession and made several more ascensions from various points in the country. In the summer of 1873, he decided to attempt a flight across the Atlantic. In collaboration with a young Pennsylvania balloonist, Washington H. Donaldson, he sought monetary backing for his venture. The publishers of a New York newspaper, the *Daily Illustrated Graphic,* agreed to finance the flight and signed a contract with the aeronauts on June 27, 1873.[109] At Wise's direction, a muslin balloon was built, 160 feet in height, including the basket and lifeboat, with a capacity of 400,000 cubic feet of gas and a lifting power of 14,000 pounds.[110] Wise, however, had a quarrel with the newspaper publishers, and the balloon started its voyage to Europe with only Washington H. Donaldson, pilot; George A. Lunt, navigator; and Alfred Ford, newspaperman and passenger, aboard.[111]

The argument was perhaps a fortunate one for the Lancaster balloonist, for the gigantic balloon, *The Daily Graphic,* crashed at New Canaan, Connecticut, 41 miles from New York City, and the project was abandoned.[112]

St. Louis was again the starting point for a flight by John Wise when, at the age of 71, he made his final voyage. At 5:00 p.m. Sunday afternoon, September 28, 1879, he began his 463rd ascension, from Lindell Park, "in the interests of meteorological science."[113] With him in the balloon *Pathfinder* was George Burr, the receiving teller at the St. Louis National Bank. Burr was a young novice who had made only one previous balloon flight.[114] The voyage boded ill from the start, for as the *Pathfinder* rose from the small clearing, its basket crashed violently against a tree and nearly spilled out the two occupants;[115] and as the crowd rushed towards the balloon, Wise had to cut loose the 1,500-foot drag rope because a number of people had taken hold of it.[116] They recovered from their near disaster, however, and soon disappeared over the horizon.

By Wednesday morning, October 1, no word had been received from the *Pathfinder* and the popular conversation was, "Have they heard from the balloonists? Nothing yet. Things begin to look serious."[117] A few reports did, however, filter back to St. Louis. On Sunday evening at 11:05, a balloon heading northeast was sighted by the night telegrapher at Miller's Station, 130 miles from Chicago on the shore of Lake Michigan; it might have been the *Pathfinder*.[118] On Monday morning, September 29, advertisements issued by W.A. Kendall, the assistant land commissioner of St. Louis, were found at Carlinville, Illinois. In the margin of each leaflet was written, "Dropped from Prof. Wise's transcontinental balloon, the Pathfinder."[119] On Wednesday, a farmer near Girard, Illinois, 73 miles from St. Louis, found a number of "Iron Mountain Railroad circulars," which Wise was known to have carried.[120]

By Friday, October 3, the report from Miller's Station was discounted, and the prevalent belief was that the two balloonists had landed within 100 miles of St. Louis. John Wise had had little confidence in the *Pathfinder,* for it was small and fragile. He was reported to have said to George Burr before the flight,

> If only one man can go, I will be that man; if two can go, you will be the other one; but I would rather leave you behind. I am old enough now to die: you are young enough to live many years.[121]

On Saturday, October 4, John Wise Jr., the grandson of the veteran balloonist, led an exploring party from St. Louis through the Girard and Macoupin County, Illinois, area. Although they spent the weekend searching in vain, the young Wise concluded optimistically that the missing balloonists were alive and safe in upper Michigan or Canada.[122]

On October 7, Louis Faber, an engineer on the Lake Shore and Michigan Southern Railroad, reported that while taking on water at Miller's Station, he and his fireman, John Rulla, sighted a balloon heading northeast toward Lake Michigan at 11:00 p.m. Sunday, September 28. This evidence confirmed the earlier report of the station telegrapher. "It was undoubtedly the Wise balloon."[123]

Rumors and theories continued to spread through the city for the next several days, but no certain evidence was found until October 24, 1879. On that afternoon, the body of a man was washed up on the southern shore of Lake Michigan, near Toleston, Indiana. Because of the decomposition and bruises, the body was unrecognizable. From the clothes and sleeve buttons initialed "G.B.," however, William E. Burr Jr. identified the dead man as his brother, George Burr, the companion of John Wise.[124] It was theorized that an accident had probably happened soon after the balloonists were over the lake, for its waters moved very slowly, and an object in the middle might not reach the shore for a year. John Wise had probably tried to land the *Pathfinder* before they reached Lake Michigan. When he expelled hydrogen from the balloon and began to descend, the brisk wind carried them out over the lake. In an attempt to gain altitude, the two men jettisoned what ballast they had; but they had let out too much gas, and the balloon sank, caught in the waters, and went down. The exact cause was a mystery, for there were no witnesses.[125] The body of John Wise himself was never found.[126] ". . . by his untimely death the country [lost] the man who [had] done more than any other American to advance the cause of aerial navigation."[127]

Balloon ascensions continued in St. Louis through the nineteenth century, and many were made from Von Der Ahe baseball park, as was one in 1890,[128] but none were so grand or so memorable as those of John Wise.

In addition to making individual private ascensions, many aeronauts also hired themselves out and gave demonstrations of their prowess at fairs, expositions, and carnivals. At the seventeenth annual St. Louis Exposition, which opened at the St. Louis Coliseum and Music Hall on September 17, 1900, Carl E. Myers exhibited his "sky cycle" and "electric airship."[129] The more successful of the two machines, the "sky cycle," was an elongated oiled silk balloon to which was attached a framework and bicycle seat on which the operator sat and manipulated pedals with his hands and feet, turning a "large white screw-like rudder" which propelled the machine through the air.[130]

On the opening night of the Exposition, he pedaled his "sky cycle" at a height of eight to ten feet above the arena floor for fifteen minutes "to the wonder and delight of the thousands of spectators," and then followed with a demonstration of his "electric airship."[131] The flights of Carl Myers were one of the four major attractions of the Exposition, which was essentially a display of merchants and manufacturers. Myers gave his performances four times a day, in rotation with the three other principal demonstrations: "Seymour's Famous 1st Regiment Band," "Hopkins' High-Class Vaudeville," and the "Electric Fountain."[132] As an added feature, his daughter, Bessie E. Myers, also piloted the machines, much to the delight of the crowd.[133]

The exhibitions of Carl Myers marked the beginning of a new century and a new era for aeronautics in St. Louis — the attempt at controlled flight. The nineteenth century had been one of free ballooning, with John Wise as its master. St. Louis would soon become one of the foremost centers of that sport in the United States and the entire world. The city owes much to John Wise for gaining its initial eminence in that area. The *Daily Missouri Republican* was true to the mark when it said of his 1859 flight:

> Under its auspices the name of our city, St. Louis, will ring from shore to shore of the continent and also of Europe.[134]

III
The Louisiana Purchase
Exposition, 1904

CONTROLLED FLIGHT was first demonstrated in St. Louis in 1904 by the airships which performed at the Louisiana Purchase Exposition, commonly known as the World's Fair. Dirigibles, however, were not a new phenomenon. Efforts to steer balloons were undertaken soon after the Montgolfiers' invention came into being.[1] But it was not until September 24, 1852, that "the first successful attempt to propel and direct a flying machine with an engine" was achieved.[2] The man who performed this feat was Henri Griffard of France. He designed a compact, single-cylinder, three-horsepower steam engine driving a three-bladed propeller. This was slung under an 88,000-cubic-foot, cigar-shaped balloon 144 feet long and 40 feet in diameter. He made several ascents and attained a top speed of seven miles per hour in still air.[3]

In 1865, Paul Hanlein of Germany used a coal-gas combustion engine to power his semi-rigid, elongated balloon.[4] Nineteen years later, Charles Renard and Arthur Krebs flew a closed circuit with the electrically propelled *La France* on August 9, 1884.[5] They used a nine-horsepower engine of 1,174 pounds, and at that time "a motor weighing only 130-4/9 pounds per horse power was . . . unprecedented."[6]

Primitive efforts continued spasmodically throughout the second half of the nineteenth century until a brilliant young Brazilian,

Photocopy by Gregory M. Franzwa

Alberto Santos-Dumont.

Alberto Santos-Dumont, became "the first to build and fly an airship in controlled, sustained flight."[7] He ascended in his airship *Number 1* from the Zoological Gardens in Paris on September 20, 1898, and rose to 1,500 feet in an impressive flight over the city.[8] In October 1901, Santos-Dumont again stunned Paris when he won the coveted Deutsch Prize of $20,000 for a round-trip flight of seven miles from St. Cloud to the Eiffel Tower within thirty minutes. After seven failures in six different airships, he piloted his *Number 6* around the course in 29 minutes and 30 seconds, averaging 14½ miles per hour.[9] When he came to St. Louis in 1904, there was universal expectation that he would be the outstanding aviator at the fair.

While Santos-Dumont was perfecting the semi-rigid airship in France, Count Ferdinand von Zeppelin, a lieutenant general in the German cavalry, built "the first rigid dirigible airship," a huge, 420-foot, linen-and-silk balloon stretched over an aluminum framework, and successfully flew it for twenty minutes on July 2, 1900, over Lake Constance on the German-Swiss border.[10] His interest in aeronautics had been awakened in in 1862 when, as an official observer from the Prussian army in the ranks of Abraham Lincoln during the Civil War, he witnessed the achievements of Thaddeus Lowe's Balloon Corps in directing artillery fire.[11] Count von Zeppelin's own success in the early years of the twentieth century was of such significance that his name was given to the class of gigantic rigid airships produced by Germany, Great Britain, and the United States over the following four decades.

Shortly after the spectacular demonstrations of Santos-Dumont and von Zeppelin on the continent, successful dirigibles were developed in the United States. Although there is some evidence that A. Leo Stevens of New York built and flew the first motor-driven, navigable airship in America in 1900,[12] and that Dr. August Greth of San Francisco made a successful airship flight on October 18, 1903,[13] the man generally credited with having built America's first truly practical airship was Captain Thomas Scott Baldwin.[14] Born in Quincy, Illinois, on June 30, 1860, Baldwin grew up as an acrobat in George De Haven's traveling circus.[15] Having turned to aerial activities at an early age, he distinguished himself by making America's first parachute jump from a balloon at Golden Gate Park, San Francisco, in 1887.[16] After performing numerous balloon exhibitions throughout the world in the 1880s and 1890s, he became interested in the idea of controlled flight. By 1903, he had constructed a semi-rigid, cigar-shaped balloon, but was still in need of a motor. In Los Angeles that summer, he came upon a motorcycle with an impressive-looking, two-cylinder, five-horsepower engine, produced by the Glenn H. Curtiss Manufacturing Company of Hammondsport, New York.[17] At that time, the later-celebrated aviator had no interest in flying, but was content to build and race motorcycles. (In 1908, Curtiss set the world's speed record for motorcycles over a measured mile course — a startling 136 miles per hour.)[18]

Baldwin persuaded Curtiss to build a motor for his airship, and by the summer of 1904, he was ready for a trial flight. On August 3, 1904, Captain Baldwin made a test run in his *California Arrow* at Oakland.

> For the first time in the United States a man ascended in a lighter-than-air craft, sailed along a predetermined course and returned to the point from which he started, while maintaining complete control of the craft throughout the flight.[19]

Because of the outstanding nature of the experiments of Baldwin, von Zeppelin, and Santos-Dumont, the officials of the Louisiana Purchase Exposition Company determined that such exploits should play a large part at the St. Louis fair in 1904.

As the one-hundredth anniversary of the Louisiana Purchase of 1803 approached, there came to be a popular appeal for a World's Fair to be held in some city within the purchase territory in commemoration of its centennial. At a meeting at the Southern Hotel in St. Louis on January 10, 1899, 84 delegates from the 14 states of the Louisiana Purchase territory came together to choose a site for the World's Fair to be held in 1903. By a vote of 76-8, St. Louis was selected. At the end of the roll call, moreover, the eight Louisiana dissenters, who had supported New Orleans, moved to make the decision unanimous.[20]

On March 12, 1901, the Louisiana Purchase Exposition Company, instituted to organize and manage the fair, was incorporated by the State of Missouri, and early in April 1901, 93 directors were elected.[21] On May 2, 1901, these directors held their first meeting and elected officers for the company. Former Governor David R. Francis was chosen president; with a secretary, treasurer, general counsel and eight vice presidents to assist him.[22]

The fair was to be financed in three principal ways. The exposition company was to raise $10,000,000, half by popular subscription among the people of St. Louis and half by municipal bonds issued by the city. In addition, Congress would appropriate the sum of $5,000,000 on condition that the St. Louis officials had raised the initial $10,000,000 of their own accord.[23] On February 6, 1901, the Exposition Company presented proof to the Secretary of the Treasury that it had secured the specified amount,[24] and Congress responded by enacting H.R. 9829, which bore the massive title,

> A bill to provide for celebrating the one hundredth anniversary of the purchase of the Louisiana territory by the United States by holding an international exhibition of arts, industries, manufactures, and the products of the soil, mine, forest, and sea, in the city of St. Louis, in the State of Missouri.[25]

The bill was passed by the House of Representatives on February 18, 1901, by a vote of 190 yeas, 42 nays, 14 answering ''present,'' and 107 not voting.[26] It was passed by the Senate by a voice vote on February 23,[27] and after conferences by the Senate and the House with some slight amendments, the act was signed by President William McKinley on March 3, 1901.[28] According to its provisions, a nine-member Louisiana Purchase Exposition Commission was set up to supervise the fair and make reports to the government as to its activities. The act also carried an appropriation from the treasury of $5,000,000,

> to aid in carrying forward such exposition, to pay the salaries of the members and the secretary of the national commission herein authorized, and such other necessary expenses as may be incurred by said commission in the discharge of its duties in connection with said exposition, [provided that no part of the $5,000,000 be used

until the entire $10,000,000 raised by the Louisiana Purchase Exposition Company is expended (except for the payment of the Commission salaries)].[29]

Thus, the Louisiana Purchase Exposition Company obtained $15,000,000 to support its endeavor. "It is one of the coincidences that the amount secured in advance for the celebration of this Centennial, is exactly what was paid for the Territory."[30]

With financial problems solved, fair officials turned to the question of a proper site within the city on which to hold the exposition. On June 28, 1901, the members of the Exposition Commission unanimously approved Forest Park as the best possible location.[31] The commission decided to use 657.36 acres in the western half of the park, plus 108.9 acres leased from Washington University, along with some 500 acres from ten other tracts, bringing the total fair area to 1,271.76 acres.[32] The total area of the four largest expositions previously held in the United States — the Centennial at Philadelphia, the World's Columbian at Chicago, the Trans-Mississippi at Omaha, and the Pan-American at Buffalo — was 1,319 acres, only a few more than that within the World's Fair grounds at St. Louis.[33] Everything pointed to an exposition that the world would not soon forget.

The theme of the Louisiana Purchase Exposition was to be "man in his full twentieth century development."[34] To this end, sixteen principal departments were set up under Frederick J.V. Skiff, director of exhibits. They were: Art, Education, Liberal Arts, Manufactures, Machinery, Electricity, Transportation, Agriculture, Horticulture, Forestry, Mines and Metallurgy, Fish and Game, Anthropology, Social Economy, Physical Culture, and Livestock.[35] In addition to these major areas, a number of special, corelated sections were established. Among these was Aeronautics.

> The exposition management felt that the time was ripe to make a signal effort in the direction of stimulating development in aerial navigation and particularly to definitely demonstrate for the information of the world, what progress had been made in this direction, and, if possible, what the immediate future might promise.[36]

Acting on a plan enunciated by F.J.V. Skiff, the directors of the Exposition Company appropriated $200,000 for aeronautic events, an unprecedented amount.[37] Of this, $100,000 was to be a grand prize "for aeronautic achievement considerably beyond anything yet attained;" $50,000 was reserved for lesser prizes; and $50,000 was set apart for other expenses.[38] A special committee, made up of two members of the board of directors of the Exposition Company, Charles W. Knapp and Nathan Frank, was organized to supervise the affairs of the Aeronautics Section, the conduct of which was placed under the general direction of Willard A. Smith, chief of the Department of Transportation Exhibits.[39] Carl E. Myers, an experienced balloonist and inventor from Frankfort, New York, was named Superintendent of Aeronautics.[40]

In order to formulate rules for the aerial contests, the officials of the exposition summoned to St. Louis a panel of world-renowned experts in aeronautics. On April 21, 1902, they met and drafted a preliminary set of rules. Present were: Skiff, Smith, Knapp and Frank of the Exposition Company; Alberto Santos-Dumont, the most celebrated aeronaut in the world; Professor A. Lawrence Rotch, a noted meteorologist from the Blue Hill Observatory of Hyde Park, Massachusetts; Charles D. Mosher, a New York yacht builder; Robert Moore of St. Louis, president of the American Society of Civil Engineers; a Professor S. Wilkins of the University of Alabama; Professor Calvin M. Woodward of the engineering department of Washington University; and Emmanuel Aime, secretary of the Paris Aero Club.[41] Two prominent American airmen, Octave Chanute and Samuel Pierpont Langley, both of whom were currently experimenting with heavier-than-air craft, were unable to attend the conference, but were later consulted.[42] Langley even told Skiff confidentially that he was interested in competing for the grand prize and might bring his celebrated "Aerodrome" to St. Louis.[43]

After discussing the matter for two days, the advisory committee sent a tentative draft to the Aero Clubs of Paris, London, Berlin, and Vienna for suggestions and modifications.[44] Alberto Santos-Dumont was so elated at the prospect of a $100,000 event that he declared: "I expect that at least 150 airships will be entered when the rules and conditions of the contest are made known."[45] The ensuing months, however, did not bear out his optimism. After many revisions, the rules were finally published, at least for the major contests, by the *St. Louis Republic* on September 4, 1904.[46] They embraced eight events for airships, "flying machines," gliders and balloons:

1) Grand Prize Contest — this was the major event of the exposition and was open to airships and "flying machines" of any description. Contestants had to make three flights over a prescribed L-shaped course, with legs of five and ten miles in length, marked by captive balloons. Each aeronaut could choose his own days for his trials, but he had to complete all three flights at an average speed of twenty miles per hour, the time being clocked by an inter-

national jury from takeoff to touchdown, and he had to land within fifty yards of the starting point without injury to himself or his machine. All trials had to be completed by September 30, 1904. As a prerequisite, each entrant must first have made a flight of one mile in length in order to qualify for the contest. The winner, if any, was to receive the grand prize of $100,000. In addition, there were four other prizes of $3,500, $3,000, $2,000, and $1,500 for second, third, fourth and fifth places respectively, on condition that each winner had made three trials and had attained a speed of at least ten miles per hour.

2) Pilotless Flying Machine Contest — a prize of $2,500 was offered for a pilotless flying machine which would make a one-mile flight along a straight course and return to its starting point in the shortest time.

3) Glider Angle Contest — a prize of $2,000 was offered for "a gliding machine mounted by an operator which shall advance in a calm or against the wind at a vertical angle most acute with the horizon."

4) Glider Stability Contest — a prize of $1,000 was offered for the glider which exhibited the best automatic stability in a series of tests which included forty flights.

5) Altitude Contest — a prize of $5,000 was offered for the balloon, airship, or "aeronautical vessel" which attained the greatest altitude, after ascending from the exposition grounds.

6) Endurance Contest — a prize of $5,000 was offered for the balloon, airship, or "aeronautical vessel" which remained the longest time in the air, after ascending from the exposition grounds.

7) Long Distance Contest — a prize of $5,000 was offered for the balloon, airship, or "aeronautical vessel" which traveled the longest distance in any direction, after ascending from the exposition grounds.

8) Washington Monument Contest — a prize of $5,000 was offered for the balloon, airship, or "aeronautical vessel" which landed closest to the Washington Monument in Washington, D.C., on condition that it ascend from the exposition grounds, travel at least 500 miles, and land east of the western boundary of Ohio.[47]

The Exposition Company thus offered at least $135,000 in prizes for its major contests alone, with the grand prize being the most attractive of all. Transportation Chief Willard A. Smith felt that the aerial activities would be the highlight of the fair.

> No such prizes were ever offered before; and the provisions in the shape of grounds, buildings, free hydrogen-gas, etc., are on the

most liberal scale. If this concourse is not in all particulars a success it will be due to the aeronauts and not to the Exposition.[48]

A. Leo Stevens, however, a prominent New York aeronaut, dis-
agreed with him. To the editor of *The Scientific American* he wrote:

> I have decided not to enter the airship contest at St. Louis. The
> speed expected is too great. The man who enters this contest has
> everything to lose and nothing to gain.
>
> The rules call for a speed of at least 20 miles per hour. This is
> impossible. The prize is perfectly safe with the Exposition Com-
> pany.
>
> I think the rules might have been modified just a little. For in-
> stance, the man making best time should be allowed to take first
> prize, second man second prize, third man third prize. There
> would then be something in sight.[49]

Time was to bear out Stevens more than Smith.

The intention of the planners of the Louisiana Purchase Exposition had been to open the fair on April 30, 1903, the centennial of
the signing of the purchase agreement. However, because many of
the pavilions, both domestic and foreign, could not be completed in
time, the opening of the exposition was postponed for one year.[50]
President Theodore Roosevelt did dedicate many of the completed
buildings on April 30, 1903, and a suitable centennial celebration
took place during the following three days.[51]

The necessary construction was completed in the ensuing months
and the exposition opened its doors one year later. President Roosevelt touched a golden telegraph key in Washington, D.C. at precisely 1:14:30 p.m. Eastern time (14½ minutes late), April 30, 1904,
to close electrical circuits and initiate the activities of the fair.[52]

> President Roosevelt's signal reached the President of the Expo-
> sition, and as the latter lifted up his hands and declared the Expo-
> sition open ten thousand flags fluttered from their masts, the
> fountains shot their spray into the air and from the caverns under
> Festival Hall the waters leaped and sent their roaring torrents
> down the cascades, the whirr of mighty machinery became the
> song of hundreds of motors and engines, two hundred thousand
> voices and scores of bands made the welkin ring, and the greatest
> of universal expositions was open.[53]

In addition to the scheduled contests, the exposition management
provided two continuous aeronautic features. The first was a display of aerial artifacts at the Transportation Building.

> The exhibit includes everything appertaining to airship construc-
> tion, methods of generating gases, and means for inflating. Then
> there are examples of dirigible balloons, aeroplanes, aerodromes,
> propellors of various shaped balloons, parachutes, landing de-

vices, instruments used in the art, and in fact samples of everything applicable to the science; truly an exposition in itself and one of unexampled interest.[54]

The second permanent attraction was a captive balloon 12,000 cubic feet in capacity, attached to a cable three-fourths of an inch thick and 1,000 feet long. For a small admission charge, spectators were taken up in its basket and given a commanding view of the exposition grounds. The balloon was operated by George Tomlinson, Louis Winholz, and Earl Pearse, assisted by A. Roy Knabenshue, a young man who was to make the most outstanding contribution to the aeronautic events of the fair,[55] as well as Harry Eugene Honeywell, a Spanish-American War veteran who would later become one of St. Louis' most celebrated balloonists.[56]

After the contest rules had been sufficiently publicized, many prospective aeronauts entered their names for the competition.

> Replies were received from 97 persons and companies. Of these, 44 designated their apparatus as "air ships;" 23 as "aeroplanes;" 3 as "flying machines;" 10 as "balloons;" 12 as "kites;" and 1 as "gliding machine." Finally, eight parties paid an entry fee of $250 for the grand contest [for the $100,000]. Two of these fees were returned when the entrants stated they paid under a misapprehension of the rules, while two other fees were returned when the apparatus of the contestants did not meet with the regulations.[57]

In order to accommodate the aerial exhibitors, an "Aeronautic Concourse" was prepared. A special area of approximately fourteen acres was set aside and enclosed by a thirty-foot fence. The lower twelve feet was an airtight wooden barrier against the wind, while the upper eighteen was of lattice work, also intended to break the force of the wind. Situated in the southeast corner of the enclosure were two interconnected airship sheds, each 180 feet long, 40 feet wide, and 30 feet high, with a twenty-foot-wide lean-to for storage and repairs running along one side of the dual hangar.[58] The exposition officials also provided an unlimited amount of free hydrogen for the contestants from a gas plant at the concourse.[59]

The distinction of being the first formal entrant in the aerial contests of the St. Louis World's Fair belongs to Gustave Whitehead of Bridgeport, Connecticut. By February 1902, he had paid his entrance fee and was making improvements on his "aeroplane flying machine," a bamboo-and-silk affair sixteen feet long, three feet wide, and three feet high. It weighed 280 pounds and was powered by a twenty-horsepower engine which operated two massive wings in bird-like fashion. "This machine, last June [1901], with an opera-

tor on board, made a safe and successful flight to a distance of one and one-half miles."[60] If this report is correct, then history has illegitimately acclaimed the Wright brothers, who made their first sustained, powered flights on December 17, 1903.

Another somewhat less promising entrant was the "Dillon-Gregg Airship," a huge metallic cylinder with a capacity of 21,000 cubic feet of gas. It was 80 feet long, 20 feet in diameter, and was said to have a lifting power of 1,500 pounds. Patented in the United States, Great Britain, Germany, France, Belgium, and Canada, it was advertised as,

> pronounced by practical mechanics and engineers the most perfect system of propulsion as applied to aerial navigation, obtaining a maximum of power and displacement, requiring a minimum of weight in its construction.[61]

The first of the contestants to appear on the exposition grounds was Marcellus McGarry of Memphis, Missouri, who arrived on May 23, 1904, with his hydrogen airship.[62] By that time, however, the officials and the public at large were looking to Alberto Santos-Dumont to provide the majority of the aerial thrills.

The young South American, whose exploits were legendary, had built his *Number 7* airship in 1902 with the specific intention of winning the grand prize of $100,000 with it. This racer was 164 feet long, 26¼ feet in diameter, and had a capacity of 44,500 cubic feet of hydrogen. It was powered by a sixty-horsepower Clement engine, driving two 16½-foot propellers — one at the bow and the other at the stern of the frame.[63] He was undoubtedly the man to beat, particularly in view of his past successes.

On May 16, 1904, however, the Exposition Committee on Aeronautics was thrown into consternation when Santos-Dumont cabled from Paris:

> Lost sixty horse power engine. Only able to get forty. Airship tried yesterday. Only goes less than twenty miles [per hour]. Cannot race until speed condition is cut down to fifteen miles per hour.[64]

The exposition officials hardly wanted to lose their star performer, so after a hasty conference, Transportation chief Willard Smith sent Santos-Dumont their answer:

> Rules changed. Prize of $50,000 is to be awarded if a speed of fifteen miles an hour is attained; $75,000 if of eighteen miles;

George J. Herwig Collection

The captive balloon at the St. Louis World's Fair hoisted paying customers on short flights throughout the duration of the exposition.

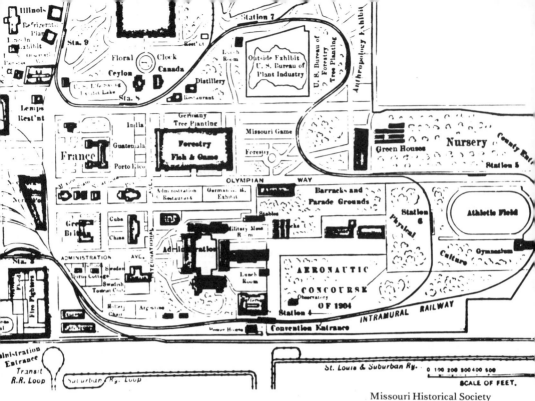

The Aeronautical Concourse of the World's Fair, where aviation history was made, was on the south side of present Millbrook Boulevard, northwest of Washington University's Brookings Hall.

$100,000 if of twenty miles. The fifteen-mile prize will be $69,000, if the flight is effected in June.[65]

As an added inducement to the entrants, the management of the fair offered a bonus of $10,000 above the standing prizes if any contestant performed a successful flight at either of these three speeds before July 1.[66] Unless a minimum of fifteen miles per hour were attained, however, no prize would be awarded at any time.[67]

Santos-Dumont arrived in New York on June 17, 1904, with his three assistants: Chapin, Gerome, and André,[68] and on June 23 he was in St. Louis.[69] His first action was to try to persuade fair officials to alter the proposed course for the grand prize trials. He preferred a straightaway ten-mile route with only one turn, while existing rules had set a triangular course, with two, time-consuming turns.[70] The managers again acceded to his wishes and scheduled his first trial for July 4.[71] He had no time to capture the bonus money with a June flight, since it would take almost a week to assemble his ship.[72]

Number 7 arrived by rail from New York on June 26 in three large

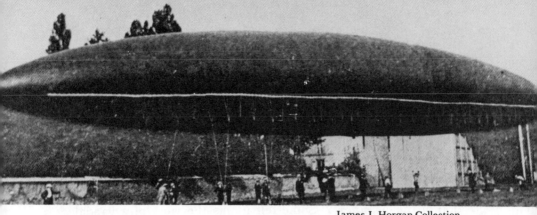

Alberto Santos-Dumont's ill-fated Number 7, *photographed prior to its destruction at the St. Louis World's Fair.*

eighteen-foot cases, each weighing 4,000 pounds.[73] The following day, Santos-Dumont directed the opening and inspection of the boxes in the presence of United States Customs officers. The hydrogen bag was made of two layers of silk cemented together, with two coats of varnish on the inside and five on the outside to make it airtight. The Brazilian intended to give it an additional coat before his trials. "It was found to be in perfect condition after the long trip from Paris."[74]

That night, "against the advice of the superintendent of aeroanautics,"[75] Santos-Dumont left the cover off the crate to let the air circulate around the envelope. At 7:00 a.m. the next day, June 28, one of the French mechanics discovered four, yard-long slashes in the gas bag. The envelope had been folded and the knife had penetrated through three pleats, making twelve rents in all.[76] A single guard had been posted in two shifts during the night. J.H. Peterson had been on duty from dusk until midnight, when he was relieved by Lucian T. Gilliam. Under questioning, Gilliam revealed that he had been absent twice during the night for short periods for cups of coffee.[77]

Police arrested, and later released, Charles F. Meyers of Warren, Massachusetts, who had been found loitering in the area, and the Exposition Company offered a reward of $1,000 for the culprit.[78] This was the third time that the Brazilian had suffered such a mishap. On May 27, 1902, his *Number 6* had been found slashed to ribbons in London, following a similar occurrence earlier that year.[79]

Santos-Dumont was understandably indignant, but he merely expressed the view that it was the work of some vandal and left for Paris July 1 without cooperating with the police or pressing the investigation.[80] He had told exposition officials that he would repair his ship and return by September, but on July 14, 1904, he told a London reporter at Le Havre that he did not intend to return to St. Louis:

> I never felt so angry and disappointed in my life. It would have taken at least two months to repair the damage, which means a loss of $8,000. I am of the opinion that the airship was wrecked by a crank and not by one of my rivals. [81]

Many theories were advanced to explain the mysterious destruction of the *Number 7*. Some felt it was the work of a vandal or a jealous rival, while among the Jefferson Guards at the exposition the rumor was prevalent that Santos-Dumont himself had slashed the envelope because he feared that he would fail in the severe trials and wished to save face. [82] It must be remembered, however, that the Brazilian airman had played a major role in formulating the rules for the contest, and that he later even succeeded in having the minimum speed lowered to a more manageable fifteen miles per hour.

A more scientific view was expressed by Wilfred de Fontvielle, who held that "the salt air encountered in crossing the ocean destroyed the elasticity of the silk and caused it to cut when unfolded." [83] This hypothesis, however, does not seem to take into consideration the nature of the rents involved and the fact that the envelope was found in perfect condition when it was inspected the day before its destruction.

The most incredible of all explanations came to light in 1907, when Harry E. Hayward, a St. Louis insurance agent, circulated a story said to have been given him by an Army officer stationed with the Jefferson Guards at the 1904 fair. He maintained that Santos-Dumont had been paid $200,000 by the Russian government to slash his own airship and withdraw from the competition in order that he might not fulfill a $1,000,000 contract with the Japanese government, with whom the Russians were then at war, to aid them with three airships for the seige of Port Arthur, on the condition that he successfully demonstrate his prowess by winning the grand prize at the St. Louis World's Fair. [84]

Rumors abounded for several years, but the bizarre event was never fully explained. It is most probable that a vandal was responsible for the destruction of *Number 7*.

The Louisiana Purchase Exposition had as yet seen no aerial activity of any nature, except for the daily operations of the captive balloon. This concession had its first test ascension on June 9, when Leon H. Archambault, a fifteen-year-old messenger boy, arose to a height of 700 feet and spoke to the crowd through a megaphone.[85]

The managers of the aeronautic events had hoped that Alberto Santos-Dumont would make his first flight on July 4, but inasmuch as he was forced to leave the fair prematurely, their hopes dimmed for a suitable aerial display for Independence Day. Hasty efforts, however, produced a balloon race that afternoon. Carl E. Myers, the Superintendent of Aeronautics at the exposition and an aerial enthusiast of long experience, made an ascension with his wife in his 20,000-cubic-foot balloon, while Tracy A. Tisdell arose in a 15,000-cubic-foot bag.[86]

Despite the light rain that was falling, both ascended briskly at 2:00 p.m. and fell off toward the southeast.[87] The showers increased to a downpour after they were aloft and consequently neither wanted to make an extensive flight, especially since the rain weighed down their balloons and caused the pilots to dispose of needed ballast. Tisdell landed in a meadow near Winstanley Park in East St. Louis, Illinois, fourteen miles from the fair grounds after seventy minutes in the air. The Myers craft descended on the rising slope of a farm near Collinsville, Illinois, twenty-two miles from St. Louis, after an hour and a half in the air. "It is an interesting fact that this is Mr. and Mrs. Myers' first ascension together, though they have been making ascensions for twenty-seven years."[88] The race was not much of a contest, and in fact, Carl Myers later revealed that it had not been a race at all, but that exposition officials had paid the balloonists a fee merely to ascend from the grounds and attract a crowd.[89]

On August 25, it was announced that Carl Myers had been relieved of his post as Superintendent of Aeronautics by Percy Hudson, assistant to Transportation chief Willard Smith.[90] A number of complaints had been registered against Myers by his subordinates and by the aeronauts on the field. It was claimed that he and his family illegally occupied rooms built on the fairgrounds at the expense of the exposition company. His unpleasantness of manner also alienated many of those who came in contact with him. In addition, many objected to his active participation in the aeronautic contests, particularly in the grand prize event, in which he was both an entrant and a judge. For these reasons, he was removed from his position of authority.[91]

His sudden dismissal, however, did not prevent him from executing a previously announced intention. On Liberal Arts Day, August 27, another dual balloon ascension took place. The contestants were Carl E. Myers, with a spherical balloon 8,000 feet in capacity, and

George Tomlinson, one of the operators of the captive balloon, with a 14,000-cubic-foot vehicle.[92] Both were aiming for the Washington Monument in Washington, D.C., and were competing for a prize of $5,000, on the condition that the winner travel at least 500 miles and land east of the western boundary of Ohio.[93]

Both started promptly at 5:00 p.m. from the Sunken Gardens in front of the Government Pavilion at the sound of a pistol shot signal. The wind carried each balloon westward, in spite of their destination. One spectator commented, "The race goes to the man who lands farthest east of Washington, Mo."[94] John Parkinson of 1219 Euclid Avenue in St. Louis had provided Tomlinson with three homing pigeons, to be released one at a time with notes on his location. By 5:00 a.m., August 28, all three had returned to their coops, but not one bore any message.[95]

Myers landed at 7:00 p.m. August 27, one mile west of St. Charles, Missouri, and only 22 miles west of the fairgrounds, farther away from his goal than when he had started. He was disappointed at not finding an eastward current and came down when he thought he saw Tomlinson land ahead of him.[96] The Syracuse balloonist, however, did discover the elusive eastward wind and sailed on through the night, landing at 5:00 p.m., August 28, seven miles southeast of Wyoming, Illinois, about 200 miles from St. Louis.[97] Neither man was eligible for the $5,000 prize, since neither had traveled 500 miles or landed east of the western border of Ohio; hence no prize was awarded and the contest remained open until November 1.[98]

On August 29, Carl Myers, undoubtedly bitter over his brusque removal from the post of Aeronautics Chief, announced that the two balloon "races" in which he had participated were in fact only hoaxes, for which payment had been made in advance. He declared that on the July 4 flight he had been merely a passenger and that his wife had acted as pilot and had received from the exposition management $250, which she divided with Tracy Tisdell. He also admitted that he and Tomlinson had been paid for their flight on August 27, but he refused to disclose the amount.[99]

Myers was a controversial figure at the World's Fair. In spite of his difficulties, he maintained his intention of competing for the grand prize. The vehicle he planned to use was his "Sky Cycle," which he had exhibited earlier in St. Louis at the exposition of 1900.[100] It was 49 feet long, with an aluminum frame suspended beneath it by a silk netting. The operator used his hands and feet to revolve pedals which turned the propeller.[101] He also brought with him his "Aerial Torpedo," a gas bag 25 feet in length, driven by an electric motor connected by wire to a switch on the ground, with which the operator directed the movements of the pilotless aircraft. "As a military vehicle it was intended to carry a bomb attached to the bottom of the framework exploded by a pre-set clockwork mechanism."[102] Despite his elaborate plans, Myers enjoyed only limited success at the fair.

On August 30, Willard A. Smith announced that eight contestants had paid $250 entrance fees for the grand prize airship race. They were: Charles Stiriz of New York City; S.M. Williams of San Francisco; Emry Davis and George Curtis of Gillespie, New York; Alva Reynolds of Los Angeles; J.C. Fremont McCauley of Fowler, Kansas; The Columbus Aerial Navigation Company of Columbus, Ohio; and Hippolyte François of St. Mande, near Paris, France.[103] In addition to these, a number of others had entered, but had not yet paid their fees.

To qualify for the supreme contest, each man had to give proof that he had made a previous flight of one mile. In addition, all had to complete their three trials for the $100,000 by September 30, at which time the contest ended. As of August 31, 1904, only two men in the United States, both San Franciscans, had qualified for the event — Captain Thomas Scott Baldwin and Dr. August Greth, both of whom had made several successful dirigible flights and both of whom had announced their intentions of competing for the grand prize.[104]

The first airship to perform at the Louisiana Purchase Exposition was operated by Thomas C. Benbow of Butte, Montana, who had arrived on the grounds on July 27, 1904.[105] His dirigible, known variously as the *Montana Butterfly*[106] or the *Montana Meteor,*[107] was a cigar-shaped bag sharply pointed at both ends with a gas capacity of 14,000 cubic feet and a length and diameter of 72 feet and 21 feet respectively. It was powered by a ten-horsepower gasoline motor which turned the four propellers attached to its light steel frame at 80 revolutions per minute. The balloon and framework weighed 270 pounds, and together with the weight of the engine (130 pounds), ballast (50 pounds), and Benbow himself (168 pounds), the entire apparatus in operation weighed 618 pounds.[108]

Shortly after 2:00 p.m. on September 6, Benbow boarded the *Meteor* in the presence of 1,000 paying spectators. Eight assistants held onto a 150-foot rope attached to the balloon, while the ship rose to a height of 125 feet and traveled for about 500 yards inside the concourse fence. It was only a captive ascension, for a slight breeze

Photocopy by Gregory M. Franzwa

Benbow's airship, Meteor, *is shown preparing for takeoff from the Aeronautical Concourse at the World's Fair. In the background is the pesky lattice fence, which managed to snag a number of the aircraft trying to sail over it.*

bothered Benbow and, in addition, he did not trust the lifting power of his ship. It was the first trial the exposition had witnessed and it marked the start of the airship activity at the fair.[109]

Two days after Benbow's demonstration, Captain Thomas Scott Baldwin arrived with his *California Arrow,* the airship destined to be the most successful of all at the St. Louis fair. This ship had a cigar-shaped, varnished Japanese silk envelope of 8,000 cubic feet capacity and was 53 feet long and 17 feet in diameter. Attached to it was a framework of spruce which in section formed an equilateral triangle, tapering to a point at both ends and braced by piano wire. Motion was provided by a two-cylinder, six-horsepower gasoline engine weighing 66 pounds. The total weight of the apparatus was 220 pounds, but the airship had a proven lifting power of 544 pounds and had attained a speed of twelve miles per hour in calm air.[110] Baldwin had been brought to St. Louis by the partnership of Dunnavant and Williams, who managed the "Over and Under the Sea" exhibit at the exposition. Under their auspices, he hoped to win the grand prize.[111]

To add to the international flavor of the contests, absent since the departure of Santos-Dumont, Francis Couteau, a French aeronaut, arrived on the grounds on September 17. His airship was a long, cigar-shaped bag, with a wooden carriage suspended beneath it, on which were mounted a powerful sixty-horsepower motor, the propeller, and the steering gear. Like the others, he was confident of capturing the $100,000.[112]

On the same day that Couteau arrived, William Avery of Chicago made the first heavier-than-air flight at the exposition.[113] He piloted a glider designed and built by Octave Chanute, the celebrated Chicago engineer and aviation enthusiast.[114] At 4:00 p.m. September 17, while two attendants ran alongside the machine to give it momentum, Avery rose to a height of five feet and sailed inside the Aeronautic Concourse for a distance of 166 yards.[115] He would later make several more flights in the stadium and the St. Louis plaza on the exposition grounds.

On September 28, ex-superintendent Carl Myers made news again when he prepared his "Aerial Torpedo" for flight at the Aeronautic Concourse. Controlled from the ground by a rheostat switch, the pilotless, hydrogen-filled balloon could rise, descend, go forward, backward, or sideways, or revolve on its axis while attaining a speed of twelve miles per hour. Myers predicted that it would revolutionize warfare if used to drop bombs on cities or army encampments.[116] In principle, his machine foreshadowed the weapons of a half-century later.

Although the deadline for the grand prize contest had been reached on September 30, the Exposition Company granted a one-month extension, in view of the fact that many contenders had arrived at the fair and were preparing for the flight, among them Hippolyte François of Paris and Alva L. Reynolds of Los Angeles.[117] All the minor contests, however, were allowed to lapse when their deadlines were reached.[118]

Alva Reynolds was the inventor of perhaps the most unorthodox "flying machine" displayed at the fair. His apparatus, called the *Man Angel,* consisted of a 3,000-cubic-foot gas bag and a framework by means of which he caused two large cambric wings to flap by manipulating levers with his hands and feet. The balloon was 30 feet long and 14 feet in diameter, and the span of the wings was 18 feet. The total weight of the machine was 250 pounds, and Reynolds anticipated optimistically that with it he could attain a speed of 20 miles per hour.[119] Like all muscle-operated ornithopters of this era, however, the *Man Angel* never made a sustained flight.

Hippolyte François, on the other hand, was the designer of a very promising airship. It was called the *Ville de St. Mande* in honor of the small French village near Paris, whose citizens had helped him build it.[120] The massive airship had a gas bag with a capacity of 65,000 cubic feet, 105 feet long and 35 feet in diameter. It was powered by a 28-horsepower motor which rested inside a framework weighing 1,474 pounds. The total weight of the airship approached two tons, by far the largest at the exposition.[121] The ship's electric motor was invented and manufactured by Prosper Lambert of Paris,[122] and on that account the airship was often referred to as the *Prosper Lambert*.[123]

While the hopeful aeronauts were readying their airships for trial, a two-day International Aeronautical Congress was held at Transportation Hall October 4-5, 1904.[124] There leading scientists and aeronauts from four countries came together, in the words of Professor C.M. Woodward of Washington University,

> to demonstrate that progress in aerial navigation was possible . . . [and] to learn, through the failure and experiments of others and a comparison of notes and results, that success cannot be hoped for except through careful study and scientific investigation.[125]

The congress opened at 10:00 a.m. October 4, and on the first day Lieutenant Colonel J.E. Capper of the British Fifth Army Balloon Corps sketched the progress of British developments in aviation. Transportation Superintendent Willard Smith then outlined the aeronautic events of the exposition; Professor A.F. Zahm of Washington, D.C., discussed air friction on the surfaces of aerial vessels; and Professor F.E. Niphur of Washington University of St. Louis read a paper entitled "Distribution of Wind Pressure on Plane Surfaces."[126] The following day, similar activities took place. Walter F. Ried of London, together with Carl E. Myers, discussed varnishes and balloon fabrics; Major B.F.S. Baden-Powell, president of the British Aeronautical Society, delivered a paper on "Kites and their Uses;" and a Captain von Tschudi of the German Army Balloon Corps sketched the progress of German aeronautics. After the fruitful two-day meeting, Loicq de Lobel, a member of the French Aeronautic Society, invited the congress to Paris for 1905.[127]

Instead of returning home, most of the international aeronautic experts remained on the grounds to witness, and in some cases to participate in, the aerial events. Most were on hand when William Avery made his first trials with Chanute's glider in the stadium on October 7, using his full equipment.[128] To launch himself into the air, the Chicago aviator mounted the glider on a small flatcar, which ran on a miniature railroad track about 100 feet long. One end of a long rope was attached to the glider and the other to a large drum, 400 feet away, which was powered by an electric motor. At Avery's

Photocopy by Gregory M. Franzwa

This glider was the only heavier-than-air machine to fly at the St. Louis World's Fair.

signal, the drum was set in motion and rapidly took up the slack in the rope. As the flatcar gained momentum, the glider raised itself into the air, the rope was released, and the machine sailed on.[129] Avery made three flights at the stadium on October 7. At 2:30 p.m. he took off, reached a height of 35 feet, and glided through the air for 175 feet. On his two other efforts, altitudes of 18 to 25 feet were reached and glides of 90 to 100 feet were attained.[130]

For the next two weeks, Avery made glides almost daily in the stadium. On October 25, however, he moved his equipment to the Plaza St. Louis because he felt he needed more room to maneuver.[131] At 3:00 p.m. October 26, he made his first trial of the biplane glider at the plaza. He reached a height of 30 feet when the rope, apparently defective, parted before his signal. The machine plunged to the ground, throwing Avery to the asphalt pavement and causing him to break his ankle.[132] His career at the fair was ended, but he had earned a creditable record. In all, William Avery made 46 flights in Octave Chanute's glider,[133] and he was the only man to fly a heavier-than-air machine at the exposition.

While Avery was making his glides at the stadium, another aeronautic event was taking place. This was kite flying, "the first contest of its kind that has ever been held."[134] According to the rules, the competition embraced two categories, based on altitude. In the first, contestants attempted to reach a height of 500 feet with an 800-foot string and maintain it for two hours, aiming at prizes of

$500, $300, and $250. In the second, contestants attempted to reach a height of one mile with a string of any length and maintain it for two hours, aiming at prizes of $800, $500, and $200.[135] The international jury, which would decide the winners, was made up of Professor C.M. Woodward of Washington University; Lieutenant Colonel J.E. Capper and Walter F. Ried of England; Professor Frank E. Niphur of Washington, D.C.; and Percy Hudson, Superintendent of Aeronautics.[136]

Heights were to be determined by means of trigonometry by spotters in the towers of the Administration Building and the Physical Culture Building who were to telephone the results to the field.[137] In the two contests there were nineteen entrants from three countries: Alexander Graham Bell, the noted inventor from Washington, D.C.; Thomas Scott Baldwin of San Francisco; William D. Marshall, J.N. Tatout, J.J. Lewis, Raymond Anglemire, Taylor Carroll, W.M. King, and J. Condon, all from St. Louis; Edward E. Harbert and Silas J. Coyne of Chicago; H.B. Bristol of Webster Groves, Missouri; A. Roy Knabenshue of Toledo, Ohio, who was later to excel in airship demonstrations; W.A. Eddy of Bayonne, New Jersey; C.S. Wardell and J.B. Wardell, a father-and-son team from Stamford, Connecticut; Carl E. Myers of Frankfort, New York; Major B.F.S. Baden-Powell of England; and an M. Crizuka of Japan.[138]

The Five Hundred Foot Contest began at 8:30 a.m. on October 17 and the Mile High Contest was held that afternoon. The judges, however, declared "no contest" for both events because of the unsatisfactory conditions and the widespread fouling. The two events were reflown on October 18 with a new rule: the contestants were each given positions 150 feet apart and were restricted to a radius of ten feet, under pain of disqualification.[139] In the Five Hundred Foot Contest there were 16 participants and only two mishaps. The kites of Major Baden-Powell and Carl Myers both broke away when their wires snapped. Baden-Powell's was soon recovered, but Myers' was not, so he offered $25 for its return. In the Mile High Contest there were nine entrants and one accident. Silas Coyne's wire broke at between 6,000 and 7,000 feet and the kite drifted out of sight; he offered a $5.00 reward for its recovery.[140]

On October 19, the international jury announced the winners. In the 500-foot class, sixteen-year-old J.B. Wardell of Stamford, Connecticut, who used a three-foot box kite, won first prize of $500. J.N. Tatout of St. Louis was second for $300; and H.B. Bristol of Webster Groves won third prize of $200. There was no winner in the Mile High class, since no one had attained that height. The three leaders were Silas J. Coyne at 3,751 feet, J.N. Tatout at 2,035 feet, and William King at 1,749 feet.[141]

In view of that fact, a number of participants petitioned the management to offer another trial of the Mile High Contest. The exposition officials acceded to their wishes, stipulating, however, that in place of cash prizes, medals of gold, silver, and bronze would be awarded to the winners.[142]

The kites of the eight entrants

Photocopy by Gregory M. Franzwa

Raymond Anglemire is shown testing his kite in the Aeronautical Concourse.

were sent up from the Plaza St. Louis at 2:00 p.m. on October 22, into a wind blowing at a brisk 20 to 25 miles per hour. Kites belonging to Eddy, Tatout, Bristol, and Lewis were torn away before they reached 400 feet. Raymond Anglemire's broke away only minutes before the two-hour time limit expired, while that belonging to Silas Coyne was lost a scant two minutes after the two-hour deadline arrived. Only the first four were eliminated, however, and those in contention at the finish were King, Harbert, Coyne, Anglemire, and Eddy (who had entered two kites).[143]

On October 25, Percy Hudson made public the results. William King of St. Louis, who used a three-foot-six-inch semi-aeroplane kite, won the gold medal with a height of 2,505 feet. Silas Coyne of Chicago won the silver medal with his altitude of 2,018 feet, and Raymond Anglemire of St. Louis reached 1,663 feet for the bronze medal. No one attained the magic height, but the contest was declared a success.[144]

In addition to these formal events, simple demonstrations of various types of kites were performed. Alexander Graham Bell exhibited his celebrated tetrahedral kite several times and on October 22 at the stadium, W.A. Eddy, himself a noted kite builder, flew Bell's invention and declared his intention of taking a picture of the fairgrounds with it.[145] Two Londoners, S.F. Cody[146] and Major Baden-Powell,[147] had each announced their intentions of demonstrating "man-carrying" kites, but their subsequent actions were not recorded.

Photocopy by Gregory M. Franzwa

Photocopy by Gregory M. Franzwa

Thomas Scott Baldwin, builder of the California Arrow. *At 210 pounds, he was too heavy to fly it.*

A. Roy Knabenshue of Toledo, destined to become the aeronautical hero of the St. Louis World's Fair.

As the kite contests were coming to a close, exhibitions of the airships were getting under way. The deadline for the $100,000 contest, which had been extended to October 31, was drawing near, however, with little hope of anyone winning the prize. Believing that airship flights would be of great interest even if they did not meet the formal conditions of the contest, the Exposition Company authorized contracts with several flyers to perform certain maneuvers in return for an undisclosed payment. The first of these contracts was with Thomas Scott Baldwin, whose *California Arrow* fulfilled the requirements in its first flight at the exposition on October 25.[148]

The *Arrow* was operated by a twenty-nine-year-old Toledo

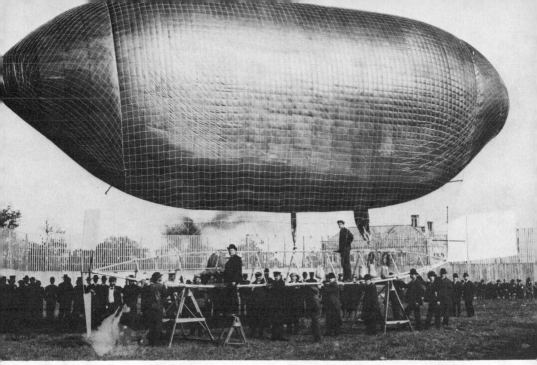

Thomas Scott Baldwin and A. Roy Knabenshue pose with the California Arrow *shortly before its historic flight. Baldwin is on the sawhorse, Knabenshue in the fuselage.*

balloonist, A. Roy Knabenshue, who had come to the fair "looking for adventure in the balloon line."[149] He soon got a job operating the the captive balloon, with which he performed a spectacular feat one Sunday in late October. He decided to make a dangerous slide down the three-quarter-inch hemp cable, citing two reasons for his intention: 1) to steel his nerves for the later career of aeronautic activities he had planned for himself, and 2) to gain added attention to aviation at the fair and perhaps induce the Exposition Company to pay him for a daily repetition of his stunt. With this in mind he ascended from the grounds while hanging onto the cable twenty feet below the basket of the captive balloon. At a height of 200 feet he began his slide, continuing down, with periodic stops, as the balloon rose to its full height of 1,000 feet. He wore no gloves, but instead bore the brunt of the friction on his heavy trousers and shoes. "At no time was I more than 200 feet high," he later wrote, "but I slid the full 1,000 feet of rope."[150] It was a thrilling demonstration, but the Exposition Company forbade further slides, deeming them "too hazardous."[151]

Knabenshue had taken no part in the development of the *Cali-*

A. Roy Knabenshue is at the controls during the first St. Louis dirigible flight — October 25, 1904.

fornia Arrow and had never before made an airship flight,[152] but he had one advantage over Thomas Scott Baldwin, the inventor of the dirigible, and that was his weight. While Baldwin weighed 210 pounds, Knabenshue weighed only 126. For this reason, the veteran San Franciscan allowed the novice from Toledo to make the flight in his place, when Knabenshue asked if he might make an ascension.[153]

At 1:52 p.m. October 25, the *California Arrow* arose from the Aeronautic Concourse into a wind of ten miles per hour. While tracing a huge figure "S" in the sky, his gasoline motor suddenly stopped as he was over the Transportation Building, and he could not get into position to restart it.[154] From that moment on, the flight continued as a normal free balloon ascension. The wind carried the *Arrow* eastward across the Mississippi River, and the airship landed at 3:23 p.m. near Chartrand School, three miles south of East St. Louis, Illinois, and fifteen miles from the exposition grounds.[155] Up to the point of the engine failure, A. Roy Knabenshue had "demonstrated the complete dirigibility of his airship," and had given St. Louis its first exhibition of controlled flight.[156]

The exposition officials were so pleased that they announced that special prizes would be awarded for subsequent airship flights.

> $500 in cash for each flight wherein the vessel sailed a distance of at least one mile from the aeronautic concourse and returned thereto with its own motive power.
>
> $250 in cash should the vessel cover a distance of at least one mile from the concourse under its own motive power and be unable to return thereto.[157]

On October 25, Superintendent of Aeronautics Hudson also announced that the deadline for the $100,000 contest had been extended once again, the new limit being November 15.[158]

The following day, the Santos-Dumont affair was brought to mind again when J.F. Osborne of 1715 Longfellow Boulevard in St. Louis announced that the airship on which he had worked all summer had been slashed by a vandal on October 20, just prior to its maiden flight. It had been left unattended in Osborne's workshop.[159] He was not the only local resident interested in the grand prize, for at least two other St. Louisans had prepared dirigibles.

J.M. O'Neall of 4422 Evans Avenue had invented a ship which was then built by L.C. Barlow of 412 South Sixth Street. It consisted of a 48-foot gas envelope to which was attached a pine framework 27 feet long, carrying the pilot's seat and a five-horsepower motor. O'Neall estimated that it would have a lifting power of 400 pounds and attain a speed of 35 to 40 miles per hour, but his success, if any, was not reported during the duration of the fair.[160]

A third hopeful St. Louisan was John Berry, who was sponsored by the Berry Aerial Navigation Company, whose directors were C.W. Laurel, J.A. Schilling, William Sutter, and Thomas W. Benoist, a man who was later to become a pioneer in the aircraft industry in St. Louis.[161] Berry's airship, the *St. Louis,* was peculiar in appearance and not at all like the conventional dirigibles of Baldwin, Benbow, and François. It consisted of a balloon of 22,000-

cubic-foot capacity which, because of its flattened appearance when inflated, resembled "two saucers placed edges together."[162] The 52-foot-long balloon was pierced at its center by a forty-foot mast of $3\frac{1}{2}$-inch brass tubing, through which ran a belt connecting the engine with two $3\frac{1}{2}$-foot basswood propellers, placed one below and one above the balloon. The engine and the mast revolved on a pivot in the basket, placed directly below the envelope, and in that manner, control and direction of the ship was achieved.[163] The directors of the Aerial Navigation Company had a difficult time in getting Berry to complete his airship, in view of the deadline for the $100,000 contest. They even brought suit against him, but the matter was settled out of court on October 29, and Berry soon had the *St. Louis* on the exposition grounds.[164]

Roy Knabenshue's success in his first flight with the *California Arrow* had spurred the other aeronauts into activity. On October 27, several thousand spectators paid an admission price of 25¢ to enter the concourse and see Thomas C. Benbow make his second attempt at flight. At 5:08 p.m. he ascended in his *Meteor,* but again it was only a captive trial, since his attendants held onto a stout rope attached to the ship. After lightening his airship by 100 pounds following his first flight, the Montana aeronaut traveled for about 3,000 feet inside the fence for nine minutes, but he still did not trust the lifting power of his vehicle enough to try a free flight.[165] It was only partially a success and did not qualify as a preliminary trial for the grand prize contest, but the crowd was pleased, even though the local press condemned Benbow for his "lack of nerve."[166]

The situation was much the same when the *Montana Meteor* made its third appearance on October 29 at 1:30 p.m. The warmth of the sun had expanded the gas in the envelope, so Benbow opened the vent to expel the excess. When he tried to ascend, however, he found that the balloon had lost too much lifting power and would not rise. Again, a large crowd had paid an admission fee to witness his failure.[167]

On October 31, the *California Arrow* showed how a real airship should perform. Captain Baldwin himself ascended at 2:00 p.m. while Knabenshue held onto the *Arrow* by its anchor rope. After letting off ballast, Baldwin called down to Knabenshue to release the rope. The noise of the engine and the cheering of the crowd, however, drowned out his voice and the order was not heard. As a result, the ship plunged suddenly downward at 2:02 p.m. and one of the aluminum propellers was broken as it hit the ground.[168] But repairs were speedily made, and the lighter Knabenshue eased the

Arrow into the air at 3:30 p.m. and made a flawless flight for 37 minutes over the exposition grounds.

> Sailing triumphantly through the air 2,000 feet above the World's Fair grounds, turning, circling, wheeling this way and that, with and against the wind, all doubts of the perfect dirigibility of the Baldwin airship were . . . removed.[169]

The young Ohio airman even released one of John Parkinson's carrier pigeons, which George Tomlinson had also used in his balloon flight on August 27. The message read: "I am now sailing over the World's Fair grounds. Time, 3:58."[170] This sparkling performance was the highlight of the Exposition. Aeronautics chief Percy Hudson said, "Knabenshue's flight vindicated the maintenance of an aeronautics department at the World's Fair."[171] The aeronaut himself added:

> Sailing an airship — such an airship, at any rate, as Tom Baldwin's Arrow — is play. It is the finest of all sports, and once on it, riding through the air high above the earth, with the vessel answering perfectly every move of the operator, you feel like you never want to come down.[172]

This flight eclipsed all previous American airship records, and Baldwin was immediately awarded the earlier-announced prize of $500 by the Exposition Company.[173]

On the following day, November 1, Knabenshue broke his own record by making a flight of 46 minutes over the exposition grounds, after ascending shortly before 2:00 p.m. At Baldwin's direction, he landed outside the concourse fence to avoid the crush of people inside. The *Arrow* was then guided over the barrier and "walked" to its shed.[174]

Because of the outstanding performance of the *California Arrow,* Knabenshue announced that he would try for a new world's distance record for airships. A fifteen-mile quadrangular course was laid out over the city:

> From the Aeronautic Concourse in a general northeasterly direction to the old water tower at East Grand avenue and North Twentieth street, thence in a general southeasterly direction to Eads bridge, thence in a general southwesterly direction to the Compton Park water, thence in a general northwesterly direction to the point of starting in the Aeronautic Concourse.[175]

At 2:06 p.m. on November 2, Roy Knabenshue took the *Arrow* into the air. At the last minute, Transportation chief Willard Smith had changed the course to a straightaway to the Compton Park reservoir, followed by a ten-mile junket over St. Louis County and a return to the concourse.[176]

The record sought, however, was not attained, for just as the aeronaut was above the Jefferson Guard headquarters, one of the valves of the gasoline engine fell off, disabling the ship and almost hitting a spectator.[177] Knabenshue called down to Percy Hudson to follow him by car, and the Aeronautics chief did his bidding, accompanied by Tom Baldwin and H.F. McGarvie, head of the Emergency Exploitation Committee at the fair. The *Arrow* landed at 2:35 p.m. in a cornfield a few miles west of the exposition grounds.

The engine was repaired and Knabenshue took off again at 3:10 p.m. However, the motor failed a second time over the fairgrounds and the wind carried the helpless ship northwest again into a potato patch seven miles from the grounds. The three men in the car sighted the drifting balloon and again followed it. The time was after 4:00 p.m. and the bag had lost a great deal of gas and ballast, so they attached three 300-foot ropes to the *Arrow* and towed it back by automobile. "It was like leading a pig to market, and it took the party four hours to make the journey to the fairgrounds."[178] Misfortune, however, followed misfortune, for when they were guiding the ship across a set of trolley wires outside the Aeronautic Concourse, their signals got confused and the ropes slipped from their grasp as the Arrow sailed off alone into the night.[179] At 8:00 the next morning, Jacob Wipke, a bartender on Clayton Road, found the airship undamaged on the farm of Henry Mildt in Fern Ridge, nine miles from the fairgrounds.

Baldwin retrieved and deflated the ship that afternoon and made plans for a record flight for November 5.[180] However, the flight never took place. After an unexplained dispute with exposition officials, Baldwin packed up the *Arrow* and shipped it to Los Angeles November 12.[181]

With A. Roy Knabenshue as its pilot, the little airship had enjoyed the greatest success of any aeronautic feature at the fair. Baldwin probably did not make any attempt for the grand prize in it because he felt that he could not attain the minimum speed of fifteen miles per hour with it. In any event, the *California Arrow* was the only truly successful dirigible at the fair, and it was a great loss to Captain Baldwin when it was destroyed in the San Francisco earthquake and fire of 1906.[182]

While A. Roy Knabenshue had been thrilling the exposition crowds, the other prospective pilots had been readying their airships to partake in the glory. T.C. Benbow attempted to make a flight on November 6, but Percy Hudson called out the exposition guards to prevent him, since it was a Sunday and the exposition

The Ville de St. Mande *was so immense it wouldn't fit in the hangar. A six-foot trench had to be dug for the fuselage.*

rules forbade airship flights when the fair was not open to the public. The Montana aeronaut said that he had been aware of the regulation, but wanted to make the ascension anyway because it was the anniversary of his first successful airship flight.[183]

Hippolyte François's airship seems to be in free flight above the Aeronautical Concourse — actually, it is tethered to a man on the ground.

Hippolyte François was also making preparations. His *Ville de St. Mande* was at that time the largest non-rigid airship ever built,[184] and because of its huge size, a trench 6 feet deep, 15 feet wide and 100 feet long had to be dug in the airship shed so that its great bulk could be housed.[185] François also had difficulty with the United States Customs officials, who demanded that he put up a $10,000 bond to ensure that the ship would be returned to its "bonded warehouse," the aerodrome.[186] The exposition managers, however, persuaded the Treasury officials to waive the bond in view of the special circumstances of his trip to America.[187] With the bulk of his problems solved, the French aeronaut made ready to take to the air. Just as he was preparing for flight, however, a leak was found in the gas bag and his first demonstration had to be postponed.[188]

While activity among the airships lagged, another aeronautic "first" was recorded at the exposition. On November 11, three men ascended in a balloon and performed the first successful demonstration of wireless telegraphy between the ground and the air in the United States.[189] They were Paul Knabenshue, the younger brother of the pilot of the *California Arrow;* A.W. McQueen, a wireless operator for the American De Forest Wireless Telegraph Company; and Will S. Forman, a reporter for the *St. Louis Globe-Democrat.* They left the exposition grounds at 3:15 p.m. in a thirty-foot balloon of 6,000-cubic-foot gas capacity. For an hour and a half, at heights varying from 1,400 feet to two miles, they received twenty messages from the station at the fairgrounds, the first of which read:

> W.S. Forman, Balloon: I congratulate the Globe-Democrat on having a reporter present to see the first wireless message ever received in a balloon. (Signed) L.Z. Harrison, Manager De Forest Company.[190]

While this historic demonstration was being undertaken, the exposition officials announced that the $100,000 airship contest, due to expire on November 15, had been extended for a third time and would last for the duration of the fair, to December 1. However, a stipulation was added,

> that each contestant who tries the course must agree before doing so that whether he wins or not he will make flights on December 2, 3 and 4 if weather permits and will not remove his ship before December 5.[191]

After months of delay, Hippolyte François finally made his first appearance on November 14. Before the largest crowd ever gathered in the concourse, the largest non-rigid airship in the world arose from the grounds at 3:42 p.m. with an American flag in its bow and a French tricolor at its stern.[192] While attendants held onto the ship by ropes, François directed maneuvers as his chief engineer, Henri Schneider, manned the engine. For 17 minutes the two men piloted the ship around the concourse until a bolt shook loose from the framework and caused one of the braces to come into the path of the left forward propeller, breaking it off and halting the demonstration.[193]

> The ascension was a captive effort, and the monster airship did not fly very high, nor very fast, nor far. The motor of the ship worked perfectly, and, while M. François declared after the flight that the dirigibility of the balloon had been proved beyond all doubt, it was not clear to the spectators whether the steering of the vessel in the air was due to the machinery or the ropes in the hands of those on the ground.
>
> The flight lacked all the sensational and interesting features and evolutions of the little Baldwin airship.[194]

Thomas C. Benbow and John Berry were also hastily getting their ships ready. To facilitate the inflation of the *St. Louis,* Berry erected a special vitriol gas plant at the concourse. He then announced that a flight of his unique vehicle was imminent.[195]

On November 15, François had completed his minor repairs and was ready to essay a second attempt at flight. Again, he intended it only as a captive ascension to test the engine and the lifting power of his balloon. While his assistants held onto the ropes, the *Ville de St. Mande* made a turn and headed toward the concourse fence. Henri Schneider, who was in the airship with François, saw that the frame in which they were standing might hit the top of the lattice-work fence, so he grabbed a megaphone and called down to the men below to let the ropes go. His assistants, however, could not understand French and only held on tighter. Seven feet of the framework crumpled as it crashed into the barrier, and the balloon sank to the ground.

As if this were not enough, while the dirigible was being taken back to its shed, a nail in the doorway caught the top of the bag and tore a large hole in it, spilling out all 65,000 cubic feet of hydrogen and instantly asphyxiating a number of sparrows which had nested in the eaves.[196] François demanded that the Exposition Company assume the cost of the repairs, and after discussion, the officials paid him $1,000.[197] Although the petulant Frenchman felt that he could have his airship ready in three days, he discovered that the damage was too extensive and he could make no further flights. The *Ville de St. Mande* was reshipped to Paris on December 24, 1904.[198]

On the day of François' last flight there were five other aeronauts on the grounds with their airships: John Berry, Thomas C. Benbow, Alva L. Reynolds, Marcellus McGarry, and A.F. Godefroy, another St. Louis inventor.   Only one was to have even partial success.[199]

On November 18, T.C. Benbow made his fourth ascent and first free flight in the *Montana Meteor* at 2:45 p.m. Thirty seconds later, his progress was arrested when his anchor, which he had neglected to haul in while busy spilling out ballast, caught in the lattice-work at the top of the fence.[200] His condition was aggravated when a ten-mile-per-hour wind suddenly sprang up and buffeted the bag against the fence and onto the network of telephone and trolley wires outside the concourse.[201] Benbow's short stint in the air provided "more thrills to the square moment for the spectators than any previous flight ever furnished."[202] With great difficulty, the errant airship was dragged off the wires and back into its hangar. The only damage, however, was a broken rudder cross-rod, some broken guy wires, and a twisted spar.[203] T.C. Benbow's harrowing experience offers much to explain why the early aeronauts feared any wind above five miles per hour.

On November 22, Benbow had completed his repairs and was ready for another attempt at free flight. At 3:08 p.m. he ascended from the concourse and sailed over the south fence "without making any entangling alliances."[204] Shortly after takeoff, however, his gas tank developed a leak and his engine stopped. The *Montana Meteor* continued on as a free balloon and landed four miles away at Jamieson and Scanlan avenues in Lindenwood in southwest St. Louis 45 minutes later.[205] Because of the scarcity of gas at the concourse, Percy Hudson, Willard Smith, and H.F. McGarvie chased after him in George Arbuckle's Winton automobile to retrieve the airship without deflating it. They towed the *Meteor* back to the grounds just as they had done with the *Arrow* earlier, and arrived at 10:00 p.m.[206] In a sense, their efforts were in vain, for Benbow left the exposition grounds on December 8 without making any further flights.[207]

John Berry began inflating his airship on November 19. Because of its unusual shape, a special scaffolding was used to hold the ship erect. The structure, however, was of rough pine planks, and after 10,000 cubic feet of gas had been pumped into the balloon, about 75 small punctures were discovered in the bag from slivers which had penetrated the silk-and-rubber envelope as it was geing inflated.[208] A few days later, a second inflation was attempted from Berry's vitriolic plant. Twelve thousand cubic feet of gas had been used before a strong wind sprang up and blew several holes in the envelope, spilling out the precious gas.[209] The third and last inflation began on December 4, with the hydrogen being obtained from the François airship by means of connecting hoses. On December 6, the *St. Louis* finally was fully inflated, but as it prepared to ascend in free flight, the wooden rim to which the envelope was connected at its equator broke from uneven strain and an eight-foot rent was opened in the gas bag. With all his efforts in vain, John Berry left the concourse on December 15.[210]

The final aerial events at the 1904 World's Fair consisted of experiments with meteorological balloons, the first ever performed in the United States.[211] They were conducted by Professor H.H. Clayton of the Blue Hill (Massachusetts) Observatory in order to record tempera-

Photocopy by Gregory M. Franzwa

Crewmen from Benbow's Montana Meteor *extricating the ungainly craft from the notorious lattice fence of the Aeronautical Concourse.*

ture, humidity, wind velocity, and altitude. Small rubber balloons with a lifting power of seven pounds were sent up from the exposition grounds, beginning in September and continuing through October, November, and December. As they ascended, the balloons expanded until they burst, falling to the earth gradually, with a silk hood slowing their descent. A card attached to each balloon offered a reward of $2.00 for its return, and nearly all were recovered. Some reached altitudes of 51,000 feet, traveled as far as 280 miles, recorded temperatures as low as -76 degrees, and attained speeds of 101 miles per hour. The experiments were eminently successful and provided a fitting climax to the aeronautic events of the fair.[212]

The Louisiana Purchase Exposition came to a close at midnight on December 1, 1904, when President David R. Francis, in the presence of 100,000 people, released a switch at the base of the Louisiana Purchase monument, causing all the lights to grow dim and fade into blackness.[213] No one denied its success or its popularity, for 18,740,073 people had attended its displays (12,804,616 paid and 5,935,457 free), an average of 100,217 per day.[214]

The most captivating events at the fair were the aeronautic activities. For the first time in the United States, wireless messages passed to a free balloon from the ground. For the first time in the world, formal kite contests were held. For the first time in the United States, experiments were conducted with meteorological balloons. For the first time in history, a mass airship contest was organized, and an American record for distance was twice set by the same dirigible. While no one won the unprecedented grand prize of $100,000, perhaps because its rules were too strict, airships provided the most telling thrills of the exposition, even though only two truly free, sustained flights were made. In addition, balloon flights, glider demonstrations, an International Aeronautic Congress, and a thorough display of the tools of aeronautics gave evidence of the complete array of aerial activity at the fair.

The total cost of the aeronautic features at the Louisiana Purchase Exposition was $45,862, most of which was spent for the outfitting of the Aeronautic Concourse. The airship sheds cost $13,888, the fence $6,559, and the two gas plants $16,052. Some $7,028 was paid out in salaries, $1,000 in prizes were awarded, and $1,335 was spent for miscellaneous items.[215]

David R. Francis, president of the Exposition Company, eloquently analyzed the significance of the aeronautic activities of the St. Louis World's Fair:

> In the estimation of many the tests and trials, seeking new attainments, conducted in connection with the exhibits of transportation and similar work of investigation carried on in connection with the other exhibit departments ranked among the principal performances of the Exposition and developed a new raison d'etre for such world gatherings.[216]

IV
The International Aeronautic
Tournament, 1907

IN 1907, ST. LOUIS WAS HOST to the James Gordon Bennett International Aeronautic Club Race, the "first ever held in the United States."[1] The Trophy, plus a cash prize of $2,500, had been donated in 1906 by James Gordon Bennett, publisher of the *New York Herald Tribune,* for an annual international long distance balloon race to be conducted by the International Aeronautic Federation.[2]

The cup itself was of solid silver, 19½ inches high and 31½ inches long. It had been executed by the House of Andre Aucoc of Paris and was valued at $2,500.

In the competition for it, every nation had the right to enter three balloons or airships with a capacity of from 13,500 to 77,000 cubic feet of gas, with an allowance of 5 percent for excess, on the condition that the pilots each belong to the aero club of the nation they represented.[3] Each aero club had to pay to the club holding the race a registration fee of $100 for every one of its entrants, with one half of the fee to be refunded for each man who actually started the race.[4] The trophy could only be held, temporarily or permanently, by an aero club or association, although the individual winner could keep the $2,500 first prize for himself, as well as one-half of the entrance fees or forfeits. The contestant finishing second was to receive one-third of these fees, and the third-place winner the remainder.[5] The cup was to be contested every year between April 1 and November 1. The Aero Club of France was to conduct the first competition, with the winning club holding the race the following year, and all expenses were to be borne by the host club.

If any organization could win the annual race three times in succession, it would have permanent possession of the Gordon Bennett Cup; the same condition would result if the cup were not challenged for five years.[6] The contest was to be purely one of distance, although it was transformable into one of duration if officials decided that atmospheric conditions warranted a test of how long the balloons could stay up rather than how far they could travel.[7] Because of the dignity and richness of the prize, as well as the international enthusiasm it evoked, the Gordon Bennett Cup became "the most famous of all balloon trophies."[8]

The first International Balloon Race was started from Paris on September 30, 1906. It was won by Lieutenant Frank P. Lahm of the United States, who bested fifteen other entrants from six other nations by traveling 402.40 miles to Flying Dales, England.[9] His victory gave the Aero Club of America the right to hold the Gordon Bennett Cup until the next competition and it gave the United States the right to be the seat of the international race for 1907.

In commemoration of Lieutenant Lahm's triumph, the Aero Club of America instituted the Lahm Aeronautic Cup contest for a $1,500 silver trophy made by Black, Starr, and Frost of New York. The competition was open to all licensed balloonists of every nation, but all trials for the cup had to begin in the United States and all contenders had to belong to the Aero Club of America. The entrant could make any number of trials individually at any time he wished, as long as he deposited a $1.00 fee[10] and notified the Aero Club of America of his intention at least twenty-four hours before each ascent.[11] (This restriction was later to prove bothersome to many of the hopefuls who started from St. Louis, particularly in 1909.)[12]

To win the cup, the entrant had to exceed the distance Lieutenant Lahm himself had traveled in winning the first International Balloon Race in 1906 — 402.40 miles. Thereafter, contestants had to exceed the record of the previous winner. Anyone who could hold the Lahm Cup for three years in succession would gain permanent possession.[13] The first man to win this trophy made his ascent from St. Louis during the aeronautic meet in October 1907.

The person who was primarily responsible for bringing the International Gordon Bennett Race to St. Louis in 1907 was Daniel C. Nugent, a local businessman who knew nothing at all about balloons.[14] While traveling from Japan to India on a trip around the world early in 1906, he met Augustus Post, the secretary of the Aero Club of America. The two became fast friends and Post invited Nugent to stop at his home in New York when he returned to the United States.

It was late in the fall of 1906 when Nugent fulfilled his promise, and by that time, Lahm had won the Gordon Bennett Cup and the Aero Club of America was investigating possible sites for the 1907 race. Post told him that Chicago, Omaha, and Denver were contesting for the honor and asked Nugent if he thought St. Louis would be interested. Although he was a neophyte in aeronautics, Nugent mentioned the matter to James E. Smith, president of the Business Men's League (forerunner of the Chamber of Commerce), when he returned to St. Louis. Realizing the prestige that would result for the city, Smith invited the Aero Club officials to visit St. Louis and investigate the possibilities.

Late in December 1906, Cortlandt Field Bishop, president of the Aero Club of America, Secretary Augustus Post, and John C. McCoy, another prominent balloonist, accepted the league's invitation and came to the city. Smith stressed three assets in his city's favor: "an appropriate site to start the races [Forest Park], a sufficient quantity and a superior quality of gas [supplied by Laclede Gas Light Company], and prizes [provided by generous members of the League]."[15] The trio had intended to go on to Chicago, Omaha, and Denver, but the advantages of St. Louis so impressed the officials that they made their decision immediately.[16] There were other factors involved:

> After a thorough examination of the country [in theory] St. Louis was selected for the international balloon races because it is central and far removed from the ocean, lakes and mountains. The city has the facilities and accommodations needed, and the public spirit to welcome the aeronauts and promote the business in hand.[17]

In order to assist the Business Men's League in conducting the race, the Aero Club of St. Louis was established in 1907. The moving spirit behind the organization and its first president was an elderly cracker magnate, Lewis D. Dozier.[18] Incorporated by the State of Missouri on May 27, 1908, and chartered for fifty years, the Aero Club's main purposes were:

> . . . to advance the development of the science of aeronautics and aerial research, and other scientific work; to encourage and organize aerial inventions and excursions, conferences, expositions, congresses and races; to develop the breeding and training of carrier pigeons; to hold, maintain, and conduct games, meets, con-

tests, expositions, and shows of airships, balloons or other inventions or constructions, designed to be propelled or travel through the air or otherwise; to maintain a club house or club houses, also garages and other houses, club grounds, electric and gas equipments and other accessories, aeronautic or otherwise, incidental to the business of the corporation upon such terms as the Board of Governors may from time to time provide. [19]

The Aero Club, a nonprofit organization, was to finance its ventures by means of a $10.00 initiation fee and annual dues of $10.00, as well as additional levies on the members as needed. [20] By the time the Gordon Bennett Race was held, the club had 400 members. [21] At that time, there were only two other aero clubs in the United States (Cincinnati and Chicago), [22] in addition to the Aero Club of America, which had been founded in 1905. [23] Because of the outstanding manner in which the Aero Club of St. Louis conducted the 1907 meet, it soon came to be "one of the strongest organizations in the country." [24]

The honorary secretary of the Aero Club was a young millionaire who was soon to become "St. Louis' foremost exponent of aviation" [25] — Albert Bond Lambert (1895-1946). He was president of the Lambert Pharmacal Company, a firm founded in 1881 by his father, Jordan W. Lambert, whose main product was an antiseptic called "Listerine." [26] His interest in flying began on one of his many business trips to Paris to set up branches there and in Hamburg, Germany, for his company. He acquired a French motorcycle in 1900 and a White Steamer automobile a few years later, and with these he used to putter around the streets of Paris. [27]

There he met Alberto Santos-Dumont, the celebrated Brazilian aeronaut, as well as Alfred Le Blanc, Lieutenant Frank P. Lahm, Courtlandt Field Bishop, Augustus Post, and many other balloonists and officials of the Aero Club of America at the Gordon Bennett Race in 1906. [28] On July 9, 1906, Lambert made his first balloon ascension from St. Cloud with his wife in a balloon piloted by E.W. Mix, an American engineer. [29] He made several more flights there, and in 1908 he was awarded his license, No. 18, issued by the Aero Club of France, thus becoming the first licensed balloonist of the Aero Club of St. Louis and one of the first in the United States. [30] This was only the beginning of a full life devoted to aviation.

In order to provide more of an incentive to the contestants of the Gordon Bennett Race, scheduled for October 21, 1907, the Aero Club and the Business Men's League arranged for prizes additional to the trophy and $2,500 provided by the *Herald Tribune* publisher. Adolphus Busch donated $1,000 for the contestant finishing second,

United Railways Company gave $750 for the third-place winner, the B. Nugent Dry Goods Company offered $500 for fourth place, and the *St. Louis Times* contributed $250 for the man finishing fifth.[31]

The Aero Club of St. Louis decided to broaden the program into an aeronautic tournament by adding two unique contests scheduled for the days after the start of the balloon race. In each event, $2,000 was to be awarded the winner and $500 the contestant who finished second.[32] The first contest was for "Dirigible balloons or airships which are lighter than air, being made so by a bag or envelope containing a gas lighter than air."[33] A three-quarter-mile triangular course was laid out from the Aero Club grounds in Forest Park north to the Frank P. Blair Monument at Lindell Boulevard, then southwest to a captive balloon over the Amateur Athletic Association grounds, and then a return to the starting point.[34]

The second event was for "Machines heavier than air, which are designed to be lifted from the ground and propelled by the pressure of planes or external surfaces of some light material against the air."[35] This was an unprecedented contest. "For the first time in history, as far as we know," commented a contemporary journalist, "there is expected to be actual 'races' between gasless flying machines at St. Louis."[36] First prize was to be awarded for the "longest or best continuous flight,"[37] in the opinion of the judges, with the runner-up receiving second prize. There was no prescribed course, only the stipulation that the machines fly at least 100 feet to be eligible for the prizes.[38]

In addition to these two special events, which were to be conducted by and paid for solely by the Aero Club of St. Louis,[39] the Aero Club of America scheduled a competition for the *Scientific American* Flying Machine Trophy. The memorial, donated by that magazine, was 32 inches high and had been made by Reed and Barton of New York, who valued it at $2,500. The award was to go to the man who could pilot a heavier-than-air machine a distance of one kilometer (3,280 feet) in a straight line, and perform further trials at the discretion of the Aero Club officials. The competition was to be annual, and if anyone could win the event three times in succession, the trophy was to be retired to that person.[40]

This contest was to be held on October 24, following the Gordon Bennett Balloon Race (October 21), and the St. Louis Aero Club dirigible (October 22) and "flying machine" (October 23) events. In addition, it was hoped that there would be several attempts at the Lahm Cup on October 25. Because this extensive aerial activity would follow the annual high-society Veiled Prophet parade and ball

(October 1) and a visit by President Theodore Roosevelt (October 2), the *St. Louis Republic* declared: "October is going to be the greatest month in St. Louis since the World's Fair."[41]

At the eastern end of Forest Park, on Kingshighway near Clayton Road, the Aero Club established its headquarters and an enclosure of wire netting 600 feet long and 300 feet wide for the start of the races. Inside the fence, a grandstand for 3,000 Aero Club members, officials, and guests was erected, while a public grandstand seating 10,000 was built across Kingshighway.[42] Public spectators were to be charged 50¢ each,[43] but Aero Club members were to be admitted free, for the 400 of them had already been assessed $35 each to cover the expenses of the tournament.[44] The club purchased 30 tons of sifted sand for ballast for the balloonists,[45] and Laclede Gaslight Company supplied free gas from its 4,000,000-cubic-foot gasometer, "one of the largest in the world."[46]

Owing to its low specific gravity, coal gas was the best commercial type available for ballooning, since it provided good lifting power for flights of long duration.[47] Of the four commercially manufactured gases, the average specific gravity of coal gas (as compared with that of air) was .440, while that of water gas was .650, that of Pintsch gas .850, and that of acetylene gas .920. Hydrogen gas was much lighter and more efficient, but it was not a commercial gas and was very expensive to produce.[48] Hence, most balloons of this period used coal gas, and the specific gravity of the variety utilized in the races at St. Louis in 1907 was an excellent .380, which was believed to be "the lightest coal gas ever produced for ballooning."[49]

These events were under the auspices of the International Aeronautic Federation, the Aero Club of America, the Aero Club of St. Louis, and the Business Men's League of St. Louis. The members of the Contest Committee for the James Gordon Bennett International Aeronautic Cup Race were Cortlandt Field Bishop, president of the Aero Club of America, chairman; Maurice Mallet, a member of the Aero Club of France; Augustus Post, secretary of the Aero Club of America; Charles J. Edwards, treasurer of the Aero Club of America; Lewis D. Dozier, president of the Aero Club of St. Louis; and Frank S. Lahm, a member of the Aero Club of America and father of the winner of the 1906 race.[50]

The members of the Contest Committee for the dirigible and "flying machine" events were Albert Bond Lambert, chairman; David R. Francis and G.H. Walker of the Aero Club of St. Louis; Cortlandt Field Bishop; and Maurice Mallet.[51] President Roosevelt authorized the Signal Corps of the United States Army to assist the contestants in every way,[52] and ten expert balloonists were sent by the service to St. Louis.[53] The ascensions were to be supervised by A. Leo Stevens of New York, "the most experienced balloonist in the United States,"[54] who had been making ascensions since the age of eleven, piling up the impressive number of 1,100 flights.[55] The official timer of the international race was Charles J. Glidden, who would use a stopwatch accurate to one-eighteenth of a second; it had been made in Switzerland at a cost of $750.[56]

In the Gordon Bennett Race, nine balloons from four nations took part: England sent one balloon, France two, Germany three, and the United States three. Spain and Italy had each entered two balloons, but because they did not technically comply with the rules of the competition, the International Aeronautic Federation barred them from the contest. Switzerland also tried to enter, but delayed its decision until after the February deadline for entries.[57]

England's lone pilot was Griffith Brewer, age 40, a veteran of sixty ascents, who had participated as an aide in the first Bennett Race in 1906. He was assisted by Lieutenant Claude M.P. Brabazon, who had been trained at the British Military Balloon School and had made fifteen free ascensions. Their balloon was the *Lotus II*, a 72,250-cubic-foot bag of varnished cotton, which had been made by the French firm of Carton-Lachambre.[58] This balloon was the same one that Alberto Santos-Dumont had used to represent the United States in the 1906 race under the name *Les Deux Ameriques*.[59] Two other British pilots had entered — C.S. Rolls and A.K. Huntington — but they both withdrew from the competition before the start of the race.[60]

France entered two balloons. Alfred Le Blanc, 40, was the pilot of the 77,000-cubic-foot varnished-cotton *Isle de France*. He was a strong contender, for he had 82 flights in his background, the longest of which had been a 630-mile voyage from Paris to the Baltic Sea in 13 hours and 20 minutes on March 16, 1907.[61] He was aided by E.W. Mix, an American engineer, the same man who had piloted the balloon in which Albert Bond Lambert had made his first ascension on July 9, 1906.[62] The other French balloon was the 79,250-cubic-foot *Anjou*, piloted by René Gasnier, 33, a veteran of 24 flights, the longest of which had been 459 miles, made in 22 hours and 8 minutes on June 18, 1907, from Brussels to Limoges. His aide was another Frenchman, Charles Levee.[63]

Germany's team of three balloons was "the most formidable offered by any of the nations presented."[64] Oscar Erbsloeh, 28, was the pilot of the *Pommern*, a 77,000-cubic-foot balloon of cotton covered with gutta-percha. He had made 53 ascensions, the longest of which had been on September 15, 1907, when he had traveled 620 miles from Brussels to Bayonne in 29 hours and 32 minutes.[65] He was to have been aided by the expert meteorologist, Professor A. Lawrence Rotch of the Blue Hill Observatory of Hyde Park, Massachusetts. At the last minute, however, the press of business kept the scientist away and in his place he sent his assistant, Henry Helm Clayton, a trained meteorologist who had performed a notable series of experiments with weather balloons at the St. Louis World's Fair in 1904.[66] Captain Hugo von Abercron, 38, had made 89 ascensions, the most of any contestant. He was the pilot of the 77,000-cubic-foot *Dusseldorf,* which he had flown in the 1906 Gordon Bennett Race. His aide was Hans Heidemann, a 45-year-old veteran of 22 balloon flights. The third German entry was the 50,000-cubic-foot *Abercron,* made of cotton covered with gutta-percha, the smallest balloon in the race. It was piloted by Paul Meckel, age 26, a silk manufacturer who had made 28 free flights.[67] His announced aide, A. von Pohlenz, never arrived, so his place was taken by Dr. Rudolph Denig of New York.[68]

The United States also entered a strong team of three balloons. Major Henry B. Hersey, a 52-year-old official inspector of the United States Weather Bureau, was the pilot of the 75,250-cubic-foot *United States.* He had made ten previous flights, one of them as aide to Lieutenant Frank P. Lahm, the winner of the 1906 Gordon Bennett Race from Paris. In the 1907 race, he was taking the place of Lieutenant Lahm, who had not sufficiently recovered from an attack of typhoid fever to compete. Hersey was an eminent meteorologist, a decided asset in a balloonist, and had accompanied Walter Wellman on his two abortive aerial polar expeditions in 1906 and 1907. His aide was Arthur T. Atherholt of Philadelphia, a member of the Aero Club of America and the Ben Franklin Aeronautic Association, the latter of which owned the largest balloon in America, the 93,000-cubic-foot *Ben Franklin.* The balloon they would use, the *United States,* was the same one Lahm and Hersey had flown to victory in 1906. It had been made by Maurice Mallet of France, a member of the contest committee for the 1907 race.[69]

The second American entry was the 77,000-cubic-foot *St. Louis,* flown by Alan R. Hawley, 38, who had made nineteen flights. He was aided by Augustus Post, secretary of the Aero Club of America.[70] They were representing the Aero Club of St. Louis, which had paid $1,200 for the balloon, as well as a $500 customs duty,[71] since it had been built in France expressly for the race by Maurice Mallet.[72] The third American entry was the 77,000-cubic-foot *America,* piloted by Captain Charles De Forrest Chandler, 34, a veteran of 21 flights, aided by John C. McCoy, vice president of the Aero Club of America.[73] This balloon, constructed of cotton by Leo Stevens, was the only American-built balloon in the race.[74]

In contrast to the international flavor of the Gordon Bennett Race, the entrants for the $2,500 dirigible contest were all Americans. Seven men had entered ten airships in the event. The favorite in the competition was the experienced Captain Thomas Scott Baldwin, who had thrilled the St. Louis crowds at the World's Fair in 1904 with his *California Arrow,* piloted by A. Roy Knabenshue.[75] For the 1907 contest, he brought two ships, the *New California Arrow* and the *Twentieth Century.*[76] One of the airships was to be piloted by Baldwin himself, while the other would be flown by Glenn Curtiss, a man who was later to make something of a name for himself in his own right.[77] Charles J. Strobel, an inventor from Toledo, Ohio, also brought two dirigibles, one to be operated by Jack Dallas and the other by Lincoln Beachey.[78]

The third contestant who had entered two ships was Cromwell Dixon from Columbus, Ohio, who at fifteen was the "youngest inventor and aeronaut of experience in the world."[79] His two dirigibles were the *Dixon Airship* and the *Sky Bicycle,* and he intended to pilot them both himself.[80] He had built both ships with his own hands, although his mother had sewn the seams of the envelopes for him. His *Sky Bicycle,* in which he had made forty flights, was reminiscent of the airship that Carl E. Myers had demonstrated in St. Louis in 1900 and 1904.[81] "The engine is the framework of an old bicycle; the motive power is his legs. He sits on the saddle and works the steering gear with a rope."[82] This amazing young aeronaut was undoubtedly the sentimental favorite among St. Louisans.

In addition to these three dual entrants, four others had entered single airships: Horace B. Wild of Chicago with his *American Eagle;* John Berry of St. Louis, who had attempted flight at the 1904 World's Fair,[83] with his *Airship America;* E. Jorgensen of Chicago with his *Jorgensen Airship;*[84] and Charles Baysdorfer of Omaha with his *Comet.*[85] The list of entries was impressive, but not all were to appear at the designated time.

In the competition for the $2,500 heavier-than-air prize, there were seven entrants, at least two of whom had expressed their intention of competing for the *Scientific American* Trophy as well.[86] They were: the *Wixon Aeroplane* of H.H. Wixon, Chicago; the *Ludlow Aeroplane* of Israel Ludlow, Norfolk; the *Gammeter Orthopter* of H.C. Gammeter, Cleveland; the *Flying Machine* of J.W. Roshon, Harrisburg, Pennsylvania; the *Orthopter* of George Francis Meyers, Columbus, Ohio; the *Flying Machine Jessie* of S. Hemstreet, Chattanooga, Tennessee; and the *Orthopter, Milwaukee Number 1,* entered by the Vacu-Aerial Navigation and Manufacturing Company of Milwaukee, and operated by Dr. Rudolph Silvester.[87] In addition to these entrants, there were a number of contestants who wished to remain anonymous.[88]

Of the seven announced entrants, four had relatively orthodox, fixed-wing vehicles, of which Ludlow's was generally representative. It was shaped "like a great box kite" and was launched into the air from a three-wheeled cart, which was used to give it momentum.[89] Three of the entrants had unorthodox, wing-flapping ornithopters, of which Gammeter's was typical. The fuselage was made of steel tubing and the wings of bamboo covered with Japanese silk. It was 12 feet long, had a wingspan of 30 feet, and weighed 290 pounds empty. The wings were moved at 75 beats per minute by a seven-horsepower Curtiss engine. When tested in its shed, however, it rose from the ground only a few inches.[90] It was reminiscent of the machine Alva L. Reynolds had attempted to demonstrate at the World's Fair in 1904 using muscle-power alone.[91] Probably none of these entrants had ever made a sustained flight, since as of December 31, 1907, only seven men in America had ever flown in powered airplanes: Wilbur and Orville Wright, A.M. Herring, F.W. Baldwin, Lieutenant Thomas Selfridge, Glenn H. Curtiss, and J.A.D. McCurdy.[92]

The entries of nine balloons, ten dirigibles, and seven airplanes gave promise that there would be on the field "a greater number of aerial craft than ever before seen in any city of the world."[93] There was more than just sport, however, in the minds of the aeronauts and the officials.

> A scientific and practical interest is connected with this programme. The races and experiments are not chiefly for amusement. Aero Clubs have been organized mainly with a purpose to determine the utility of balloons and flying machines. If they are but dangerous toys, and without principles of value as vehicles of transportation, the clubs desire to get at the proofs.[94]

By mid-October, many of the contestants had arrived in St. Louis. At the headquarters of the Aero Club of America in New York on October 12, Cortlandt Field Bishop had directed the official drawing of positions for the countries in the Gordon Bennett Race. It was determined that the order of start would be Germany, England, the

United States, and France, and that the same rotation would continue until all the balloons had ascended.[95] At a meeting of the contest committee at the Jefferson Hotel in St. Louis on October 16, the individual order of ascension was chosen. Even though C.S. Rolls and A.K. Huntington were not expected, places were assigned to them since they had paid their fees. Thus, the order of start was: 1) Erbsloeh and Clayton (Germany), *Pommern;* 2) Rolls (England), withdrawn; 3) Hersey and Atherholt (United States), *United States;* 4) Le Blanc and Mix (France), *Isle de France;* 5) Abercron and Heidemann (Germany), *Dusseldorf;* 6) Brewer and Brabazon (England), *Lotus II;* 7) Chandler and McCoy (United States), *America;* 8) Gasnier and Levee (France), *Anjou;* 9) Meckel and Denig (Germany), *Abercron;* 10) Huntington (England), withdrawn; 11) Hawley and Post (United States), *St. Louis.*[96]

A few of the contestants had expressed their intention of making trial ascents before the race to test the gas and wind conditions. Earlier during 1907, there had been four flights by members of the Aero Club of America from St. Louis, and three of the men involved were entered in the Gordon Bennett Race. Each was no doubt testing the "feel" of the city. On January 1, 1907, J.C. McCoy and Alan R. Hawley ascended in the 1,000-cubic-meter *Orient* from St. Louis and landed 86 miles away at Pearl, Illinois. On April 26, Hawley went up alone in the *Orient* and sailed 60 miles to Carrollton, Illinois. On April 30, J.C. McCoy and Captain Charles De Forrest Chandler ascended in the 2,200-cubic-meter *America* in competition for the Lahm Cup. They failed to exceed Lahm's record of 402.40 miles, however, and landed 135 miles away in Golconda, Illinois. On May 2, Alan R. Hawley and A. Leo Stevens made a flight in the *Orient* from St. Louis, but they were forced down seven miles away in Collinsville, Illinois, by varying air currents which caused them to cross and recross the same river eight times at about the same spot. Hawley, Chandler, and McCoy were each entered in the International Race and probably gained useful information on the atmospheric conditions around St. Louis through these four flights.[97]

On October 14, 1907, McCoy and Chandler scheduled still another trial flight from the city, but their ascension was postponed when several punctures were discovered in their 35,000-cubic-foot *Psyche,* which had just arrived from New York.[98] Repairs were quickly made and they ascended from the Laclede Gas Plant at Second and Rutger streets at 1:42 p.m. October 15, landing 87 miles away at Jacksonville, Illinois, at 5:15 p.m. The flight was intended as a test of the lifting power of the coal gas, which they found to be of excellent quality.[99]

Perhaps impressed with the success of their flight in the *Psyche,* Chandler and McCoy decided to try for the Lahm Cup. After registering their intention and depositing a $1.00 fee with the Aero Club of America, they ascended from the Second and Rutger street plant at 4:15 p.m. October 17, in the 78,000-cubic-foot Signal Corps balloon *United States No. 10,* carrying 1,600 pounds of ballast and a good supply of canned provisions.[100] Almost before this balloon was out of sight, Alan Hawley and Augustus Post got away at 6:35 p.m. in the 35,000-cubic-foot *Stevens No. 21* on a routine trial flight.[101] The two ascensions were witnessed by many of the Gordon Bennett contestants, as well as a large crowd of spectators. The *Stevens No. 21* landed twelve hours later at 6:30 a.m. at Boggstown, Indiana, only 225 miles away, for the two aeronauts had taken only 280 pounds of ballast and did not expect a long flight.[102] During the trip they kept a diary and made several interesting entries:

> 9:10 — Gunshot fired: scared us pretty bad for a while. I don't think it was fired maliciously, but it is a poor way to greet a balloonist.
>
> 10:41 — Drag rope tore off front fence of cottage. Woman came out and said something; couldn't understand her; didn't particularly want to.
>
> 11:00 — Sullivan, at an elevation of 600 feet, drag rope struck roof of Masonic Home. Some one came out and yelled: "This is the Masonic Home 135 miles from St. Louis."[103]

At 1:30 p.m. October 18, the *United States No. 10* landed three miles from Walton, Roane County, West Virginia, in the foothills of the Alleghenies.[104] Its official distance was 473.56 miles, a new Lahm Cup record.[105] For the first time, Lieutenant Frank P. Lahm's mark of 402.40 miles had been exceeded. The two men said they could have gone as far as the Atlantic Ocean, but they had descended deliberately in order to have time to return to St. Louis for the Gordon Bennett Race, since they knew they had broken Lahm's record.[106] There was some question as to who had been the pilot of the balloon, but the cup was awarded to Captain Charles De Forrest Chandler, since the balloon was Army property and, according to War Department regulations, could only ascend with an Army officer in charge.[107] If this distance of 473.56 miles was not exceeded in Lahm Cup competition for three years, then Chandler would be awarded permanent possession of the trophy.[108]

Before word was received that Chandler and McCoy had won the

Lahm Cup, the last of the preliminary trial flights had begun. Oscar Erbsloeh and his aide Hans Heidemann ascended from Second and Rutger streets at 12:55 p.m. October 18 in the *Psyche,* the balloon in which Chandler and McCoy had flown to Jacksonville, Illinois, four days earlier. A strong wind was blowing at the time of the ascent and the balloon nearly hit a smokestack as it was rising. Heidemann, however, used great presence of mind and deftly cut away three large sand bags hanging near the top of the basket. The *Psyche* shot up out of danger and landed four hours later at Red Bud, Illinois, 37 miles from St. Louis.[109] The arrival that night of Paul Meckel, the last of the Gordon Bennett entrants, gave evidence that the great international race was about to get under way.[110]

Simultaneous inflation of all the balloons began at 9:30 a.m. October 21, with the time of the start scheduled for 4:00 p.m. that afternoon.[111] The total capacity of the bags was almost 700,000 cubic feet, but the efficient Laclede system proceeded at the rate of 600,000 cubic feet of coal gas per hour.[112] The contestants, officials, and public hoped for unprecedented performances. A local newspaper commented:

> From the records made in the trial flights last week, especially that of the United States No. 10, piloted by Capt. Charles De Forrest Chandler and J.C. McCoy, and from the long-distance trips made by the foreign contestants in former races, it is expected that the battle beginning this afternoon will be the hardest fought in the history of the sport, and flights of unusually long distances are expected of all nine contestants.[113]

The accuracy of this prediction was to be well borne out by the results. On the basis of previous performances, "Oscar Erbsloeh of the German contingent probably would be the favorite,"[114] but in a straw ballot on October 19, the guardsmen of the Jefferson Barracks selected: 1) McCoy and Chandler, 2) Erbsloeh and Clayton, 3) Le Blanc and Mix, 4) Hersey and Atherholt, and 5) Gasnier and Levee.[115] Hawley and Hersey declared their intentions of having their flights in the Gordon Bennett Race count as trials for the Lahm Cup as well,[116] but the officials of the Aero Club of America asked them to abandon the dual-purpose idea in order not to detract from the dignity and spirit of the Gordon Bennett Race, the major event.[117]

At a meeting of pilots and aides with the contest committee on October 20, each man was given a number of packets addressed to the Hotel Jefferson in St. Louis and to the headquarters of the Aero Club of America in New York. The balloonists were to record their

The start of the 1907 Gordon Bennett International Balloon Race.

position, the temperature, wind direction and velocity, as well as the condition of the ship. These cards were to be thrown over the side every two hours, and the people finding them were directed to mail them from a post office.[118] Upon descending, each pilot was to record his exact landing spot and time and secure notarized affidavits as to its truth from the residents of the area. A sealed Richard barograph was placed in each balloon to record altitude and determine if a balloon landed at any time during its flight. The United States Geological Survey in Washington was to compute the distances of each balloon from St. Louis to the recorded landing point.[119] On October 17, Professor C.M. Woodward of Washington University reckoned the exact position of the starting point: latitude 38°37'38", longitude 90°15'53".[120]

On the morning of October 21, the weather was fair and mild, with a brisk twelve-mile-per-hour breeze blowing. The wind, however, came from the southeast, an ill sign for long flights, since such a wind is not of long duration and would soon have brought the balloons back over St. Louis again with precious time, gas, and ballast lost. But in the afternoon it shifted and blew steadily from the southwest, with only intermittant gusts from the southeast.[121] Just before the start of the race, Leo Stevens sent up a twelve-foot test balloon, which headed north and then bore off eastward.

The saffron-colored *Pommern* was the first to depart, at precisely 4:00:25 p.m., as the Jefferson Barracks band played the "Wacht Am Rhein." The soldiers in attendance then carried the *United States*, piloted by a nervous Major Henry Hersey, to the same spot and it ascended at 4:05 while the crowd cheered wildly and the band played the "Star Spangled Banner." The glossy-yellow *Isle de France* ascended at 4:10, rose straight up without dropping ballast, and fell off to the west to the tune of the "Marseillaise." While the band again played the German anthem, the *Dusseldorf* arose sluggishly at 4:15, dumped ballast, and headed northwest. At 4:19 the *Lotus II*, "a time-worn and storm-beaten looking affair,"[122] was saluted warmly by the crowd as it ascended to the tune of "God Save the King." This balloon headed toward the grandstand and the pilots hastily had to dump forty pounds of precious ballast to get away unscathed.

The recent Lahm Cup winners were next off at 4:24, and they had the enthusiastic crowd on its feet. Their balloon, the *America,* had narrowly escaped destruction by spontaneous combustion in shipment from New York. When it was unpacked on October 17, it was discovered that the varnish, which had recently been applied, had heated in several places, turning the fabric brown. "It is said that if unpacking had been delayed another hour the balloon would have been destroyed."[123] The *America* made a poor start in the Gordon Bennett because it was over-ballasted. About 100 pounds of sand had to be thrown over the side before it was able to make its ascension.

The *Anjou* was "by far the best appearing on the grounds."[124] At 79,250 cubic feet, it was also the largest balloon in the race, and only narrowly got under the limit by using the 5 percent degree of grace allowed by the contest committee. At 4:30 it dashed gracefully upward as the band again played the "Marseillaise." Next was the *Abercron,* which has just been rechristened the *Tschudl.* Peculiar in shape, "it resembled an apple, with the top flat."[125] The two Germans got a good start at 4:35 and headed westward without wasting ballast.

The *St. Louis* was the last to ascend. It got the best reaction from the crowd, but made the poorest start. Heavily ballasted, the bag at first refused to move, and then dragged along the ground for fifty yards. It was carried back to the starting point, ballast was ejected, and it rose nicely at 4:41 as the Barracks guardsmen for the

Thomas Scott Baldwin's New California Arrow.

third time played the "Star Spangled Banner."[126]

In addition to a food supply varying from oranges to brandy for 36-40 hours, each balloon took up similar basic equipment.

> All carried the same instruments, which included a compass, statoscope, an instrument for ascertaining whether the balloon is ascending or descending; barograph, charts, maps, rule, electric flashlight, life belt, water, anchor, sand scoop and megaphone.[127]

For the most part, the ascensions went smoothly and on schedule, and the pageantry was well appreciated by the crowd.

> Nine huge gas bags, clumsy looking enough, rose stately and slowly over the heads of the 100,000, while throughout the city 400,000 more bent their necks, pointed their noses to the sky and watched the bags move and move [sic] into the clouds and grow dim and disappear.[128]

While St. Louis waited for progress reports on the race, it turned to the next event on the program, the airship exhibitions. A crowd of 20,000 assembled at the balloon grounds in Forest Park on October 22 to witness trial flights for the dirigible races, which had been rescheduled for October 23. Fifteen-year-old Cromwell Dixon was the first to perform. He ascended in his *Sky Bicycle* and pedaled over the grounds for 25 minutes before his legs grew tired and he drifted with the wind eastward across the Mississippi River, landing an hour later at 5:00 p.m. at Venice, Illinois, eleven miles from the concourse. His mother followed him by car and they deflated the ship and returned to St. Louis that night.[129]

Captain Thomas Scott Baldwin made two short flights, circling,

Jack Dallas taking off in a Strobel airship. Moments later he crashed into telephone and trolley wires on Kingshighway, suffering only minor damage to himself and his aircraft.

diving and turning with the *New California Arrow* in the same manner in which A. Roy Knabenshue successfully demonstrated the old *California Arrow* at the 1904 World's Fair.[130] He was followed by Jack Dallas, flying one of the airships of Charles J. Strobel. The engine stopped at a height of 500 feet after a few minutes, and as he expelled gas to descend, the dirigible gained momentum and plunged onto the network of telephone and trolley wires on Kingshighway. He was extricated from his predicament, which was reminiscent of that of Thomas C. Benbow at the World's Fair,[131] by two "trouble wagons" from United Railways, with only slight damage to his ship.[132]

On October 22, the contest committee of the Aero Club of St. Louis revised the rules for the dirigible race. In place of the triangular course originally set, a new route was laid out "from a line in the aero enclosure straight to Blair Monument, Forest Park, rounding a captive balloon or other goal located there and return, crossing the line of start."[133] The distance from the grounds to the monument was 3,400 feet, or in some cases 3,450, owing to the positions of the airships on the field, making the round trip of the full course between 6,800 and 6,900 feet.[134] In place of the previously announced awards of $2,000 for the winner and $500 for second place, prizes of $1,500, $750, and $250 were to be awarded for first, second, and third places. Each contestant was to have three trials, with his best time counting, and the airships were to depart from the concourse at three-minute intervals.[135]

When the races were held, before a crowd of 100,000 on October 23, only five of the entrants took part, and only three finished the course. Cromwell Dixon did not participate in the competition for the prizes;[136] Glenn Curtiss was on the field, but Baldwin did not want him to fly;[137] and E. Jorgensen and John Berry withdrew from the race because they felt the wind was too strong.[138] Horace B. Wild attempted a flight in the *Comet,* but his engine broke down and he drifted back over the crowd and landed south of the concourse.[139] Charles Baysdorfer, the owner, then ascended in the same ship, but he also experienced difficulty and crashed after a slow dive from a height of 150 feet, causing $100 in damage to the airship and almost killing himself.[140]

There were, however, three successful contestants. Thomas Scott Baldwin faced Jack Dallas and Lincoln Beachey, both of whom were his former pupils.[141] Dallas' airship broke down on his first two trials. On the first, he circled the captive balloon at Blair Monument, but on the return trip his motor stopped and he drifted helplessly over the line in a time of 8 minutes and 50 seconds. The identical thing occurred on his second attempt, which took him 7 minutes and 15 seconds to accomplish. On his third trial, however, he made a successful run and posted a time of 6 minutes and 10 seconds.[142]

Captain Baldwin, the favorite in the race, made a sluggish time of 9 minutes and 30 seconds on his first flight. On his second trial, moreover, a strong headwind forced him to abandon his effort before he even reached the monument. This failure induced him to transfer the gas envelope of the *New California Arrow,* which he had

Thomas Scott Baldwin lifts his New California Arrow *out of Forest Park, before a packed grandstand.*

been using, to the framework of the more powerful *Twentieth Century*. With this he made his third trial, but he was only able to circle the route in 7 minutes and 5 seconds, almost a full minute slower than Dallas.[143]

Lincoln Beachey posted the mediocre time of 7 minutes and 15 seconds on his first flight, and waived a second trial. On his last attempt, however, he amazed the crowd and shamed his rivals when he completed the circuit at relatively "blazing" speed in the time of 4 minutes and 40 seconds to win the competition.[144]

Charles J. Strobel, who owned the airships flown by Lincoln Beachey and Jack Dallas, collected first and second prizes of $1,500 and $750 respectively.[145] Thomas Scott Baldwin, who had finished a poor third, received $250.[146] In addition, a special purse of $375 was given to Cromwell Dixon in appreciation for his excellent performance.[147] Within four years, "the youngest aviator in the United States" would be killed when he crashed from a height of 100 feet at the International Fair Grounds in Spokane, Washington, on October 2, 1911.[148]

These dirigible events were the last of the tournament, for there were no airplane flights, either for the $2,500 Aero Club of St. Louis prize or for the *Scientific American* Flying Machine Trophy. Israel Ludlow and H.H. Wixon of Chicago both brought their primitive "flying machines" to the field, but neither was able to rise from the ground. The trophy and the cash prize were not awarded.[149]

There were, however, two additional aerial events that were not on the program. A contingent from the Blue Hill Observatory — A. Lawrence Rotch, Henry Helm Clayton, and S.P. Ferguson — sent aloft 25 six-foot meteorological balloons during the month of October,[150] and the Blanke-Werner Candy Company released several hundred small balloons which bore tags reading:

> October 22, 1907. Balloon week, St. Louis, Mo. To the finder of this tag: Return this tag either in person or by mail and receive in return a handsome box of our fine, delicious chocolates and Nadja caramels mixed. P.S. — Not good after October 26, 1907.[151]

By October 23, the results of the Gordon Bennett International Race, which had been started two days earlier, were tentatively known. The *Pommern* and the *Isle de France* were so close, however, that the winner had to be determined by the United States Geological Survey. The German balloon won the race and broke John Wise's American record[152] with a flight of 873.4 miles to Asbury Park, New Jersey. The French balloon was second, with a distance of 867.4 miles to Herbertsville, New Jersey,[153] but in their losing effort Le Blanc and Mix set a new world's duration record of 44 hours and 3 minutes.[154] Both bags had been forced to descend when they reached the sea. In all, eight balloons exceeded Lahm's 1906 winning distance of 402.40 miles, and the ninth, the *Lotus II,* probably also would have, but it was compelled to descend when its pilot, Griffith Brewer, became ill.[155] The official results were:

1) *Pommern* (Germany) — Oscar Erbsloeh, pilot, and Henry Helm Clayton, aide. 873.4 miles to Asbury Park, New Jersey.

2) *Isle de France* (France) — Alfred Le Blanc, pilot, and E.W. Mix, aide. 867.4 miles to Herbertsville, New Jersey.[156]

3) *Dusseldorf* (Germany) — Hugo von Abercron, pilot, and Hans Heidemann, aide. 797.352 miles to Dover, Delaware.

4) *America* (United States) — J.C. McCoy, pilot, and Charles De Forrest Chandler, aide. 726.418 miles to Pautuxent, Maryland.

5) *St. Louis* (United States) — Alan R. Hawley, pilot, and Augustus Post, aide. 714.500 miles to Westminster, Maryland.

6) *Tschudl/Abercron* (Germany) — Paul Meckel, pilot, and Rudolph Denig, aide. 690.547 miles to Manassas, Virginia.

7) *Anjou* (France) — René Gasnier, pilot, and Charles Levee, aide. 672.794 miles to Mineral, Virginia.

8) *United States* (United States) — Henry B. Hersey, pilot, and Arthur T. Atherholt, aide. 623.950 miles to Tyneside, Ontario, Canada.

9)*Lotus II* (England) — Griffith Brewer, pilot, and Claude Brabazon, aide. 360.670 miles to Sabina, Ohio.[157]

H.H. Clayton felt that the Germans and French did so well because:

> (1) they had studied and practiced the technique of ballooning; (2) they were well equipped; and (3) they were guided by expert advice. These are the things which are likely to win in any contest.[158]

Oscar Erbsloeh won the prize of $2,500, and the James Gordon Bennett International Aeronautic Cup was awarded to his club, the Berliner Luft-Schiffer Verband (Aero Club of Berlin), which would conduct the race in 1908. Le Blanc won the $1,000 second prize, donated by the Anheuser-Busch Brewing Company; Abercron the $750 United Railways purse for third place; McCoy the $500 fourth prize, provided by the B. Nugent Dry Goods Company; and Hawley the *St. Louis Times* prize of $250 for fifth place.[159]

The Aero Club of St. Louis and the Business Men's League bore all the expenses of the meet. They spent a total of $25,000: $1,200 for the balloon *St. Louis,* $5,000 for prizes, $2,500 for the grandstands and fencing, $1,000 for the coal gas, $1,500 for Laclede Gas Light Company's expense in laying the pipeline, $500 for maintaining the club house, and $13,300 for miscellaneous items, including rooms at the Hotel Jefferson for all the contestants.[160] The tournament was, in effect, a losing venture financially, for the grandstand receipts were $1,800 on October 21, $300 on October 22, and $1,500 on October 23, for a total of $3,600, of which $700 went to the League and the remainder to the Aero Club.[161]

The accomplishments of the meet, however, and the enthusiasm aroused were well worth the expense. At least five new records were set: 1) an American balloon distance record; 2) a world's balloon endurance mark; 3) a new record for prompt inflation and starting; 4) the unprecedented achievement of uniformly long flights by all the contestants; and 5) a new speed record for dirigibles.[162]

Morris A. Heimann, a St. Louis manufacturer and sportsman, was so enthusiastic that he ordered a 35,000-cubic-foot balloon for $1,500 from A. Leo Stevens, which he intended to name the *Melba* after his daughter. In so doing he became the first individual St. Louisan ever to own a balloon.[163] The excitement also stimulated Adolphus Busch to offer a $1,000 trophy for an annual balloon race to be started from St. Louis.[164]

The 1907 Gordon Bennett Race was deemed "the greatest aeronautical contest ever held both from the length of the trips of each contesting balloon and the duration of time.''[165] The week of aerial events was the most spectacular St. Louis, and perhaps the world, had seen up to that time. Lewis D. Dozier, president of the Aero Club of St. Louis, said:

> The international race is without doubt the greatest that St. Louis has had since the world's fair. There has never been anything like it in the country. The interest that the race aroused was remarkable and far beyond our expectations. All classes and every kind of people got enthusiastic over ballooning this week and it is the intention of the Aero Club of St. Louis to keep up the work. We will continue as an organization, only on a greater basis as an organization with some experience and the one that pulled off the greatest international balloon race ever held.[166]

The later activities of the Aero Club were to give full complement to his high expectations.

V
Centennial Week, 1909

O N JULY 5, 1808, A PETITION to incorporate St. Louis as a town
was drawn up, and two days later it received 80 signatures out
of a possible 101 of the "taxable inhabitants."[1] Elections were
held, a municipal government was established, and the incorporation was formally enacted on November 9, 1809.[2] The 100th anniversary of this event was celebrated from October 3 to October 9,
1909 — Centennial Week. The St. Louis Centennial Association,
of which Mayor Frederick H. Kreismann was president and Walter
B. Stevens secretary, directed the program for the entire week.[3]
The officials planned parades, luncheons, banquets, balls, concerts,
receptions, naval demonstrations, and aerial activities. This last
item was to be the highlight of the week. St. Louis would witness
balloon races, dirigible maneuvers, and for the first time in its history, sustained airplane flights.

It is well known that Orville Wright made "the first sustained
flight of an engine-driven, heavier-than-air, man-carrying flying
machine" on December 17, 1903.[4] He and his brother, however,
achieved their goal because a number of eminent men had laid the
groundwork for them. In England in the first half of the nineteenth
century, Sir George Cayley, William Samuel Henson, and John
Stringfellow developed theories of heavier-than-air flight and experimented with models.[5] In France, Clement Ader made flights in

three full-sized monoplanes in the 1890s, but was never able to gain control over his erratic machines.[6] Germany's Otto Lilienthal executed 2,000 glider flights before he was killed in a crash on October 10, 1896.[7] In the United States, John J. Montgomery made "the first successful glider flight in America" in 1883,[8] and Octave Chanute and A.M. Herring continued in his tradition, followed by the unfortunate fiascoes of Samuel Pierpont Langley.[9] The most famous of the successors of the Wright brothers made his first flight in the spring of 1908 and on July 4 of that year became the first man to win the *Scientific American* Flying Machine Trophy with the first public airplane flight in the United States.[10] He was Glenn Hammond Curtiss, the man who would be the most outstanding performer during Centennial Week, 1909.

In the interim since the 1907 aeronautic tournament, St. Louis had witnessed a significant amount of aerial activity. On September 8, 1908, Albert Bond Lambert, who had recently been elected to the St. Louis City Council, made his twelfth balloon flight and his first in the United States. He ascended in a 35,000-cubic-foot nameless balloon with Harry Eugene Honeywell, a local balloon manufacturer. They left the Laclede Gas plant at Second and Rutger streets at 4:52 p.m. and landed at Creve Coeur Lake, twenty miles west of the city, at 7:00 p.m.[11]

Less than a month later, Dr. Frederick J. Fielding, president of the Aero Club of San Antonio, asked Honeywell to build and pilot a balloon for him for a trip across the Atlantic Ocean. It was to be the largest balloon ever constructed, for it would be 85 feet in diameter and 300,000 cubic feet in capacity at minimum.[12] The further developments of this venture, however, were not reported.

During the same year, Morris A. Heimann, the first St. Louisan to have his own private balloon,[13] set out in his new 40,000-cubic-foot *Melba* in an attempt to exceed Oscar Erbsloeh's American record of 873.4 miles.[14] With Jack Bennett, a former British Army Balloon Corpsman, as pilot, the *Melba* arose from Second and Rutger streets at 3:15 p.m. October 13, 1908, but only sailed 26 miles before it landed at Wood River, Illinois at 4:30. Heimann, like Honeywell, was a balloon manufacturer, but this was his first ascension.[15]

A third St. Louis balloon maker who was active in 1908 was John Berry, who had unsuccessfully tried to demonstrate airships at the World's Fair in 1904 and at the aeronautic tournament in 1907.[16] He constructed a 40,000-cubic-foot spherical balloon with special propellers attached and ascended in this "dirigible" from Second and

Rutger at 9:30 a.m. August 16, 1908. On its maiden voyage the ship sailed only 21 miles to Troy, Illinois, where it landed at 1:30 p.m. The propellers, which Berry turned by hand, had only caused the balloon to spin and had added no speed or efficiency to the ship.[17]

The most spectacular flight of the year was made by Albert Bond Lambert and H.E. Honeywell. Lambert invited the balloon manufacturer to make a trip with him so that he could show Honeywell how to use a drag rope, a technique the drug tycoon had acquired in France. Lambert later recalled:[18]

> Captain Honeywell returned the compliment by equipping our outfit with a blower to force air into the gas bag after loss of gas. The idea originated with Captain Honeywell and the scheme was successful.[19]

They made their ascension from the Laclede Gas plant in the 60,000-cubic-foot oiled-cotton *Yankee* at 12:28 p.m. November 18, 1908. The day before, they had notified the Aero Club of America of their intention to try for the Lahm Cup by attempting to exceed Captain Charles De Forrest Chandler's record of 473.56 miles, established on a flight from St. Louis on October 17-18, 1907.[20] In addition to carrying fifty 45-pound bags of sand, the *Yankee* was well equipped for a long journey.

> Lambert took with him a good stock of provisions. In the stock were two fried chickens, twelve sandwiches, one pint of brandy, three quarts of water and two quarts of hot coffee in the thermos bottle. He also carried a number of aerial navigation instruments, including a statoscope, aerostat, aneroid barometer and Osram flashlight.[21]

The millionaire councilman suffered some criticism because of his avid interest in aeronautics. A contemporary newspaper cartoon depicted Democratic party workers marching down a road marked "To organization for coming spring election" and carrying signs which read "For Municipal Improvement" while Albert Bond Lambert hovered in a balloon above them, shouting, "Get busy boys, I'll be back soon."[22]

On its maiden voyage the *Yankee* traveled about 450 miles and landed at 7:00 a.m. November 19, in a cotton field on M.L. Arendale's plantation, seven miles from Tiger, Georgia.[23] During the night, Lambert himself later remembered, they had become lost and by daybreak did not know their position.

> I guessed Tennessee and Kentucky; Honeywell guessed Arkansas. Just after sun-up we were flying very low over the tree tops, speed about fifteen miles an hour. Not far ahead was a man in a field lazily leaning on a hoe. We were going to cross directly overhead.

"Here's our chance to find out where we are," said Honeywell. He yelled as loudly as he could: "What State and County are we in?" Man on the ground: "Where are you going?" Honeywell: "Why don't you answer my question?" Man: "Why don't you answer mine?"[24]

A few hours later they landed safely, but failed to capture the Lahm Cup. This trip was Lambert's thirteenth and was marred by another "unlucky" occurrence. Their balloon developed a leak and they had to make an emergency landing at Boyd, Illinois, 70 miles from St. Louis, to repair it, a factor which further reduced their distance.[25] Chandler's record, however, was to be broken in a flight from St. Louis the following year.

In July 1909, a rival organization was established to challenge the Aero Club of St. Louis for local aeronautic leadership. Morris A. Heimann was the promoter of this group, the Aero Club of South St. Louis, whose purpose was "to make ballooning a common sport and at the same time to boom South St. Louis.[26] Heimann donated his three balloons to the club — the 40,000-cubic-foot *Melba,* the 78,000-cubic-foot *South St. Louis,* and the 17,000-cubic-foot, one-man *South St. Louis, Jr.,* the smallest balloon in the city. The last two he had built at his factory at Thirteenth and Rutger streets, which was to serve as the new club's headquarters. A $5.00 membership fee from the 300 members would be devoted solely to buying gas for the balloons.[27]

John Berry, who had donated his *University City,* was the official pilot of the club, which intended to affiliate with the Aero Club of America as soon as possible.[28] The president of the new organization was Charles Nugent of B. Nugent and Company Dry Goods, and the vice president was Charles F. Wenneker, head of the Million Population Club of St. Louis. Heimann refused to accept office, but became a member of the executive committee.[29] Despite the elaborateness of the unit, the Aero Club of South St. Louis was never able to attain the stature of the original Aero Club of St. Louis.

In the same month that the newcomer was established, it clashed with its rival. Morris A. Heimann announced that John Berry would ascend in the *Melba* on July 18, 1909, with Julia Hoerner, who would thus become the first woman to ascend in a balloon from St. Louis.[30] H.E. Honeywell, however, a member of the Aero Club of St. Louis, snatched the chauvinistic "honor" from Berry and Heimann. On the inaugural flight of his 39,000-cubic-foot *Missouri,* he left the Rutger Street gas plant at 11:10 a.m. July 16, with his wife and Ada Miller, along with a "mystery woman" who later identified

Morris A. Heimann, right, before takeoff of the Melba *from the Laclede plant at Second and Rutger streets. Julia Hoerner is in the basket.*

herself as Mary Van Fertig. They landed at 4:05 p.m., 76 miles away at Washington, Missouri.[31] Julia Hoerner did make a flight on July 20 with John Berry in the *Melba,* sailing only to Belleville, Illinois.[32] The Aero Club of St. Louis, however, had won the laurels. A local newspaper commented:

> The ascension of Honeywell and the consequent blasting of Heimann's plans, adds another link to the merry little war waged on Heimann by the aristocratic members of the Aero Club [of St. Louis.][33]

No one remembered, however, that a Mr. S. Hobart had scored the "first" sixty-eight years earlier when he ascended from Fourth and Market streets with a fourteen-year-old Miss Day on October 9, 1841.[34] The Dozier-Lambert forces would clash again with the Heimann-Nugent crew during Centennial Week, in a continuation of their rivalry.

The aeronautic activities of the centennial celebration were under the auspices of the Aero Club of St. Louis, which had been authorized by the Centennial Association to spend $14,000 for the aerial events.[35] To assure the success of the exhibition, the club intended to bring noted aviators to St. Louis during the week. Albert Bond Lambert, chairman of the contest committee, declared:

> I have the greatest hopes of getting Curtiss for the fall flights, and no effort will be spared to have him operate an aeroplane which is owned by a local club. Our officials, who will meet in New York next week, think they have struck upon the best plan of assuring his coming, that is, by buying his air craft. We offered the Wright brothers $7,500 for one of their planes. They have treated our offer with only lukewarm promises.
>
> Since the favorable outlook in the matter of getting Curtiss, we have ceased worrying over the Wright brothers, although our offer still stands. Their presence would be a big drawing card. They have proven their craft to be one of the world's greatest. A contest between the Wright brothers and Curtiss would be the most interesting aviation contest imaginable.
>
> We stand ready to offer Curtiss the sum promised the Wright brothers. If they do not consider it favorably, we are ready to go as far in the pecuniary matter as our deliberations in New York will allow us. We intend to go into the matter to win, and we hope to return to St. Louis with an absolute promise from Curtiss, and, perhaps, Bleriot.[36]

Curtiss was currently the biggest name in aviation, for he had won the James Gordon Bennett International Aviation Cup for airplanes (not to be confused with the James Gordon Bennett International Aeronautic Cup for balloons) in the speed event at the first International Air Meet at Rheims, France, August 22-29, 1909.[37] This was "the date when flying came of age"[38] and Glenn Curtiss had been the star.

In an attempt to assist the Aero Club, the *St. Louis Post-Dispatch* cabled Curtiss, then exhibiting his prowess in Brescia, Italy:

> Could you fly in St. Louis at Centennial Celebration, Oct. 4 to 9 and at what figure.[39]

The aviator answered immediately:

> Expect to be engaged early in October. Like to fly your city three days six thousand.[40]

Lewis D. Dozier, president of the Aero Club, David R. Francis, and G.H. Walker were in New York conferring with Curtiss' partner, A.M. Herring,[41] but Albert Bond Lambert, who was in charge of the aerial program, decided not to leave the negotiations completely to them. On September 9, he wired Curtiss of his acceptance of the offer made through the *Post-Dispatch*.[42] On September 21 the Aero Club officials signed a formal contract with the aviator in New York, whereby he was to receive $6,000 for four flights, weather permitting, on October 6, 7, 8, and 9, 1909.[43] The elaborate plan of buying Curtiss' airplane did not have to be carried out.

Efforts were also made to secure the services of the Wright brothers, Hubert Latham, Henri Farman, and Louis Bleriot,[44] but all proved unavailable. The Wrights declared that they were "not in the exhibition business"[45] and announced on September 24 that they would enjoin the foreign aviators if they attempted to fly in the United States:

> If these machines are brought to this country for the purpose of making flights we will file suit against the owners. Both the Bleriot machine and the Farman machine are infringements on our patents.[46]

Despite the threat of court action, the Aero Club contracted with J.W. Curzon of Jackson, Mississippi, the following day for exhibitions by his Farman biplane, a replica of the machine in which Henri Farman himself had won the $20,000 distance prize and the $10,000 duration prize at the Rheims meet with a 118-mile flight lasting four hours.[47] The airplane was to be piloted by François Osmont, one of Farman's students, and Curzon was to receive $2,000 for bringing the ship to St. Louis and $1,000 for each day on which he made a sustained flight, on the condition that his total fee not exceed $5,000.[48]

A week earlier, on September 17, Vice President Daniel C. Nugent of the Aero Club of St. Louis had secured Mark O. Anthony of New York, who was financed by the Calcium Light Company, for an exhibition of his "wireless dirigible," a machine similar to the "Aerial Torpedo" demonstrated by Carl E. Myers at the World's Fair.[49] This airship, powered by a small motor which was controlled from the ground by electricity, was 35 feet long, with a gas capacity of 1,200 cubic feet and a lifting power of 35 pounds.[50]

> The wireless airship is intended primarily to be of aid at life saving stations on the coast. It will be cast adrift during storms from the station, and when above a storm-tossed ship the operator on shore will so manipulate the currents as to cause the [pilotless] airship to drop a rope, which will lead to shore. The inventor says also the airship will be of inestimable benefit in war to beleaguered cities.

> The controlling levers and valves are manipulated by currents of varying strength from a switchboard below. The craft can be made to describe circles in the air, rise to different altitudes and return to the starting point.[51]

A number of local inventors also expressed their intentions of exhibiting machines during Centennial Week. Frederick Van Barolom, the son of the president of the National Bank of Commerce, built an airplane at his home at 1 Westmoreland Place and planned to fly it during the celebration if he could find a suitable engine.[52] It was a monoplane 7 feet long and 26 feet in span, with a single propeller.[53] Hugh A. Robinson of 1526 North Whittier Street, a member of the Aero Club, perfected his third airplane at the shops of the Dorris Automobile Company, where he was employed. Patterned after the Latham monoplane, it was 34 feet long and had a wing area of 240 square feet. The machine weighed 600 pounds and, propelled by a 25-horsepower motor, it was expected to attain a speed of forty miles per hour.[54] John H. Tully and M. Dettmar of St. Louis built a biplane for the celebration and, like Van Barolom, sought a suitable engine for it.[55] Two Chicago inventors also constructed planes for the centennial — Edward E. Harbert (who had earlier exhibited kites at the World's Fair)[56] and F.N. Mahan.[57] While Curtiss and Osmont, as well as Anthony, were to fly on contract, the Centennial Association, prompted by the large number of amateur efforts, laid out a course in Forest Park and offered a cash prize for the airplane making the longest continuous flight in a contest slated for October 8.[58]

Although the airplane exhibitions were to be the highlight of the week, the main event of the centennial was a balloon race in three classes, scheduled for October 4. The first feature was a contest for advertising balloons, which were to be sent up at 2:30 p.m. that afternoon. The idea was conceived by Albert Bond Lambert, and it would be the first event of its kind ever held.[59] Twenty-four 3,000-cubic-foot balloons would be sent off, sponsored by such companies as Anheuser-Busch Brewing Company; Scruggs, Vandervoort, and Barney Dry Goods Company; Brown Shoe Company; and Halsey Automobile Company. Attached to the pilotless balloons were water-filled tin buckets, punctured to release their ballast in droplets.[60] The Aero Club offered five prizes for the balloons traveling the farthest distances,[61] and a reward of $10.00 was pledged to those who found and returned the bags as they landed.[62]

At 3:00 p.m. the St. Louis Centennial Cup Race for 40,000-cubic-foot balloons was to start. First prize was the Centennial Cup, with the Aero Club of St. Louis Trophy for the man who finished second. There were three entries: the 40,000-cubic-foot *Missouri,* owned by the Aero Club of St. Louis; the 35,000-cubic-foot *Indianapolis,* owned by the Aero Club of Indiana; and the 40,000-cubic-foot *Peoria,* owned by the Air Craft Club of Peoria, Illinois.[63]

At 4:30 the long-distance race for 80,000-cubic-foot balloons was scheduled to start. For the first five finishers, prizes of $600, $400, $300, $200, and $100 were to be awarded, plus a trophy for the balloon which stayed aloft longest. In this event there were seven entries, each of which was 80,000 cubic feet in capacity: the *St. Louis III,* owned by the Aero Club of St. Louis and piloted by Sylvester Louis Von Phul; the *Centennial,* owned and piloted by H.E. Honeywell of the Aero Club of St. Louis; the *University City,* owned and piloted by John Berry, a member of both rival St. Louis aero clubs; the *Hoosier,* owned by the Aero Club of Indiana and piloted by Charles Walsh of New York; the *Cleveland,* owned and piloted by J.H. Wade Jr., of Cleveland; the *New York,* owned and piloted by Clifford B. Harmon of New York; and the *Pommery,* owned and piloted by Nathan H. Arnold of New York.[64] These three balloon contests were to start from the Aero Club's newly established grounds at Chouteau and Newstead Avenues. The entrants in the long-distance event intended to have their records apply for the Lahm Cup as well.[65]

The third phase of the aerial program was for dirigibles. A triangular course was laid out in Forest Park from the Aero Club enclosure near Art Hill to the Mounted Police Station to the Frank P. Blair monument and return,[66] and the Aero Club officials offered a prize of $1,000 for the winner and $500 for the contestant who completed the route in the second-fastest time.[67] There were four entrants, each of whom had flown in St. Louis in years past: the veteran Thomas Scott Baldwin brought a 12,000-cubic-foot dirigible, powered by a 25-horsepower motor; A. Roy Knabenshue one of 8,000 cubic feet with a four-horsepower bicycle engine; Lincoln Beachey his 9,000-cubic-foot ship with a motor similar to Knabenshue's;[68] and seventeen-year-old Cromwell Dixon brought his 8,000-cubic-foot, 17-horsepower airship, with a spare Curtiss engine of twenty horsepower.[69]

In addition to these four contestants, L.S. Flateau of 5258 Maple Avenue in St. Louis was also involved in the area of dirigibles. He built a model of a revolutionary aluminum-hulled airship which he intended to construct in the near future. The 65,000-cubic-foot cylindrical metal shell was to be kept aloft with air heated to 200 degrees Fahrenheit by four Bunsen burners. A powerful engine was to drive four propellers and move the ship through the air. In spite of the tremendous amount of weight involved, "Mr. Flateau has no doubt that the hot air will be able to sustain the aluminum shell, the engine and carriage."[70] An avid engineer and scientist, he had patented 78 inventions and stood eighth on the list of living inventors for number of patents granted.[71]

While preparations were being made for the centennial, independent aeronautic activities took place in the city. Due to the efforts of Albert Bond Lambert, Missouri became "the only state that has its national guard equipped with an aero detachment."[72] This unit, Company A of the Missouri National Guard, held its first test session on September 5, 1909, when Lambert ascended in the *Missouri* from the Aero Club grounds at Chouteau and Taylor Avenues, and made a short flight to Camp Thelma, one mile from the Meramec Highlands near Fenton, Missouri.[73] The flight was not only a practice drill for the 22 members of the Balloon Corps,[74] but also a phase of the continuing rivalry with the Aero Club of South St. Louis.

That same afternoon, Captain Jack Bennett of the South St. Louis group made a flight in Morris Heimann's tiny *South St. Louis, Jr.,* from the Laclede plant at Second and Rutger streets.[75] The gas for the balloon cost only $15.00 and the bag was inflated to its 17,000-cubic-foot capacity in twenty minutes, while the average 80,000-cubic-foot long distance balloon required more than two hours to inflate.[76] During his flight, Bennett distributed 10,000 circulars advertising Centennial Week and the South St. Louis Aero Club, and landed 15 miles from Potosi, Missouri, a few hours after takeoff. His distance of 70 miles was slightly farther than Lambert's, and thereby Morris Heimann won a wager of $300 he had placed with his own aeronautic organization.[77]

This newly-established club made a bid for recognition when its chief pilot, John Berry, ascended in his *University City* from the Rutger Street gas works on September 19, with Dr. George C. Schwarz of Peoria as his aide. They were attempting to break Charles Chandler's Lahm Cup record of 473.56 miles, but sailed only 300 miles to Benton, Wisconsin. The flight was the first Schwarz had ever made. Berry, however, was a veteran, and this was his third attempt at the Lahm Cup, which he hoped to capture during the centennial races.[78]

On Sunday, October 3, 1909, the bells of 444 churches signaled the opening of Centennial Week.[79] On the following morning, "Welcome Day" (in honor of the visiting mayors),[80] preparations were made for the three scheduled balloon races. The huge gas retort at the St. Louis Aero Club grounds at Chouteau and Newstead had been filled with 4,000,000 cubic feet of hydrogen, although only 1,500,000 cubic feet would be needed for the participants.[81] Jefferson Barracks guardsmen had been detailed to assist in the inflation, and grandstands had been erected for the Aero Club members and their guests. There was no charge for the public, as there had been in previous contests, for every event of the entire week was free.[82] At that time, the Aero Club of St. Louis had 624 active members, only six of whom were licensed balloonists: James W. Bemis, John Berry, H. Eugene Honeywell, Albert Bond Lambert, Sylvester Louis Von Phul, and Harlow B. Spencer. Five of them were to serve as pilots in the balloon races and one was chairman of the contest committee.[83] There were 5,000 people gathered inside the enclosure at the start of the race and at least 150,000 more in the immediate environs.[84]

The members of the Balloon Corps of the Missouri National Guard filled the business balloons and began to liberate them at 2:30 p.m. The first to ascend was that of the Norvell-Shapleigh Company, but the roar that greeted it was nothing compared to that given Anheuser-Busch's *Budweiser* balloon. Attached to it was a clothing-store dummy bearing the inscription "L.D. Dozier," playing on the ironical fact that the president of the Aero Club of St. Louis was terror-stricken when faced with flight and had never made a balloon ascension.

> For the benefit of the uninitiated, if there be any such, it may be explained that, like a good general, the president of the Aero Club remains in the rear, directing operations through his aides-de-camp, instead of personally leading the charge against the enemies of the air, preferring to stay on terra firma rather than ascend to coela infirma.
>
> In other words, Mr. Dozier, the most famous patron and pro-

ducer of aeronautics in the world, not barring Emperor William, of
Germany, or President Faure of France, wears shoes with nine-
inch spikes in them rather than fly in the face of fate by going up
or down in a balloon.

> This wise determination has been the source of endless jest and
> merriment to his friends, who fail to remember that it long ago
> ceased to be the function of commanders of armies to lead charges,
> and, that the best precedents are inexorable in their dictation that
> the general commanding shall remain far to the rear, watching
> everything, seeing everything, directing everything, but above all
> things not exposing his precious self to anything more dangerous
> in the way of aeronautics than Knabenshue cocktails. [85]

Shortly thereafter, the entrants in the Centennial Cup Race were
sent aloft. There were only two contestants, for the *Indianapolis*
had withdrawn, thereby assuring that each would win a trophy.
The first of the 40,000-cubic-foot bags to ascend was the *Peoria* at
3:58 p.m., with James W. Bemis as pilot and E.G. Smith as his
aide. At 4:02 Harlow B. Spencer and James P. Deniver followed in
the *Missouri*.

> The two small balloons, in getting away without difficulty, set the
> successful examples. All of the large balloons, which went up
> afterwards, were equally as fortunate. There was no suggestion of
> accident during the day. [86]

These two pilots had just received their licenses, and this was their
first race. [87]

The contestants for the long-distance Lahm Cup Race then prepared to ascend.

> On the space between the pyramid stands were anchored eight
> great yellow balloons, looking like huge grape-fruit, their silken
> sides shining in the sun, their surfaces pulsating. . . . To furnish
> gas for inflation a long iron pipe lay like a huge devil's darning-
> needle down the center of the boulevard of balloons. From this
> main ran branches, each feeding an apparently insatiable yellow
> monster of silk and cord. [88]

The first to ascend was the *Cleveland,* piloted by J.H. Wade Jr.,
who was aided by A.H. Morgan, the nephew of the well-known fi-
nancier. [89] They took off at 4:40 p.m., heading southwest and clearing the housetops by fifty feet. S. Louis Von Phul and J.M. O'Reilly
were next off in the *St. Louis III* at 4:48 as the Barracks band played,
perhaps prophetically, "I Don't Know Where I'm Going, but I'm
On My Way." They were followed at 4:52 by Harry Eugene Honeywell and J.W. Tolland in the *Centennial*. The fourth entry was
piloted by Nathan H. Arnold of New York, who had been aboard the
St. Louis II when it fell into the North Sea in the Gordon Bennett

Race from Berlin in 1908.[90] Assisted by M. Leroy Taylor, he arose in the *Pommery* at 4:58.

A few minutes later, Clifford B. Harmon and Augustus Post of the Aero Club of America got away in the *New York,* the most expensive balloon in the race. The *University City* then made its ascension at 5:15 with John Berry and W.C. Fox, as the band played "There'll be a Hot Time in the Old Town Tonight." Berry was the favorite in the race, for he had recently won the first National Balloon Race, held at Indianapolis on June 5, 1909. With Paul McCullough as his aide, he had sailed the *"U. City"* 377.92 miles to Fort Payne, Alabama, in 25 hours and 35 minutes. In the same contest, Albert Bond Lambert and H.E. Honeywell had finished second with a distance of 328.5 miles.[91] Berry was also the sentimental hopeful, for his well-patched balloon was the oldest in the race.

At 5:20 H.H. McGill and J.E. Schauer ascended in the *Indiana.* This was a late entry in addition to the previously announced seven. McGill had wanted to make a unique entrance into St. Louis and had ascended from his home city of Indianapolis on September 30 with five passengers in his basket. The wind did not favor his plan, however, and he landed October 1 at White Plains, Kentucky, and shipped the balloon to St. Louis.[92] Although McGill had made 342 ascensions, he had never qualified as an official pilot. Lambert, Harmon, and Post had wired the Aero Club of America in New York on October 3 for an emergency license for him, but it had not arrived by the time of the start. In the contest, therefore, McGill had to race as a free-lance pilot, and could receive no prizes if he won, although he himself contended that he would be eligible if his license arrived before the end of the race.[93]

The last of the balloons, the *Hoosier,* took off at 5:47. The acting pilot, Dr. P.M. Crume, was in much the same position as McGill, except that he had no hope of receiving a license before the finish of the race. The *Hoosier* was to have been piloted by Charles Walsh, but he failed to arrive, so his aide, Dr. Crume, became the pilot and appointed Dr. L.E. Custer to assist him.[94] A ninth large balloon, the *South St. Louis,* piloted by Morris A. Heimann with Jack Bennett, made an independent ascension from the Laclede Gas plant at Second and Rutger and did not participate in the race.[95] The officials of the Aero Club of St. Louis had barred Heimann from the competition by refusing to allow him to use the facilities at their grounds for the start of the race. The furious balloon manufacturer, who, unlike his opposite number, Lewis D. Dozier, was an avid balloonist, decided to make the flight anyway for the Lahm Cup, even though he was not eligible for the Aero Club of St. Louis prizes.[96]

Each of the huge balloons was well-equipped for forty hours of flight. The stockpile in the *St. Louis III* was representative.

> Von Phul and O'Reilly took with them a case of beer, two gallons of mineral water, a can of malted milk, four cans of self-heating soup, 12 cans of sardines, three jars of jelly and a box of cookies.[97]

As the balloons sailed onward for the next two days, St. Louisans gathered at Forest Park for airplane and airship flights. The Centennial officials, at the suggestion of G.H. Walker, had adopted a color code to signal the people of the city in regard to the aerial activity for each day. Downtown buildings and street cars were to display flags with various meanings: red — airplanes will fly; white — dirigibles will fly; orange — wireless dirigible will fly; black — all flights canceled; black and white — previous signal canceled. On the grounds in Forest Park, pennants were to be displayed to show which particular airman would fly: red — Curtiss; blue — Osmont; purple — Anthony; white — Baldwin; green — Beachey; orange — Knabenshue.[98]

The 31-year-old Glenn Curtiss arrived in St. Louis on October 6. A local newspaper described him:

> The young American aviator is tall, slender, and stoops, or "jukes" forward with some of the birds he emulates. In his dark eyes there is that odd bird-like look: the look that is common to deep thinkers and students; the look that belongs to men who are always peering into the future, not idly regarding the present or the past.[99]

He brought with him two planes, both exact replicas of the machine in which he had won the speed classic at Rheims. Each biplane had a 32-foot wingspread and was powered by a 25-horsepower engine. Curtiss had built one of the planes on order for A.P. Warner of New York, who paid $7,500 for the machine.[100]

On October 4, St. Louis' Hugh Robinson brought his airplane to Forest Park for trials, but it did not have sufficient power to rise from the ground. On the same day, it was announced that Frederick Van Barolom would be unable to participate in the airplane races on October 8 because he had no suitable engine for his monoplane.[101]

On October 6, François Osmont made an attempt to fly Curzon's Farman biplane. The effort was a timid, half-hearted one, and Osmont shut his engine off just as he war reaching takeoff speed, using the excuses that "he feared collision with the trees; the ground was too rough, the crowd too close."[102] His failure delighted the airship pilots, who scoffed:

> We're out of date, passed by the times, ostlers of aviation, eh? You'd better hitch up the old gas bag to her, Frenchy! Airship bird, eh? Well, she acts like an ugly automobile.[103]

Lincoln Beachey then made a short flight 600 feet over the trees Osmont had feared so much,[104] just as Roy Knabenshue had done with his dirigible earlier that day.[105]

By the following morning, the results of the balloon races were known. In the Centennial Cup Race for 40,000-cubic-foot bags, the *Peoria* took first place and the trophy. James W. Bemis of St. Louis and George E. Smith of Peoria sailed 115 miles to Levins, Illinois. Harlow B. Spencer and James P. Deniver of St. Louis won the Aero Club of St. Louis Cup in the *Missouri* with a flight of 100 miles to Hibernia, Missouri.[106]

The long-distance race for 80,000-cubic-foot balloons was remarkable in that the contestants who finished first and second departed within five minutes of each other, yet one landed in Minnesota and the other in Alabama. The race was won by S. Louis Von Phul and Joseph M. O'Reilly in the *St. Louis III,* which traveled 540 miles to Mille Lac, Minnesota, in 40 hours and 24 minutes. They broke the Lahm Cup record of 473.56 miles and also won the first prize of $600 given by the Aero Club of St. Louis.[107] H. Eugene Honeywell and J.W. Tolland traveled 488 miles to Silas, Alabama, in the *Centennial* to win second prize of $400. J.H. Wade Jr. and A.H. Morgan sailed the *Cleveland* 459 miles to Alexander City, Alabama, and took third place for $300. The *University City,* with John Berry and W.C. Fox, won $200 with its flight of 202 miles to Mooresville, Missouri. Nathan H. Arnold and Leroy Taylor sailed 177 miles to Knobel, Arkansas, in the *Pommery;*[108] they won fifth place for $100 and Arnold also collected a $500 wager from Clifford Harmon, who finished sixth.[109]

Caught in crosswinds, the *New York,* with Clifford B. Harmon and Augustus Post, traveled only 146 miles to Edina, Missouri, but it took them 48 hours and 26 minutes to do so, and won them the endurance cup. This broke the record of 44 hours and 3 minutes set by Alfred Le Blanc and E.W. Mix in the 1907 Gordon Bennett Race from St. Louis,[110] and it stood for decades as an American duration record for balloons.[111] Harmon and Post also scored another first when they reached an altitude of 24,200 feet, another American record.[112]

Two of the eight contestants in the race were disqualified. Drs. P.M. Crume and J.H. Custer sailed 123 miles to Russellville, Missouri, in 17 hours and 24 minutes in the *Hoosier,* but since Crume had no pilot's license he was ineligible for any prizes.[113] H.H. McGill and J.E. Schauer actually finished in second place with a flight of 523 miles in the *Indiana* to Albany, Minnesota.[114] McGill was disqualified, however, not because he had no license, for it did arrive before the race ended,[115] but because he had started the race out of turn. He had been the seventh to make his ascension, instead of taking his alloted position of third.[116]

The ninth large balloon, which was contending only for the Lahm Cup, had problems of its own. A farmer mistook the *South St. Louis* for one of the advertising balloons and fired several shots at it, hoping for the $10.00 reward. Heiman and Bennett, therefore, landed as quickly as possible, coming down at Laredo, Missouri, 205 miles from St. Louis. The furious promoter of the South St. Louis Aero Club declared:

> They might have known the farmers would shoot at those little balloons in order to bring them to earth. It was placing the balloonists in unnecessary danger. There is danger enough in the sport itself without adding to it. Even if none of the aeronauts were hurt by a bullet, it would have been very easy to cause a leak that might lead to a serious accident.[117]

The advertising balloon race, upon which Heimann had vented his wrath, was won by the Halsey Automobile Company, whose balloon landed 80 miles away in Vergennes, Illinois. Each of the 24 bags was returned, and distances ranged down to that of the Ely-Walker Dry Goods Company, whose balloon finished last with a distance of 26 miles to Freeburg, Illinois.[118]

All of the balloonists in the long-distance race had intended their flights as trials for the Lahm Cup,[119] and three of them — Von Phul, McGill, and Honeywell — had exceeded Charles Chandler's record of 473.56 miles. Not one of them, however, was awarded the cup. Von Phul had failed to mail a letter he had written to the Aero Club of America announcing his intention,[120] and McGill neither registered with the Aero Club nor had a suitable license.[121] Harry Eugene Honeywell had sent in his $1.00 fee six months in advance, but he had told Augustus Post, secretary of the Aero Club of America, only verbally before the start of the race of his intention to make a Lahm Cup trial.[122] The Aero Club of America was still discussing his case when a new contender, A. Holland Forbes, solved the dilemma by setting a legitimate record far in excess of Honeywell's.

Meanwhile, aerial activity was increasing at Forest Park.

> The first aeroplane flight ever seen west of Dayton, O., took place at 6:21 a.m. Thursday [October 7, 1909], when Glenn Curtiss, watched by not more than fifteen persons, made two short trips

at the aviation field in Forest Park.[123]

After a run of 385 feet, he leaped into the air, reached a height of 20 to 35 feet, made a turn, and came down because the morning mist still obscured the trees. He then took off again and made a short hop back to his tent.[124] At dusk Curtiss made a third flight. This time a crowd of 300,000 waited for three hours to see him fly sixty yards, before his gas line clogged and the plane bumped to the ground. "The time of the flight was scarcely four seconds, yet it was flight — flight surpassingly beautiful and graceful while it lasted."[125]

The dirigibles were also in action that afternoon, making test flights for the race, which was scheduled for "St. Louis Day," October 9.[126] Knabenshue, Baldwin, and Beachey each made trial spins over Art Hill between 4:00 and 5:30, with the two younger aeronauts engaging in an impromptu race from the Art Museum to the enclosure, which Beachey won by a few seconds.[127] Osmont circled a three-quarter-mile course three times on the ground at dusk, but failed to get into the air.[128] Robinson was also on the field, but by the time he was ready, it was too dark to fly. Dixon had intended to test his airship with the others, but it had been damaged in transit and he was busy with repairs.[129]

The events of the following day, October 8, were essentially the same. Glenn Curtiss made his fourth flight of the week at 7:41 a.m., speeding at 30 miles per hour above the trees for 1 minute and 30 seconds for three-quarters of a mile before a crowd of only 300 persons, most of whom were Aero Club members and guests. Shortly thereafter, J.W. Curzon took the controls of his Farman biplane but was only able to rise four feet from the ground.[130]

Curtiss made another flight at dusk, rising 25 feet above the trees in a 40-second jaunt for 750 yards as a crowd of between 50,000 and 60,000 looked on. François Osmont then mounted the Farman and sped down the track for 400 feet, bouncing twice into the air and down again. As he drove the airplane back toward his tent in humiliation and disgust, he struck a small rise in the ground and cracked a wheel stanchion, ending further attempts at flight. Curzon, the owner, was furious and screamed at Osmont, who could neither speak nor understand English. Osmont, the pilot, replied with a torrent of words at Curzon, who could neither speak nor understand French. While their exchange was taking place, Hugh Robinson made a takeoff run in his monoplane, but his engine was not powerful enough to lift him into the air.

Each of the three airplanes was bothered somewhat by the wind. For that reason, they made most of their attempts to fly at dawn or

Glenn Curtiss flew this biplane over Forest Park for 90 seconds on the morning of October 8, 1909.

at dusk, when the wind was calmest, since they would not fly in any breeze over three miles per hour.[131] The highlight of the afternoon, in addition to Curtiss' relatively lengthy flight, came shortly after 5:00 o'clock when three airship pilots, Baldwin, Beachey, and Knabenshue, took to the air at the same time and circled over the park for six minutes. Cromwell Dixon made no flights because he was still repairing his damaged dirigible, and M.O. Anthony refused to demonstrate his "wireless dirigible" because the wind was too strong.[132]

A stiff seventeen-mile-an-hour wind canceled all flights on October 9, and showers drove all but 5,000 optimistic people from Forest Park. At about 5:00 p.m., however, the rain ceased and the breeze dropped, and Curtiss consented to fly. He was only in the air for 75 seconds, but he reached a speed of forty miles per hour and traveled for eight-tenths of a mile.[133] Declared the aviator: "This flight I have just made is the kind I have been waiting to make since I came."[134] The high wind, nevertheless, did prevent the four dirigible pilots from participating in their scheduled race, and the Aero Club would allow them no extension in time, so the prizes of $1,000 and $500 were not awarded.[135]

Glenn Curtiss made his seventh and last flight of the meet on October 10. Even though the Aero Club would not sanction the Sunday exhibition, he took off at 6:40 a.m. before a small crowd of 100 persons. The flight only lasted 1 minute and 21 seconds but it was his best of the week. He reached a speed of 40 miles per hour and a height of 60 feet as he circled over the park and returned almost to the exact starting point.[136]

That afternoon the aviator made a tour of potential airfield sites with L.D. Dozier, Albert Bond Lambert, G.H. Walker, and other officials of the Aero Club. Because of Curtiss' victory at Rheims in August 1909, the United States was to be the site of the 1910 James Gordon Bennett International Aviation Cup speed classic.[137] In addition, Edgar W. Mix had just won the 1909 James Gordon Bennett International Aeronautic Cup balloon race at Zurich, thereby bringing that event also to the United States for 1910. St. Louis intended to bid for the honor of staging both contests,[138] but it needed to develop suitable facilities, particularly for the accommodation of heavier-than-air craft. The Forest Park field was too cramped and had too many trees for safe airplane flights, so the Aero Club appropriated $20,000 for the establishment of a proper airfield.[139] With Glenn Curtiss, the officials visited Kinloch Race Track, a site near Shaw's Garden, and a tract of land along St. Charles Rock Road. The flier recommended the expansion of the present field at Forest Park, but the Aero Club leaders maintained their interest in Kinloch Park and shortly thereafter developed it into a permanent airfield.[140]

Curtiss waited in vain to fly on October 11, but the wind was too high, so he pocketed his $6,000 and left that night to keep a commitment in Chicago.[141] The wind had also prevented the four airship pilots from making flights on October 10. Beachey and Knabenshue left that night for a meet in Birmingham, and Baldwin and Dixon, who had made no flight during the week, remained in St. Louis to observe the upcoming aerial events.[142] J.W. Curzon made no further attempts at flight after François Osmont damaged his biplane on October 8. He left a few days later with his $2,000 fee, although he had earned no bonuses for sustained flight.[143] Mark O. Anthony did not exhibit his "wireless dirigible" during the week, and the airplane race, scheduled for October 8, was also canceled because "the only eligible machines were unable to fly that day."[144] Despite the number of failures, Aero Club President L.D. Dozier was satisfied.

> It would have been better had we been able to have the flights the first part of the week. The weather then was ideal, and if the events had taken place at that time there would have been no difficulty. As it was, the wind and rain stopped some of the features. On the whole the programme was carried out well, and interesting flights were given. The club feels that the exhibitions were worthy of Centennial Week.[145]

St. Louis had not yet, however, closed its 1909 aeronautic season. A. Holland Forbes, acting president of the Aero Club of America, and Max C. Fleischmann, former mayor of Cincinnati, arrived in the city on October 11 for the purpose of making a trial flight for the Lahm Cup in the *New York*, which Forbes owned jointly with Clifford B. Harmon.[146] Although a number of balloonists had had trouble with the entrance and notification requirements during the previous week, Forbes, the acting Aero Club president, was worry-free: "All I have to do to register for the Lahm Cup is to hand myself a dollar."[147] The *New York* left the Rutger Street gas plant at 5:35 p.m. October 12, 1909,[148] and succeeded in its venture. A. Holland Forbes broke Charles Chandler's standing record of 473.56 miles, established in a flight from St. Louis in 1907,[149] and he also eliminated the claims of H.E. Honeywell, S. Louis Von Phul, and H.H. McGill. The *New York* traveled 697.17 miles to twenty miles south of Richmond, Virginia, in 19 hours and 15 minutes to win the Lahm Cup.[150]

Albert Bond Lambert and S. Louis Von Phul, who had earlier

announced their intention to attempt to break Chandler's record, were unswerved by Forbes' success. At 5:30 p.m. October 15, they ascended from Rutger Street in the *St. Louis III,* the same balloon which Honeywell had built and Von Phul had flown in the long distance race during Centennial Week. A stiff 28-mile-per-hour wind was blowing at the time of their ascent, and but for their deft work in tossing three sand bags over the side, they would have been blown onto a network of telephone lines.[151] The two made an excellent flight and narrowly missed exceeding Forbes' newly-established Lahm Cup record. They traveled 685 miles in 15 hours and 29 minutes, landing in a tree near Ridgeville, South Carolina, 30 miles west of Charleston.[152] The St. Louis balloonists failed to win the trophy, and to make matters worse, while Councilman Lambert was sailing over the countryside, the St. Louis City Council voted down his pet measure, a bill "intended to permit electric signs to extend across the sidewalks."[153] Their flight, however, did establish a new American balloon speed record of 44 miles per hour.[154]

The free exhibitions of Centennial Week and the Lahm Cup trials which followed were proud products of the Aero Club of St. Louis. Although the scheduled airplane and dirigible races did not materialize, there were three successful balloon races, more than a dozen airship flights, and seven genuinely thrilling, although by modern standards somewhat short, airplane flights by Glenn Curtiss, the first ever performed in St. Louis. With eager expectation, the Aero Club looked forward to activity even more outstanding in 1910.

VI
The International Aeronautic
Tournament, 1910

IN 1910 THE AERO CLUB OF ST. LOUIS experienced the greatest
year in its history. The organization took part in two airplane
meets, an international balloon race, a convention of aero clubs, a
national aero show, the staging of a spectacular flight over the Mississippi River, and the establishment of the first permanent airfield
in St. Louis.

The initial activity of the year was the first American convention
of aero clubs. At the request of the St. Louis unit, fourteen organizations from all parts of the country came together for the first time on
January 29, 1910. Albert Bond Lambert was one of the men appointed to the Racing Committee to arrange sanctioned air meets, and it
was felt that he could use his influence to secure for his city the
James Gordon Bennett International Balloon Race.[1]

Since Edgar W. Mix had won the 1909 Gordon Bennett from Zurich, the United States was to be the site of the contest in 1910.
St. Louis, Omaha, Denver, and Kansas City were bidding for the
event.[2] In April, however, the Aero Club of America announced
that, because of the outstanding success of the 1907 contest, St.
Louis had won the honor for 1910. The international race was scheduled to start on October 17 at 4:00 p.m., since on that night and
those immediately following there would be a full moon, which
would be of aid to the balloonists.[3]

A month earlier, it had been announced that Lewis D. Dozier, president of the 700-member Aero Club of St. Louis, "the largest and most active club in the country,"[4] had resigned after nearly three years as chief of the organization. He would stay on, however, as one of the vice presidents of the club, and in his place, Albert Bond Lambert, who had been first vice president, was elected to head the organization.[5] No better man could have been chosen to guide the group during its most productive year.

In 1910 the Aero Club operated four separate airfields: Camp #1, "Spherical Ascension Grounds" at Chouteau Avenue between Taylor and Newstead; Camp #2, "Jumping Grounds," on the block circled by West Pine, Sarah, Vandeventer, and Laclede; Camp #3, "Temporary Practice Field" at Washington Park, near East St. Louis, Illinois; and Camp #4, "Permanent Aviation Field and Dirigible Harbor" at Kinloch Park, Missouri.[6] The Chouteau Avenue balloon grounds was to be the site of the Gordon Bennett Race on October 17,[7] and at the Washington Park field an aviation meet for novices was conducted by the Aero Club in July 1910.[8] The tournament was deemed a success, although it saw "no real flying."[9] It did, however, stimulate the building of aircraft by many residents of the city.

Hugh A. Robinson and Frederick Van Barolom perfected the monoplanes that they had attempted to demonstrate during Centennial Week in 1909.[10] In addition, W.F. Zeller, William Frank, Clarence Williams, Mark Fisher, Will Y. Haggart, W. Fears, Alfred Kuhne,[11] and "many St. Louis automobile chauffers"[12] were building planes during the spring and summer of 1910 and readying them for trials.

Arthur Cornell, a St. Louis carpenter who resided at 2109 O'Fallon Street, constructed an airplane of cypress and wrought iron, 22 feet long and 3 feet wide. Its unique feature was that it had both a horizontal propeller 7 feet 6 inches long on the top of its fuselage, and a vertical propeller 5 feet 6 inches long in its nose.[13] Daniel J. Piskerski, owner of the Union Machine Works at 1413 North Tenth Street, built a monoplane of his own design, but he failed in his first attempt to fly it at Calvary Cemetery before a crowd of 200 spectators on September 8, 1910.[14] J.J. De Praslin came all the way from Nicaragua expecting to buy a Farman biplane in St. Louis. When he found none for sale, he had one built in John Berry's garage at 1025 North Vandeventer Avenue. The machine was 40 feet long, 14 feet high, and had a wingspan of 32 feet. The fuselage and the Gnome engine, which he had shipped from France, together cost $6,000.[15]

Albert Bond Lambert, left, and Orville Wright. This photo is captioned "Aviation Meet, Kinloch Field, St. Louis, 1910," but there is no record of Wright visiting at that time. Lambert did fly with Wright that year, but at Dayton, Ohio, and that probably was where this photo was made.

The last significant young airplane builder was Tom W. Benoist, who constructed his third biplane in 1910.[16] He had been working at aeronautics since the World's Fair, when he had been financially interested in John Berry's unsuccessful dirigible,[17] but, although he had built three airplanes on his own, he had never made a flight.[18] This hiatus was filled on September 18, 1910, when Benoist became "the first resident of St. Louis to drive an aeroplane."[19] The flight was also the first to take place at the new Kinloch Field and was made not in one of Benoist's own planes, but in a Curtiss biplane he had purchased from Howard Gill. During his short hop, he reached a height of 50 feet and traveled 150 yards.[20] Although he was St. Louis' first actual pilot, Tom Benoist was not the first resident of the city to fly in an airplane. E. Percy Noel, secretary of the

Aero Club of St. Louis, earned that distinction on April 8, 1910, when he went up as a passenger with Glenn Curtiss at Memphis, Tennessee.[21] A few months later, Albert Bond Lambert made a flight with Orville Wright at Dayton, Ohio,[22] and his brother, J.D. Wooster Lambert became the third St. Louisan to fly when he took a trip of 9 minutes and 37-3/5 seconds with Claude Grahame-White at the Harvard-Boston air meet on September 12.[23] Thomas W. Benoist was to become, however, St. Louis' most enterprising aviator and its first great airplane manufacturer.

Kinloch Park, the setting for his first flight, had been selected as the site for the Aero Club's permanent aviation field shortly after the close of the 1909 centennial celebration.[24] Located twelve miles from downtown St. Louis, the former racetrack soon came to be called Lambert Field because the Aero Club president had been so influential in its development for aeronautics.[25] This nomenclature, however, did not catch on in nearly the degree as that applied to a different airfield in the 1920s, the city's current municipal airport.

The primary purpose of the establishment of the field was the conducting of an international aeronautic tournament, scheduled for October 8-18, 1910.[26] This would not be the first such meet held in the United States, for the Aero Club of California had achieved that distinction earlier that year at Dominguez Field, Los Angeles, January 10-20.[27] The Aero Club of St. Louis, nevertheless, meant to distinguish itself by staging an even greater contest. In so doing, it gained the honor of becoming the only aero club in the United States to possess its own permanent aviation field — Lambert Field/Kinloch Park.[28]

Before the great venture got under way, St. Louis witnessed one of the most sensational events in its aeronautic history. As a prelude to the great October tournament, the *St. Louis Post-Dispatch,* in cooperation with a local citizens' committee headed by Edward Devoy and Albert Bond Lambert, made arrangements for Clifford B. Harmon, the New York aviator who had set an American balloon endurance record during Centennial Week,[29] to make a flight down the Mississippi River at St. Louis. A contract was signed in New York in August 1910, and at the same time, Harmon agreed to bring with him Thomas Scott Baldwin, another veteran who had often appeared in St. Louis.[30] Shortly thereafter, however, the New York aeronaut crashed both of his biplanes and wired the newspaper, canceling his flights:

> My disappointment that I am not to be the first to fly in an aeroplane over the Mississippi is far greater than that of any individual

in St. Louis. I know only too well how hospitable your people are, hence my regret.[31]

The *Post-Dispatch* then made the same offer, a cash award of $2,500, to the Wright brothers, but they were occupied with other activities.[32] Thomas Scott Baldwin, however, did agree to make the river flight in place of Harmon, on the condition only that his expenses be paid. The *Post-Dispatch* was to assume the financial burdens of the aviator and the Citizens' Committee was to pay the ground costs.[33]

Officials prepared an airfield near the river to accommodate his plane. A tract of land 3,500 feet long and 500 feet wide, adjacent to Bellefontaine Cemetery in North St. Louis, was leased. The weeds were cut, sheds were erected, it was enclosed by an 8,000-foot fence, and arrangements were made for 25 men from the First Regiment of the Missouri National Guard to assist the airman and 300 policemen to handle the crowds.[34] Unlike those at the scheduled Kinloch meet, Baldwin's would be free to the public.[35]

On September 8, Captain Baldwin arrived with his two mechanics, Jay Stafford and Carl Moulfield, and began to assemble his airplane, which had been shipped from Long Island and had reached St. Louis the preceding day.[36] His homemade machine, named the *Red Devil,* was a Curtiss-type biplane and could attain a speed of 55 miles per hour.[37] The route he was to fly was from the aviation field at 6700 North Broadway overland to Merchants' Bridge, then downriver over McKinley and Eads bridges to a landing on the east side at Cahokia Ferry, opposite Pestalozzi Street. If weather and wind conditions permitted, he was to make a return trip by the same course, but flying under Eads Bridge. The distance was seven miles each way, and Baldwin estimated that it would take him about ten minutes for each leg.[38]

Before he undertook the daring stunt, the New York pilot, who at 205 pounds was still "the heaviest successful aviator,"[39] performed a number of trial flights at the North St. Louis field. On September 9 at 5:55 p.m., he took his first short hop, and then at 6:10, in the presence of 300 spectators, Baldwin made "the first aeroplane flight in a closed circuit ever accomplished within the limits of St. Louis," and he did it in a twenty-mile-per-hour wind.[40] He made two three-quarter-mile circles of the field in three minutes at a height of 70 feet and a speed of 55 miles per hour.[41]

After a short test run at 3:57 p.m. on September 10, the *Red Devil* left the airfield at 5:24 and headed for Merchants' Bridge one mile away. At a height of 150 feet in a brisk, eighteen-mile-per-hour

The St. Louis Republic *ran this montage of Baldwin and his* Red Devil *on the day after his famous flight beneath Eads Bridge.*

wind. Baldwin then turned south and flew over the Mississippi River for six miles. While passing over Eads Bridge, he ran into a dead calm which caused his ship to drop 100 feet in an unexpected thrill for the 200,000 spectators who lined both banks and swarmed upon the bridges. After only ten minutes of flying, he landed at Cahokia Ferry on the eastern bank and rested for 22 minutes to take on water and inspect the *Red Devil.* He then took off and headed upriver for Eads Bridge and the most hazardous part of his trip.

> I was sweeping onward at nearly a mile a minute. There was but one thing to do—make sure of my ground and go straight ahead.
> Now the bridge was just ahead of me. I did not dare look up to see the crowd, nor turn to the right nor left to see the people on the levees. A thoughtless or careless second might dash me against one of the piers, and end my flying career. Of course, you don't have much time to think about such things when you are sweeping through the air.

I recall now that I saw the outline of two black piers ahead of me and the steel framework above me, but it was all over in a second. There was a moment of exhilaration when I realized that I had successfully passed under the bridge, and that I was then on the last lap of my first flight of consequence.[42]

The east span of Eads Bridge is 502 feet wide and 65 feet high, and the *Red Devil,* with its 38-foot wingspan, made a perfect bull's-eye. This feat was surpassed a few moments later when the veteran aviator passed under the east span of McKinley Bridge, 500 feet wide and 65 feet above the water. After a nine-minute, wind-aided return flight, Baldwin landed his ship, having covered the fourteen-mile round trip in a flying time of nineteen minutes, averaging 43 miles per hour.[43] This had been an exhibition St. Louis would not soon forget, for it was "the best demonstration of a heavier-than-air flying machine ever seen in the Mississippi Valley,"[44] and the first extensive flight to take place in the city. Captain Baldwin, one of the few men licensed to pilot balloons, dirigibles, and airplanes,[45] had had long experience exhibiting his prowess over St. Louis and it was fitting that he should make such a sensational flight. After four more daring displays the following day at the North St. Louis field in a twenty-mile-per-hour wind,[46] he was given two $1,500 checks by the *Post-Dispatch* and the Citizens' Committee and was promised a gold medal by the Aero Club of St. Louis.[47] On September 13, he left for New York, vowing to return for the Kinloch meet. While praising the exploits of the aviator, the *Globe-Democrat* editorialized:

> Next month St. Louis will offer the greatest aeronautic programme, including the international balloon race for 1910, ever arranged in any country. The present exhibitions of Capt. Baldwin are but a skirmish line suggestion of what is coming.[48]

At Kinloch Park, three hangars were built at a cost of $300 apiece,[49] grandstands were erected to seat 100,000 spectators, and $1,500 worth of telephone and telegraph lines were laid for the press.[50] To attract a sufficient number of aviators, the Aero Club of St. Louis offered prizes aggregating $25,000 for a program of ten events: "Bomb throwing, altitude flights, endurance flights, speed races, fancy flying, quick turning, slow flying, accurate landing, quick starting and special feats."[51] These contests were to be conducted daily between 2:00 and 5:00 p.m., except for October 17, the date of the Gordon Bennett Race. The most innovative feature was to be the attacks on the helpless battleship *"Doughnaut,"* a 300-foot-long and 50-foot-wide model of the latest floating fortress. The airmen were to hurl plaster bombs at it from heights ranging from 200 to 1,000 feet, with a prize of $1,000 going to the most accurate marksman.[52]

Albert Bond Lambert made arrangements with A. Roy Knabenshue, the one-time dirigible jockey who had risen to become manager of the Wright Exposition Company, for six of the Wright fliers to appear at the meet: Walter Brookins, Arch Hoxsey, Ralph Johnstone, P.O. Parmelee, A.L. Welch, and J. Clifford Turpin.[53] Brookins was the senior Wright pilot and the most capable member of their team, even though he was only twenty years old.[54] Hoxsey and Johnstone were known as the "Star Dust Twins" because of the skill of their performances.[55] The one was "an immaculate dandy, balancing his pince-nez elegantly," the other "a clown and inveterate vaudeville performer."[56] These three young luminaries of the Wright Company were great friends, but were bitter rivals in the air, each always trying to outdo the other. Despite their considerable abilities, however, the three were not even licensed pilots, and the Aero Club of America named Albert Bond Lambert to observe their flights officially during the meet so that they could qualify properly.[57] The Wrights paid their pilots $20 per week, with a bonus of $50 for every flight they made; all prizes won, however, went to the brothers. This was a profitable arrangement, for in 1910, its first year of operation, the Wright Exposition Company made a net profit of $100,000.[58]

As the primary drawing card of the meet, Lambert secured the services of Alfred Le Blanc, the famed balloonist and aviator who stood "at the very top of the list of great French airmen."[59] The British ace, Alexander Ogilvie, also agreed to appear. Both he and the Frenchman would make their American heavier-than-air debuts at St. Louis, although Le Blanc had participated in the International Balloon Race in 1907.[60]

Tom W. Benoist was to represent the Aero Club of St. Louis at the meet with his new Gill-Curtiss biplane, and H.E. Honeywell and J.W. Tolland of St. Louis planned to demonstrate their new semi-rigid dirigible.[61] This made a total of nine airplanes and one airship entered in the daily contests.

Because of the great expense of the meet, the Aero Club charged an admission fee of 50¢ per person for pavilion seats and $1.00 for the grandstand. The parking rate was $1.00 per car and $1.00 per passenger (a charge which included a grandstand seat). Street cars went to the airfield from all points of the city for a fare of 10¢.[62] These cars were scheduled to carry signal flags of either red, denoting "flights today," or white, denoting "no flights today,"[63]

Arch Hoxsey landed at Kinloch Field October 8, 1910, after setting a nonstop long distance record from Springfield, Illinois. He dove for the benefit of the photographers before landing.

but manager Knabenshue canceled them as unnecessary, saying, "Our men will fly any day, rain or shine, wind or calm."[64]

The great aviation meet opened on October 8 in grandiose fashion. Arch Hoxsey set an American cross-country nonstop distance record with a flight from the grounds of the Illinois State Fair at Springfield. His distance was 87 miles, breaking the previous record of 86, set by Walter Brookins on September 29 on one leg of his flight in the same plane from Chicago to the fair grounds.[65] Despite its glamor, the flight was marred by mishap. A special train with a white-painted roof had been detailed to guide Hoxsey to St. Louis. The aviator's watch, however, was six minutes fast and he took off from the field at 11:54 a.m. instead of at noon as scheduled. Lookouts at the depot missed his departure and the train finally pulled out at 12:12, speeding at 70 miles per hour to catch him. The result still would have been fortunate had not the Wright pilot become confused at the junction of the Alton and McKinley tracks at Carlinville and taken the wrong ones. The upshot of the affair was a complete failure for the train, which never sighted the aviator. Hoxsey also missed a large tar paper smoke signal at Kinloch Field and finally landed at 2:39 p.m. at St. Louis Country Club, interrupting two startled elderly gentlemen engaged in a round of golf. He got five gallons of gas, plus suitable directions, and arrived at Kinloch Park at 3:30 p.m.[66] It was a comedy of errors, but a record nonstop flight nonetheless. The Wrights charged no additional fee for the demonstration, for it was their compliment "in appreciation for what St. Louis has done for aviation."[67]

There were twelve other flights on the opening day of the meet in the presence of a disappointing crowd of 8,000 spectators. The character and length of these exhibitions set the stage for the flights of the rest of the week. They were:

J. Clifford Turpin, up 2:00 p.m., down 2:07; altitude, 300 feet. Walter Brookins, up 2:01, down 2:10, altitude 800 ft. Walter Brookins, up 2:36, down 2:39; to sight Hoxsey. Walter Brookins, up 3:02, down 3:23; to sight Hoxsey. A.L. Welch, up 3:13, down 3:25. Arch Hoxsey sighted, 3:21, down 3:30; left Springfield 12:00 n. Walter Brookins, up 4:24½, down 4:36; bomb-throwing. Ogilvie, up 4:42½, down 5:01; figure eights. Arch Hoxsey, up 4:50, down 5:03; with passenger [Andrew Drew]. Walter Brookins, up 5:00, down 5:19½; vol plane. Walter Brookins, up 3:50, down 4:01; with Ogilvie. Hoxsey, up 4:03, down 4:07½. A.L. Welch, up 4:10, down 4:18; bomb-throwing.

Total time up — Turpin, 7 minutes; Brookins, 1 hour 15 minutes; Welch, 20 minutes; Hoxsey, 3 hours 17 minutes; Ogilvie, 18½ minutes.[68]

Shortly after Hoxsey had arrived, "the most exciting flight of the afternoon" was made when Walter Brookins took up Alexander Ogilvie at 3:50 for an eleven-minute flight in his Wright biplane. It was the first time St. Louisans had witnessed a passenger riding in an airplane.[69] It was hoped that the enthusiasm generated by the inaugural events would draw larger crowds in succeeding days.

On the second day of the meet 75,000 people, most of whom remained in the free area outside the fence,[70] watched fifteen flights by five different aviators.[71] The feature of the afternoon was a nine-mile cross-country race between Arch Hoxsey and Walter Brookins over a triangular course for a prize of $1,000. Both pilots "revved up" their Wright biplanes as three Signal Corpsmen held the tails of each plane. At the signal of a "bomb shot" at precisely 3:58:30 p.m., both aviators roared into the air. Averaging nearly one mile per minute, the two Wright rivals crossed the finish line in a dead heat 9 minutes and 21 seconds later, and the race was rescheduled for October 12.[72] The crowd-pleasing event of the day came shortly after 4:30, when four of the Wright pilots took to the air at one time: Turpin, Hoxsey, Brookins, and Welch. Shortly thereafter, the day's program ended when twenty-year-old Walter Brookins executed a spiral glide from several hundred feet in the air, landing fifteen seconds after 5:00 p.m.[73]

Missouri Historical Society

Percy Noel, flying a Wright biplane, took this picture of Ralph Johnstone seconds before Johnstone decided to wave to the crowd. As he did, a gust of wind hit his own Wright craft and it crashed from a height of 20 feet. Johnstone recovered and returned to Kinloch before the meet was over.

Missouri Historical Society

Among the ten flights witnessed by the 5,000 paying spectators on October 10 was a three-minute trip by Ralph Johnstone, cut short by a crash from a height of twenty feet. The cause of the accident was pilot error, for as he took his hands off the controls to wave, a puff of wind caught his fragile biplane and pushed it sideways to the ground.[74] The Wright star was hospitalized with bruises on his legs and ankles, but soon recovered and rejoined the competition. That same afternoon, James H. White set up his camera equipment and began shooting motion pictures of the flights.[75] This film was later known as the "death reel" because almost all of the aviators depicted died in plane crashes within the next eighteen months.[76]

The most long-remembered event of the entire meet occurred on October 11, when Colonel Theodore Roosevelt made a visit to St. Louis and to Kinloch Park. Arch Hoxsey had telegraphed the former president at Hot Springs, Arkansas, on October 9, inviting him to make a flight when he came to the city, but Roosevelt had not replied.[77] When "TR" arrived at the airfield, Albert Bond Lambert presented Hoxsey, who seized the opportunity.

"Col. Roosevelt, our birthdays fall on October 27," he said, "and as a result, I feel that I have somewhat of a lien on your indulgence. I want you to take a short spin with me in the air. You can, with perfect safety, trust yourself in my hands."

Col. Roosevelt pushed his hat back on his head and asked, "Now?"

"Yes," replied Hoxsey, "this is as good a time as we can ever get. It is calm and ideal flying machine weather. Will you go?"[78]

The ebullient ex-president needed little urging. A crowd of 30,000 saw the Wright biplane take off at 4:01 p.m. and execute curves and "figure eights" for 3 minutes and 20 seconds at a height of fifty feet. Roosevelt waved so enthusiastically that Hoxsey had to caution him to remain still and hold onto the braces. Said Teddy on landing: "Bully. There's nothing like it. I wish I could have stayed up longer."[79] It was only fitting that such a man would be the first president to fly.[80]

Roosevelt's exhibition was understandably the highlight of the afternoon, and it overshadowed significant achievements. A.L. Welch was in the air before the former president arrived and after he had departed. When Welch finally landed at 5:03 p.m., with scarcely a drop of gasoline in his tanks and deafened from the engine noise, he had set a new American endurance record of 3 hours, 11 minutes, and 55 seconds, breaking by 6 minutes and 15 seconds the record Ralph Johnstone had established at Boston a month

Arch Hoxsey adjusts his goggles before giving the first airplane ride to a United States president. The honoree was Theodore Roosevelt.

earlier.[81] Alfred Le Blanc made three flights in his trim Bleriot monoplane. Brookins hit the *"Doughnaut"* with one of his two plaster bombs, and also carried Lieutenant Hart of the Signal Corps for 25 minutes and 40 seconds to a height of 2,500 feet in the longest and highest passenger flight to take place at Kinloch Park.[82] Aero Club president Albert Bond Lambert, in preparation for his pilot's license, then made a nine-minute flight with Arch Hoxsey.[83] It was a most eventful day.

On October 12, a crowd of 12,000 saw fifteen flights by seven aviators. Le Blanc flew circles around the Wright biplanes with his Bleriot XI monoplane, one of three he had brought to the United States for the James Gordon Bennett International Aviation Trophy Race on October 29 at Belmont, New York. The French ace claimed that he had touched 80 miles per hour, although no measured course had been set up to test him.[84] Ralph Johnstone got up from his hospital bed, against the advice of Roy Knabenshue, to make a five-

Pioneer aviators dropped plaster "bombs" on a mockup of a battleship during the Kinloch air meet.

minute flight. The cross-country race was re-run and Hoxsey nipped Brookins in a tight finish. Albert Bond Lambert then made the third flight of his career, a short spin with Arch Hoxsey, who allowed him to pilot the biplane for a few minutes.[85] At the close of the day's program, five planes got into the air at the same time.[86]

That same afternoon, Tom Benoist, who was to have flown at the Kinloch meet, was injured at an air tournament in Amarillo, Texas. While tinkering with his Gill-Curtiss biplane on the ground, he was struck on the head by the propeller, causing him to suffer a slight brain concussion and the loss of three toes of his right foot as well. He had gone to Texas to fulfill a contract for his friend, Howard Gill, who had been too ill to attend.[87] The St. Louis pilot, however, soon recovered, and continued his aerial career.

Among the eleven flights on October 13 were Lambert's fourth trip and A. Roy Knabenshue's first appearance in a plane. Although he was the manager of the Wright Company, he had never ridden an airplane. Brookins took him up for 10½ minutes and also cut circles with Johnstone and Hoxsey. The "Star Dust Twins" each made speed runs over the measured mile, with Arch Hoxsey recording the faster time of 1 minute and 21-2/5 seconds.[88] Le Blanc refused to pilot his racer over the course because it was the thirteenth of the month.[89]

The superstitious Frenchman had no qualms on October 14. "A red barn marked the start and a white paper arrow head the finish at the press stand.''[90] As he roared over the measured-mile course, Albert Lambert timed him at 53 seconds flat, a new American speed record of 68 miles per hour, barely under James Radley's world record of 74 miles per hour.[91] J. Clifford Turpin tried to break Welch's endurance record with the same plane Welch had used, but he had to land after 1 hour, 28 minutes, and 20 seconds when the pistons of his engine ''froze'' from lack of oil.[92] The day's events came to an end after fourteen flights when Ralph Johnstone made a spiral glide into a ''dead stick'' landing from a height of 3,000 feet.[93]

That evening, Aero Club president Lambert, who had taken his fifth flying lesson that day with Arch Hoxsey, issued a plea for more support for the meet. He reckoned that the gross expenses of the tournament would exceed $45,000. The current receipts were sufficient to pay for the aviators' prizes, but he hoped that spectators would turn out heavily for the last two days of the meet, scheduled to end on October 16, so that the Aero Club could liquidate the ground expenses. ''Pay your way through the gates,'' urged Lambert, ''and discourage the parasites who seek adjoining fields to deadbeat their way.''[94]

A crowd of 18,000 took his exhortation to heart on October 15, but a large number of ''parasites'' were also on hand. Fifteen flights were made that day. Albert Bond Lambert had his sixth ride, and Ralph Johnstone set a new St. Louis altitude mark of 4,500 feet.[95] Everyone got an unexpected thrill when 64-year-old Lewis D. Dozier, vice president, former president and organizer of the Aero Club of St. Louis, finally lost his reputation[96] and made his first flight of any kind in his life. Walter Brookins lured him into a biplane to pose for a motion picture. For effect, he started the engine, and then asked Dozier if he would like to go up for a short trip. The Aero Club executive was hardly enthusiastic but he agreed to the venture. The flight was 3 minutes and 40 seconds of sheer terror for him. Walter Brookins later described the trip:

> Dozier was holding on tight, very tight, when we made the circle and approached the grandstand. Banners, handkerchiefs, and hats were waving. I said: ''Wave to the crowd; show them you are not nervous.'' ''All right,'' said Dozier, but he didn't stir. ''Wave!'' said I, as we again approached. ''All right,'' said Dozier, but he didn't even change his expression. On the third lap I yelled emphatically, ''Wave, this is your last chance!'' I then glanced over and saw Mr. Dozier holding on to the upright with four fingers, and waving his thumb.[97]

A crowd of 35,000 paid $16,000 on October 16 to witness the

A smiling and confident Lewis D. Dozier sits next to young Walter Brookins, unaware of Brookins' intent to give the flight-shy business executive his first, terror-filled airplane ride.

closing events of the Kinloch air meet.[98] The large turnout liquidated the expenses of the Aero Club and gave promise for another meet in 1911, since it at first appeared that there would be a surplus in the treasury.[99] Johnstone and Brookins raced cross-country three miles and back in the main event of the day. "Almost at the finish Johnstone executed a skillful maneuver, flying under Brookins, and so getting ahead of him."[100] There were sixteen flights on the final day, and the meet ended when Ralph Johnstone touched the ground at 5:12 p.m.[101] That night, all the fliers packed up their machines and shipped them to New York for the Belmont meet, which was to begin on October 22.[102]

The "Star Dust Twins" had only a few more weeks to live. Ralph Johnstone died in a plane crash at Denver on November 17 after a reckless spiral glide.[103] Arch Hoxsey was killed at Los Angeles on December 31 when he crashed while trying for an altitude record.[104]

They were only two of the 37 well-known aviators who died in airplane crashes in 1910.[105]

St. Louis could hardly have asked for a more stirring aerial tournament. Although the crowds did not occupy the grandstand in as great a number as expected, the paid attendance for the nine-day exhibition was 63,210,[106] and the meet was something of a financial success. The fliers did not always adhere to the program, but the people did not mind. Although P.O. Parmelee failed to accompany the Wright team, and neither Tom Benoist nor H.E. Honeywell were able to exhibit their St. Louis-built machines, Alfred Le Blanc, Alexander Ogilvie and the five pilots of the Wright Company amassed a total of 127 flights, among which were new American records for speed, distance, and endurance. Despite the smashing success of the Aero Club's first major airplane tournament, the climax was yet to come. On October 17, St. Louis turned its attention to the James Gordon Bennett International Balloon Race.

Ten large 70,000- to 77,000-cubic-foot balloons from four nations were to take part in the contest: three each from the United States and Germany and two each from France and Switzerland.[107] Fourteen pilots had been expected to enter the competition, including Count von Moltke from Denmark,[108] but only ten materialized. The American team had been chosen with a national elimination race from Indianspolis on September 17. The first three finishers had been: Alan R. Hawley and Augustus Post, who had sailed 453 miles in the *America II;* H.E. Honeywell and J.D. Wooster Lambert (the brother of the Aero Club president), 379.5 miles in the *Centennial;* and J.H. Wade Jr., and A.H. Morgan, 371 miles in the *Buckeye.*[109] Two days before the Gordon Bennett was to start, however, Wade suddenly withdrew from the race to attend his grandmother's funeral. Sylvester Louis Von Phul of St. Louis, who had finished fourth at Indianapolis, was named to replace him on the American team.[110]

The Aero Club's ascension grounds at Chouteau and Newstead had been doubled in size for the race by the leasing of adjacent property at a cost of $1,000.[111] Two thousand seats at $1.50 each were erected on the field, with a special section reserved for the Aero Club members and guests,[112] and the residents of the area reaped a monetary harvest by selling "wildcat" seats outside the enclosure at prices ranging from 10¢ to 25¢.[113] Laclede Gaslight Company laid a sixteen-inch pipeline from its plant at Second and Rutger streets to the grounds and conveyed a coal gas of .387 specific gravity.[114] James Gordon Bennett, publisher of the *New York Herald Tribune,*

The Million Population Club, *last place balloon in the international competition in St. Louis in October 1910, also flew in the National Balloon Race in Indianapolis a month earlier, when this picture was taken.*

provided a $2,500 trophy for the winning club and a cash prize of $3,000 to be divided among the first three finishers.[115] In addition, August A. Busch donated $500 and the Aero Club of St. Louis $250 for fourth and fifth places respectively.[116] The International Contest Committee was made up of Cortlandt Field Bishop, Pierre Gasnier, Albert Bond Lambert, Lewis D. Dozier, and Frank S. Lahm.[117] On October 13 in New York, this panel presided over the allotment of the starting positions. The rotation selected was France, the United States, Switzerland, and Germany.[118]

On October 17 at 4:40:29 p.m., the first ascension took place in the presence of 25,000 spectators. This cambric balloon, the *Condor,* was piloted by Jacques Faure of France, who was assisted by E.G. Schmolck. As the Jefferson Barracks Band played the national anthem, St. Louis' *Million Population Club,* a Honeywell-built cambric balloon, arose at 4:52:45 with S. Louis Von Phul and J.M. O'Reilly in charge. Switzerland's rubber *Azurea* then took to the air at 5:07:05, piloted by E. Messner and Leon Giraudan. Seven minutes and ten seconds later, the *Harburg III* made its ascension, with Lieutenant Leopold Vogt in command, aided by the German-speaking William F. Assmann of St. Louis.

Next came the *Isle de France* at 5:23:30. It was piloted by Alfred Le Blanc, who had been runner-up in two previous Gordon Bennetts and had recently distinguished himself with heavier-than-air craft at Kinloch Park. This "double-threat" airman was the favorite in the race. "He is regarded as having more experience in long distance flying than any of his opponents and he is regarded as the best individual selection by a group of experts."[119] This time, however, the experts would be proven fallible. His aide was Walter de Mumm, scion of the celebrated family of French winemakers.

The sixth starter, at 5:25:40, was the *St. Louis IV,* piloted by

Harry Eugene Honeywell with J.W. Tolland, both of whom were representing the Aero Club of St. Louis. This balloon, and the *Million Population Club,* each of which was a product of Honeywell's handiwork, had been left uncovered on the grounds during the preceding night, and a horde of grasshoppers had eaten fifteen holes in the tasty linen fabric of the two envelopes.[120] Both were patched and made their ascensions on cue, but the strange accident would affect their behavior during the race.

At 5:26:55 the *Helvetia* took to the air, with Colonel Theodore Schaek and A. Armbruster in its basket. Colonel Schaek, president of the Aero Club of Switzerland, was deemed a strong contender, for he held the world's endurance record of 73 hours, set in the Berlin Gordon Bennett Race of 1908.[121] In eighth position, the *Dusseldorf II* ascended at 5:35:55, controlled by Hans Gericke and Samuel F. Perkins. Alan Hawley, "the dean of American aeronauts,"[122] and his customary companion, Augustus Post, let go in the *America II* at 5:45:56. The final entry, the glistening *Germania,* arose at 5:54:30, at the bidding of Hugo von Abercron and August Blanckertz. This balloon was the most colorful of all, for it had been covered with a coating of aluminum dust to deflect the rays of the sun and thus prevent the expansion and subsequent weakening of the gas.[123] This ingenious tactic was to bear rich fruit.

St. Louis was well represented in the race, for it provided five of the twenty pilots and aides (Honeywell, Von Phul, Tolland, O'Reilly, and Assmann).[124] In a lethargic ten-mile-per-hour wind, the first five balloons headed west-northwest, while the rest veered off toward the north, both of which were favorable courses giving promise of extremely long flights, uninterrupted by mountains or the sea. The two French and three American balloons carried "blowers" similar to that used by Lambert and Honeywell in their flight in the *Yankee* in 1908.[125]

> This machine connects with the bag by a tube, and has a fan-like wheel by which air can be forced into the bag to keep it continually inflated as the gas leaked out.[126]

In addition to such technical innovations, the balloons carried interesting items in preparation for extensive flights:

> Pate de fois gras, caviar, compressed oxygen, lime stoves, grapefruit, champagne, Rhein wine, claret, beer, whiskey, cigars to be chewed but not smoked, mattresses, chairs, tables, playing cards, skillets, revolvers, soups in self-heating cans and straw to keep the feet warm.[127]

Special precautions were taken against thirst and frostbite.

Each aeronaut, when asked if he expected to carry liquor, replied in the negative, but then added "Except for some bottles of," and then gave the name of some liquor. Col. Schaek was emphatic in stating he would carry no liquor "except two quart bottles of whiskey.[128]

Within two days after the start of the race, most of the results were known. Seven of the balloons had sped on over Canada, but three had been forced to land south of the Great Lakes: the *Million Population Club,* the *St. Louis IV,* and the *Condor,* all of which suffered gas leakage.[129] The most eventful trip was that of the *Harburg III,* for when it descended rapidly from 18,000 feet into Lake Nepissing, Ontario, the balloon struck the water with such force that William Assmann broke his left arm and sprained his right wrist.[130]

By October 22, all the balloons were accounted for except the *America II.*[131] Hawley and Post had landed in the wilds of Quebec after a flight of almost 48 hours and had had to travel for four days on foot before they came across a party of four French-Canadian fur trappers who took them by canoe to the settlement of St. Ambrose, where they telegraphed word of their landing to St. Louis. During the preceding week, search parties from the American and Canadian governments, the Aero Club of America, the Aero Club of St. Louis, the United States Revenue Cutter Service, the United States Army Signal Corps, and the Hudson's Bay Company had combed the wilds looking for them.[132] Their distance was first reported as 1,355 miles, which would have broken Count Henry de la Vaulx's ten-year-old world's record of 1,193 miles.[133] A War Department survey, however, determined the distance to be 1,172.9 miles. This was a new American record, for it bettered Oscar Erbsloeh's mark of 873.4 miles, a standard achieved in the 1907 Gordon Bennett from St. Louis.[134] It was also a new Lahm Cup record, breaking the one set by A. Holland Forbes in a 697.17-mile flight from St. Louis in 1909.[135] Alan Hawley thus won both the James Gordon Bennett International Aeronautic Cup and the Lahm Aeronautic Cup, for he had registered his intention to try for the latter, even though the Aero Club of America had discouraged such a dual purpose idea in the 1907 Bennett Race from St. Louis.[136] As a result of his excellent flight, Hawley also won permanent possession of the Lahm Cup, since his mileage stood unexceeded for the requisite three years. In fact, it lasted until 1976 as the American distance record for Class A-10 (unrestricted size) balloons.[137]

Recent developments in balloon technology have made possible flights of enormous distances. In the three-year period from 1978 to 1981, balloonists crossed the United States, the North American continent, and both the Atlantic and Pacific oceans. As of 1984, the last major unattained achievement was a flight around the world.[138]

The official results of the 1910 International Balloon Race were:

1) *America II* (United States) — Alan R. Hawley, pilot, and Augustus Post, aide. 1,172.9 miles to Lake Tschotogama, Quebec.

2) *Dusseldorf II* (Germany) — Lieutenant Hans Gericke, pilot, and Samuel F. Perkins, aide. 1,127.5 miles to Kiskisink, Quebec.

3) *Germania* (Germany) — Hugo von Abercron, pilot, and August Blanckertz, aide. 1,068.8 miles to Coocoocahe, Quebec.

4) *Helvetia* (Switzerland) — Colonel Theodore Schaek, pilot, and A. Armbruster, aide. 826.0 miles to Ville Marie, Quebec.

5) *Harburg III* (Germany) — Lieutenant Leopold Vogt, pilot, and William Assmann, aide. 758.4 miles to Gull Island, Lake Nepissing, Ontario.

6) *Azurea* (Switzerland) — Captain E. Messner, pilot, and Leon Giraudan, aide. 747.9 miles to a point 22 miles northeast of Biscotasing, Ontario.

7) *Isle de France* (France) — Alfred Le Blanc, pilot, and Walter de Mumm, aide. 718.7 miles to a point three miles north of Pogamasing, Ontario.

8) *St. Louis IV* (United States) — H.E. Honeywell, pilot, and J.W. Tolland, aide. 551.3 miles to Hillman, Michigan.

9) *Condor* (France) — Jacques Faure, pilot, and E.G. Schmolck, aide. 408.2 miles to Two Rivers, Wisconsin.

10) *Million Population Club* (United States) — S. Louis Von Phul, pilot, and J.M. O'Reilly, aide. 316.3 miles to a point 6½ miles north of Racine, Wisconsin.[139]

A total of $3,750 had been donated for prizes, to which the Aero Club of America added $600, one half of the fees of the original twelve entrants. Hawley received $1,400, in addition to winning the Gordon Bennett Cup for the Aero Club of America and the Lahm Cup for himself. Gericke received $1,200, von Abercron $1,000, Schaek $500, and Vogt $250.[140]

One month after the start of this race, the Aero Club conducted its last activity for the year, the first National Aero Show, November 17-24.[141] Eighty entrants, representing aero clubs, aeronautic industries, and private initiative exhibited their wares at the Coliseum, Jefferson and Washington avenues. Several different types of aircraft were on display: Tom Benoist's Gill-Curtiss, with which he had had his recent accident at Amarillo, a Wright biplane, a Farman biplane, a nickel-plated Curtiss biplane, and two Bleriot monoplanes.[142] The Farman biplane may have belonged to J.D. Wooster

Lambert, who had purchased one for $6,000 and was to take flying lessons in New York from Claude Grahame-White, the British ace who had formerly owned the plane.[143] John Berry built a Demoiselle monoplane for the show, and also exhibited a large balloon, which he intended to take to Mount McKinley.[144] J.J. Prince built a Bleriot at a carriage factory on South Grand Boulevard; a man named Swift constructed a wing-flapping ornithopter to bring to the show; and Thomas Scott Baldwin displayed his celebrated *Red Devil,* the plane in which he had flown over the Mississippi two months earlier.[145]

The only mishap at the exposition occurred when the 40,000-cubic-foot *Missouri,* which had been improperly suspended from the Coliseum ceiling, exploded with a loud report and collapsed.[146] Model airplane contests were held each day and a prize of $5.00 was awarded for the best daily flight of more than 100 feet, with "grand prizes" of $10,00, $5.00, and $2.50 for those who made the most flights over fifty feet during the entire show. One of the entrants was Samuel Lambert, the sixteen-year-old nephew of the president of the Aero Club,[147] who would later play a vital role in the air industry of St. Louis.[148]

The main feature of the show was the "man-carrying" kite demonstrations of Samuel F. Perkins, the same person who had assisted Hans Gericke in the Gordon Bennett Race. With his apparatus, he set two kiting marks. On November 23, he sent Helene Mallard up to a height of 40 feet over Forest Park in a chair attached to the kite. She was the first woman ever to make such a flight.[149] On November 30, Perkins himself broke the world's altitude record when he soared to 300 feet on his kite.[150] The demonstration was a fitting close to a golden year for the Aero Club of St. Louis.

The Kinloch meet was the first substantial air tournament conducted by the Aero Club. The total receipts for the nine-day program were $38,315.61. The club had spent $27,297.00 for prizes and $11,264.16 for advertising, and thus lost $245.55 on the venture. To cover expenses of $4,138.82 for the James Gordon Bennett International Aeronautic Cup Race, the Aero Club collected only $533.65 in gate admissions, a loss of $3,605.17.[151] The organization, therefore, sustained a deficit of $3,850.72 for the entire tournament, but there was no discouragement. St. Louis immediately placed its bid with the Aero Club of America for the 1911 Gordon Bennett Race,[152] and plans were made for another air meet in conjunction with it.

If one had to select the greatest year in the entire history of aviation in St. Louis, that choice could only be 1910. This was the Aero Club's "finest hour."

VII
Fairground and Kinloch, 1911

ENCOURAGED BY THE SUCCESS of its previous ventures, particularly those of 1910, the Aero Club of St. Louis decided to stage two air meets in 1911. Although the city's aviation fame came from free ballooning, both tournaments would concentrate on heavier-than-air craft, in keeping with the latest developments in aviation. St. Louis had put in its bid for the annual Gordon Bennett Race, but it lost out to Kansas City.[1] Pilots from the Aero Club of St. Louis, however, swept the first three places in the National Elimination Race, also held at Kansas City, on July 10: Frank P. Lahm in the *St. Louis IV,* John Berry in the *Million Population Club,* and William Assmann in the *Miss Sophia.*[2] All three thereby earned places on the American team for the international race, in which they finished second, fourth, and fifth, respectively.[3]

Albert Bond Lambert, the vigorous president of the Aero Club of St. Louis, realized one of his many ambitions when he finally earned an official pilot's license in September 1911.[4] He had made his first airplane flight with Orville Wright the year before and had had several lessons from Arch Hoxsey at the Kinloch meet in 1910.[5] Walter Brookins coached him during the summer and autumn of 1911 as he completed his requirements. The Aero Club of America expected certain qualifications of its licensed airplane pilots:

Applicants must pass the three following tests:

Albert Bond Lambert, St. Louis industrialist, became the first St. Louisan to win a pilot's license.

(A) Two distance tests, each consisting in covering, without touching the ground, a closed circuit not less than five kilometers in length (length measured as indicated below).

(B) An altitude test consisting in rising to a minimum height of 50 metres above the starting point.

(C) The (B) test may be made at the same time as one of the (A) tests.

The course over which the aviator shall accomplish the aforesaid two circuits must be indicated by two posts situated not more than 500 metres from each other.

After each turn made around a post the aviator will change his direction so as to leave the other post on his other side. The circuit will thus consist of an uninterrupted series of figure eights, each circle of the figure alternately encircling one of the posts. The distance credited over the course covered between two turns shall be the distance separating the two posts.

For each of these three tests the landing shall be made:

(1) By stopping the motor not later than the time when the machine touches the ground.

(2) At a distance of less than 50 metres from a point designated by the applicant before the test.

Landings must be made properly and the official observer shall indicate in his report the way in which they were made, the issue of the license being always discretionary.

Official observers must be chosen from a list drawn up by the governing organization of each country.[6]

Lambert received License Number 61 from the Aero Club of America.[7] In so doing he became one of only five men in the United States to hold both official balloon and airplane licenses,[8] as well as the first St. Louisan[9] and the only president of an aero club to possess an airplane pilot's license.[10] He himself could thus take a more active part in the air festivities of 1911.

The Aero Club's first air meet of the year took place October 1-8 at Fairground Park. This 128-acre tract in North St. Louis, used as a drill field during the Civil War and later as an exposition site and a race track, had been formally dedicated a municipal park by Mayor Frederick H. Kreismann on October 9, 1909, the final day of Centennial Week.[11] The exhibitions there were to be free of charge, since the public had a disinclination to pay for what it could see for nothing.

At all past aviation meets where an admission fee has been charged the outside crowd has greatly outnumbered the inside crowd. . . . Empty grandstand seats are the rule rather than the exception at aviation meets.[12]

The 700-member Aero Club would not be bothered by the expense of the tournament. "The one hundred millionaires included in its membership would feel guilty of professionalism, perhaps, unless called upon to make up a deficit."[13] While there may not have been quite that many men of extreme wealth in the organization, aeronautics in these early days was very much a rich man's game, as names like Alberto Santos-Dumont, A.H. Morgan, Walter de Mumm, Clifford B. Harmon, and Albert Bond Lambert attest.

The aerial activities were to be the main feature of an entire week of free public entertainment in the city. Also included in these events of "Festival Week" were the annual Veiled Prophet parade and ball, a marathon foot race, a national automobile show at Forest Park Highlands, and motor boat races on the Mississippi River.[14]

Fairground Park had been selected in place of the Kinloch airfield because it was in the city itself and was thus much more accessible to the public.[15]

President William Howard Taft had declared his intention of visiting St. Louis during the autumn of 1911, and it was hoped that, because of Theodore Roosevelt's precedent in 1910,[16] Taft might be persuaded to make an airplane flight.[17] (Apparently no one remembered that "Big Bill" weighed over 300 pounds and that the heaviest passenger ever carried up to that time had weighed a relatively dainty 241."[18] The president made his visit, however, not during "Festival Week," but on September 23. Albert Von Hoffmann, a St. Louis air enthusiast, invited him, nevertheless, to make a balloon ascension with him from University City. Taft declined and from the safety of a box seat at a baseball game in League Park he watched Von Hoffmann and his two small sons as they sailed over the city with John Berry in the *Million Population Club* to East Madison, Illinois, where they landed 2½ hours later.[19]

On the evening before the president's arrival, the first aviation fatality at Kinloch Park took place. Raymond J. Raymond, a twenty-five-year-old Greek immigrant, was killed while cranking the engine of the monoplane owned by his employer, Amedee V. Rayburn Jr. "He was completely scalped and suffered a compound fracture of the skull when struck by the propeller, which began to whirl prematurely."[20] More than 2,000 flights had been made in the eighteen months that Kinloch airfield had been open before this first fatality.[21] The tragedy, nonetheless, did not dampen the enthusiasm of the aviators for the coming activities.

The star of the Fairground meet was to be Walter Brookins, the sole survivor of the celebrated "Big Three" of American aviation who had been the mainstays of the powerful Wright team.[22] When the Wright brothers learned of their pilot's negotiations with the Pioneer Aeroplane and Exhibition Company of St. Louis, they made their position clear:

> We call your attention to the fact that Mr. Brookins is bound to fly for The Wright Company if he flies at all, and that if he attempts to fly for others, without first obtaining our consent, we will have him enjoined.[23]

Perhaps disgruntled over shabby treatment by the brothers, Brookins broke with them and launched out on his own.[24] On September 15, 1911, Albert Bond Lambert, together with C.J. Shea of the Pioneer Aeroplane and Exhibition Company, signed a contract with him whereby Pioneer would furnish the aviator with a Wright biplane and that he would be paid $3,000 for flights on October 1, 7, and 8.[25] Four days later, Brookins signed another agreement with Pioneer whereby he would fly for the company for six months in return for 50 percent of the gross earnings he might receive from his exhibitions.[26] His later success made the venture a profitable one for both parties.

A number of other aviators were scheduled to appear at Fairground: Andrew Drew and Tom Benoist of St. Louis, John D. Cooper, Charles Zornes, Sax Ganz, C.O. Prowse, and Hillery Beachey, the brother of the Toledo aeronaut who had flown dirigibles in St. Louis in 1907 and 1909.[27] In addition, several pupils from Tom Benoist's flying school intended to exhibit their fledgling talents: Harry Rafferty, John Woodlief, Alfred Boullet, B.N. Elsk, and Charles Griffin.[28] Contests for rapid starting, speed, altitude, target bombing, and accurate landing were planned, as well as the usual aerobatics by all participants.[29]

A stand had been erected on the field to display colored flags designating the aviators in the air: Brookins, blue; Drew, red; Benoist, white; Cooper, green; Zornes, pink; Ganz, purple; Prowse, black and white; Beachey, brown; and Benoist's students, purple and white.[30] The climax of the meet was to take place on October 7 and 8, when Hugh Robinson of St. Louis, who had experimented with monoplanes in 1909 and 1910,[31] would demonstrate his Curtiss hydroplane on the Mississippi.[32]

The meet was to have opened on October 1 with a flight by Walter Brookins from Forsyth Junction to Fairground Park, but wind and rain prevented the stunt. Because of the great number of people who had braved the inclement weather and stood eight to ten feet deep around the former one-mile racetrack, Brookins did make two flights over the field. The first lasted from 4:15 p.m. to 4:31 and the second from 4:35 to 4:47.[33] The temporary airfield proved greatly inferior to the Aero Club's permanent aviation park. Although Kinloch Field had in 1910 been "pronounced by aviators the finest field they had ever ascended from,"[34] the ex-Wright ace was not pleased with Fairground, since it had an uneven surface and offered little room for takeoff.

> I would not attempt to carry a passenger from this site. But, in nice weather, I think we will have a good meet. The water in the lagoons is quite a few inches deep and will allow of aliting in the lagoons without damage to the machines.[35]

No formal flying was scheduled for October 2-3 because of the opening of the auto show and the Veiled Prophet pageant on those days.[36] Walter Brookins, however, kept interest in the aerial activities aroused by giving flying lessons and short exhibitions at Kinloch Park.[37]

Walter Brookins straps two 50-pound sacks of mail to his biplane, then took off on the first airmail flight in the city. The date: October 2, 1911.

On October 4, the young aviator took part in the most memorable event of the 1911 meet.

> Walter Brookins established a world's record . . . in carrying 5,000 pieces of mail by "Aerial Post" from Kinloch Aviation Field to Fairground, a distance of twelve miles, in ten minutes and fifteen seconds.[38]

On October 2, Postmaster T.J. Akins of St. Louis had been authorized by Postmaster General Frank H. Hitchcock to collect and deliver mail by airplane on October 4, 5, 6, and 7 to demonstrate the feasibility of such service.[39] St. Louisans who wished to participate in the stunt had been directed to mark all outbound letters, "Please save and send by Aerial Post."[40] The postal officials then canceled each of the 5,000 pieces of mail with a special stamp reading, "Aeroplane Station No. 1, St. Louis, Mo. Aviation Field. October 4, 1911."[41] Two fifty-pound sacks of mail were rushed to Kinloch Park and strapped to the wings of Brookins' biplane. He took off at 4:17:27 p.m. and landed at 4:32, after circling over Fairground Park for four minutes for the benefit of the 25,000 spectators. Postman F.W. Hageymeyer then took the two mailbags off the wing and sent them by car to the downtown post office for outbound shipment and delivery.

> It is said that hundreds of the thousands of post cards and letters
> contained in the sacks contained this greeting, "Greetings, this is
> the first post card to be sent from St. Louis by Aeroplane Post."[42]

Walter Brookins, who at different times had held every airplane record in the world,[43] was only two weeks late in adding another to his list. The first man to carry official mail by airplane was Earl Ovington, who had flown it ten miles from Nassau Boulevard to Garden City Estates during an air meet on Long Island from September 23 to October 2, 1911. This was the birth of airmail in the United States.[44] Brookins, nonetheless, gave St. Louis the distance record by two miles.[45]

Three stations were established as terminals for the mail flights during the following three days: Kinloch No. 1, Fairground No. 1 at the western end of the park, and Fairground No. 2 at the eastern terminus. Only those cards and letters bearing the words "Aerial Route" in the lower left corner and deposited in a special box at Vandeventer Avenue and Natural Bridge Road would be carried by plane between the stations.[46]

Brookins' historic demonstration had been made in a strong wind which canceled the formal speed, altitude, and accuracy events. Several pilots, however, did attempt to take to the air on October 4. W.H. Blakely rose only a few feet in his fragile machine, and W.C. Robinson failed in his efforts to take off in a plane owned by Alfred Kuhne of St. Louis. Walter Brookins made a second flight of ten minutes and Tom Benoist was readying his biplane when darkness closed in on him.[47]

Earlier in the afternoon, a crowd of 25,000 had witnessed a crash by Hillery Beachey from a height of fifty feet after only a few minutes of flight. He was rushed unconscious to Mullanphy Hospital, as a frenzied mob converged on his broken plane for souvenirs. The aircraft was a Curtiss-type biplane which had been built by Morris A. Heimann and Beachey at Heimann's factory at Thirteenth and Rutger streets. The mishap occurred because the plane was in improper balance. The Toledo aviator, who had been paid $5.00 per minute for his time in the air, soon recovered from his injuries but made no flights during the meet.[48]

Had it not been for the daring of Walter Brookins, the 20,000 spectators at Fairground on October 5 would have spent the afternoon without witnessing a flight. A steady wind again proved too strong for the amateurs and again prevented the scheduled events. A brisk breeze overturned W.C. Robinson's Farman biplane after it made a short jump into the air, but the aviator was thrown to the ground unhurt. Brookins then made two five-minute circuits of the field in spite of severe buffeting by the wind. On his first trip he carried another bag of airmail between the two stations at the park.

> Notwithstanding the fact that the mail was only carried the circuit of the field, the sack was filled with thousands of missives which had been sent especially to be carried by aeroplane.[49]

Again on October 6, Walter Brookins found himself the only performer, as high winds and occasional raindrops canceled the aerial program. An impatient crowd of 10,000 saw him make two short flights in his wind-jostled Wright biplane. On landing, he gave his assessment of the situation:

> Two things have hindered the St. Louis meet this week. The starting and landing places in this park are rough, and air currents have been adverse. I believe I have encountered every kind of bad air current in existence this week.[50]

Aero Club President Albert Bond Lambert had more trouble in keeping the aviators on the ground than in getting them into the air.

> Robinson and Kearney came to me and asked to be allowed to fly, but the winds and air stratas are too treacherous for them to risk their lives. Each is ambitious for a record and inclined to underrate the dangers of the air. Robinson and Kearney and Blakely have been wild to make flights.[51]

Inclement weather and a thirty-mile-per-hour wind again prevented the scheduled events on October 7. Hugh Robinson was to have carried mail between Missouri and Illinois in his Curtiss hydroplane over the Mississippi River, but the wind proved too strong. His scheduled race with Hugo K. Kippert's *Missouri III* motorboat for a $1,000 wager over a 2½-mile course, with the boat receiving a one-mile handicap, was also canceled.[52] The "Idol of Chicago," George W. Beatty, who held three world's passenger-carrying records, had contracted to fly solo for one hour over Fairground Park for $5.00 per minute. His flight was put off, as well as a five-mile speed race for a $200 prize donated by the Anheuser-Busch Brewing Company.[53] The winner of the fifteen-mile "marathon" foot race from Kirkwood to Fairground was to have been carried across the finish line by plane, but this feature, too, had been canceled because of the wind.[54] A disappointed Albert Bond Lambert declared:

Missouri Historical Society

*Hugh Robinson ascended from the Mississippi River in this
Curtiss seaplane on October 8, 1911. Here he accepts a sack of mail,
which he flew to the east side, then back to Missouri again. This
was the first seaplane flight in St. Louis.*

> We have had a week of phenomenally unfavorable weather for
> the performance of what promised to be one of the best aviation
> programmes ever planned in this part of the country.
>
> Our contracts for $4,500 worth of aviation events expired to-day
> [October 8], without a performance of any note, owing to the
> wretched weather through the week. We hope, however, if the
> weather is favorable to-day, to make up to some extent for the dis-
> appointment of the week by offering special prizes aggregating
> $800 for flights by the aviators who are still on the grounds.[55]

A crowd of 50,000 persons, the largest of the week, gathered at
Fairground Park on October 8 for the closing events of the meet.
The day was chilly but free of buffeting winds. George Beatty had
been scheduled to fly from 2:30 to 5:30 for $5 per minute, but his
engine went dead after two and one-fifth minutes of flight, and he
was paid only $11.00.[56] Brookins made five flights over the field,

and during one trip he dropped a mail sack from a height of 1,000 feet to demonstrate the efficacy of rural deliveries. "At all times did he have his machine under perfect control and his landings were as light as the snowfall."[57] Andrew Drew made a five-minute flight over the field, and Horace Kearney rose to a great height and flew over the city for several minutes, as thousands of residents came out of their houses to watch him. Three bombs were then set off to announce the close of the Fairground air meet.[58]

On the Mississippi River, Hugh Robinson performed as expected, although the *Missouri III* did not appear for the scheduled race. Robinson ascended in his Curtiss seaplane at 10:38 a.m. from the foot of North Market Street. He headed downstream and sailed over Eads Bridge at a height of 750 feet. In a more extensive repetition of Thomas Scott Baldwin's *Red Devil* flight of 1910,[59] Robinson then turned north and flew under Eads Bridge, over McKinley Bridge, and under Merchants' Bridge. Turning south, he steered the hydroplane under Merchants' Bridge a second time, and under McKinley Bridge, as he touched the water for the sixth time during the demonstration. This was the first time St. Louis had seen a seaplane in flight. "Robinson soared for more than twenty minutes and never in the history of aviation in St. Louis has a more entertaining flight been witnessed."[60] He had carried a sack of mail to the Illinois side of the river, but no arrangements had been made to leave it there, so he brought the bag back with him to the St. Louis post office.[61]

Immediately thereafter, the St. Louis aviator collected a $1,000 stipend from the Aero Club for the flight,[62] and then departed for Minnesota to make an unprecedented air trip down the Mississippi River from Minneapolis to New Orleans. This daring venture had been proposed by Albert Bond Lambert in the spring of 1911. In mid-September, the Trans-Mississippi Valley Flying Association had been formed, and it had solicited $15,000 from Minneapolis, St. Louis, Memphis, New Orleans, and other communities along the route to pay the expenses of the undertaking. Hugh Robinson was to start the flight on October 13 under the auspices of the Curtiss Exhibition Company.[63]

Robinson's river jaunt on October 8 brought down the curtain on the "Festival Week" air meet. Albert Bond Lambert declared:

> We hope the success of the first free aviation meet ever held in any large city in America will attain for St. Louis the reputation of being the capital of aviation.[64]

The Aero Club president exaggerated the achievements of the Fairground meet, for wind and rain had canceled much of the scheduled program. What little flying had been done, nevertheless, was of major significance, particularly the carrying of official United States airmail. Only the prowess of twenty-one-year-old Walter Brookins kept the tournament from being a complete disaster. He was also to play a primary part in the Aero Club's second air meet of 1911.

The Aero Club of St. Louis scheduled a broader tournament for October 14-21 at Kinloch Park, its permanent aviation field. Among the featured events on the program were several nine-mile cross-country races for a prize of $500, daily altitude contests for $250, quick-starting tests for $200, target bombing for $100, accurate-landing contests for $200, and the traditional acrobatics by all the entrants.[65] In contrast to the free Fairground meet, the Kinloch tournament was to carry an admission charge of 50¢ per person and a parking rate of $1.00 per car and 50¢ per passenger (a fee which included a grandstand seat).[66]

On September 5, 1911, Albert Bond Lambert signed an agreement with A. Roy Knabenshue, manager of the Wright Company, whereby the Wrights would supply three pilots and biplanes in return for 25 percent of the gross receipts of the meet.[67] The three aviators — Howard Gill, J. Clifford Turpin, and P.O. Parmelee — were to fly every day but October 15, because of the rule of the Wright Company against Sunday flights.[68] Also entered were Dr. Henry Walden of Mineola, Long Island, with his picturesque Antoinette monoplane; Amedee V. Rayburn Jr. of St. Louis with his Bleriot monoplane; Horace Kearney and John D. Cooper of St. Louis with Curtiss biplanes; Alfred Elton and Andrew Drew of St. Louis with Wright biplanes; George Beatty; and Walter Brookins.[69] Bad blood had existed between Brookins and the Wrights since he had become an independent flier. Said the former Wright ace: "I don't know what the events are, but I herewith challenge any of the Wright team in any form of flying competition they can think of."[70]

Wilbur Wright made his first visit to St. Louis on October 10 to make final arrangements for the tournament. After Albert Bond Lambert had shown him the Aero Club's facilities, the great pioneer paid the city a supreme compliment:

> I was very much pleased with Kinloch field, and I think it an admirable place for a meet. I also have been watching the enthusiasm of St. Louisans in aviation, and am glad to say I think no other city in the country has displayed more general interest.[71]

St. Louis maintained its reputation with the Kinloch meet of 1911 but only after a stubborn battle with public apathy.

Only six aviators participated in the opening events on October 14 before a meager crowd of 5,000. Clifford Turpin made the first flight shortly after 2:30 p.m. George Beatty then took off on a passenger flight with a young woman who wore a purple gown and a mask to match. When they landed, she was whisked away in a car parked on the field, and the curious crowd never learned her identity.[72] The mystery did not bother George Beatty, who charged $25 for each flight and at a recent meet in Chicago had earned more than $7,000 by flying passengers several hours each day.[73] Such a fee was not exhorbitant, however, for on September 6, 1910, Marie Campbell had paid Claude Grahame-White $1,000 for a few minutes' ride at the Harvard-Boston meet.[74]

Andrew Drew won the quick-starting contest by taking off with a run of only 179 feet. The St. Louisan also won the accurate-landing event by stopping 47 feet away from his target. Howard Gill placed second in both contests. The main event of the day was a nine-mile race form Kinloch Park to St. Stanislaus Seminary, a Jesuit novitiate, and back. P.O. Parmelee bested J. Clifford Turpin by one-half mile in a time of 8 minutes and 53-3/5 seconds. The only mishap of the afternoon occurred when George Beatty was unable to take off with Fred Essen, a prominent St. Louis County Republican leader, who proved too heavy for the light engine.[75] Andrew Drew won his third event by dropping two croquet balls within 26 feet of the target; for the third time, Howard Gill placed second to him with a distance of 29 feet.[76] The day's events closed with a short flight by Harry Walden in his trim Antoinette monoplane.[77]

Choppy air currents made flying hazardous on October 15, and all formal events were canceled.

> The wind shot across the field in such powerful puffs the aviators hesitated at mounting skyward. Flights were limited to plain sailing, but appeared spectacular because of the continual flopping of the machines in the whirling wind.[78]

Albert Elton, Andrew Drew, and George Beatty made short hops, and Walter Brookins braved the breeze to drop several "bombs" from a height of 400 feet. Dr. Henry Walden was forced down into a corn field and broke part of the landing gear on his monoplane. A small crowd of men then forgot its manners and attacked the plane for souvenirs, but Aero Club officials successfully fought off the mob and preserved the aircraft.[79] It was feared that the weather might wipe out the Kinloch program as it had the Fairground activities of the preceding week.

Winds of 17 to 24 miles per hour again hampered flying on October 16 and kept the crowds from the field. P.O. Parmelee won the nine-mile race to the novitiate and back, bucking the buffeting currents to record a time of 12 minutes and 57 seconds and earn his second $500 purse. J. Clifford Turpin was runner-up with a time of 13 minutes and 11 seconds. Howard Gill, the third member of the Wright team, won two $250 prizes by taking off in a distance of 101 feet and by landing only eight feet from his target. The lone passenger carried that afternoon was Albert Elton, who flew in a biplane piloted by Andrew Drew. A nearly fatal accident occurred when a wheel fell off Howard Gill's airplane at a height of fifty feet and almost hit Hillery and Lincoln Beachey, who were standing near the hangars. After Gill had jolted to a landing, he explained:

> My mechanic must have forgotten to tighten the bolts. The force of
> a blow from the wheel falling from such a height would be suf-
> ficient to put a man out of commission I believe. [80]

At 5:00 p.m., spectators were permitted on the field, where Clifford Turpin gave them a lecture on aeronautics while seated in his plane. Shortly thereafter, Andrew Drew made the closing flight of the day, performing circles, "figure eights," and "ocean waves," at a height of 200 feet.[81]

The first conversation between a pilot and his passenger by "aerophone" took place on October 17. Bernays Johnson, the foster son of former Missouri Lieutenant Governor Charles P. Johnson, invented a contrivance to make conversation possible above the engine noise. The device consisted of an ordinary telephone box and and two football helmets, to the earpieces of which special receiving discs were attached, as well as speaking tubes at the mouth. Both helmets were connected by wire to the box. Johnson explained:

> The principle of the apparatus is merely to intensify the human
> voice in its natural key. The whirr of the engine is a deep bass,
> while the human voice is comparatively shrill. Though you can
> hear both noises while in the air, the voice is easily distinguishable
> from the constant buzz.[82]

The mechanism was primitive, but it was a first step toward the development of the intercom. Bernays Johnson led the stilted conversation in a flight with Howard Gill over Kinloch Field:

> Hello, Gill; don't go so high. We're not high. Say, Gill, are we
> falling? No; only doing the spiral. Gee, Gill, but it is cold up here.
> It is the wind that makes you think so.[83]

Three other biplanes were in the air at the same time as Gill and Johnson. James W. Bemis, a director of the Aero Club of St. Louis, flew with Walter Brookins; Knox Taussig with Andrew Drew; and P.O. Parmelee climbed to a height of 3,500 feet and then spiraled to the ground.[84] In the nine-mile race, J. Clifford Turpin won out over P.O. Parmelee, who had won the event twice before. Howard Gill attempted an endurance record, but had to land after only 24 minutes because of the rough wind.[85] Andrew Drew then equaled the world's record in the accurate-landing contest when he came down four feet from the mark.[86]

In a demonstration of aerial bombing, Louis Spindler went up with Walter Brookins and dropped one of his homemade iron bombs. The missile tore a five-foot hole in the ground and its report could be heard a mile away. The day's events closed when Dr. Henry Walden made a repeat of his performance of October 15 and again had to land his monoplane in a ditch because of lack of power. The landing gear, propeller, and tail were demolished, and although he himself was unhurt, Walden had all he could do to ward off the souvenir hunters who immediately surrounded his plane. Because of the sparseness of the crowds and the laxity of the support for the tournament — the result, perhaps, of poor weather and spectator fear of further disappointment — the Aero Club officials canceled the formal program for the next two days.[87]

Nonscheduled events, however, did take place. On October 18, P.O. Parmelee broke the American altitude record by climbing to a height of 7,500 feet in a flight which lasted 35 minutes. Albert Bond Lambert declared the record official and then, with Walter Brookins as passenger, made a seven-minute flight himself, his first since obtaining his pilot's license.[88] More than a dozen passengers were carried aloft, among them Zoe Schotten, a society debutante, and Master Gabriel, a three-foot-tall midget actor, noted as the first midget to fly by the record-conscious officials.[89]

Significant achievements were also attained on October 19, even though the regular events had been suspended. For the second time within a year, the American endurance record for airplanes was established at Kinloch Park.[90] Howard Gill took off in his Wright biplane at 12:49:50 p.m. and landed 4 hours, 16 minutes, and 40 seconds later, after having made countless circuits of the field and nearby countryside at heights ranging from 300 to 1,500 feet. He had taken a pocketful of chewing gum and chocolate candy with him and was determined to stay up until his plane ran out of gas. He exceeded the former mark by 14 minutes and 40 seconds, and came down because he thought he saw Roy Knabenshue signaling him, even though he still had five gallons of gas remaining.[91] Said Gill on landing: "It was tiresome."[92]

At 3:45 p.m., P.O. Parmelee took off in an attempt to better his performance of the previous day by breaking Roland Garros' world's altitude record of 13,946 feet. He only reached 4,500 feet, however, and descended when he became lost in the clouds. He also staged an impromptu race with Turpin, but only on an unofficial basis. Five passenger flights were made, but none of the regular events were held and no prizes were awarded for the performances.[93] Because of the two-day moratorium to encourage popular support, the prizes of the contests for the remaining two days of the meet were increased: $2,000 for the cross-country race, $1,000 for the altitude contest, and $500 each for the quick-starting, accurate-landing, target-bombing, and pursuit-racing tests.[94]

Inclement weather, however, continued to plague the Aero Club. Rain forced the cancelation of the program on October 20,[95] but ironically it did not prevent the outbreak of a devastating fire. That night, the Benoist Aircraft Company at 6664 Delmar Avenue in University City was totally destroyed after an unexplained explosion. Five airplanes, two extra engines, and the main manufacturing machinery went up in smoke. Tom Benoist estimated his loss at $20,000, with only $2,000 in insurance coverage.[96] The pioneer manufacturer, nevertheless, did not abandon hope and was soon operating as usual.

A drizzling rain and a chilling temperature of 38 degrees again forced a postponement of the program on October 21. That same day, the Aero Club received word that Hugh Robinson had abandoned the Minneapolis-New Orleans hydroplane flight which he had begun on October 17 (four days late). He needed $20,000 for expenses, and the towns along the river had raised a sufficient fund for him. They began to withdraw their commitments, however, when the aviator refused to give definite dates for his arrival, since his movements depended on wind and weather conditions. When Robinson reached Rock Island, Illinois, 371 miles from his starting point, he sent a telegram in desperation to Albert Bond Lambert, demanding that the Aero Club of St. Louis, his home organization, increase its $500 subscription:

> Unless St. Louis guarantees $2,000 will end flight here. Answer immediately.[97]

The Aero Club president evidently regard the demand as impudent, and responded:

> Your telegram demanding $2,000 and threat to end flight at Rock Island just received. As the sum we have raised for you does not amount to $2,000 we withdraw any and all guarantees we had for you to arrive here on your way to New Orleans.[98]

The St. Louis aviator carried out his threat and ended his flight at Rock Island. The venture cost the Curtiss Exhibition Company an estimated $5,000.[99]

Two weeks earlier, St. Louis had been denied its chance to greet another long-distance flier, Calbreath P. Rodgers, who was on his way to becoming the first man to pilot an airplane across the United States.[100] He had been scheduled to stop at St. Louis, but instead had leaped from Springfield, Illinois, to Marshall, Missouri, where he had landed on October 10. In so doing, he set a new cross-country distance record of 1,398 miles, breaking the previous record of 1,265 miles,[101] which Harry N. Atwood had established with a flight from St. Louis to New York City from August 14 to 25, 1911.[102]

The Kinloch air meet came to a close on October 22. After two crash landings of his Antoinette monoplane earlier in the week, Dr. Henry Walden finally enjoyed a successful and extensive ten-minute flight at an altitude of 300 feet. "His machine, heretofore considered only a probability, flew as steady as the perfected Wright biplanes."[103] Albert Bond Lambert made a short flight, and Parmelee, Kearney, Elton, and Brookins carried passengers. None of the scheduled events took place, since the tournament had officially ended the previous day, but in the main feature of the afternoon, Parmelee and Elton demonstrated the practicability of aerial reconaissance. The two pilots discovered a detachment of National Guardsmen who had hidden themselves in a cornfield, and they dropped plaster bombs on them from a height of 500 feet. The tournament came to a close in rather spectacular fashion when Charles Zornes of Walla Walla, Washington, allowed his crippled *Red Wing* biplane to be soaked with gasoline and set on fire at the airfield.[104]

Most of the aviators then crated their machines and left the city, but a number of them remained. For the next few months, weekly air meets were staged at Kinloch Park for an admission charge of 25¢. Lambert, Gill, Beatty, Walden, and several other pilots shared the receipts equally, using the money primarily to pay for gasoline. On October 28, Howard Gill distinguished himself by setting a new American record for passenger poundage when he carried aloft the 255-pound Fred B. Murphy, bettering the previous record by 14 pounds. The flight also established a new mark for total weight carried — 416 pounds, as opposed to the previous high of 410.[105] Kinloch Park remained the center of such activity until heavy snows prevented further flying.

In its two air meets of 1911, the Aero Club of St. Louis upheld its reputation as the most active organization in the country. Although the Fairground tournament had been largely washed away by foul weather, which had also affected much of the Kinloch program, new records had been established and new aircraft and equipment had made their appearance. The dual meet was hardly a worthy successor to the broad program undertaken in 1910, but it was a noteworthy tribute to the energy and talents of Albert Bond Lambert.

VIII
The National Balloon Race, 1914

I N 1914, THE AERO CLUB of St. Louis conducted its first major balloon race in four years. Sporadic heavier-than-air activity progressed at Kinloch Park and Tom Benoist continued his airplane manufacturing concern in the city. The pioneer aviation industrialist had even scored a historic "first" on March 1, 1912, when he participated in the first parachute jump ever made from an airplane.[1] The idea for the stunt was conceived by Benoist, who also built the biplane that was used for the flight.[2] Tony Jannus and Albert Berry, the son of John Berry (the celebrated St. Louis balloon pilot and manufacturer), took off from Kinloch Field at 2:30 that afternoon and flew 17 miles to Jefferson Barracks in South St. Louis, over which the jump was to be made.

> The parachute, by means of which Berry hoped to reach the ground in safety, was encased in a funnel-shaped tube, which was attached to the front bar of the aeroplane. It was held in the tube by rubber bands which would break under the weight of Berry's body.[3]

The entire Barracks Company was on the field when Captain Berry leaped from the plane at a height of 1,500 feet. He landed softly on the parade ground and was carried off on the shoulders of the guardsmen. No announcement of the demonstration had been made since it had been deferred on two previous occasions because of bad weather, and the aviators did not want to disappoint the pub-

Aviation history again was made over the City of Flight on March 1, 1912, when Capt. Albert Berry, right, made the first parachute jump from an airplane. The Benoist biplane, built in St. Louis, was piloted by Tony Jannus. The parachute was carried in the cone-like device in the undercarriage, held in by rubber bands which broke under the weight of the jumper.

lic a third time. Berry himself was a veteran "chutist," for he had made several jumps from balloons and had no apprehensions about a safe landing.[4] He was, however, the first man ever to parachute from an airplane, although the first jump with a free-type backpack parachute (later adopted as the standard) was not to be made until April 28, 1919.[5]

> By his daring, skill and courage, Capt. Berry proved the parachute to be a practical device. Yet the irony of it was that many brave airmen would lose their lives during WWI for the failure of their governments to provide parachutes for leaping from a burning plane.[6]

In October of 1913, the United States won the James Gordon Bennett International Balloon Race for the fourth time in seven years.[7] The only two Americans in the race, Ralph Upson in the *Goodyear* and St. Louis' Harry Eugene Honeywell in the *Uncle Sam,* finished first and second respectively.[8] Because of the victory, the United States was to be the host for the 1914 international race, and Upson and Honeywell were automatically granted positions on the three-man-American team. St. Louis made its customary bid for the Gordon Bennett Race, offering $5,000 in prizes for the contestants,[9] but it again lost out to Kansas City, as it had in 1911.[10]

In March of 1914, however, the Contest Committee of the Aero Club of America awarded St. Louis the annual National Balloon Race for that year, an elimination contest to choose the third duo for the American international team. Oakland, California, and Portland, Oregon, had each offered $3,500 in prizes for the event, but St. Louis won the honor because of its central location, even though it had put up only $3,000.[11] Again the favorable geography of the city was a factor in its aeronautic success.

The race was scheduled to start at 5:00 p.m. on July 11, 1914, at the balloon grounds of the Aero Club of St. Louis at Priester's Park at Grand Avenue and Meramec Street.[12] The amphitheater on the field had a seating capacity of 8,000, and the Aero Club was to charge an admission ranging from 25¢ for standing room outside the enclosure to $1.00 for the best seats in the grandstand.[13] The ascension site itself was a circular area 420 feet in diameter, under which was a network of gas mains to provide simultaneous inflation for all the balloons.[14] Laclede Gas Company was to direct the inflating of the balloons, and each bag was to have ten soldiers from the Jefferson Barracks in attendance.[15] Albert Bond Lambert was to be the official starter, and he would represent the Aero Club of America, under whose auspices the race was to be conducted, since he was a member and an official pilot of the organization. Robert Nolker, president of the Aero Club of St. Louis, was to represent the local unit.[16]

The eleven entrants made the St. Louis contest the largest national race ever held up to that time, and it was expected that new records would be established as a result of: 1) the central location of the city, 2) the superior quality of the gas available, and 3) the favorable atmospheric conditions which were predicted.[17] The contestants also remembered that St. Louis had been the starting point for the flights which had established the three standing American records for distance, duration, and speed:[18] Alan Hawley's 1,172.9-mile voyage to Lake Tschotogama, Quebec, October 17-19, 1910;[19] Clifford B. Harmon's flight of 48 hours and 26 minutes to Edina, Missouri, October 4-5, 1909;[20] and Albert Bond Lambert's 44-mile-per-hour trip to Ridgeville, South Carolina, October 15-16, 1909.[21]

Of the eleven who had entered the National Balloon Race, five pilots were St. Louisans. John Berry, "the dean of the balloonists,"[22] would fly the *Aero Club of St. Louis,* with sixteen-year-old Albert Von Hoffmann Jr., the youngest aeronaut in the race, as his aide. Representing the Million Population Club of the city was Captain William Assmann, a veteran of long experience. One of his most creditable flights had been an unsuccessful attempt at the Lahm Cup in a 725-mile trip with J.M. O'Reilly in the *Million Population II,* October 9-10, 1913.[23] He was to pilot the *Miss Sophia,* a balloon he had named after his daughter. Assmann would be the only man in the race to fly alone, since his small and aged balloon had insufficient lifting power for two people.[24]

E.S. Cole of St. Louis had made only 21 flights, but he held the distance record for balloons of 40,000-cubic-foot capacity, established on a 375-mile flight in 1910.[25] With R.E. Emerson as his aide, he would pilot the 80,000-cubic-foot *San Francisco 1915.* St. Louis' Paul H. McCullough had entered every national race except the 1913 contest from Kansas City, when he had been obliged to serve as an observer of the 1,000-mile Great Lake Flying Boat Cruise on the same date. His aide was William H. Trefta and their entry was the *Uncle Sam,* in which H.E. Honeywell had finished second in the 1913 Gordon Bennett Race. Honeywell himself was the fifth St. Louisan entered in the race, but since he had already earned a place on the international team, he withdrew so that McCullough might pilot the balloon he had intended to use.[26]

Captain R.A.D. Preston of Akron, Ohio, was the favorite in the race, for he had finished first in the 1913 national contest from Kansas City and had aided Ralph Upson, winner of that year's Gordon Bennett Race from Paris. With his aide, M.D. Tremelin, he would pilot the rubberized 80,000-cubic-foot *Goodyear,* the same balloon he and Upson had flown to victory the preceding year.

The father and son team of Warren and Herbert Rasor from Brookville, Ohio, had entered the competition and would fly the 80,000-cubic-foot *Hoosier.* Arthur T. Atherholt and Philip Sharples represented the Aero Club of Pennsylvania and would compete in the *Pennsylvania.* Atherholt was a veteran of more than 100 flights, the most interesting of which had been in the 1912 Gordon Bennett Race from Stuttgart, when he landed near St. Petersburg, Russia, and was jailed as a spy.[27] His aide on that flight, John Watts, was himself entered in the national race, and with W.F. Comstock he was to pilot the *Kansas City III.* Dr. Jerome Kingsbury and C.L.

Wynne of New York represented the Aero Club of America with the 80,000-cubic-foot *America III.* The eleventh entrant, Roy Donaldson of Springfield, Illinois, was forced to withdraw when his balloon, the *Springfield,* was lost in the race from Portland, Oregon, a few weeks before the St. Louis contest.[28]

There were thus nine contenders, all vying for the honor of representing the United States in the international race at Kansas City in October. In addition, Albert Von Hoffmann Sr. offered a trophy for the winner,[29] and the Aero Club of St. Louis provided $400 for the first prize, $300 for second, $200 for third, and $100 for fourth place, as well as $150 expense money for each pilot.[30]

Aero Club President Robert Nolker presided at a banquet for the pilots and their aides at the Hotel Jefferson on July 10. Starting positions were drawn and each pilot was presented with an electric searchlight as a gift from the host club.[31] The following morning, simultaneous inflation of the nine balloons was undertaken at Priester's Park, with the efficient Laclede gasometer pumping at the rate of 160,000 cubic feet per hour.[32]

By mid-afternoon, the entrants stood ready, with a meager crowd of only 4,000 on hand, a far cry from the throngs of 1907, 1909, and 1910. "The balloons were anchored in the center of the grounds and resembled giant mushrooms which had sprung up since noon."[33] The temperature was an incredible 111 degrees,[34] an ill omen for the balloonists. Because heat caused the gas to expand, the capacity of a balloon was lessened 1 percent per degree of heat, which meant a difference of 800 cubic feet at each step above the seasonal normal for the balloons in the national race, and therefore diminished the chances for extensive flights.[35] The excessive heat was to have a telling effect on the St. Louis race.

At 4:15 p.m., the *Hoosier,* which was scheduled to be the first to ascend, suddenly burst and expelled 80,000 cubic feet of gas into the atmosphere. "Just as it was inflated to capacity there was a sound as if someone had struck a bass drum, and the *Hoosier* came down in a heap."[36] The balloon had been damaged in the Dayton flood in 1913 and the water had deteriorated the silken fabric and made it too weak to stand the strain.[37] The disappointed, but somewhat relieved, Warren Rasor, who was to have piloted the balloon, declared: "It was mighty lucky for me that the *Hoosier* did her collapsing act before I cut loose."[38]

H.E. Honeywell released a small pilot balloon at 4:36 p.m. to test the wind direction and velocity. It shot straight up and remained motionless in the calm air at a height of 1,000 feet. At precisely

4:59:40, Albert Bond Lambert shouted, "Go!", Dr. Kingsbury yelled, "Hands off!" to the soldiers, and the *America III* made its ascension, as the Jefferson Barracks Band played the "Star Spangled Banner." At intervals of about five minutes, the next seven balloons took to the air while the band played appropriate selections and the sparse crowd cheered enthusiastically.[39] The *San Francisco 1915* was the most fully equipped, for it carried a wireless telegraph in order to receive government weather bulletins and reports on the other balloons.[40] Berry and Von Hoffmann took four carrier pigeons with them in the *Aero Club of St. Louis,* two of which were to be released in flight and two on landing. Despite the extreme heat on the field, all the balloonists had heavy overcoats and mufflers with them in preparation for freezing temperatures above the clouds.

The favorite in the race had also drawn the coveted last position of start, where it could gauge the wind conditions and take advantage of the evening coolness to contract its gas and conserve its lifting power. The *Goodyear* made the final ascension at 5:35:40.[41] Each balloon carried nearly a ton of sand ballast,[42] as well as suitable provisions. All headed south or southwest, except the *Kansas City III,* which caught in a counter-current and fell off to the northeast.[43] But for the destruction of the *Hoosier,* all the ascensions proceeded smoothly and on schedule.

The unusual atmospheric conditions and excessive heat harassed the contestants throughout the race. The pilots made futile attempts to get into a favorable air current and wasted precious gas and ballast in shifting up and down, without gaining distance. Several balloons hovered over St. Louis throughout the night and some crossed and re-crossed the city at altitudes of 200 to 17,000 feet in a vain search for strong wind. A thunderstorm the following day only compounded their aggravation.[44]

The abnormal weather produced flights of uniquely short distances. All the balloons landed July 12 in either Illinois, Indiana, or Kentucky. The only occurrence out of the ordinary was the landing of John Watts and W.F. Comstock in the *Kansas City III.* At the termination of their flight, they sent a telegram to the Aero Club of Kansas City: "Landed 2:20, two miles north Enfield. Not seriously hurt. Fell 1,000 feet into a tree."[45] By the evening of July 12, all but one of the balloons had reported their final positions. The following day, news of the *San Francisco 1915* reached the city, but the outcome of the race was unchanged. The favorite had upheld the prediction of the experts and had nearly doubled the distances of the other seven contenders. The results were:

1) *Goodyear* — R.A.D. Preston, pilot, and M.D. Tremelin, aide. 300 miles to Constance, Kentucky.

2) *Pennsylvania* — Arthur T. Atherholt, pilot, and Philip Sharples, aide. 160 miles to Rockville, Indiana.

3) *Uncle Sam* — Paul H. McCullough, pilot, and William H. Trefta, aide, 155 miles to Lewis, Indiana.

4) *Aero Club of St. Louis* — John Berry, pilot, and Albert Von Hoffmann Jr., aide. 150 miles to Terre Haute, Indiana.

5) *America III* — Dr. Jerome Kingsbury, pilot, and C.L. Wynne, aide. 138 miles to Princeton, Indiana.

6) *Miss Sophia* — William Assmann, pilot. 132 miles to Flat Rock, Illinois.

7) *San Francisco 1915* — E.S. Cole, pilot, and R.E. Emerson, aide. 115 miles to McLeansboro, Illinois.

8) *Kansas City III* — John Watts, pilot, and W.F. Comstock, aide. 110 miles to Enfield, Illinois.[46]

R.A.D. Preston, therefore, won the right to represent the United States with Ralph Upson and Harry Eugene Honeywell in the James Gordon Bennett International Balloon Race at Kansas City in October 1914. That contest, however, was never held. The war clouds already rising in Europe canceled the Gordon Bennett Races for the next six years.[47]

The national race at St. Louis had been a disappointment from the standpoints of both the interest aroused and the performances shown. The sizzling temperatures were primarily responsible for these misfortunes, but it had been necessary to stage the event in mid-summer, since the international race was customarily contested in the fall. St. Louis was to witness one more National Balloon Race in its history. It would be one which was more in keeping with the city's high aeronautical reputation.

IX
The Army-Navy and
National Balloon Races, 1919

IN THE YEAR FOLLOWING the end of the Great War, St. Louis moved into its readjustment by once again turning to the aeronautic activity which had made the city one of the primary air centers in the United States. In 1919, balloon racing returned to St. Louis in the form of two significant events. They were conducted by the Missouri Aeronautical Society, the successor to the Aero Club of St. Louis. The society had been formed at St. Louis in April 1917,[1] for the purpose of training balloon pilots for wartime service. During the next 1½ years, the organization's adjunct, the Missouri Aeronautical Reserve Corps, under the command of the ever-active Major Albert Bond Lambert, "qualified 354 students, made more than 1,500 ascensions and used 34,000,000 cubic feet of gas."[2] The society was to conduct both the Army-Navy and the National Balloon Races in 1919.

> The military championship of the United States is the goal in the army and navy race, while the open championship of the United States is the honor sought in the national race.[3]

The inter-service event was scheduled to start on September 26, 1919, from the grounds of the Missouri Aeronautical Society at Meramec Park (formerly Priester's Park) at Grand Boulevard and Meramec Street. This contest was to be "the first of its kind ever held in this country" and it was planned as an annual affair.[4] Captain Charles J. Glidden of the Army Air Service was to be the official starter, and Lieutenant Commander Zachary Lansdowne of the Navy, who had been the official American observer on the British *R-34,* which in July 1919 had become the first dirigible to cross the Atlantic Ocean,[5] was to be the referee. Major Albert Bond Lambert was to officiate, and Major Thomas Scott Baldwin, the celebrated balloon, airship, and airplane pilot, would observe the race on behalf of the United States government.[6]

Each branch of the service had entered three contestants, all vying for military prestige, as well as a silver trophy, which would be awarded to the winning department.[7] Each of the six balloons, valued at $2,000 apiece, was the property of the Missouri Aeronautical Society, which would defray the expenses of the entire affair.[8] The three Army teams consisted of: Lieutenant Colonel Jacob W. Wuest and Second Lieutenant William E. Huffman, Fort Omaha, Nebraska; Second Lieutenant Isaac H. Coulter and Second Lieutenant Harold K. Hine, Brooks Field, San Antonio, Texas; Captain E.P. Phillips and First Lieutenant Byron T. Burt, Langley Field, Virginia. The Naval contingent was composed of: Lieutenant H.W. Hoyt and Ensign F.W. Reichelderfer, Akron, Ohio; Ensign J.H. Stevens and Lieutenant W.R. Reed, Pensacola, Florida; Lieutenant Junior Grade R. Emerson and Ensign F.L. Sloman, Washington, D.C.[9]

The Army balloon carried white canvas banners depicting in red letters the fields they represented, along with the numbers 1, 2, and 3. The Naval craft conveyed similar information in blue lettering, but were numbered 50, 52, and 54. Although all the participants were skilled balloonists, First Lieutenant Burt was the only man to have seen front-line service during the war. He had been awarded the Distinguished Service Cross for saving the life of his assistant, who had been caught in the rigging of their observation balloon during the battle of the Argonne Forest.[10]

At a luncheon for the pilots and aides at the Hotel Jefferson on September 25, the order of start was determined and the rules of the competition were discussed. Lieutenant Colonel Wuest, the ranking officer present, won the choice by successfully calling ''heads'' as Captain Glidden flipped a coin.[11] The Army graciously gave the Navy first place, but its motive was pragmatic.

> This is an advantage for the army in that the army can observe wind conditions from the first balloon in the air, and they have the further advantage of gas contraction, which occurs late in the evening on the ground, and every minute on the ground is gas conservation.[12]

Major Lambert had earlier explained a unique feature of the rules of the race.

A contestant may alight to make adjustments, observations or inquiries if he likes, and then resume the flight, or he may alight, for instance, for breakfast at a farmhouse, or to await the rising of the sun so that his gas will expand, or to take on ballast and then resume the flight. There is one thing he must not do — take on gas.

The contestants will be given the greatest latitude to cover distance. That is the aim of this race. In other races they could not land and resume the flight, they could not so much as allow their guide rope to touch the ground. This will not be a nonstop flight race. The contestant, therefore, will be in the race until his gas gives out or an accident prevents his arising on the gas originally taken on.[13]

Despite this liberal policy, the entrants would choose the traditional nonstop plan as the best practical course, since a landing required the expulsion of irreplaceable gas and a consequent loss of lifting power.

The simultaneous inflation of the six 50,000-cubic-foot competing balloons and a lone 40,000-cubic-foot pilot balloon began on September 26 at 1:30 p.m., with the Laclede gasometer pumping at the rate of 130,000 cubic feet per hour.[14] Preliminary exhibitions were staged before the start of the race. The Twelfth Balloon Company of Fort Omaha demonstrated 5,000-cubic-foot, one-man "jumping balloons," as well as midair transfers from one balloon to another.[15] Gunner J.H. Hykes of the Navy also sent aloft a number of three-foot "sounding balloons" to test meteorological conditions,[16] just as Professor H.H. Clayton had done at the World's Fair and again in 1907.[17] A captive Cacquot balloon was moored to an Army truck on the field and rode at a height of 500 feet to indicate the wind direction. It was hauled down several times during the afternoon to take up venturesome photographers.[18]

Chairs for 3,000 spectators had been erected at Meramec Park, and space for 500 automobiles was available.[19] A charge of $1.00 per person was levied for admission to the grounds. This fee had been determined upon as a measure of restriction and not for revenue, since the Missouri Aeronautical Society did not desire a particularly large crowd.[20]

Several thousand spectators, nevertheless, were on hand when the ascensions began. The pilot balloon arose promptly at 6:00 p.m., with Captain A.C. McKinley of the Army Air Service and Gunner J.H. Hykes of the Navy aboard. Its purpose was to demonstrate the direction and velocity of the wind, but it made an inauspicious start when it fouled on a wire on the north fence of the park and dragged up several posts before it broke loose. The formal contestants then followed at five-minute intervals, all heading northwest. Lieutenant Hoyt and Ensign Reichelderfer of Akron in the *Navy #54* had been scheduled to ascend third at 6:15, but they were eliminated before the start because their balloon was leaking too severely.[21] The five others arose on cue.

The supplies taken by the military aeronauts seemed ascetic in comparision to the exotic provisions normally borne in civilian races. "Each contestant carried sandwiches, coffee and water sufficient to last two days. They wore regular uniforms and trench coats."[22] In addition, the Naval balloons were each equipped with wireless radios to receive weather information from Arlington Station in Washington, D.C.[23] Instead of returning to St. Louis after the race, all contestants were directed to proceed immediately to their assigned stations.[24]

The three-to-two advantage the Army obtained over the Navy was dissolved only ten minutes after the last balloon had ascended. Lieutenant Colonel Wuest and Second Lieutenant Huffman of Fort Omaha in the *Army #2* were forced to land at 6:40 p.m. on Olive Street Road between Spring Avenue and Hanley Road in St. Louis County because their balloon also suffered from excessive leakage.[25] Of the seven balloons, only the *Navy #50* and the *Army #3* enjoyed relatively routine flights. Several hours after the unusual leaks had damaged two of the starters, the pilot balloon landed neatly on a sandbar in the Mississippi River one-half mile south of the Wisconsin border.[26] Lieutenant Emerson and Ensign Sloman of Washington crossed Lake Michigan in the *Navy #52,* but were brought roughly to earth at 10:20 a.m. September 27, when their drag rope caught in a tree and caused the balloon to rip itself open as it came to the ground.[27] Captain Phillips and First Lieutenant Burt of Langley Field in the *Army #1* experienced the most eventful trip of the seven. They were caught in a gale while over Lake Michigan on the morning of September 27 and were blown down into the water five miles north of the Door Peninsula. After battling ten-foot waves for nearly two hours, they were finally rescued by a small lake steamer, but their balloon was lost.[28] The *Navy #50,* the *Army #1,* and the *Navy #52* achieved distances so close that Major Lambert requested the War and Navy Departments to reckon the official measurements and determine the winner. Said Lambert:

> As far as we can tell with the aid of small maps and a compass,

the army and navy balloons that landed in Michigan are about tied. The approximate distance covered was 490 miles.[29]

The Geological Survey in Washington computed the distances of the four contestants who had actually competed in the race, and on October 9 announced the results:

1) *Army #1* — Captain E.P. Phillips, pilot, and First Lieutenant Byron T. Burt, aide. 491.8 miles to Door Peninsula, Michigan.

2) *Navy #52* — Lieutenant R. Emerson, pilot, and Ensign F.L. Sloman, aide. 486.4 miles to a point two miles northwest of Stittsville, Michigan.

3) *Navy #50* — Ensign J.H. Stevens, pilot, and Lieutenant W.R. Reed, aide. 479 miles to a point four miles north of Menominee, Michigan.

4) *Army #3* — Second Lieutenant Isaac H. Coulter, pilot, and Second Lieutenant Harold K. Hine, aide. 470 miles to a point eleven miles north of Green Bay, Wisconsin.[30]

The Army, therefore, was awarded the silver trophy for besting the Navy. St. Louisans took particular pleasure in the victory, for the winner was one of their own. Captain Phillips was a resident of St. Louis County and had been the principal of Maplewood High School.[31] The Missouri Aeronautical Society had spent $20,000 for the military event, including $6,000 for the loss of three balloons.[32] The club considered the expense minimal, however, and eagerly looked forward to the next event on its program.

At a reunion on July 15, 1919, of more than fifty officers, instructors, and civilians connected with the Missouri Aeronautical Society's World War I balloon school, Major Albert Bond Lambert had announced that St. Louis had been selected by the Aero Club of America as the site for the annual National Balloon Race, which would start on October 1.[33] The contest was to be conducted by the society under the auspices of the Aero Club of America in accordance with the rules of the International Aeronautic Federation. The local organization would supply free gas for the entrants, provide each of the balloonists with $100 for personal expenses, and donate prizes of $500 for first place, $300 for second, and $200 for third, "or the equivalent in silver plate."[34] Ordinarily, the national race served as an elimination test to select the three-man American team for the annual James Gordon Bennett International Aeronautic Cup Race,[35] but because of the war, the international trophy was not contested from 1914 to 1919.[36] The St. Louis race, therefore, would determine only the national champion for 1919.

The ten entrants, many of whom had performed in St. Louis in the past, selected their starting positions by lot on September 29 at the Missouri Aeronautical Society grounds at Meramec Park. Captain Elmer G. Marchuetz and Lieutenant Charles S. Powell of St. Louis would be the first to start. They were to ascend at 6:00 p.m., October 1, in the *Missouri Aeronautical Reserve*. Five minutes later, Captain Paul J. McCullough and Bernard Von Hoffmann of St. Louis would arise in *The 84*. The third starter was to be the *City of St. Louis,* piloted by William Assmann, with Joseph M. O'Reilly as his aide. Next would be Ralph Upson and Ward T. Van Orman from Akron, Ohio, in the *Goodyear*. At 6:20, Captain Carl Dammann and Lieutenant Edward J. Verheyden of St. Louis would ascend in the *Wichita Aero Club*. They would be followed by Captain John S. McKibben and Ensign Joseph F. McGuire of Murphysboro, Illinois, in the *Murphysboro*. The seventh starter would be the *Ohio,* with the father-and-son team of Captain Warren and Herbert H. Rasor of Brookville, Ohio, aboard. Captain Ernest S. Cole and Leo C. Ferrenbach of St. Louis would then ascend in the *St. Louis V*. The *Kansas City* would be next, piloted by St. Louis' veteran Harry Eugene Honeywell, aided by Harry Worthington of Kansas City. The final balloon, scheduled to depart at 6:45, would be the *America,* with Lieutenant Joseph S. Batt and Joe Torrey II of the Aero Club of America in charge.[37]

The Missouri Aeronautical Society conducted the traditional prerace banquet for pilots and aides at the Racquet Club on September 30. Majors Albert Bond Lambert and Thomas Scott Baldwin spoke briefly, as well as James W. Bemis, president of the society; Captain Charles J. Glidden, the official starter of the race; and George M. Meyer, president of the Aero Club of Kansas City. Glidden made the prediction that "pony dirigible balloons" for pleasure purposes would be selling on the market within a year for $1,000, and that weekend trips of 1,000 miles would be possible.[38] The rules were discussed, and it was explained that under International Aeronautic Federation regulations, emergency landings of up to fifteen minutes in length were permitted, but only when unavoidable.[39] As in the Army-Navy Balloon Race earlier in the week, this privilege would not be exercised.

A thorough inspection of all the balloons began on the morning of October 1 in order to prevent a recurrence of the incident during the previous contest, when two balloons had been forced out of the race because of gas leaks. Everything was apparently found in suitable condition, and the inflation of the balloons, which required 770,000 cubic feet of gas, began at 11:00 a.m.[40] One contender must

There were wide open spaces at Meramec Park, South Grand and Meramec, at the start of the National Balloon Race on October 1, 1919.

have been only cursorily inspected, for its defects were to make themselves apparent during the race. That morning, the United States Weather Bureau in Washington issued for the contest a special forecast which was to have ominous significance:

> Moderately southerly winds at surface, fresh south-southwest winds aloft; conditions will become unfavorable for free ballooning late tonight and Thursday [October 2], when there will be showers and thunderstorms to the east and north of St. Louis.[41]

A crowd of several thousand had congregated at Meramec Park when Lieutenant James T. Neely of Philadelphia and James B. Jordan of Oklahoma City ascended at 5:55 p.m. in a 40,000-cubic-foot pilot balloon to test the wind direction and velocity.[42] At five-minute intervals thereafter, each of the balloons arose and fell off toward the north in a steady wind. Captain John S. McKibben's *Murphysboro* was of radically light material and he himself had stripped the balloon of all but the essential provisions in an attempt to obtain maximum efficiency.[43] In direct contrast was Ralph Upson's *Goodyear,* whose bright green basket was protected with large, rubber, air-filled pontoons to absorb the landing shock.

> The other balloonists "went light," carrying only the necessaries, but Upson, the crack dirigible navigator, went equipped with everything for a pleasant voyage, including a hammock in which he may rest and read, electric lights, an extra heavy drag rope, maps and implements galore, cold cream to protect his complexion

from sunburn, ax, shotgun, fishing tackle — in fact, full equipment for hunting and fishing should he happen to come down somewhere in the wilds of the United States or Canada. He took at least twenty pounds more equipment than any others, and carried forty bags, thirty pounds each, of ballast.[44]

The excellent caliber of his balloon was to prove the efficacy of his philosophy.

Each balloon in the race was of 80,000-cubic-foot capacity, except the Rasors' 50,000-cubic-foot *Ohio*[45] and McKibben's 78,000-cubic-foot *Murphysboro*.[46] William Assmann's *City of St. Louis* suffered severe leakage and had to expend a great deal of sand ballast to arise, but the other nine entrants ascended smoothly and on schedule. At 6:45 p.m., the *America,* the last contestant, took to the air.[47] Said Major Lambert: "It was a wonderful start. You do not often see ten balloons get off in a race in such a perfect manner."[48]

The results of the contest were reminiscent of the St. Louis Gordon Bennett Race of 1910, since more than half of the balloons landed well into Canada. By October 3, all but three of the pilots had reported their final positions. Lieutenant Neely descended in the small pilot balloon at the Great Lakes Naval Training Center, 280 miles from St. Louis. Although he was not a contestant, he bettered the distances of three of the formal entrants, who had used 80,000-cubic-foot balloons. Batt and Torrey took the *America* only 220 miles to Leland, Illinois, and Marcheutz and Powell landed their *Missouri Aeronautical Reserve* at Roselle, Illinois, 250 miles from the city. Assmann and O'Reilly tried to steer their crippled *City of St. Louis* across Lake Michigan at a height of 10,000 feet, but they could find no current. They descended 265 miles from St. Louis at Winnetaka, Illinois, with the battered balloon falling to pieces as they landed.[49]

Captain John McKibben had been determined to beat Ralph Upson, but he was obliged to land the *Murphysboro* near Georgian Bay, 90 miles north of Toronto and 700 miles from St. Louis after a flight of 17 hours and 22 minutes.[50] The Rasors landed the *Ohio* at 12:21 p.m. October 2, eight miles east of Perry Sound, Ontario. Although their balloon had a capacity of only 50,000 cubic feet, they traveled a creditable 750 miles from the city.[51] Despite the fact that they had twelve sacks of ballast and a stable amount of gas remaining, they descended because the *Ohio* was heading away from civilization and the sixty-five-year-old Captain Warren Rasor did not feel physically able to endure the rigors of the Canadian wilds.[52] Honeywell downed the *Kansas City* at 6:00 p.m. October 2, two and one-half miles north of Cardinal Canal, Ontario, recording a distance of 892 miles. Ralph Upson, however, bettered the mark by piloting his well-stocked *Goodyear* 1,050 miles to Dunbar, Quebec, landing there on October 2 at 8:55 p.m.[53]

McCullough and Von Hoffmann finally reported their position on October 5. They had landed *The 84* near Ferris Township, Ontario, forty miles north of Perry Sound, on October 2, and had hiked for three days before they reached Waubamik, Ontario, and telegraphed St. Louis. Their distance of 800 miles did not surpass Upson's, but it was sufficient for third place. Before returning to St. Louis, the determined pilots expressed their intention of retracing their route and recovering their balloon.[54]

Cole and Ferrenbach had a similar experience with the *St. Louis V*. They ran into storms over Saginaw Bay and fought the weather at heights ranging from 700 to 20,000 feet (where they had difficulty in breathing). At 5:00 p.m. on October 2, they landed 32 miles east of Lamable, Ontario, something less than 800 miles from St. Louis, and had to walk for three days before they reached civilization.[55] The two St. Louisans made no mention of returning to the wilds for their balloon.

By October 9, Dammann and Verheyden in the *Wichita Aero Club* had still not reported, but the St. Louis officials continued to express optimism, remembering that Alan Hawley and Augustus Post had been missing for ten days before they walked out of the Canadian woods with a new American distance record in 1910.[56] On October 10, however, Major Lambert received a telegram from W.J. Simpson, who had found the *Wichita* near his home six days earlier:

> Picked up balloon near Cove Island, Lake Huron, Oct. 4. Brought wreckage to Tobermonary. No trace of men. Number on basket "53;" on balloon, "83."[57]

Search parties combed the wilderness near the Ontario community, 650 miles from St. Louis, for the next several days, while seaplanes and patrol boats investigated the inlets, coves, and islands of Lake Huron. Their inquiries uncovered the fact that a party of fishermen had seen the balloon floating in the lake on October 2, but had taken it for a schooner.[58] On October 15, an Eagle Boat crew from the Great Lakes Naval Training Station found the body of twenty-three-year-old Lieutenant Edward J. Verheyden of 5244 Theodosia Avenue, St. Louis, in Lake Huron off Cape Hurd.[59] On October 21, the body of twenty-seven-year-old Captain Carl W. Dammann of 3614 Hartford Street, St. Louis, washed up on the lake shore at Pine Tree Harbor, near Tobermory, Ontario.[60] They had apparently been

The ill-fated Wichita Aero Club, *about to cast off for the National Balloon Race.*

caught in a storm and forced down into the treacherous waters of Lake Huron, a fate similar to that which John Wise and George Burr had suffered in 1879 over Lake Michigan.[61]

The tragic culmination of the race mellowed the enthusiasm generated by Ralph Upson's impressive victory. Because of its central geographical position, its superior facilities, and the spirit of its citizens, St. Louis was the capital of American balloon racing, but it had never before witnessed two major races in such close conjunction. The hand of Albert Bond Lambert was again in evidence as the Missouri Aeronautical Society carried on in the tradition outlined by the Aero Club of St. Louis in the first decade of the twentieth century.

X
The International Air Races, 1923

S T. LOUIS WITNESSED IN 1923 the most grandiose aeronautic endeavor in its history. In October of that year, the city was host to the National Aero Congress, the convention of the National Aeronautic Association, the Air Institute of the Aeronautical Chamber of Commerce of America,[1] a $5,000,000 exposition of aircraft and accessories,[2] and nine air races for prizes totaling $13,300.[3] That such a comprehensive "heavier-than-air" program should be staged in the "center of free ballooning"[4] was due to the efforts of a "new breed" of aerial enthusiasts, along with the assistance of the ever-present Albert Bond Lambert.

The initiative in securing this air festival was taken by the Flying Club of St. Louis. This organization had been formed in January 1921 for two purposes: to bring more closely together the 400 St. Louisans who had served as pilots and observers in World War I and to carry on the work commenced by the Aero Club of St. Louis and the Missouri Aeronautical Society.[5] The seed of determination had been implanted in President Randall Foster and the other officials of the club at a Lions Club meeting on October 19, 1922, when Colonel C.G. Hall, the commanding officer at Scott Field in Belleville, Illinois, gave a vivid description of the recent National Air Races at Detroit. Two days later, Foster consulted Joseph Pulitzer, the publisher of the *St. Louis Post-Dispatch,* as to the advisability of making an effort to secure the 1923 races for St. Louis.[6]

The newspaper executive, together with his brothers Herbert and Ralph, had donated a trophy for the annual high-speed race which had been the highlight of the three previous National Air Races.[7] At his direction, a citizens' committee was formed, consisting of thirty representative businessmen, headed by W. Frank Carter. This group assumed the obligation of underwriting the contests and negotiated with representatives of the Army and Navy, as well as the National Aeronautic Association (the successor of the Aero Club of America), which had been formed in 1922 to supervise and foster aerial developments.[8] On June 25, 1923, the NAA awarded the National Air Races to St. Louis.[9] The citizens' committee then dissolved and formed the St. Louis Aeronautic Corporation and the St. Louis Air Board to conduct the meet.[10]

The St. Louis Aeronautic Corporation was a holding company which was chartered for fifty years by the State of Missouri in May 1923. Its purposes were:

> To conduct the business of manufacturing, buying, selling and dealing generally in all kinds of machines, appliances, goods and merchandise, to purchase, lease or otherwise acquire and own lands for aeronautic purposes; and to construct all needful improvements thereon; to own and operate an aeronautic field for use in all kinds of aerial navigation; to conduct aeronautic meets, races, conventions, and exhibitions, and to do any and all things that may be necessary or incidental to its said principal business as above set out.[11]

Its aim was to raise money for the needs of the program, and to this end, it was capitalized at $200,000, in the form of four thousand $50 shares.[12] Benjamin F. Bush was president of the corporation, W. Frank Carter and Carl F.G. Meyer vice presidents, and Arthur B. Birge general manager and secretary. The board of directors included Joseph Pulitzer and Major Albert Bond Lambert.[13]

The St. Louis Air Board was also established to assist in the financing and business management of the tournament. It was to be the trustee for all properties acquired and was to defray the ground expenses in conjunction with the Aeronautic Corporation. W. Frank Carter was chairman of the group, assisted by Benjamin F. Bush, director general, and Arthur B. Birge, general manager.[14]

The Flying Club of St. Louis was reorganized, with membership open only to those who held a $50 share of stock in the St. Louis Aeronautic Corporation and who paid an additional $10 in dues. The revenue provided by the members of the club would finance the air meet. It was to lease all necessary property for the races, in cooperation with the two newly-created organizations.[15] The Flying Club was also to serve in more of a "grass roots" capacity, in that many of its members would offer their services as officials and judges of the activities. President Foster was chairman of the Race Committee and Major Lambert, ably assisting the "youngsters," headed the Contest Committee.[16] Working with them would be the formal representative of the National Aeronautic Association, B. Russell Shaw,[17] and the official observer of the International Aeronautic Federation, Colonel Frank P. Lahm, who as a lieutenant had won the first James Gordon Bennett International Balloon Race from Paris seventeen years earlier.[18]

In addition to the conducting of the air meet in 1923, these three organizations labored for the establishment of a permanent airport for St. Louis.[19]

> It is interesting to note that the first idea of W. Frank Carter, Joseph Pulitzer, Maj. A. B. Lambert and others, was to raise $45,000.00 to provide for the holding of the International Air Races, Aero Congress, Air Institute, and Aeronautical Exposition at Scott Field, 35 miles away from St. Louis.[20]

Since the distance was too great, however, the officials began to look elsewhere for a suitable location. Major Lambert made available the St. Louis Flying Field in Bridgeton, six miles west of the city limits, which he had been maintaining at his own expense under a $2,000-per-year lease from Mrs. Mary Jane Weldon.[21] This field had been acquired on June 18, 1920, by the Missouri Aeronautical Society "for establishing airplane service between St. Louis and other cities."[22] The St. Louis Aeronautic Corporation took control of the 183-acre Weldon tract for $73,200[23] and leased 316 acres of adjoining land for $19,358.[24] These additional tracts were only on a short-term basis. (The 54-acre Ferguson Farm, for example, was leased for $2,250 from August 15 to October 10, 1923.)[25]

It was the purpose of the Air Board and the Aeronautic Corporation "to provide St. Louis with the most modern, the largest, and the most completely equipped airport in the middle west."[26] To this end, more than $130,000 was spent in grading the field and erecting the necessary buildings and facilities.[27] Nearly one square mile of earth was leveled and sown with rye. Four steel hangars, each 132 feet long and 120 feet wide and with a capacity of 25 airplanes each, were constructed, along with a machine shop, a 10,000-gallon gasoline tank, and a 10,000-gallon water tank.[28] Six miles of woven wire fencing was strung, and a creek at one end of the field was completely covered. Three sixty-foot pylons were set up to mark the

Mighty jets thunder out of Lambert Field every few minutes today, but in the early fall of 1923 it was a hay field.

racing course[29] at a cost of $1,870.54.[30] A grandstand seating 53,000 was built, bleachers for 12,000, parking space for 25,000 cars was cleared, and ample provision for 100,000 spectators was made.[31]

> Over 150 mules, twenty tractors and dirt removers and 200 men have been employed in making the field level enough for ships landing at 150 miles an hour to glide safely over the field as if they were on a billiard table.[32]

The efforts of the Flying Club, Air Board, and Aeronautic Corporation in establishing a permanent air terminal in St. Louis assisted the city immeasurably in earning a reputation as the "Aerial Crossroads of America."

> Located in the very center of the north and south mid-continental air route and a focal point for flying from all directions, St. Louis starts with a geographical advantage that is unequalled. With a modern flying field, an aroused civic interest in aeronautics and such a location, St. Louis looms large on the air map of the United States. . . . Rewards, far greater than now imaginable, will come to St. Louis as a return for its progressiveness.[33]

When the officials began laying plans for the meet in the spring of 1923, their original intention had been to stage only the Pulitzer Trophy Race.[34] Their quickened enthusiasm, however, resulted in a broad aerial program. Nine contests were planned, eight of them

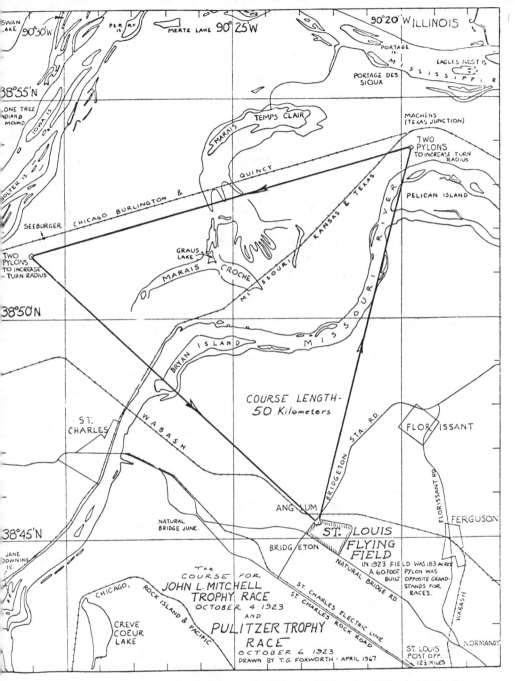

Western Historical Manuscript Collection, University of Missouri-St. Louis

The race course for the 1923 Pulitzer Trophy was about 10 miles per leg of the equilateral triangle.

to be flown over a triangular course 50 kilometers (31.07 miles) in circuit, marked by three pylons, one on the field, another just north

of the Missouri River near Texas Junction, and the third just southwest of the Mississippi River near the Seeberger Station on the
Burlington Railroad.[35]

The competition format was established as follows:

1) "On to St. Louis" Race — Open to civilian pilots with any type
of airplane, this contest was designed to encourage attendance at
the meet by air. Competing planes had to be flown to the Bridgeton
airfield from at least 200 miles away. The winner was to be determined on a point scale in four categories: a) Average speed based on
total elapsed time — a maximum of 100 points would be awarded on
the basis of 150 miles per hour; for each mile per hour less, one
point would be deducted, with no points given for average speeds
of less than 50 miles per hour. b) Distance covered — ten points
would be awarded for each additional 100 miles above a basic 500-
mile requirement. c) Passengers carried — ten points would be
given for each passenger, up to a total of 100 points (ten passengers). d) Engine horsepower — a maximum of 200 points would be
awarded to the plane completing the flight with an engine of 30
horsepower or less; for every ten additional horsepower, five points
would be deducted, the minimum being fifteen points (for 400
horsepower and above). The flights in this competition had to be
made between September 20 and 30, 1923. The winner was to receive the St. Louis Senior Chamber of Commerce Trophy and a cash
prize of $500, with awards of $250, $150, and $100 for second,
third, and fourth places. The St. Louis Junior Chamber of Commerce Trophy would be given to the pilot who flew the greatest
distance.[36]

2) Flying Club of St. Louis Trophy Race — Open only to civilian
pilots with two-seater airplanes having engines of 90 horsepower or
less, this annual contest was designed to give low-powered aircraft
a fair chance in competition. All planes had to carry a load of 340
pounds evenly distributed in the two cockpits, consisting of a pilot
and a passenger, with sufficient sand ballast, if necessary, to bring
their weight up to the required amount. The distance of the race
was to be 150 kilometers (93.21 miles), three times around the circuit. A minimum of four, up to a maximum of sixty entrants could
compete for prizes of $500, $300, and $200, as well as a trophy for
the winner.[37]

3) Liberty Engine Builders' Trophy Race — Open only to military
pilots, this contest was designed to encourage the development of
more efficient observation-type airplanes. In addition to the two-
man, 340-pound crew, the planes had to carry a "contest load"

based on the size of the engine they used. The distance of the race was to be 300 kilometers (186.42 miles), six circuits of the course. A trophy and prizes of $800, $500, and $200 were offered for a minimum of four and a maximum of forty entrants.[38]

4) Aviation Club of Detroit Trophy Race — Open only to civilian fliers, this annual contest was designed to encourage the development of light commercial aircraft. Each plane had to have an engine of less than 220 horsepower and carry two 170-pound passengers, or the equivalent in sand ballast. Prizes were to be awarded in two categories, speed and efficiency, with the latter based on a figure of merit determined by dividing the weight carried by the engine horsepower and multiplying the result by the average speed over the 250 kilometers (155.34 miles) of the race. Any number between six and forty could compete for prizes of $500, $300, and $200 in each class.[39]

5) Merchants Exchange of St. Louis Trophy Race — Open to both civilian and military pilots, this event was intended to stimulate the development of large commercial aircraft and military bombers capable of carrying a "payload" of 2,000 pounds. In addition to a two-man, 340-pound crew, each plane had to carry a "contest load" based on its engine size, as in the Liberty Engine Builders' Trophy Race. The distance was to be 300 kilometers (186.42 miles), and prizes of $1,000, $700, and $300 were offered for a minimum of four and a maximum of forty contestants.[40]

6) Mulvihill Model Trophy Contest — Open to members of the Junior Flying League of the National Aeronautic Association, this annual event was designed simply to stimulate the building of model airplanes. The only restrictions were that the plane be powered by rubber bands and have a span of less than 40 inches. Each entrant was to be allowed three trials of his model, and the contest was to be solely one of duration. The winner would receive a cup donated by B.V. Mulvihill, the vice president of the NAA, with $400 being divided among the first seven finishers.[41]

7) *Detroit News* Air Mail Trophy Race — Open only to United States Air Mail pilots, this race was designed to allow them to exhibit their prowess to the public and to publicize the service. Any number from four to forty could participate in the 300-kilometer (186.42-mile) contest, and prizes of $800, $500, and $200 awaited the winners.[42]

8) John L. Mitchell Trophy Race — Open only to pilots of the First Pursuit Group of the Army Air Service, this annual contest was staged in memory of an Army flier who had died during World

War I. The trophy was donated by his brother, the celebrated Brigadier General William (''Billy'') Mitchell, then assistant chief of the Army Air Services. The distance of the race was 200 kilometers (124.27 miles) and the winner would receive the memorial cup.[43]

9) Pulitzer Trophy Race — Open to civilian and military pilots alike, this contest was designed to stimulate the production of high-speed aircraft. Valued at $5,000, the trophy had been donated to the NAA in May 1916 by Joseph, Herbert, and Ralph Pulitzer, the publishers of the *St. Louis Post-Dispatch* and the *New York World,* for a four-fold purpose:

> . . . to quicken American interest in the science that Americans first developed and gave to mankind; to induce the equipment of military and civilian aviators for national defense; to demonstrate the practical uses of airplanes for the transportation of passengers and mail, and to open the first transcontinental aerial highway.[44]

The original intention of the donors was the staging of an annual transcontinental race for the trophy, but World War I prevented any competition until 1920, by which time the plans had evolved into a contest of pure speed. The distance of the race was to be 200 kilometers (124.27 miles), and the winner would receive a gold plaque, $2,000, and custody of the Pulitzer Trophy for one year. Second and third finishers were to receive $1,500 and $500 respectively.[45] This contest would be the highlight of the St. Louis meet.

The prizes for these nine events aggregated $13,300,[46] a far cry from the lush fruits offered in the first decade of the century, but sufficient to attract a suitable array of aviators. By late September, 1923, there were 119 entrants for the contests: 20 in the ''On to St. Louis'' Race, 8 in the Flying Club of St. Louis Trophy Race, 15 in the Liberty Engine Builders' Trophy Race, 9 in the Aviation Club of Detroit Trophy Race, 10 in the Merchants Exchange of St. Louis Trophy Race, 27 in the Mulvihill Model Trophy Contest, 16 in the *Detroit News* Air Mail Trophy Race, 6 in the John L. Mitchell Trophy Race, and 8 in the Pulitzer Trophy Race.[47] In the eight major races, the only St. Louisans entered were Major William B. Robertson and his brother Frank, the operators of the fledgling Robertson Aircraft Corporation, who were slated to compete for the trophies offered by the aero clubs of St. Louis and Detroit.[48] The races became international in character when Sadi-Lecointe of France expressed his intention of participating in the Pulitzer Race[49] and Mario Fossati and Brack-Papa of Italy formally entered their 800-horsepower Fiat racers in the speed classic.[50]

There was more than just sport involved in the contests at the meet, particularly with regard to the Pulitzer event. A contemporary magazine editorialized:

> The race is a laboratory experiment, a very expensive but essential device to push air equipment and personnel to their highest efforts. The public should accept the races in the spirit of a scientific as well as a sporting event and should take care to put itself on the real issues involved.[51]

The officials of the meet staged a thorough campaign to publicize the races.

> The main towns within a 150-mile radius of the city are being placarded with 24-sheet posters. Streamers are being strung across the main highways. Billboards are being covered with news of the races. Automobiles are carrying stickers. Trolley cars will give directions to the field. Within 150 miles of St. Louis, automobile clubs will paint directions as to how to reach St. Louis Field. Aircraft manufacturers from all over the United States are routing exhibits to the aeronautical exhibition. The Curtiss Airplane Company has loaned a ship, in which speakers will fly to many towns within a 150-mile radius, distributing handbills and delivering speeches at fairs, Rotary Clubs, Chamber of Commerce meetings and other clubs.[52]

This effort was graphically aided by the Sperry Gyroscope Corporation, which loaned its 450,000,000-candlepower searchlight, which could throw its beam a distance of 100 miles.[53]

The St. Louis Air Board secured not only a sufficient amount of capable aviators, but also a significant number of distinguished guests to observe the air festivities: Secretary of War John H. Weeks, Secretary of the Navy Edwin Denby, Secretary of Commerce Herbert Hoover, Postmaster General Harry S. New, a surfeit of senators and congressmen, General John J. Pershing, Brigadier General William Mitchell, Orville Wright, Glenn Curtiss, President Howard Coffin of the NAA, Major General Mason M. Patrick, chief of the Army Air Service, Rear Admiral William A. Moffett, chief of the Naval Bureau of Aeronautics, Eddie Rickenbacker, and several other civic leaders, industrialists, and public officials,[54] as well as air attachés and observers from England, France, Japan, Italy, Czechoslovakia, Siam, Brazil, Peru, Canada, and the Philippines.[55]

Because of heavy rains on September 30, which left St. Louis Flying Field covered with pools of water, the three-day meet, scheduled to open on October 1, was postponed until October 4.[56] As a result, an additional $40,000 had to be spent for the extended

This poster, 21" by 14", decorated store windows within a 150-mile radius of St. Louis for weeks prior to the 1923 Air Races.

overhead expenditures and a re-rolling of the airfield to bring it into a condition of safety for the aviators.[57] The delay, however, gave the fliers more time to prepare for the contests and permitted the public to turn its undivided attention to the congresses and conventions then taking place.

The National Aeronautic Association, "the largest aeronautic body of its kind in the world,"[58] held its annual convention at the Hotel Statler on October 1. The delegates discussed the organization's program of air legislation, publicity, and activity, and re-elected Howard Coffin president, although he resigned the following day in favor of Frederick B. Patterson, the head of Dayton's National Cash Register Company.[59] At the Third Annual Aero Congress, also in the Statler on October 1, Howard Coffin, General Patrick, Admiral Moffett, and Assistant Secretary of War Dwight Davis (a St. Louisan) spoke on such varied topics as the regulation of civilian pilots to eliminate irresponsible stunting and the American Legion's program for limiting air armaments.[60]

The following day, the Second National Air Institute convened and papers were delivered by aeronautical engineers, scientists, and public officials on such subjects as the uses of aircraft, the United States Air Mail Service, and the future of commercial aviation.[61] Three days earlier, thousands of St. Louisans had poured over St. Louis Flying Field, inspecting the $5,000,000 exposition of airplanes, dirigibles, parachutes, instruments, bombs, and aerial accessories which had been brought together under an immense tent.[62] The enthusiasm they displayed was only a prelude of what was to come.

Before the formal events got under way, two "monsters" paid visits to St. Louis and received the homage of the crowd. On October 2, the Navy's ZR-1 landed at the Bridgeton airfield. This gigantic airship was the first American-built rigid dirigible[63] and was "the largest aircraft in the world."[64] Constructed with a framework of duraluminum, the airship was 680 feet long, 78 feet in diameter, and had a gas capacity of 2,150,000 cubic feet. (In comparison, a large championship-racing spherical balloon held about 80,000 cubic feet of gas.) The ZR-1 was powered by six Packard engines and had a lifting power of 103,000 pounds and a cruising range of 4,500 miles. The pride of the Navy cost $1,500,000, plus an additional $2,000,000 for a steel-and-concrete hangar 962 feet long, 348 feet wide, and 200 feet high, at Lakehurst, New Jersey.[65] The unique feature of the ZR-1, besides its unprecedented size, was the fact that it was the first airship in history to use nonflammable helium

Over 100 Army and Navy enlisted men grabbed lines dropped from the Navy's ZR-1 as she docked at Lambert Field. This photo was made at dawn, October 2, 1923.

gas[66] (at a cost of $175 per thousand cubic feet)[67] rather than the customary, highly flammable hydrogen. Its initial test flight had been made at Lakehurst on September 4, 1923, but the flight to St. Louis was its longest run.[68]

With a crew of 42, the *ZR-1* left its New Jersey housing at 6:59 a.m. on October 1 and hove into sight over St. Louis at 3:30 a.m. the following morning. After cruising over the city until dawn, the ship circled leisurely over the airfield and began to descend.

> Then ropes were dropped from the hold, and cables, with pulleys, were lowered from the forward cabin. Another set of lines was dropped from the rear. One hundred and twenty enlisted men of the Army and Navy caught the spider web of ropes. While the holders of the two long cables, running on pulleys, drew her nose slowly earthward, the more numerous holders of many lines, branching from ropes let down from a hold on the interior of the ship, spread themselves over the surrounding ground and stabilized the position of the great craft, just over the heads of the soldiers and the assembled civilians. . . . After the landing had been effected, the men remained at the ropes and served as the ship's anchor throughout her stay.[69]

Only a few hundred people were on the field when the airship

The ZR-1, *later re-christened the* Shenandoah, *dwarfed everything else at Lambert Field. The Wabash Railroad is in the foreground, with Bridgeton Station Road running from left to right (northeast to southwest). Natural Bridge Road runs diagonally across the upper right corner of this photo.*

landed, but the crowd swelled to 7,000 when its presence became known.[70] Although the crew of the dirigible had planned to spend most of the day at St. Louis, strengthening breezes and a tenuous mooring forced its departure at 9:40 a.m., after less than three hours at anchor.[71] With Admiral Moffett aboard, the *ZR-1* returned to Lakehurst, landing there on October 3 at 6:48 a.m. after a round-trip flight of 2,200 miles in an elapsed time of 47 hours and 49 minutes.[72]

The thousands of St. Louisans who witnessed its graceful flight over the city would never forget the impressive majesty of its performance. Within two years, however, tragedy was to strike the *ZR-1*, which had been christened the *Shenandoah* on October 10, 1923.[73] The great airship broke up in a storm over Marietta, Ohio, on September 3, 1925, with the loss of 14 lives.[74] The uproar that Brigadier General Billy Mitchell raised over this catastrophe (as

Western Historical Manuscript Collection, University of Missouri-St. Louis

An enterprising newspaper photographer got this shot of the giant Barling Bomber over St. Louis.

well as over a military seaplane crash two days earlier) was directly responsible for his celebrated court martial.[75]

The second "monster" to appear at the St. Louis air meet was the Army's answer to the *ZR-1* — the Barling Bomber, "the largest airplane in the world."[76] Powered by four tractor and two pusher engines, the gigantic triplane was 65 feet long, 28 feet high, and had a wingspan of 120 feet[77] (the exact distance of the first sustained heavier-than-air flight).[78] A contemporary journal commented:

> The arrival of the Barling Bomber at the St. Louis airport was in a way the most remarkable event of a week's crowded aerial demonstrations. To say that this six-engined triplane is huge, does not in the least convey the impression it creates on the ground or in flight. "Monumental" would perhaps best express it.[79]

The Barling Bomber remained at the St. Louis airfield throughout the week, stupefying the thousands who inspected it. The pride of the Army weighed 27,132 pounds empty, and with its gross weight

The Barling Bomber was the largest plane ever built at the time. The three wings had a span of 120 feet, only 35 feet shorter than today's DC-10. The little plane at right is the Sperry "Messenger," also known as the "Flivver," with which Lawrence Sperry won fourth prize in the "On-To-St.-Louis Race."

of 42,569 pounds it could reach 95.5 miles per hour. The ship cost $500,000 to construct and, like the *Shenandoah,* required a special hangar at a cost of $700,000.[80] Little flying was done after its maiden flight on August 22, 1923, however, because when officials in Washington requested that it be flown a mere 400 miles from Dayton, Ohio, to the capital for exhibition purposes, the bomber was unable to climb high enough to clear the Appalachian Mountains. After lying in disrepair for five years, the Barling was surreptitiously destroyed in 1928 at the order of General H.H. Arnold, so that no public outcry would be made over the million-dollar waste of the taxpayers' money.[81] The cantankerous "beast," nevertheless, had been one of the memorable features of the St. Louis air meet.

The first of the formal events of the 1923 International Air Races came to a close on September 30, when the time limit for the "On to St. Louis" Race expired. C.S. ("Casey") Jones earned the victory by piling up 216 points, the best of the eleven who finished the competition. The exhibition manager of the Curtiss Airplane Corporation flew a Curtiss "Oriole" biplane, carrying Ladislas d'Orey as a passenger, 900 miles from Garden City, Long Island. He started his flight at 10:42 a.m., September 27, and arrived at the Bridgeton airfield at 9:42 a.m., September 29, after three stops in Pennsylvania, Ohio, and Illinois.[82] Jones scored no points for speed (he averaged less than the required 50 miles per hour), 40 points for distance (he traveled 900 miles), 10 points for passengers (he carried one), and 166 points for engine horsepower (he had a 98.5-horsepower Curtiss OX-5 engine).[83] He won first prize of $500 and the St. Louis Senior Chamber of Commerce Trophy. H.F. Cole flew a Thomas-Morse pursuit plane from Pembina, Minnesota, to take second prize of $250 with a point score of 215, one behind the winner. W.W. Meyer carried four passengers from Chicago in a Heath-

Favorite biplane to win third place for $150, and Lawrence Sperry won the $100 fourth prize by piloting his "Messenger" from Washington, D.C.[84] "Casey" Jones had also tied for the Junior Chamber of Commerce Trophy with the longest distance. The magnanimous winner, however, withdrew in favor of H.F. Cole, who had also flown 900 miles.[85]

Although rain prevented the major races from taking place at St. Louis Flying Field on October 1, 2, and 3, the Mulvihill Model Trophy Contest was conducted at 2:30 p.m. on October 3. Only twelve entrants competed in the event, nine from Chicago and three from St. Louis, while soggy weather kept fifteen others away.[86] The Chicagoans, all members of the Illinois Model Aero Club, put their hosts to shame by sweeping the seven cash prizes and capturing the first nine places. Sixteen-year-old E.J. Lange, the president of the club, fittingly won the trophy and $100 by keeping his model aloft for 4 minutes and 22.6 seconds. Most of the contestants were under eighteen, but 38-year-old Walter L. Brook of Chicago, who had been building models since 1907, also participated in the event and finished eighth with a time of 1 minute and 36 seconds. All of the Chicagoans made flights of more than one and one-half minutes, while the three St. Louisans finished tenth, eleventh, and twelfth, with dismal records of 37.2, 20.8, and 17.8 seconds, respectively. Said President Lange:

> Our club has been in existence for eleven years, and we have learned a lot about model airplanes. But we hope to get a lot of competition from St. Louis in the future. We will help your boys if we can, and we will get a licking from you yet — but you'll have to go some to give it to us.[87]

A crowd of 19,000 spectators gathered at the Bridgeton airfield on October 4 for the first formal races of the meet.[88] Before the contests got under way, however, the dean of St. Louis aviation was honored, Major Albert Bond Lambert. He was the man primarily responsible for putting St. Louis on the world's air map and for bringing about the city's newly-established airfield. Katherine Perkins, the daughter of Colonel Albert T. Perkins, a member of the St. Louis Air Board, dedicated the field and presented it to Major General Mason M. Patrich, chief of the AAS. She declared:

> The field is finished. I dedicate it as the Lambert-St. Louis Flying Field. I turn it over to your command for the races, sir. All contestants are present and accounted for.[89]

With that, the Flying Club of St. Louis Trophy Race opened the official program at the field. Seven contestants took part in the

Western Historical Manuscript Collection, University of Missouri-St. Louis

Contestants roar around the pylons during the Flying Club of St. Louis Race.

event, a 150-kilometer race for light planes with engines of 90 horse-power or less. Edmond T. Allen was the eighth entrant, but he failed to appear.[90] The seven contestants got into the air at 11:00 a.m., and "Casey" Jones jumped into the lead in his "Oriole." He led for the entire first lap of the 50-kilometer course, with Lawrence B. Sperry close behind in his "Messenger," followed by R.P. Hewitt's Farman "Sport," Walter E. Lees' Hartzell FC1, Perry Hutton's Laird "Swallow," St. Louisan William B. Robertson's "Special," and Tex La Grone's Rogers "Day." On the second lap, Sperry, who was "hedge-hopping" at a height of 20 feet, took the lead from Jones, but he was overtaken by Lees at the start of the third and final lap. The rest of the field trailed behind the three leaders, with Tex La Grone three miles back. In the home stretch of the last lap, Sperry was only 200 yards behind Lees when he was forced down by ignition trouble. He made swift repairs and was able to complete the race. Lees crossed the finish line at 12:04:50 p.m. with a total time of 62 minutes and 37.02 seconds, an average speed of 89.31 miles per hour, for which he won the trophy and $500. Perry Hutton was second at 86.77 miles per hour for $300. "Casey" Jones was third for $200, at a speed of 85.28 miles per hour. Robertson was fourth at 83.95, La Grone fifth at 81.05, Hewitt sixth at 78.43, and Sperry last, his average dropping from 87.65 miles per hour for two laps to 71.95 for the entire race.[91] It was a fine opening event and was well appreciated by the enthusiastic crowd.

The second contest of the day started at 12:45 p.m. for the John L. Mitchell Trophy. The six entrants were all Army pilots from the First Pursuit Group and each flew a 300-horsepower Thomas-Morse MB3, the standard equipment of that unit. Since the planes were identical, the race was simply a test of pilot skill for four laps of the 50-kilometer course. They took off singly and turned the first pylon in the order in which they left the field. First Lieutenant T.W. Blackburn led for the first three laps, with First Lieutenant G.P. Tourtellot, First Lieutenant T.K. Matthews, and Captain Burt E. Skeel pressing him throughout. Shortly after they began the final circuit, Matthews experienced fuel line trouble and was forced out of the race. The contenders jockeyed for position and Captain Skeel took the lead. He was able to maintain his edge and finished first with a time of 50 minutes and 54.95 seconds, averaging 146.45 miles per hour. Lieutenant Tourtellot ran out of gas 300 feet from the finish line but was able to sustain his glide and placed second at 143.21 miles per hour, 47 seconds ahead of Lieutenant Blackburn, the early leader, who averaged 141.13 miles per hour. First Lieutenant J.T. Johnson was fourth at 139.20 miles per hour and Captain V.B. Dixon last at 138.94. It was fitting that Captain Skeel won the event, for he was the commanding officer of the unit, the only pursuit group in the AAS.[92]

The Liberty Engine Builders' Trophy Race was the final contest of opening day. The 300-kilometer event for regulation two-place observation planes began at 2:30 p.m. Twelve Army pilots, a Marine, and a Naval officer were entered in the race, but one withdrew before the start and four more made forced landings. Ensign D.C. Allen in the Navy's 18T triplane had been expected to win the race, but he experienced the only accident of the day when the crankshaft of his engine broke and he had to dive sharply for the ground from a height of 500 feet in order to avoid crashing into the grandstand. The plane bounced along the field for fifty feet and flipped over on its back, but Allen and his mechanic, Chief Machinists Mate T.G. Hughes, crawled out unhurt. Two planes ran out of gas and one other contestant experienced engine trouble, but their landings were not nearly so spectacular. After the customary nip-and-tuck battle for the lead, First Lieutenant C. McMullen crossed the line first with his 450-horsepower Fokker CO4 biplane in a time of 80

Lieut. C. McMullen flew this Fokker CO4 biplane to victory in the Liberty Engine Builders' Trophy Race, averaging 139.03 miles per hour.

minutes and 26.84 seconds, averaging 139.03 miles per hour to win the trophy and a cash prize of $800. First Lieutenant H.K. Ramey took second for $500 with a speed of 137.54 miles per hour, and First Lieutenant L.H. Smith finished third at 135.35 for $200. Such peak performances had never before graced an opening day.[93]

A crowd of 25,000 was assembled at Lambert Field for the two events scheduled for October 5.[94] The Aviation Club of Detroit Trophy Race for light commercial planes began at 11:00 a.m. Four of the seven starters in the 250-kilometer contest were forced down before the end of the race, so the three finishers each received prizes. Both Major William B. Robertson and his brother Frank had to land when water mixed with the gasoline in their engines. Lieutenant H.R. Harris had difficulty with the timing gear in his engine, and J.L. Burns suffered burned-out bearings. The contest was a two-fold affair, with prizes for speed and efficiency, the latter being determined by dividing the payload by the engine horsepower and multiplying the result by the speed attained. Jack Atkinson won the race in a Bellanca monoplane with an average speed of 94.28 miles per hour, earning the trophy and $500 for his achievement. Perry Hutton placed second for $300 at 87.03 miles per hour in a Liard "Swallow." C.S. ("Casey") Jones was the third of the finishers, winning $200 for speeding his "Oriole" at an average of 82.69 miles per hour for the five laps. The three men finished in the same order on the efficiency scale: Atkinson had a figure of merit of 674.84 for $500, Hutton 300.42 for $300, and Jones 285.55 for $200.

> Owing to the length of the course and the relative low speed of the contestants this race was not particularly thrilling from the public viewpoint, but it was very instructive to the technician. . . . It was just a steady grind, with the fittest surviving.[95]

At 2:00 p.m. the 300-kilometer Merchants Exchange of St. Louis Trophy Race got under way. The event was intended for large capacity "freight or passenger" airplanes, but with one exception, the entrants were all military bombers. There were ten contestants, seven from the Army and three from the Navy. Two of the Army pilots failed to start and each of the services lost a contestant due to engine trouble during the race. First Lieutenant H.L. George won the trophy and $1,000 with a twin-engine Martin bomber, averaging 114.28 miles per hour for 97 minutes and 52.21 seconds. The Navy won second prize of $700, with Lieutenant M.A. Shur piloting a single-engine Douglas bomber at an average speed of 107.62 miles per hour. The Marine Corps took third honors and $300 for First Lieutenant W.S. Hallenberg's 105.44-mile-per-hour performance in a Martin bomber. The only commercial plane in the race, First Lieutenant H.G. Crocker's Fokker T2, finished last, averaging 94.46 miles per hour.[96]

On October 6, 85,000 people paid admission to the grandstand and there were 20,000 more in the immediate environs, for this was the day the Pulitzer speed classic was to be contested.[97] The spectators also came to witness the *Detroit News* Air Mail Trophy Race, which started at 11:00 a.m. Fifteen mail pilots, all flying standard United States Air Mail biplanes, started the event, a 300-kilometer, six-lap contest. The only occurrence of note came when the judges ruled that J.H. Knight had failed to cross the starting line properly as he began the race and would be disqualified unless he made a seventh lap. Lieutenant Russell L. Maughan then took off in a Curtiss fighter, pulled abreast of Knight, and after gesticulating wildly for several minutes, communicated the message to him. The mail pilot crossed the finish line in third place, but then executed the additional lap, which caused him to finish "out of the money" in fifth place. J.F. Moore won the trophy and a prize of $800 for averaging 124.98 miles per hour, completing the course several miles ahead of the field. D.C. Smith finished five minutes after Moore and won $500 with a speed of 120.83 miles per hour. P.F. Collins averaged 120.09 to win third prize of $200.

> That the mail pilots possess flying ability to a superior degree was amply demonstrated to the public at St. Louis, for the way they handled their ships, particularly around the pylons, was unexcelled during the entire meet. Their flying skill was also allied with good judgment, particularly when two or three pilots would turn a pylon together, for not one of them ever interfered with the maneuver of a mate.
>
> The proverbial reliability of the Air Mail ships was also demonstrated, for this was the only event during the races where not a single contestant had a forced landing outside of the airport.[98]

The Pulitzer Trophy Race was the contest everyone had come to see, for it was to be a test of pure speed among the fastest ships available. The Navy had entered four pilots, two in 700-horsepower Wright torpedo bombers and two in 500-horsepower Curtiss fighters. This branch of the service had spent a large portion of its air appropriation on the development of the two airplanes, sacrificing everything for engine efficiency and speed. The Army fielded three entrants, two with Curtiss racers and one with a 500-horsepower Verville Sperry, the only monoplane in the race. Each of the Army's planes had flown in the 1922 Pulitzer Race at Detroit, and few improvements had been made on them, since the AAS had spent most of its 1923 appropriation for the development of the Barling and Martin bombers.[99] The great speed event was to be a test of the favored Army, resting somewhat on its laurels, against the underdog Navy, well-prepared with powerful equipment. It was also to be a battle between Curtiss and Wright, the pioneer manufacturers, for supreme honors in the industrial field.[100]

To reduce as much as possible the chances of accident, it was decided to pair the contestants and run the race in heats. First Lieutenant L.H. Sanderson of the Marine Corps was first into the air with a red Navy-Wright torpedo bomber. He circled the field behind the starting point, climbed to 4,000 feet, and then dove straight for the first pylon at the starting line. He flashed by the timers at 2:31 p.m. and streaked out of sight. A moment later, First Lieutenant J.D. Corkill of the Army took to the air in a black Army Curtiss racer. From 3,000 feet he, too, made a diving start to obtain maximum speed and chased after Sanderson. The Marine pilot completed the first of four 50-kilometer laps in 8 minutes and 5.58 seconds at an average speed of 230.33 miles per hour, and finished his entire run in 32 minutes and 24.59 seconds, averaging 230.06 miles per hour. Corkill lagged all the way, turning in a time of 34 minutes and 26 seconds, averaging 216.45 miles per hour. As he was circling to land, Lieutenant Sanderson found himself out of gas and had to set his ship down in a haystack just off the field. The racer was demolished, but the Marine pilot suffered only a sprained ankle.[101]

In the second heat, Lieutenant Alford J. Williams in a blue Navy-Curtiss R2C1 was pitted against First Lieutenant Alexander Pearson in the slate-colored Verville Sperry monoplane. "The planes were barely away before the Navy's Williams began to sink the Army grey."[102] With a deafening roar, he gathered momentum in a diving start and swept directly over the crowd at an incredible 280 miles per hour, passing out of sight in 20 seconds. Lieutenant Pearson then took off, but he never finished the first leg of the course. His propeller was in improper balance and he had to turn back to the airfield and land.[103]

When Pearson withdrew, the contest committee decided to start the third and last heat with Williams still in the air. Lieutenant S.W. Callaway in a red Navy-Wright torpedo-bomber was first off, followed by Lieutenant Harold J. Brow in a blue Navy-Curtiss R2C1 and Lieutenant Walter Miller in a black Army-Curtiss racer. Lieutenant Al Williams completed the course in 30 minutes and 36.01 seconds, averaging 243.67 miles per hour. The blackouts he suffered in the steep banking turns confused him to such a degree that

Western Historical Manuscript Collection, University of Missouri-St. Louis

Army First Lieutenant Alexander Pearson flew a graceful Verville Sperry R-3 monoplane in the Pulitzer Trophy Race, managing to turn the first pylon before being forced down by an imbalanced propeller.

he lost count of the laps and made a fifth circuit of the route. It then remained to be seen whether his time would be beaten. It was not. He had won the Pulitzer Trophy.

One of the most remarkable features of the race was the consistency of the three pairs of sister ships which participated in the 124.27-mile race. Navy Lieutenants Williams and Brow took first and second places (worth $1,500 and $1,000 respectively) in Curtiss R2C1 racers. Brow averaged 241.78 miles per hour, less than two miles per hour slower than Williams' speed. Marine Corps Lieutenant Sanderson and Naval Lieutenant Callaway took third and fourth places with Wright torpedo-bombers, Sanderson averaging 230.06 miles per hour (for $500) and Callaway 230.00. Army First Lieutenants Miller and Corkill finished fifth and sixth in Curtiss racers. Miller flew at 218.91 miles per hour and Corkill at 216.45.[104]

It was a great day for the Navy and for Curtiss. Al Williams had established new world's speed records for both 100- and 200-kilometer closed circuit courses: 243.812 and 243.673 miles per hour respectively.[105] Said Orville Wright: "I never thought it would be possible."[106] The Navy swept the first four places, but each of the

Navy Lieutenant Alford J. Williams averaged 243.67 miles per hour in his Curtiss R2C-1, to win the 1923 Pulitzer Trophy Race.

six contestants had bettered Army Lieutenant Russell L. Maughan's standing record of 205.9 miles per hour, which he had set in the Pulitzer Race at Detroit in 1922.[107]

When Williams was asked how it felt to be "speed king" of the world, he replied:

> It feels funny and you can say for me that I felt funny when it was all happening. I knew I was making great speed, but I did not know just what it was. I crossed the starting line with my indicator showing 280 mi./hr. I kept her wide open, but my speed dropped some, and somewhere in the third lap I went "woozy." I felt just like I was asleep. It was those turns that did it. I couldn't see, so I jerked off my goggles, but that didn't help any it seemed. I was all mixed up and lost track of the laps. Sure was "woozy." I knew things were mixed up so I went around again to make sure.[108]

The Pulitzer performance was a perfect climax to an unprecedented air meet. The International Air Races, however, had been "international" in name only, for none of the expected foreign entrants appeared for competition.[109] They could have added but little to the widespread activity. In addition to the formal program, countless flights and demonstrations were performed by planes and pilots of all types. Among the visiting airmen, listed an obscure #59 on a roster drawn up by *Aviation* magazine, was "C.A. Lindbergh in Curtiss JN4, OX5, from Minneapolis, Minn."[110] On this, his first trip to St. Louis, Charles Lindbergh had been involved in one of the few accidents at the meet. He flew his friend Bud Gurney over Lambert Field — Gurney wanted to make an exhibition parachute jump. The chute opened successfully, but Gurney landed awry and broke his left shoulder.[111]

The St. Louis Flying Club, the Air Board, and the Aeronautic Corporation delivered yeoman performances in 1923. The International Air Races can only be described in superlatives. While the 1859 balloon voyage of John Wise was probably the most significant flight ever made from St. Louis, and 1910 the city's most productive aeronautic year, the 1923 air meet was surely its most grandiose aerial gathering. In all, 375 aircraft appeared at the tournament: 204 from the Army Air Service, 25 from the Navy, 130 civilian ships, and 16 from the Post Office Department. A total of 355,834.30 miles was flown cross-country in connections with the meet, along with 18,273.52 miles at Lambert Field itself. In those 374,107.82 flying miles not a single serious accident took place.[112] The tournament was a success in every respect, including financial, which was something of a record in itself, since most meets in the past had produced monetary deficits. A contemporary account noted:

> This perhaps will be the most lasting consequence of the St. Louis meet. If aviation races can attract crowds of one hundred thousand people and take in one hundred and fifty thousand dollars in receipts, these events may become more frequent.[113]

The St. Louis Aeronautic Corporation collected $329,133.14 to stage the International Air Races: $171,225.00 in stock subscriptions, $138,319.78 from ticket sales, $11,381.49 from advertising and program sales, $492.00 in entry fees, $1,839.81 from concessions, and $5,875.06 in miscellaneous donations. The total cost of the meet was $315,416.57, the greatest part of which represented ground expenses of $172,756.29 for the development of Lambert-St. Louis Flying Field. Its purposes accomplished, the corporation liquidated itself on February 28, 1924, having made a profit of $13,716.57.[114] Many men could share the credit for the success of the meet, but the highest praise belonged to Arthur B. Birge, the general manager of the Aeronautic Corporation and the Air Board, who had been "the effective power that translated into action the decisions of the officers."[115]

> The International Air Meet held in St. Louis the first week in October was without exaggeration by far the biggest and best aeronautical demonstration ever held, not only in this country, but in the world. By reason of the attendance, the multiplicity of the events, the number and variety of the aircraft present, the able management and the unprecedented record of not a single serious accident in 300,000 mi. flown, the St. Louis meet was truly in a class by itself.[116]

XI
The *Spirit of St. Louis*, 1927

ONE OF THE MOST MOMENTOUS FLIGHTS of all time took place in 1927. When Charles Augustus Lindbergh became the first man to fly nonstop alone from New York to Paris, he found himself an international idol and provided an immeasurable stimulus for commercial aviation. The unprecedented accomplishment also boosted St. Louis another notch higher on the ladder of aeronautic greatness, for the young adventurer had matured at Lambert Field and had received the enthusiastic financial cooperation of a number of businessmen in the city. The dramatic venture was both the climax of and the prelude to a storybook career.

Charles A. Lindbergh Jr. was born in Detroit, Michigan, on February 4, 1902. He entered a family which was distinguished in its own right. His grandfather, Ola Mansson, had been a prominent social reformer in the Swedish *Riksdag* and a close friend of the crown prince, who had become King Charles XV in 1859. Disgusted with the antiquated class structure of his native country, however, Mansson emigrated to Sauk Center, Minnesota, that year and changed his somewhat common name to August Lindbergh.[1] He had an additional motive for altering his residence and surname, for he had been one of the directors of the Bank of Sweden and was then under prosecution for embezzlement.[2]

Charles Augustus Lindbergh Sr. was born in Stockholm in 1859.

In keeping with the Swedish custom, his surname had been Olsson, but he, too, changed it to Lindbergh, following his father's example.[3] He received a law degree from the University of Michigan and, after his first wife died of cancer, he married Evangeline Lodge Land in 1901. Their only son was born the following year.

The senior Lindbergh took up the practice of law in Little Falls, Minnesota, and in 1906 he was elected to congress from the state's monolithically Republican Sixth District. Like his father before him in the *Riksdag,* he earned a reputation as a progressive reformer, and served for five consecutive terms as a member of the House of Representatives.[4]

The junior Lindbergh, who soon dropped that addendum from his name, was raised in Little Falls. His parents were estranged soon after his birth, and he spent most of his time with his mother, to whom he had an extraordinarily strong attachment.[5] He reached his full height of 6 feet 3 inches late in high school, and after graduation, he began to think of aviation as a career.[6] In September 1920, Lindbergh enrolled as a freshman at the University of Wisconsin to take its highly reputed mechanical engineering courses. His chief forms of recreation were shooting with the ROTC pistol and rifle teams and buzzing through the streets of Madison on his Excelsior motorcycle, in a manner reminiscent of an earlier aeronautic enthusiast who in 1900 had exhibited one of the first motorcycles Paris had ever seen — Albert Bond Lambert.[7]

Lindbergh had gazed upon his first airplane in Washington, D.C. in 1912, but although he had been fascinated with flying since that date, he "had never been near enough to a plane to touch it."[8] Wisconsin offered little in the area of aeronautical engineering and he felt that his grades were too poor for him to measure up to the requirements at a more air-minded school (namely, Massachusetts Institute of Technology), so he looked elsewhere for more practical experience. He later wrote:[9]

> Soon after the start of my third semester at Wisconsin I decided to study aeronautics in earnest, and if, after becoming better acquainted with the subject, it appeared to have a good future, I intended to take it up as a life work. I remained at the University of Wisconsin long enough to finish the first half of my sophomore year. Then about the end of March 1922, I left Madison on my motorcycle en route to Lincoln, Nebraska, where I had enrolled as a flying student with the Nebraska Aircraft Corporation.[10]

On April 9, 1922, he made his first flight. Lindbergh and sixteen-year-old Harlan "Bud" Gurney squeezed into the front cockpit of a Lincoln Standard, while Otto Timm piloted the ship from the rear.[11]

By the end of May, he had received eight hours of instruction from Timm and I.O. Biffle and was ready to solo. The course, however, had cost $500 and Lindbergh had spent an additional $150 on food and lodging. He was unable to raise the necessary bond to cover possible breakage, so he could not make his solo flight.[12] Moreover, before his ten-hour course of instruction could be completed, the corporation liquidated its flying school and sold its only trainer to Erold G. Bahl, who was planning a barnstorming tour through southeastern Nebraska. Lindbergh persuaded Bahl to let him go along as mechanic and helper, and he thus got his first taste of cross-country flying.[13]

Barnstorming was a common practice in the early 1920s. Many former wartime pilots and "airplane bums" went from town to town throughout the country giving any sufficiently courageous residents a five- or ten-minute spin for $5.00 apiece.[14] "Slim" Lindbergh, who had acquired his nickname while training at Lincoln,[15] learned many things on his junket with Bahl, among them the perilous practice of "wing walking."[16] He then returned to Lincoln in June 1922 for his remaining two hours of flying instruction. In the same month, he made his first parachute jump, after tutorship by Charlie Harden, a celebrated exhibition jumper. On his first attempt, Lindbergh performed a difficult "double drop" with two parachutes. After the first opened, he cut it away and opened the second halfway to the ground.[17] The thrilling demonstration earned him immediate prestige among the airmen at the field.

After "wing walking" and parachute jumping his way through several flying circuses, where he was billed as "Daredevil Lindbergh,"[18] the young aviator went to Americus, Georgia, to attend a government auction in April 1923. There he bought his first airplane, a Curtiss "Jenny" with a 90-horsepower OX-5 engine, for $500. (The wartime trainers had originally cost $10,000 apiece.)[19] He still had not made a solo flight "although at that time the fact was strictly confidential."[20] He then "barnstormed" through the South and up into the Midwest, where he attended the St. Louis International Air Races in October 1923, along with a swarm of other visiting airmen.[21]

Eager for further instruction, Lindbergh turned to the Army as a means of achieving "a college education in flying."[22] He entered the Army Air Service Training School at Brooks Field, San Antonio, on March 15, 1924, and was formally enrolled as a cadet four days later. "It was the first school he had ever attended which fully engaged him and to which he devoted, willingly, his best efforts"[23] By this time, "Slim" Lindbergh had 325 hours of flying time, while

George J. Herwig Collection

Lindbergh chose this portrait in uniform as his passport photo. He carried it with him during the flight to Paris.

most of the other 103 students in his class had none.[24] They received 75 hours of training in 150-horsepower "Jennies" at Brooks, along with suitable ground instruction and classroom studies. With a final few hours in de Haviland DH-4s, the 33 students who had weathered the primary course were sent to the advanced school at Kelly Field, San Antonio, in September 1924.[25]

Here the fledgling airmen flew MB-3 and SE-5 scout planes, twin-engine Martin bombers, TW-3 observation planes, and tiny Sperry "Messengers." On March 6, 1925, nine days before he was to graduate, Lindbergh made his first emergency parachute jump. While staging a mock attack on a DH-4B with his SE-5 in formation with eight others, Cadet Lindbergh collided with Lieutenant C.D. McAllister, who was piloting another of the small scout planes. Both parachuted to safety. "Never before had anyone escaped alive from a collision of airplanes in the air."[26] As a result of the accident, "Slim" Lindbergh automatically became a member of the exclusive Caterpillar Club. This organization had been founded on October 20, 1922, by Lieutenant H.R. Harris of the AAS, who "on that day made the first forced jump in the Air Service in which a chute saved a life."[27] The Caterpillar Club was dedicated to the silkworm, the insect to which every emergency jumper owed his life, and only those who made such leaps could claim membership.[28]

Of the initial 104 cadets, only 18 were graduated from the advanced flying school at Kelley Field as second lieutenants on March 15, 1925. Although he had always been a poor student, Charles Lindbergh was second in his class at Brooks Field and first at Kelley.[29] Like most of the others, he promptly resigned from the active service in order to retain his freedom as a member of the Air Service Reserve Corps.[30] After obtaining a Lincoln Standard OX-5 biplane at Lambert Field, he went on a barnstorming tour of the Midwest for the next several weeks. His prowess with an airplane earned him a reputation as "one of the best all-around stunt fliers in the country, fearing nothing that is possible to be accomplished in the air."[31]

> Lindbergh was not only a master of every standard stunt — the "falling leaf," the Immelmann, loops and spins and barrel rolls — he had also a specialty of his own. He climbed thousands of feet into the air, then dove straight downward at a terrific speed until [everyone] was sure he must crash, having passed the last possible point at which a pullout was possible. Then he did pull out, so near the earth that his wheels sometimes brushed tall grasses.[32]

During the summer of 1925, the Post Office Department was advertising a number of airmail routes for private operators. One of the bidders was Robertson Aircraft Corporation of St. Louis, which had offered Lindbergh the job of chief pilot if its bid were accepted. In October of that year, Robertson was awarded the Chicago-St. Louis mail route. While awaiting the inauguration of the run, Lindbergh took a position as an instructor in the company's flying school.[33] At Lambert Field on June 2, 1925, he had to make his

Lindbergh saw this view many times — Lambert Field immediately after takeoff. The building at far left is a log cabin clubhouse. In front of it are two airmail hangars. The structures in the foreground are the National Guard hangars. The farmhouse where Lindbergh lived while carrying the mail is in the grove of trees. The view, made in 1925, is to the southwest. The stabilizer of the photographer's plane projects into the photo from the left.

second emergency parachute jump when he found himself unable to recover from a tailspin he had purposely initiated while testing a four-place OXX-6 Plywood Special.[34] He was now a double member of the Caterpillar Club.

During the winter, Lindbergh remained at the airfield instructing students and gaining experience for himself. In November 1925 he enlisted in the 110th Observation Squadron of the 35th Division of the Missouri National Guard, and was commissioned a First Lieutenant soon afterward.[35] The unit had been organized by his ''boss,'' Major William B. Robertson, on June 23, 1923, and was one of the first in the country.[36] ''Slim'' Lindbergh was active in the group and in 1926 was promoted to the rank of captain.[37]

A photographer stood on the vaulted roof of the westernmost airmail hangar to photograph the Robertson Aircraft Corp. offices in 1927. Lindbergh's rooming house is beneath the "X."

Equipped with five Liberty-engine de Haviland DH-4s and four Curtiss "Orioles," William and Frank Robertson began their Chicago-St. Louis airmail operation on April 15, 1926.[38] Despite their prolific faults, the de Havillands were the workhorses of the route.

> These were called "flaming coffins" by pilots because their fuel tanks, set between engine and cockpit, were likely to explode in crash landings. Moreover, their landing speed was dangerously high; their landing gear was so weak it broke frequently on rough runways; they were so heavy they couldn't climb out of small fields; visibility from their cockpits was poor; and they had, as pilots said, "the gliding angle of a brick."[39]

Charles Lindbergh, Philip Love, and Thomas Nelson were the only three regular pilots of the mail run. As chief, "Slim" Lindbergh had the honor of making the inaugural flight:

> On April fifteenth at 5:50 a.m. I took-off from the Air Mail Field at Maywood on the first southbound flight, and that afternoon we sent two ships north with the inauguration mail from St. Louis, Springfield and Peoria.[40]

Robertson Aircraft Corporation had bid something under $3.00 per pound for the route,[41] and was paid only for the mail actually carried. The great volume transported on April 15, 1926, gave portent for a bright future with high profits.

> But after the first day's heavy load, swollen with letters of enthusiasts and collectors, interest declined. Men's minds turned back

where [illegible handwriting] Roomed [illegible] for his trip to Paris 1926

George J. Herwig Collection

Lindbergh could walk to work during his airmail days. The early Lambert Field buildings are visible behind this photo of his rooming house. All structures in this picture were destroyed years ago.

to routine business; the air mail saves a few hours at most; it's seldom really worth the extra cost per letter. Week after week, we've carried the limp and nearly empty sacks back and forth with a regularity in which we take great pride. Whether the mail compartment contains ten letters or ten thousand is beside the point. We have faith in the future. Some day we know the sacks will fill.[42]

As a mail pilot, Lindbergh was paid a salary of $350 per month, with flying allowances which brought the sum to $450.[43] The Robertson contract called for five round trips each week, but even though the bags often outweighed the mail, the company pilots made their connections on 98 percent of their flights in the first five months of operation.[44] Under Lindbergh's supervision, from April of 1926 until February 1927, the mail service between St. Louis and Chicago involved 589 trips, only 14 of which were not com-

The Robertsons' fleet of notorious de Havilland DH-4 aircraft, which flew the mail between St. Louis and Chicago.

pleted, generally as the result of foul weather.[45]

The chief pilot himself was responsible for at least two of these failures. On September 16[46] and November 3, 1926, fog over Chicago's Maywood Field forced him to make emergency parachute jumps.[47] On both occasions when his "wooden bird" had failed, he brought the mail ignominiously through by "iron horse." He had now become the only four-time member of the Caterpillar Club.[48] There is some evidence indicating that Major William B. Robertson fired Lindbergh, who had suffered four crashes within twenty months, after he had wrecked his second mail plane. Philip Love and Thomas Nelson, however, resigned in protest, and Robertson was forced to re-hire his chief pilot.[49]

During his frequent hops between St. Louis and Chicago, Lindbergh found time to occupy himself with his inner thoughts. It was on such a trip in September 1926 that the idea for a transatlantic flight first struck him.

> Why shouldn't I fly from New York to Paris? I'm almost twenty-five. I have more than four years of aviation behind me, and close to two thousand hours in the air. I've barnstormed over half of the forty-eight states. I've flown my mail through the worst of nights. I know the wind currents of the Rocky Mountains and the storms of the Mississippi Valley as few pilots know them. During my year at Brooks and Kelly as a flying cadet, I learned the basic elements of navigation. I'm a Captain in the 110th Observation Squadron of Missouri's National Guard. Why am I not qualified for such a flight? . . . As I attempted them [my previous goals], I can — I will attempt that too. I'll organize a flight to Paris.[50]

Such a prospect had first been brought to public attention on May 22, 1919, when Raymond Orteig, an air-minded Frenchman who owned the Lafayette and Brevoort Hotels in New York City, offered a prize of $25,000

> to be awarded to the first aviator who shall cross the Atlantic in a land or water aircraft (heavier-than-air) from Paris or the shores of

Lindbergh boards a Robertson DH-4 for the Chicago run. Twice he had to make emergency parachute jumps.

France to New York, or from New York to Paris or the shores of France, without stop.[51]

The donor stipulated that the flight be made within five years, but when the prize still lay unclaimed in 1924, he renewed it for a similar period.[52] The entrants had to provide a sixty-day advance notice of their intention to attempt the crossing, and the flight had to be made under the rules of the National Aeronautic Association and the International Aeronautic Federation[53]

By the time Charles Lindbergh was ready to embark upon his odyssey, the Atlantic had been crossed eight times by air. From May 17 to 27, 1919, the United States Navy seaplane *NC-4* with a crew of three flew from Trepassy, Newfoundland, to Lisbon, Portugal, by way of the Azores.[54] A few weeks later, the first nonstop crossing was made by Captain John Alcock and Lieutenant Arthur Whitten Brown of England in a twin-engine Vickers-Vimy biplane.

Lindbergh was Robertson's chief pilot during his airmail days; his two colleagues were Thomas Nelson, left, and Phil Love.

They flew from St. John's, Newfoundland, to Clifden, Ireland, June 14-15, 1919, and received the *London Daily Mail's* prize of 10,000 pounds, as well as knighthood from King George V.[55] In July of the same year, the British rigid dirigible *R-34,* commanded by Major G.H. Scott, made a round trip from England to the United States and back.[56] In August 1924, the United States Army "Round-the-World" fliers spanned the Atlantic from England to the United States by way of Greenland in the *New Orleans* and the *Chicago.*[57] The fifth crossing was made in October of that same year, when the German-built American rigid airship *ZR-3* (later christened the *Los Angeles)* sailed 5,066 miles in 81 hours and 17 minutes from Friedrichshafen, Germany, to Lakehurst, New Jersey.[58]

In addition to those five spannings of the North Atlantic, there were three "pre-Lindbergh" crossings of the South Atlantic. Commander Ramon Franco flew from Los Palos, Spain, to Pernambuco,

The NC-4 became the first airplane to cross the Atlantic Ocean, in 1919. The three-engine Navy biplane paid a promotional visit to the St. Louis riverfront in 1926.

Brazil, on January 30-31, 1926. On February 24, 1927, Commander Francesco de Pinedo completed an extensive flight from Italy to Pernambuco; and on March 18, 1927, Major Sarmento Beires of Portugal ended a 1,715-mile flight from Bolama in Portuguese Guinea to Brazil.[59] The Orteig Prize, nevertheless, remained untouched, for none of the eight transatlantic flights had been nonstop from New York to Paris.

After mulling over the various possibilities, Captain Lindbergh decided that a single-engine monoplane would offer him the best chance for success. A biplane would have too much air resistance and a ship with two or three engines would increase the likelihood of engine failure.[60] With these characteristics in view, his mind settled on one specific airplane — the Wright-Bellanca.

> If only I had the Bellanca, . . . there are all kinds of records I could break for demonstration. . . . Judging from the accounts I've read, it's the most efficient plane ever built. It could break the world's endurance record, and the transcontinental, and set a dozen marks for range and speed and weight. Possibly — my mind is startled at its thought — I could fly nonstop between New York and Paris.[61]

This airplane was owned by the Wright Aeronautical Corporation, and if that company would not finance him, he would need at least $10,000 to purchase the plane himself, if it were for sale.[62] Financial backers were essential. If he could attract initial investment, a successful flight would pay for itself with the Orteig Prize. To sway

St. Louis businessmen, he prepared an outline of five advantages to be attained by a transatlantic flight:

1) Revive St. Louis' interest in aviation;
2) Advertise St. Louis as an aviation city;
3) Aid in making America first in the air;
4) Promote nation-wide interest in aviation;
5) Demonstrate perfection of modern equipment.[63]

A few days after the transoceanic idea first struck him, Captain Lindbergh approached Earl Thompson, an insurance executive who owned a golden-winged Laird "Swallow" and who had taken a few flying lessons from him at Lambert Field. Lindbergh explained his needs and offered to put up $2,000 himself if Thompson would help him gather a sufficient number of backers for the flight. The insurance man suggested a Fokker trimotor for the venture, but the mail pilot noted its prohibitive cost ($90,000) and also elaborated on the advantages of a single-engine monoplane. Thompson was hesitant, but interested.[64]

A week later, Lindbergh took his case to Major Albert Bond Lambert, the dean of St. Louis aviation. The proposal, as expected, whetted his insatiable aeronautic appetite, and he donated $1,000, on the condition that the young aviator secure a suitable number of other supporters. His prospects brightening, Lindbergh next visited Major William B. Robertson, who was enthusiastic, but could then promise no money for the venture because his company was in financial difficulty of its own. He did offer his chief pilot the use of his name, however, and gave him time off the mail run to make arrangements for the flight.[65] Robertson would ultimately contribute financially to the endeavor.

In December 1926 Lindbergh met with Harry Hall Knight, a prominent stockbroker who was president of the Flying Club of St. Louis. When the would-be transatlantic flier said that he needed almost $15,000, Knight called in Harold M. Bixby, president of the State National Bank and head of the Chamber of Commerce. After some discussion, they told Lindbergh that they would handle all his financial problems. The airman later described his reaction:

> I stop, I start, and turn automatically as I drive back to Lambert Field. I'm conscious of neither time nor distance. Then I'm really going to fly to Paris! It's no longer just an idea, no longer simply a plan in my mind. I feel like a child on Christmas morning, seeing all that he's longed for suddenly piled, dazzling, before him, not knowing which object to pick up first. My most difficult problems are solved — organization and finance.[66]

Knight and Bixby, the primary coordinators of the venture, se-

Prior to leaving for Roosevelt Field and fame, Lindbergh posed with Harry Hall Knight, left, and E. Lansing Ray, right, two of his backers. The third man is unidentified.

cured the interest of four more men in addition to Earl Thompson and Majors Lambert and Robertson: E. Lansing Ray, the publisher of the *St. Louis Globe-Democrat,* Harry F. Knight, the senior broker of the family, and J.D. Wooster Lambert and Frank Robertson, the younger brothers of St. Louis' two eminent aviation pioneers.[67] These nine men provided Charles Lindbergh with the use of their names and potential influence, as well as the necessary finances. Harold Bixby remembered:

> We had a thousand dollars from Albert B. Lambert, and $2,000 from Lindbergh, as well as a thousand from Bill and Frank Robertson, and five hundred from Earl Thompson. We borrowed $10,500 on the endorsement of Harry Knight and me.[68]

While his organization was developing, Lindbergh himself searched for a suitable airplane. Negotiations collapsed with the Wright Aeronautical Corporation, which sold the Wright-Bellanca monoplane to its designer, Giuseppe Bellanca of the Columbia Aircraft Corporation. This firm agreed to sell the plane to Lindbergh for $15,000, but only on the condition that its directors choose the pilot for the transatlantic flight.[69] The firmly resolute aviator then turned elsewhere. The Fokker and Travel Air companies also rejected the gangling youth, refusing to stake their reputations on a possible failure.[70]

The only manufacturer to show any real interest was Ryan Airlines, a small company on the San Diego waterfront. Lindbergh arrived at the factory on February 23, 1927. He consulted with President B.F. Mahoney, who set the price at $10,580 for one of his monoplanes and a Wright Whirlwind engine, with all special equipment extra, at cost.[71] After contacting Harry H. Knight by wire, Lindbergh placed a formal order for the plane on February 28, 1927.[72] The airplane had been christened even before it reached the drawing board. At a meeting of the financial backers of the flight in early February, after preliminary contact with Ryan had been made, Harold Bixby had suggested the title *Spirit of St. Louis*.[73] The name was indeed apropos, and Lindbergh himself was the first to agree.

The transatlantic aircraft, a slight modification of Ryan's basic M-2 design, was given the model designation NYP (New York-Paris). It was a high-wing monoplane with a length of 27 feet 8 inches, a height of 9 feet 10 inches, and a span of 46 feet. The *Spirit of St. Louis* had an empty weight of 2,150 pounds and a designed gross weight of 5,130 pounds. Its maximum speed was 129 miles per hour, with a landing speed varying from 49 to 71 miles per hour, depending upon its load.[74] The ship had a capacity of 451 gallons of gas and 25 gallons of oil. Its engine was a 223-horsepower Wright Whirlwind J-5C. At an ideal economical speed of 97 miles per hour, the *Spirit* had a range of 4,210 miles.[75] The plane's fuselage was of welded steel tubing covered with fabric and its wings were of wood, wire, and cloth. All of its flying instruments were made by the Pioneer Instrument Company of Brooklyn, New York.[76]

> Lighted instrument panel with earth inductor compass, altimeter, tachometer, turn and bank indicator, airspeed indicator, 8-day clock, oil pressure, oil temperature, air pressure, fore and aft level, and transverse level gauges. This was probably the most advanced single engine instrument panel in 1927.[77]

Lindbergh worked closely with Ryan's chief engineer, Donald Hall, throughout his stay in San Diego. Their excellent teamwork produced a finished airplane in record time. The mail pilot stressed the necessity of lightness, speed, and range: "I think we ought to

The brand new Spirit of St. Louis *leaves the Ryan Airlines factory in San Diego, only 60 days after construction started.*

give first consideration to efficiency in flight; second, to protection in a crack-up; third, to pilot comfort.''[78]

At a ship's store in San Pedro, Lindbergh bought the necessary maps and charts that he needed for the flight. He would fly a great circle course from New York to Paris, a distance of 3,610 miles, according to his Mercator projection.[79] The flier made dangerous sacrifices for maximum efficiency. He would carry no parachute (it weighed 20 pounds), no navigation lights, no fuel gauges, no radio, and no sextant — weight was of the essence.[80] He even considered jettisoning his landing gear after takeoff, but Harry Knight forbade it.[81]

Late in March 1927, Lindbergh formally registered with the National Aeronautic Association in competition for the Orteig Prize.[82] He was not alone in his intentions, for five other planes were readying for a transatlantic flight: Lieutenant Commander Noel Davis and Stanton Wooster in a Keystone ''Pathfinder'' trimotor biplane, *The American Legion;* Commander (later Admiral) Richard E. Byrd in a Fokker trimotor, the *America;* Clarence Chamberlain in the Wright-Bellanca *Columbia;* René Fonck in a twin-engine Sikorsky biplane; and Captain Charles Nungesser and Lieutenant François Coli in a single-engine Levasseur biplane, *L'Oiseau Blanc* (The White Bird). Charles Lindbergh was the only one who intended to fly alone.[83]

Lindbergh bids farewell to the crew who built his airplane, prior to his record-breaking nonstop flight from San Diego to St. Louis.

The *Spirit of St. Louis* was completed on April 28, 1927, only sixty days after the order had been placed.[84] Harry Hall Knight had given Lindbergh a cashier's check for $15,000, dated February 18, 1927, to cover the expenses of the undertaking.[85] The pilot had spent $13,500 in San Diego for the plane, with engine and full equipment.[86]

On April 22, 1927, the Aeronautics Board of the Department of Commerce granted license number N-X 211 for the *Spirit of St. Louis.* Six days later, the silver-painted monoplane made its first flight, attaining an impressive speed of 128 miles per hour, but with a load of only 400 pounds.[87] After several more test flights, the *Spirit* was ready for its shakedown cruise. Lindbergh took off from Rockwell Field, San Diego, at 3:55 p.m. May 10, on his hop across the country. At 8:00 Central Standard Time the next morning, the trim aircraft appeared over St. Louis, three hours ahead of schedule. The young aviator had traveled the 1,500 miles in 14 hours and 5 minutes, "the longest nonstop flight ever made across country by one man."[88] He had navigated solely by dead reckoning, as he would on the Atlantic flight, and had guided himself with Rand McNally railroad maps, which he had purchased in a San Diego drugstore for 50¢ apiece.[89]

> I set a straight line for St. Louis and flew by the compass all the way. My flying time was better than 100 miles an hour most of the way, and my altitude was 5,000 to 6,000 feet, except when crossing the Rocky Mountains, when I went up to 13,000. I had moonlight to fly by until about 2 a.m. The crossing of the Rockies was at a point north of Santa Fe, New Mexico. The line I took was such a straight one that I didn't see a city or a large town until I reached Jefferson City this morning [May 11].[90]

After spending the day with Harry Hall Knight and the other

A boyish-looking Charles A. Lindbergh poses before leaving St. Louis for his epochal flight across the Atlantic Ocean.

eight members of the Spirit of St. Louis Organization, his group of financial backers, Lindbergh took off at 8:12 a.m. May 12, and landed at Curtiss Field, Long Island, 7 hours and 25 minutes later. He had crossed the continent, a distance of 2,500 miles, in a flying time of 21 hours and 30 minutes,[91] chopping 5 hours and 20 minutes off the previous transcontinental record, set in 1923 by Lieutenants John A. MacReady and Oakley G. Kelly.[92] Said the *New York Times:* "His time is the quickest ever made from coast to coast and it is the only time a pilot has flown such a distance alone."[93] His prestige soared, and critics now began to take him seriously.

When Lindbergh arrived in New York, two other planes were already there, waiting to cross the ocean — Commander Byrd's *America* and Clarence Chamberlain's *Columbia.*[94] On May 8, Charles Nungesser and François Coli had left Le Bourget Field in *L'Oiseau Blanc* bound for New York. They were never heard from again. Two days later, the world knew of their failure, for they had carried only enough gasoline for forty hours of flight. Search parties, however, continued looking for them.[95] The tragic consequences of the French attempt jeopardized the American flights then in preparation. On May 10, the State Department released an announcement:

> The American ambassador to France, the Hon. Myron T. Herrick, has cabled the State Department that the French people are deeply moved and anxious over the lack of news of the missing aviators. Out of regard for their present state of anxiety he feels that the take-off of a transatlantic flight from the United States at this time, when the fate of the French aviators is still in doubt, might be misunderstood and misinterpreted.[96]

In the preceding eight months, transatlantic attempts had killed six men and injured three others. Nungesser and Coli were lost at sea.[97] On September 21, 1926, Captain René Fonck had crashed his overloaded Sikorsky trimotor shortly after takeoff from Roosevelt Field, Long Island. Although he himself was unhurt, the resulting fire killed two of his crewmen, Jacob Islamoff and Charles Clavier.[98] On April 16, 1927, the trimotor *America* overturned on landing after its first test flight, injuring three men, including Byrd himself.[99] On April 26, Davis and Wooster were killed when their *American Legion* crashed in flames after taking off on a test flight from Langley Field, Virginia.[100] None of the three pilots who gathered on Long Island in mid-May 1927 were unaware of the dangers they faced.

Most observers rated Commander Byrd the favorite in the "race," with Chamberlain second, and Lindbergh "a dark horse of great possibilities."[101] Captain Lindbergh, however, felt that his more formidable competitor was Clarence Chamberlain, who was flying the plane he himself had unsuccessfully tried to buy.[102] In preparation for the flight, this Wright-Bellanca *Columbia* had set a world's endurance record April 12-13 by flying continuously for 51 hours, 11 minutes, and 25 seconds, more than enough time to cross the ocean nonstop.[103] It was an impressive show of strength.

Of all the prospective Atlantic fliers, Lindbergh was by far the most popular. "No one ever more perfectly personified youthful adventure than this young knight of the air . . . He was easily the lion of the hour."[104] Dubbed, to his disgust, "Lucky Lindy" and "The Flying Fool,"[105] the shy mail pilot wilted at the excessive publicity he received and condemned the sensationalism of the press.

Accuracy, I've learned, is secondary to circulation — a thing to be sacrificed, when occasion arises, to a degree depending on the standards of each paper. But accuracy means something to me. It's vital to my sense of values. I've learned not to trust people who are inaccurate. Every aviator knows that if mechanics are inaccurate, aircraft crash. If pilots are inaccurate, they get lost — sometimes killed. In my profession life itself depends on accuracy.[106]

Various factors delayed each of the prospective transatlantic flights. The Nungesser-Coli tragedy resulted in a temporizing of their plans, and when the fliers felt that it was prudent to take off, bad weather grounded all attempts. Commander Byrd also needed additional time to test his *America*.[107] The Bellanca camp was stalled by a personal quarrel between financial backer Charles Levine and proposed navigator Lloyd Bertaud, which resulted in a court suit by Bertaud enjoining the plane from flying without him.[108] Lindbergh himself was worried about the Orteig Prize, for he would not be eligible until sixty days after his formal entrance. This waiting period would not expire until the end of May, and by then it might be too late. He telephoned Harry Hall Knight in St. Louis, who said, "To hell with the money. When you're ready to take off, go ahead."[109] Such spirit made him ever thankful that he had found such generous businessmen in St. Louis to finance him.

. . . my partners haven't interfered with my plans in any way. They've stuck to Bixby's original proposition that they'll take care of the finances, and leave the technical end of the flight to me.[110]

On May 19, a drizzling rain darkened New York, but Lindbergh got word that the weather was clearing over the Atlantic. He resolved that he would start the following morning. The young aviator went to bed at midnight, but so many thoughts passed through his mind that he was unable to sleep. He arose at 2:15 a.m. and went out to the airfield.[111] The slight drizzle had driven all but 200 people from Curtiss Field.[112] At 4:15 a.m. the *Spirit of St. Louis* was towed tail-first to nearby Roosevelt Field. This airfield had been leased by Commander Byrd, but he had graciously invited Lindbergh to use its facilities, since its runway was much more suitable than that on Curtiss Field.[113]

Captain Lindbergh was to carry only thirty pounds of the bare essentials on the flight: two flashlights, a first aid kit, a ball of string, a hunting knife, four red flares sealed in rubber tubes, waterproof matches, charts and maps, a needle, five cans of Army rations, two air cushions, two canteens (one with four quarts of water for emergency and the other with one quart for drinking during the flight), an Armburst Cup for condensing the moisture from breath into drinking water, and an inflatable rubber life raft.[114] The only food he was to take, besides the Army rations, would be five sandwiches (two of ham, two of roast beef, and one of hard-boiled eggs).[115]

Rain delayed his takeoff until shortly before 8:00 a.m. The *Spirit* rested at the western end of Roosevelt Field, facing east, toward Paris. The takeoff would be made with a dangerous five-mile-per-hour tail wind, but if Lindbergh were to take off westward, into the wind, he would have to pass over the hangars and blocks of houses beyond, with no chance to survive a crash. As it was, he would have to clear a menacing stand of trees and telephone wires at the eastern end of the field.[116] The crowd had swelled to 500 and watched as the last of the 451 gallons of gas was pumped into the plane. The *Spirit of St. Louis* then weighed 5,250 pounds,[117] 750 more pounds than ever before.[118] The takeoff would be made more hazardous by the fact that Lindbergh had to fly blind. His two main fuel tanks were situated in the nose of the *Spirit* and a homemade periscope was his only means of forward vision, although he had a clear view through the side windows of the cockpit.[119]

At 7:54 a.m., May 20, 1927, the *Spirit of St. Louis* began to roll down the runway of Roosevelt Field.

> Inside sat a tall youngster, eyes glued to the instrument board or darting ahead for swift glances at the runway, his face drawn with the intensity of his purpose.
>
> Death lay but a few seconds ahead of him if his skill failed or his courage faltered. For moments, as the heavy plane rose from the ground, dropped down, staggered again into the air and fell, he gambled for his life against a hazard which had already killed [six] men.
>
> And then slowly, so slowly that those watching it stood fascinated, as if by his indomitable will alone, the young pilot lifted his plane. It dipped and then rose with renewed speed, climbing heavily but steadily toward the distant trees.
>
> The spirit of unconquerable youth had won and "Slim" Lindbergh was on his way to Paris.[120]

The silver monoplane had taken off in a distance of 3,800 feet[121] and had cleared the threatening wires by twenty feet.[122] It was then in its true element.

> The *Spirit of St. Louis* is no longer an unruly mechanical device, as it was during the takeoff; . . . rather, it seems to form an extension of my own body, ready to follow my wish as the hand follows the mind's desire — instinctively, without command.[123]

At a speed of 100 miles per hour, the *Spirit* passed over New York,

The New York Times.

"All the News That's Fit to Print."

THE WEATHER

VOL. LXXVI...No. 25,319. • • •   NEW YORK, SATURDAY, MAY 21, 1927   TWO CENTS

LINDBERGH SPEEDS ACROSS NORTH ATLANTIC, KEEPING TO SCHEDULE OF 100 MILES AN HOUR; SIGHTED PASSING ST. JOHN'S, N. F., AT 7:15 P.M.

LOWMAN GETS POST AS ANDREWS QUITS IN BIG DRY SHIFT

Mellon, in Same Stroke, Names Chief Chemist Doran Commissioner in Place of Haynes.

STEP TO CHECK FRICTION

Andrews Will Retire Aug. 1 With Work Completed—Haynes Is Forced Out in Shake-Up.

MOVE SATISFIES ALL SIDES

Both Haynses Are on Record as Prohibition Advocates and Are Acceptable to Dry League.

SINCLAIR SENTENCED TO 3 MONTHS IN JAIL

Oil Man Is Also Ordered to Pay $500 Fine for Refusing to Reply to Senators.

APPEALS AND GIVES BOND

Littleton Argues in Vain That His Client Exercised His Constitutional Rights.

'Too Old,' Says Hughes at 65, To Run for the Presidency

LINDBERGH LEAVES NEW YORK AT 7:52 A. M.

With Cool Determination He Braves Death to Get Off in the Misty Dawn, Winning Out by Luck and Skill.

PLANE FALTERS AND THEN RISES AND IS OFF

Hundreds Gasp as Unconquerable Youth by Sheer Wizardry Lifts Machine Carrying 5,200-Pound Load, With Failure a Few Yards Off.

By RUSSELL OWEN

CAPTAIN CHARLES A. LINDBERGH.
The First American Flyer to Start on the Flight Between New York and Paris.

LINDBERGH'S STORY FOR THE TIMES

When next heard from, Lindbergh will write the story of his great exploit especially for readers of The Times and certain associated world newspapers. It will appear in New York exclusively in The Times.

BELLANCA FLIGHT HELD BACK BY WIND

Hop, Set for Dawn, Is Called Off After All Preparations—Bertaud Well Thrown Out.

LONE FLIGHT GRIPS FRENCH IMAGINATION

Lindbergh's Ocean Hop Appeals to Paris as Nothing Else Could Have Done.

GETS HIS BEARINGS IN NEWFOUNDLAND

With the First Leg of His Flight to Paris Over, He Puts to Sea and Heads for Ireland

ALL OF THE "BREAKS" ARE IN HIS FAVOR

Fog Disperses, Weather Clears and Gentle Following Winds Help to Speed Him Along on His Hazardous Venture.

ST. JOHN'S, N. F., May 20—Captain Lindbergh's airplane passed over St. John's at 8:15 o'clock tonight [7:15 New York Daylight Saving Time].

Leaves American Continent

SYDNEY, N. S., May 20—Captain Lindbergh got his last sight of the American continent at 5 o'clock [4 o'clock Eastern Daylight Saving Time] this afternoon.

Strung Well in His Favor

ST. JOHN'S, N. F., Saturday, May 21—Strong westerly winds.

Smokes Over Nova Scotia Coast

YARMOUTH, N. S., May 20—Captain Lindbergh passed over New Truxlet.

Lindbergh Keeps to Schedule.

George J. Herwig Collection

America and the rest of the world awaited news of the intrepid transatlantic flier.

Connecticut, Rhode Island, Massachusetts, and then "homed in" on its great circle course as it headed over its first stretch of ocean.

Here Captain Lindbergh brought his plane down to a height of ten feet to take efficient advantage of the cushion of air on the water. The tension necessary to maintain stability, however, proved too demanding and he soon moved to a safer height of 100 feet.[124] While over Newfoundland, he deliberately deviated from his route to fly over St. John's so that he might be sighted and that word of his progress might be known.[125] He was spotted there at 7:15 p.m. (EST).[126] Ahead lay almost 2,000 miles of Atlantic Ocean.

Clouds and haze forced him up to 10,000 feet as he started over the sea. Here the greatest agony of the journey began to afflict him. "I never knew what the desire to sleep meant to me before this flight."[127] Left to his own thoughts, he reflected on his past career and considered larger matters.

> It's hard to be an agnostic up here in the *Spirit of St. Louis,* aware of the failty of man's devices, a part of the immense between its earth and stars. . . . [The universe] and man conscious of it all — a worldly audience to what if not to God?[128]

Captain Lindbergh had often stayed awake for more than forty hours at a time,[129] but it had never seemed so difficult. He held his hand in the slipstream to guide air blasts into his face, but to little avail. Shortly before the end of the twenty-seventh hour, he found some ammonia capsules in his small first aid kit and broke one open to revive himself. His senses were so dull, however, that he could not even smell it.[130] A few minutes later, all thoughts of sleep left him. He sighted a group of fishing boats, flew low over them, and shouted, "Which way is Ireland?" The stunned fishermen were too startled to reply.[131] Shortly thereafter, he passed over Valentia and Dingle Bay on the southwest coast of the Emerald Isle. Although his earth inductor and liquid compasses had both been rendered useless in a magnetic storm at the end of the fifteenth hour,[132] he was only three miles off his great circle course when he sighted Ireland.[133] His joy was boundless.

> Ireland, England, France, Paris! The night at Paris! *This* night at Paris — less than six hours from now — *France and Paris!* It's like a fairy tale. Yesterday I walked on Roosevelt Field; today I'll walk on Le Bourget.[134]

He came upon the coast of France near the end of the thirty-second hour and for the first time began to lay his future plans. One hour later, at 4:20 p.m. (EST), he ate one of his sandwiches, his first food since takeoff. He was about to throw its waxed paper wrapping out the window, but the sight of the beautifully patterned countryside was so exquisite that he shoved the paper into a bag, lest he defile the panorama beneath him.[135] Lindbergh then paid tribute in his mind to the faultless machine which had transported him across the vastness of the sea.

> The *Spirit of St. Louis* is a wonderful plane. It's like a living crea-ture, gliding along smoothly, happily, as though a successful flight means as much to it as to me, as though we shared our ex-perience together, each feeling beauty, life, and death as keenly, each dependent on the other's loyalty. *We* have made this flight across the ocean, not *I* or *it*.[136]

Le Bourget Field was not marked on any of his maps. He knew only that it was northeast of Paris.[137] He passed over what he thought might be the airport, but it was not as well lighted as he had expected, so he flew on for five more minutes. Sighting only black-ness ahead, he turned back and decided to land on the dimly-lit field. It was Le Bourget. The exhausted pilot touched down at 10:24 p.m. (Paris time), May 21, and 100,000 Frenchmen, alerted to his imminent arrival, were there to greet him.[138]

> After the plane stopped rolling I turned it around and started to taxi back to the lights. The entire field ahead, however, was cover-ed with thousands of people running towards my ship. When the first few arrived, I attempted to get them to hold the rest of the crowd back, away from the plane, but apparently no one could un-derstand, or would have been able to conform to my request if he had. . . . Speaking was impossible; no words could be heard in the uproar and nobody apparently cared to hear any.[139]

The official time for the flight between New York and Paris, according to the barograph of the National Aeronautic Association which Lindbergh had carried, was 33 hours, 30 minutes, and 29.8 seconds.[140] When the *Spirit* landed, it had 85 gallons of gasoline and 14½ gallons of oil left in its tanks, an amount sufficient to travel another 1,040 miles.[141] On the 3,610-mile trip, Lindbergh had averaged about 107 miles per hour, consuming approximately one gallon of gasoline every ten miles.[142] The operating expenses for the flight, including gasoline, oil, and deterioration, approxi-mated $175.[143]

Various statements are attributed to Captain Lindbergh on step-ping out of his plane. According to the *New York Times,* he said, "Well, I made it."[144] Another newspaper records him saying, "Well, here we are; I am very happy."[145] A third contemporary account seems more convincing.

> "I'm Charles Lindbergh," he said when he landed — when some-one asked him later why he said this, for there had been so many other statements accredited to him, he answered: "Yes, that's what I said because I was afraid they might think I was somebody else."[146]

Charles Lindbergh himself recalls that, on hearing the snap of wood and the tearing of fabric around him, his first words to the French were: "Are there any mechanics here?"[147]

The tumultuous crowd was distracted when Lindbergh's flying helmet found itself on the head of newspaperman Harry Wheeler, who was promptly inundated by a flow of well-wishers. Two French aviators, a Lieutenant Detroyat and a civilian pilot named Delage, were then able to spirit the new hero away to safety.[148] After two hours of pushing through the swarming throng, he finally reached Ambassador Myron T. Herrick at the edge of the airfield.

The *Spirit of St. Louis* had been placed in a locked hangar and Captain Lindbergh insisted on viewing it immediately to survey the damage done by the enthusiastic crowd which had poured over it.

> It was a great shock to me to see my plane. The sides of the fuselage were full of gaping holes, and some souvenir hunter had pulled a lubrication fitting right off one of the rocker-arm housings on my engine. But in spite of surface appearances, careful inspection showed that no serious damage had been done. A few hours of work would make my plane airworthy again.[149]

One treasured item stolen from the cockpit was his logbook; the loss of which he bitterly regretted.[150] The actions of the well-meaning but frenzied mob spoiled for a time the welcome France had prepared for him. The transatlantic pilot, however, had only one immediate desire. After supper and a press interview at the American embassy, he was finally able to ease his gnawing need for sleep.

> Paris clocks marked 4:15 in the morning before I went to bed. It was sixty-three hours since I had slept.[151]

In the ensuing days, weeks, months, and years, the young airman experienced the unprecedented worship of people the world over. From President Doumergue of France he received the Chevalier Cross of the Legion of Honor, the first ever awarded to an American citizen.[152] On May 28, he flew the *Spirit* to Brussels, where King Albert presented him with the Order of Chevalier of the Royal Order of Leopold.[153] The following day, King George V of England decorated him with the Air Force Cross.[154] Everywhere hundreds of thousands turned out to pay homage to him. In a time when tariff problems and war debts had rent great rifts in international relations, the personable young American single-handedly revived an atmosphere of harmony among nations. Ambassador Herrick capsuled the best explanation of this "Lindbergh Phenomenon." On May 22, he cabled President Calvin Coolidge:

> If we had deliberately sought a type to represent the youth, the intrepid adventure of America, and the immortal bravery of Nun-

CONGRATULATIONS!
St. Louis Committee

St. Louis Globe-Democrat.

VOL. 53—NO. 3 —FIRST SECTION   ST. LOUIS, SUNDAY MORNING, MAY 22, 1927.   PRICE 10 CENTS

LINDBERGH FLEW 1000 MILES THROUGH SLEET STORM; COULD HAVE REMAINED IN AIR NINE MORE HOURS

CITY HOLIDAY PROPOSED TO HONOR HERO

President Neun of Board of Aldermen Urges That Mayor Proclaim Day of Celebration.

"LIM" EXPECTED HERE BY PLANE

Committee of Backers Thinks Move to Advance Flying Would Please Lindbergh Most of All.

Backer of Lindbergh Project Tells of Struggle for Funds

Contribution of Globe-Democrat, Only Newspaper to Support Flight, Helped Make Trip Possible, Says Harry H. Knight.

St. Louis Roll of Honor

HERE are the eight St. Louisans who, in association with the Globe-Democrat, made Lindbergh's flight possible.

CAPT. CHARLES A. LINDBERGH, who backed himself to the extent of his entire savings, $2000.

HAROLD M. BIXBY, vice president of the State National Bank and president of the Chamber of Commerce.

HARRY F. KNIGHT, of the banking firm of Knight, Dysart & Gamble.

HARRY HALL KNIGHT, president of the St. Louis Flying Club, associated with Knight, Dysart & Gamble, and son of Harry F. Knight.

MAJ. A. B. LAMBERT, long identified with aviation in St. Louis and head of the Chamber of Commerce Committee on Aeronautics.

J. D. WOOSTER LAMBERT, vice president of the Lambert Pharmacal Company.

MAJ. WILLIAM B. ROBERTSON, head of the Robertson Aircraft Corporation, for whom Capt. Lindbergh formerly flew as an air mail pilot.

EARL C. THOMPSON, vice president of the Indemnity Company of America.

I Knew He'd Do It If It Were Possible, Says Hero's Mother

Spartan Like Composure of Mrs. Lindbergh Broken by Tears.

Lindbergh, Smiling Happily, Scorns Sleep Until He Describes Flight

By CARLYLE MacDONALD

Staff Correspondent of the Globe-Democrat and New York Times

PARIS, May 22.—Capt. Lindbergh was discovered at the American Embassy at 9:30 o'clock this morning.

HE DID

New York to Give Lindbergh Greatest Reception Yet Staged

His Will Excel Even That of Queen and Channel Swimmer's.

25,000 Joy-Mad Storm Police to Greet Lindbergh

Overran Guards in Tumultuous Welcome to St. Louisan.

Lindbergh Averaged 107 1-2 Miles an Hour for 3600-Mile Hop

Took 33 Hours and 30 Minutes for Trans-Atlantic Hop.

DIDN'T KNOW FLIGHT WOULD BE SO SHORT

St. Louisan Ate Only One and a Half of His Four Sandwiches in Making 3600-Mile Hop from New York to Paris in 33½ Hours.

Lindbergh's Own Story to Appear Exclusively in the Globe-Democrat

CAPT. CHARLES A. LINDBERGH was too exhausted after his arrival in Paris late last night to do more than indicate his experiences during the flight. After he settles today he will narrate the full story of his remarkable exploit for readers of Sunday's GLOBE-DEMOCRAT.

By EDWIN L. JAMES

Special Cable to the Globe-Democrat and New York Times

Paris Crowds Waited for Lindbergh With Feverish Anxiety

James Describes Dramatic Scenes at Hero's Landing Place.

George J. Herwig Collection

E. Lansing Ray, publisher of the St. Louis Globe-Democrat, *was one of Lindbergh's backers; he devoted virtually his entire front page to coverage of the flight. So did almost all the other daily newspapers of the Western world.*

Lindbergh flies the Spirit of St. Louis *over the Seine River in Paris, during a demonstration flight.*

gesser and Coli, we could not have fared as well as in this boy of divine genius and simple courage.[155]

On June 4, 1927, Captain Lindbergh sailed for home on the naval cruiser *Memphis,* with the *Spirit of St. Louis* crated on deck.[156]

It is probable that when Lindbergh reached America he got the greatest welcome any man in history has ever received; certainly the greatest when judged by numbers; and by far the greatest in its freedom from that unkind emotion which in such cases usually springs from one people's triumph over another.[157]

President Coolidge decorated him with the Distinguished Flying Cross and Postmaster General Harry S. New presented him with an airmail stamp depicting the *Spirit of St. Louis,* the first time any living American had been so honored.[158] At the Hotel Brevoort in New York City on June 16, he was awarded the $25,000 Orteig Prize, for the donor himself had officially waived the sixty-day notification requirement, which the young flier had not observed.[159] The following day, Lindbergh returned in triumph to St. Louis,

An estimated 7.5 million people honored Lindbergh upon his return to New York. This blizzard of 1,800 tons of confetti fell on June 13, during a parade which was six miles long. It was led by 10,000 troops; 200 planes flew overhead. The New York celebration lasted four days.

George J. Herwig Collection

Lindbergh never forgot his backers. He is shown with Harold Bixby upon the flyer's triumphant return to St. Louis.

where the city feted him and Secretary of War Dwight Davis commissioned him a colonel in the Missouri National Guard.[160]

Charles Lindbergh received more than 15,000 articles from 69

The parade down Olive Street on June 18, 1927, was an exuberant one, with many troops required to keep the surging crowds from their hero. Lindbergh rode in an open car with St. Louis Mayor Victor J. Miller.

On the side of the lorry:

35th DIV. AIR COR

Trans-Atlantic Flyer
His name:
In Paris—"Le Fou Volante
(the flying fool)
In New York—"Lucky."
In St Louis—"Just —
SLIM."

SLIM BEAT E[

NO—THIS IS NOT THE BELLANCA.

The Air Guard manifested its pride in the lettering on the side of their lorry — a unit of the Lindbergh welcoming parade.

countries in recognition of his achievement.[161] The young flier was awarded the Wilson Medal and $25,000 from the Woodrow Wilson Foundation for his contribution to international friendship, as well as a similar amount of money from the Vacuum Oil Company, whose gasoline he had used. Colonel Lindbergh, however, generally refused to commercialize on the flight. He declined a $50,000 cigarette endorsement, a home in Flushing Meadows, New York, and several motion picture contracts, one of which entailed a reported $5,000,000.[162] He received countless medals, municipal keys, honorary memberships, models of the *Spirit,* portraits of himself, and trinkets of all descriptions. The Missouri Historical Society received permission from the flier to exhibit the vast collection at the Jefferson Memorial in St. Louis for a period of ten days, beginning June 25, 1927. Approximately 80,000 people visited the display during that time, and it aroused such interest that the society requested Lindbergh's permission to exhibit the trophies indefinitely. He con-

Crowds on
Art Hill to meet
"Slim" after his
return from Paris
1927

No St. Louisan who watched the flyover of the Spirit of St. Louis *from Art Hill on June 19, 1927, ever forgot the emotional experience. St. Louis' City Art Museum is in the background.*

sented and the collection has been there since.[163] The members of the Spirit of St. Louis Organization magnanimously refused to accept any share in the flier's awards.[164]

The supreme compliment, and the one Lindbergh perhaps cherished most, was the Medal of Honor. H.R. 3190 was passed unanimously by the House of Representatives on December 10, 1927,[165] and by the Senate two days later.[166] On December 14, President Coolidge signed the resolution,[167] which honored

> Col. Charles A. Lindbergh, United States Army Air Corps Reserve, for displaying heroic courage and skill as a navigator, at the risk of his life, by his nonstop flight in his plane, the *Spirit of St. Louis,* from New York to Paris, France, on May 20, 1927, by which he not only achieved the greatest individual triumph of

any American citizen, but demonstrated that travel across the ocean by aircraft was possible.[168]

Charles Lindbergh was not the first man to fly across the Atlantic, yet no one remembers those who preceded him: The *NC-4,* Alcock and Brown, the *R-34* the Army "Round-the-World" crew, the *ZR-3,* Franco, Pinado, and Beires. The distinctive feature of Lindbergh's flight was that it was nonstop solo from New York to Paris, with the crowning highlight of a perfect "hit" by dead reckoning alone.[169] This accomplishment was no fluke, for Charles Lindbergh had 2,000 hours of flying time to his credit and was a consummate pilot of wide experience. The adulation he received for his achievement was unparalleled. Chamberlain made his Atlantic flight in June of 1927,[170] and Byrd a month later,[171] but the reception they experienced was paltry indeed when compared with that enjoyed by Lindbergh.

After a short hop around the country in June and July, which included a junket into Canada, the newly-elevated colonel took an extensive tour in the *Spirit of St. Louis* throughout every one of the 48 states under the auspices of the Guggenheim Fund for the Promotion of Aeronautics. The trip lasted from July 20 to October 23, 1927, during which time he covered 22,000 miles in the flying time of 260 hours and 45 minutes, making stops at 82 cities and arriving late only once (at Portland, Maine, because of fog).[172] On December 13, he flew to Mexico City at the request of Ambassador Dwight Morrow and President Plutarcho Calles. He then made a goodwill tour of the Central American Republics, and later returned to Mexico several times on his own, marrying the ambassador's daughter, Ann Morrow, in 1929.[173] On April 30, 1928, the *Spirit of St. Louis* made its last flight, a 725-mile trip from Lambert Field, St. Louis, to Bolling Field, Washington, D.C. There it was presented to the Smithsonian Institution. In the one year and two days of its active existence, the silver monoplane had made 174 flights and logged a total flying time of 489 hours and 28 minutes.[174]

The incredible hysteria generated by the young aviator was perhaps primarily the result of his uniquely unspoiled personality.

> He was quiet. He was modest. He seemed to be shy. He had a sweet, winning smile. He was, basically, the stuff of which heroes are made. Every mother saw in him the perfect son, every woman the perfect mate. Yet to every man he symbolized all that is manly and noble and brave.[175]

Undoubtedly the most significant result of the transatlantic flight of the *Spirit of St. Louis* was an unprecedented stimulus to aeronautics in the United States, a phenomenon known as the "Lindbergh Boom."

> The Lindbergh flight acted like adrenalin in the blood stream of American aviation. In a single year after Lindbergh's flight, applications for pilot licenses in the United States jumped from 1,800 to 5,500. In 1928 the nation's airline operators doubled their mileage, trebled their mail load, and quadrupled the number of passengers they had carried in 1927. And airline stocks boomed.[176]

The transatlantic flight of May 20-21, 1927, was only a spectacular prelude to Charles Lindbergh's aeronautic contributions. In 1928 he took a position as technical adviser to Transcontinental Air Transport (forerunner of Trans World Airlines),[177] and during the 1930s he also laid out several transoceanic routes for Pan American Airlines.[178] After the kidnap-murder of his son in 1932, Lindbergh disappeared into complete seclusion, but arose into controversy shortly before the outbreak of World War II. From 1936 to 1938 he made frequent visits to Germany, fraternized with leading government officials, and was even decorated by Hermann Goering.[179] Lindbergh was widely vilified in the American press for his actions, for few knew that he had been making secret reports on German air strength to Major General H.H. Arnold, chief of the United States Army Air Corps. General Arnold later wrote:

> Lindbergh gave me the most accurate picture of the Luftwaffe, its equipment, leaders, apparent plans, training methods, and present defects that I had so far received.[180]

His prominent activities with the isolationist America First Committee in 1941 also caused him much criticism, and his antisemitic outbursts ended the mass adulation which was once his.[181] When the United States entered the war, however, he lent his capable talents to the development of superior aircraft, and even shot down two Japanese "Zeros" as a civilian in the Pacific.[182] Commissioned a brigadier general in the Air Force Reserve in 1954, Charles Lindbergh later served as a consultant to Pan American World Airways.[183] He died of cancer at his home in Kipahulu, Maui, Hawaii on August 26, 1974.[184]

When the young airmail pilot made his earthshaking flight of May 20-21, 1927, he flew not as a St. Louisan, but as an American. Although the city had provided him with generous financial backers, he had only resided there for two years, and the results derived from his unprecedented achievement affected the entire nation, rather than just one metropolis. Yet the city was paid a timeless tribute in honor of its contribution to the venture in the title of the airplane which made it possible — the *Spirit of St. Louis*.

XII
The International Balloon Race, 1929

THE JAMES GORDON BENNETT International Balloon Race
came to St. Louis for the third time in 1929. The original trophy,
donated in 1906 by the publisher of the *New York Herald Tribune,*
had been taken out of circulation in 1924, when Ernest Demuyter
of Belgium won the international contest for the third straight year,
thus earning for himself permanent possession of the cup. The people of Belgium then purchased a trophy by popular subscription and
entrusted it to the Aero Club of France so that the annual contest
could continue.[1] The United States, however, gained permanent
possession of this cup when its pilots scored successive victories in
1926, 1927, and 1928.[2] A third trophy was donated by the Board of
Commerce of Detroit, the site of the 1928 contest, and it would be
placed in competition for the first time at St. Louis in 1929.[3] Even
though the actual Gordon Bennett Cup was no longer contested, the
annual event was still called the Gordon Bennett Race.[4]

Orville Wright, chairman of the Contest Committee of the National Aeronautic Association, announced on December 18, 1928,
that the city which had conducted the international affair in 1907 and
1910 would again host the competition in 1929. The event was to be
sponsored by the Air Board of the St. Louis Chamber of Commerce.
Stanley Clarke, Air Board head, would be chairman of the Contest

Committee; Mayor Victor Miller, honorary chairman; Major Albert Bond Lambert and E.B. Meissner, vice chairmen; and W.W. Smith, treasurer. They planned to raise $10,000 to $15,000 to defray the expenses of the race.[5]

The contest was scheduled to start on September 28, 1929, from a field at 8900 South Broadway, just south of Mannion's Park.[6] The Air Board's original intention had been to stage the contest at Scott Field, Belleville, Illinois,[7] but this proposal was abandoned in favor of a site within St. Louis itself. Special mains were laid by Laclede Gas Light Company to the Broadway field to convey coal gas for the balloons. The ascension site was divided into two sections separated by a wire fence, one area for the balloons and the tents of the officials and the press, and the other for the expected 40,000 spectators.[8] Although an admission fee had been levied at many of the earlier contests conducted in the city, the 1929 race was to be free of charge to the public.[9]

The judges for the event would be Francis Murphy, president of the St. Louis Balloon Pilots' Association; Elmer Marchuetz of St. Louis, a former wartime balloonist; Arthur Hoskins, a member of the Air Board; and Augustus Post, a prominent New York balloonist and former officer of the Aero Club of America. He and Alan R. Hawley, the referee for the race, held the standing American balloon distance record of 1,172.9 miles, a feat they had accomplished in the 1910 Gordon Bennett Race from St. Louis.[10] Major Albert Bond Lambert, the official representative of the National Aeronautic Association, would be the starter, and Carl F.G. Meyer, former president of the St. Louis Chamber of Commerce, the timer. Captain Paul McCullough, a noted local balloonist, was to serve as "official measurer of balloons."[11]

The Air Board offered prizes aggregating $3,000. In addition to one year's possession of the trophy, the winner would receive a cash prize of $1,000. The second-place finisher would win $800, and there were awards of $600, $400, and $200 for third, fourth, and fifth places.[12] The contest officials also provided $500 in expense money for each of the foreign crews, along with a stipend of $100 for each of the Americans. Alan Hawley offered an additional $500 for anyone who exceeded his standing distance record.[13]

Six nations entered balloons in the competition, but the United States was the only country to field a full complement of three entrants. Heading the American team was Ward T. Van Orman of Akron, who would pilot the *Goodyear VIII,* with Alan MacCracken as his aide. A four-time winner of the National Balloon Race, Van Orman was a veteran of long experience and had won the Gordon Bennett Race in 1926, starting the American victory string.[14] Representing the United States Army was Captain William Kepner, assisted by Captain L.J. Powell, both of whom were stationed at Scott Field. Kepner had won his place on the 1929 American team by virtue of his victory in the 1928 contest at Detroit, when he had won permanent possession of the second international trophy for the United States.[15] The third American entrant was the Naval balloon, piloted by Lieutenants T.G.W. Settle and Winfield Bushnell, who had earned their position in the contest by winning the National Balloon Race from Pittsburgh earlier in the spring.[16]

Germany had entered two balloons in the international event. The *Stadt Essen* was to be piloted by Erich Leimkugel, a 52-year-old chemist who would make his initial appearance in Gordon Bennett competition even though he had been ballooning for twenty years. He had been named to start in the 1914 international race, but World War I had intervened and canceled the contest. He was to be aided by 33-year-old Georg Froebel.[17] The other German entrant, the *Barmen,* would be piloted by Dr. Hugo Kaulen Jr., who at twenty-six was the youngest man in the race. The son of a former Gordon Bennett contender, he had made his first flight at the age of nine, and was a balloonist of some repute. His aide, Fritz Ebener, was a 35-year-old war hero who had been ballooning for four years.[18]

Four nations entered one balloon apiece. From Denmark came Lieutenant Georg Schenstrom and S.A.U. Rasmussen in the *Danmark.*[19] France sent the *Lafayette,* with Georges Blanchet of Paris and Howard Scholle of New York. In contrast to Kaulen, Blanchet was the oldest man in the race and the dean of all the pilots. He had made his first ascension in 1893 at the age of nineteen and had executed approximately 500 flights since that time, including four futile attempts at the Gordon Bennett Cup.[20]

Representing Argentina, a nation which rarely entered the competition, was D. Eduardo Bradley, a twenty-year balloon veteran who held the distinction of being the only man ever to pilot a balloon over the Andes Mountains, a feat he had accomplished in 1916. He was secretary of the Aero Club of Argentina and his nation's Secretary of Civil Aeronautics. With Francisco J. Cadaval, Bradley would pilot the *Argentina* in the St. Louis race.[21] From Belgium came the powerful Ernest Demuyter, who would sail the *Belgica* with Frans Lecharlier as his aide. Demuyter was the favorite in the race, for he had won the international contest in 1920, 1922, 1923,

Inflation is nearly complete for the 1929 James Gordon Bennett International Balloon Race, launched from a field at 8900 South Broadway.

and 1924, his last series of victories earning him permanent possession of the original Gordon Bennett Trophy.[22] No other man had even won the event more than once.[23] This consummate achievement was more than adequate testimony to the fact that championship ballooning was not simply a matter of luck.

The customary pre-race banquet was held at the Hotel Jefferson on September 26. Each contest was introduced to the 300 assembled aeronautic enthusiasts and Chamber of Commerce members, with the German and Franco-Belgian consuls presenting the representatives of their nations. The starting positions for the race were then selected. With Albert Bond Lambert presiding, Danny Miller, a fifteen-year-old Eagle Scout who had accompanied the Naval crew from Lakehurst, New Jersey, drew the pilots' names from a bowl and handed the slips to Augustus Post, who read each name aloud. The balloonists then came forward one by one and chose a sealed envelope containing a starting number. Erich Leimkugel was unfortunate enough to draw first place, while Georges Blanchet won the coveted ninth position.[24]

> To start last is a distinct advantage for there is a forty-five minute differential between the taking off of the first and last balloons during which the air cools noticeably, changing the density of the inflating gas.[25]

George Logan, vice chairman of the Air Board, spoke at the dinner, along with Alan Hawley and Augustus Post, who favored the audience with reminiscences of their wide ballooning experience. Major Lambert used the occasion to expatiate on his favorite subject.

> The free balloon is elementary to the training of balloon observers and dirigible pilots. Just as long as lighter-than-air craft is a factor in national defense and an increasing development of civilian aviation, free ballooning will continue. Cities should get behind it and help build up the lighter-than-air service.[26]

His words were more prophetic than he realized, for with the demise of the dirigible after a series of tragic crashes during the next decade, the sport he loved would fade from the scene.

A crew of 120 Army balloon technicians from Scott Field, commanded by Captain Douglas Johnson, began to inflate the balloons at 7:00 a.m., September 28.[27] Each bag had a capacity of 80,000 cubic feet, and the Laclede gasometer pumped coal gas simultaneously into the nine entrants at a rate of 100,000 cubic feet per hour. During the inflation, each balloon was secured to the ground with 120 forty-pound sandbags. Full inflation was delayed until just before the 4:00 p.m. start, when the balloons were "topped off" to capacity.[28] Paul McCullough recorded the official measurements of the bags; each averaged fifty feet in equatorial diameter with 80,000 cubic feet of coal gas.[29]

At 3:12 p.m. Harry Eugene Honeywell, the veteran St. Louis balloonist, ascended in a pilot balloon to test the wind direction for the formal contestants. With him were his daughter, Mrs. C.E. Brown of Evansville, Indiana; Arthur Hoskins, one of the judges of the race; and Elmer Doerr, a local businessman.[30] The breeze was so negligible that it took them nearly three hours to reach Lambert Field, twenty miles away, where they landed at 6:05 p.m.[31] The stifling heat would also be a factor in the race, for the temperature at the Broadway ascension grounds exceeded ninety degrees. A crowd of 20,000 had gathered for the start of the contest, while thousands more watched from the adjacent hillsides.[32] A detachment of troops from Jefferson Barracks and the 138th Infantry kept them in order and rigidly enforced the smoking prohibition.[33]

Shortly before the race began, the three new American balloons were formally christened. Helen Frampton performed the ceremony for the *Goodyear VIII;* Myrtle McGrew Lambert, daughter of the official starter, for the Army's entrant, the *Scott Field;* and Mrs. Thomas G.W. Settle, wife of the Naval pilot, for the Navy's nameless contender.[34] At precisely 4:00 p.m., the eighteenth annual James Gordon Bennett International Balloon Race was begun. The

Missouri Historical Society

By the time the 80,000-cubic-foot bags were full an enormous crowd had assembled to watch the start of the race.

date was coincidentally the fiftieth anniversary of the final, fatal flight of John Wise.[35]

The musicians' union band played "Die Wacht Am Rhein" as the yellowish *Stadt Essen* took to the air with Leimkugel and Froebal aboard. Next came the alabaster-white *Goodyear VIII* with Van Orman and MacCracken, as the band piped "Yankee Doodle." The *Argentina* followed, making the quietest ascension of all, for Bradley and Cadaval had no local partisans to cheer them onward. They got away a few seconds ahead of time, but all the rest of the ascensions were at precise five-minute intervals.[36]

At 4:15 Schenstrom and Rasmussen arose on schedule in the *Danmark*. The Danish aide had nearly missed the flight, for he had not arrived in St. Louis until 1:30 that afternoon. Kaulen and Ebener then arose in the yellow-colored *Barmen*. Five minutes later, Demuyter and Lecharlier followed in the *Belgica,* the same balloon which had won four previous Gordon Bennett Races.[37] The Belgian balloon must have startled the crowd somewhat, for it sailed away with the letters of its name reversed in mirror fashion.

> A workman who had turned the bag inside out to make minor repairs had forgotten to turn it back and the condition was not noted until the bag was partially inflated. The noted Belgian balloonist declared it made no difference.[38]

The musicians played the "Star Spangled Banner" as the seventh contestant, the Naval balloon, sailed off at 4:30 with Lieutenants Settle and Bushnell aboard. Captains Kepner and Powell were next away in the *Scott Field,* as the band played the Army classic, "The Old Grey Mare." The *Lafayette* completed the ascensions at 4:40 p.m., with Georges Blanchet, who cut a dapper figure in checkered breeches and a plaid cap, and Howard Scholle.[39]

Each balloon headed northwest in the slight breeze, and the bags were visible for hours, strung out in a line at various altitudes, each seeking a strong current.

> A dirigible balloon, plowing rings around the floating bags, and a tri-motored airplane which fished about all the lighter-than-air craft, added to the sunset air show enjoyed by people in nearly all parts of the city.[40]

Each of the nine balloons had carried essentially the same equipment: 1,000-1,500 pounds of sand ballast, food and water for five days, navigation instruments, and radios to receive the weather bulletins which KMOX would broadcast hourly in English, German, French, Danish, and Spanish. The three American balloons had a special flotation apparatus attached to their baskets in case of a water landing, and the *Scott Field, Goodyear VIII, Barmen,* and *Argentina* carried pneumatic rubber boats as well. Cartons of cigarettes were plainly visible in many of the wicker baskets, for although smoking was strictly forbidden in flight, the pilots took them on the chance that they might land in an area remote from civilization, a not unlikely possibility in light of the results of previous St. Louis races. Each crew had been given ten telegraph blanks addressed to the Air Board, and was directed to toss them overboard during the flight with notations on its position. On landing, the pilots were to notify the St. Louis officials of their exact location as soon as possible.[41]

None of the contestants had any hopes for a record. The unseasonably hot weather and the negligible wind boded ill for long flights. When Erich Leimkugel had seen the pessimistic weather report, he had declared: "Ach, we stay over St. Louis all night."[42]

His prediction was hopelessly accurate. After drifting lazily over the city for several hours, the balloons all landed the following day.

Missouri Historical Society

Ward T. Van Orman gave a parting wave as his heavily-ballasted Goodyear VIII *cast off. He and his copilot, Alan A. MacCracken, were later declared the winners of the race with a flight of 341 miles.*

The only eventful occurrence concerned the *Argentina*. Eduardo Bradley was hospitalized with a crushed knee when his balloon struck a tree near Fairbanks, Indiana, and tossed him out of the basket, along with his aide, Francisco Cadaval, who escaped unscathed.[43] The race was a clean sweep for the American team, with the Belgian ace leading the foreign entrants. The first two finishers were so close that an official government survey had to decide the winner. Ward Van Orman had won his second international race by only three miles. The records of the nine contestants were:

1) *Goodyear VIII* (United States) — Ward T. Van Orman, pilot; and Alan MacCracken, aide. 341 miles to a point three miles southeast of Troy, Ohio.

2) *Scott Field* (United States) — Captain William E. Kepner, pilot; and Captain James F. Powell, aide. 338 miles to a point two miles north of Neptune, Ohio.

3) Naval Balloon (United States) — Lieutenant Thomas G.W. Settle, pilot; and Lieutenant Winfield Bushnell, aide. 304 miles to a point ten miles southwest of Eaton, Ohio.

4) *Belgica* (Belgium) — Captain Ernest Demuyter, pilot; and Frans Lecharlier, aide. 226 miles to Corydon, Indiana.

5) *Danmark* (Denmark) — Georg Schenstrom, pilot; and S.A.U. Rasmussen, aide. 209 miles to a point five miles southeast of Bedford, Indiana.

6) *Lafayette* (France) — Georges Blanchet, pilot; and Howard Scholle, aide. 200 miles to Stinesville, Indiana.

7) *Barmen* (Germany) — Hugo Kaulen Jr., pilot; and Fritz Ebener, aide. 171 miles to a point four miles southeast of Melvin, Illinois.

8) *Stadt Essen* (Germany) — Erich Leimkugel, pilot; and Georg Froebel, aide. 169 miles to Catlin, Illinois.

9) *Argentina* (Argentina) — Dr. Eduardo Bradley, pilot; and Francisco J. Cadaval, aide. 155 miles to Fairbanks, Indiana.[44]

The 1929 International Balloon Race was reminiscent of the national contest at St. Louis fifteen years earlier, when poor wind and excessive heat had also resulted in disappointing distances.[45] The records turned in by the nine contestants were the lowest in the history of Gordon Bennett competition, "exceeding" the previous low established in 1913, when the winning distance was 384 miles.[46] This contest was the last major balloon race held in St. Louis. Only two more American cities were to host the international event — Cleveland in 1930 and Chicago in 1933.[47]

The era of the gas bag was rapidly drawing to a close. The final

Gordon Bennett Race was conducted at Warsaw, Poland, September 15-18, 1935, when Z. Burnzynski and W. Wysocki took first place with a distance of 1,025 miles. This victory, the third straight for Poland, gained for that nation permanent possession of the international trophy.[48] The original James Gordon Bennett International Aeronautic Cup had endured from 1906 to 1924, the Belgian trophy from 1925 to 1928, and the Detroit cup from 1929 to 1935. The race continued for three more years (without American participation) in Warsaw (1936), Brussels (1937), and Liége (1938), but the invasion of Poland canceled the 1939 event, which had been scheduled for Warsaw.[49]

After an interruption of 45 years, the Gordon Bennett classic was resurrected in 1983 with a race from Paris sanctioned by the International Aeronautic Federation.[50] A new trophy was donated by the Aero Club of the Polish People's Republic and the Lodz newspaper *Glos Robotniczy*.[51] The revival of sport ballooning in the past decade gives promise that this contest, traditionally the greatest of balloon races, will continue.

St. Louis still retains an unmatched record of having hosted three Gordon Bennett races, more than any other American city. Detroit held two; and Kansas City, Birmingham, Cleveland, and Chicago one each.[52] Although the American team had made a fine showing in the 1929 St. Louis race, the city's reputation as the nation's center of free balloon racing suffered a setback because of the poor results. The St. Louis Air Board had gladly spent $22,500 to sponsor the event, but the officials must have lamented that the contest was not a copy of the glorious days of 1907 and 1910.

XIII
The Saint Louis Air Races and
International Aerobatic Competition, 1937

IN COMMEMORATION of the tenth anniversary of Charles A. Lindbergh's transatlantic achievement, St. Louis was host to a three-day program of air racing and aerobatics from May 29 through 31, 1937. The meet was sponsored by the St. Louis Air Race Association, headed by attorney George B. Logan. This organization, made up of sixty-three businessmen and flying enthusiasts, had raised $53,000 to defray the expenses of the tournament and offered $15,500 in prizes for a broad program of events.[1]

A somewhat more sensational memorial derby had been planned by the French government. In September 1936, Air Minister Pierre Cot had announced that a purse of 3,000,000 francs ($135,000) would be provided for a transatlantic air race from New York to Paris during the summer of 1937.[2] Colonel Lindbergh had not been consulted by the French officials, and he, along with a number of American aeronautics authorities, vigorously protested, lest the competition be a repetition of the Dole Pineapple Company California-to-Hawaii Race of August 1927, when six fatalities had resulted from planes crashing into the sea.[3] Twenty-two pilots, however, entered the French contest before Colonel John Monroe Johnson, assistant secretary of commerce in charge of aeronautics, announced on May 17, 1937, that the United States government would not permit the race to be held. Said Johnson:

We are trying to encourage transatlantic flying, but we don't want to jeopardize it. . . . The Commerce Department is charged with the duty of safety in the air and this race is a highly hazardous undertaking. There will be no race.[4]

The St. Louis officials planned a memorial of less mammoth proportion, but one equally as stimulating and perhaps even more crowd-pleasing. Five races were scheduled, each over a five-mile triangular course marked by checkered pylons. Among the more prominent entrants were Roger Don Rae, American air racing's top flier and leading money-winner in 1936;[5] Art Chester, two-time Brock Trophy ace and former holder of the world's 100-kilometer speed record; and Colonel Roscoe Turner, twice winner of the Bendix Trophy[6] (who, as it turned out, was unable to participate in the St. Louis events).

The highlight of the meet was to be the International Aerobatic Competition, the first such contest ever conducted. Each contestant had to perform, without repetition, a ten-minute program of stunts previously selected from a list of eighty-four maneuvers drawn up by the National Aeronautic Association. The four highest scorers of the first two days of the tournament would compete against each other on the final day for a trophy and a first prize of $2,000.[7] Entrance into this competition was solely by invitation, an honor which the contest committee afforded to eight pilots:[8] Captain Alexander de Papana, Rumania's leading aviator, aerobatic champion, and Olympic flying ace, who was an expert bobsledder and tennis player as well,[9] and one of those who had entered the outlawed Anniversary Air Race;[10] Tex Rankin, a forty-year-old Hollywood movie stunter; Paul Mantz, another veteran movie flier, who was also technical advisor to Amelia Earhart; Roger Don Rae, one of America's top all around fliers; Captain Leonard Povey, American-born chief instructor in the Cuban Air Force;[11] and Mike Murphy and Lieutenant Joseph C. Mackey, two rising contenders.[12] The eighth entrant was slated to represent the Canadian Flying Clubs' Association, but was not selected in time for the competition.[13]

In addition to the racing and aerobatics, a wide range of aerial activity was scheduled: formation flying by the Army and Navy, parachute jumping, and informal stunting. One of the most unusual features of the meet would be the performances of Earl "Batman" Stein of Findlay, Ohio, who employed bat-like "wings" of cloth attached to his arms and legs to check his descent during his daring delayed parachute jumps.[14]

In contrast to the extensive 50-kilometer (31.07-mile) course at the 1923 air meet, the five-mile triangular course for the 1937 races would be in view of the spectators at all times. Grandstands for 15,000 people were erected at Lambert-St. Louis Municipal Airport, the scene of the tournament, and preparations were made to accommodate crowds of 40,000.[15] Admission prices were set at $2.20 for a reserved grandstand seat, $1.10 for an unreserved place, 65¢ for adult standing room, and 25¢ per child for a similar position. Owners of property west of the field anticipated an overflow crowd and had set up chairs which they planned to offer for 40¢ each.[16]

Arch League, chief dispatcher at the airport, would supervise all flights from the control tower,[17] and James Rowan Ewing, promoter of the tournament, would manage and direct the entire show.[18] A panel of judges would scrutinize the contestants and determine the winners: Major Alford J. Williams of New York, chairman, the man who had established the world speed record of 243.812 miles per hour as a Navy lieutenant in the Pulitzer Trophy Race at St. Louis in 1923;[19] Major James H. Doolittle, St. Louis' celebrated air ace, who would earn even greater distinction during World War II; Lieutenant Colonel Philip R. Love of St. Louis, who had served with Lindbergh on Robertson Aircraft Corporation's Chicago-St. Louis mail run a decade earlier;[20] and Billie Parker of Bartlesville, Oklahoma, and John H. Livingston of Waterloo, Iowa, two wealthy aviation enthusiasts. A substitute judge would be Ben O. Howard of Chicago, president of the Professional Pilots' Association.[21] Colonel Lindbergh himself had been invited, but he had cabled his regrets from his hideaway in England.[22]

After the traditional pre-race banquet at the Coronado Hotel the previous night, the tournament got underway on May 29. Spectators began arriving at the field at 7:00 a.m. to inspect the planes and view the preliminary flying. There were two minor accidents among the morning's test flights. At 11:00 Captain Leonard Povey of the Cuban Air Force suffered engine failure in his yellow biplane shortly after takeoff and was forced to land in an oatfield one quarter of a mile south of Lambert Field. The racer was towed back to firm ground and Povey then took to the air and returned safely to the airport. Forty-five minutes later, Jim Malone, a veteran St. Louis pilot, brushed the wingtip of his tiny red racer on the ground as he was coasting at 70 miles per hour over the center of the airfield, but he only skimmed off a bit of replaceable fabric.[23]

Intermittant bursts of sunshine spread through the dark, broken clouds as the formal program opened at 1:05 p.m. A twenty-six piece band, conducted by Max Steindel, first cellist of the St. Louis

Symphony Orchestra, struck up the "Star Spangled Banner" before a meager crowd of 5,000 spectators. Although the onlookers swelled to 12,000 later in the day, the attendance was a disappointment to Ralph Page, the airport manager, who had predicted 22,500. Mayor Bernard F. Dickmann initiated the inaugural speeches and was followed by promoter James Rowan Ewing, St. Louis Air Race Association chairman George B. Logan, and Charles F. Horner, president of the National Aeronautic Association.[24]

The first formal event of the tournament was a non-flying dressage in which five pilots paraded their trim racers before the grandstand. The event was won by Art Chester of Los Angeles, whose blunt-nosed, cream-colored "Jeep" was adjudged the smartest-looking aircraft in the show.[25] At 1:15, seven biplanes from the Fifteenth Observation Squadron from Scott Field soared over the field in an impressive graduated formation. Just as they landed at the southern end of the field and taxied over to the National Guard Hangar, ten Naval Reserve planes got ready to take to the air. Then followed a spectacular display of informal stunting by Jim Malone, the only St. Louisan in the tournament.

> Notwithstanding the aspect of comedy, it was a skillful exhibition of flying, with the yellow wings of the monoplane skimming the ground on a dozen occasions. Missing the pylon in the center of the field by a scant margin, hedge-hopping close to roof tops, injecting simulated peril into each maneuver, Malone kept the fans on the edges of their chairs for 10 minutes. He drew a large measure of applause at the end of his flight.[26]

At 2:42 the first race was begun, a fifty-mile contest for planes with engines of less than 397 cubic inches. This event proved the most sensational of the meet, for on the eighth lap, Roger Don Rae of Lansing, Michigan, piloting a yellow-and-brown Folkerts Special, the *Miss Detroit,* experienced a spectacular crash. At a height of fifty feet, Rae was speeding over the airfield at 250 miles per hour 300 yards behind the leader when three birds sprang into the air from the bushes beneath him. One of them crashed into the wooden propeller, breaking it off at the hub.

The plane nosed down sharply, but the Michigan aviator, who did not know what had hit him, fought desperately for control, succeeded in raising the racer's nose, and set the ship down on its belly in a cloud of dust in the center of the airfield. An ambulance rushed across the field, and the pilot, stunned from a slight brain concussion and bleeding freely from severe scalp and facial wounds, was taken to the nearby Naval Reserve dispensary, where Dr. Samuel

An alert Post-Dispatch *photographer captured the crash of Roger Don Rae's racing plane, skidding to a halt in front of the Lambert Field grandstand.*

Bassett quickly treated his injuries. Rae and his wife rode past the grandstand in an open car later that afternoon, but his flying at the meet was ended, even though he had planned to participate in the aerobatic and parachuting events. His $8,000 racer was almost totally destroyed, but his mechanics declared that it would be ready for the National Air Races at Cleveland in the fall.

Disastrous accidents were taken in stride by such pilots as Roger Rae. Only three months earlier, on February 28, he had been forced into a wreck when his engine failed on takeoff in a race at Daytona Beach. Rae's fellow aviators praised his magnificent handling of the *Miss Detroit* in his latest crisis. Hollywood stunter Tex Rankin said, ''It was the greatest piece of headwork I've ever seen.''[27] Because of the excellence of his emergency actions, Rae's name was prominently mentioned for the John D. Brock Trophy, an award to be given to the outstanding flier of the meet.[28]

The opening race was won by Art Chester in his Menasco-engined ''Jeep.'' He had led throughout, although hotly pursued by Roger Don Rae. Chester averaged 253.5 miles per hour over the fifty-mile route to pick up first prize of $900. S. J. Wittmann of Oshkosh,

Wisconsin, finished second for $500, and St. Louis' Jim Malone was third and last in his snubnosed "Red Midget," for $300. Both Wittmann and Malone had been lapped by the speedier front-runners. Because only three contestants finished the race, the full purse of $2,000 was not entirely divided.[29]

Shortly after 4:00, the second race of the day began, another $2,000, fifty-mile contest, but for larger planes, with engines of less than 559 cubic inches. The event was a nip-and-tuck battle between Marion McKeen of Los Angeles in a scarlet, low-wing Brown Special monoplane; and Gus Gotch of Los Angeles in a Schoenfeldt Special, with the field of three trailing most of the time. McKeen won the contest, averaging a flat 240 miles per hour for $900. Gotch finished a scant 43 yards behind him at 239.9 miles per hour for $500. Art Chester added $300 to his earlier winnings by piloting his "Jeep" to third place at a speed of 227.8 miles per hour. R.A. Kling of Lamont, Illinois, was fourth at 210.7 miles per hour for $200; and S.J. Wittmann of Oshkosh finished last for $100.[30]

Four men were scheduled to perform in the aerobatic competition, but Captain Leonard Povey deferred his flight because of engine trouble, although he was able to stage an informal exhibition of stunting to test his ship. The three other contestants one by one executed their pre-selected routines of loops, spins, barrel rolls, figure eights, dives, turns, and similar gyrations as the spellbound spectators craned their necks attentively upward. Movie stunter Paul Mantz was awarded 209 points by the judges to lead the competition, and Mike Murphy of Kokomo, Indiana, scored 97 points for his second-place performance. Hounded by engine difficulty, Lieutenant Joseph C. Mackey was able to keep his plane in the air for only 2½ of his allotted ten minutes, but he still managed to score 79 points. He trailed the field.[31]

Because of a 22-mile-per-hour wind, the scheduled target parachute jumps were postponed, but a number of other events did take place. The Linco Trio, composed of Lieutenant Mackey, Carl Middleton, and Edward S. Leach, executed a demonstration of "smoke aerobatics." The three planes rolled, dove, and looped in unison, while trailing an ostentatious wake of white smoke. Colonel Art Goebel of Oklahoma performed a similar exhibition solo, but also demonstrated the effectiveness of two-way radio at the same time, with his words being carried to the crowd by loudspeaker. Earl "Batman" Stein, a veteran of 250 jumps, exhibited a singularly thrilling display by leaping from a plane at an altitude of 10,000 feet, streaking downward at 90 miles an hour with his cloth "wings" flapping, bringing gasps to the gaping crowd, and finally pulling the ripcord of his parachute at a height of 5,000 feet. The impact of his landing was so severe that he was rendered unconscious for several minutes. The formal program of opening day came to a close with a mass parachute jump by six young men from the doorless aperture of a trimotored transport 2,500 feet over the field. All landed safely, but a few narrowly missed coming down on the dangerous concrete runways.[32]

Western Historical Manuscript Collection, University of Missouri-St. Louis

Earl Stein, the "Batman," shows his wingspread upon landing after a 10,000-foot jump.

One of the most significant events of the tournament came at dusk that afternoon when most of the crowd had departed. The feat was performed by Louise Thaden, winner of the 1936 Bendix Trophy for transcontinental flying, as well as the 1936 Harmon Trophy as the nation's outstanding aviatrix. She had announced her intention of attempting to break the women's American 100-kilometer (62.14 miles) speed record for commercial planes, then held by the celebrated Amelia Earhart Putnam at 174 miles per hour. She was to have undertaken the flight earlier in the afternoon, but her sealed barograph, the official speed recording device, was late in arriving. The officials expected that she would wait until the following day, but to their surprise, and that of the 100 remaining spectators at Lambert Field, Mrs. Thaden took off at 6:35 p.m. and headed for Scott Field, Belleville, Illinois, 50 kilometers away. ". . . I was all hepped up," she said later, "and so I waited until the whole program was over and then decided to make it."[33]

Less than twenty minutes later, her green Beechcraft cabin monoplane returned. Louise Thaden had established a new record of 197.9 miles per hour for the 100-kilometer round trip. For her achievement, the eminent aviatrix was awarded the Phil de Catesby Ball Memorial Trophy and a cash prize of $250.[34] It was a stirring climax to an impressive opening day.

Amelia Earhart herself was never able to challenge Mrs. Thaden's record, for a week earlier, on May 21, she had begun her fateful west-east circumnavigation of the globe, a flight which was to end in mysterious disaster when she and her navigator, Fred

Louise Thaden broke the speed record for women with a flight at 197.9 miles per hour.

Noonan, disappeared in the Pacific Ocean on July 2, short of Howland Island.[35]

Governor Lloyd Stark of Missouri formally opened the second day's events on May 30 at 1:15 p.m. Jim Malone again displayed his prowess at impromptu stunting, and the Army and Navy contingents repeated their formation flying for the crowd. Louise Thaden also took part in the opening ceremonies and flew over the field in a blue-winged biplane to receive a well-deserved ovation from the spectators. Gathered in the grandstand was a crowd of 40,000 people,[36] perhaps lured in the macabre hope of witnessing another spectacular crash, but more probably drawn by the broad program successfully performed the previous day. Whatever their motive, their Sunday afternoon was well spent.

The first race of the day was a fifty-mile free-for-all sprint. The start was somewhat inauspicious, for Art Chester, who was favored to win the event, experienced engine failure just as his plane reached a height of twelve feet in the air.

> Fighting desperately for control, Chester landed on the grass and bumped to a dizzy halt, the wings of his ship grazing the ground several times, but escaping damage. Had his engine quit 10 seconds later, with a forced landing "in the rough" the only course open to him, it might have been a different story.[37]

R.A. Kling of Lemont, Illinois, won the ten-lap race and $900 with an average speed of 233.7 miles per hour. Because he could not fully retract his landing gear, Kling had to fly in the rather odd position of having one gear down and the other tucked under the belly of his biplane. At the end of the race he also had difficulty in getting the wheels locked in their landing position. He circled the field three times as fire trucks and ambulances made anxious preparations below, but he finally succeeded and landed without incident. Marion McKeen finished second at 229.2 miles per hour for $500, and S.J. Wittmann was a distant last at 202.1 miles per hour for $300.[38]

The second race of the afternoon was a forty-mile contest for commercial planes, sponsored by oil baron Frank Phillips, who put up a trophy and a purse of $1,000 for the event. Art Chester easily bested the three other competitors by averaging 192.2 miles per hour with his wasp-like green biplane. Robert Glass of Dallas was second at 164.3 miles per hour and Jack Gatz of Wichita was third at 156.3, with Marion McKeen trailing the field at 126 miles per hour.[39]

Shortly before the contest had taken place came one of the most sensational surprises of the meet.

> Moving like a supercharged bullet, Maj. Alexander de Seversky flew over the field at 3:19 p.m. and thrilled the crowd with a series of rolls, turns and dives in his silver-colored "mystery" ship.
>
> Observers expressed the opinion the Russian-born American manufacturer touched 350 miles an hour as he streaked before the crowded grand stands, and, after nosing the ship upward, climbed to 1,500 feet in the twinkling of an eye.[40]

The impressive aircraft was probably a P-35, an all-metal, low-wing monoplane which the major, who had lost a leg during World War I, had himself designed.[41] So closely was the United States government guarding the refinements of the progressive ship that permission was denied de Seversky to land at the airport. Instead he returned to Scott Field, where the plane was placed under guard, and later he flew back to Lambert Field in a National Guard biplane.[42]

In the day's acrobatics, Rumania's Captain Alexander de Papana proved his international repute by logging a score of 257 with an impressive show of skillful maneuvers. Hollywood stunter Tex Rankin finished second with 238 points, and Captain Leonard Povey, the American-born Cuban, earned a total of 196 for his demonstration. Lieutenant Joseph Mackey, who had suffered engine trouble the previous day, was allowed to finish his ten-minute program and thus raised his total to 196 points, tying Povey for fourth place.[43] The finalists would compete the following day for the trophy, title, and cash prizes.

Parachuting provided a prominent part of the program on the second day of the meet. Faye Lucille Cox of Los Angeles was the major attraction. The foremost woman "chutist" in the country, Mrs. Cox had made a total of 319 jumps and gave a brilliant performance even though she was still recuperating from a broken arm, suffered when she had landed in a tree a few weeks earlier.[44] She bailed out at 5,700 feet and plummeted downward, scattering flour to simulate a trail of smoke. Delayed jumps were her specialty and she stunned the crowd by falling 5,000 feet before she opened her parachute, at which point the spectators uttered an audible sigh of relief, in unison.

A formal contest was also held and five jumpers participated, each trying to land as close as possible to a 100-foot circle in the center of the airfield by spilling the wind from his parachute to shift his position. Leonard Moore of Norwood, Ohio, took first place by landing 175 feet from the center of the target. "Whitey" Rauner of Cincinnati was second, followed by Verne Stewart of Elgin, Illinois, Merlyn C. Cox, the husband of the celebrated delayed-jumper, and John Wickum of Chicago.[45] Their exciting exhibitions provided a fine finish to a full program.

The opening ceremonies on May 31, the third and final day of the tournament, were again graced by eight Naval Reserve biplanes and seven Army ships from Scott Field, flying in serpentine and "V" formations. A crowd of 22,000 paying spectators occupied the grandstand, while 10,000 more watched from outside the fence.[46]

In the lone race of the day, a fifty-mile event sponsored by the Missouri Brewers' Association, Gus J. Gotch of Los Angeles lapped the field in his Schoenfeldt Special to win $900 by averaging 251.6 miles per hour. Marion McKeen was second at 212.3 for $500, S.J. Wittmann third for $300, and R.A. Kling won $200 with his last-place showing of 164.7 miles per hour.[47]

Transport ships and stock model commercial planes paraded slowly at a height of 500 feet above the field between 1:30 and 2:00 in a display of the current aircraft in use. Mike Murphy then took off from the roof of an automobile in a demonstration of "how not to fly." After bouncing on the ground, he zoomed straight up, did a "wingover" into a tailspin, and held the crowd spellbound with his acrobatic monoplane, all the while trailing a wake of white chemical smoke. "Batman" Stein followed with a repeat of his performance of opening day by parachuting from a height of 10,000 feet.[48]

Target jumping was again a feature of the program as seven parachutists competed for prizes aggregating the odd total of $322. Merlyn C. Cox demonstrated that he was still the head of his household by winning first prize of $146 with a jump of only 98 feet from the center of the circle, an exemplary performance with the barely controllable parachutes of that era. "Air meet officials described his effort as usually good; seldom does a jumper hang up a better mark."[49] Second prize of $81 went to "Whitey" Rauner for 144 feet, and Leonard Moore took third place for $48 with 325 feet. Verne Stewart landed 438 feet from the center of the traget for fourth place and $32, and Mitchell Lakonski pocketed $15 for fifth place with a distance of 454 feet. Two other entrants landed "out of the money."[50]

The climax of the entire meet came with the finals of the International Aerobatic Competition. Although the concluding tests had been originally scheduled for only the four highest finishers of the preliminary performances, a fourth-place tie between Povey and Mackey at 196 earned each a slot in the finals with de Papana (257), Rankin (238), and Mantz (209). While freedom of choice had rested with the contestants in the elimination trials, the judges selected the stunts to be performed in the deciding test from the NAA master list.[51] The competition was won by forty-year-old Tex Rankin, "the dean of American stunt flyers,"[52] who had survived fifteen crashes over a long career as a movie pilot and flying instructor.

> Precision in the execution of the aerial maneuvers was the important factor in the competition, with showmanship and safety also counting. Rankin went through his final routine with the skill that comes of long practice and, while losing 25 points for performing at too high an altitude, he gained ground with one especially difficult maneuver in which he flew his ship on one side and then the other, performed a "one and a half" slow roll and recovered precisely flying on his other side.[53]

With this breathtaking exhibition in his silvery, low-wing monoplane, Rankin tallied a total of 282.7 points to win $2,000 and permanent possession of a handsome gold-and-onyx trophy, as well as the title "king of the world's acrobatic flyers."[54] Captain Alexander de Papana displayed a more extensive repertoire with his German biplane, but in the opinion of the judges he was not as precise as Rankin. The Rumanian scored 269.4 points to take second place for $1,000. Disaster almost overtook Paul Mantz, another movie stunter, for, as he neared the crest of an outside loop and started a slow roll, his plane caught fire. The flames flickered out as he continued his turn in the air, however, and he took third place, a shade behind de Papana, with 268.4 points for $600. Povey and Mackey were again far back with scores of 191 and 189 for $400 and $250 respectively.[55] The excellent performances of these international aviators provided a stirring climax to the program, which then concluded with a mass jump from a transport by nine parachutists.[56]

In the closing ceremonies on the field, the winners of the various contests were presented with their trophies and cash prizes. Ob-

Alexander de Papana of Rumania circles the center pylon during the finals of the International Aerobatic Competition.

servers had correctly predicted two days earlier the recipient of the John D. Brock Trophy. Roger Don Rae, who had crashed his speedy *Miss Detroit* in full view of 12,000 spectators after a bizarre accident on the opening day of the meet, was awarded the cup as the standing pilot of the tournament. His skillful handling of the emergency earned him the well-deserved respect of all who had witnessed it. [57]

The St. Louis Air Races and International Aerobatic Competition was the last great aeronautic program contest in the city. It was St. Louis' only major aerial activity in the preceding thirty years in which the active hand of Major Albert Bond Lambert was not prominently in evidence. The retired drug tycoon was then devoting his full energies to the St. Louis Police Board, of which he had been a member since 1933, as well as watching closely the development of Lambert-St. Louis Municipal Airport. [58] There is little doubt, however, that the dean of St. Louis aviation was one of the sixty-three businessmen and flying enthusiasts who had raised $53,000 to cover the expenses of the tournament. [59]

Unlike St. Louis' last major balloon race, the Gordon Bennett contest of 1929, which had been something of a disappointment, its final air meet was a success in every respect, with California contestants collaring most of the honors. The three-day program, packed with impressive aerial activity of every description, had been completely in accord with the city's high aeronautic repute. St. Louis' reputation as a leading air center after 1937 would be furthered by its aircraft industries, which had already been long in operation.

Part Three:
Air Industries

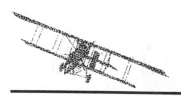

XIV
The Minor Industries, 1858-1945

AMONG THE MORE PROMINENT FACTORS responsible for St. Louis' air leadership were its varied aeronautic industries. While not all of them reached the size or significance of the Robertson, Curtiss-Wright, or McDonnell undertakings, even the relatively "minor" enterprises had important functions in the city's air life. Moreover, they assisted its economic growth in no small measure and made lasting contributions to all phases of military, civil, and commercial aviation.

The first area in which St. Louis sustained air industry was, quite naturally, that of ballooning. One of the city's earliest pioneers in that field was the Ericsson Hydrogen Balloon Company, which in 1858 was at least engaged in the staging of regular exhibitions throughout the Midwest, if not the actual building of the gas bags themselves.[1] It was not until the turn of the century, however, that balloon construction in St. Louis saw further development.

At the Louisiana Purchase Exposition of 1904, many residents of the city attempted to exhibit their prowess with machines of their own making. Perhaps the most important was John Berry, whose Aerial Navigation Company had built a unique airship, the 22,000-cubic-foot *St. Louis,* in which he himself failed to effect a successful ascension.[2] For the next several years, as a prominent member of the Aero Clubs of both St. Louis and South St. Louis, he continued

Museum of Science and Natural Histo

The cover from Maurice A. Heimann's 1908 catalog.

to construct and experiment with lighter-than-air craft, among them the much-traveled *University City*[3] and an inefficient spherical "dirigible" with attached propellers of his own design,[4] with occasional forays into the heavier-than-air field.[5]

A more industrious manufacturer was Morris A. Heimann, the colorful promoter of the Aero Club of South St. Louis, who built and sold several balloons and airships at his cabinet and appliance factory at Thirteenth and Rutger streets. In 1908, he fabricated the "largest balloon in the world,"[6] the 110-000-cubic-foot *Chicago* for C.A. Coey of that city. By the following year, he had constructed the racing-size *South St. Louis* and the tiny *South St. Louis, Jr.,* both of which he turned over to the organization he had founded to rival the Dozier-Lambert unit.[7] During the next few years, his shop completed several more balloons, as well as at least one airplane, which Heimann constructed in 1911 in cooperation with Hillery Beachey.[8] As a balloon manufacturer, pilot, and enthusiast, Morris Heimann enriched St. Louis with his positive contributions to the sport in the early years of the twentieth century.

Another, more celebrated pioneer balloon builder was Harry

Eugene Honeywell. He was a veteran of the Spanish-American War and had served with Admiral Dewey at Manila. Honeywell came to St. Louis during the World's Fair and got his first aeronautical experience when he took part in the operation there of the captive balloon.[9] Having executed his initial free balloon ascension in 1905, Honeywell began to manufacture the vehicles shortly thereafter at his home in the city. One of his earliest contracts, in 1908, was for a 300,000-cubic-foot balloon in which Dr. Frederick A. Fielding planned to cross the Atlantic Ocean.[10] The commitment was either not undertaken or unsuccessfully effected, for the further developments of the venture went unreported.

During the following year, the young manufacturer, then a lieutenant in the aero detachment of the Signal Corps of the Missouri National Guard (the only such air unit in the United States at that time),[11] was engaged in building three 5,000-cubic-foot balloons for the government, which was to conduct scientific tests with them at Fort Weed, New York.[12] In 1910, two Honeywell-built balloons, the *Million Population Club* and the *St. Louis IV,* took part in the Gordon Bennett Race,[13] and he himself also constructed a semi-rigid dirigible for the tournament,[14] although it failed to make its appearance at Kinloch Park. By 1911, H.E. Honeywell had "the largest balloon factory in the United States"[15] and was enjoying unlimited prosperity.

Although he achieved noteworthy success as a balloon manufacturer and as late as 1928 was still constructing gas bags for himself and other practitioners of the sport,[16] Honeywell earned his international reputation primarily in the capacity of a balloon pilot. By the time of his death in 1940, he had made more than 600 flights, participated in more than 35 major races, covered more than 25,000 miles in the air, and was widely known as "the dean of American balloonists."[17] Among his more notable accomplishments were victories in the 1922 Gordon Bennett contest and the National Balloon Races of 1912, 1916, and 1920, with runner-up honors in fifteen major competitions.[18] He was St. Louis' foremost balloonist and the equal of any in the world. Because it had men like Harry Eugene Honeywell in its ranks, the city could declare itself unchallenged as the center of free ballooning in the United States.

St. Louis also kept pace in heavier-than-air activities. As progress in that phase of flight developed, the city was well represented by its first truly great industrialist, Thomas Wesley Benoist. Born in Irondale, Missouri, on December 29, 1874, he spent his early years in the lead mines of that area and migrated to St. Louis in 1893,

The nation's first exclusive aeronautical supply store was at 3932 Olive Street. It was operated by Thomas W. Benoist. This photo was taken in 1909.

where he became an apprentice molder at the Buck Stove Foundry.[19] The reserved and mild-tempered youth, who had a liking for political history and applied science, got his first aeronautical experience as one of the directors of the Berry Aerial Navigation Company, which financed the building of John Berry's abortive airship at the Louisiana Purchase Exposition of 1904.[20]

During the same year, Benoist made his first free balloon flight, but for a time was too occupied with other matters to pursue the avocation in depth. He was then working for Harry Turner's Mississippi Valley Auto Company, but in 1907, he and his brother Charles opened their own auto supply company at 3932 Olive Street, right in the heart of "Automobile Row." In the spring of 1908, Tom Benoist made a permanent entrance into the field of aviation when he converted the shop into the Aeronautic Supply Company, popularly known as "Aerosco."[21] This was the first supply house for airplane parts and accessories in the nation,[22] as evidenced by contemporary advertisements, which described the firm as "First in All

Benoist about the time of his first flight, in 1910, at Kinloch Field.

America.''[23]

For a time, Benoist sold only makeshift material, such as bicycle wheels, motorcycle parts, and piano wire, but these were the only aircraft articles available and were eagerly sought by would-be aviators.[24] By mid-1910, the company had acquired an international reputation and was shipping aeronautical supplies to Japan, Cuba, and Canada, as well as to all parts of the United States.[25] By that time, moreover, Aerosco's materials were somewhat more sophisticated and it even offered complete airplanes. Benoist's stock ranged from a simple $2,200 Santos-Dumont monoplane with a 30-horsepower Darrac engine to a luxurious $12,000 two-place Antoinette monoplane with a 100-horsepower Antoinette engine. A Curtiss biplane sold for $5,000, a Wright Flyer for $7,500, a Farman biplane for $8,000, a more plebian Antoinette monoplane for $7,500, and a Benoist biplane for a modest $3,000, each equipped with a suitable engine.[26] During 1910, more than seventeen airplanes from this large supply of both domestic and foreign craft were sold.[27]

The pioneer industrialist had begun making his own aircraft in 1909 at his factory at 6664 Delmar Boulevard in University City, and by May of the following year, he had completed three rudimentary biplanes of his own design.[28] At that time, however, he was only a builder and not a flier; he had yet to make his first flight. This he accomplished at Kinloch Park on September 18, 1910, in a Curtiss biplane he had purchased from Howard Gill. In so doing, he became the first St. Louisan to pilot an airplane and the first to use the Aero Club's newly-opened airfield.[29] He was to have exhibited the biplane at the International Air Meet at the field the following month, but he appeared instead in Amarillo, Texas, to substitute for Gill, who had suddenly fallen ill. There Benoist was hospitalized after a bizarre accident on October 12. While he was making minor repairs on the engine, he was struck on the head by the propeller, which caused him both a slight brain concussion and the loss of three toes from his right foot as well.[30] The young St. Louisan made a rapid recovery and soon resumed his aerial affairs.

During 1910, the year which witnessed the immense expansion of St. Louis aeronautics, a number of other firms within the city were engaged to some extent in the aviation industry. The Phoenix Auto Supply Company at 3974-76 Olive Street, supported by the slogan, ''If It's Good We Carry It,'' offered a substantial line of airplane and balloon, as well as automobile, motorcycle and motorboat parts.[31] The Aeromotion Company of America at 1611 Wright Building distributed Paris-made rotary Gnome engines at $2,600 for a 50-

horsepower model and $4,800 for one of 100 horsepower.[32] The Carter Carburetor Company at 921-941 North Market Street exhorted St. Louis pilots to "stop puttering with the commonplace" and purchase one of its "Featherweight" items, the "lightest carb on earth or in the air."[33] Even the Missouri Tent and Awning Company at 210 Chestnut Street advertised, "Canvas work for aeroplanes solicited."[34] At that time, however, the only large-scale operator in the city who was building his own planes was Tom W. Benoist.

While he continued to manufacture pusher-type biplanes at his Delmar Boulevard factory, he widened the scope of his endeavors during the winter of 1910-1911 by opening a flying school at Kinloch Field, the first in the city.[35] Benoist was soon joined by Tony Jannus, who became his chief pilot, along with Hugh Robinson and Jack Henning, the latter a graduate of the prestigious Wright school at Dayton, Ohio. Just as in the case of his Aeronautic Supply Company, the fame of the Benoist Flying School was so widespread that he attracted students from all over the United States, and from Europe and Asia as well.[36] At the Fairground air meet in October 1911, a number of these students exhibited their talents, or at least attempted to do so, for wind and wet weather canceled the bulk of the program.[37]

In the autumn of that year and through 1914, Tom Benoist showed another aspect of his aerial versatility when he periodically went on exhibition tours of stunt flying throughout Missouri, Illinois, Indiana, Ohio, and much of the Midwest.[38] With him at times were Tony Jannus, John D. Cooper, Horace Kearney, and a number of others, among whom were at least two of his students, John Woodlief (a 1911 pupil)[39] and William H. Bleakley (a 1913 pupil).[40]

Somewhat in competition with Benoist during these years was the Pioneer Aeroplane and Exhibition Company of St. Louis, which was capitalized at $12,000 and chartered for fifty years by the State of Missouri on July 12, 1911, for "Manufacturing and Business Purposes."[41] While the company did little, if any, manufacturing, its business affairs were active. Under the presidency of C.J. Shea, Pioneer hired Walter Brookins in September 1911, and supplied him with a Wright biplane for the Fairground tournament, while at the same time, the company contracted with the aviator on a "fifty-fifty" basis to make exhibitions under its auspices for the following six months.[42] For the next two years, Shea and his organization provided airplanes and engaged airmen for several air meets as additional evidence, with Tom Benoist, of St. Louis' activity in the exhibition field of aviation.[43]

The city's initial aeronautic entrepreneur had suffered a second setback on October 20, 1911. On that night, the Benoist Aircraft Company's factory at 6664 Delmar Boulevard was completely gutted by a raging fire which followed a mysterious explosion. Unfortunately, Benoist was insured for only $2,000. He lost five planes, two extra engines, and the main manufacturing machinery — a loss estimated at $20,000.[44] It was then that he probably occupied the building at 6628 Delmar Boulevard,[45] where he was soon able to continue as usual, after his widespread enterprises helped him recoup his losses.

While the Aero Club of St. Louis' Kinloch Field was in active existence from 1910 to 1913, the energetic Tom Benoist was in continuous operation there. It was the headquarters of his flying school and the testing ground for his airplanes. At that airfield about 1913, Major Frank L. Lane of the United States Army, along with Benoist and Jannus, successfully tested the first rapid-fire gun designed expressly for an airplane.[46] At Kinloch a year earlier, Tom Benoist, W.C. Lineback, and Albert Berry developed an innovative method of packing a parachute, which Berry demonstrated on March 1, 1912, over Jefferson Barracks in the world's first such jump from an airplane, a Benoist model piloted by Tony Jannus.[47]

Two months later, Tom Benoist brought out a type of aircraft familiar to Europe but new to the United States. While most American planes of that day had an open framework with a pusher engine in the rear, this progressive biplane had a fuselage completely covered with fabric from nose to tail, along with a tractor engine in the nose. Tested successfully at Kinloch Park, it was a giant step forward in the science of aeronautics and justly deserved the $4,500 prize awarded at the Chicago air meet of 1912, when the plane carried five passengers, including pilot Tony Jannus.[48]

In such an airplane, with a red arrow painted through the letters of the name "Benoist" on its side, Jannus participated in another St. Louis "first" when he swooped low over the thousands of visitors at the St. Louis Fair on St. Charles Rock Road on September 24, 1912, landed near the refreshment stand, and delivered on order four cases of Lemp's beer, the first consignment of freight ever to go by air.[49] The stunt was merely one more product of the inventive mind of Tom Benoist.

His enthusiastic endeavors and satisfying successes made his name, at least in aeronautical circles, a quasi-household word, albeit a somewhat unpronounceable one. A contemporary trade journal attempted to correct the situation with a limerick by A.C.

Beech:

> There is a plane builder — Benoist,
> Whose feelings have grown very raw,
>   Because his name's spoken
>   In French very broken,
> When it always should rhyme with "wah-wah." [50]

Although his aerial activities were legion, St. Louis' pioneer industrialist was primarily known for his developments with hydroplanes and flying boats. The first successful takeoff from water had been executed by Henri Fabre near Martigues, France, on March 28, 1910, but it was not until Glenn Curtiss equaled the feat on January 26, 1911, in San Francisco Bay, that the maneuver had been performed a second time. [51] The Benoist Aircraft Company was, therefore, among the first to enter the field when it began experimenting on the Mississippi River in June 1912 with a company plane to which floats had been attached. [52] In order to publicize the corporation's developments in this area and attract favorable attention, [53] Tony Jannus made a spectacular flight down the Missouri and Mississippi Rivers in a Benoist tractor hydroplane with a six-cylinder, 75-horsepower Roberts engine. [54] He started at Omaha on November 6, 1912, and arrived at his destination in New Orleans on December 16, with a well-traveled case of Lemp's beer and a side of bacon for the mayor. [55] This was a new world's hydroplane distance record of 1,973 miles, completed in 39 days with an actual flying time of 31 hours and 43 minutes. [56]

Finding himself cramped at his factory at 6628 Delmar, Tom Benoist expanded his operations in 1913 and began building his seaplanes at the shops of the St. Louis Car Company, to which E.B. Meissner of that organization had graciously given him access. [57] There he devised a method of completely encasing a plane in a water-tight hull, and he scored a coup on Glenn Curtiss by introducing that spring the first true flying boat, while his chief rival was still perfecting the pontoon-equipped hydroplane. [58]

Their competition continued in the development of a twin-engine flying boat capable of spanning the Atlantic Ocean. Benoist completed his model, with a massive 75-foot wingspan, at the car company in 1913, but an over-anxious mechanic put the ship through a premature trial run and crashed it beyond repair. [59] Curtiss finished his machine that year and tested it successfully, but World War I prevented any immediate attempt to put the ocean-crossing scheme into operation. [60] This flying boat, in 1919, did become the first aircraft to span the Atlantic. [61]

In the front cockpit of this huge, twin-engined flying boat are its designer, Tom Benoist, left; Edwin B. Meissner, head of St. Louis Car Company, where it was built; and pilot Tony Jannus, right. Identity of the others is lost.

In the realm of water aircraft, Tom Benoist earned his principal aeronautical repute. For one specific accomplishment in that area, history particularly remembers him. Impressed with Benoist's seaplane developments, especially as evidenced by the momentous river trek, P.E. Fansler of St. Petersburg, Florida, contacted the airman in regard to the establishment of an airline in his area. Negotiations between the St. Louis aviator and Florida businessmen in 1913 resulted in the crystallization of the project.[62]

On January 1, 1914, the St. Petersburg-Tampa Airboat Line, Passenger and Express Service began carrying customers and freight the 21 miles across Tampa Bay. This was "the first sustained, scheduled air-passenger service in the United States, and probably in the world."[63] An auction was held to determine the first passenger who would make the trip with pilot Tony Jannus, a flight across the bay to Tampa. St. Petersburg Mayor A.C. Pheil won the honor for $400.[64]

The company began operations with a single, two-place biplane Benoist Type XIV flying boat, which was 26 feet long and, powered

St. Petersburg-Tampa
AIRBOAT LINE

Fast Passenger and Express Service

SCHEDULE:

Lv. St. Petersburg	10:00 A.M.
Arrive Tampa	10:30 A.M.
Leave Tampa	11:00 A.M.
Ar. St. Petersburg	11:30 A.M.
Lv. St. Petersburg	2:00 P.M.
Arrive Tampa	2:30 P.M.
Leave Tampa	3:00 P.M.
Ar. St. Petersburg	3:30 P.M.

Special Flight Trips

Can be arranged through any of our agents or by communicating directly with the St. Petersburg Hangar. Trips covering any distance over all-water routes and from the waters' surface to several thousand feet high AT PAS—SENGERS' REQUEST.

A minimum charge of $15 per Special Flight.

JANUARY 1, 1914

Rates: $5.00 Per Trip.   **Round Trip $10.**   **Booking for Passage in Advance.**

NOTE--Passengers are allowed a weight of 200 pounds GROSS including hand baggage, excess charged at $5.00 per 100 pounds, minimum charge 25 cents. EXPRESS RATES, for packages, suit cases, mail matter, etc., $5.00 per hundred pounds, minimum charge 25 cents. Express carried from hangar to hangar only, delivery and receipt by shipper.

Tickets on Sale at Hangars or

CITY NEWS STAND
F. C. WEST, Prop.

271 CENTRAL AVENUE   ST. PETERSBURG, FLORIDA

Courtesy Florida Aviation History Society

This flyer advertised the nation's first scheduled airline, owned and operated by St. Louis' Tom Benoist.

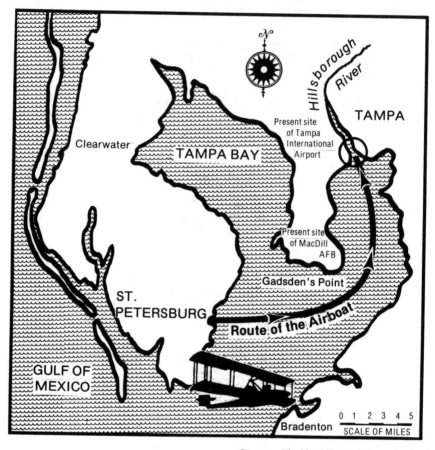

Courtesy Florida Aviation History Society

Benoist's Airboat didn't go far — about 21 miles one way. The flight took about 20 minutes.

by a 75-horsepower Roberts engine, could reach a maximum speed of 64 miles per hour.[65] The world's first scheduled airline offered two round trips daily between the two cities. The morning flight left St. Petersburg at 10:00 and arrived at Tampa at 10:30, leaving that point at 11:00 and arriving back at its starting point one-half hour later. The afternoon flight left at 2:00 and completed its two-way run at 3:30. The passenger rate was $5.00 one way and $10.00 for a round trip, with freight charges of $5.00 per 100 pounds.[66]

During the first ten days of operations with "Boat No. 44," Tony Jannus made 26 round trips, carried 52 passengers, and covered 682 miles in an actual flying time of 12 hours, 42 minutes, and 30 seconds.[67] Two more flying boats,[68] constructed at the Benoist Air-

St. Louisan Tony Jannus shown shortly after takeoff on January 1, 1914, the world's first flight of a scheduled airline.

The hangar of the St. Petersburg-Tampa Airboat Line had a sign identifying it also as the "Benoist School of Aviation." The Florida Aviation History Society is raising funds to reconstruct the building on the exact site.

Jannus posed in the cockpit with George S. Gandy, builder of St. Petersburg's Gandy Bridge, in the winter of 1914.

craft Company's factory at 6628 Delmar Boulevard,[69] were added on January 15 and manned by Roger Jannus (the brother of Benoist's chief pilot) and Weldon B. Cooke.[70] The St. Petersburg-Tampa Airboat Line functioned from January 1 to April 27, 1914, carrying passengers, express, and mail.[71] During that period, the flying boats flew a total of 1,205 passengers some 11,000 miles[72] and lost only four days as a result of bad weather, lack of customers, and engine trouble.[73] The line was subsidized by the Chambers of Commerce of the two cities but, with the end of the tourist season as well as the novelty of the phenomenon, the expenses became prohibitive.[74] After four months of operation, Benoist terminated his airline, along with the flying school he had also maintained in that area,[75] and moved back to St. Louis. Although it had only a brief life, the historic enterprise had effected an unprecedented accomplishment and foreshadowed the day when scheduled airlines would routinely function throughout the world.

Jannus banks the Airboat IV *gracefully over the waters of Tampa Bay. The Florida Aviation History Society, with the aid of the Smithsonian Institution, has replicated the original craft and makes occasional demonstration flights.* *

Once again in the city of his aeronautical awakening, Tom W. Benoist continued to manufacture land biplanes as well as flying boats at his Delmar Boulevard plant, and in the spring of 1914 he opened a seaplane flying school at the Carondelet Motor Boat Club on the Mississippi River, offering students a comprehensive course of instruction for $350.[76] Although he had enjoyed bountiful prosperity in St. Louis, the aerial entrepreneur received an irresistible offer from Sandusky, Ohio, the home of the Roberts Aircraft Motor Company, whose engines he had long used in his planes, so

*Photos pertaining to the St. Petersburg-Tampa Airboat Line are taken from a publication by that name issued by the Florida Aviation History Society, and available from them for $6 postpaid: Box 127, Indian Rocks Beach FL 33535.

he moved his entire operation there in 1916.[77]

The Benoist saga ended abruptly on June 14, 1917. While riding in an open streetcar to his factory in Sandusky, the 42-year-old industrialist swayed outward as the car made a sharp turn and struck his head on a telephone pole. Three hours later he was dead.[78] "Short, slender, wiry, with a wry, humorous grin and keen, smiling eyes,"[79] the aeronautical salesman, manufacturer, showman, instructor, and transporter had given St. Louis, the nation, and the world unprecedented accomplishments. Had the great genius lived out a normal existence, he would surely have ranked as the equal of Curtiss, Martin, Boeing, Douglas, or McDonnell.

After his departure, St. Louis was at a loss for continuous air industry. Unfortunately, it took a world war to provide the necessary stimulus. On April 6, 1917, the Aviation Section of the Signal Corps of the United States Army (the predecessor of the Army Air Corps and the United States Air Force), could count in its ranks only 65 officers, 1,087 enlisted men, and 55 training planes, none of which was fit for combat.[80] America was then fourteenth among world air powers,[81] below China, Spain, and Bulgaria.[82] As a result, a comprehensive program to recruit airmen and provide airplanes was undertaken.

To fill the latter gap, the Joint Army and Navy Technical Aircraft Board presented the Secretaries of War and Navy on May 25 with an ambitious procurement plan: 3,500 Curtiss JN-4 "Jenny" trainers, 1,700 de Haviland battle and observation planes, 600 "Spad" pursuit ships (standard equipment of the French), 600 SE-5s (the British equivalent of the "Spad"), 600 Sopwith scout planes (another British design), 200 Curtiss R-4s (an advanced trainer), and 175 Farman seaplanes.[83] By August 1917, Congress had appropriated $695,000,000 (not all of which would be spent) for aviation purposes.[84] With specific objectives in mind and the money to carry them out, the government began to search for suitable manufacturers.

In the autumn of 1917, Washington officials met with a number of St. Louis businessmen to form a company in the city to produce airplanes. Among those consulted were A. J. Siegel, who as president of Huttig Sash and Door Company was familiar with the handling of such airframe woods as fir, spruce, and pine, and Edwin B. Meissner, who as vice president of St. Louis Car Company had the facilities for making the metal fittings to supplement the wooden elements in airplanes, some experience in aircraft manufacturing (gained with Tom Benoist), and a large shop and assembly room

Edwin D. Meissner, of the St. Louis Car Company, is in the front cockpit of this JN-4D "Jenny."

easily converted for airplane production. An agreement was reached and the St. Louis Aircraft Corporation was formed, with A.J. Siegel as president, E.B. Meissner as vice president, and Ralph Siegel as secretary.[85]

Early in 1918, the company was awarded its first government contract, an order for two-place, open-cockpit Curtiss JN-4D "Jenny" biplane trainers. By the end of May, the competed planes were coming off the assembly line of the reconverted factory of the car company. Shortly before November 11, employment at the plant reached a peak of 900 and the shop was turning out 30 trainers per week.[86] A total of 450 "Jennies" were built by St. Louis Aircraft before the armistice canceled its second subcontract for 200 more and halted its production.[87]

American industry manufactured a total of 5,034 service planes and 8,860 trainers during World War I.[88] The city of St. Louis produced more than $1,000,000 worth of aviation goods during the war and ranked fifth among the centers of production in the United States (approximately tied with Sacramento; Springfield, Massachusetts; and Ithaca, New York; but after Dayton, Buffalo, Detroit, and New York City).[89] The St. Louis Aircraft Corporation, which hoped to continue in the postwar years,[90] was responsible for the greatest part of that achievement, with balloon production, primarily by H.E. Honeywell,[91] probably accounting for the rest.

As might have been expected, St. Louis made significant contributions to the war effort in the lighter-than-air field. Shortly after the United States entered the conflict, the Missouri Aeronautical

Society, prompted by Albert Bond Lambert, was organized for the specific purpose of operating a balloon school "to train aviators for Government service."[92] The society was headed by James Bemis, a long-time St. Louis balloonist, together with S.J. Buckingham as secretary and John G. Lonsdale as treasurer. Lambert himself held no office in the organization because he expected an imminent Army commission, after which he would have been unable to make a contract with the government in regard to the school.[93]

On May 4, 1917, the first contingent of students, eleven St. Louis youths, made formal application to join the Missouri Aeronautical Reserve Corps, the designation of the unit to which they would belong as members of the Missouri Aeronautical Society's training school.[94] The entrance requirements were quite stiff, for each had to be between the ages of 21 and 30 and have a college education.[95] The instructors were all licensed balloonists and had long been active in St. Louis aeronautics: Albert Bond Lambert, in command; James Bemis and Joseph O'Reilly, second in command; E.S. Cole, William Assmann, H.E. Honeywell, John Berry, Paul McCullough, and Harlow B. Spencer. The initial equipment of the corps consisted of five balloons and baskets, one dummy balloon, four aneroid barometers, four statoscopes, and several compasses, maps, and charts. Instruction in the handling of the balloons would be given at Meramec Park at Grand Avenue and Meramec Street, with training in kite ballooning conducted at a field at 8000 South Broadway. All instructors would hold the rank of first lieutenant and all students that of second lieutenant. Upon completion of the course, which lasted from six to eight weeks, the graduates were to have the choice of either going into active service or entering the Officers' Reserve Corps as balloon instructors themselves.[96]

The man who had conceived the idea for the balloon school to help the war effort had also been quick to offer assistance in an earlier government emergency. When war was threatening between the United States and Mexico over the activities of President Victoriano Huerta, Albert Bond Lambert, organizer of the United States Aviation Reserve Corps, wired Secretary of War Lindley Garrison and Secretary of the Navy Josephus Daniels on April 20, 1914, that 45 of the airmen who had enlisted in his unit were ready for immediate action. In addition to Lambert himself, eight of the members were St. Louisans: Tom Benoist, Anthony Jannus, Hugh Robinson, Hillery Beachey, William H. Bleakley, William Assmann, Paul McCullough, and H.E. Honeywell (the last three of whom were balloonists). Each reserve pilot was to be equipped with either a dirigible or an airplane, six of which St. Louis would provide.[97] The plan never came to fruition, however, for the crisis ended on April 27, 1914, when Presidents Wilson and Huerta accepted the mediation of Argentina, Brazil, and Chile in their dispute.[98]

Lambert's balloon school, on the other hand, did come to pass. The St. Louis unit of the Missouri Aeronautical Reserve Corps commenced training on May 15, 1917, at Meramec Park. Lambert and McCullough each made two basket-filled ascensions in order to give each of the eleven students a practical lesson in ballooning.[99] Through the efforts of Albert Bond Lambert, the War Department officially recognized the school as a training station for the United States Army Aeronautical Corps on June 5,[100] and from that date began to defray its expenses, which up to that time had been borne by the magnanimous Lambert himself.[101] This balloon school was the first the Army had ever sanctioned.[102]

The unit operated at Meramec Park from May 1917 to May 1918, when it was moved to Camp John Wise in San Antonio, Texas.[103] Lambert, by then a major, continued to supervise the training until the end of the war.[104] During the year and one-half of its existence, the Missouri Aeronautical Society Balloon School qualified 354 pilots and observers (93 of whom were St. Louisans), had as many as 40 balloons in service at once, made more than 1,500 ascensions, and used more than 34,000,000 cubic feet of gas.[105] Without the zeal of its commanding officer, whose action in establishing it had been characteristic of his aerial enthusiasm, the Army's first balloon school might never have come into existence.

In the immediate postwar years, the air industry in St. Louis was dominated by the Robertson Aircraft Corporation.[106] A number of other companies, however, were established during that period. In 1926, the Bridgeton Aircraft Corporation began operations with three airplanes at Lambert Field.[107] For the next two or three years, the firm offered sightseeing tours of the city, distributed "Eaglerock" biplanes for the Alexander Aircraft Corporation of Denver, Colorado, and maintained a modest flying school.[108]

An establishment of similar activity was formed during the summer of 1927. This was the Von Hoffmann Aircraft Company, founded by two long-time St. Louis balloonists and aviators, Albert Von Hoffmann and his son Bernard.[109] Until the early 1930s, the company conducted an air taxi service from Lambert Field, operated a prosperous flying school, practiced aerial photography for hire, and for a time distributed in the Missouri area such airplanes as the Ryan "Brougham," the Alexander "Eaglerock," the Whittesley

Washington University Archives

The graceful "Cardinal," low-cost personal plane manufactured by St. Louis Aircraft Company. This is one of the first models, built in the late 1920s.

"Avian," and the St. Louis "Cardinal."[110]

This last, appropriately-named model was produced by the St. Louis Aircraft Corporation, a subsidiary of the St. Louis Car Company, which introduced it at the Detroit Air Show in 1929.[111] The "Cardinal" was a two-place, high-wing cabin monoplane intended primarily for the private owner. The plane had a wingspan of 32 feet and its fuselage was constructed of welded steel tubing covered with fabric, with a spacious cabin furnished in leather.[112] In addition to manufacturing airplanes, St. Louis Aircraft was also the area distributor for the American "Eagle,"[113] a $2,450 three-place open biplane.[114] The production of the popular "Cardinal" lasted until 1933,[115] after which time the corporation sustained itself with a variety of aerial products.

One of the largest of the "minor" St. Louis industries was the B.F. Mahoney Aircraft Corporation. This firm, known until 1927 as Ryan Airlines, had built Charles A. Lindbergh's *Spirit of St. Louis,*[116] and after his celebrated achievement, Mahoney Aircraft was reaping a prosperous harvest by producing an airplane almost identical in appearance to the *Spirit,* at its San Diego plant. This model was the $9,700 Ryan B-1 "Brougham," a five-place, fabric-covered, high-wing cabin monoplane powered by a Wright 220 Whirlwind engine. The plane had a top speed of 126 miles per hour, a service ceiling of 16,000 feet, and a normal range of 700 miles.[117] Lindbergh's transatlantic hop had made the airplane design so popular that orders for it poured in from all over the world. By the spring of 1928, a year after the sensational flight, the San Diego plant had shipped three of its models to Australia, one each to Rome and Paris, and was in the process of completing orders from Mexico City and Warsaw, Poland.[118] Domestic and foreign demand for the "Brougham" was so great that the company had an urgent need for expansion.

Lindbergh's success proved advantageous to the builder of his airplane also, and sales of the Ryan "Brougham" boomed. This one is a mail plane from the Robertson Aircraft fleet, photographed at Lambert Field about 1928.

As early as June 1927, negotiations had begun between B.F. Mahoney, president of the corporation, and Harold M. Bixby, president of the St. Louis Chamber of Commerce and one of the financial backers of Lindbergh's flight.[119] The latter's persuasion was effective and on December 31, 1927, Mahoney announced that, while his San Diego factory, airline, and flying school would continue to function, the company's main base would be moved to St. Louis.[120] Construction of a $50,000 plant at Lambert Field was begun in January 1928,[121] and production of the Ryan B-1 "Brougham" was slated to begin on August 1 of that year, at an initial rate of 25 per month.[122] Mahoney himself announced that his decision to relocate in St. Louis was motivated "by the Lindbergh flights, by the central location of St. Louis, and by the city's plans for establishing a municipal airport."[123]

A Missouri corporation, capitalized at $500,000, was chartered to finance the firm.[124] B.F. Mahoney was to continue as president of the company, and Phil De Catesby Ball, owner of the St. Louis Browns baseball team, was to be chairman of the board of directors, along with wealthy St. Louisans Harry Hall Knight and Harold M. Bixby, the last two of whom had provided the greatest part of the monetary backing for Charles Lindbergh.[125]

In 1929, the company supplemented its B-1 series with the B-5 "Brougham," a six-place, 300-horsepower cabin monoplane designed for use by corporations and private owners who needed a ruggedly constructed plane capable of taking off from small, rough fields.[126] Late in the same year, the firm added the six-place, Wasp-powered B-7 "Brougham," designed particularly for airlines, organizations, or individuals demanding a plane with high speed, good performance, and suitable comfort.[127] Mahoney Aircraft produced several hundred of these three models of the basic high-wing monoplane design at Lambert Field before its parent company, the Detroit Aircraft Corporation, moved the entire assembly facility out of St. Louis and into Detroit early in 1930.[128] For the two years that St. Louis had housed its facilities, the company had enjoyed substantial prosperity and contributed to the city's success as a true center of air industry.

Shortly before Mahoney's departure, St. Louis was host to the International Aircraft Exposition, held in the St. Louis Arena, February 15-23, 1930. The Aeronautical Chamber of Commerce of America had selected the city as the site for the exhibition because it was a noted air center, its people were air-minded, and it had facilities spacious enough to house the display.[129] A total of 170 aircraft concerns (among them Curtiss-Wright, Keystone, Travelair, Cessna, Stinson, and Fairchild) exhibited their products in the three buildings of the Arena complex. The estimated value of the flying equipment was $2,500,000, including 87 airplanes, a number greater by 25 than that of any previous exposition.[130]

In addition to the static display, there were a number of rousing aerial activities in conjunction with the exhibit. On February 16, D.S. "Barney" Zimmerly, a test pilot for the Nicholas-Beazley Airplane Company of Marshall, Missouri, broke the world's altitude record for light planes, then held by Germany's Paul Baumer at 22,250 feet. Flying a Barling NB-3 low-wing monoplane, Zimmerly took off from a clearing in Forest Park opposite the Arena at 2:25 p.m. and reached the record altitude of 27,250 feet in a flight which lasted two hours and eight minutes.[131] Two days later, Major Philip Love, one of Charles Lindbergh's original teammates on the mail run between Chicago and St. Louis,[132] set something of a world's record when he accomplished the unprecedented feat of performing three "outside loops" in succession while carrying a passenger in a Waco biplane over Lambert Field.[133]

Such spectacular demonstrations heightened interest in the International Aircraft Exposition itself. Between February 15 and February 30, 1930, 150,000 visitors crowded the Arena halls to view the aeronautical equipment.[134] The impressive exhibit, reminiscent of a similar display held in the city in 1910,[135] and the enthusiasm it aroused was significant evidence as to the importance of St. Louis in the area of air industry.

In the year following the great exposition, Monocoupe Corporation, a company with characteristics not unlike Mahoney Aircraft, began functioning at Lambert Field, near the growing Curtiss-

Wright factory which then dominated the St. Louis aerial industrial scene.[136] Three years earlier, in 1928, the Central States Aviation Company had started manufacturing at Moline, Illinois, a revolutionary airplane in the personal aircraft field. This was the "Monocoupe," so called because of the two outstanding features of its design — a monoplane wing (a departure from the more widespread biplane configuration), and a side-by-side arrangement of its two seats in the manner of the "coupe" style of automobile. (This was a departure from the traditional tandem arrangement.)[137] The 1928 "Monocoupe," then known as Model 60 (because of the horsepower of its engine), was 30 feet in span, 19 feet 9 inches in length, and was powered by a Velie engine which enabled it to attain a top speed of 102 miles per hour. Constructed of fabric-covered welded steel tubing, the ship was modestly priced at $2,675.[138] Central States Aircraft, which had been reorganized under the name Mono Aircraft, Inc. in 1929,[139] continued to operate at Moline until 1931, when it was again reorganized and moved to St. Louis as the Monocoupe Corporation.[140]

For the next twenty years, the company continued to manufacture the "Monocoupe," the airplane which for a time held the record for the longest continuous production of a single basic American design, until surpassed in the late 1950s by the Beech Model 18[141] By 1931, however, when it established its base at Lambert Field, the corporation was also turning out the "Monopreps," a tiny trainer, and the "Monocoach," a four-place cabin monoplane.[142]

In 1934, the company experienced a third reorganization when it was taken over by the Lambert Aircraft Corporation, which Sam Lambert, the nephew of St. Louis' foremost aerial enthusiast, had organized at the municipal airport.[143] Lambert Aircraft continued production of the three earlier models and in August 1934 constructed its most celebrated single airplane, a modified "Monocoupe" produced on order for Colonel Charles A. Lindbergh. Costing $7,600, the plane was similar to the Model 90 the company was then manufacturing, with special features such as a blister cowl, more cockpit leg room, and a treated glass-paneled windshield, together with a 145-horsepower Warner Super-Scarab engine.[144] The aviator made no flights of consequence in it, but he used it extensively as his personal plane. In August 1940, Lindbergh donated his unique "Monocoupe 145" to the Missouri Historical Society, the depository of his enormous collection of awards and momentos. There it remained crated until students of Parks College of Aeronautical Technology of St. Louis University restored it in 1962

Lindbergh's "Monocoupe" was donated to the Missouri Historical Society, kept for awhile at the National Museum of Transport (where this photo was taken in 1977), and now hangs in the passenger terminal at Lambert Field.

and put it on permanent display at the St. Louis Museum of Transport.[145]

Late in 1935, Lambert Aircraft added a fourth airplane to its successful production line — the "Monosport," a low-wing monoplane with a ninety-horsepower engine, enabling it to cruise at 115 miles per hour for a range of 575 miles.[146] That same year, the president of the company, Clare Bunch, set an official national altitude record for planes weighing less than 1,300 pounds when he took a 990-pound "Monocoupe," with company vice president B.L. Carter along, to a height of 19,000 feet over Lambert Field on October 12, 1935.[147] It was in that year also that the corporation introduced its most popular version of the "Monocoupe," the Model 90-A, a $3,825 airplane powered by a ninety-horsepower Lambert engine.[148]

Lambert Aircraft Corporation continued to produce its series of immensely popular monoplanes in St. Louis until 1940, when the entire operation was transferred to Orlando, Florida.[149] During the ten years it had functioned at Lambert Field, the company had assured the city's success as a center of air industry and had provided an immeasurable stimulus to private civil aviation as well.

During Monocoupe-Lambert's tenure at the airport, St. Louis Aircraft Corporation had also been manufacturing aerial equipment. After its "Cardinal" had been taken out of production in 1933, the firm engaged in a number of industrial projects for the next several years. In 1934, the firm manufactured a wide variety of parts for the Air Corps, including airplane skis, and its engineering department was experimenting with aircraft designs for both the Army and the

Navy.[150] It continued to produce parts during the following year.[151] Early in 1936 the company submitted a proposal to manufacture a primary trainer for the Air Corps,[152] which probably did not accept it for production.

In its search for a primary trainer on which to base its expanding training programs in the late 1930s, however, the government did consider St. Louis Aircraft's Model PT-1W, a conventional biplane with tandem open cockpits and a 225-horsepower Wright uncowled radial engine in an all-metal fuselage. This airplane had the distinction of being the "last original biplane design" submitted to the Army.[153] One example, designated the XPT-15, was bought in 1939,[154] followed by an evaluation batch of thirteen YPT-15s delivered in 1940.[155] Although somewhat archaic in comparison to the sleek low-wing monoplanes then in predominant use, the excellence of the model was attested by the very fact that the Army Air Corps was seriously interested in it.

St. Louis Aircraft was at that time also manufacturing a wide line of aircraft parts, including C-6, C-8, and C-9 balloon cars, blowers for observation balloons, airplane skis, and fuel tanks, as well as experimenting with its PT-LM-4, a two-place, open-cockpit, all-metal, monoplane acrobatic trainer.[156] During World War II, the corporation manufactured much the same equipment,[157] experimented ineffectively with troop-cargo gliders,[158] and completed production subcontracts for 350 Fairchild PT-23 two-place, low-wing, all-metal monoplane trainers, as well as thirteen Fairchild PT-19s by 1945.[159]

With the onset of the war, the aviation industry in St. Louis mushroomed into epic proportions, a phenomenon repeated all across the nation. The city's "Big Three" in airframe production were Curtiss-Wright, McDonnell, and Robertson, but a number of other plants engaged in widespread manufacturing of aircraft, parts, and flying accessories.

The most important of the "minor" industries was the Laister-Kauffmann Aircraft Corporation. When Germany startled the world by 1941 by introducing the use of gliders in its invasion of Crete, Jack Laister, a veteran St. Louis glider enthusiast, immediately put himself to work and submitted a design for a training model to the Army Technical Service Command. The preliminary draft was accepted and he was given a contract to build four experimental ships.[160]

A corporation was formed, and with a staff of three men, Laister began manufacturing the two-place training gliders at a building at

The erecting shop of St. Louis Aircraft, showing PT-23s in various stages of assembly in 1943, the height of World War II.

7710 Ivory Street, in September 1941.[161] Designated the TG-4, the trainer was 50 feet in span and 22 feet long. The company ultimately delivered three of the experimental models (XTG-4) to the Army Air Forces[162] and completed two contracts, each for 75 ships, of the production version (TG-4A),[163] as well as constructing three evaluation examples of the Coeppingen-designed TG-20, a one-man trainer.[164]

Laister-Kauffmann's success in the field of training gliders was so marked that the company was awarded a subcontract to manufacture a much larger, troop-carrying glider in December 1942, at which time the firm moved its base to the Arena at 5660 Oakland Avenue.[165] Known as the CG-4A, this cargo glider was a high-wing, fabric-covered ship of mixed wood and metal construction, and measured 48 feet 4 inches in length with a wingspan of 83 feet 8 inches. It could accommodate fifteen fully-equipped troops, including two serving as pilots, or a standard Army jeep, a one-quarter ton truck with a four-man crew, or a 75-millimeter howitzer and crew. The CG-4A was the most widely-used glider of the war.

It participated in the invasions of Sicily and France, as well as those of Burma and other areas of the Pacific Theater. The ship had been designed by the Waco Aircraft Company of Troy, Ohio, but fifteen other firms were engaged in its production, among them the Laister-Kauffmann Aircraft Corporation, which manufactured 310 of them during the war (of a total of 12,393 delivered).[166]

By February 1945, the St. Louis concern had plants at the Oakland Avenue Arena and at 3850 Laclede Avenue, with general offices at 6376 Laclede, and it was employing 1,300 people. Laister-Kauffmann was one of the largest of the companies in the nation engaged solely in the production of gliders. By that date, the firm was working on $1,747,273 in contracts to manufacture the CG-4A and to design the CG-10A, which was to be its proudest achievement.[167]

Named the "Trojan Horse," the CG-10A had the largest cargo space and payload of any glider ever developed in the United States up to that time. Jack Laister had been drafting the design since 1942, but he only achieved success late in 1944. The massive high-wing wooden ship was 67 feet long with a wingspan of 105 feet. It had a "cavernous" cargo interior 30 feet long, 7 feet high and 8½ feet wide, accessible through the huge "clamshell" doors under the tail. The "Trojan Horse" could carry six tons of air freight, an amount four times the capacity of the popular CG-4A. It could accommodate 42 fully-equipped troops, or a 2½-ton truck, or a 155-millimeter howitzer. It was the largest all-wood plane the Army had ever accepted.[168] After the initial prototype (XCG-10A),[169] only ten were delivered, however, before the end of the war forced the abandonment of the program.[170]

While Laister-Kauffmann Aircraft Corporation produced hundreds of gliders for the war effort, several St. Louis companies, most of them converted for that purpose, manufactured a broad variety of aircraft parts, equipment, and accessories. By February 1945, a total of 98 firms within the city were working on $82,119,483 in contracts for aviation supplies.[171] The Kilgen Organ Company at 4632 West Florissant Avenue was building turret seats, navigator tables, and berths for combat planes on a $125,000 government contract. The American Stove Company had a $3,800,000 order from the Air Technical Service Command for auxiliary fuel tanks which could be jettisoned in emergencies. Society Brand Hat Company was using its facilities to manufacture $183,320 worth of summer flying helmets. Emerson Electric Manufacturing Company at 1842 Washington Avenue had a $5,500,000 order for airplane engines. Anheuser-Busch Brewing Company at 721 Pestalozzi Street was making wing parts and rudder equipment worth $15,000.[172]

Just as in the cities of the rest of the United States, St. Louis' industries were using their full potential for the strengthening of the nation's air might. Only five plants were actually producing complete airframes (Curtiss-Wright, McDonnell, Robertson, Laister-Kauffmann, and St. Louis Aircraft), but a legion of firms was engaged in turning out aircraft components of all descriptions.

On August 14, 1945, the government canceled nine billion dollars worth of its nationwide contracts for aerial equipment.[173] With that, the aviation industry in St. Louis all but came to a standstill. Curtiss-Wright withdrew from the city, the emergency wartime plants returned to the manufacture of peacetime goods, Robertson and Laister-Kauffmann halted their glider production, the St. Louis Aircraft Corporation closed its doors,[174] and St. Louis itself aeronautically became a one-company (McDonnell Aircraft) city.

The many aircraft plants and aeronautical enterprises which had from time to time made St. Louis their home from 1858 to 1945 contributed substantially to the city's economic and aerial well-being. A portion of them seemed relatively insignificant, at least from a national viewpoint, in that they produced few planes or functioned for only a short time. Such operations, however, as the Benoist Aircraft Company, Monocoupe-Lambert, and even H.E. Honeywell's balloon firm can only be called "minor industries" in comparison to the much broader and more important Robertson, Curtiss-Wright, and McDonnell complexes, which loomed much larger in that field in the city. The smaller companies, nevertheless, were important in their own right, for without them St. Louis could have laid no true claim to consideration as a vibrant center of air industry.

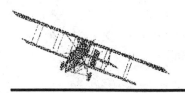

XV
Robertson and Curtiss, 1919-1945

AMONG THE MOST IMPORTANT of the air industries of St. Louis was the complex which included the Robertson Aircraft Corporation, the Curtiss-Robertson Airplane Manufacturing Company, and the Curtiss-Wright Corporation. Its significance was of such maximum moment that without these three units, the city would not have been the center of lasting air industry that it is.

The story of the Robertson Aircraft Corporation is not unlike that of the Benoist Aircraft Company, for each became involved in a multitude of aeronautical enterprises. Both William (1893-1943) and Frank (1898-1934) Robertson, the founders of the firm, learned to fly in the Army during World War I, although they saw no active combat, inasmuch as the Armistice canceled their orders for overseas duty.[1] After the two were mustered out in February 1919,[2] they tried the secular business world for a time, but their taste for flying determined their careers. In April 1919 they borrowed $1,800 from their father, purchased a war surplus "Jenny," painted "Robertson Aircraft Company" on its side, and began their flying operations.[3]

A typical example of their initial activity was an exhibition of stunting by Lieutenant William B. Robertson, before a crowd of several thousand people at Creve Coeur Lake on August 22, 1920.

St. Louis Post-Dispatch

Major William Bryan Robertson, St. Louis aviation pioneer.

In the modest air show that day, he executed loops, Immelmann turns, tailspins, and nosedives, climaxing his routine with an impressive "falling leaf" by dropping with a dead engine from a height of 300 feet to treetop level, restarting the engine, and landing gracefully on the shore.[4]

The brothers maintained their headquarters at the Forest Park airmail field, and when the mail service was abandoned in 1920, they purchased the hangar and its related equipment.[5] In February 1921, the fledgling concern was formally incorporated by the State of Missouri with an initial capitalization of $15,000, most of which was represented by their Curtiss "Jenny," an extra 90-horsepower OX-5 engine, and their airfield facilities.[6] William B. Robertson became president of the corporation and his brother Frank vice president.[7]

By 1922, Robertson Aircraft Corporation was operating from the St. Louis Flying Field, which Bill Robertson had helped establish in 1920[8] and on which he had landed the first plane shortly thereafter,[9] as well as at Forest Park. They maintained hangars and repair shops at each location and owned an impressive fleet of seven airplanes (five Curtiss "Jennies," one Curtiss "Oriole," and one Sturtevant biplane). The company was enjoying a prosperous business of carrying sightseers, hauling passengers on short hops throughout the Midwest, and "barnstorming" at county fairs and similar gatherings. During that year, the brothers made 5,000 flights, flew 35,000 air miles, and carried 1,000 passengers and 3,000 pounds of freight. Their rates averaged 50¢ to $1.00 per mile

George J. Herwig Collection

The hangar-headquarters of the Missouri Air National Guard.

for inter-city trips, with a flat rate of 35¢ per pound of freight.[10] The company's reputation and its bank account were growing rapidly.

During the following year, the elder Robertson, the driving force behind the young corporation, organized a number of his wartime associates and aeronautically inclined acquaintances into a military flying unit. On June 23, 1923, the Army recognized it as the 110th Observation Squadron, 35th Division Aviation, Missouri National Guard. William B. Robertson, with the rank of major, was its first commanding officer, holding that post until 1924.[11] The unit trained at Lambert Field in Curtiss "Jennies" through the 1920s, advanced to Douglas O-38 observation planes in the 1930s, saw service with Bell P-39 "Airacobras" and Curtiss P-40 "Warhawks" in the Pacific during World War II, used Republic F-84F "Thunderstreaks" in the 1950s,[12] and continued its training with North American F-100 "Super Sabres" in the 1960s.[13] Major Robertson's zeal in founding and nurturing the squadron was in large part responsible for its initial success and later eminence. It was fitting that he be commemorated when the unit's headquarters at Lambert Field was formally dedicated on May 17, 1959, as "Robertson Air National Guard Base."[14]

In the same manner as Tom W. Benoist, William and Frank Robertson, along with their younger brother Dan, operated a flying school, which they had opened shortly after they began their aerial activities.[15] As a special offer for June, July, and August, 1925, the company reduced its price for a two-week course, which guaranteed "to teach a student to fly and successfully operate an airplane by

The Von Hoffmann (left) and Robertson hangars at Lambert Field during the early 1930s.

himself, regardless of the number of flying hours required,'' to $100.[16] The response was so overwhelming, however, that the Robertsons decided to continue the low rate indefinitely. By December 1925 the company had graduated 49 students from its school and proudly reported ''that not one of them has ever blown a tire, nosed over, or broken a propeller. . . .''[17]

During the previous year, the corporation had leased four 120' by 66' hangars at Lambert Field as its base of operations. In 1924, the Robertsons made 1,926 sightseeing, stunt, and shuttle-service flights for a total of 33,705 air miles with 1,200 passengers and several hundred pounds of freight.[18] Like Tom Benoist's Aerosco, the brothers also maintained at that time a large stock of aerial parts and supplies of all descriptions. Shortly after World War I, they virtually cornered the market on airplane engines by purchasing several hundred 90-horsepower OX-5s, the most popular model of that era, from government surplus.[19] By 1924, the company had also acquired 35 airplanes, which it was refitting in its repair shops and offering for sale.[20] Despite a costly fire that year which destroyed their main hangar and $60,000 worth of airplanes and accessories, painfully recalling Benoist's severe conflagration of 1911,[21] the company recovered quickly and continued its operations.[22]

Even though it suffered a second fire the following year, the firm managed to maintain assets of $250,000.[23] In 1925 Robertson Aircraft Corporation had in stock an aerial armada of 333 ready-to-fly airplanes of all types: ''Standards,'' ''Jennies'' (ranging in price from $750 for the airframe alone to $1,500 for a model with a 150-horsepower Hispano-Suiza engine), ''Canucks'' (Canadian version of the ''Jenny''), ''Orioles,'' DH-4s, ''Spads,'' and many others. A contemporary advertisement urged buyers to ''Come in and take your pick.''[24] During that year, the company sold 76 planes and was employing 22 full-time mechanics to rebuild its ships and ready them for delivery.[25]

In cooperation with the Nicholas-Beazley Airplane Company of Marshall, Missouri,[26] the corporation had also purchased by that time 450 government-surplus "Standards," in which it had planned to install new controls, struts, fittings, gas tanks, instruments, landing gear, and accessories as part of its customary reconditioning procedure.[27] The company then had supply warehouses at San Antonio, Houston, New Orleans, Fort Wayne, Kansas City, and St. Louis.[28] The operation was so vast that in December 1925 the concern increased its capitalization to $500,000.[29] By 1926, Robertson Aircraft was "as well known as any aviation organization in the United States."[30] Its high repute was due in large part to the fact that it was the nation's largest aeronautical supply house.[31]

The fame the young company achieved so rapidly came equally as a result of its activities in the airmail area. Sustained service of official United States airmail had begun on May 15, 1918, from New York to Washington,[32] with St. Louis joining the program for a time shortly thereafter.[33] For the next eight years, the airmail was managed and maintained directly by the government. By 1924, however, it was felt that the service had suitably matured and that private operation of the endeavor would be both feasible and proper. Congress responded with Representative Clyde Kelly's "bill to encourage commercial aviation and to authorize the postmaster general to contract for air mail service." The most important clause (Section 4) of the measure stipulated:

> That the Postmaster General is authorized to contract with any individual, firm, or corporation for the transportation of air mail by aircraft between such points as he may designate at a rate not to exceed four-fifths of the revenues derived from such first-class mail.[34]

The House of Representatives passed the resolution (H.R. 7064) on December 18, 1924, by a vote of 292-15, with 125 not voting.[35] The Senate followed by acclamation on January 27, 1925,[36] and President Coolidge signed it into law six days later.[37] The Kelly Act was "the starting gun for commercial aviation."[38]

In mid-1925 Postmaster General Harry S. New placed nationwide advertisements for the first eight feeder routes of the novel system. On October 7, he opened the bids and awarded the contracts. Only five of the routes were consigned, however, for the bids and potential operators for the remaining three were found unsatisfactory.[39] Contract Air Mail Route #1 (Boston-New York) went to Colonial Airlines, CAM-3 (Chicago-Dallas and Fort Worth) to National Air Transport, CAM-4 (Salt Lake City-Los Angeles) to Western Air

Express, CAM-5 (Elko, Nevada-Pasco, Washington) to Varney Speed Lines, and CAM-2 (Chicago-St. Louis) to Robertson Aircraft Corporation, which bested both National Air Transport and General Airways to win the honor.[40] Said Postmaster General New on October 7, 1925:

> The awarding of contracts this day for the carrying of mail by air transport over five routes in widely separated sections of the country marks an epoch in the history of the American post office. Upon the result of the enterprise this day entered depends the future of aerial transport in the United States.[41]

The Robertsons won their bid by agreeing to carry mail for 67.5% of the postage income.[42] By that time, the brothers were well qualified to handle their task. William had accumulated 2,500 hours in the air and Frank 2,000.[43] Their capable management of their supply house, flying school, and aerial taxi service had earned them an enviable reputation in aeronautical circles. It was fitting that their corporation was one of the five firms selected to initiate the unique program.

The Robertsons, occupied with administration and management, did not fly the mail ships themselves, but instead hired three pilots to perform that task: Philip Love, Thomas Nelson, and the lanky Charles Lindbergh, who would soon make history of his own. With five 450-horsepower de Havilland DH-4s and four 160-horsepower Curtiss "Orioles,"[44] the company began the operation on April 15, 1926. As chief pilot, Lindbergh had the honor of making the inaugural flight from Maywood Field, Chicago, to Lambert Field, St. Louis.[45]

Robertson Aircraft Corporation offered daily service over the 278-mile route, except for Saturday and Sunday northbound and Sunday and Monday southbound. The morning plane left Chicago at approximately 6 o'clock (when the overnight mail plane arrived there from New York), and after stops at Peoria and Springfield, arrived in St. Louis at 9:15. The afternoon plane left St. Louis at 4:00, and with stops at Springfield and Peoria, arrived in Chicago at 7:15.[46] From late autumn to early spring, the morning flight began and the evening flight ended in dangerous darkness. Within two years after the service was initiated, however, bright beacon searchlights were stationed every ten miles over the route, and at twenty-mile intervals lighted emergency landing fields, each manned by a caretaker, were situated, all at government expense.[47] Despite the many hazards they encountered, the Robertson pilots, like those on the earlier St. Louis-Chicago run,[48] were remarkably efficient in the performance of their duty. During the first five months of the operation they completed 98 percent of their flights.[49]

George J. Herwig Collection

Insets of Philip Love (left) and a baby-faced Charles A. Lindbergh, are in this photo of Robertson's DH-4 mail planes. Lindbergh was the chief pilot.

When the novelty of the service wore off after a few weeks, the volume of mail measurably declined and the canvas sacks often outweighed their contents.[50] Most private contractors lost money during the first year of operation. While the average income of all the routes was 42.9¢ per mile, the average cost ranged from 50¢ to 85¢ per mile.[51] During its first full year of airmail activity, from April 15, 1926 to April 15, 1927, the Robertson Aircraft Corporation received $71,664.83 from the Post Office Department for carrying the mail.[52] That sum, the fifth highest of the thirteen contractors then in operation, probably did not cover the firm's expenditures. Government action in regard to better rates and more favorable subsidies, together with an increase in public utilization of the service, earned more equitable profits for the carriers in the ensuing years.

At the time that it acquired CAM-2, Robertson Aircraft had a book value of $200,000.[53] Although his mail run had depleted his resources somewhat, William Robertson decided to expand his enterprises by entering the area of actual airframe manufacturing itself. During the summer of 1927, Major Robertson, along with Harry Hall Knight and Harold M. Bixby (who were then also engaged in persuading Mahoney Aircraft to settle in St. Louis),[54] conferred in New York with President Clement M. Keys of the Curtiss Airplane and Motor Company as to the feasibility of constructing private planes in St. Louis.[55] Impressed by the current "Lindbergh Boom" which was giving great impetus to that phase of the aircraft industry, Keys gave his assent to the project in the autumn of 1927.[56]

The proposed company would construct a three-place cabin monoplane which Curtiss engineers were already designing. It was known as the Curtiss "Robin." The celebrated manufacturing concern had long been building military planes for the government at its two plants in Buffalo and Garden City, New York. Curtiss executives, however, felt that it would be more practical and less cumbersome to open a new branch in St. Louis rather than to utilize their existing factories to manufacture their offering for the commercial field.[57]

An industrial survey of the St. Louis area was initiated on October 6, 1927, for the location of the new Curtiss subsidiary, which was to be called the Curtiss Robertson Airplane Manufacturing Company.[58] Early the following year, a Missouri corporation was capitalized at $500,000 to handle the venture,[59] with the Curtiss-Keys group holding 50 percent of the stock.[60] On January 28, 1928, William Robertson resigned from his position with Robertson Aircraft to head the new company. He remained a member of the board of directors, but his brother Frank assumed the presidency in his stead.[61]

On the same day, Robertson Flying Services, under Frank Robertson, was brought into being to assume control of the company's flying school, aerial photography operation, and general service functions. Robertson Aircraft Corporation, also under the younger brother, was to continue as a separate entity and would devote itself primarily to the Chicago-St. Louis airmail run.[62] Despite the loss of Major Robertson, the company maintained its varied interests and enjoyed considerable prosperity.

The celebrated Robertson warehouse was as bountiful as ever. In February 1928, Frank Robertson consummated an earlier agreement which may have been a major factor in attracting the Curtiss interests to St. Louis. The young executive gained a financial windfall when he sold to the incipient Curtiss-Robertson concern "virtually the [world's] entire remaining stock" of old, reliable, 90-horsepower OX-5 engines, 1,142 in all, for $400,000. They were to be fully reconditioned and turned over for use in the proposed

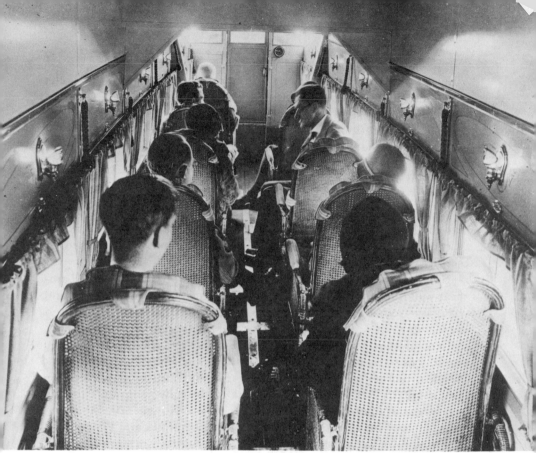

The cabin of a new Ford Trimotor, photographed at Lambert Field during the early 1930s.

"Robin."[63]

CAM-2 was also beginning to show a profit for the corporation. Using five de Havillands, three Douglas biplanes, a "Standard," and a Waco, company pilots carried 34,772 pounds of mail and ten passengers between St. Louis and Chicago in 1927, for a gross income from the government of $138,714.26.[64] On April 6, 1928, the corporation expanded its service over the route by signing a contract with the American Express Company for the rapid transit of air freight between the two cities. The rates were lower than for regular airmail (25¢ per quarter-pound, with a minimum charge of $1.00), and the medium was thereby expected to attract a large business in such items as photograph and film transport when it went into operation on May 1.[65] On April 1, 1928, Robertson Aircraft had taken measures to step up its passenger service and was averaging three per day over the mail run by that time.[66]

The notable achievements and bright prospects of the young airline attracted the attention of a number of financiers from St. Louis and Detroit. In the spring of 1928 the Robertsons sold CAM-2 to Arnold Stifel, a local stockbroker, and his associates for $300,000, a handsome profit on their original investment of $30,000.[67] Keeping its initial name, Robertson Aircraft Corporation was then reorganized at a capitalization of $1,000,000. Arnold Stifel became president of the company, Frank Robertson vice president, and H.H. Perkins secretary-treasurer. Major William Robertson, still president of the Curtiss-Robertson concern, took a position on the board of directors.[68] Fortified with new money and new leadership, the corporation moved quickly to expand its mail and passenger service.

Stifel planned to spend $250,000 on the company's base at Lambert Field to provide improved hangars, ticket offices, express and baggage rooms, a lunch counter, and a waiting room. Increased passenger, mail, and freight service was scheduled, and to that end, a fleet of fourteen huge, all-metal Ford trimotors, worth $50,000 each, was to be acquired.[69] Four of the luxurious ships, the largest single order ever placed with Ford up to that time, were delivered in August 1928.[70] The inaugural flights of the new program with the twelve-passenger "giants" took place on August 20. A round trip between St. Louis and Chicago, via Springfield and Peoria, was scheduled for each day but Sunday. Such flights were to carry only special mail, with the regular airmail departing on the customary morning and evening hops in the aging de Havillands.[71]

On August 1, 1928, new mail rates had gone into effect. Instead of a flat 10¢ per ounce, the government set the rate at 5¢ for the first one-half ounce, plus 10¢ for each additional ounce.[72] That day, the poundage on Robertson's CAM-2 rose 350 percent to 229 pounds, but the volume was expected to decrease to about 150 pounds daily after the novelty had passed. This was still a 100 percent improvement over the pre-August situation.[73] Public usage and profits were progressing.

Under the auspices of Arnold Stifel (or perhaps shortly before the company's reorganization), Robertson Aircraft acquired a new mail line in mid-1928, Contract Air Mail Route #28 — St. Louis to Omaha via Kansas City. In preparation for the new service, slated to begin on January 1, 1929, the corporation purchased one of Von Hoffmann Aircraft Company's two hangars at Lambert Field for $25,000, and placed orders with various manufacturers for 18 airplanes for $225,000, among them two Travel Air OX-5s, two Ryan "Broughams,"[74] and three Stearman monoplanes, the last equipped to carry 500 pounds of mail with space for four passengers.[75] The actions of Robertson Aircraft were repeated throughout the nation. In such a manner did airlines emerge and, with increased public support, grow into the vast operations of a later era.

Arnold Stifel and his associates had hardly commenced activity with their new concern when it was again reorganized. On October 6, 1928, the huge Universal Aviation Corporation, capitalized at $7,000,000, came into existence under Louis H. Piper of Minneapolis.[76] It was formed by the merger of fourteen substantial aircraft companies, among them Robertson Aircraft Corporation.[77] The new firm would make its headquarters in St. Louis, a central point from which it could supervise its subsidiaries efficiently.[78]

At the birth of Universal, Frank Robertson regained the presidency of his company from Arnold Stifel. With the giant corporation's plans for coast-to-coast airline service, he had hopes of acquiring two additional mail routes: Chicago-Atlanta and St. Louis-Evansville, Indiana.[79] Although these desires failed to materialize, activity on CAM-2 increased substantially in 1928. During that year, Robertson Aircraft carried 56,300 pounds of mail over that route, as well as 2,492 passengers between St. Louis and Chicago, and St. Louis and Kansas City.[80]

In addition to assuming control of Robertson's mail runs, Universal Aviation acquired the company's flying school at Lambert Field, renaming it Universal Flying School. By 1929 the new managers offered a broad curriculum of courses leading toward several licenses: a program for private pilots for $545, for limited commercial pilots for $1,265, for transport pilots for $3,945, for mechanics for $200, for aviation welders for $125, and even a correspondence course on general aeronautical data for $75[81] — quite a change from the simple lessons Robertson had offered for $100 during the summer of 1925. This school at St. Louis' municipal airfield was one of ten throughout the country which Universal had taken over by 1929.[82] Dan Robertson, the least known of the three celebrated brothers, continued to head the St. Louis flying school until early in 1929, and then departed on February 7 of that year for Mexico City to become the personal pilot for wealthy aviation promoter Eduardo y Turbide.[83]

Frank Robertson had also by that time left his position as head of the family operation. His successor to the presidency of Robertson Aircraft Corporation was H.H. Perkins, formerly secretary-treasurer of the firm at the Stifel reorganization. On March 27, 1929, Perkins made public a list of impressive statistics concerning Robertson Air-

One of two new Fokker Trimotors was christened on May 1, 1929, marking the inaugural flight of the St. Louis-Omaha airmail run. Mayor Victor Miller is in the foregound (in the light coat).

craft. From April 15, 1926, to January 1, 1929, company pilots had carried 120,735 pounds of mail over CAM-2 between St. Louis and Chicago. They had flown 372,815 air miles of a scheduled total of 384,850, for an outstanding efficiency performance of 97.02 percent, the highest of the 24 private airmail lines then in operation. Only rain, snow, sleet, and fog had prevented a perfect score.[84]

While it continued to improve its mail and passenger service over CAM-2, Universal's subsidiary inaugurated its second route, CAM-28, from St. Louis to Omaha via Kansas City on May 1, 1929, four months after its announced opening. Two six-place Fokker trimotors initiated the service, at rates of $32 one way to Kansas City, with a $60 charge for a round trip, and $48 one way to Omaha, with a $90 fee for a round trip from St. Louis.[85] Within a few months, Universal pushed its line to the West Coast, and on October 1, 1929, the city's first night airmail flight to that area was undertaken.[86] St. Louis was rapidly assuming a position of key importance in the field of commercial aviation.

As the growing airlines throughout the nation crystallized into a permanent and vital facet of the American scene, immense corporations merged together to control the vast industry. The first of the real giants was Aviation Corporation (Avco), a $200,000,000 holding company which was formed on May 17, 1929, under Graham Grosvenor of New York. Among the firms of which it assumed control was Universal Aviation Corporation and all of its subsidiaries, including Robertson Aircraft Corporation.[87] On February 8, 1930, Avco's operating unit, American Airways (later American Airlines) came into existence.[88] The various routes of the Robertson-Universal enterprise were then made part of American's widespread system, which eventually included a network of 6,293 miles from the Northeast through the Midwest to the Pacific Coast.[89]

By that time, Major William B. Robertson, the founder of the concern which in only ten years had grown to become one of the key components of the world's largest airline system, was engaged in completing his stint in the manufacturing end of the aircraft industry. The firm he headed, the Curtiss-Robertson Airplane Manufacturing Company, was then the proud producer of a highly successful airplane — the Curtiss "Robin."

The first two prototypes of the model had been built at the Curtiss factory on Long Island in the spring of 1928. The requisite tools and dies were then shipped to St. Louis to continue the operation.[90] Production at the new $60,000 Curtiss-Robertson plant had been slated to begin on April 1 of that year,[91] but it did not actually commence until July,[92] and the first St. Louis-built "Robin" took to the air on August 7, 1928, in time to publicize the airport bond issue being voted upon that same day.[93]

At times it is difficult to determine the origin of the names manufacturers give to the aircraft they produce. Such is not the case with the "Robin," for it logically joined the "bird series" Curtiss was constructing during that era, represented by the "Oriole," the "Falcon," the "Hawk," and the "Condor."[94] The title was in keeping with the personality of the plane, for while the "Hawk" was intended for the screaming pursuit of enemy aircraft, the "Robin" was a peaceful ship dedicated to roaming the countryside and serving civil aviators.

Designed for the private owner, the "Robin" was a three-place, high-wing cabin monoplane with a fabric-covered, tubular-steel fuselage. The original version was 25 feet 10 inches long, 7 feet 10 inches high, and 41 feet in span, and it was powered by a 90-horsepower Curtiss OX-5 engine. The "OX-5 Robin," as it was termed, had a fuel capacity of 50 gallons in its two wing tanks, giving a a range of 556 miles at a cruising speed of 90 miles per hour, ten miles per hour less than its maximum speed.[95] This model sold for $3,800,[96] a relatively modest price for 1928, and the plane proved popular and its sales were widespread. "A common color was orange, with black trim, and the Robin was a handsome airplane — no sweeping 'jet' lines, but a look of rugged and honest simplicity."[97] The original Curtiss "Robin" was "the only serious attempt to design a truly 'modern' airplane for the war surplus OX-5."[98]

Two other versions of the model were also produced in quantity by Curtiss-Robertson. Late in 1928, the "Challenger Robin" was introduced. Its dimensions were much the same as the OX-5 model, but it was equipped with a 170-horsepower Curtiss Challenger engine, which greatly increased its overall performance and raised its price to $7,500.[99] The company even sold a half-dozen of these planes rigged with twin floats for water service.[100]

The third version, begun in 1929, was called the "J-6 Robin," for it was outfitted with a 165-horsepower Wright Whirlwind J-6 engine. Its basic configuration was almost identical to the earlier two models but, like the "Challenger Robin," it could attain a top speed of 118 miles per hour and its performance was much more efficient than the original "OX-5 Robin."[101]

Late in 1929 the company began production of a four-place "Robin" equipped with a 185-horsepower Challenger engine and priced at $7,995. The Depression was rapidly spreading over the nation, however, and few of these more luxurious models were sold before production of the ship ceased entirely.[102]

In the year and one-half that the "Robin" was manufactured, from August 1928 to December 1929, a total of 749 planes were constructed (most of them with OX-5 engines), a record for the mass production of a single basic design.[103] Along with the "Monocoupe," the "Brougham," and a few other models, the "Robin" enjoyed unbridled popularity during the "Lindbergh Boom" and was sought by private aviators throughout the country. The success of the ship made it the pride of Curtiss-Robertson and solidified the endeavors of that corporation.

One of the primary factors responsible for the peculiar popularity of the "Robin" was the widespread publicity it received as a result of its spectacular achievements. The first notable accomplishment came on December 17, 1928, when Dale Jackson, a test pilot for Curtiss-Robertson, dizzily executed in succession the record number of 417 barrel rolls in an "OX-5 Robin" over Lambert Field.[104] He would later use a "Robin" to establish more impressive marks in another aeronautical area. Five months after Jackson's exhibition, Laurie Younge of Jacksonville, Florida, set a solo non-refueling endurance record of 25 hours and 5 minutes in another "Robin." [105] It was in this aspect of aerial activity that the plane was to receive its most celebrated accolades.

In the late 1920s and early 1930s, an unprecedented craze of endurance flying gripped American aviation. The competition was begun in earnest when Major Carl A. Spaatz and Captain Ira C. Eaker (both to become generals a decade later) circled a fuel-laden Fokker trimotor, named the *Question Mark* (for their uncertainty as to its potential), over Los Angeles for 150 hours, 40 minutes and 15 seconds, from January 1 to January 7, 1929.[106] This score was bettered on May 26 of that same year, when Reginald Robbins and James Kelly landed their Ryan B-1 "Brougham" *Fort Worth* with a new record of 172 hours, more than a full week in the air.[107] Little more than a month later, Byron K. Newcomb and Roy L. Mitchell took off in their Stinson SM-1, *City of Cleveland*, on June 29, 1929, and came down 174 hours and 59 minutes later with the endurance crown.[108] Even as they landed, however, Loran W. Mendall and Ronald B. Reinhart were already tearing the laurels from their grasp. The two pilots completed their attempt at Culver City, California, in their *Angeleno* biplane on July 12 with a new mark of 246 hours, 43 minutes, and 32 seconds.[109] It was this record that two St. Louisans set out to surpass.

The very next day, Dale "Red" Jackson and Forrest "Obie" O'Brine, both test pilots for the Curtiss-Robertson Airplane Manufacturing Company, took to the air in the *St. Louis Robin #1* at Lambert Field in the presence of 1,000 spectators at 7:17 a.m. July 13, 1929. The flight was primarily intended as a test for the plane's 170-horsepower Challenger engine, but the fliers declared that they might also essay an endurance attempt.[110] Their airplane was a standard "Challenger Robin," except for a few superficial changes: a catwalk had been fitted from the cockpit to the engine to permit periodic inspection and assist in the necessary refueling; and the two rear seats had been removed for the installation of an extra 125-gallon gasoline tank, upon which were placed blankets and a mattress where one flyer could rest as the other piloted the ship from the single bucket seat in the front of the cabin. The two had flipped a coin to determine who would win the chair for the first four-hour shift. O'Brine won and it was he who piloted the plane at takeoff.[111]

Their refueling "tanker" was another "Challenger Robin," flown by C. Ray Wassall and P.V. "Shorty" Chaffee. At regular intervals, Wassall pulled his ship above the *St. Louis Robin #1* and Chaffee lowered the refueling hose to one of the endurance fliers,

St. Louis Post-Dispatch

A Post-Dispatch *staff photographer made this photo on July 26, 1929, of Forrest O'Brine on a catwalk servicing the engine of his Curtiss "Robin," as it was setting a new world endurance record above Lambert Field. The plane is being flown by his partner, Dale Jackson. O'Brine is not wearing a parachute.*

together with a bucket containing sandwiches, cold chicken, fruit, coffee, milk, newspapers, and any desired messages.[112] Jackson and O'Brine made a total of 77 contacts with Wassall and Chaffee, 48 of them for refueling. In their two and one-half weeks in the air, they covered 25,200 miles and used 3,590 gallons of gasoline.[113]

For a time, the *St. Louis Robin #1* was accompanied by the *Missouri Robin,* flown by Joseph Hammer, a mail pilot, and W. Gentry Shelton, a wealthy air enthusiast. They had taken off from Lambert Field on July 17 but were forced down by an oil leak on July 22 after 117 hours and 18 minutes in the air.[114] Two other crews in separate cities had also joined the duration derby by that time. The Houston duo, however, suffered engine failure after 233 hours, and the Minneapolis pilots were killed when their plane crashed in its 156th hour.[115] Jackson and O'Brine continued their seemingly endless circuit over St. Louis city and county.

They had their hopes set on the 500-hour mark, but Major William

Robertson, the sponsor of the flight, ordered them down on the eighteenth day, explaining that the

> objects of the test flight have been fully accomplished, as the Curtiss Challenger motor has more than proved itself, and the Robin airplane has proved itself, and the technical data that was wanted has been secured.[116]

Jackson and O'Brine obediently came down at Lambert Field at 7:38:30 p.m. July 30, 1929, with a new world's endurance record of 420 hours, 21 minutes, and 30 seconds,[117] almost double the previous mark and a notable contrast with the two earlier duration scores recorded in St. Louis: A.L. Welch's performance of 3 hours, 11 minutes, and 55 seconds on October 11, 1910, at Kinloch Park,[118] and Howard Gill's mark of 4 hours, 16 minutes, and 40 seconds at the same airfield on October 19, 1911.[119]

Jackson and O'Brine had another motive for landing short of their goal. On July 29, their close friend George Lea Lambert, the son of St. Louis' foremost aviation promoter, suffered a fatal crash at the municipal airport while giving an aerobatic flying lesson to one of the students of the Von Hoffmann Flying School, where he was company vice president. Although the endurance fliers did not witness the accident, they read of it in the newspapers delivered to them and expressed their intention of attending the funeral.[120]

For their momentous achievement, Dale Jackson and Forrest O'Brine were well paid. The Curtiss Airplane and Motor Company gave them $100 for each hour above the Mendall-Reinhart mark of 246 hours, 43 minutes, and 32 seconds. Famous-Barr department store and the B.F. Goodrich Company each offered them $100 for every day above the previous record, and similar contributions came from several other establishments in the city, together with numerous contracts for personal appearances at state fairs and vaudeville houses. In addition, the two pilots continued to draw their normal salary from Curtiss-Robertson, with the customary "overtime" bonuses. In all, Jackson and O'Brine received more than $31,255 before they had even completed their flight.[121]

The impressive record of 420 hours, 21 minutes, and 30 seconds stood for nearly a year before John and Kenneth Hunter of Sparta, Illinois, kept their second-hand Stinson "Detroiter" *City of Chicago* in the air from June 11 to July 4, 1930, for a time of 553 hours, 41 minutes, and 30 seconds. The endeavor was a family affair in every respect, for their two brothers, Walter and Albert, manned the refueling ship. The Hunters had hoped to stay up even longer, but an overheated engine forced them down. They had, nevertheless,

The Hunter family endurance team, from left: Albert, John, Irene, Kenneth, and Walter, in front of their City of Chicago *after they had captured a world record in 1930.*

gained the crown they sought.[122]

Not to be outdone, Dale Jackson and Forrest O'Brine set out 2½ weeks later to win back their title. The two took to the air at Lambert Field on July 21, 1930, at 7:11 a.m. in the *Greater St. Louis,* a "Challenger Robin" which Major Robertson had given them as a reward for their earlier feat. Unlike the 1929 effort, this attempt was not sponsored by the aircraft manufacturer, for they had left their test pilot positions and were operating on their own under the auspices of the Shamrock Oil and Gasoline Company, which would pay them $100 for each hour above the Hunters' mark. They had hoped to pass the 1,000-hour barrier, but a broken crankcase forced them down on August 17 at 6:39:30 a.m. The *Greater St. Louis* had, however, set a new world's record of 647 hours, 28 minutes, and 30 seconds.[123]

Although 25,000 expectant bystanders had greeted them at Lambert Field on July 30, 1929,[124] a surprised crowd of only 300 was on hand when they landed on August 17, 1930, with their second re-

Jackson and O'Brine are about to take off for their second world endurance record, again in a Curtiss "Robin."

cord. As earlier, nevertheless, the venture had been a lucrative one. In addition to the Shamrock greenery ($9,300), the pilots received $1,500 for the Movietone News rights to their flight, as well as several thousand dollars in contracts from state fairs throughout the Midwest — more than $39,000 in all. The reward was worthy of their achievement, for in addition to setting a world's endurance record, Jackson and O'Brine became the only fliers, at least of that era, to regain the duration crown after having once lost it. [125]

The wondrous "Robin" and its reliable Challenger engine had been the prime reasons for their impressive endurance feats. The ship was also responsible for the last great endurance flight of that decade. From June 4 to July 1, 1935, Fred and Algene Key of Meridian, Mississippi, piloted their Curtiss "Robin" *Ole Miss* to a new record of 653 hours and 34 minutes, barely surpassing the mark established by the St. Louisans five years earlier. [126] The indomitable Jackson and O'Brine might have attempted a third assault at the title had they been able. Dale Jackson, however, had been killed in a plane crash during an air race in Miami, Florida, on January 6, 1932. Captain Forrest O'Brine would suffer the same fate while taking off in a dive bomber at El Paso, Texas, on June 19, 1944. [127] During the age of the duration derbies, they had been the greatest of all.

Douglas ("Wrong Way") Corrigan starts his 9-year-old "Robin" down the runway of New York's Floyd Bennett Field enroute to Ireland nonstop in mid-August 1938.

While its endurance accomplishments gained the "Robin" its most notable fame, the plane was also involved in an event equally spectacular. In 1938, Douglas Corrigan used a nine-year-old "J-6 Robin" when he made his controversial crossing of the Atlantic Ocean.[128] The Bureau of Air Commerce had refused to sanction his planned transoceanic flight, so Corrigan solemnly announced that he would make a transcontinental hop from New York to Los Angeles instead. He took off from New York, however, and arrived in Dublin, Ireland, 28 hours and 13 minutes later, stoutly maintaining that his compass had been 180 degrees in error and that cloud cover had prevented him from realizing that he was over water and not land. For his "mistake" the aviator served a token five-day flying suspension aboard ship on his return home, and forever thereafter was known as "Wrong Way" Corrigan. [129]

While the "Robin" was its most celebrated product, Curtiss-Robertson had another horse in its stable. The second model the company constructed was the "Thrush," which was unveiled in 1929, its production overlapping that of its predecessor.[130] It was essentially a six-place "Robin," for its outward appearance was much the same. The "Thrush" was a high-wing cabin monoplane with a fuselage of fabric-covered "duralumin." It was 32 feet 4 inches long, 9 feet 3 inches high, and 48 feet in span. It was powered by a 170-horsepower Curtiss Challenger engine. The maximum speed of the ship was 110 miles per hour and at a cruising rate of 94 miles per hour it had a range of 1,015 miles. [131]

Three prototypes were built at the Curtiss factory on Long Island in June 1929, and after testing, production was initiated at St. Louis.[132] During the winter of 1929-1930, however, Curtiss-Robertson, which employed 508 people then,[133] fabricated only ten "Thrushes" before the program was canceled.[134] Its listed price of $10,000[135] was a bit too high for the sportsmen of a nation in the midst of economic collapse.

In the same month that the "Thrush" had been developed, a major reorganization of the company had taken place. On June 26, 1929, Curtiss Airplane and Motor Company merged with Wright Aeronautical Corporation, thereby ironically drawing together the names of aviation's foremost antagonists (although neither was personally affiliated with the venture) into the $70,000,000 Curtiss-Wright Corporation.[136] Among the twelve prominent subsidiaries involved in the transaction were Keystone Aircraft, Travel Air, Moth Aircraft, and Curtiss-Robertson.[137] In the power shake-up which followed, the Curtiss-Robertson Airplane Manufacturing Company and the Travel Air Company were combined in 1930 under the name Curtiss-Wright Airplane Company to produce commercial aircraft in St. Louis. Walter Beech became president of the new firm, with Ralph Damon and William B. Robertson vice presidents.[138] Under this management the St. Louis plant continued its output of civil aircraft.

In the spring of 1930, perhaps after a disagreement with the other executives, Major Robertson withdrew from the organization and joined his brother Frank to form the Robertson Airplane Service Company. In April of that year they began a daily air passenger service from St. Louis to New Orleans using Ryan "Broughams."[139] They maintained headquarters at Lambert Field, the post office address of which was then "Robertson, Missouri." This unusual situation had been brought about during the summer of 1929, when the 400 residents of Anglum, the town in which Robertson Aircraft Corporation and a portion of the airfield was located, drew up a petition to have their village renamed in honor of the Robertson brothers, who had "put it on the map." On November 1, 1929, the Post Office Department had complied with their request.[140] It was a fitting gesture to one of the greatest aeronautical families of St. Louis.

The Robertsons continued to operate their airline through the Mississippi Valley and late in 1930 set about securing a lucrative airmail contract over the same route. The Post Office Department expressed its interest in establishing the service in that area, but before they could consummate the agreement, the brothers ran

Laura Ingalls and her de Havilland "Gipsy Moth," after performing 714 consecutive barrel rolls over Lambert Field in August 1930.

St. Louis Post-Dispatch

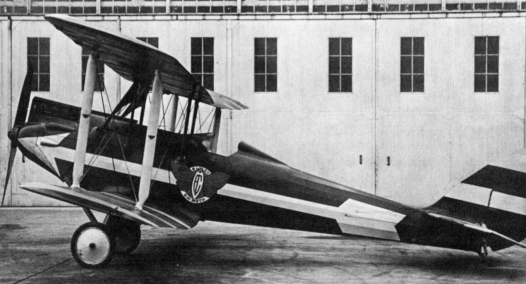

afoul of American Airways (the very company which had purchased their two previous routes). American prevailed and won the contract.[141]

After his brother Frank died of tuberculosis in 1934,[142] Major William Robertson opened a small flying school at St. Louis' municipal airport and continued to bid unsuccessfully on Midwestern mail routes as they were laid out for contract.[143] It was not until World War II that he returned to the manufacturing aspect of the aircraft industry.

During the Depression, that phase of aviation had suffered severe setbacks, inasmuch as governments, airlines, and private individuals found it increasingly difficult to afford such expensive items as airplanes. In order to boost the sale of its products, Curtiss-Wright established in 1930 the Curtiss-Wright Sales Corporation, the first such group to enter the field of aviation. Based on current practices in the automotive industry, the organization conducted a thorough market analysis of the entire country and divided the nation into sectional patterns of franchised dealerships. With the Sales Corporation in charge of distribution the Curtiss-Wright plant in St. Louis became its prime supplier of aircraft designed for private use.[144]

Even before this unit had been brought into existence, the St. Louis factory was producing for that market a model it had acquired in a roundabout manner. In 1925 England's de Havilland Aircraft Company had introduced the DH-60 "Moth," a two-place, tandem biplane trainer powered by an 85-horsepower "Gipsy" engine. The unique feature of the ship was its unusual stability, resulting from automatic "wing slots" which made it practically spin-proof and stall-proof.

In 1928 Moth Aircraft Company of Lowell, Massachusetts, was organized to manufacture an American version of the plane under a license agreement with de Havilland. When the Curtiss-Wright Corporation was formed in 1929, Moth Aircraft was absorbed and production of the ship was moved to the Curtiss-Wright plant at St. Louis the following year. Priced at $4,500, the plane suffered a sales slump as the Depression deepened, and it was discontinued in 1931. Between 1928 and 1931, however, some 168 "Moths" were built at both the Lowell and St. Louis factories.[145]

It was a popular ship, with safety and stability its primary advantages. These characteristics were fully in evidence on May 3, 1930, when Laura Ingalls, St. Louis' first licensed woman transport pilot, executed the women's world record number of 344 loops in succession over Lambert Field with a "Gipsy Moth," stopping only when she ran out of gas after her one-hour performance.[146]

By far the most successful of Curtiss-Wright's efforts during that era was the CW-1 "Junior," a fragile-looking, two-place open monoplane with a single pusher engine mounted above its parasol

Walter Beech with the Curtiss "Junior."

wing. Introduced in 1931, the ship was practically a powered glider, for it was light, smooth, and slow, and served equally well as a trainer or a simple pleasure craft. Two amphibian prototypes were even produced, but test results were unsatisfactory and that version was abandoned. The original model, however, enjoyed widespread popularity, particularly among coyote hunters of the Southwest.[147] The major factor in its success was its extremely low price — the "Junior" came fully equipped for only $1,450.[148] A total of 265 were built and sold before it was taken out of production at the end of 1931.[149]

The "Junior" was the least costly of an extensive series of private aircraft Curtiss-Wright had unveiled at the National Air Show in Detroit in 1931. The company offered four models in the medium-price range: the "Sport Trainer," a two-place open biplane with a Warner Scarab engine; the "Light Sport," a three-place open biplane with a Kinner B-5 or Warner Scarab engine; the "Sportsman," another three-place open biplane, but powered by a 240-horsepower Wright Whirlwind engine; and the "Sedan," a four-place cabin monoplane available with a variety of engines.[150] The most expensive ship in the series was the luxurious eight-place "Travel Air," which retailed at $26,000.[151]

In addition to providing the private owner with a broad choice of planes, Curtiss-Wright's St. Louis plant also catered to the commercial transport operators. In 1930 the company introduced its first effort in that area, the "Kingbird," an eight-place, twin-engine cabin monoplane. Among its purchasers were Eastern Airlines and the United States Marines. The Turkish government also bought two or three examples of the model,[152] perhaps as the result of the services of Major William B. Robertson in laying the foundation for that nation's aviation development program.[153] Although only fifteen were built, the "Kingbird" was an excellent airplane and was one of the first twin-engine models used in carrier airline operations.[154]

The company's second commercial endeavor was undertaken in 1932 with the appearance of the T-32 "Condor," an improved version of an earlier Curtiss design. It was a large, streamlined, twin-engine cabin biplane with a capacity for fifteen passengers and a crew of three.[155] The spacious airliner made its debut at the precise moment for the Depression-racked St. Louis plant. George Ebert, a company accountant (later comptroller), remembered:

> We had about $1,200 in the bank — half the money needed for one week's payroll but there wasn't a man in the organization who would have been willing to fold his hands and say "quits."
>
> Eastern Airlines was our first customer. We asked for and received 25 percent cash in advance on the signing of their contract. This gave us the necessary financial support essential for the purchase of materials and at least enough to tide us over a few payrolls. The Goddess of Luck certainly must have been smiling down on us because shortly after receiving Eastern's contract, we sold American Airlines. The same down payment was asked for and received and we progressed one stop further in this memorable and hectic transaction.
>
> I can recall the day when Ralph Damon, who was at that time president of our organization, obtained an order from the U.S. Army for two Condors to be delivered in thirty days. We all wondered how he was going to do it. But, Eastern Airlines agreed to lend us two of their ships already on the production line and after incorporating the necessary Army changes, we were able to deliver as per contract — on the nose.

"Condors" in production at the St. Louis factory of Curtiss-Wright Corporation.

Thus, by an intricate pattern of shift and shuffle, all three contracts were signed and completed successfully and we wound up our first year of Condor sales with all bills paid and $100,000 in the bank.[156]

A total of 44 "Condors" were produced in St. Louis.[157] While most served with Eastern and American Airlines, where the ship was known as "the luxury liner of the '30's,"[158] several were fitted for various other tasks. A few BT-32 bomber versions of the "Condor" were constructed and sold to the Chinese and Colombian governments. Three cargo models (CT-32) were purchased by the Argentine Navy and several others saw wide use throughout Central and South America. Admiral Richard E. Byrd utilized a "Condor" (#41) for his second trip to Antarctica and was so impressed with its performance that he secured two more from the United States Navy for his next expedition. In 1934, a specially-built, twelve-place AT-32 "Condor" became the first production sleeper plane in history when American Airways made some half-dozen a prominent part of its system.[159] Its reputation grew and its sales boomed.

The death knell of this fabric-covered biplane, however, was sounded with the advent of the all-metal monoplane. Production ceased in 1935, and many of the ships, particularly those owned by Eastern Airlines, were returned to St. Louis to be converted into cargo ships for use in England and on the Continent [160] (where several were used for night flights of fresh fruit and vegetables from Holland to London).[161] Hardly any airplane of that era was such a world traveler: North America, South America, Europe, Asia, and even Antarctica. It was one of the finest airliners of its day.

Although the company intensified its efforts in the commercial field, the St. Louis plant also made additional developments in the personal area. While continuing production on such models as the "Sedan" in 1933, Curtiss-Wright brought out four new ships that year, all designed for the private owner: the "Sport," a three-place open biplane with a 175-horsepower Wright Whirlwind engine; the "Speedwing," another three-place open biplane, but equipped with a 250-horsepower Whirlwind; the "Special Speedwing," a similar model with a 330-horsepower Whirlwind; and the "Special Speedwing De Luxe," a two-place open biplane with a potent 420-horsepower Wright Whirlwind engine.[162]

Even though the St. Louis plant specialized in the production of civil and commercial aircraft, its parent company had long been celebrated for its output of military planes. In 1932 St. Louis undertook its first project in that area. This model was the "Osprey," a two-place attack, pursuit, and observation plane powered by a 420-horsepower Whirlwind. The ship was designed primarily for the export market, and late in the year, 90 employees were added to the 200 already working at the factory to hasten the planes to the South American governments which had ordered them.[163]

During the mid-1930s, the aircraft industry was proceeding briskly with developments of all-metal monoplanes. Curtiss-Wright, too, engaged in extensive experiments in that field. In 1935 the St. Louis plant contracted with the Department of Commerce to design and build an all-metal airplane for private and sportsmen pilots' use. Early in the engineering stages, however, the military possibilities of the ship became apparent. A single model, designated the CW-19L "Coupe," was delivered to the Commerce Department, thus terminating the contract. That airplane, however, became the forerunner of Curtiss-Wright's extensive "19 Series."[164]

In 1936, the CW-19R made its debut. This ship was a two-place, all-metal, low-wing monoplane military trainer mounting two machine guns and a pair of bomb racks. A total of sixteen were built and sold to South American governments.[165] During the next few

George J. Herwig Collection

The first of the 1933 Curtiss "Condors" warming up before the new Lambert Field terminal building on March 13, 1933.

years, the basic design of the extremely versatile "Model 19," as a land plane, a seaplane, or amphibian, was produced in several versions: a commercial sport plane, a commercial trainer, an advanced military trainer, an observation ship, a photo-reconaissance vehicle, a pursuit ship, and a light bomber.[166]

Foreign governments throughout the world expressed interest in the plane, but they requested that the non-retractable feature of its landing gear be eliminated in order to streamline the ship for greater speed and altitude capabilities. In 1938 the model was improved and redesignated the CW-21, a single-seat, all-metal, low-wing monoplane interceptor with fully retractable landing gear. Powered by a 1,000-horsepower Wright Cyclone, the CW-21 "Demon," as it was termed, could reach a top speed of 315 miles per hour and cruise for 630 miles at a service ceiling of 34,000 feet.

The first foreign order came from the Chinese government, and in 1939 three complete planes, a set of tools and drawings, and 32 sets of components were delivered. The following year the Netherlands East Indies requested 24 examples of a modified version, the CW-21B, but only 17 were delivered before war broke out in the Pacific. Based in Java, the CW-21B "Demon" experienced its first military action on February 3, 1942, but almost all were destroyed on the ground during the next few days. Only three other "Demons" were built at the St. Louis factory. These were delivered to the American Volunteer Group at Rangoon, but all three crashed in the Chinese mountains on their way to Kunming on December 23, 1941.[167]

St. Louis' Curtiss-Wright Airplane Company, which in 1936 had been renamed the St. Louis Airplane Division of Curtiss-Wright Corporation,[168] began to concentrate strictly on military aircraft in the mid-1930s. Its last personal models, the "Sport" and the

"Speedwing," were discontinued in 1936, following the demise of the "Condor."[169] During the previous year[170] the St. Louis plant had also built the "Courtney Amphibian," a large, single-engine biplane flying boat equipped with tricycle gear for land use. It was designed by Captain Frank Courtney, a celebrated RAF war ace, who was a close friend of Richard Hoyt, the Curtiss-Wright board chairman. Courtney persuaded Hoyt to give his model a trial.[171] Two prototypes were constructed at the St. Louis plant (one of which was sold to the Japanese, who took numerous pictures of the nearly-empty factory when delivery was made in 1936),[172] but the model did not hold great promise, so the novel ship died in its experimental stage.

One of the company's more permanent and more successful designers was George A. Page Jr., who in 1943 became director of engineering for the entire airplane division of the Curtiss-Wright Corporation. From his headquarters in St. Louis he was credited with designing some sixty models for the company.[173] Perhaps his most celebrated achievement was the C-46 "Commando," the cargo-carrying bulwark of the war effort.

The basic draft of the model, designated the CW-20, crystallized in 1936 after three years of study. The ship was intended as a commercial airliner, for it had a capacity of 36 passengers (twice as many as any liner then in existence) plus a crew of five. The company planned to built twenty-five units, but tooled for fifty in the hope of repeated orders.[174]

The prototype of the CW-20, built at St. Louis, made its first flight at Lambert Field on March 26, 1940, piloted by Eddie Allen.[175] Powered by two 1,750-horsepower Wright Cyclone engines, the all-metal monoplane was 76 feet 4 inches long, 21 feet 9 inches high, and 108 feet 1 inch in span.[176] It was "the largest twin-engine transport in the world."[177] In addition, the liner incorporated several novel features: a tell-tale system of warning lights to announce faulty engine operation, oil pressure, landing gear, and gasoline supply; special soundproofing material in its fuselage construction; and de-icers on its wings and tail.[178] It was by far the most impressive and advanced ship in its class.

Soon after its maiden flight, the Army, then looking for a suitable cargo and troop transport, ordered twenty-five militarized versions of the would-be airliner under the designation C-46. While this contract was being completed, the single CW-20 prototype was purchased in October 1941 for evaluation under the designation C-55.[179] Subsequently, this solitary model was sent to Great Britain under

The St. Louis Post-Dispatch *ran this photo of a hangar full of Curtiss "Commando" troop transports being assembled in the Buffalo, New York, Curtiss-Wright plant. Similar lines were in operation at other Curtiss plants in St. Louis, Louisville, and New Orleans.*

the Lend-Lease program. Early in 1942 it made a transatlantic crossing in the swift time of 9 hours and 40 minutes.[180] As it drew near the coast of England, however, the C-55 (CW-20) was almost shot down as an "unidentified flying object" by air raid spotters, who had never seen such a huge ship and who had not been told of its impending arrival. Quick work by the headquarters staff, who were expecting the plane, prevented its destruction.[181] The C-55 was put to good use by the British, who named it the *St. Louis* in honor of the city where it had been built. It served ably in Malta, Gibraltar, and the Mediterranean area in general, and was even used at times by Prime Minister Winston Churchill himself.[182]

The first of the production C-46s, with two 2,000-horsepower Pratt and Whitney engines and a cargo capacity of 40 equipped troops or 45,000 pounds, came off the assembly lines of the Curtiss-Wright plant at St. Louis in May 1942.[183] A modified version, designated the C-46A, was the first model produced in quantity. The Curtiss-Wright factory at Buffalo built 1,039 "Commandos" of this type, its Louisville division 438, and the St. Louis plant a total of twelve.[184] Buffalo remained the main source of "Commando" production during the war, while St. Louis concentrated on the manufacture of parts for the ship, and also completed seventeen of the C-46E version (with a stepped windscreen and larger cargo door), the last delivered on July 27, 1945.[185] The C-46 "Commando" was the workhorse of the Troop Carrier Command during World War II.

It served in every theater of action, but gained lasting fame for its "Over-the-Hump" operations in the critical China-Burma area.[186]

While the "Commando" was "St. Louis' biggest war baby"[187] and the pride of Curtiss-Wright, an earlier associate of that firm was engaged in manufacturing the city's other most noted wartime aeronautic product. He was Major William B. Robertson, who had abandoned his airline and flying school to emulate Jack Laister[188] in the production of cargo and troop gliders. Between 1942 and 1945, Robertson Aircraft Corporation acquired, in succession, three subcontracts for the 15-place Waco CG-4A glider,[189] and by February 1945 held $3,172,876 in orders for the model from the Air Technical Service Command.[190] Ultimately, the company manufactured at least 170 of the ships,[191] together with a large amount of parts for other aircraft.[192]

Ironically, the city's greatest native aviation operator met his death in a CG-4A built by his own company. The tragedy occurred at 3:55 p.m. Sunday, August 1, 1943, in the first public demonstration of the "all St. Louis-built glider."[193] *Time's* account was stark:

> A plywood Army glider was released from its tow plane over St. Louis' Municipal Airport. A wing cracked, shredded into splinters. The glider plummeted crazily 1,500 ft. to earth. Debris and bodies were thrown 50 ft. into the air. All ten passengers were killed instantly.[194]

A crowd of 5,000, including the wives of the victims, had witnessed "the worst air disaster in the history of St. Louis."[195] Crushed to death in the crash were: William Dee Becker, St. Louis' reform mayor; Major William B. Robertson, president of Robertson Aircraft Corporation, builders of the fatal glider; Harold A. Krueger, vice-president and chief engineer of Robertson Aircraft; Thomas N. Dysart, president of the St. Louis Chamber of Commerce; Max H. Doyne, Director of Public Utilities; Charles L. Cunningham, deputy comptroller for the city; Henry L. Mueller, presiding judge of the St. Louis County Court; Lieutenant Colonel Paul H. Hazelton of the local AAF group; Captain Milton C. Klugh, pilot of the ship; and John M. Davis, a private first class in the 71st Troop Carrier Command. No one escaped alive.

Although the catastrophe all but wiped out City Hall and took the lives of significant industrialists and military personnel, it might have been even more costly. Three other men had been scheduled to make the flight: Major Ralph W. Page, onetime manager of Lambert Field who was then commanding officer of the AAF Service Command at the airport, who was busy with other matters and had excused himself at the last moment; Girard Varnum, president of the St. Louis County Chamber of Commerce, who had been occupied with arrangements for the funeral of his mother-in-law; and Major Albert Bond Lambert, St. Louis' most celebrated aerial enthusiast, who had stopped momentarily at an Army hangar at the airfield and had missed the takeoff of the ill-fated glider. [196]

Immediately after the disaster, the Army grounded every glider in its possession pending a complete examination into the cause of the crash. [197] The inspectors made a thorough investigation and determined that the accident resulted from a defective fitting joining the right wing to the fuselage. Less than half as thick as it should have been, the fitting had snapped and caused the wing to break off sharply, sending the body of the ship into a straight nose dive to the ground. [198]

In spite of the disaster, Robertson Aircraft Corporation continued its output of aircraft until 1945, along with the city's four other wartime airframe producers: Curtiss-Wright, McDonnell, Laister-Kauffmann, and St. Louis Aircraft. [199] Of them all, the St. Louis Airplane Division of Curtiss-Wright Corporation was by far the largest and most active.

During the late 1930s the company maintained its production of the versatile "19 Series" and the models emanating from that design, among them the CW-21 interceptor and the CW-22 advanced trainer (both intended primarily for the export market), together with the CW-23 pursuit ship for the United States Army. [200] With the coming of the war and the increase in government contracts, the St. Louis plant expanded rapidly. Ground was broken for new buildings at Lambert Field on November 19, 1940, and the factory space was increased to 1,247,100 square feet by 1942, with employment plans for approximately 13,000 workers [201] (a substantial increase over the plant's January 1940 total of 481 people). [202]

During the war years the advantages of St. Louis as an industrial center became prominently apparent. A contemporary trade journal commented:

> For military purposes, the Curtiss-St. Louis plant is ideally situated. It rests in the heart of the nation, the Alleghenies and the Appalachians forming protective walls to the east and the Rockies, an equally strong barrier on the west. Here, the Missouri climate is not rigorous but remains uniformly good throughout the year, not so hot as to deprive workers of their energy, nor so cold as to make working conditions difficult. It is, in all respects, *strategic St. Louis.* [203]

St. Louis Post-Dispatch

Moments after this picture was made, at about 3:45 p.m. Sunday, August 1, 1943, these men were dead. The wing of the St. Louis-built CG-4A glider fell off at 1,500 feet, in front of a packed and horrified grandstand. From left: Capt. Milton C. Klugh, pilot; Charles L. Cunningham, deputy St. Louis controller; Lt. Col. Paul H. Hazelton, of the Army Air Forces Materiel Command; Max H. Doyne, director of public utilities for the City of St. Louis; Harold A. Krueger, vice president and chief engineer of Robertson Aircraft, builder of the glider; Henry L. Mueller, St. Louis County's presiding judge, Major William B. Robertson, president of the building firm; Thomas N. Dysart, president of the St. Louis Chamber of Commerce; and William Dee Becker, mayor of St. Louis. One other man, Pvt. J.M. Davis, the plane's mechanic, also was killed.

In 1941, the St. Louis Airplane Division concentrated on the SNC-1 trainer, a modified version of the CW-22 ''Falcon,'' for the Navy, together with the AT-9, a twin-engine advanced transition trainer so versatile and reliable that the Army termed it the ''Jeep.'' [204] In that year the plant completed 234 aircraft of those types for military service. [205]

St. Louis Post-Dispatch

AT-9 "Jeep" trainers, left, destined for Army service, roll from Curtiss-Wright's St. Louis assembly line. At right is a row of single-engine Navy trainers.

During the following year the St. Louis factory manufactured a total of 997 aircraft, among them the SNC-1 "Falcon" and the AT-9 "Jeep," together with the A-25 dive-bomber, the Army counterpart to the Navy's SB2C "Helldiver."[206] By February 1945, Curtiss-Wright's St. Louis Division had more than one-half billion dollars worth of standing contracts for aircraft production: $250,548,141 for the C-46 "Commando" transport, $229,456,922 for the A-25 "Helldiver" divebomber, $10,378,206 for the AT-9 "Jeep" trainer, and unpublicized amounts for experimental models.[207] In addition, the company had $1,025,000 in contracts from the Air Technical Service Command for such aircraft parts as high-pressure cylinders, oil tubes, valve caps, and compressors.[208] The Curtiss-Wright complex had the greatest amount of orders of any firm then doing business with the government in St. Louis. (The United States Cartridge Company stood second with $427,133,121 in contracts for small arms and ammunition.)[209]

In addition to major production on four aircraft during the war, the St. Louis plant also made significant experiments with two other models, the unique C-76 "Caravan" and the even more unusual SP-55 "Ascender."

St. Louis Post-Dispatch

Families of Curtiss-Wright employees were allowed to tour the St. Louis plant on November 7, 1943, to examine the Army's A-25 dive-bomber.

During the early months of the war there was fear in military circles that Germany might land assault troops on American beaches. To guard against this eventuality, the Army needed a cargo plane to bring personnel and supplies quickly to any trouble spot which might develop. The aircraft had to be spacious and swift, yet capable of landing in whatever emergency fields were available (specifically, a 1,200-foot clearing over a 50-foot obstacle). It also had to be constructed with a minimum use of strategic materials (aluminum). When Curtiss-Wright undertook the project it found that the choicest aircraft woods were slated for the English "Mosquito" and the cargo and troop glider program. The firm finally settled on plywood, out of which it fabricated at St. Louis the twin-engine, high-wing monoplane C-76 "Caravan."[210]

The unusual ship made its first flight at Lambert Field on January 5, 1943.[211] The Army placed orders for 2,800, half to be built at the

Curtiss-Wright plants at St. Louis and Louisville, and half on sub-contract by Higgins Aircraft at New Orleans.[212] By mid-1943, Louisville had built twenty of the ships and St. Louis five,[213] when the Army began to realize that assault by sea was improbable. With the need for it having ceased to exist, production of the "Caravan," a satisfactory ship in every other respect, was halted after only twenty-five had been constructed.[214]

A more imaginative project was the CW-24, designated the XP-55 "Ascender" by the Army. One of the most radical fighter designs of the war period, the "Ascender" was a single-seat, all-metal, low-wing monoplane, whose deeply swept-back wing, 1,275-horsepower pusher engine, and nose elevators made it appear to be flying backwards. This "tail-first" ship had several distinct advantages over conventional fighters: improved forward visibility for the pilot; better firing power due to the the lack of need for a synchronizing mechanism to fire through the propeller; increased speed (377.5 miles per hour); and less danger to the pilot from engine fire.[215]

The prototype CW-24 was tested extensively in 169 flights at Muroc Field (later Edwards Air Force Base) between November 1941 and May 1942, and on July 10 of the latter year Curtiss-Wright received an order for three of the ships, under the designation XP-55. The St. Louis plant built the planes and delivered them in 1943 and 1944.[216] During the official inspection trials, however, control problems and stalling tendencies developed. The ship had been designed for a 2,000-horsepower Continental engine, but that powerplant proved unavailable. The forced usage of the 1,275-horsepower engine resulted in poor performance. The Army felt that the disadvantages of the "Ascender" did not justify its unorthodox design, and the project was abandoned in 1944.[217]

During World War II the Curtiss-Wright Corporation constructed a total of 26,269 airplanes[218] at its four main factories at Buffalo, Columbus, St. Louis, and Louisville. St. Louis ranked third in company production with a tally of 2,436 planes produced,[219] primarily A-25 "Helldivers" (900), AT-9 "Jeeps" (791), SNC-1 "Falcons" (505), and C-46 "Commandos" (57).[220] With the severe cutback in government contracts near the end of the war, economic considerations forced the Curtiss-Wright Corporation to confine its operations to a more limited number of plants. In 1945, the St. Louis Division closed its doors and Curtiss-Wright withdrew from the city.[221]

During the quarter-century of the tenure of the Robertson, Curtiss-Robertson, and Curtiss-Wright corporations in St. Louis, thousands of aircraft were produced, as well as airlines formed, passengers and freight carried, and flying students taught. Almost limitless in influence, these related companies had significant effects on the field of aviation in the city, the nation, and countries throughout the world. Without them St. Louis could have made no noteworthy name as a center of air industry. With them its eminence in that area was realized.

XVI
McDonnell, 1939-1965

A FTER WORLD WAR II, St. Louis became a "one-company" city in the field of aircraft industry. Within a short time, however, that firm — McDonnell Aircraft Corporation — rose to a position of virtually unequaled excellence in the domain of jet fighter and aerospace production, and during the first quarter-century of its existence manufactured almost as many aircraft as had been produced by all the previous concerns in the city's history. The impressive record accomplished by the corporation was largely the work of one man — the company founder, James Smith McDonnell Jr.

Born in Denver, Colorado, on April 9, 1899, he spent his early years in Little Rock, Arkansas, and enrolled at Princeton University in 1917. After a three-month stint in the Army, McDonnell returned to the school to finish his physics program and received the degree of Bachelor of Science in 1921.[1] Upon graduating, he determined that his maximum potential could best be realized in the field of aviation. Thereupon he entered the Massachusetts Institute of Technology, one of the few schools in the nation offering an advanced degree in aeronautical engineering.[2]

After two years of graduate study, he turned to the practical aspect of flight and gained an appointment to the Army Air Corps Flying School at Brooks Field, Texas, in 1923. The following year,

McDonnell completed his training at Kelly Field and was commissoned a second lieutenant,[3] antedating by one year another young Army-trained airman who would also make aviation history from St. Louis.[4] Lieutenant McDonnell immediately resigned his active-duty commission to complete his program at MIT, graduating with a class of four in 1925 with the degree of Master of Science. James S. McDonnell was then one of the few fully equipped aeronautical engineers in the United States, having had advanced training in both the theory and practice of flight.[5]

McDonnell Douglas Corp.

James Smith McDonnell as a young aviator.

Outfitted with such qualifications, he had little difficulty in securing his first position, even while still at MIT. It was an engineering post with the Huff-Daland Company of Ogdensburg, New York, in 1924. After a few months, however, he moved on to Consolidated Aircraft in Buffalo and then to Detroit and the Stout Metal Airplane Company, a subsidiary of Ford Motor, in May 1925.[6] There he contributed to the development of that firm's celebrated all-metal trimotor, but he was personally fired by Henry Ford Sr. for committing the unpardonable sin of wearing knickers to work.[7]

The young engineer, however, had benefited from the experience he had gained in the design of metal aircraft and easily blended his talents into the operations of Hamilton Metalplane Company in Milwaukee. He quickly rose to the position of chief engineer, and in 1927 he collaborated with company President Thomas F. Hamilton in the design of the "Metalplane," one of the most successful passenger-mail transports of the period.[8] Although McDonnell's future was secure at Hamilton, an intriguing proposition launched him on his own the following year.

In 1928 aviation promoter Harry F. Guggenheim made public his plans for a $100,000 Safe Airplane Competition. The award would be won by the plane which executed in the best manner the performance requisites:

a. Minimum flying speed 35 mph. b. Minimum gliding speed 38 mph. c. Top speed of 110 mph. d. Initial climb rate of 400 ft. a minute. e. Landing run of 100 ft. f. Approach over an obstruction 35 ft. high, and coming to rest 300 ft. from the base of the obstruction. g. Take off in 300 ft. h. Take off over an obstruction 35 ft. high in a distance of 500 ft. from the base of obstruction. i. Flattest glide at 8° to the horizontal. j. Steepest glide at 16° to the horizontal.[9]

McDonnell's imagination was stirred by the proposal, and in private he designed a tandem, two-place, single-engine, low-wing monoplane incorporating the latest research on wing slots and flaps for safety and stability. So enthused did he become at the prospect of winning the prize and producing the design in quantity that in the spring of 1928 he formed his own company — J.S. McDonnell and Associates. The "associates" were J.W. Cowling (later a designer for Lockheed Aircraft) and C.I. Zakhartchenko (later chief helicopter designer for McDonnell Aircraft). The project had the cooperation of Thomas Hamilton, who helped them build their tiny plane at his Milwaukee plant. McDonnell named the ship the "Doodlebug."[10]

The contest trial took place at Mitchell Field, Long Island, so the young engineer flew his entry east from Milwaukee in mid-1929. In the first official tests, the "Doodlebug" (complete with red and green flashlights taped to its wingtips)[11] performed magnificently. It repeatedly took off in a scant time of eight seconds in a distance of 180 feet, attained a maximum speed of 110 miles per hour, flew safely at 35 miles per hour, and landed in a mere 40 feet.

Troublesome difficulties, however, developed during the test flight on November 22, 1929. McDonnell eased the ship along at a height of 2,700 feet above the watchful contest judges and then put it into a dive. At 2,200 feet the stabilizer failed, fouled the tail mechanisms, and completely destroyed rudder and elevator control. "The *Bug* increased its diving angle past the vertical and both McDonnell and the contest officials were astonished an almost perfect outside loop!"[12]

The pilot was on the point of parachuting from the berserk aircraft when he decided to gamble and attempt to ride it down. The jammed controls broke loose, he righted the ship, and assisted by the plane's inherently stable characteristics, he brought it safely to the ground. As he landed, however, the wheels snagged on some concrete blocks on the airfield and the "Doodlebug" was badly damaged.[13] Despite the fact that a greater tragedy had been averted, the Guggenheim officials, needless to say, were hardly im-

The "Doodlebug" aloft.

pressed with the aircraft's safety features.

J.S. McDonnell and Associates then returned to Milwaukee for repairs on the ship. The "Doodlebug" was restored to health, but as the company president was flying it back to New York, the engine "smeared," strewing parts all over the countryside. Again McDonnell managed a safe landing, but his participation in the competition was ended.[14] The contest was ultimately won by the Curtiss "Tanager," a cabin biplane which bested the field of fifteen to win the $100,000 Safe Airplane award.[15]

The hapless J.S. McDonnell and Associates disbanded in 1930, and the "Doodlebug" designer then participated in the formation of the Airtransport Engineering Company. After a year of searching for funds in a Depression-ridden investment market, however, the company collapsed and McDonnell moved on to the Great Lakes Aircraft Corporation in Cleveland.[16] Two years later, in 1933, he joined the Glenn L. Martin Company in Baltimore and spent a fruitful five and one-half years with that firm, rising to the eminent position of chief project engineer of the landplane division.[17] Late in 1938 McDonnell felt he was ready to strike out on his third attempt at founding his own company. This time he was successful.

During the winter and spring of 1939 the forty-year-old entrepreneur scoured the country for a suitable site for the establishment of his organization. After a lengthy survey, he selected St. Louis. His reasons were logical:

> The entire airplane industry was too concentrated on the eastern seaboard and the west coast. I felt that the Government, in giving contracts, would look with approval on the dispersion of the in-

dustry. I knew I couldn't afford to build an airport, yet newly developed planes would need longer and longer runways. I wanted an industrial center where I could find skilled people in the 300 different trades involved in an airplane factory, and I wanted a place where I could find some local financing.[18]

Seven months after he had left Martin Aircraft, he had found his location and the requisite finances. With $30,000 of his savings and $135,000 of invested capital[19] ($5,000 of which came from Laurence S. Rockefeller, who proffered it after a half-hour interview with the persuasive James S. McDonnell),[20] the venturesome engineer formed McDonnell Aircraft Corporation on July 6, 1939. On that day he occupied 1,700 square feet of office space on the second floor of an American Airlines building on the north side of Lambert Field with one employee (Louis Ritter), a typewriter, two Army cots, some office furniture, and no contracts.[22]

Three months later the staff stood at fifteen, but no orders had yet been received.[23] By June 1940 employment had risen to thirty-two, and the company occupied its first factory, a building with 37,400 square feet of floor space at Lambert Field.[24] That same month the struggling firm witnessed its first success, a $3,000 award from the Army Air Corps for a piston-and-jet, twin-engine, 550-mile-per-hour pursuit plane design submitted in a competition.[25] At the same time, a winning fighter design brought $9,900 from the Navy.[26] The hoped-for production orders, however, did not follow. At least it had a start, and the long, lean period was drawing to a close. At the end of its first fiscal year of operation, nevertheless, discounting the two "contest prizes," the corporation's ledger read: 0 sales, 0 earnings, and 0 backlog.[27]

The prewar arms buildup gave the necessary stimulus to the young company. In August 1940 McDonnell Aircraft Corporation received its first manufacturing order, a subcontract for $7,672 worth of small parts for Stinson observation planes.[28] The following month, the Army Air Corps, intrigued with the firm's pioneering efforts, award MAC a $20,000 contract for jet propulsion experimentation.[29] That early research laid the groundwork for the company's greatest achievements in its later history.

During World War II, McDonnell Aircraft worked primarily on subcontracts for airframes and parts for aircraft designed by other companies. In December 1940 the corporation received its first major orders: $1,343,577 for tail assemblies for the Douglas C-47 "Skytrain" twin-engine transport, and $1,381,875 for engine cowlings for the Douglas A-20 "Havoc" twin-engine light bomber.[30]

The first offices of McDonnell Aircraft Corporation were on the second floor of this structure, the original American Airlines building on the north edge of Lambert Field.

While engaged in completing this task, the firm received its first production airplane subcontract, a $15,288,608 order for Fairchild AT-21 "Gunner" gunnery trainers.[31] McDonnell's St. Louis factory was becoming so overcrowded by that time, however, that the company decided to open a branch in Memphis in 1942 to produce the twin-engine trainers. The Tennessee plant delivered its first "Gunner" in February 1944, and by the end of the year had constructed 30 airplanes,[32] when further work was canceled and the factory turned to the manufacturing of pressurized fuselages for the Boeing B-29 "Superfortress"[33] until it was closed in October 1945.[34]

By February 1945 McDonnell Aircraft was the largest supplier of airplane parts in St. Louis, for it then held $33,882,290 in orders for various components of Douglas and Boeing aircraft.[35] During the war, McDonnell manufactured some 7,000,000 pounds of aircraft materials on subcontract: 59,000 gun turret pieces for the Consolidated B-24, pressurized fuselage sections for the Boeing B-29, and 60,000 parts for the Douglas A-20 and C-47, as well as 30 complete Fairchild AT-21s.[36] The work performed grossed $60,000,000 (on which earnings after taxes were three-fourths of one percent). The McDonnell operation embraced twenty buildings in both St. Louis and Memphis, with a combined total floor area of 760,000 square feet. Company employment at its peak reached 5,212 (of whom about 60 percent were women).[37] It was an admirable record

A wartime scene inside the McDonnell plant, where workmen are making subassembles for the FD-1.

for a corporation not yet six years old.

While subcontracts had been the firm's main contribution to the war effort, McDonnell engineers had not been idle with proposals of their own, and during the war years, several of those ideas materialized in significant products. On July 29, 1941,[38] the company received a contract from the Army Air Force for two prototypes of "the first airplane of an all-McDonnell design."[39] This ship was the XP-67, a single-seat, twin-engine bomber-destroyer 44 feet 9½ inches long and 55 feet in span, armed with six 37-millimeter cannon. The first model was completed on December 1, 1943, but a week later, it was severely damaged when fires started in its engine nacelles owing to a malfunction in the exhaust manifold. The XP-67 was repaired and made its first flight on January 6, 1944, but engine trouble necessitated an emergency landing after it was in the air only six minutes. During further trials in the spring and summer of 1944, the ship was sluggish and unstable, and seemed under-

McDonnell's AT-21 "Gunner" assembly line in their Memphis plant early in 1944.

powered, in that it was unable to attain its designed speed of 472 miles per hour. The official performance tests were slated for late September 1944, but on September 6, the XP-67 was irreparably damaged by fire in its hangar. This accident, plus the unsatisfactory performance in the preliminary trials, resulted in the cancelation of the second prototype and of the entire program as well.[40]

The XP-67 was the first and last piston airplane McDonnell Aircraft ever developed for the government. The company's future lay in another area. By the time of the bomber-destroyer's demise, the St. Louis firm was already underway on its first successful model, the forerunner of its celebrated "Spook Series" of jet fighters.

Because of his company's progressive research in jet propulsion, James McDonnell received a significant telephone call on December 31, 1942, inviting him to come to Washington the next day for high-level conferences on a revolutionary new aircraft. He went eagerly, and on January 1, 1943, was asked to develop the first jet-propelled, carrier-based fighter for the Navy.[41]

This was the XFD-1 "Phantom," a single-seat, twin-jet fighter 37 feet 3 inches long and 40 feet 9 inches in span, designed to operate at 15,000 feet with an endurance of forty-five minutes at speeds approaching 500 miles per hour.[42] Studies were made of powerplant arrangements of two, six, eight, and ten engines, but it was felt that two 19-inch, 1,600-pound thrust Westinghouse "Yankee" engines in the wing roots would provide maximum efficiency.[43] On August 30, 1943, the Navy ordered three prototypes of the XFD-1.[44]

The first "Phantom" was completed in January 1945, but just one Westinghouse 19X-2B engine was then available for installation. McDonnell Aircraft had such confidence in the ship, however, that it scheduled the inaugural test flight for January 26, 1945, with only one engine.[45] The XFD-1 left the ground for the first time quite unofficially during taxi trials that day when it ardently hopped six feet into the air and flew for several yards before the startled Wood-

McDonnell's only piston-powered war plane, the XP-67, flew early in 1944.

ward Burks, McDonnell's chief test pilot, brought it back to the ground. Later in the afternoon the ship executed two half-hour stints in the air at somewhat higher altitudes before company and government officials.[46]

Intensive tests in the next six weeks showed the "Phantom" to be vastly superior to any fighter then in service. It could climb to 20,000 feet at a rate of 5,000 feet per minute and speed along at 420 knots for 750 miles. Impressed with its capabilities, the Navy awarded McDonnell on March 17, 1945, "BuAer Contract No. 6242," an order for 100 "Phantoms," redesignated FH-1. V-J Day, however, forced military cutbacks, but rather than abandon the new plane entirely, the Navy reduced its order from 100 to 30 planes. Initial delivery began on schedule in January 1946.[47]

McDonnell's first production aircraft of its own design was noted for three particular accomplishments: 1) in the spring of 1945 it became the first Naval airplane to attain a speed of 500 miles per hour;[48] 2) on July 21, 1946, a "Phantom" piloted by Lieutenant Commander James J. Davidson became the first jet airplane to take off from and land on an aircraft carrier (the *U.S.S. Franklin D. Roosevelt);*[49] and 3) on May 5, 1948, Navy Squadron VF 17-A, equipped with sixteen FH-1 "Phantoms" aboard the *U.S.S. Saipan,* became the first complete carrier-based jet fighter squadron in the world.[50]

The remarkable performance of the ship had prompted the Navy to order an additional 30 planes late in 1946.[51] The sixtieth and last of the production FH-1 "Phantoms" was delivered on schedule on May 27, 1948.[52] This airplane was McDonnell's first great accomplishment, and in its day it was "the most effective interceptor . . . in naval operations."[53]

During the war McDonnell Aircraft Corporation also experimented with two exotic aerial vehicles. The first was the RTV-2 "Gargoyle," a radio-controlled flying bomb 10 feet 1½ inches long and 8 feet 6 inches in span.[54] On September 3, 1944, the Navy awarded the firm a development contract for a small number of the guided missiles,[55] but in March 1946 the program was reoriented and the "Gargoyle" was limited to testing and research operations.[56] During the same period, MAC experimented with the eleven-foot XDD-1 "Katydid" target drone, but was unable to secure a production contract for it.[57]

It was also during World War II that McDonnell Aircraft turned its mind to helicopter development. In May 1944 the Navy awarded an experimental contract to the firm for the world's first twin-engine helicopter, the 5½-ton XHJD-1 "Whirlaway."[58] This novel craft made its first public appearance at Lambert Field on October 26, 1946,[59] but despite its progressive features, the "Whirlaway" never graduated into the production stage. In the ensuing years, MAC would design several more unique rotary-wing aircraft, all with the same fate.

In the heavy cutback of governmental expenditures after the war, many burgeoning aircraft companies were severely crippled. McDonnell was one of those affected. Although the firm managed to gross $6,562,001.27 in sales during fiscal year 1946, it sustained a net loss (for the only time in the first 26 years of its existence) of $226,134.24. As of June 30, 1946, however, the corporation did have $1,161,962.39 in working capital, more than enough to enable it to continue its fighter production and dabble in experimental research.[60]

MAC was then situated in the 48.8-acre, 1.5-million-square-foot factory which it had taken over from Curtiss-Wright in 1945 when that firm withdrew from the city.[61] McDonnell's employment was rising and the company was fast becoming a prominent part of the aircraft industry.

Even as its first successful fighter was being born, a successor was being conceived. In March 1945, the same month in which McDonnell received the production order for the FH-1 "Phantom," it was awarded an experimental contract by the Navy for two XF2H-1 "Banshee" prototypes.[62] This ship was only slightly larger (41 feet 6 inches in span and 38 feet 11½ inches in length) than its predecessor, but its more powerful engines (two 3,000-pound-thrust Westinghouse 24Cs) and its highly polished, super-smooth finish enabled it to streak through the air at 630 miles per

The FH-1 "Phantom," first of the "spook" series, was a spectacular performer which laid the foundation for the later success of the young and aggressive company. It is shown over west St. Louis County in 1945.

hour.[63] "The Banshee was the airplane that 'made' the young McDonnell Aircraft Corp."[64]

The ship made its first flight at Lambert Field on January 11, 1947, with chief test pilot Robert M. Edholm at the controls.[65] The Navy was pleased with its performance and granted a production contract for 56 F2H-1 models in May 1947, the first of which was delivered precisely one year later.[66]

Like its predecessor, the "Banshee" gained many distinctions. On August 6, 1949, the first American use of a pilot ejection seat for an emergency escape was made by Lieutenant J.L. Fruin in an F2H-1 while traveling at more than 500 miles per hour over Walterboro, South Carolina.[67] In the same month, the plane established world's altitude record for jet fighters at 52,000 feet.[68] During the Korean War, the carrier-based, twin-jet ship bombed, strafed, and flew photographic missions, earning particular fame for its action against the bridges of Toko-Ri.[69] By 1956 several "Banshees" had been placed on duty with the Royal Canadian Navy, under the terms of the Mutual Defense Atlantic Pact, thereby becoming Canada's first carrier-based jets.[70]

A total of 895 "Banshees" were produced[71] in seven different versions: the F2H-1 day fighter, in use prior to 1950; the F2H-2, a heavier and more powerful model for the Korean War; the F2H-2B, the first fighter with atomic capabilities; the F2H-2P photo-reconaissance model; the F2H-2N night fighter; the F2H-3 all-weather fighter; and the F2H-4, which incorporated the latest radar equipment.[72] The last plane was delivered on schedule on October 31, 1953,[73] completing a program worth $320,000,000 in cumulative sales.[74] During its period, the "Banshee" was

> the fastest [630 miles per hour], longest-range [absolute range of 2,000 miles and a combat radius of 600 miles], fastest-climbing [9,000 feet per minute], and highest-ceilinged [52,000 feet] carrier fighter in the world and that is championship in the toughest aircraft design field available.[75]

During the years of "Banshee" production, McDonnell Aircraft was working on a number of other projects. In response to the Army Air Force's need for bomber protection, the company submitted a design for a tiny parasite fighter and in October 1945 was granted an experimental contract to produce the XF-85 "Goblin."[76] One of the smallest jet aircraft ever built, the ship was 15 feet long, 8 feet high, and 21 feet 1 inch in wingspan, and with its single 3,000-pound-thrust Westinghouse J34 engine it could attain the creditable speed of 648 miles per hour.[77] The unique "Goblin," looking much like an angry, plump bumblebee, was designed to nestle in the bomb bay of a B-29 or B-36, zip out and destroy any attackers, and return again to its mother ship via special docking hooks.[78]

The first flight tests were held at Muroc Field, California, on August 23, 1948, when the XF-85 was dropped seven times from a B-29, executed three returns (the first ever by an airplane in its class), and made four desert landings.[79] Despite its impressive performance, the Air Force deemed the radical parasite-fighter plan unsuitable, particularly with the end of the B-36 era and the rise of smaller and faster jet bombers — the "Goblin" now had nothing to guard. In October 1949 the project was abandoned[80] after only two XF-85 prototypes had been built.[81]

Shortly after the parasite program had been undertaken, MAC introduced its second effort in the rotary-wing area. In June 1946 the company received an experimental contract from the Air Force for a helicopter with jet engines.[82] The result was the XH-20 "Little Henry," the world's first ramjet helicopter.[83] The tiny, single-seat aircraft, with a small McDonnell-built engine at each end of its 18½-foot rotor, was 12 feet 6 inches long and 7 feet high and could reach a speed of fifty miles per hour.[84] The original "Little Henry," however, was the only one of its kind, for like that of the "Whirlaway," the project never left the experimental stage.[85]

In the same month that the St. Louis corporation received the

McDonnell Douglas Corp.

McDonnell's F2H-2 "Banshee" performed superbly during the Korean War and was termed "the plane that made the company."

order for its innovative jet helicopter — June 1946 — it was also awarded an experimental contract by the Air Force for two prototypes of a long-range, twin-jet penetration fighter.[86] This ship, the XF-88 "Voodoo," was 54 feet 1½ inches long and 39 feet 8 inches in span and could attain a speed of 647 miles per hour for a range of 1,725 miles.[87] It made its first flight trials on October 20, 1948, but the Air Force, pinched for funds by budget reductions, canceled further development in 1950.[88] The "Voodoo," however, was down but not out. It would come to life again two years later.

In January 1949, while it was still producing the "Banshee," experimenting with the "Voodoo," and delving into helicopter and missile research, McDonnell Aircraft began the development of its third Navy jet fighter-interceptor, the XF3H-1 "Demon."[89] The plane had only one engine, a departure from MAC's customary designs, but the Navy wanted it that way. The "Demon" made its first flight at Lambert Field on August 7, 1951.[90] Impressed with the ship's performance, the Navy responded with a production contract on October 3, 1951, and converted the general order into a specific procurement contract for 150 F3H-1 "Demons" (at $1,068,324 each) on August 29, 1952.[91] Despite its auspicious start, the "Demon" would prove to be the only blot on the sparkling record of McDonnell's first quarter-century.

The F3H-1 was originally a 22,000-pound, short-range interceptor. During the Korean emergency in 1951, however, the Navy was hard-pressed to meet the powerful MIG-15 on an even basis and decided to redesign the "Demon" as a medium-range, all-weather fighter. This meant adding 7,000 pounds to the plane's weight, and some feared that the Westinghouse J40-22 engine would be unable

McDonnell Douglas Corp.

McDonnell's F3H "Demon" proved to be a worthy airframe to continue the successes established by the FH and F2H. The engine manufacturer, however, couldn't power it properly.

to bear the load. In April 1952 President James S. McDonnell fired off a letter to Washington, warning that the result would be a "disappointingly underpowered combination."[92] He requested a more powerful engine, but none was available. While Westinghouse continued development on its improved version, the J40-24, the Navy installed the disputed J40-22 as an "interim engine" in the heavier "Demon," designated the F3H-1N.[93] McDonnell's doubts materialized. The consequences were disastrous.

By mid-1955 six of the underpowered airplanes had crashed (none in Korean combat), killing two pilots. On September 24 of that year, the Navy announced that of 56 F3H-1Ns which had been delivered, 21 (worth a total of $28,350,000) were being permanently grounded; the remaining 29 were to be backfitted with more powerful Allison J-71 engines (at a cost of $4,300,000 each), converting them into the model McDonnell was already producing under the designation F3H-2N.[94] Shocked at the fiasco, the *St. Louis Globe-Democrat* editorialized:

> McDonnell Aircraft Corporation made the airframe for the ships and installed the engines, but had nothing to do with the manufacture or design of the power plants. There is evidence McDonnell lodged a protest about the engines with the Navy. But [the] Navy went ahead with the program anyhow. The engines are a product of Westinghouse. They are reported simply not powerful

enough to operate these planes. Whether this is the fault of Westinghouse, or of Navy specifications, needs to be determined. Let's get the facts. Somebody bungled badly. It was a deadly big-scale mistake.[95]

Congress, as expected, reacted immediately. On September 26, Representative Frank Karsten of St. Louis asked Chet Holafield (D-California) chairman of the House Military Operations Subcommittee, to begin an investigation of the disaster.[96] That same day, Senator Stuart Symington of Missouri made an identical request of the Senate Military Preparedness Subcommittee, then chaired by Lyndon B. Johnson (D-Texas).[97] During October and November of 1955, thorough hearings took place in Washington. What the probes brought out was a story of men under pressure whose haste had resulted in costly errors. After the testimony, Congressman Holafield summed up the case:

> Undoubtedly there was waste in this program, as there is in any development of a new plane or weapon. I've seen no evidence of fraud or improper action. . . . Mistakes were made honestly under the pressure of the Korean emergency. Navy officers simply were caught in a gamble . . . to push ahead in search of a plane equal to the MIG, or to wait until assured their new plane would be a success.[98]

Although no blame was formally placed, the Navy was probably the most at fault — it had made the decision to risk operation with the questionable engine. The powerplant manufacturer perhaps shared some responsibility, but it was penalized excessively. "The flop cost Westinghouse all its Govt. jet contracts, millions of potential profits and a big chunk of prestige."[99] McDonnell emerged from the scuffle bruised, but largely unscathed. The company president's early protest had saved its reputation.

The 21 F3H-1Ns deemed unsuitable for backfitting with Allison J-71 engines (because of the prohibitive cost) were shipped (not flown) to various Naval installations around the country to serve as ground trainers and armament research vehicles, surely among the most expensive in history.[100] The remaining 29 of the faulty "Demons" were equipped with suitable engines and joined the carrier fleet. The Navy reckoned its loss on the entire fiasco at $265 million.[101]

In spite of the catastrophic ordeal, McDonnell continued to receive production contracts for the ship, which it fulfilled in several versions. In all, 519 "Demons" were delivered to the Navy by November 1959.[102] Despite its notoriety, the "Demon" proved a capable plane once its engine problems were corrected, and it even earned a number of distinctions. It was the first airplane designed for missile armament rather than machine gun or cannon.[103] One of its series (an infamous F3H-1N), delivered on December 29, 1954, was the 1,000th airplane the company produced.[104] The ship acquitted itself in a particularly admirable manner during the critical operations in Lebanon and Quemoy-Matsu in 1958 as the mainstay of the American fleet.[105] After a decade of activity, the last "Demmons" were phased out of service on September 21, 1964, to make way for a faster and more effective carrier fighter, another McDonnell product — the F-4B "Phantom II."[106]

During the early stages of the "Demon" program, MAC had also been developing a number of experimental aircraft. In June 1951 the company was granted a contract by the Army to begin work on a revolutionary model combining the principles of both the airplane and the helicopter.[107] Designated the XV-1 "Convertiplane," it was powered by McDonnell-built pressure jets mounted at each rotor tip.[108] The prototype was introduced in February 1954, and on April 29, 1955, the XV-1 became the first aircraft ever to achieve full conversion from helicopter to airplane flight.[109] In the following month it gained another distinction by establishing an unofficial world's speed record for helicopters at 200 miles per hour.[110] Despite the high promise of the model, the Army canceled the program after only two prototypes had been built, and the "Convertiplanes" were ultimately presented to the Smithsonian Institution and the Army Aviation Center Museum.[111]

During the same period, McDonnell also experimented with another rotary-winged ship, the Model 120 "Flying Crane," designated the XHCH-1 by the Navy in August 1952.[112] Although the sturdy jet-rotored craft was capable of carrying a useful load which exceeded its own empty weight,[113] the Navy decided against pursuit of the project and the "Flying Crane" went the way of the three previous McDonnell helicopters.

At the time the company was developing this model, it was in its most prosperous year. During fiscal 1952, MAC reported sales of $81,771,092, netting the firm a handsome profit of $3,064,243. The company then employed more than 14,000 personnel and it had an impressive backlog in excess of $460,000,000.[114] In keeping with its customary procedure, the corporation was developing new and more powerful aircraft to succeed those it was then producing.

Although McDonnell's mainstay through three healthy production contracts had been the United States Navy, the company sought to interest the Air Force as well. The Korean War brought the op-

McDonnell Douglas Corp.

The U.S. Air Force became a prime McDonnell customer with the purchase of the F-101 "Voodoo."

portunity. In search of a long-range fighter-interceptor to counter the potent MIG-15, the Air Force hearkened back to McDonnell's XF-88 "Voodoo" which it had abandoned in 1950, and granted the company a production award for an improved version, designated the F-101, in September 1952.[115]

First flown at Edwards Air Force Base, California, in the autumn of 1954,[116] the "Voodoo" became fully operational in 1957,[117] when it proceeded to establish numerous world records. On November 27, 1957, the twin-jet fighter streaked from Los Angeles to New York and back in the brisk time of 6 hours and 46 minutes for a new transcontinental round trip record. On December 12, 1957, the supersonic ship established the world's absolute speed record for airplanes by passing through the requisite 15/25-kilometer straightaway course at 1207.6 miles per hour. Two years later, the F-101 "Voodoo" established two more world's records: the 1,000-kilometer closed course mark of 700.47 miles per hour, executed on April 8, 1959; and the 500-kilometer closed course record of 816.279 miles per hour, established on April 15, 1959.[118] It was the fastest and most powerful fighter-interceptor of its day.

The "Voodoo" was the first airplane to be utilized by all three major Air Force units: the Strategic Air Command, the Tactical Air

Robert C. Little, McDonnell's chief test pilot, is shown in 1958 as he was about to put the new F4H-1 "Phantom II" through its paces. The plane became McDonnell's most famous and is still being flown throughout the world. Little is now a vice president of McDonnell Aircraft Co.

Command, and the Air Defense Command.[119] In May 1956, during tests at Bikini Atoll, it earned the dubious distinction of becoming the first airplane ever to be exposed in flight to an H-bomb explosion.[120] Like an earlier McDonnell "spook," the ship gained international experience when the United States transferred 66 missile-carrying F-101Bs to the Royal Canadian Air Force in 1961.[121] While its exploits were many, the "Voodoo's" most celebrated achievement came about in the fall of 1962 when it brought back evidence in detailed photographs of the Russian missile buildup in Cuba and thereby alerted the nation and the world to a major Soviet threat.[122]

MAC produced a total of 819 supersonic F-101s in three versions — long-range attack fighter, interceptor, and photo-reconaissance.[123] The versatile "Voodoo" served the Air Force admirably and rewarded McDonnell Aircraft as well, for the company grossed more than one billion dollars on the entire project.[124]

As early as 1953, the St. Louis firm had begun work on its latest supersonic jet fighter, the two-place, twin-engine, long-range, high-altitude F4H-1 "Phantom II."[125] On May 27, 1958, the swift ship, piloted by Robert C. Little, made its initial flight at Lambert Field,[126] and later in the same year it won McDonnell a production contract from the Navy by bettering the Chance-Vought F8U-3 "Crusader" in formal performance trials.[127] In December 1960 the fighter-interceptor model (later designated the F-4B) became operational with fleet squadrons,[128] and in April 1962 the reconaissance version (later designated the RF-4B) initiated its training with the Marines.[129]

By that date the remarkable "Phantom II" had established fifteen world's records, among them: highest altitude for an airplane (98,557 feet — December 6, 1959); greatest speed over a 500-kilometer closed course (1,216.76 miles per hour — September 5, 1960); greatest speed over a 1,000-kilometer closed course (1,390.24 miles per hour — September 25, 1960); Los Angeles-New York transcontinental record (170 minutes — May 24, 1961); greatest speed over a three-kilometer straightaway course at a restricted altitude of 328 feet (902.769 miles per hour — August 28, 1961); absolute speed record for airplanes over a 15/25-kilometer straightaway course (1,606.3 miles per hour — November 22, 1961); highest sustained altitude in level flight (66,443.8 feet — December 5, 1961); and eight time-to-climb marks, the latest for 30,000 meters or 98,425 feet (371.43 seconds — April 12, 1962).[130]

The "Phantom II's" high performance and adaptability drew the attention of both Secretary of Defense Robert McNamara and the Air Force, which wished to improve its tactical fighter capability. In 1961 the McDonnell F4H-1 was pitted against the Republic F-105 and the Convair F-106, both then in production, and it clearly demonstrated its superiority. In a decision without precedent, the Air Force phased out the F-105, a stunning blow to Republic, curtailed the F-106, and placed an order for 1,000 new versions, designated the F-110 (later F-4C) of the Navy's F4H-1.[131] The "Phantom II" thereby became the first American airplane ever to achieve tri-service acceptance.[132]

Characterized as "the Free World's fastest and highest-flying airplane,"[133] the versatile ship could carry several "Sparrow III," "Bullpup," and "Sidewinder" missiles, along with a multi-ton load

The F4 high above the Missouri River in Missouri, photographed in June 1965.

of conventional bombs, rockets, napalm, or nuclear devices, to 92 percent of the earth's surface without refueling.[134] McDonnell developed four versions of the F-4 — interceptor, fighter-bomber, and two reconaissance models [135] (each worth more than $1,000,000 to MAC)[136] — and by November 14, 1964, the date when the company delivered its 3,000th airplane (an F-4C), it had produced 717 Phantom IIs,[137] and was turning them out at a rate of at least one per day on government contracts calling for more than 2,000 of the planes for the Navy, the Marines, and the Air Force.[138] In February 1965 the United States even sold a large number of F-4s (to be equipped with Rolls-Royce engines) to Great Britain, a maneuver which resulted in mass protest demonstrations by British aircraft workers and almost brought down the tenuous Wilson government.[139]

The swept-wing, drooped-nose fighter-bomber-interceptor was by far McDonnell's most successful airplane. By the mid-1960s, selection was underway for the next generation — the multi-service TFX (F-111), designed to surpass speeds of 2,000 miles per hour. McDonnell Aircraft, in cooperation with Douglas Aircraft, bid on the supersonic fighter, but lost to General Dynamics, which received the order amidst much controversy.[140] The St. Louis firm did, however, salvage a subcontract in November 1962 for a specially designed cockpit for the TFX.[141] The two-man module is a self-contained, sealed compartment which can be blasted from the fuselage of the aircraft in 1/100th of a second through the use of an "exploding wire" which acts like a welder's torch to cut the cockpit free instantaneously and parachute it to the ground. By means of this sealed module, emergency ejections can be made with maximum safety at extreme speeds.[142]

In addition to its jet fighter production, McDonnell Aircraft was working, with various degrees of success, on a number of other projects at that time. About 1958, the company spent $13,000,000 of its own funds to develop a four-engine turbojet transport designed for possible use by the Air Force and/or private corporations. Designated the "McDonnell 220," the trim little ship was adaptable for seating from eight to twelve passengers and could reach a speed of 570 miles per hour.[143] There were no buyers, and the unwanted prototype was ignominiously relegated to hangar, while company executives took their own trips in a Lockheed "Jetstar."[144]

In 1962 McDonnell entered the area of short-takeoff-and-landing (STOL) aircraft when it made an agreement with Société Anonyme des Ateliers d'Aviation Louis Breguet of France, by which it acquired exclusive Western-hemisphere sales rights to that firm's Breguet 941 prototype.[145] This ship, which the St. Louis corporation redesignated the "McDonnell 188E," was a four-engine transport capable of flying at a top speed of 240 miles per hour, yet was still highly controllable and safe at the extremely low speed of 57 miles per hour. Its main feature, however, was its STOL characteristic, for with an eight-ton payload it could land with a run of less than 100 yards (a maneuver which it accomplished by instantly reversing its propellers).[146] This vehicle would have particular advantages in a jungle area, such as Viet Nam, where only tiny dirt landing fields were available. With this in mind, McDonnell Aircraft is currently (1965) attempting to persuade the Air Force to purchase its STOL 188E.[147]

With its traditional diversification, MAC was also keeping pace with aeronautic progress by continuing research and experimentation with guided missiles. The company's interest in the field began during World War II with the "Gargoyle" and the "Katydid," but both of those models failed to reach the production stage. McDonnell's first significant accomplishment in that area came in 1951, when the firm was awarded a subcontract to produce the airframe and ramjet engine for the Navy's surface-to-air "Talos,"[148] a project for which Bendix Corporation was the designer and prime contractor.[149] The program proved to be the longest in which McDonnell had yet participated, for by 1962 the firm was still turning out the basic components for the missile, and the contract was expected to continue through 1966.[150]

A direct outgrowth of the "Talos" was the Navy's "Typhoon," a faster and more efficient surface-to-air missile for which Bendix was again the designer and prime contractor and McDonnell the airframe and ramjet producer.[151] Despite the high performance of the vehicle, the Navy canceled further development in 1963 after only a few prototypes had been constructed and tested.[152]

The next product in McDonnell's line of pilotless, radio-controlled craft was the intriguing GAM-72 "Quail," on which the company began work in 1958 for the Air Force. Designed to be launched in "coveys" from the bomb bay of a B-52 "Stratofortress," the short, squat "Quails," which incredibly appeared and behaved as B-52s to enemy radar, serving as decoy missiles to draw firepower away from the actual bombers. The GAM-72 thereby greatly increased the penetration capability of the nuclear-armed bomber force it augmented.[153] In the few years of active production, probably several hundred of the vehicles were constructed.[154] McDonnell delivered the last "Quail" of its $186,000,000 contract to the Strategic Air Command on May 28, 1962.[155]

Among the most advanced of McDonnell's missile developments was the Model 122 "Alpha Draco," the first ballistic missile of its own design, which was intended for experiments in hypersonic aerodynamics. The company received a contract from the Air Force in 1954 to construct three of the pencil-shaped vehicles, all of which were launched from Cape Canaveral in 1959.[156] The "Alpha Draco" achieved unprecedented speeds in excess of Mach 5 (approximately 3,700 miles per hour) in level flight within the atmosphere itself. The innovative design proved to be a breakthrough in the development of aerospace vehicles capable of atmospheric-maneuvering flight at hypersonic speeds.[157] From the successful Model 122, it was but a short step to McDonnell's most celebrated undertaking — Project Mercury.

During 1956 and 1957, the National Advisory Committee for Aeronautics (NACA) began serious consideration of the possibilities of utilizing current ballistic missile boosters to provide the necessary velocities and altitudes for manned orbital and space flight.[158] Further studies crystallized Project Mercury, the purpose of which was threefold: 1) to place a manned space capsule in orbital flight around the earth; 2) to investigate man's performance capabilities

McDonnell Douglas Corp.

McDonnell's "Alpha Draco" ballistic missile achieved speeds of Mach 5, paved the way for Project Mercury, America's first venture into manned space flight.

and his ability to survive in a space environment; and 3) to recover the capsule and man safely.[159]

On November 7, 1958, a contractors' briefing was held at Langley Research Center, Virginia, to explain the program and its needs to some forty prospective bidders on the project.[160] More detailed specifications were then distributed to twenty manufacturers who had stated their firm intention to bid for the contract,[161] but only eleven (AVCO, Chance Vought, Convair, Douglas, Grumman, Lockheed, Martin, McDonnell, North American, Northrup, and Republic) had actually done so by the deadline of December 11, 1958.[162] The St. Louis firm, which had begun formulating its design in 1957 and had poured $900,000 of its own funds into capsule research in anticipation of the government's needs, won the honor of becoming the prime contractor for the project.[163] On February 13, 1959, the National Aeronautics and Space Administration (which had superseded NACA on October 1, 1958) signed a contract with MAC for the design and construction of 12 (later raised to 20) manned orbital Mercury spacecraft.[164]

The vehicle McDonnell produced was a titanium capsule shaped like a television picture tube. It was approximately nine feet high and six feet in diameter at its base, with a seventeen-foot escape tower to propel it away from the booster missile in case of emer-

An ebullient J.S. McDonnell drove President John F. Kennedy, left, and his nephew, Sanford ("Sandy") McDonnell, through his plant. Sandy McDonnell now is chairman of the board of McDonnell Douglas Corporation.

gency during the critical first few seconds after launch.[165] The first was delivered to NASA on April 1, 1960, little more than a year after the order was placed.[166]

After the capsules had undergone six preliminary test flights (including a suborbital ballistic firing on January 31, 1961, with a chimpanzee named Ham as pilot),[167] Alan B. Shepard Jr. made the "free world's first manned space flight" on May 5, 1961, with *Freedom 7* (capsule #7) on a suborbital mission lasting 15 minutes and 22 seconds and reaching a height of 116 miles.[168] This feat was duplicated on July 21, 1961, by Virgil I. Grissom with *Liberty Bell* (capsule #11), which was lost on recovery at sea when the side hatch opened prematurely while the astronaut was awaiting helicopter pickup.[169]

Tests also proceeded on the orbital phase of Project Mercury. After a successful orbit of an empty capsule on September 13, 1961, and two circuits by a chimpanzee named Enos on November 29,

McDonnell Douglas Corp.

The Freedom 7 *Mercury capsule, which carried Alan Shepard on America's first manned space flight.*

1961,[170] John H. Glenn Jr. executed the "free world's first orbital flight" in a 3.25-circuit mission lasting 4 hours, 55 minutes, and 23 seconds on February 20, 1962.[171] As *Time* reported:

Just after John Glenn's *Friendship* 7 [capsule #13] plunked safely into the sea, a wiry, inconspicuous-looking man in rimless glasses hustled out of the Mercury control tower blockhouse at Cape Canaveral to telephone St. Louis. Moments later, 22,000 workers at the McDonnell Aircraft plant laid down their slide rules and wrenches to hear the boss's long-distance words piped over the public address system. Said James Smith McDonnell, 62: "This is Mac calling all the team!" Then, after exulting over the orbital shot and praising the "great teamwork" that accomplished it, he signed off: "My congratulations to you all."[172]

That flight completed the initial assignment of Project Mercury. The subsequent launchings were primarily for additional knowledge of the little-known realm of outer space. On May 24, 1962, Malcolm Scott Carpenter made a 3.25-orbit flight in *Aurora 7* (capsule #18) and on October 3 of the same year, Walter M. Shirra rode *Sigma 7* (capsule #16) on a 6.17-orbit mission. Project Mercury concluded with the impressive 23.23-orbit flight of Leroy Gordon Cooper in *Faith 7* (capsule

J.S. McDonnell, left, and Astronaut (now U.S. Senator) John H. Glenn Jr., in March 1962, after Glenn's Project Mercury flight.

#20) on May 15-16, 1963.[173] The program resulted in prestige for the United States, valuable information for American scientists, and $138,335,000 for prime contractor McDonnell Aircraft (although the firm realized only a modest 3.7 percent profit before taxes).[174] With the outstanding success of Project Mercury it was quite natural that the St. Louis corporation be selected to manufacture the vehicles for the second phase of America's manned space efforts — Project Gemini.

This undertaking was the intermediate stage between Project Mercury and Project Apollo, the actual landing of a man on the moon, slated for 1970 but accomplished in 1969.[175] Gemini's objective was fourfold: 1) to evaluate astronaut performance in space environment for periods of a week or more; 2) to demonstrate rendezvous and docking techniques in orbit by uniting with an Agena target module, a maneuver for which Apollo personnel had practical use; 3) to demonstrate controlled re-entry and landing; and 4) to utilize the two-seat capacity of the spacecraft for astronaut

McDonnell Douglas Corp.

The Gemini capsule.

training.[176]

On December 7, 1961, even before Project Mercury had accomplished its primary object, NASA announced that McDonnell Aircraft would be the prime contractor for the two-man capsule for Project Gemini (named for the constellation featuring the celestial "Twins," Castor and Pollux).[177] On March 29, 1963, the St. Louis firm was awarded a $456,650,062 contract to construct thirteen bell-shaped, Mercury-like titanium capsules 12 feet high and 7½ feet in diameter at the base.[178] Profits on the venture were to be much more handsome than those of its predecessor,* with McDonnell standing to realize a gain of as much as 15 percent.[179]

The first Gemini spacecraft, an unmanned empty shell, was blasted into successful orbital ballistic flight (with no recovery planned or attempted) on April 8, 1964.[180] Foul weather, booster problems, and mechanical difficulties plagued the program. By December 1964 Project Gemini was nearly 18 months behind schedule.[181] The second and final unmanned capsule, crammed with a variety of instruments, including two electronic "black boxes" simulating astronauts, was launched atop a "Titan II" booster at 9:03:59 a.m. (EST) on January 19, 1965, at Cape Canaveral (at that time re-named Cape Kennedy). During its suborbital flight, which lasted a brief 19 minutes and 13 seconds, the 6,900-pound spacecraft reached a height of 98.9 miles and a speed of 16,000 miles per hour, and traveled 2,155 miles downrange before parachuting into the Atlantic Ocean.[182] Deemed a success by its observers, the test opened the way for the first manned Gemini three-orbit flight, with Virgil I. Grissom and John Young aboard, scheduled for April 1965.[183] A total of ten manned missions is planned, at approximate intervals of three months.[184] By the time the project is completed, McDonnell will undoubtedly have another one in hand.

During the period in which it was engaged in spacecraft production for both Mercury and Gemini, the company was also occupied with a project of a related nature called ASSET (an acronym for the ponderous Aerothermodynamic/Elastic Structural Systems Environmental Tests).[185] A direct outgrowth of the successful "Alpha Draco" of 1959,[186] the ASSET vehicle is an unmanned, non-orbiting glider designed to obtain data on the re-entry problems of winged spacecraft.[187]

McDonnell received its initial contract for the program in June 1960 from the Dynamics Laboratory, Aeronautical Systems Division of the Air Force Systems Command,[188] and began construction of the vehicles in 1961.[189] The craft was shaped somewhat like a winged ice cream cone. It was 69 inches long, 55 inches in span, and was constructed of heat-resistant (up to 4,000 Fahrenheit) exotic

*The author is now approaching mid-1965, when this doctoral dissertation was completed. He was, therefore, addressing in the future tense material which, in the year of publication (1984), is regarded as ancient history.

metals (molybdenum, columbium, titanium, zirconia, graphite, and one cryptically labeled L-605). The $16,000,000 contract called for a total of six ASSET gliders: four aerothermodynamic structural vehicles (ASV — "to investigate various concepts and to obtain flight environment data on materials, surface coatings, surface temperatures, and pressure distribution,") and two aerothermoelastic vehicles (AEV — "to obtain data on thermal effects on structural response and aeroelastic instabilities").[190]

The first ASSET vehicle (ASV-1) was launched successfully from Cape Kennedy into a ballistic suborbital trajectory on September 18, 1963, and recovered after a 900-mile flight down the Atlantic Missile Range during which it reached an altitude of 38 miles and a speed of 11,000 miles per hour.[191] During the next fifteen months, four more of the sensor-crammed metallic gliders (ASV-2, ASV-4, AEV-1, and AEV-2) plowed through the atmosphere at hypersonic speeds,[192] with the last vehicle (ASV-4) completing the project (although it was lost at sea) on February 23, 1965.[193]

As a result of MAC's impressive developments in the "Alpha Draco" and ASSET programs, it was announced by the Pentagon on November 12, 1964, that the company had been

McDonnell Douglas Corp.

McDonnell's ASSET perches atop its launch vehicle at Cape Canaveral, Florida, on September 9, 1963.

awarded a contract worth $40,000,000 (with an initial down payment of $3,500,000) for research for the Air Force on an even more sophisticated "boost-glide re-entry vehicle,"[194] a project on which the corporation had been working quietly since the spring of 1963.[195] The future of McDonnell Aircraft lies in such studies and the fruits they bear.

During its first quarter-century of operation, the corporation experienced a measure of success almost unprecedented in the aircraft industry. From July 6, 1939, to June 30, 1964, McDonnell grossed $4,723,476,295 in total sales, paid out $1,744,319,588 in salaries, and netted after taxes $140,107,635 (of which it retained $114,537,163, or 81.7 percent for growth).[196] On its silver anniversary, the company sprawled over a 383-acre, 5,300,000-square-foot complex of 106 buildings, valued at $75,000,000, at Lambert Field and throughout the St. Louis area, with scattered outposts across the nation.[197] With employment at 34,858,[198] and a weekly payroll in excess of $5,000,000, the company was by far the largest single employer in Missouri.[199] MAC stood at the most prosperous peak in its eventful history, and prospects for the future were extremely bright, for as of June 30, 1964, the corporation had a backlog of $1,184,149,765 (tenuously asterisked, however, "subject to termination, reduction, or stretch out, at the convenience of the government").[200]

In no small way was McDonnell Aircraft Corporation's phenomenal rise due to James Smith McDonnell Jr. himself. "Mr. Mac," as he was known to his "teammates," was the dynamic force behind the company's extensive and farsighted operations. Aptly described as "the man with the slide rule mind,"[201] he once even used that device to calculate how much eggnog per person should be served at the company Christmas party to ensure "conviviality without rowdiness" — twelve ounces.[202] It was an example typical of his ingenuity.

Although James McDonnell described himself as "just a practicing Scotsman,"[203] his actions contradicted the stereotype. His philanthropies include $400,000 to St. Louis' planetarium (named in his honor), $200,000 to Country Day School, and $100,000 each to Washington, St. Louis, and Princeton Universities.[204] Among his more notable awards was the prestigious 1963 Daniel Guggenheim Medal (previously received by such men as Orville Wright, Charles Lindbergh, and James H. Doolittle) "for lifetime contributions of outstanding nature on the design and development of military aircraft and for pioneer work in space technology."[205]

On July 23, 1962, James McDonnell stepped down from the company presidency in favor of David S. Lewis, but he remained to guide the firm from his post as chairman of the board of directors and chief executive officer.[206] He died on August 22, 1980, at the age of 81.[207]

From the XP-67 through the ghostly gallery to Project Gemini and the "boost-glide re-entry vehicles" of the future, his company has been the mainstay of St. Louis aviation for nearly forty years. Had there been no McDonnell Aircraft Corporation, the city's status as a major air center would have terminated in 1945. Because there has been and is such a vital aeronautical component within its borders, St. Louis' reputation as a significant synosure of aerial achievement has reached unprecedented peaks. With McDonnell that stature is secure.

Conclusion

FOR MORE THAN A CENTURY, St. Louis has held a prominent position as a noteworthy center of every aspect of aviation. The legion of airmen associated with the city were major factors responsible for its high aerial repute. Great aeronauts like John Wise and Thomas Scott Baldwin laid the foundation by their pioneer accomplishments. Great aviators like Al Williams and Charles Lindbergh added further to its fame. Great astronauts like John Glenn and Walter Shirra carried its name literally around the world.

Of all the airmen in the city's history, the most outstanding was Albert Bond Lambert, its own native son. His guiding hand secured the balloon races and aeronautic tournaments the Aero Club staged in the first decade of the twentieth century. His able mind planned and supervised the development of the city's initial airfields and ascension grounds. Most of all, his generosity and supreme dedication maintained and improved the Bridgeton-Anglum cornfield which grew into Lambert-St. Louis International Airport, justly named in his honor. From 1907 to 1946, the period which witnessed the city's aeronautic foundation and maturation, he was active in almost every aspect of aviation affecting St. Louis. No man loomed larger than he on the pages of the city's air history.

While Major Lambert was the city's foremost aerial enthusiast,

St. Louis was not lacking in others of eminent stature: John Berry, Harry Eugene Honeywell, Thomas Wesley Benoist, William and Frank Robertson, James Smith McDonnell. Such men trafficked in every phase of flight, from spherical balloons, to flying boats, to hypersonic spacecraft. They assisted immeasurably in the building of their city's high aeronautical repute.

The spirit of the St. Louisans themselves was in no small way responsible for the city's aeronautic greatness. They supported its balloon races, air shows, and aerial tournaments, major and minor alike. They passed its airport bond issues and paid for the improvement of its aeronautic facilities. They peopled its aircraft plants and turned out its innovative products. Perhaps more than residents of other cities, St. Louisans have traditionally displayed a more than ordinary interest in things aeronautical.

St. Louis' air leaders and its residents themselves were necessary components to its establishment as a significant air center. They complemented the natural geography of the city itself — its central location: a boon to ballooning, a convenient site for air meets, a focal point for commercial airlines, an advantage for industry.

The city's favorable geographic location, the enthusiasm of its air leaders, and the spirit of its citizens were the touchstones of its aeronautic success. These three factors combined to bring the city superior air facilities, sensational air activities, and significant air industries. Experienced in every facet of aviation, St. Louis has earned an aerial reputation the equal of any city in the world. It is, indeed, the City of Flight.

Chronology

May 31, 1830 — Dr. Claude G. Brun files a patent in St. Louis County Court for a muscle-powered device for propelling balloons.

May 17, 1836 — Richard Clayton makes a six-mile balloon flight from Fourth and Market streets.

July 1-2, 1859 — John Wise, John La Mountain, O.A. Gager, and William Hyde establish a world's distance record for balloons by traveling 826 miles in the *Atlantic* from St. Louis to Henderson, New York, in 19 hours and 40 minutes.

April 30-December 1, 1904 — Louisiana Purchase Exposition management offers $200,000 purse for aeronautics, including a grand prize of $100,000. Captive and free balloon ascensions, glider exhibitions, kite competitions (first ever held), aeronautic congress (first ever conducted), wireless telegraphy from ground to balloon (first ever demonstrated), meteorological balloon experiments (first ever staged), and dirigible flights. Spectacular, but somewhat of a disappointment in that few prizes are awarded. A. Roy Knabenshue is highlight of the fair by demonstrating sustained controlled flight in the *California Arrow,* for the first time in St. Louis.

Mid-1907 — Aero Club of St. Louis is founded by Lewis D. Dozier.

October 17-18, 1907 — Captain Charles De Forrest Chandler and John C. McCoy become the first to win the Lahm Cup with a 473.56-mile flight in the *United States No. 10* from St. Louis to Walton, West Virginia.

October 21, 1907 — Start of the James Gordon Bennett International Balloon Race from Forest Park, first ever held in the United States. Won by Oscar Erbsloeh and H.H. Clayton in the *Pommern* with a new American distance record of 873.4

miles. Runner-up *Isle de France,* with Alfred Le Blanc and E.W. Mix, sets world's endurance record of 44 hours and 3 minutes.

October 23, 1907 — Dirigible races conducted in Forest Park in conjunction with Gordon Bennett Race. Won by Lincoln Beachey. Scheduled heavier-than-air flights fail to materialize.

Spring 1908 — Thomas W. Benoist founds the Aeronautical Supply Company, first of its kind in the United States.

September 8, 1908 — Albert Bond Lambert makes his first balloon flight in the *United States,* a twenty-mile trip with H.E. Honeywell from the Rutger Street plant of Laclede Gas to Creve Coeur Lake.

June 5, 1909 — John Berry of St. Louis wins first National Balloon Race, held at Indianapolis.

July 1909 — Aero Club of South St. Louis founded by Morris A. Heimann.

Mid-1909 — Due to the efforts of Albert Bond Lambert, Missouri becomes the only state to have its National Guard equipped with an aerial detachment. Unit holds its first test ascension September 5 at Chouteau and Taylor avenues.

October 4, 1909 — Start of Centennial Balloon Races from grounds at Chouteau and Newstead Avenues. Major event won by S. Louis Von Phul and Joseph M. O'Reilly in the *St. Louis III* with a 540-mile flight to Mille Lac, Minnesota. Clifford B. Harmon and Augustus Post set endurance record of 48 hours and 26 minutes in a 146-mile flight to Edina, Missouri, in the *New York.*

October 7, 1909 — Glenn Curtiss makes first airplane flight to take place in St. Louis. It lasts only a few seconds, but crowds of up to 300,000 watch his performances in Forest Park throughout the week. Dirigible maneuvers held concurrently, but wind and rain cancel much of the program.

October 12-13, 1909 — A. Holland Forbes and Max C. Fleischmann win the Lahm Cup from Charles De Forrest Chandler, with a 697.17-mile flight in the *New York* from St. Louis to Richmond, Virginia.

October 15-16, 1909 — Albert Bond Lambert and S. Louis Von Phul set official American balloon speed record of 44 miles per hour with a 685-mile flight to Ridgeville, South Carolina, in 15 hours and 29 minutes in the *St. Louis III.*

Mid-1910 — Kinloch Park airfield is established by the Aero Club of St. Louis.

July 1910 — Air meet for novices staged at Washington Park, East St. Louis, Illinois, by the Aero Club of St. Louis.

September 10, 1910 — Thomas Scott Baldwin makes St. Louis's first extensive airplane flight with an impressive trip over and under the Mississippi River bridges in his *Red Devil.*

September 18, 1910 — Tom Benoist becomes first St. Louisan to pilot an airplane and the first to use the new Kinloch Park airfield.

October 8, 1910 — Inaugural issue of *Aero,* the first weekly aeronautical magazine in the United States, is published in St. Louis by E. Percy Noel of the Aero Club.

October 8-16, 1910 — International Air Meet at Kinloch Park. Arch Hoxsey sets nonstop cross-country record of 87 miles from Springfield, Illinois, to St. Louis. Theodore Roosevelt becomes first U.S. president to fly in an airplane. A.L. Welch sets world's endurance record of 3 hours, 11 minutes, and 55 seconds. Alfred Le Blanc sets American speed record of 68 miles per hour.

October 17, 1910 — Start of the James Gordon Bennett International Balloon Race from Chouteau and Newstead avenues. Alan R. Hawley and Augustus Post set new American distance record of 1,172.9 miles to Lake Tschotogama, Quebec, in the *America II* to win the Gordon Bennett Cup. They also win permanent possession of the Lahm Cup, since their mark will remain unbeaten for the requisite three years.

November 17-24, 1910 — First National Air Show is held at the Coliseum. Eighty exhibitors display their aeronautic wares. In conjunction with the show, Helene Mallard becomes the first woman ever to ascend in a "man-carrying" kite, in Forest Park.

July 10, 1911 — St. Louis pilots Frank P. Lahm, John Berry, and William Assmann sweep first three places in the National Balloon Race at Kansas City.

August 14-25, 1911 — Harry N. Atwood establishes cross-country record of 1,265 miles in an airplane flight from St. Louis to New York City.

September 1911 — Albert Bond Lambert is granted License No. 61 by the Aero Club of America to become one of the five men in the United States holding both official balloon and airplane licenses, as well as the first St. Louisan and the first president of an aero club licensed to pilot an airplane.

October 1-8, 1911 — Air meet at Fairground Park. Official United States mail is carried by plane for the second time in history. Walter Brookins stars, despite the fact that high wind and rain washes away most of the program.

October 14-21, 1911 — Air meet at Kinloch Park. Principle of the intercom or "aerophone" is demonstrated for the first time by Bernays Johnson and Howard Gill. Andrew Drew equals world's record in accurate landing by stopping four feet from his target. Haward Gill sets American endurance record of 4 hours, 16 minutes, and 40 seconds. P.O. Parmalee establishes American altitude record of 7,500 feet.

October 28, 1911 — Howard Gill sets new American record for passenger poundage by carrying aloft the 255-pound Fred Murphy at Kinloch Park. Flight also sets total weight record of 416 pounds.

March 1, 1912 — Albert Berry makes world's first parachute jump from an airplane, over Jefferson Barracks in South St. Louis.

September 24, 1912 — With a Benoist biplane, Tony Jannus delivers four cases of Lemp's beer to the St. Louis Fair — the first consignment of freight to go by air.

November 6-December 16, 1912 — Tony Jannus establishes the world's hydroplane distance record of 1,973 miles with a Benoist biplane flying boat on a flight down the Missouri-Mississippi river system from Omaha to New Orleans.

Mid-1913 — Major Frank L. Lane, Tom Benoist, and Tony Jannus demonstrate at Kinloch Park the first rapid-fire machine gun designed expressly for airplanes.

January 1, 1914 — Tom Benoist and Tony Jannus inaugurate the world's first scheduled airline, the St. Petersburg-Tampa Airboat Line, Passenger and Express Service. During the next four months, 1,205 passengers and several tons of freight are flown across Tampa Bay between the two cities.

July 11, 1914 — Start of the National Balloon race at Priester's Park. Excessive heat (111°) results in poor distances. R.A.D. Preston wins contest in the *Goodyear* by traveling 300 miles to Constance, Kentucky.

May 1917-November 1918 — Missouri Aeronautical Society's balloon school under Albert Bond Lambert trains 354 pilots and observers for wartime service.

April 1919 — Air Mail Field established at Forest Park. Service begins in the following year, but only lasts until 1921.

September 26, 1919 — Start of the first Army-Navy Balloon Race at Meramec Park. Won by Captain E.P. Phillips and First Lieutenant Byron T. Burt in *Army #1* with a 491.8-mile flight to Door Peninsula, Michigan.

October 1, 1919 — Start of the National Balloon Race at Meramec Park. Won by Ralph Upson and Ward T. Van Orman with 1,050-mile flight to Dunbar, Quebec, in the *Goodyear.*

June 18, 1920 — Missouri Aeronautical Society leases 160-acre cornfield on Natural Bridge Road to establish an airfield. Later grows into Lambert-St. Louis International Airport.

October 3-6, 1923 — International Air Races held at Lambert Field. Lieutenant Al Williams sets world's speed record of 243.812 miles per hour in the Pulitzer Trophy Race. Eight other major events. The *ZR-1* (later the *Shenandoah),* the largest dirigible in the world, and the Barling Bomber, the largest airplane in the world, make appearances.

October 7, 1925 — Robertson Aircraft Corporation is awarded CAM-2 from Chicago to St. Louis, one of the first five airmail routes granted to private operators by the Post Office Department.

May 20-21, 1927 — Charles Lindbergh becomes the first man to fly nonstop solo from New York to Paris in a flight of 33 hours, 30 minutes, and 29.8 seconds in the *Spirit of St. Louis.*

August 7, 1928 — First "Robin" comes off the production line of the Curtiss-Robertson Airplane Manufacturing Company, which will produce a record 749 more during the next 1½ years. A $2,000,000 airport bond issue is passed the same day by a margin of five to one.

December 17, 1928 — Dale Jackson executes record number of 417 barrel rolls in succession in an "OX-5 Robin" over Lambert Field.

July 13-30, 1929 — Dale Jackson and Forrest O'Brine set world's endurance record of 420 hours, 21 minutes, and 30 seconds in the *St. Louis Robin #1.*

September 28, 1929 — Start of the International Balloon Race at ascension grounds at 8900 South Broadway. Won by Ward T. Van Orman and Alan MacCracken with a 341-mile flight in the *Goodyear VIII* to Troy, Ohio. Lowest winning distance in the history of the Gordon Bennett Race. Last major balloon race held in St. Louis.

February 15-23, 1930 — International Aircraft Exposition held in the Arena. 170 aviation companies display exhibits. In conjunction with the show, two record performances take place: D.S. "Barney" Zimmerly sets world's altitude mark for light planes by climbing to 27,250 feet in a Barling NB-3 over Forest Park; Philip Love executes record number of three outside loops in succession in a Waco biplane with a passenger over Lambert Field.

May 3, 1930 — Laura Ingalls, St. Louis' first licensed woman transport pilot, performs the women's world record number of 344 loops in succession with a "Gipsy Moth" over Lambert Field.

July 12, 1930 — Lambert-St. Louis Municipal Airport formally dedicated by Admiral Richard E. Byrd.

July 21-August 17, 1930 — Dale Jackson and Forrest O'Brine establish the world's endurance record of 647 hours, 28 minutes, and 30 seconds in the *Greater St. Louis,* a "Challenger Robin," to become the only pilots to regain the duration crown after having once lost it.

October 12, 1935 — Clare Bunch, president of the Lambert Aircraft Corporation, sets national altitude record for planes weighing less than 1,300 pounds by taking his "Monocoupe," with company vice president B.L. Carter, to a height of 19,000 feet over Lambert Field.

May 29-31, 1937 — St. Louis Air Races and International Aerobatic Competition (first ever held) staged at Lambert Field in commemoration of the tenth anniversary of Lindbergh's transatlantic flight. Five major races in addition to the aerobatic contest. Louise Thaden sets women's 100-kilometer speed mark of 197.9 miles per hour. City's last major air meet.

July 6, 1939 — McDonnell Aircraft Corporation founded at Lambert Field by James Smith McDonnell Jr.

March 26, 1940 — The CW-20, prototype of the Curtiss C-46 "Commando," the largest twin-engine transport of its era, makes its initial flight at Lambert Field.

August 1, 1943 — Tragic glider crash at Lambert Field kills Mayor William Dee Becker, Major William B. Robertson, and eight other civic, political, industrial and military figures. Worst air disaster in the city's history.

June 1946 — McDonnell Aircraft receives contract from the Air Force to build the XH-20 "Little Henry," the world's first ramjet helicopter.

July 21, 1946 — McDonnell FH-1 "Phantom" becomes first jet airplane to take off from and land on an aircraft carrier, the *U.S.S. Franklin D. Roosevelt.* The "Phantom" is also the first Naval airplane to exceed 500 miles per hour.

October 26, 1946 — McDonnell XHJD-1 "Whirlaway," the world's first twin-engine helicopter, makes its inaugural flight at Lambert Field.

November 12, 1946 — Major Albert Bond Lambert, the dean of aviation in St. Louis, dies in his sleep of heart disease.

August 23, 1948 — McDonnell XF-85 "Goblin" jet parasite fighter makes successful return to its B-29 mother ship. First time such a maneuver performed.

August 1949 — McDonnell F2H "Banshee" sets altitude record of 52,000 feet.

April 29, 1955 — McDonnell XV-1 "Convertiplane" becomes first aircraft ever to achieve full conversion from helicopter to airplane flight. Later sets unofficial helicopter speed record of 200 miles per hour.

March 10, 1956 — Striking new barrel-vaulted terminal building at Lambert Field is formally dedicated by Mayor Raymond R. Tucker.

December 12, 1957 — McDonnell F-101 "Voodoo" establishes world's absolute speed record for airplanes at 1,207.6 miles per hour. Eventually holds five other transcontinental and closed-course speed records.

November 22, 1961 — McDonnell F4H "Phantom II" establishes world's absolute speed record for airplanes at 1,606.3 miles per hour. Eventually holds fourteen other speed, altitude, and time-to-climb records.

February 20, 1962 — John Glenn becomes first American to orbit the earth, using a McDonnell Mercury space capsule christened *Friendship 7.*

March 23, 1965 — First manned orbital flight of McDonnell Gemini space capsule is launched, with Virgil I. Grissom and John Young as crew.

Spring 1965 — Parks Metropolitan Airport, Cahokia, Illinois, is scheduled to open as St. Louis' first secondary municipal airport.

Glossary

Aeronaut — the pilot of a balloon, airship, or other lighter-than-air craft.

Airframe — the wooden or metal structure of an airplane without its engine or powerplant. Most aircraft manufacturers who settled in St. Louis were airframe producers. Only Monocoupe-Lambert and McDonnell Aircraft did any significant engine production.

Airship — a gas-filled lighter-than-air craft, generally cigar-shaped, to which was attached a framework housing the pilot (aeronaut) and an engine or engines to control the flight. Also called a dirigible because it achieved steerable flight.

Amphibian — an airplane equipped with a boat-like hull and retractable wheels enabling it, like an alligator or a frog, to operate from both land and water.

Astronaut — the pilot of a space capsule or other vehicle capable of traveling through space. The term was coined with the advent of McDonnell's Project Mercury.

Aviator — the pilot of an airplane or other heavier-than-air machine, as opposed to the aeronaut, whose realm was lighter-than-air craft.

Ballast — an essential component for controlling a free balloon. The usual ballast was several hundred pounds of sand, customarily in forty-pound bags. By tossing it out by the handful, a pilot could ascend in search of a favorable current.

Balloon — a spherical, gas-filled bag, generally of varnished silk or rubberized cotton, to which was attached a basket, usually of wicker, for pilot and provisions. Borne by the wind, such vehicles could only be controlled in respect to vertical motion: to ascend, the aeronaut tossed out sand ballast; to descend, he expelled gas from a special valve at the top of the bag. A medium-size balloon in the early 1900s held about 40,000 cubic feet of coal gas (the most popular variety) or hydrogen; championship racing balloons of that era averaged 80,000 cubic feet in capacity.

Barograph — an instrument used by aeronauts and aviators alike to record the altitudes at which they flew. The device measured atmospheric pressure and was required equipment on all official flights as insurance against unauthorized landings.

Biplane — an airplane with two wings, one above the other. The earliest airplanes were of this type, since the dual wing supplied added lift to supplement the weak engines of that era. Many were manufactured until well into the 1930s. A monoplane has only one wing, a triplane three, and a quadriplane four. (There were such craft.)

Cowling — the metal cover enclosing the engine of an airplane.

Drag rope — a device used by balloonists to regulate the altitude at which they flew. Frequently more than 1,000 feet long, the rope dangled from the basket in flight. Often it trailed along on the ground smashing into houses, fences, trees, or whatever else was in its path.

Fuselage — the body of an airplane; the basic structure to which its wings and control surfaces are attached.

Hypersonic speed — a velocity in excess of Mach 5, approximately 3,700 miles per hour at sea level.

Mach number — named after Austrian physicist Ernst Mach (1838-1916), this designation represents the ratio of the speed of an aircraft (or other body) to the speed of sound in the surrounding atmosphere. For subsonic speeds the Mach number is less than one (for instance, .82); for supersonic speeds it is greater than one (for instance, 1.47). Mach 1 at sea level is 738 miles per hour.

Ornithopter — a "flying machine" propelled by flapping wings in the manner of a bird. Also called an orthopter. No muscle-powered machine of this type ever made a sustained flight. The first human-powered aircraft to make a sustained flight was the *Gossamer Condor,* a pedal-powered monoplane designed by Paul MacCready of Pasadena, California, which flew a prescribed 1.5-mile figure-eight course near Shafter, California, in August 1977. Another MacCready design, the *Gossamer Albatross,* spanned the English Channel on June 13, 1979.

Prototype — the first experimental model (full-size) of an aircraft intended for production in quantity. If the potential buyer (for instance, the government) is satisfied with the performance of the prototype, he orders it in quantity; if he is not, the project usually terminates in its experimental stage.

Pusher engine — a piston-driven engine facing the rear of an airplane which pushes it through the air. A tractor engine (the more predominant variety since World War I) is located in the nose or on the wing of an airplane and pulls it through the air.

Rip panel — a device by which a balloonist may instantly deflate the balloon on landing, especially on windy days, to avoid being dragged all over the countryside.

Statoscope — an instrument which indicated whether a balloon was ascending or descending; it was often difficult to determine that from the pilot's vantage point.

Supersonic speed — a speed in excess of 738 miles per hour at sea level (the speed of sound, which is Mach 1).

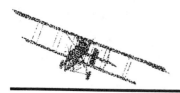

Publisher's Afterword

IT MUST HAVE BEEN in the early 1970s when I first came across Jim Horgan's dissertation, "City of Flight." I was in the Pius XII Library of Saint Louis University for some reason long forgotten, and I can't even recall whether I happened across the volume on the shelves accidentally or whether I was making a deliberate search for things pertaining to flight in St. Louis. For whatever reason, I was drawn to it.

I skimmed it in utter fascination that afternoon, and the next time I was in the library I read it through — all 600 pages of it. It was no less captivating to me then than it is today, and I determined that someday, somehow, I would publish that dissertation.

While I was busy with my growing publishing company, thoughts of the book wouldn't go away. The lines of force which led to its publication started to be drawn in the spring of 1979. I had been commissioned to prepare the biography of the late General Leif J. Sverdrup, and in the course of the research I was attracted to a company founded by that great man — Midcoast Aviation. That firm, or rather its predecessor, had been floundering in the late 1960s, and in 1971 the general himself persuaded John T. Tucker to leave his lucrative presidency of Butler Aviation to return to St. Louis and revive the ailing company.

Sverdrup had almost unerring judgment in people, and it was obvious during the course of my two-hour interview that his confidence in young John Tucker was well placed. (Tucker was only 34 when he assumed the Butler presidency.)

Sverdrup had known Tucker as a boy, for he is the son of the late Raymond R. Tucker, now coming to be regarded as the best mayor St. Louis has ever had and the only one to have served three terms. The elder Tucker and Sverdrup were friends during those years, as Sverdrup's engineering firm, Sverdrup and Parcel, flashed to international prominence. Ray Tucker, an engineering professor, had a high regard for the general, and the feeling was mutual.

Midcoast Aviation

John Tucker

As I left John Tucker's office on March 6, 1979, I was enthralled by a collection of some 200 photographs mounted in the corridors of the Midcoast office and terminal buildings. They constituted a dramatic pictorial essay on the history of aviation in St. Louis. John Tucker obviously was interested in the subject. Later, as our friendship grew, I discussed with him the possibility of issuing the best of those photos as a portfolio for the Midcoast clientele. Little came from those talks.

When I stopped in at the Pius Library in the fall of 1983 the Horgan manuscript was no longer on the shelves. It had been put on microfilm and the original typescript had been destroyed. I determined then and there to issue that book, and soon, so I tracked down Dr. Horgan. He now is chairman of the social science division of Saint Leo College in Saint Leo, Florida, in the Tampa Bay area. I contacted him and received his blessing, although he was flabbergasted that anyone would want to issue his work in book form 19 years after it had been laid to rest.

Recalling his interest in aviation history, I decided to contact John Tucker again. I told him that it would not be economically feasible for The Patrice Press to undertake the publishing venture alone. He agreed to sponsor the book because he felt the people of St. Louis were forgetting about the tremendous contribution their forebears have made to aviation. He said, "We'll fund this project because it needs to be done."

Tucker and I and two of his employees then drove to Natural Bridge and McDonnell boulevards, the address of the nearest White Castle restaurant. There we consummated the arrangement in a quasi-religious ritual almost as ancient as St. Louis itself. He downed four bellybombers; I had three.

The list of people to be thanked by me is growing almost daily. Right at the top is Jim Horgan himself. He offered to do some updating on the manuscript, but I asked that this not appear in the text. (Most of it is in this afterword or the annotation.) He re-examined the manuscript, edited it again, had it copied for me, and rushed it to St. Louis. He provided some photos I didn't have and couldn't get. He did everything I asked him to do, cheerfully and with enthusiasm.

Then there is the Midcoast staff. Stacy Weaks, a veritible encyclo-pedia on the history of business aviation and Lambert Field, studied the manuscript himself and was impressed with its thoroughness. Linda Plummer proofread the entire manuscript; and Tucker's cheerful, gracious executive secretary, Catherine Wolfe, facilitated communications among us all — certainly no easy task.

Duane R. Sneddeker, curator of photographs at Missouri His-torical Society, and his staff were available whenever I needed them, and that was often on short notice. So was Anne Kenney, curator of the Western Historical Manuscript Collection, Thomas Jefferson Library, University of Missouri/St. Louis. Beryl Manne, head of archives at Washington University's John M. Olin Library, who had helped so generously in my research for the Sverdrup bio-graphy, came through again with her photographic archives of the St. Louis Car Company's rich aviation history.

My friend, David Lipman, managing editor of the *St. Louis Post-Dispatch,* allowed me to use his newspaper's vast reference library (the "morgue"), where I was helped by Nancy Stoddard, the librar-ian, and especially by Marie C. Jones of that department.

Betty Burnett helped on numerous aspects of the publication and prepared the index for the book. My wife Laura proofread the gal-leys and managed to catch errors that somehow eluded others.

Gary Lucy's dramatic rendering of the photo on p. 140 under-scores the growing sentiment that he is Missouri's finest living illus-trator. Others who helped by providing pictures are credited beneath those photos. All have my gratitude.

Here is a brief update on some of the remarkable things that have happened in this City of Flight in the 19 years since Horgan finished (or thought he had finished) his work. He describes what has happened to ballooning:

Nikki Caplan and St. Louis Ballooning Today

Competitive sport ballooning returned to St. Louis in December 1973, when Nikki Caplan took the lead in organizing the Forest Park Balloon Race, the city's first contest since it hosted the 1929 James Gordon Bennett Cup Race. "We scoured the Midwest," she said, "and came up with nine balloons."[1] The contest was a "hare and hounds race" for hot-air balloons. Trailing a long identifying banner, the "hare" took off a few minutes before the eight "hounds," which then chased the "hare" across the Mississippi River to Jersey County, Illinois. The winners, for landing closest to the quarry, were Jerry Kinkade and copilot Wayne Shaw. The race has been an annual event in the city since that time.[2]

With Robert Esch and other ballooning enthusiasts, she helped form the Gateway Aerostatic Association in 1974 to promote the revival of the sport. The fiftieth anniversary of Charles A. Lindbergh's flight provided the occasion for a commemorative balloon race, organized by Donald Sarno and Henry Fett in May 1977.[3]

Subsequently, Caplan and her husband Donald, who operate a sales-repair-school and charter service called BalloonPort of St. Louis, organized the McDonnell Douglas Aero Classic for gas balloons in 1982 and 1983. Sanctioned by the Balloon Federation of America, the event recalled a feature of the 1904 World's Fair, for the destination of the contestants was the Washington Monument in the District of Columbia.

The most eventful flight of the 1982 race was made by Col. Joseph Kittinger and his copilot Robert Snow in the *Rosie O'Grady*. Like Alan Hawley and Augustus Post in the 1910 Gordon Bennett Race, they were blown northeastward into the wilds of Canada, coming down 45 miles north of Lake St. John in Quebec Province. "We got a call in the middle of the night," remembered Nikki Caplan. "The message was that Kittinger was being chased by a buffalo. Imagine the image that popped into our minds." The balloonists were being tracked by a "Buffalo," an aircraft of the Canadian Air Rescue, which summoned a helicopter to pick up the adventurers after a few hours on the ground.

What was truly extraordinary about the flight was their distance: 1,172.3 miles, a nearly exact duplication of Hawley and Post's 1,172.898 miles to Lake Tschotogama. For contest purposes, unfortunately, it was too far in the wrong direction. The winners were the celebrated Ben Abruzzo (a member of both record-setting crews who had crossed the Atlantic Ocean in 1978 and the Pacific in 1981) and his copilot Ron Clark (who had also crossed the Pacific).

BalloonPort Photo

Nikki Caplan

After a northeastward flight of 457.4 miles in the *Benihana,* they came down near Clare, Michigan, but closer to the Washington Monument than any of the ten other contenders.[4] Kittinger later distinguished himself by becoming the first balloonist to achieve a solo crossing of the Atlantic, September 14-18, 1984.[5]

The winds were also fickle for the 1983 contest, just as they had been in 1904, when Carl Myers landed in St. Charles, Missouri, farther away from the monument than when he started. But the McDonnell Douglas Aero Classic judges had anticipated the situation and provided two alternate targets for the five entrants: the towns of either Piedmont or Ozark, Missouri. The winners were Fred Krieg and his daughter Angela, who flew the *Destiny* southward to a landing eight miles from Piedmont, 113.5 miles from St. Louis.[6]

Nikki Caplan herself is St. Louis' foremost modern balloonist. She holds the women's world's distance record for gas balloons in the AA-6 through AA-15 class. With C. Jane Buckles as copilot, she sailed 843.59 miles from Albuquerque, New Mexico, to Duncombe, Iowa, on October 6-8, 1982,[7] in the 35,000-cubic-foot helium balloon *City of St. Louis.*[8] The equipment and provisions they carried on that flight illustrate that while today's scientific instruments are more sophisticat-

ed, ballooning has changed little from the adventuresome days
of John Wise:

> 720 lbs. of sand ballast in 30-lb. bags; two 30-lb. 12 v. batteries;
> 2 20 lb. 12 v. batteries; 5 lbs. of misc. "C", "D", "A" and
> "AAA" batteries; "Cool" Light sticks.
>
> Aircraft transceiver; transponder; encoding altimeter; electron-
> ic variometer and altimeter; mechanical altimeter and rate-of-
> climb indicator; VOR (navigation); ELT; FM transceiver; elec-
> tronic envelope and ambient temperature indicator; AM-FM
> receiver; compass; sealed recording Winter barograph; 2 oxy-
> gen cylinders, regulator and masks; life jackets; fire extinguish-
> er; navigation lights; 200' drag line; 2 80 lb. cargo chutes;
> Porta-Potty; sleeping bag; U.S. flag.
>
> Complete sets (U.S.A.) of sectionals; WAC charts; low altitude
> navigation charts; flight log; plotter; calculator; aircraft papers;
> balloon mail.
>
> Tins of fruit cocktail; chocolate pudding; Vienna sausages;
> chicken salad; tomato, apple and grapefruit juice; wheatstone
> crackers; Cadbury chocolate bars; Gorp trail mix; string cheese;
> instant coffee; hot chocolate; Coffee Mate (creamer); 8 quarts
> of water; paper plates and paper towels; plastic cups and uten-
> sils; ice pick; knife; Wet Ones; coffee pot; miniature propane
> stove; personal ditty bags containg a "change"; cold weather
> gear; toothbrush; lip balm; cigarettes.
>
> Emergency equipment: strobe light; flare gun; mirror; whistle;
> pliers; screwdriver; duct tape; spare line; carabineers; snaffles;
> electrical tape; Band-Aids; vitamins; salt tablets; aspirin;
> Sine-Aid; Sun Screen; Cutter's insect repellant; saline solution.[9]

These excerpts from the log of the *City of St. Louis* chronicle
the highlights of their record flight:

> 7:31 PM (October 6) Launch from Cutter Field, Albuquerque,
> N.M.
>
> 7:39 PM Altitude 7,200. Ballast count 22. Track N. North of
> launch site.
>
> 9:15 PM Tracking toward Santa Fe. Thermos of coffee ready for
> nite watch.
>
> 4:20 AM Altitude 11,340. Track 075°. Speed 22. Jane up.
> Nikki asleep. Crew contact.
>
> 8:45 AM Altitude 10,440. Speed 17. 45 mi east of Dalhart, TX.
>
> 1:45 PM Altitude 9,600. N. Buffalo, OK. Valve 2 sec. Crew
> contact. Req'd weather info. Long range crew contact with
> weather report. New front expected thru KS FR AM. (We

Nikki Caplan, left, and copilot C. Jane Buckles in the City of St. Louis, *enroute to a new world's distance record. They were photographed near Albuquerque, New Mexico, on October 6, 1982.*

plan to land before!)

5:50 PM   Altitude 5,610. Ballast count 9. Hutchinson, KS. Dropped battery in field with chute. Contacted crew to retrieve.

Midnight   Near Omaha. Nikki woke to rain. Clear skies but raining on us. Soaked! No p'ptn on surface! Climbed above thin cloud layer. Tho cold, we continued to climb??

2:20 AM   Altitude 10,500. Track 060°. Speed 26.2. Very cold and wet.

4:50 AM Altitude 2,700. 2-3 miles NE Jefferson AP. Damp.

6:29 AM (October 8) Landed! Bushy Creek State Preserve, Duncombe, Iowa. Duration 35 hours, 16 minues. Distance 843.59 statute miles. 1,357.63 km.[10]

For this achievement and her other "outstanding contributions to gas ballooning," Nikki Caplan was awarded the 1983 *Diplome Montgolfier* by the International Aeronautic Federation.[11] Because of her second-place standing among American competitive balloonists (according to a formula developed by the Balloon Federation of America), Caplan won the right to represent the United States (along with Ben Abruzzo and Robert Penny) in the 1984 James Gordon Bennett Cup Race from Zurich, Switzerland.[12]

Ballooning is once again established in St. Louis, and the revival of the city's reputation is due in no small measure to the accomplishments of the exuberant Nikki Caplan.

Notes

1. Telephone conversation between the author and Nikki Caplan, August 24, 1984.
2. Telephone conversation between the author and Nikki Caplan, September 4, 1984.
3. Letter to the author from Nikki Caplan, September 10, 1984.
4. Telephone conversations between the author and Nikki Caplan, September 13, and Donald Caplan, September 14, and letter to the author with the official results, September 14, 1984.
5. *St. Petersburg Times,* September 19, 1984.
6. Telephone conversations between the author and Nikki Caplan, September 4 and 13, and letter to the author with the official results, September 14, 1984.
7. The flight was officially made on October 7-8, since balloon records are reckoned according to Greenwich Mean Time.
8. Telephone conversation between the author and Debra Spaeth, Operations chairman of the Balloon Federation of America, August 31, 1984.
9. Letter to the author from Nikki Caplan, September 6, 1984.
10. Flight log of the *City of St. Louis,* a copy of which was sent to the author by Nikki Caplan on September 6, 1984.

A row of Army Air Corps aviation cadets stands inspection before their biplanes at Parks Air College (now Parks College of Saint Louis University), sometime during World War II.

11. Telephone conversation between the author and Debra Spaeth, August 31, 1984.
12. Telephone conversation between the author and Nikki Caplan, September 4, 1984.

Horgan's study is limited to aerial activity on the Missouri side of the Mississippi River, with scant reference to activity in nearby Illinois. Parks College was founded on August 1, 1927, less than three months after Lindbergh's transatlantic flight, by Oliver L. Parks, a St. Louis automobile salesman and pilot. His "college" at Lambert Field consisted of a rented hangar housing two biplanes, plus himself as the faculty. The following year he moved flight operations to Cahokia, across the Mississippi River from downtown St. Louis. In 1940, with war clouds gathering, the government asked Parks to increase his pilot training capacity from 400 to 7,000 students per year, and to do it within 90 days. Parks came through, and his facility ultimately made pilots of 37,000 cadets from 1940 through 1945 — 10 percent of all the U.S. Army Air Corps pilots — plus another 2,000 mechanics.

The school today has 18 brick buildings on campus, plus 18 late model Cessna training planes. Current enrollment (1984) is 1,050 students. A branch operation is maintained at Spirit of St. Louis County Airport in Chesterfield. Parks donated his college to Saint Louis University in 1946, and it remains a branch of that institution today.

Most of the smaller airfields in St. Louis County had perished even before the Horgan manuscript was completed. One which sur-

Midcoast Aviation

St. Louis Downtown-Parks Airport, its name changed in September 1984 from Bi-State Parks Airport, now serves a growing clientele from the central city. Formerly the Curtiss-Steinberg Airport, then Parks Metropolitan, the field developed when flight operations were discontinued at the campus of nearby Parks College.

vived, and continues today as a healthy private facility, is Gene Taylor's Weiss Airport. Another, which fell upon hard times in the 1970s, is Spirit of St. Louis — recently resuscitated by St. Louis County and now a burgeoning secondary airport. It serves west St. Louis County.

Parks Airport as such is only a single grass strip on the campus. The old Curtiss-Steinberg facility, northeast of the college and also in Cahokia, became an arm of the Bi-State Development Agency. It serves the downtown St. Louis area as a secondary field today. In September 1984 the name was changed to St. Louis Downtown-Parks Airport. Midcoast has a major facility there, both in the hangars and in the striking new terminal building.

Nowhere has change been more evident than at Lambert Field. After the dissertation was done a decision was announced: henceforth it would be known as "St. Louis International Airport." A surprising howl emerged from St. Louis, and the dismayed officials quietly changed it to "Lambert-St. Louis International Airport."

Midcoast is the principal tenant of the new terminal building at St. Louis Downtown, in Cahokia. The firm also owns several hangars there for maintenance and outfitting of business aircraft.

The howls died away. St. Louisans were aware of their aviation history, as well as human nature; they could live with that. Despite the pretentious nature of the name, it is still known, and probably always will be known as "Lambert Field."

Probably the most controversial aviation issue ever to hit Missouri transpired in the early 1970s. The postwar baby boom was in full flower then, and the North County had become densely developed with row after row of low-cost single family homes. They had encroached to the very edges of Lambert Field, and it appeared as if there was no room for future airport expansion.

The St. Louis consulting engineering firm of Horner and Shifrin was commissioned to study the problem. They recommended several sites for a new airport, their preference being in the Columbia-Waterloo area of Illinois, across the river from south St. Louis County.

The concept drew several powerful backers: downtown St. Louis interests, the State of Illinois, the Federal Aviation Administration, the *St. Louis Post-Dispatch,* and the mayor of the City of St. Louis, Alfonso J. Cervantes.

Virtually everyone else was against the project. The powerful presence of the United States government seemed to make the chances for retention of Lambert Field nil, but Wallace ("Buck") Persons, a St. Louis industrialist, fought back. He provided persistent leadership which coalesced the various independent Lambert Field advocates into a single fighting force. G. Duncan Bauman, publisher of the *St. Louis Globe-Democrat,* brought his paper into the fray. Lawrence Roos, St. Louis County Supervisor, and the Missouri delegation in Washington exerted enormous pressure on the administration. In 1977 President Jimmy Carter's secretary of transportation, Brock Adams, withdrew federal support for the Columbia-Waterloo scheme and the battle was over. Many felt that Cervantes' position in favor of an Illinois airport was a major factor in his failure to gain nomination for a third term.

In the meantime, federal dollars have been flowing into Lambert almost as rapidly as they can be spent. David Leigh, the longtime airport manager, has retired and his job now is held by Leonard L. Griggs Jr., who has become known as one of the foremost airport adminstrators in America. There has been no time since his arrival that there has not been a major construction project underway at Lambert Field. The runways have been improved, lengthened, and their lighting updated. The terminal facilities have been dramatically expanded.

A new international wing has been built, served by Airport Terminal Services, a Midcoast Aviation subsidiary. The "old" TWA hangar, built in the mid-1950s, was demolished in 1984 to make room for the mile-long "Concourse D," which stretches far to the east along Interstate Highway 70 from the 1955 terminal building. TWA plans to build a new hangar still further to the east. That firm also plans to add a $1 million customs and immigration unit to its portion of the international wing. The airport is expected to jump from the 14th busiest in America in 1983 to 6th place in 1984, as a result of the expansion.

Lambert's traffic jumped from 11 million passengers in 1982 to more than 20 million two years later, and from 291,000 takeoffs and landings to more than 400,000 in the same years. Among American airports, only Newark is growing faster.

TWA, whose financial problems in the past decade read like the Perils of Pauline, named St. Louis its principal domestic "hub" in 1982, and with some tough new top management seems to be turning the corner into steady profitability. Nearly 10 percent of its

TWA flies a fleet of Lockheed 1011 wide-bodied trijets from its St. Louis hub.

28,000 employees now call St. Louis home, and Lambert is now handling about one fifth of the airline's total capacity. Challenges to the St. Louis operation by both American and Eastern were turned away, but one that has not been turned away, and one which the company still regards as threatening, is that mounted by Ozark.

The *TWA Skyliner* for October 11, 1982, carried a quote that surprised more than a few Ozark executives: "If there's a potential troublesome rival for TWA at St. Louis, it's the hometowner that's quietly been there all along: Ozark."

Ozark? Yes, little Ozark Airlines, founded 34 years ago with four Douglas DC-3s, which will move into Concourse D, with its extended "people mover," sometime in 1985.

Ozark's first flight, Number 2 to Chicago, took off at 6:58 on Tuesday morning, September 26, 1950. One person boarded at St. Louis, none in Springfield, one in Decatur, and none in Champaign-Urbana. Four thousand more would fly Ozark that year, and with six additional cities in 1951, the passenger total grew to 49,354.

In 1965 Ozark passed the million-passenger mark for the first time, and purchased its first jet — a Douglas DC-9. That same year the line bought 21 FH-227B Fairchild-Hiller prop-jets, and the handwriting was on the wall for the old DC-3s. The last of the durable tail-draggers was traded away late that year.

Deregulation was a frightening aspect to many airlines, but "little" Ozark used it to increase its route miles an astounding 86 percent in 1978. It became a coast-to-coast airline in 1982, with the addition of San Diego, and in 1984 the cities of Greensboro, North Carolina, and Jacksonville, Florida, were added to the network. The airline now serves 66 cities in 25 states.

Ozark Airlines

*Ozark Airlines started operations in 1950 with four DC-3s (above),
now is an all-jet airline flying DC-9s (below).*

Ozark Airlines

The fleet now includes 45 DC-9 jets, and before the year is out it
will have two of the McDonnell Douglas MD-80s. As of June 1984
there were 3,980 people in the service of the firm, with a monthly
payroll of nearly $15 million.

In 1984, TWA accounted for 58 percent of Lambert Field's
traffic, but Ozark is responsible for a solid 25 percent of the daily
flights.

And what of McDonnell? When Horgan left them in 1965, Mr.
Mac was still struggling unsuccessfully with the idea of getting into
the commercial aspects of aviation, as a hedge against the day when
military sales might fall off. McDonnell had been trying hard to
crack that market, and produced a design which had striking simil-
arities with one offered almost simultaneously by Douglas Aircraft, a Long Beach firm. It happened to be coincidental — it was

McDonnell Douglas Corp.

These two Scotsmen were among aviation's greatest pioneers. James S. McDonnell, left, and Donald W. Douglas are shown in a moment of conviviality.

just the way the plane had to be built to solve the problems then confronting the airlines. McDonnell tried to get Donald Douglas to enter into a joint manufacturing agreement for the plane; Douglas would have no part of that. And the airlines would continue to have no part of McDonnell. Douglas had a track record in commercial aviation; McDonnell did not. So it fell to Douglas to produce the DC-9. That was in the spring of 1963. Of Mr. Mac, Douglas said, "He'll be back."

Three years later things seemed to be at a peak for the California giant. Then came a strange turnaround. The company went from black to red ink; buckets of it. The aerospace rumor mill crackled and McDonnell's eyebrows arched. He had asked his people to keep an eye on Douglas and they had done so. The word was out in 1966 — Douglas was scheduled for a loss of $75 million. They could not survive it.

Six firms vied for the ailing company. McDonnell, with his brother William A. McDonnell at his side, delivered his pitch personally. Bill McDonnell, a financial wizard, is credited with gaining much of the financing needed by the company through its period of rapid growth. He thought that he could assemble the funding needed for this move, too.

McDonnell Douglas Corp.

The DC-10 now is carrying on the tradition established by the old DC-3.

McDonnell Douglas Corp.

McDonnell Douglas is now producing the military derivative of the DC-10 for the armed forces, known as the KC-10.

One by one the other bidders fell away. Mr. Mac decided to make a final proposal. On Friday, January 13, 1967, the negotiating committee made its recommendation for the St. Louis company. The affiliation was approved by the U.S. Department of Justice on Friday, April 28, 1967, and the following Monday morning McDonnell Douglas Corporation opened for business.

At that time McDonnell employed 45,000 people and Douglas 80,000. One year later, on April 25, 1968, McDonnell Douglas made the dramatic announcement that it was proceeding with plans for a new wide-bodied trijet. It would be known as the DC-10.

When the 1970 annual report was issued, the name of David Sloan

McDonnell Douglas Corp.

McDonnell Aircraft's F-15 "Eagle," an astounding airplane which has given America air superiority over all other nations. In 1984 the U.S. Air Force selected the F-15E as its primary dual-role fighter, with initial operating capability scheduled for late 1988.

McDonnell Douglas Corp.

The U.S. Navy has selected the F/A-18 "Hornet" as its principal carrier-based fighter. It can be catapulted or landed with virtually no wind across the carrier deck.

McDonnell Douglas Corp.

More than 3,000 "Harpoon" anti-ship missiles have been delivered, most of them to the U.S. Navy.

McDonnell Douglas Corp.

The McDonnell Douglas AV-8B "Harrier II," a vertical-short takeoff and landing (V-STOL) airplane, manufactured since 1969 under license from Britain's Hawker-Siddeley Aviation, Ltd. The plane is now entering service with the U.S Marine Corps.

McDonnell Douglas Corp.

The McDonnell Douglas "Delta Super 8" launch vehicle is used consistently by governments and private corporations for sending satellites into orbit. It first went into service on May 13, 1960, and has been upgraded from a 500-pound payload to a capacity of more than 3,000 pounds. The ancillary Payload Assist Module (PAM) has been used as an upper stage, not only with the "Delta" but also on the Space Shuttle.

Lewis was missing. Mac's hand-picked successor had bolted the traces to take a job heading General Dynamics Corporation, which has since become America's largest defense contractor. Lewis had a major change in mind; he moved the world headquarters to St. Louis. There are no manufacturing facilities here, but St. Louis is now the home of the two largest defense companies in the nation. Sanford ("Sandy") McDonnell, son of William A. McDonnell, replaced Lewis as president. He now serves as chairman and chief executive officer.

McDonnell Douglas Corp.

McDonnell Douglas inherited the AH-64 "Apache" attack heli-copter when it purchased Hughes Aircraft in 1984.

By 1974 34 airlines around the world had ordered the DC-10, and the twin-finned F-15 "Eagle" had been delivered to the U.S. Air Force. The "Eagle" broke all world time-to-climb records, some of them having been set by McDonnell's F-4 "Phantom" and some by Russian aircraft. The F-15 flew from a standstill on the runway to 39,370 feet in 59.38 seconds; and to 98,425 feet in 3 minutes, 27.80 seconds. The fighters logged more than a million flight hours in 1984, while the F/A-18 "Hornet," put into operational service in 1983, chalked up more than 80,000. The U.S. Navy and the Marine Corps hope to buy 1,377 of the carrier-based "Hornet," and other nations have added significantly to that number. The U.S. Marine Corps also hopes to purchase 328 AV-8B "Harrier IIs," fighter aircraft which can take off and land vertically from shortened run-ways or from battlefields. They will replace five squadrons of Mc-Donnell Douglas A-4 "Skyhawk" attack aircraft and three squad-rons of AV-8A "Harriers."

The company's "Harpoon" has become the most widely used anti-ship missile in the U.S. Navy. It was operational on 223 ships and submarines and 209 airplanes at the end of 1983. On May 4, 1984, the company turned the 3,000th "Harpoon" over to the Navy.

Resistance to McDonnell as a commercial aircraft builder disappeared with the merger with Douglas Aircraft. The new 150-passenger, fuel-efficient MD-80 twinjet has drawn orders from airlines all over the world.

The "Tomahawk" cruise missile is being produced in the McDonnell Douglas plant at Titusville, Florida.

On August 30, 1984, a McDonnell Douglas engineer, Charles Walker, became the first industry-sponsored astronaut to fly on a space shuttle mission. His job was to operate the Electrophoresis Operations in Space (EOS) device for several hours during the mission. Materials separated aloft in the weightless atmosphere are to be used by an MDC partner for clinical testing of the first space-manufactured product.

And after years of heartbreakingly bad luck in trying to produce an acceptable helicopter, MDC got into the business the same way it entered commercial aviation — it bought in. Hughes Helicopters, Inc., was acquired in January 1984. The U.S. Army plans to purchase 515 of the AH-64A "Apache" attack helicopters, with a program value of more than $7 billion. The aircraft will be made at the Hughes plant in California.

The sons of James Smith McDonnell now are in important management positions — John F. McDonnell is president of McDonnell Douglas Corporation and James S. McDonnell III is corporate vice president-marketing.

It is hard to imagine that back in the late 1940s the suggestion was

Missouri Air National Guard

The F-100 "Super Sabre" (above), which the Missouri Air Guard used in Viet Nam, now has been replaced by the powerful F-4 "Phantom," shown below over the downtown St. Louis riverfront.

Missouri Air National Guard

made that, since Lambert Field was getting so crowded, Mac ought to take his company elsewhere. The late Aloys P. Kaufmann, then mayor of St. Louis, led the drive to persuade the growing firm to move from the city-owned Lambert Field. And every Monday morning the young assistant city editor of the *St. Louis Globe-Democrat*, G. Duncan Bauman, would argue for the right to run yet another story on the foolishness of the dispute. He had heard that Jim Mc-Donnell was looking to Arkansas for a plant site; that would never do. Finally Al Kaufmann caved in and started looking to the then-undeveloped south side of Lambert Field for expansion of the airport; hencefort he would leave McDonnell alone.

Today the giant McDonnell Douglas occupies almost the whole of the north boundary of the airport, from Lindbergh Boulevard along what is now James S. McDonnell Boulevard (formerly Brown Road) to the point where the latter thoroughfare curves to the south, along what used to be Airport Road. It remains the largest employer in Missouri. Its production schedules today would amaze even its founder, and he has been gone but four years. And somewhere, deep within the growing complex of structures at Lambert Field, plans are being hatched for projects which will continue the economic health and technological supremacy of the organization well into the 21st century.

And what of Maj. Robertson's Air National Guard? The 1927 hangar is long gone and there are new facilities northwest of the Lambert Field terminal building for that durable institution. By the time of completion of Dr. Horgan's dissertation, their F-84 "Thunderstreaks" were being phased out and the F-100C "Super Sabre" was being employed as the principal strike aircraft. That is the plane which served the Guard so well in 1970, when it entered the Viet Nam conflict.

The Air Guard started replacing that plane with the F-4 "Phantom" in October 1978, and that tough, powerful fighter is still being flown daily. Security reasons preclude disclosure of either personnel or aircraft strength, but there is no secret about the Guard's high morale, or its dedication to continued training to maintain its high profile and combat readiness.

There is one aspect of this heritage which has not been covered, and that is business aviation. After the second World War there were a number of small operations at Lambert Field and elsewhere. Sophisticated performance was rare, but there was some. Edgar M. Queeny, founder of Monsanto Company, commissioned one firm to recondition a DC-3 and the resultant *Prairie Wings* was a landmark of opulence and good taste.

But when business aviation is discussed today, that translates to mean Midcoast Aviation, Inc., for that firm currently is doing nearly 90 percent of that type of work here these days.

When John Tucker took over that troubled firm, there were 17 employees, a rapidly diminishing customer base, a tough competitor at Lambert Field, and transient movements of about 800 planes per

Midcoast Aviation

Prairie Wings, *a DC-3 luxuriously outfitted for Edgar M. Queeny, chairman of Monsanto Company.*

month. Tucker immediately began attracting key people from Remmert-Werner, Rockwell, Butler Aviation, and other companies. Within months the firm had turned its first profit in years.

The following year, Midcoast established Airport Terminal Services, Inc., to provide refueling, ground, and turnaround services for international airlines and large charter carriers at Lambert's new international wing. Through another subsidiary, Airport Commuter Services, thousands of commuter aircraft are served at Lambert's main terminal building.

Two more 15,000-square-foot hangars were added in 1978, another 6,000 square feet of office space and shops, four more acres of ramp, and a 100,000-gallon fuel storage plant. Midcoast spent more than $3,500,000 on its Lambert Field installation from 1975 through 1978.

In 1978 the company opened an aviation service facility at Bi-State Parks Airport, and the following year began a $1.5-million construction program there. Two new 15,000-square-foot hangars were built, 1,000 square feet of offices and shops were added, and an existing hangar was purchased.

In 1980 ATS won a contract to service the 747s and DC-10s of the Military Air Lift Command. St. Louis is a MALC transfer point for the U.S, Europe, and the Orient.

Midcoast was named by Canadair Challenger and Falcon as a completion center for their business jets. In 1982 the firm installed the first Sperry Electronic Flight Instrument System (EFIS) in a Canadair Challenger in the Midcoast Completion Center. There,

Midcoast Aviation

*Vehicles from Airport Terminal Services, Inc., a Midcoast sub-
sidiary, swarm about a British Caledonian trijet, preparing it for
nonstop service from Lambert Field to England.*

The Midcoast facility is located on the southeast corner of Lambert Field. The TWA hangar in the upper portion of this 1984 photo is no more; it has been replaced by "Concourse D," a mile-long wing of the airport terminal building developed largely to serve passengers of St. Louis-based Ozark Airlines.

too, the first 3,000-hour inspection on a Falcon 50 business jet was performed by Midcoast. The company executes all Standard Depot Level Maintenance procedures on all Navy and Marine CT-39 Sabreliners.

In 1984 Midcoast became the first Fixed Base Operator in a 10-state area to receive the Defense Quality Excellence Award of the U.S. Department of Defense. The 33,000 readers of *Professional Pilot* magazine have voted the company the top aviation service operator in the Midwest annually since 1975.

Today Midcoast operates a total of 12 hangars, two general aviation terminal buildings, and a major office building — totaling 238,000 square feet — on 68½ acres of land. More than 500 people are on the payroll, some 25,000 to 30,000 private passengers on 5,000 to 6,000 business aircraft are served each month, and the company enjoys an annual revenue of $33 million.

Midcoast is equipped to rebuild, virtually from the tires up, the major makes of business aircraft flying today. It is authorized by the manufacturers as their official service station for Lockheed JetStar, Hawker-Siddeley HS125 jet, Bell 206 jet helicopter, Dassault Falcon 10-20-50 jet, Piper Cheyenne and Swearingen Merlin turboprops and their engines. They are also staffed with specialists for Sabreliner, Gulfstream I-II-III, KingAir, Citation, Lear, MU2, Westwind, and most other aircraft.

The company works two shifts regularly — 8 a.m. to midnight daily and 10 a.m. to 6 p.m. weekends. Specialists are on hand to provide support to Midcoast clients in the field. Technicians work on a

Midcoast Aviation

The interior of this new business jet was designed and installed by Midcoast personnel.

Midcoast Aviation

Midcoast technicians recently applied a gleaming paint job to this "Falcon 10" business jet.

dazzling array of avionics from nearly three dozen manufacturers. They often take unfinished airframes from a factory and install decorator interiors of their own design.

Within that growing young company, as with the aerospace giant to the north, there is a special feeling of teamwork — Jim McDonnell liked to refer to his employees as "teammates." There is a spirit of camaraderie at Lambert Field which seems to be almost unique. The "teammate" concept could apply to all connected with aviation in St. Louis, for all contributed to the aerial successes of this pioneering city. From powerful aeronautical executives to South St. Louis homemakers who vote "yes" when the bond issues appear on the ballot; from editorial writers to kids working on the tarmac; from soaring gas balloonists to propane-fired hot air jockeys; from Tom Baldwin in his *Red Devil* to the astronauts — all did their part, all helped pave the way for this old, river-anchored city to emerge, truly, as the City of Flight.

Gregory M. Franzwa
The Patrice Press

October 1, 1984

Bibliography

PRIMARY SOURCES
MANUSCRIPTS AND DOCUMENTARY COLLECTIONS

Aeronautics Papers. 2 Volumes: 1830-1939 and 1940-   Missouri Historical Society Archives.
Miscellaneous manuscripts and documents on all phases of aviation in St. Louis.

Curtiss-Wright Papers. Missouri Historical Society Library.
Typewritten summary of company activities during the 1930s.

David Francis Collection. 2 Volumes: 1902 and 1904. Missouri Historical Society Archives.
Miscellaneous manuscripts and documents of the Louisiana Purchase Exposition, some of which pertain to aeronautical activities at the fair.

International Air Race Papers, 1923. Missouri Historical Society Library.
Miscellaneous manuscripts and documents dealing primarily with the background and organization of that air meet.

Albert Bond Lambert Aeronautical Papers. 2 Volumes, Missouri Historical Society Archives.
Miscellaneous manuscripts and documents, primarily on Lambert Field.

Lambert-St. Louis Municipal Airport Papers. Missouri Historical Society Library.
Miscellaneous manuscripts and documents pertaining to all phases of the airport's development.

GOVERNMENT DOCUMENTS

Civil Aeronautics Board. *Handbook of Airline Statistics.* Washington: United States Government Printing Office, 1963.

Congressional Globe. 31 Congress, 2 Session.
A reference to John Wise.

Congressional Record. 56 Congress, 1-2 Sessions. 68 Congress, 2 Session. 70 Congress, 1 Session.
References to the Louisiana Purchase Exposition, the Kelly Air Mail Act, and Charles Lindbergh, respectively.

Grimwood, James M. *Project Mercury: A Chronology.*
Washington: National Aeronautics and Space Administration, 1963.

Holly, Irving Brinton, Jr. *United States Army in World War II, Special Studies: Buying Aircraft: Matériel Procurement for the Army Air Forces.* Washington: Office of the Chief of Military History, Department of the Army, 1964.

United States Senate, Committee on Aeronautical and Space Sciences. *Report on Project Mercury: Man-in-Space Program of the National Aeronautics and Space Administration.* Report No. 1014, 86 Congress, 1 Session, December 1, 1959.

MEMOIRS AND BOOKS

Arnold, General H.H. *Global Mission.* New York: Harper and Brothers, 1949.
Relates to St. Louis in that he gives anecdotes on the Barling Bomber, which appeared in the city in 1923, and also exonerates Charles Lindbergh from any charge of collaboration with the Nazis in the 1930s.

Francis, David R. *The Universal Exposition of 1904.* 2 Volumes. St. Louis: Louisiana Purchase Exposition Company, 1913.
Francis was president of the 1904 World's Fair. Volume I contains detailed descriptions of all the exhibits and events, including the aerial activities, while Volume II contains financial statements and illustrations.

Lindbergh, Charles A. *The Spirit of St. Louis.* New York: Charles Scribner's Sons, 1953.
No better book has been written on his 1927 flight. Contains details on the background and story of that achievement, with flashbacks on his earlier career. It won the Pulitzer Prize for Autobiography in 1954.

_____. "We." New York: Grosset and Dunlap, 1927.
Contains much the same material as his later book, but was written in a period of only six weeks during the summer of 1927, and is therefore rough and unpolished.

Stevens, Walter B. *St. Louis: One Hundred Years in a Week.* St. Louis: St. Louis Centennial Association, 1910.
Stevens was the secretary of the Centennial Association. Here he recounts the events of Centennial Week, 1909, basing himself primarily on local newspaper accounts.

Wise, John. *A System of Aeronautics.* Philadelphia: Joseph A. Speed, 1850.
One of the first learned studies ever written on aeronautics, this book treats of the subject in three parts: a history of ballooning, memoirs of the author's first fifteen years of experience in that field, and techniques on the manufacture of balloons.

_____. *Through the Air.* Philadelphia: To-day Printing and Publishing Company, 1873.

An expansion of his earlier work, this book is in part a literal reprint of his previous study, but recounts the author's forty years of experience in ballooning, including his record-breaking flight from St. Louis in 1859.

PROGRAMS AND PAMPHLETS

Aero Club of America, 1911. New York: Aero Club of America, 1911.

Articles of incorporation, bylaws, contest and license rules, records of major races, and general regulations of the organization.

Aero Club of St. Louis: Purposes - Results, 1907-1910. St. Louis, 1910.

Summary of the organization's activities during its first three years of existence.

The Airport Bond Issue and What It Means to St. Louis. St. Louis, 1942.

Articles of Incorporation, Bylaws, Officers and Members: Aero Club of St. Louis, 1909. St. Louis: Aero Club of St. Louis, 1909.

In addition, this handbook also has the results of the 1907 and 1909 balloon races staged by that organization.

Aviation: What It Means to You. St. Louis: Universal Aviation Schools, 1929.

A brochure on Universal's flying schools, including the unit in St. Louis.

The Curtiss-Robertson Airplane Mfg. Co., Division of Curtiss-Wright. New York: Curtiss-Wright Sales Corporation, 1930.

A brochure describing the three types of ''Robins'' the company then was producing.

Daily Official Program, World's Fair, Louisiana Purchase Exposition, St. Louis, USA. Number 184, November 30, 1904. St. Louis: The Model Printery, 1904.

This issue describes the machines of four aeronauts appearing at the fair.

Industrial Club of St. Louis. *Air Transport Facilities in the St. Louis District.* St. Louis, c. 1930.

A leaflet on the history and current facilities of the airports in the St. Louis area.

M.A. Heimann Manufacturing Co.: Designers and Manufacturers of Balloons and Airships. St. Louis, c. 1909.

An advertising brochure.

McDonnell Annual Reports: 1946, 1962, 1963, 1964. St. Louis: McDonnell Aircraft Corporation, 1946, 1962, 1963, 1964.

NASA-McDonnell Gemini Spacecraft. St. Louis: McDonnell Aircraft Corporation, c. 1962.

Description of the capsule and the purposes of the program.

Official Program for the Second Competition for the Gordon Bennett Aeronautic Cup, Forest Park, St. Louis, U.S.A., October, 1907. St. Louis: Lesar-Gould Advertising and Publishing Company, 1907.

Official Souvenir Program, October 1st-8th, 1911. St. Louis: Aero Club of St. Louis, 1911.

Preview of the Fairground Park air meet.

Program for Ceremonies Inaugurating U.S. Air-Mail Service, Forest Park Aerial Field, August 16, 1920, St. Louis, Missouri, U.S.A. St. Louis, 1920.

Also contains a history of the events leading up to the establishment of the airfield.

Report on Nation-Wide Survey of Status of Municipal Post-War Airport Plans. St. Louis, 1945.

Rules and Entry Blank, International Air Races, St. Louis, U.S.A., October 1, 2, 3, 1923. St. Louis, 1923.

St. Louis Aeronautic Corporation. *St. Louis: The Aerial Crossroads of America.* St. Louis, 1923.
A short pamphlet on the SLAC, its purposes, the 1923 air races, and the need for a permanent airport.

Shaw, B. Russell, *International Air Races: Report of the Contest Committee, Lambert-St. Louis Field, St. Louis, Mo., October 3, 4, 5, 6, 1923.* St. Louis, 1923.
Official report of the results of the races.

Skiff, Frederick J.V., and Smith, Willard A. *Universal Exposition, Saint Louis, 1904: Rules and Regulations Governing the Aeronautic Competition — Supplementary Rules Issued August 1903.* St. Louis: Department of Transportation Exhibits, 1903.

Stevens, Walter B. *Centennial of the Incorporation of St. Louis: Official Program of the Celebration, October 3-9, 1909.* St. Louis: Woodward and Tiernan Printing Company, 1909.

Souvenir from the St. Louis Pilgrimage of the Million Population Club, St. Louis to Indianapolis, Ind., to Attend Elimination Balloon Races, September 16th, 17th, 18th, 1910. St. Louis, 1910.

Welcome Home!! St. Louis, 1927.
Program of the banquet held for Charles A. Lindbergh at the Hotel Chase, June 18, 1927.

SCRAPBOOKS

Morris A. Heimann Collection. Missouri Historical Society Library.
Newspaper clippings on the activities of local balloonists, including Heimann himself, during the years 1909-1919.

Joseph M. O'Reilly Scrapbook. Missouri Historical Society Library.
Newspaper clippings on the activities of local balloonists, including O'Reilly himself, during the years 1909-1941.

Scrapbook of Aviation Activities in St. Louis. 2 Volumes. Missouri Historical Society Library.
Miscellaneous newspaper clippings, primarily on the municipal airport.

Scrapbook of Balloon Activities in St. Louis. 2 Volumes. Missouri Historical Society Library.
Newspaper clippings on various balloon events.

PERIODICALS

"Activities at the Flying Fields and Hydro Havens — Missouri: Kinloch," *Aero and Hydro,* Vol. V, No. 19 (February 8, 1913), 343.

"Aerial Navigation," *World's Fair Bulletin,* Vol. 3, No. 4 (February 1902), 20-21.
Announcement of the $200,000 purse for aeronautics at the fair.

"Aero Club Ascensions, 1907," *American Magazine of Aeronautics,* Vol. I, No. 4 (October 1907), 11.

"Aero Club of America," *American Aeronaut,* Vol. I, No. 3 (October 1909), 136.

"Aero Club of St. Louis," *Aero,* Vol. I, No. 1 (October 8, 1910), 16.
Lists the four airfields then used by the club.

"Aero Club of St. Louis," *Aero,* Vol. I, No. 5 (November 5, 1910), 18.
Lists the four airfields then used by the club.

Aeronautus. "The History of Airships," *American Magazine of Aeronautics,* Vol. I, No. 4 (October 1907), 25-27. Also discusses contemporary airship activity.

"Air Liner Travels 682 Miles First 10 Days," *Aero and Hydro,* Vol. VII, No. 17 (January 24, 1914), 213-213.
Notes on Tom Benoist's St. Petersburg-Tampa Airboat Line.

"Air Mail Contract Payments," *Aviation,* Vol. XXII, No. 21 (May 23, 1927), 1078.
Lists the income received by the thirteen private contractors in operation from April 15, 1926, to April 15, 1927, including Robertson Aircraft.

"Air Mail Facts and Figures," *Aviation,* Vol. XXIII, No. 8 (August 22, 1927), 419.

"Air Mail Planes at St. Louis," *Aviation,* Vol. XV, No. 12 (September 17, 1923), 339.

"Airplanes, Engines, and Propellers for Over 100,000 Warplanes Produced by Curtiss-Wright," *The Curtiss Wright-er,* Vol. 5, No. 12 (March 23, 1945), 1.

"Airports and Airways: St. Louis, Mo.," *Aviation,* Vol. XXIII, No. 18 (October 31, 1927), 1067-1068.
Notes on the proposed Lambert-St. Louis Municipal Airport.

"Airports and Airways: St. Louis, Mo.," *Aviation,* Vol. XXIII, No. 24 (December 12, 1927), 1426-1427.
Notes on the proposed Lambert-St. Louis Municipal Airport.

"Airports and Airways: St. Louis, Mo.," *Aviation,* Vol. XXIII, No. 25 (December 19, 1927), 1488.
Notes on the proposed Lambert-St. Louis Municipal Airport.

"Airports and Airways: St. Louis, Mo.," *Aviation,* Vol. XXIV, No. 3 (January 16, 1928), 162-163.
Notes on the proposed Lambert-St. Louis Municipal Airport.

"Airports and Airways: St. Louis, Mo.," *Aviation,* Vol. XXIV, No. 6 (February 6, 1928), 344-345.
Notes on the proposed Lambert-St. Louis Municipal Airport.

"Airports and Airways: St. Louis, Mo.," *Aviation,* Vol. XXIV, No. 9 (February 27, 1928), 540-541.
Notes on Robertson Aircraft Corporation.

"Airports and Airways: St. Louis, Mo.," *Aviation,* Vol. XXIV, No. 12 (March 19, 1928), 738.
Notes on Robertson Aircraft Corporation.

Alexander, George. "First Successful Gemini Mission Points to Manned Flight in 1964," *Aviation Week & Space Technology,* Vol. 80, No. 15 (April 13, 1964), 29-30.

_____. "GT-2 Success Brings Go-Ahead Order for First Manned Gemini," *Aviation Week & Space Technology,* Vol. 82, No. 4 (January 25, 1965), 30-31.

"American Aero Calendar," *Aeronautics,* Vol 6, No. 4 (April 1910), 128.

"America Wins Gordon Bennett Balloon Race," *Aviation,* Vol. XXIII, No. 13 (September 26, 1927), 726.

"American Aeronautical Accomplishments in 1923," *Aviation,* Vol. XVI, No. 2 (January 14, 1924), 38-39.

"Announcement," *Aviation,* Vol. XV, No. 12 (September 17, 1923), 340-341.
Notes on the St. Louis International Air Races.

"Arch Hoxsey Flies to St. Louis Meet," *Aero,* Vol. I, No. 2 (October 15, 1910), 11-13, 20.

"Army and Navy Entries in the Pulitzer Trophy Race," *Aviation,* Vol. XV, No. 14 (October 1, 1923), 400-403.

"Army and Navy Pilots in the St. Louis Races," *Aviation,* Vol. XV, No. 14 (October 1, 1923), 404-407.

"Army Pilots Named for St. Louis Air Races," *Aviation,* Vol. XV, No. 11 (September 10, 1923), 304.

"The Ascender," *Curtiss Fly Leaf,* Vol. XXVIII, No. 1 (January-February, 1945), 14.

"ASSET No. 5 Flight Resounding Success," *McDonnell Airscoop,* Vol. XXIII, No. 11 (December 1964), 1-2.

"ASSET No. 3," *McDonnell Airscoop,* Vol. XXIII, No. 7 (August 1964), 4.

"ASSET No. 2 Being Readied For Launch," *McDonnell Airscoop,* Vol. XXIII, No. 2 (March 1964), 1, 8.

"Authorized Official Program of the Fifth International Balloon Race," *Aero,* Vol. I, Extra (October 17, 1910).

"Aviation: Demon on the Ground," *Time,* Vol. LXVI, No. 19 (November 7, 1955), 101.

"The Backbone of Our Future Air Fleet," *Aviation,* Vol. XV, No. 17 (October 22, 1923), 507-512.

"Balloon Championship," *Fly,* Vol. I, No. 9 (July 1909), 9.
Notes on the first National Balloon Race, won by John Berry of St. Louis.

"The Barling Bomber," *Aeronautical Digest,* Vol. 3, No. 4 (October 1923), 249, 284.

"Belgium Again Wins Gordon Bennett Race," *Aviation,* Vol. XV, No. 15 (October 8, 1923), 438-439.

"Belgium Wins G.B. Cup," *Aviation,* Vol. XVI, No. 25 (June 23, 1924), 671.

"Benoist 1914 Flying Boat Described," *Aero and Hydro,* Vol. VII, No. 2 (October 11, 1913), 17.

"Benoist School Moves to Florida," *Aero and Hydro,* Vol. VII, No. 14 (January 3, 1914), 165.

"Benoist's Aero-Boat Line Running Smoothly," *Aero and Hydro,* Vol. VII, No. 15 (January 10, 1914), 177-178.

"B.F. Mahoney Aircraft Corp. to Move its Factory to St. Louis," *Aviation,* Vol. XXIV, No. 3 (January 16, 1928), 158.

Birge, Arthur B. "Concerning the St. Louis Aeronautic Corporation," *America at Work,* Vol. VII, No. 7 (September 5, 1923), 18, 32.

_____. "Progress of Construction Work on St. Louis Field," *Aviation,* Vol. XV, No. 11 (September 10, 1923), 307-308.

"A Brief Epitome," *World's Fair Bulletin,* Vol. 2, No. 9 (July 1901), 4-7.
Summary of the activities surrounding the Louisiana Purchase Exposition since its conception.

"Brookins Wins $10,000 in New Wright," *Aero,* Vol. I, No. 1, (October 8, 1910), 7-8.

"B. Russell Shaw & Co. To Re-Design and Improve Airport at St. Louis," *Aviation,* Vol. XXIV, No. 11 (March 12, 1928), 640.

Bush, B.F. " 'On-to-St. Louis,' " *Civic Review* (August 1923), 3-8.

" 'The California Arrow,' " *World's Fair Bulletin,* Vol. 6, No. 1 (November 1904), 18-20.

"Capt. Burt E. Skeel Wins Mitchell Trophy Race," *Aviation,* Vol. XV, No. 16 (October 15, 1923), 478-479.

Carter, W. Frank. "The Value of Airports," *Civic Review* (August 1923), 2.
An exhortation for the development of one for St. Louis.

_____."What a City Owes to Aviation," *America at Work,* Vol. VII, No. 7 September 5, 1923), 11-13, 34.

_____. "What St. Louis Flying Field Means to St. Louis," *The Cherry Diamond* (September 1923), 13-15.

"C-46 Final Assembly Here!" *The Curtiss Wright-er,* Vol. 4, No. 51 (December 22, 1944), 1.

"Change in Army Entrants in St. Louis Races," *Aviation,* Vol. XV, No. 15 (October 8, 1923), 451.

"The Chicago-St. Louis Air Mail Line," *Aviation,* Vol. XX, No. 14 (April 5, 1926), 499.
Discusses CAM-2 and its operator, Robertson Aircraft.

Clayton, Henry Helm. "The Use of Air Currents in Ballooning," *American Aeronaut,* Vol. I, No. 4 (February-March 1908), 111-115.
Clayton was a member of the German crew which won the 1907 Gordon Bennett Race at St. Louis, and he bases his article on that flight.

"Club News," *Aeronautics,* Vol. 6, No. 4 (April 1910), 142.
Notes on the Aero Club of St. Louis.

"Col. Roosevelt Rides With Arch Hoxsey," *Aero,* Vol. I, No. 2 (October 15, 1910), 9-10.

"The Coming Contests," *America at Work,* Vol. VII, No. 7 (September 5, 1923), 22.

"Coming Events in Flying," *Aeronautics,* Vol. 6, No. 5 (May 1910), 170.

"Corporations: The Problems of Westinghouse," *Time,* Vol. LXVI, No. 17 (October 24, 1955), 98-99.
The difficulties discussed are those of the McDonnell "Demon."

"Curtiss Condors Never Grow Too Old To Fly," *Curtiss Fly Leaf,* Vol. XXVIII, No. 3 (May-June 1945), 10-12.

"The Curtiss Jeep (AT-9)," *The Curtiss Wright-er,* Vol. 3, No. 53 (December 17, 1943), 5.

"Daring Feats of Acrobats & Aeronauts," *The Scientific American* (July 16, 1859), 39.
Story on John Wise's flight from St. Louis to Henderson, New York.

"Dates Ahead," *Aero,* Vol. I, No. 1 (October 8, 1910), 5.
A calendar listing the aeronautic events of 1910.

De Fonvielle, Wilfred. "A Year's Progress in Flying," *Harper's Weekly,* Vol. XLVIII, No. 2495 (October 15, 1904), 1582-1585.
This article contains an interesting explanation of the mysterious destruction of Alberto Santos-Dumont's airship at the World's Fair. De Fonvielle suggests that the salt air encountered in the ocean crossing weakened the varnished silk envelope and caused it to split when exposed to the dry St. Louis air.

"Distinguished Guests to Attend International Air Races," *Civic Review* (August 1923), 8.

"Distribution of American Eagle Granted to St. Louis Aircraft Co.," *Aviation,* Vol. XXIV, No. 9 (February 27, 1928), 517.

"E.J. Lange Wins Mulvihill Model Trophy Contest," *Aviation,* Vol. XV, No. 16 (October 15, 1923), 484.

"Elimination Race Results," *Aero,* Vol. I, No. 2 (October 15, 1910), 6, 20.

"Expansion," *Curtiss Fly Leaf,* Vol. XXIV, No. 1 (January-February 1941), 3-12, 26.

"$55,650 Offered at Belmont Park," *Aero,* Vol. I, No. 1 (October 8, 1910), 20.

"First Gnome in St. Louis," *Aero,* Vol. I, No. 1 (October 8, 1910), 16.
A "Gnome" was an engine made in Paris.

"First Trial Flights of Naval Airship ZR-1," *Aviation,* Vol. XV, No. 11 (September 10, 1923), 311.
This rigid dirigible appeared at the International Air Races.

"Flight of the ZR-1," *Aeronautical Digest,* Vol. 3, No. 4 (October 1923), 232-236, 282-283.

"Flying Machine and Airship Competitions at St. Louis," *American Magazine of Aeronautics,* Vol. I, No. 4 (October 1907), 8.

Forden, Samuel W. "Manufacture of Coal Gas For Balloons," *American Aeronaut,* Vol. I, No. 5 (May 1908), 182-184.
Forden was associated with St. Louis' Laclede Gaslight Company.

"Former Gordon Bennett Aeronautic Cup Contests at a Glance," *Aero and Hydro,* Vol. VII, No. 3 (October 18, 1913), 26.

Foster, John Jr. "Design Analysis of the Curtiss Commando," *Aviation* (August 1943), 130-153.

Foster, Randall. "Program for the St. Louis Meet," *Aeronautical Digest,* Vol. 3, No. 4 (October 1923), 241-242.

Foy, John J. "Curtiss-St. Louis: The Milestone Builder," *Curtiss Fly Leaf,* Vol. XXV, No. 1 (January-February 1942), 3-13.
Gives a short history of the company and discusses the products the plant was currently producing.

"France Extols Lindbergh's Education," *The Literary Digest,* Vol. XCIII, No. 13 (June 25, 1927), 19.

Gammeter, H.C. "The Gammeter Orthopter," *American Magazine of Aeronautics,* Vol. 1, No. 4 (October 1907), pp. 15-16.

"The Gordon Bennett Balloon Races," *Aviation,* Vol. XXIII, No. 9 (August 29, 1927), 479-480.

"The Gordon Bennett in October," *American Aeronaut,* Vol. I, No. 4 (February-March 1908), 127.

"Gordon Bennett Race," *American Magazine of Aeronautics,* Vol. I, No. 4 (October 1907), 4-8.

"Historical Notes and Comments," *Missouri Historical Review,* Vol. XXII, No. 1 (October 1927), 105-106.
A note on Charles A. Lindbergh.

"Historical Notes and Comments," *Missouri Historical Review,* Vol. XXIII, No. 3 (April 1929), 490.
The first licensed air passenger and express line in Missouri began in November 1928.

"Historical Notes and Comments," *Missouri Historical Review,* Vol. XXIV, No. 2 (January 1930), 312-313.
"Anglum, Missouri" officially became "Robertson, Missouri" on November 1, 1929.

"Historical Notes and Comments," *Missouri Historical Review,* Vol. XXVIII, No. 4 (July 1934), 315.
A large bronze tablet commemorating Charles Lindbergh's transatlantic flight was unveiled at Lambert Field on May 20, 1934.

"Historical Notes and Comments," *Missouri Historical Review,* Vol. XLIII, No. 2 (January 1949), 176.
A plaque in memory of Albert Bond Lambert was unveiled at Soldiers' Memorial on October 15, 1948.

Hoskins, Arthur C. "St. Louis as a Dirigible Center to Rehabilitate Free Ballooning," *Aeronautical Digest,* Vol. 3, No. 4 (October 1923), 242, 288.

"Hoxsey Leads Flying," *Aero,* Vol. I, No. 2 (October 15, 1910), 9-10.

Hyde, William. "The Great Balloon Experiment: Details and Incidents of the Trip," *Glimpses of the Past.* Vol. IX, No. 4 (October-December 1942), 93-111.
A reprint of the story Hyde wrote for the *Daily Missouri Republican,* July 7, 1859, on his flight with John Wise in the *Atlantic.*

"Independence Day Celebrated With Patriotic Ceremonies July 4th," *World's Fair Bulletin,* Vol. 5, No. 10 (August 1904), 2-7.
Contains an account of the balloon race which was held that day.

"International Balloon Race," *Aero,* Vol. I, No. 1 (October 8, 1910), 5.

"In the Slip Stream," *Aero and Hydro,* Vol. V, No. 19 (February 8, 1913), 345.
Contains a limerick about Tom Benoist.

"J. Atkinson Wins Country Club of Detroit Trophy Race," *Aviation,* Vol. XV, No. 16 (October 15, 1923), 481-482.

"J.F. Moore Wins Air Mail Trophy Race," *Aviation,* Vol. XV, No. 16 (October 15, 1923), 474-476.

"John Nelson Named Vice President of the B.F. Mahoney Aircraft Co.," *Aviation,* Vol. XXIV, No. 9 (February 27, 1928), 526.

Kiel, (Mayor) Henry W. "Invitation to the International Air Races and Aeronautical Exhibition October 1, 2, and 3," *Civic Review* (August 1923), 1.

_____. "Welcome to St. Louis," *America at Work,* Vol. VII, No. 7 (September 5, 1923), 16, 22.

Klemin, Alexander. "Notes on the Guggenheim Safety Competition," *Aviation,* Vol. XXIV, No. 4 (January 23, 1928), 246-254.
James S. McDonnell entered his "Doodlebug" in this contest.

Lambert, Major Albert Bond. "St. Louis — on World's Air Map for 16 Years," *St. Louis Post-Dispatch,* September 30, 1923, Sunday Magazine, 3.

_____, and Robertson, Major William B. "Early History of Aeronautics in St. Louis," *Missouri Historical Society Collections,* Vol. V, No. 3 (June 1928), 237-255.
Major Lambert reviews, somewhat inaccurately as to specific names and dates, St. Louis' aviation history from 1904 to 1923. Major Robertson discusses American commercial aviation.

"Last St. Louis-Built Curtiss Commando," *The Curtiss Wright-er,* Vol. 5, No. 30 (July 27, 1945), 1.

"Last Two Demons Retired From Fleet With Ceremonies," *McDonnell Airscoop,* Vol. XXIII, No. 11 (December 1964), 8.

"A Letter from Leo Stevens," *The Scientific American,* Vol. XC, No. 13 (March 26, 1904), 251.
A letter to the editor from a prominent aeronaut who criticizes the rules for the airship contest at the St. Louis World's Fair.

"Lieut. A.J. Williams Wins Pulitzer Trophy Race," *Aviation,* Vol. XV, No. 16 (October 15, 1923), 468-474.

"Lieut. C. McMullen Wins Liberty Engine Builders' Trophy," *Aviation,* Vol. XV, No. 16 (October 15, 1923), 479-480.

"Lieut. H.L. George Wins Merchants' Exchange Trophy Race," *Aviation,* Vol. XV, No. 16 (October 15, 1923), 482-484.

"Lindbergh Backers Will Finance New Mahoney Factory at St. Louis," *Aviation,* Vol. XXIV, No. 4 (January 23, 1928), 210.

"Maj. Robertson Resigns to Head Curtiss-Robertson Airplane Mfg. Co.," *Aviation,* Vol. XXIV, No. 7 (February 13, 1928), 398.

"Manufacturer's Specifications on American Commercial Airplanes and Seaplanes as Compiled by Aviation," *Aviation,* Vol. XXIV, No. 6 (February 26, 1928), 326-327.

"Many Machines Building at St. Louis," *Aeronautics,* Vol. 6, No. 5 (May 1910), 165.

"McDonnell's 3000th Plane, an F-4C Phantom, Delivered November 14," *McDonnell Airscoop,* Vol. XXIII, No. 11 (December 1964), 2.

"Mr. Mac Receives Guggenheim Medal," *McDonnell Airscoop,* Vol. XXIII, No. 1 (February 1964), 1-2.

"Mercury's Father," *Time* (March 9, 1962), 86.
Story on James S. McDonnell and John Glenn's orbital flight in *Friendship 7.*

"The N.A.A. Annual Convention," *Aviation,* Vol. XV, No. 17 (October 22, 1923), 513-516.
It was held in St. Louis in conjunction with the International Air Races.

"The New Air Mail Contracts," *Aviation,* Vol. XIX, No. 16 (October 19, 1925), 552.
Robertson Aircraft Corporation received one of the five original contracts.

"New York-Paris Flight a Reality," *Aviation,* Vol. XXII, No. 22 (May 30, 1927), 1120-1122.

"The New York-Paris Flight Projects," *Aviation,* Vol. XXII, No. 17 (April 25, 1927), 823-825.
A discussion of the six crews then making preparations for transatlantic attempts.

"News of the Month," *Aerial Age,* Vol. 16, No. 5 (May 1923), 241-242.
Discusses the upcoming St. Louis meet.

"News Released on CW's XP-55 'Ascender,'" *The Curtiss Wright-er,* Vol. 5, No. 6 (February 9, 1945), 1.

Noel, E. Percy. "First American Convention of Aero Clubs," *Aeronautics,* Vol. 6, No. 3 (March 1910), 87-88.
Noel was then secretary of the Aero Club of St. Louis. Meeting was held in St. Louis.

"No Pulitzer Races This Year," *Aviation,* Vol. XX, No. 21 (May 24, 1926), 779.
An editorial on the reasons for the cancellation of the contest, which was held annually from 1920 to 1925.

"Official World and American Air Records," *Aviation,* Vol. XXIII, No. 16 (October 17, 1923), 947-949.

"On-to-St. Louis Race Won by C.S. Jones," *Aviation,* Vol. XV, No. 16 (October 15, 1923), 476-477.

"On the Management Front at Curtiss-St. Louis," *Curtiss Fly Leaf,* Vol. XXV, No. 1 (January-February 1942), 25.

Osborn, Earl D. "St. Louis — Wichita and Denver Air Centers," *Aviation,* Vol. XXII, No. 25 (June 20, 1927), 1386-1388.
This article contains a short discussion of Robertson Aircraft Corporation.

Osborn, Robert R. "On the Atlantic Flight Preparations," *Aviation,* Vol. XXII, No. 21 (May 23, 1927), 1082-1084.
A discussion of the activities of Lindbergh, Byrd, and Chamberlain.

"Our Own Story of the St. Louis Air Race Meet," *Aviation,* Vol. XV, No. 16 (October 15, 1923), 468-489.

Packer, Ed. "Car-Line Airport," *Aviation Maintenance & Operations* (June 1948), 60.
A story on Ross Airport.

Patterson, Lieutenant T.T. "Navy Wins Two Most Coveted Trophies," *U.S. Air Service,* Vol. 8, No. 11 (November 1923), 11-14.
A story on the Pulitzer Trophy and Schneider Cup Races of 1923.

"Phantom World Records," *McDonnell Airscoop,* Vol. XXIII, No. 6 (July 1964), p. 7.

Post, Augustus. "Aero Club of America," *Fly,* Vol. I, No. 1 (November 1908), 10-11.

_____. "Air Sailing and Motoring," *American Aeronaut,* Vol. I, No. 4 (February-March 1908), 116-118.

"Prince-Bleriot Nearly Ready," *Aero,* Vol. I, No. 1 (October 8, 1910), 10.
This plane was being built in St. Louis.

"Prizes Presented to Contestants at Smoker," *Aviation,* Vol. XV, No. 17 (October 22, 1923), 519-520.

"Program and Entries for the St. Louis Air Meet," *Aviation,* Vol. XV, No. 14 (October 1, 1923), 393-399.

"Progress and Comment," *Aeronautical Digest,* Vol. 4, No. 3 (March 1924), 169.
A story on the Barling Bomber, which appeared at the International Air Races in St. Louis in 1923.

"Progress of Second National Air Institute," *Aviation,* Vol. XV, No. 14 (October 1, 1923), 411.

"Progress Report on St. Louis Race Activities," *Aviation,* Vol. XV, No. 12 (September 17, 1923), 336-338.

"Quick Facts on the Curtiss Plant in Strategic St. Louis," *Curtiss Fly Leaf,* Vol. XXV, No. 1 (January-February 1942), 24, 29-30.

"Report of Balloonist," *World's Fair Bulletin,* Vol. 5, No. 10 (August 1904), 40.
Contains the results of the July 4 balloon race.

"Robertson Aircraft Co. Prospers," *Aviation,* Vol. XIX, No. 26 (December 28, 1925), 919-920.

"Robertson Aircraft Corp. to Erect Factory," *Aviation,* Vol. XXIII, No. 7 (August 15, 1927), 374.

"Robertson Gets Chicago-St. Louis Mail Contract," *Aviation,* Vol. XIX, No. 17, (October 26, 1925), 596.

Rodgers, Thomas L. "Recollections of St. Louis — 1857-1860," *Glimpses of the Past,* Vol. IX, No. 4 (October-December 1942), 118-119.
A few notes on the 1859 flight of John Wise.

"Rulers of Three Nations Confer Honors Upon Captain Charles A. Lindbergh," *Aviation,* Vol. XXII, No. 23 (June 6, 1927), 1216-1217.
Discusses the awards given to Lindbergh in France, Belgium, and England.

"Ryan Brougham Monoplane," *Aviation,* Vol. XXIII, No. 20 (November 14, 1927), 1173-1175.

"The Saga of the 'St. Louis,'" *The Curtiss Wright-er,* Vol. 3, No. 53 (December 17, 1943), 3.
This was the CW-20, the St. Louis-built prototype of the C-46 "Commando," which the British named after the city of its origin.

"St. Louis," *Aeronautical Digest,* Vol. 3, No. 4 (October 1923), 238-240.
An article on the International Air Races.

"St. Louis as an Airport," *Aviation,* Vol. XV, No. 14 (October 1, 1923), 391.

"St. Louis Balloon History," *Aero,* Vol. I, No. 2 (October 15, 1910), 17-18.

"St. Louis Balloon Pilots Win First Three Places," *Aero,* Vol. II, No. 16 (July 22, 1911, 345-346.
Story on the 1911 National Balloon Race at Kansas City.

"St. Louis-Built Curtiss planes and Year in Which First of Model Was Completed," *The Curtiss Wright-er,* Vol. 5, No. 29 (July 20, 1945), 2-3.

"St. Louis Gets Balloon Race," *Aeronautics,* Vol. 6, No. 4 (April 1910), 138.

"St. Louis May Ask for Race Next Year," *Aero and Hydro,* Vol. VII, No. 4 (October 25, 1913), 38.
Concerns the Gordon Bennett Race, which the United States won in 1913 and was scheduled to host in 1914. Because of the war, however, that year's contest was not held.

"St. Louis Meet Opens With a Rush to Lambert Field," *Aero,* Vol. I, No. 1 (October 8, 1910), 3-5.

"St. Louis News," *Aviation,* Vol. XV, No. 20 (November 12, 1923), 603.

"St. Louis — 1923," *Aviation,* Vol. XV, No. 16 (October 15, 1923), 467.

"St. Louis Races Financial Statement," *Aviation,* Vol. XVI, No. 13 (March 31, 1924), 342.

"St. Louis Ready for International Air Races," *Aviation,* Vol. XV, No. 14 (October 1, 1923), 392-393.

"St. Louis — The Aerial Magnet," *Aviation,* Vol. XV, No. 11 (September 10, 1923), 301.

"St. Louis — The First Metropolis of the Sky," *Sterling Magazine,* Vol. 3, No. 3 (October 1911).
Article on the 1911 air meet at Fairground Park.

"Santos-Dumont Coming," *World's Fair Bulletin,* Vol. 3, No. 6 (April 1902), 31-32.
This article contains a short history of airships.

"Santos-Dumont in St. Louis," *World's Fair Bulletin,* Vol. 3, No. 7 (May 1902), 2-4.

"Sensational Balloon Voyage and Other St. Louis Reminiscences," *Glimpses of the Past,* Vol. IX, No. 4 (October-December 1942), 92.
Some contemporary notes on the 1859 flight of John Wise.

"Side Lights on the St. Louis Meet," *Aviation,* Vol. XV, No. 15 (October 8, 1923), 443-444.

Smith, Willard A. "Transportation Exhibits," *World's Fair Bulletin,* Vol. 5, No. 3 (January 1904), 7-9.

_____. "The Transportation Exhibits," *Harper's Weekly,* Vol. XLVIII, No. 2471 (April 30, 1904), 680.

"Summer's Balloon Races Grow More Important," *Aero and Hydro,* Vol. VII, No. 26 (March 28, 1914), 321.

"Ten in International Spherical Race," *Aero,* Vol. I, No. 2 (October 15, 1910), 5-6.

"That Brookins 'Kid,'" *Aero,* Vol. I, No. 2 (October 15, 1910), 10.

"13 Years Ago and Today at Curtiss-St. Louis," *Curtiss Fly Leaf,* Vol. XXV, No. 1 (January-February 1942), 14-15, 29.

Tinker, Clifford A. "Washington," *Aeronautical Digest,* Vol. 3, No. 4 (October 1923), 237-283.
Story on airship *ZR-1,* which visited St. Louis in 1923.

"To Teach Advanced Flying," *Aviation,* Vol. XXIII, No. 19 (November 7, 1927), 1120.
A note on Von Hoffmann Aircraft Company.

"Transport: Stunt Flight," *Time,* Vol. XXIX, No. 2 (May 31, 1937), 45-46.
Story on the abortive plans for a transatlantic race on the tenth anniversary of Lindbergh's flight.

Twining, H. La V. "The Los Angeles Aero Meet," *Aeronautics,* Vol. 6, No. 3 (March 1910), 80-81.
Story on the first formal air meet conducted in the United States.

"Uncle Sam's Second Flying Hop Across the Pond," *The Literary Digest,* Vol. XCIII, No. 13 (June 25, 1927), 37-48.
Story on the Chamberlain-Levine transatlantic success.

"U.S. at War," *Time,* Vol. XLII, No. 6 (August 9, 1943), 20
Story on the glider crash at Lambert Field which killed Mayor William Dee Becker, Major William B. Robertson, and eight others.

"Value of Ballooning to Aviation," *Aero and Hydro,* Vol. VII, No. 4 (October 25, 1913), 46.

Van Zandt, Lieutenant J. Parker. "Greatest Air Meet in History of Aviation," *U.S. Air Service,* Vol. 8, No. 11 (November 1923), 25-28.
An account of the St. Louis International Air Races.

_____. "The 1923 Pulitzer Air Classic," *U.S. Air Service,* Vol. 8, No. 11 (November 1923), 15-21.

"Von Hoffmann Aircraft Appointed Alexander Eaglerock Distributor," *Aviation,* Vol. XXIII, No. 25 (December 19, 1927), 1475.

"Von Hoffmann Aircraft Co. to Distribute B.F. Mahoney Planes," *Aviation,* Vol. XXIII, No. 16 (October 17, 1927), 954.

"Voodoo World Records," *McDonnell Airscoop,* Vol. XXIII, No. 6 (July 1964), 7.

"W.E. Lees Wins Flying Club of St. Louis Trophy," *Aviation,* Vol. XV, No. 16 (October 15, 1923), 477.

Wellman, Walter. "Long Distance Balloon Racing," *McClure's Magazine,* Vol. XVII, No. 3 (July 1901), 203-214.
Contains a note on Count Henry de la Vaulx's 1900 flight of 1,193 miles which broke the world mark John Wise had set in 1859 from St. Louis.

"Why the World Makes Lindbergh Its Hero," *The Literary Digest,* Vol. XCIII, No. 13 (June 25, 1927), 5-11.

"With the Balloonists," *Aeronautics,* Vol. 6, No. 3 (March 1910), 102.

"The World's Aero Records," *Aeronautics,* Vol. 6, No. 3 (March 1910), 93.

"World's Airplane Records Recognized by the F.A.I..," *Aviation,* Vol. XV, No. 14 (October 1, 1923), 410-411.

"The World's Fair Postponed," *World's Fair Bulletin,* Vol. 3, No. 8 (June 1902), 3-5.

"The World's High Speed Records," *Aeronautical Digest,* Vol. 3, No. 4 (October 1923), 243-245.

"World's Maximum Speed Record Broken," *Aviation,* Vol. XV, No. 20 (November 12, 1923), 598-599.
Article on Al Williams' Pulitzer performance in St. Louis.

"ZR-1 Completes St. Louis Flight," *Aviation,* Vol. XV, No. 15 (October 8, 1923), 445.

"ZR1 Makes Successful 2,200 Mile Flight," *Aviation*, Vol. XV, No. 16 (October 15, 1923), 490-491.

ADVERTISEMENTS

"Aeromotion Company of America," *Aero*, Vol. I, No. 2 (October 15, 1910), 32. This firm and all those which follow were components of the aircraft industry in St. Louis.

"Aeronautical Supply Company," *Aero*, Vol. I, No. 1 (October 8, 1910), 24.

"Carter Carburetor Company," *Aero*, Vol. I, No. 2 (October 15, 1910), 21.

"French American Balloon Company," *Aero*, Vol. I, No. 2 (October 15, 1910), 19.

"John Berry Auto Repair Company," *Aero*, Vol. I, No. 2 (October 15, 1910), 23.

"Missouri Tent and Awning Company," *Aero*, Vol. I, No. 2 (October 15, 1910), 23.

"The New Benoist Flying Boat," *Aero and Hydro*, Vol. V, No. 19 (February 8, 1913), inside cover.

"Phoenix Auto Supply Company," *Aero*, Vol. I, No. 2 (October 15, 1910), 31.

"Robertson Aircraft Corporation," *Aviation*, Vol. XIX, No. 3 (July 20, 1925), 79.

NEWSPAPERS

Daily Missouri Republican. July-October 1841; January-August 1859.

Missouri Republican. May 1836.

The Missouri Republican. September-October 1879.

New York Times. May 1927; September-October 1929; August 1974; May 1980; October 1981.

St. Louis Aviation News. Vol. I, No. 1 (October 1946).

St. Louis Globe-Democrat. September 1900; May-December 1904; September-October 1907; February-November 1908; August-November 1910; September-October 1911; March 1912; October 1913; April, June-July, 1914; May-June 1917; July, September-October 1919; September-October 1923; October-November 1927; January, April-October, December 1928; January-October, December 1929; January-March, May, August 1930; July 1932; October 1935; May-June 1937; February 1940; July-August 1943; January, April, June, 1944; February, December 1945; March, October-December 1946; January, July 1947; July 1949; September 1955; June-December 1963; January-December 1964; January-February 1965.

St. Louis Post-Dispatch. August, November-December 1904; September-October 1907; July, September-October 1909; September-October 1910; June-July 1914; July, September-October 1919; May-June, August-October 1920; September 1923; May 1927; August 1928; May, September-October 1929; May-June 1937; August 1942; October 1943; June 1944; July, November 1946; March 1949; April 1950; June-December 1963; January-December 1964; January-February 1965.

St. Louis Republic. January 1899; September-October 1900; June 1901; April 1902; May-December 1904; September-October 1907; November 1908; September-October 1909; July-December 1910; September-October 1911; May-June 1917.

St. Louis Star. July 1909.

St. Louis Star-Times. August 1935; August 1946; September 1947.

St. Louis Times. July 1909; October 1911; May 1914.

St. Petersburg Times. August 1978; June 1979; August 1980; October 1981; June 1983.

SECONDARY SOURCES
BOOKS

Bennitt, Mark, and Stockbridge, Frank Parker, *et. al., History of the Louisiana Purchase Exposition.* St. Louis: Universal Exposition Company, 1905.
Bennitt was manager of the General Press Bureau of the exposition; Stockbridge was managing editor. This well-illustrated book is a complete history of the 1904 World's Fair in one volume.

Buel, J.W. *Louisiana and the Fair.* Volumes 4, 9, and 10. St. Louis: World's Progress Publishing Company, 1905.
Official, or at least quasi-official, history of the 1904 World's Fair in 10 volumes.

Cooke, David C. *The Story of Aviation.* New York: Archer House, 1958.
A general history, with particular emphasis on United States Army and Naval activity.

Cunningham, William Glenn. *The Aircraft Industry: A Study in Industrial Location.* Los Angeles: Lorris A. Morrison, 1951.
Detailed coverage on the whole of the United States, including hard-to-find statistics on St. Louis.

Davis, Kenneth S. *The Hero: Charles A. Lindbergh and the American Dream.* Garden City: Doubleday, 1959.
By far the best secondary work on Lindbergh. Covers his entire life to date, with great accuracy, objectivity, and detail.

De la Croix, Robert. *They Flew the Atlantic.* Translated by Edward Fitzgerald. New York: W.W. Norton, 1958. Coverage extends from the earliest attempts at the turn of the century to the rash of crossings in the late 1920s and early 1930s.

Dene, Shafto. *Trail Blazing in the Skies.* Akron: Goodyear Tire and Rubber Company, 1943.
Story of the United States airmail, including Robertson Aircraft's CAM-2.

Donovan, Frank. *The Early Eagles.* New York: Dodd, Mead, 1962.
Good treatment and analysis of Lindbergh's flight.

Fife, George Buchanan. *Lindbergh, The Lone Eagle: His Life and Achievements.* New York: A.L. Burt Company, 1927.
One of a number of studies which appeared shortly after the flight. Reasonably well done, with several facts later authors seem to omit.

Garber, Paul E. *The National Aeronautical Collections.* Washington: The Smithsonian Institution, 1956.
Garber was then curator of the National Air Museum. His book is a general history of aviation, with particular emphasis on the events depicted and aircraft exhibited in the museum.

Green, William. *War Planes of the Second World War.* Volume 4: *Fighters.* Garden City: Hanover House, 1961.
Detailed summaries, arranged according to manufacturer, of every major airplane of the period.

Josephy, Alvin M., Jr., *et. al.* (editors). *The American Heritage History of Flight.* New York: Simon and Schuster, 1962.
An excellent comprehensive history from primitive mythology to Project Mercury.

Juptner, Joseph P. *U.S. Civil Aircraft.* Volume 1: *ATC 1-ATC 100.* Los Angeles: Aero Publishers, Inc., 1962.
Detailed histories of each airplane.

_____. *U.S. Civil Aircraft.* Volume 2: *ATC 101-ATC 200.* Los Angeles: Aero Publishers, Inc., 1964.

Kelly, Charles J., Jr. *The Sky's the Limit: The History of the Airlines.* New York: Coward-McCann, 1963.
A comprehensive history of the United States airlines by the former special counsel to the Civil Aeronautics Board.

Lipsner, Captain Benjamin B. *The Airmail: Jennies to Jets.* Chicago: Wilcox and Follett Company, 1951.
A history of the mail service from 1918 to 1948 by its first superintendent, with particular stress on the early years, based on his own reminiscences.

Morris, Lloyd, and Smith, Kendall. *Ceiling Unlimited: The Story of American Aviation from Kitty Hawk to Supersonics.* New York: Macmillan, 1958.
An excellent general history.

Neville, Leslie E., and Silsbee, Nathaniel F. *Jet Propulsion Progress.* New York: McGraw-Hill, 1948.
The authors cite some interesting anecdotes on the McDonnell "Phantom."

Scamehorn, Howard L. *Balloons to Jets: A Century of Aeronautics in Illinois, 1855-1955.* Chicago: Henry Regnery Company, 1957.
Doctoral dissertation at Southern Illinois University. Scamehorn treats of many things related to the air history of St. Louis, particularly Robertson Aircraft Corporation.

Scott, John D. *Vickers: A History.* London: Weidenfield and Nicolsen, 1962.
A general history of the company. Summarizes the Alcock-Brown nonstop transatlantic flight of 1919, made in a Vickers-Vimy bomber.

Shamburger, Page. *Tracks Across the Sky: The Story of the Pioneers of the U.S. Air Mail.* New York: J.B. Lippincott, 1964.
Some treatment of Lindbergh and Robertson.

Smith, Henry Ladd. *Airways: The History of Commercial Aviation in the United States.* New York: Alfred A. Knopf, 1942.
Excellent coverage on Robertson Aircraft Corporation.

Swanborough, F.G., and Bowers, Peter M. *United States Military Aircraft Since 1909.* London: Putnam, 1963.
Technical data and histories of all major American military planes.

Ward, Baldwin H., *et. al.* (editors). *Flight — A Pictorial History of Aviation.* New York: Simon and Schuster, 1953.
A general history, valuable for its information on every major event in the history of aviation.

PROGRAMS AND PAMPHLETS

Airshow Program Committee. *40th Anniversary of the 110th Tac. Ftr. Squadron, Missouri Air National Guard and Progress of General Aviation in St. Louis.* Wood River, Illinois: East 10 Publishing Company, 1963.
This program contains a history of the unit (founded by Major William B. Robertson), a chronology of the air history of St. Louis, a summary of the development of Lambert Field, and a capsule history of McDonnell Aircraft. Partially inaccurate in respect to certain specific events and dates.

Beauregard, Nettie H. *Lindbergh's Decorations and Trophies.* St. Louis: Missouri Historical Society, 1935.

Dedication Program Committee. *The Robertson Air National Guard Base. Saint Louis: Dedication, 17 May 1959.* St. Louis, 1959.
Contains a history of the 110th Squadron.

Facilities . . . McDonnell Aircraft. St. Louis: McDonnell Aircraft Corporation, c. 1959.

First in Flight. New York: Curtiss-Wright Corporation, c. 1949.

The Future is at McDonnell. St. Louis: McDonnell Aircraft Corporation, c. 1961.
Pamphlet explaining the history and facilities of the company.

Goodyear Aeronautics Department. *Free Ballooning.* Akron: Goodyear Tire and Rubber Company, 1919.
A general history.

Look to Parks. East St. Louis, Illinois: Parks College of Aeronautical Technology of Saint Louis University, c. 1949.
A brochure on Parks Air College.

McDonnell Aircraft Corporation: Achievements, 1939-1956. St. Louis: McDonnell Aircraft Corporation, 1956.
Particularly useful for specific dates, for it is arranged as a chronology.

McDonnell: The First 25 Years, 1939-1964. St. Louis: McDonnell Aircraft Corporation, 1964.

110th Bombardment Squadron, 131st Bombardment Wing, Missouri Air National Guard: 30th Anniversary Year, 1923-1953. St. Louis, 1953.
A history of the unit.

Program for Dinner in Honor of Major Albert Bond Lambert, Given by Air Board, St. Louis Chamber of Commerce, Tuesday, January 31, 1928, Chase Hotel. St. Louis, 1928.
Contained in this program is a chronology of 32 events in the air history of St. Louis. Partially inaccurate.

Quigley, Martin, *et. al. St. Louis: A Fond Look Back.* St. Louis: The First National Bank in St. Louis, 1956.
A short pictorial history, with some data on air events.

St. Louis is Rich in Aviation History and a Pioneer in Many of its Phases. St. Louis, c. 1942.
A chronology of the city's air history in the files of the Missouri Historical Society. May have been written by Albert Bond Lambert. Partially inaccurate as to specific dates.

Sheppler, Robert. *Aviation Instruments: A Brief History*. Davenport, Iowa: Bendix Corporation, 1962.

A reprint in pamphlet form of four articles from the *American Aviation Historical Society Journal*. Makes reference to the instruments in Lindberg's *Spirit of St. Louis.*

"25th Anniversary Plant Tour Fact Sheets."

A mimeographed collection of statistics prepared for McDonnell tour guides for the company's open house held on July 4, 1964.

You and McDonnell: A Handbook for Employees. St. Louis: McDonnell Aircraft Corporation, 1963.

Contains a history of the company.

PERIODICALS

"Air Mail From St. Louis in 1859," *Missouri Historical Review,* Vol. XXVI, No. 4 (July 1932), 429-430.

"Air Mail Service in St. Louis," *Bulletin of the Missouri Historical Society,* Vol. XIII, No. 3 (April 1957), 351-352.

Bonney, Walter T. "The Heritage of Kitty Hawk: Part VII," *Pegasus* (August 1956), 10-15.

A story on Tom Benoist.

Bowers, Peter M. "The Sixty Best Commercial Airplanes, 1927-1936," *Air Progress,* August/September 1963, 18-40, 94-95.

"Central States Aero Historians Meeting," *Wingfoot Lighter-Than-Air Society Bulletin,* Vol. 11, No. 9 (July-August 1964), 4-5.

Anecdotes on dirigible pilots at the 1904 World's Fair.

"Col. Lindbergh's 'Lambert 145 Monocoupe' — 1934." *Flying* (August 1963), 67.

Cross, Roy. "Men and Ships," *Model Airplane News* (January 1959), 13, 62-63.

"Do You Know or Don't You?" *Missouri Historical Review,* Vol. XXXI, No. 1 (October 1936), 72.

Albert Bond Lambert established the Army's first balloon school on April 6, 1917, at St. Louis.

"Fifty Years of St. Louis Through One Man's Camera," *Bulletin of the Missouri Historical Society,* Vol. XIII, No. 1 (October 1956), 64-65.

Some notes on air events.

"First Parachute Landing from an Airplane," *American Aviation Historical Society Journal,* Vol. 9, No. 2 (Summer 1964), 142-143.

Executed at St. Louis by Albert Berry on March 1, 1912.

"Flying," *Time,* Vol. 84, No. 14 (October 2, 1964), 81.

Story on the revival of the National Air Races, which had been outlawed in 1949 by the CAA as too hazardous.

Forden, Leslie N. "Whatever Became of . . . the Curtiss Robin." Undated magazine clipping from the scrapbook of L.J. Sutorius.

"Historical Notes and Comments," *Missouri Historical Review,* Vol. XXIV, No. 1 (October 1931), 101.

First mail carried by plane in St. Louis was on October 5, 1911.

"Historical Notes and Comments," *Missouri Historical Review,* Vol. XXVI, No. 2 (January 1932), 198.
Walter Brookins made the city's first airmail flight.

"A History of the U.S. Army Air Corps," *Aviation,* Vol. XXI, No. 5 (August 2, 1926), 170-173.

"How to Prosper on Low Profits," *Business Week* (January 1, 1955), 70-71.
A story on McDonnell Aircraft Corporation.

Ingells, Douglas J. "The Sport of Wings," *Pegasus* (August 1956), 1-4.
Notes on various air races.

Key, William C. "25 Years of Scheduled Air Transport," *Pegasus* (January 1952), 1-15.

Lange, Dana. "A History of St. Louis — Volume I," *Public School Messenger,* Vol. 28, No. 9 (November 20, 1930), 1-100.

"Lindbergh's *Spirit of St. Louis,*" *Air Progress,* Special Edition, 1952, 54-55.
A detailed drawing.

"McDonnell — A Fabulous Saga of Men and Jets," *St. Louis Commerce* (June 1956), 68-76.

"McDonnell Banshee," *Aero Digest,* Vol. 65, No. 3 (September 1952), 22-38.
An excellent history of the company, particularly on the early activities of J.S. McDonnell himself.

"McDonnell Celebrates Its 25th Birthday," *McDonnell Airscoop,* Vol. XXIII, No. 6 (July 1964), 1-8.
A review of the first 25 years of the company's history.

"Modest Wizard," *Newsweek* (January 26, 1959), 79.
A story on James S. McDonnell.

"Monocoupe Club," *Antique Airplane Association News* (March 1963).
An article on Lindbergh's "Monocoupe" from the files of the Missouri Historical Society.

Morehouse, Harold E. "Flight from the Water," *American Aviation Historical Society Journal,* Vol. 9, No. 3 (Fall 1964), 172-178.
The article covers the activity of Tom Benoist in the realm of flying boats.

"News and Comment," *Bulletin of the Missouri Historical Society,* Vol. IX, No. 2 (January 1953), 204-205.
Aero magazine, the first weekly of its kind, began in St. Louis in 1910.

Nye, Willis. "Lincoln Beachey, Balloonist," *American Aviation Historical Society Journal,* Vol. 9, No. 1 (Spring 1964), 56-57.

"An Outline of Aviation," *The Literary Digest,* Vol. XCIII, No. 13 (June 25, 1927), 9-10.

"Parks — The 'Airline' School," *Air Trails Pictorial* (September 1948), 34-35, 76.

"Personalities," *Forbes* (March 1, 1962), 17.
A story on James S. McDonnell.

Plehinger, Russell. "Endurance Flying: The Pilots and Planes," *American Aviation Historical Society Journal,* Vol. 9, No. 4 (Winter 1964), 280-287.

"A Portfolio of Early Aviation Pictures," *Bulletin of the Missouri Historical Society,* Vol. VIII, No. 4 (July 1952), 377-379.
Accompanying text on highlights of the air history of St. Louis.

Rolfe, Douglas. "Air Progress: The McDonnell Story," *Air Trails,* Vol. XXIV, No. 6 (September 1950), 28-29.

Ross, Walter. "What Became of Charles Lindbergh?" *Reader's Digest,* Vol. 84, No. 502 (February 1964), 91-96.

Scamehorn, Howard Lee. "Thomas Scott Baldwin: The Columbus of the Air," *Journal of the Illinois State Historical Society,* Vol. XLIX, No. 2 (Summer 1956), 162-189.

Schloss, Leon. "A Requiem for Roosevelt Field," *Pegasus* (May 1952), 1-15.

Wadell, L.S. "The Airborne Story," *Pegasus* (June 1954), 1-15.

Whalen, Richard J. "Banshee, Demon, Voodoo, Phanton — and Bingo!" *Fortune,* Vol. LXX, No. 5 (November 1964), 136-139, 256-262.
An excellent story on McDonnell Aircraft.

White, Edward J. "A Century of Transportation in Missouri," *Missouri Historical Review,* Vol. XV, No. 1 (October, 1920), 158-162.

"Yesterday's Wings: The Monocoupe," *The AOPA Pilot* (February 1963), 76-77.

Young, Pearl I. "Airships and Balloons at the St. Louis Fair, 1904 — Parts I, II, III," *Wingfoot Lighter-Than-Air Society Bulletin,* Vol. 11, Nos. 4, 5, 6 (February, March, April, 1964), 2-5; 2-4, 8; 2-6.

NEWSPAPERS

"Air Story of St. Louis," *St. Louis Globe-Democrat.* November 3, 1929-February 16, 1930.
An excellent 16-part story on St. Louis air activities from 1904 to 1910. It appeared weekly in the Sunday "Aviation" section.

Althoff, Shirley. "The Busy World of Scott Air Force Base," *St. Louis Globe-Democrat,* April 12, 1964, Sunday Magazine, 6-10.

"Ballooning in St. Louis Long Ago," *St. Louis Post-Dispatch,* July 16, 1949.

Bothwell, Dick. "Antique Aircraft Passes Dry Land Test," *St. Petersburg Times,* January 9, 1964, 1-B, 11-B.
Story on the ceremonies commemorating the fiftieth anniversary of the opening of Tom Benoist's historic airline.

Brashear, Lee. "Early Birdman," *St. Louis Globe-Democrat,* June 15, 1952.
An excellent story on the life of Tom Benoist.

Briggs, Bob. "The Fabulous Phantom," *St. Louis Globe-Democrat,* May 3, 1964, Sunday Magazine, 4-8.

Brown, David. "Air Race," *St. Louis Globe-Democrat,* October 13, 1963, Sunday Magazine, 6-9.
Story on the current activities of the Aero Club of St. Louis.

_____. "Jennys to Jets," *St. Louis Globe-Democrat,* June 16, 1963, Sunday Magazine, 4-7, 19.

Childs, M.W. "Interesting St. Louisans: Major Albert Bond Lambert," *St. Louis Post-Dispatch,* September 21, 1930, Sunday Magazine, 5.

Douty, Esther M. "Greatest Balloon Trip Ever Made," *The* (Cleveland) *Plain Dealer,* July 5, 1959, 1B, 8B.
Story on John Wise's *Atlantic* on the occasion of the 100th anniversary of the flight.

Jones, Richard M. "The Airport," *St. Louis Post-Dispatch*, July 19, 1964, Sunday Magazine, 18-21.

_____. "Battle in Gumbo Bottoms," *St. Louis Post-Dispatch*, October 11, 1964, Sunday Magazine, 42-43.
Story on the dispute between the owners of Lobmaster Sky Ranch and the developers of the Spirit of St. Louis Airport.

"Laclede Gas Co. Grew Rapidly in Last 25 Years," *St. Louis Post-Dispatch*, Bicentennial Edition, February 16, 1964, 19M.

"Laclede Gas Fueled St. Louis' March to a Brighter Era," *St. Louis Globe-Democrat*, Bicentennial Edition, February 29-March 1, 1964, 11W.

"Looking Backward," *St. Louis Globe-Democrat*, August 18, 1963, Sunday Magazine.
A note on the Jackson-O'Brine 647-hour endurance flight of 1930, cited inaccurately as 1929.

"Looking Backward," *St. Louis Globe-Democrat*, January 12, 1964, Sunday Magazine, 13.
A note on Charles Lindbergh's airmail activities in St. Louis.

Magrath, Christy C. "Wings of Old Kinloch," *The* (Berkeley, Missouri) *Public News*, June 25, 1953, 2.
An excellent story on Tom Benoist and the activity at Kinloch Field.

"Maj. A.B. Lambert Dies in His Sleep; Pioneer St. Louis Aviation Backer," *St. Louis Post-Dispatch*, November 12, 1946, 1, 6.

"New Lambert-St. Louis Air Terminal," *St. Louis Post-Dispatch*, March 11, 1956, Part 8, 1-15.

Olson, Clarence E. "Phantoms on the Assembly Line," *St. Louis Post-Dispatch*, March 22, 1964, Sunday Magazine, 16-17.

Schafers, Ted. "McDonnell Aircraft Marks 25th Year," *St. Louis Globe-Democrat*, July 4-5, 1964, 1F.

Terry, Dickson. "McDonnell Aims for the Moon," *St. Louis Post-Dispatch*, June 24, 1962, 1I.

Wagner, Theodore P. "Flying High With Old-Time Pilots," *St. Louis Post-Dispatch*, June 2, 1963. 1J.
Story on the reunion of members of the 110th Squadron of the Missouri Air National Guard on its fortieth anniversary.

_____. "Pioneer St. Louis Pilot Looks Back," *St. Louis Post-Dispatch*, December 10, 1958.
Reminiscences of C. Ray Wassall.

_____. "St. Louis a Leader Since 1904 in Development of Aviation," *St. Louis Post-Dispatch*, Bicentennial Edition, February 16, 1964, 3V, 6V.

Wallin, David R. "McDonnell Corp. Young But a Leader in Space Age," *St. Louis Post-Dispatch*, Bicentennial Edition, February 16, 1964, 3T.

Warner, Jay M. "When St. Louis Had Gas Pains," *St. Louis Globe-Democrat*, January 8, 1950.

"Weather Halts Benoist Flying Boat Testing," *St. Petersburg Times*, January 10, 1964, 1B, 11B.
Story on the ceremonies commemorating the fiftieth anniversary of the opening of Tom Benoist's historic airline.

Woo, William. "He Flashes Across the Sky Like a Streak," *St. Louis Post-Dispatch,* August 18, 1963, 3G.

TELEVISION DOCUMENTARIES

Guggenheim, Charles, and Associates, Inc. (producers). "A Bicentennial Tribute: St. Louis, 1764-1964." KSD-TV, February 16, 1964, 9:00-10:30 p.m.

──────────. "City of Flight." KETC-TV, June 5, 1963, 9:30-10:30 p.m.

McDonnell Aircraft Corporation (producer). "The First 25 Years at McDonnell." KMOX-TV, July 7, 1964, 6:30-7:00 p.m.

REFERENCE WORKS

Aeronautical Chamber of Commerce of America. *The Aircraft Year Books for 1930, 1931, 1932, 1933, 1935.* New York: D. Van Nostrand, 1930, 1931, 1932, 1933, 1935.
Especially valuable for information on aircraft industries.

Aircraft Year Books, 1919, 1920, 1921. New York: Manufacturers' Aircraft Association, 1919, 1920, 1921.

Aircraft Year Books, 1922, 1924, 1925, 1926, 1927, 1928, 1929. New York: Aeronautical Chamber of Commerce of America, 1922, 1924, 1925, 1926, 1927, 1928, 1929.

Appleton's Cyclopedia of American Biography. Volume VI. New York: D. Appleton and Company, 1889.
On John Wise.

Aviation Week. *29th Annual Airport and Business Flying Directory.* New York: McGraw-Hill, 1961.
Information on airports in the St. Louis area.

Chilton Aero Directory and Catalogue, 1929. Philadelphia: Chilton Class Journal Company, 1929.
Information on aircraft industries.

Civic Union of St. Louis. *Who's Who in St. Louis, 1930-1931.* St. Louis: Civic Union of St. Louis, 1930.

Combs, Vice Admiral Thomas S., and Russell, Rear Admiral James S. *United States Naval Aviation, 1910-1960.* Washington: Department of the Navy, 1960.
A chronology of major events, with many references to the products of McDonnell Aircraft.

Encyclopedia Britannica. Volumes I-II. Chicago: Encyclopedia Britannica, Inc., 1954.
General information on airships, balloons, and civil aviation.

Fahey, James C. *U.S. Army Aircraft, 1908-1946.* Falls Church, Virginia: Ships and Aircraft, 1964.
Excellent for hard-to-find production statistics on every airplane accepted by the Army between those dates.

Jane's All the World's Aircraft, 1962-1963. London, 1963.
The classic work in its field.

Larkin, Samuel T. (editor). *Who's Who in Saint Louis, 1928-1929.* St. Louis: Civic Union of St. Louis, 1928.

Malone, Dumas (editor). *Dictionary of American Biography*. Volume XX. New York: Charles Scribner's Sons, 1936.
On John Wise.

Mingos, Howard (editor). *The Aircraft Year Books for 1936, 1937, 1938, 1939, 1940, 1941, 1942*. New York: Aeronautical Chamber of Commerce of America, 1936, 1937, 1938, 1939, 1940, 1941, 1942.

_____. *The Aircraft Year Books for 1943, 1944, 1945, 1946*. New York: Lanciar Publishers, Inc., 1943, 1944, 1945, 1946.

National Committee to Observe the 50th Anniversary of Powered Flight. *Fifty Years of Powered Flight: 1903-1953 — A Reference Book of Significant Air Achievements*. Toledo: Admaster Creations Company, 1952.
A general chronology.

The National Cyclopaedia of American Biography. Volume I. New York: James T. White and Company, 1898.
On John Wise.

Shrader, Welman A. *Fifty Years of Flight: A Chronicle of the Aviation Industry in America, 1903-1953*. Cleveland: Eaton Manufacturing Company, 1953.
A general chronology.

Notes

CHAPTER I

1. *Missouri Republican,* May 19, 1836, p. 2. See Chapter II, p. 41.
2. *Daily Missouri Republican,* August 17, 1841, and October 14, 1841. See Chapter II, p. 41.
3. *Ibid.,* June 29, 1859, p. 3. See Chapter II, p. 46.
4. John Wise, *Through the Air* (Philadelphia: To-day Printing and Publishing Company, 1873), p. 490.
5. *The Missouri Republican,* September 28, 1879, p. 3. See Chapter II, p. 52.
6. "Ballooning in St. Louis Long Ago, *St. Louis Post-Dispatch,* July 16, 1949, See Chapter II, p. 53.
7. *St. Louis Globe-Democrat,* October 10, 1907, p. 2. See Chapter IV, p. 97.
8. "Laclede Gas Fueled St. Louis' March to a Brighter Era," *St. Louis Globe-Democrat,* Bicentennial Edition, February 29-March 1, 1964, p. 11W.
9. *Official Program of the Second Competition of the Gordon Bennett Aeronautic Cup, St. Louis, U.S.A.,* October 1907 (St. Louis, 1907), p. 17.
10. *St. Louis Post-Dispatch,* October 27, 1907, p. 12.
11. *St. Louis Globe-Democrat,* October 18, 1907, p. 1. See Chapter IV, p. 103.
12. *St. Louis Republic,* November 19, 1908, p. 1. See Chapter V, pp. 116-117.
13. *Ibid.,* October 13, 1909, p. 9. See Chapter V, p. 133.
14. *St. Louis Republic,* October 3, 1909, Part V., p. 14. See Chapter V, p. 124.
15. "Ten in International Spherical Race," *Aero,* Vol. I, No. 2 (October 15, 1910), p. 5. See Chapter VI, p. 151.
16. *St. Louis Republic,* October 18, 1910, p. 2.
17. *St. Louis Post-Dispatch,* July 6, 1914, p. 7. See Chapter VIII, p. 176.
18. *St. Louis Globe-Democrat,* July 5, 1914, p. 12.
19. *St. Louis Star-Times,* August 9, 1935. See Chapter XIV, pp. 290-291.
20. *St. Louis Post-Dispatch,* September 26, 1919, p. 1. See Chapter IX, p. 181.

21. *Ibid.,* October 2, 1919, p. 1. See Chapter IX, p. 187.
22. "Laclede Gas Co. Grew Rapidly in Last 25 Years," *St. Louis Post-Dispatch,* Bicentennial Edition, February 16, 1964, p. 19M. See Chapter XII, p. 251.
23. *St. Louis Republic,* October 11, 1909, p. 1. See Chapter V, p. 132.
24. Christy C. Magrath, "Wings of Old Kinloch," *The* (Berkeley, Missouri) *Public News,* June 25, 1953, p. 2. See Chapter VI, p. 141.
25. *St. Louis Globe-Democrat,* October 3, 1910, p. 3.
26. Magrath, p. 2.
27. *Aeronautics Papers, 1830-1939,* Missouri Historical Society Archives.
28. Majors Albert Bond Lambert and William B. Robertson, "Early History of Aeronautics in St. Louis," *Missouri Historical Society Collections,* Vol. V., No. 3 (June 1928), p. 242.
29. "A Portfolio of Early Aviation Pictures," *Bulletin of the Missouri Historical Society,* Vol. VIIII, No. 4 (July 1952), p. 378.
30. "Air Story of St. Louis," *St. Louis Globe-Democrat.* February 16, 1930, p. 13s.
31. *St. Louis Globe-Democrat,* September 7, 1910, p. 1. See Chapter VI, p. 139.
32. *St. Louis Republic,* October 10, 1909, Part I, p. 7. See Chapter VII, p. 159.
33. *St. Louis Post-Dispatch,* August 15, 1920, p. 14B.
34. *Program of the Inauguration of U.S. Air Mail Service, Forest Park Aerial Field, Saint Louis, Missouri, U.S.A., August 16, 1920* (St. Louis, 1920), p. 3. Cited hereafter as *Air Mail Program, 1920.*
35. *Idem.*
36. *Aircraft Year Book, 1920* (New York: Manufacturers Aircraft Association, 1920), p. 301.
37. *Air Mail Program, 1920,* p. 3.
38. *St. Louis Post-Dispatch,* August 15, 1920, p. 14B.
39. *Air Mail Program, 1920,* p. 4.
40. *St. Louis Post-Dispatch,* August 16, 1920, p. 1.
41. *Air Mail Program, 1920,* p. 4.
42. *St. Louis Post-Dispatch,* September 21, 1920, p. 15.
43. Captain Benjamin B. Lipsner, *The Airmail: Jennies to Jets,* (Chicago: Wilcox and Follett Company, 1951), p. 194.
44. *Aircraft Year Book, 1922* (New York: Aeronautical Chamber of Commerce of America, 1922), p. 27.
45. *St. Louis Post-Dispatch,* June 18, 1920, p. 11. The original size of the field is cited variously as 169 acres in "Lambert-St. Louis Municipal Airport, St. Louis, Missouri," *Aeronautics Papers, 1830-1939.* Missouri Historical Society Archives, p. 1, and 170 acres in "A Brief Summary Relative to the Early History of the Lambert-St. Louis Municipal Airport," *Albert Bond Lambert Aeronautical Papers,* Missouri Historical Society Archives, p. 1.
46. *St. Louis Post-Dispatch,* June 18, 1920, p. 11.
47. "A Brief Summary Relative to the Early History of the Lambert-St. Louis Municipal Airport," p. 1.
48. See Chapter X, pp. 193-194.
49. W. Frank Carter, "What St. Louis Field Means to St. Louis," *The Cherry Diamond,* September 1923, p. 13.
50. "Stockholders' Report: St. Louis Aeronautic Corporation, February 28, 1924," *International Air Race Papers, 1923,* Missouri Historical Society Library.

51. "Side Lights of the St. Louis Meet," *Aviation,* Vol. XV, No. 16 (October 15, 1923), p. 487.
52. Letter from Mrs. Mary Jane Weldon to Major Albert Bond Lambert, *Aeronautics Papers, 1830-1939,* Missouri Historical Society Archives.
53. "Airports and Airways: St. Louis, Mo.," *Aviation,* Vol. XXIII, No. 24 (December 12, 1927), p. 1426.
54. *Souvenir Program, 40th Anniversary of the 110th Tac. Ftr. Squadron, Missouri Air National Guard, and Progress of General Aviation in St. Louis* St. Louis, 1963), p. 6. Cited hereafter as *Souvenir Program, 1963.*
55. *Aircraft Year Book, 1922,* p. 26.
56. *St. Louis Globe-Democrat,* July 1, 1928, pp. 8-9.
57. *Ibid.,* p. 8.
58. "A Brief Summary Relative to the Early History of the Lambert-St. Louis Municipal Airport," p. 3.
59. "Airports and Airways: St. Louis, Mo.," *Aviation,* Vol. XXIII, No. 24 (December 12, 1927), p. 1426.
60. *Souvenir Program, 1963,* p. 20.
61. "Airports and Airways: St. Louis, Mo.," *Aviation,* Vol. XXIV, No. 3 (January 16, 1928), p. 162.
62. "A Brief Summary Relative to the Early History of the Lambert-St. Louis Municipal Airport," pp. 2-4.
63. *St. Louis Post-Dispatch,* August 7, 1928, p. 3.
64. *St. Louis Globe-Democrat,* August 9, 1928, p. 2.
65. *St. Louis Post-Dispatch,* August 9, 1928, p. 6.
66. *St. Louis Globe-Democrat,* August 9, 1928, p. 2.
67. *St. Louis Globe-Democrat,* January 29, 1929.
68. "Lambert-St. Louis Municipal Airport, St. Louis, Missouri," p. 2.
69. Industrial Club of St. Louis, *Air Transport Facilities in the St. Louis District* (St. Louis, c. 1930), unpaginated leaflet.
70. *St. Louis Globe-Democrat,* October 12, 1928.
71. *St. Louis Globe-Democrat,* June 9, 1929.
72. Henry Ladd Smith, *Airways: The History of Commercial Aviation in the United States* (New York: Alfred A. Knopf, 1942), p. 391.
73. *Industrial Club of St. Louis leaflet.*
74. *St. Louis Post-Dispatch,* July 14, 1932.
75. *Idem.*
76. "Lambert-St. Louis Municipal Airport, St. Louis, Missouri," pp. 3-4.
77. "Lambert-St. Louis Municipal Airport, St. Louis, Missouri," pp. 3-5.
78. Quoted in *Lambert-St. Louis Municipal Airport Papers,* Missouri Historical Society Library.
79. *Albert Bond Lambert Aeronautical Papers,* Missouri Historical Society Archives.
80. *Lambert-St. Louis Municipal Airport Papers.*
81. *St. Louis Post-Dispatch,* October 5, 1943, p. 4A.
82. *Lambert-St. Louis Municipal Airport Papers.*
83. "Airport Commission," *Albert Bond Lambert Aeronautical Papers,* Missouri Historical Society Archives, p. 1.
84. *Lambert-St. Louis Municipal Airport Papers.*
85. *Albert Bond Lambert Aeronautical Papers.*
86. *The Airport Bond Issue And What It Means to St. Louis* (St. Louis, 1942), pp. 2-4.

87. *St. Louis Post-Dispatch,* August 5, 1942, p. 1.
88. *St. Louis Post-Dispatch,* August 2, 1942, p. 1D.
89. *St. Louis Globe-Democrat,* December 6, 1945.
90. *Lambert-St. Louis Municipal Airport Papers.*
91. *St. Louis Post-Dispatch,* October 5, 1943, p. 1A.
92. Albert Bond Lambert, "Summary of the Status of the Airport Situation in the St. Louis Area, October 1946," *Albert Bond Lambert Aeronautical Papers,* Missouri Historical Society Archives, p. 2.
93. *Report on the Nation-Wide Survey of Status of Municipal Post-War Airport Plans* (St. Louis, 1945), p. 32.
94. *St. Louis Globe-Democrat,* April 29, 1944.
95. *Albert Bond Lambert Aeronautical Papers.*
96. *Report on the Nation-Wide Survey of Status of Municipal Post-War Airport Plans,* p. 34.
97. *St. Louis Globe-Democrat,* November 28, 1946.
98. *Ibid.,* January 16, 1947.
99. *Ibid.,* July 19, 1947.
100. *St. Louis Globe-Democrat,* March 22, 1946, p. 3A.
101. *St. Louis Post-Dispatch,* July 1, 1946.
102. Ed Packer, "Car Line Airport," *Aviation Maintenance & Operations,* June 1948, p. 60.
103. *St. Louis Globe-Democrat,* July 19, 1947.
104. *St. Louis Post-Dispatch,* April 16, 1950.
105. Letter from Milton M. Kinsey, president of the St. Louis Board of Public Service, to all members of the City Airport Commission, May 6, 1946, *Albert Bond Lambert Aeronautical Papers,* Missouri Historical Society Archives.
106. *St. Louis Aviation News,* Vol. I, No. 1 (October 1946), p. 4.
107. *Ibid.,* p. 7.
108. *St. Louis Star-Times,* August 27, 1946, p. 11.
109. *St. Louis Post-Dispatch,* November 12, 1946, p. 1.
110. *St. Louis Globe-Democrat,* November 1, 1946, p. 1.
111. *St. Louis Post-Dispatch,* November 2, 1946, p. 4A.
112. *St. Louis Star-Times,* September 9, 1947.
113. "New Lambert-St. Louis Air Terminal," *St. Louis Post-Dispatch,* Sunday Magazine, Part 8, pp. 3, 6.
114. "Air Terminal Building Soars, Swoops," *St. Louis Globe-Democrat,* Bicentennial Edition, February 29-March 1, 1964, p. 15V.
115. "New Lambert-St. Louis Air Terminal," p. 6.
116. "New Lambert-St. Louis Air Terminal," p. 6. According to *Aviation Week, 29th Annual Airport and Business Flying Directory* (New York: McGraw-Hill, 1961), p. 133, however, the longest runway at Lambert Field in 1961 was 7,600 feet long, earning the airport an FAA rating of Class 6 (based on a longest runway length of 6,700-7,699 feet).
117. *Aviation Week,* p. 133.
118. *Idem.*
119. *St. Louis Globe-Democrat,* August 13, 1964, p. 3A.
120. *St. Louis Post-Dispatch,* October 15, 1964, p. 2C.
121. *Ibid.,* July 16, 1964, p. 22A.
122. *St. Louis Globe-Democrat,* August 1-2, 1964, p. 3A.
123. *St. Louis Post-Dispatch,* September 16, 1964, p. 12A.

124. *St. Louis Globe-Democrat,* August 21, 1964, p. 2A.
125. Richard M. Jones, "Battle in the Gumbo Bottoms," *St. Louis Post-Dispatch,* Sunday Magazine, October 11, 1964, p. 42.
126. *St. Louis Post-Dispatch,* September 16, 1964, p. 12A.
127. Quoted in *St. Louis Globe-Democrat,* November 6, 1964, p. 5B.
128. *Ibid.,* September 9, 1964, p. 10A.
129. *Ibid.,* November 9, 1964, p. 10A.
130. *Ibid.,* August 2, 1963, p. 2A.
131. *Ibid.,* July 18-19, 1964.
132. *St. Louis Post-Dispatch,* July 12, 1964, p. 1.
133. David Brown, "Empty Airfield," *St. Louis Globe-Democrat,* June 7, 1964, p. 8.
134. *St. Louis Globe-Democrat,* March 2, 1930, p. 3s.
135. Brown, p. 9.
136. *St. Louis Aviation News,* Vol. I, No. 1 (October 1946), p. 1.
137. *St. Louis Globe-Democrat,* July 16, 1949.
138. *St. Louis Post-Dispatch,* July 10, 1964, p. 5A.
139. Brown, p. 9.
140. *St. Louis Post-Dispatch,* November 10, 1964, p. 3A.
141. Brown, p. 9.
142. *St. Louis Globe-Democrat,* May 30-31, 1964, p. 2F.
143. *St. Louis Post-Dispatch,* July 11, 1964, p. 1.
144. *St. Louis Globe-Democrat,* November 15-16, 1964, p. 3A.
145. *Ibid.,* November 11, 1964, p. 14A.
146. *St. Louis Post-Dispatch,* November 10, 1964, p. 3A.
147. *St. Louis Post-Dispatch,* December 29, 1964, p. 8A.
148. *St. Louis Globe-Democrat,* November 26, 1964, p. 3A.
149. *Ibid.,* January 1, 1965, p. 12B.
150. *St. Louis Post-Dispatch,* November 29, 1964, p. 15A.
151. *St. Louis Globe-Democrat,* December 29, 1964, p. 3A.
152. *St. Louis Post-Dispatch,* October 18, 1964, p. 1.
153. *St. Louis Globe-Democrat,* November 5, 1964, p. 11A.
154. Quoted in *St. Louis Globe-Democrat,* November 19, 1964, p. 1.
155. *Ibid.,* May 30-31, 1964, p. 2F.
156. *St. Louis Post-Dispatch,* November 17, 1964, p. 1.
157. *Ibid.,* December 5, 1964, p. 3A.
158. *St. Louis Post-Dispatch,* May 15, 1964, p. 6A.
159. *St. Louis Globe-Democrat,* November 18, 1964, p. 1.
160. *St. Louis Post-Dispatch,* December 23, 1964, p. 3A.
161. *Ibid.,* November 12, 1964, p. 3A.
162. *Ibid.,* December 16, 1964, p. 3B.
163. *St. Louis Globe-Democrat,* February 3, 1965, p. 3A.
164. *St. Louis Post-Dispatch,* January 20, 1965, p. 20A.
165. *Ibid.,* January 7, 1965, p. 3A.
166. *St. Louis Globe-Democrat,* October 28, 1964, p. 6A.
167. *Ibid.,* December 11, 1964, p. 15A.
168. Letter to the author from David E. Leigh, manager of Lambert-St. Louis Municipal Airport, December 11, 1964.
169. *St. Louis Globe-Democrat,* January 23-24, 1965, p. 4A.

CHAPTER II

1. Baldwin H. Ward, *et. al.* (editors), *Flight: A Pictorial History of Aviation* (New York: Simon ？ id Schuster, 1953), p. 14.
2. Goodyear Aeronautics Department, *Free Ballooning* (Akron: Goodyear Tire and Rubber Company, 1919), p. 25.
3. Ward, p. 14.
4. Goodyear Aeronautics Department, p. 25.
5. Alvin M. Josephy Jr., *et. al.* (editors) *The American Heritage History of Flight* (New York: Simon and Schuster, 1962), p. 41.
6. Goodyear Aeronautics Department, p. 29.
7. Paul E. Garber, *The National Aeronautical Collections* (Washington: The Smithsonian Institution, 1956), p. 17.
8. Garber, p. 17.
9. Ward, p. 14.
10. Josephy, p. 41.
11. *Ibid.,* p. 44.
12. Frank Donovan, *The Early Eagles* (New York: Dodd, Mead, 1962), p. 28.
13. Garber, p. 19.
14. Josephy, p. 73.
15. Ward, p. 15.
16. John Wise, *Through the Air* (Philadelphia: To-day Printing and Publishing Company, 1873), p. 42.
17. "Certificate of Dr. C.G. Brun," *Aeronautics Papers, 1830-1939,* Missouri Historical Society Archives. This document is written in French, but a translation accompanies it.
18. *Missouri Republican,* May 10, 1836, p. 2.
19. *Ibid.,* May 19, 1836, p. 2.
20. *Daily Missouri Republican,* July 27, 1841, p. 3.
21. *Daily Missouri Republican,* August 16, 1841, p. 2.
22. *Ibid.,* October 14, 1841, p. 2.
23. *Idem.*
24. Howard L. Scamehorn, *Balloons to Jets: A Century of Aeronautics in Illinois, 1855-1955* (Chicago: Henry Regnery Company, 1857), p. 9.
25. *Ibid.,* p. 8.
26. Wise, *Through the Air,* p. 27.
27. *Idem.*
28. *Ibid.,* p. 28.
29. *Ibid.,* p. 31.
30. Josephy, p. 44.
31. John Wise, *A System of Aeronautics* (Philadelphia: Joseph A. Speed, 1850), p. 148.
32. *Ibid.,* pp. 149-151.
33. Wise, *Through the Air,* p. 254.
34. *Ibid.,* p. 255.
35. *Ibid.,* p. 258.
36. Wise, *A System of Aeronautics,* p. 156.
37. *Ibid.,* pp. 192-193.
38. *Ibid.,* pp. 195-198.

39. Josephy, p. 44.
40. Donovan, pp. 28-29.
41. Josephy, p. 44.
42. Wise, *Through the Air,* p. 358.
43. Wise, *A System of Aeronautics,* p. 237.
44. Wise, *Through the Air,* p. 358.
45. Wise, *A System of Aeronautics,* pp. 244-246.
46. *Ibid.,* pp. 257-258.
47. Wise, *Through the Air,* p. 391.
48. *Congressional Globe,* 31 Congress, 2 Session, p. 132.
49. Wise, *Through the Air,* p. 430.
50. This name is also spelled LaMountain, Lamountain, and Lamountane.
51. Wise, *Through the Air,* p. 489.
52. *Ibid.,* p. 490.
53. *Daily Missouri Republican,* June 19, 1859, p. 3.
54. *Ibid.,* June 30, 1859, p. 3.
55. Wise, *Through the Air,* pp. 489-490.
56. "Daring Feats of Acrobats & Aeronauts," *The Scientific American,* New Series, Vol. 1, No. 3 (July 16, 1859), #9.
57. *Daily Missouri Republican,* July 2, 1859, p. 3.
58. Wise, *Through the Air,* p. 490.
59. *Daily Missouri Republican,* June 29, 1859, p. 3.
60. *Idem.*
61. *Ibid.,* July 2, 1859, p. 2.
62. Wise, *Through the Air,* p. 490.
63. *Daily Missouri Republican,* June 30, 1859, p. 3.
64. *Ibid.,* July 7, 1859, p. 2. This issue contains William Hyde's personal account of the trip.
65. *Idem.*
66. *Ibid.,* July 2, 1859, p. 2.
67. Captain Benjamin B. Lipsner, *The Airmail: Jennies to Jets* (Chicago: Wilcox and Follett Company, 1951), p. 288.
68. "Air Mail From St. Louis in 1859," *Missouri Historical Review,* Vol. XXVI, No. 4 (July 1932), pp. 429-430. See also Bob Doty, "Tippecanoe and Flyers Too," *Pegasus,* February 1956, p. 13.
69. "Daring Feats of Acrobats & Aeronauts," p. 39.
70. *Daily Missouri Republican,* July 7, 1859, p. 2.
71. Wise, *Through the Air,* p. 493.
72. *Daily Missouri Republican,* July 7, 1859, p. 2.
73. *Ibid.,* July 2, 1859, p. 2.
74. Wise, *Through the Air,* p. 494.
75. *Daily Missouri Republican,* July 7, 1859, p. 2.
76. Wise, *Through the Air,* p. 507.
77. "Daring Feats of Acrobats & Aeronauts," p. 39.
78. *Daily Missouri Republican,* July 4, 1859, p. 2.
79. *Idem.*
80. *St. Louis Globe-Democrat,* October 23, 1907, p. 2. This issue has an excellent map which shows the route of the *Atlantic's* flight and is marked with relative distances from St. Louis.
81. *Daily Missouri Republican,* July 7, 1859, p. 2.

82. Wise, *Through the Air,* p. 503.
83. *Ibid.,* p. 508.
84. The mail was ultimately recovered and sent by train to New York City. "Air Mail From St. Louis in 1859," pp. 429-430.
85. Wise, *Through the Air,* p. 513.
86. *Daily Missouri Republican,* July 7, 1859, p. 2.
87. *Ibid.,* July 6, 1859, p. 2.
88. *Daily Missouri Republican,* July 7, 1859, p. 2.
89. Wise, *Through the Air,* p. 519.
90. *Daily Missouri Republican,* July 7, 1859, p. 2.
91. *Idem.*
92. Josephy, p. 59.
93. "Ballooning in St. Louis Long Ago," *St. Louis Post-Dispatch,* July 16, 1949.
94. A. Lawrence Rotch, "The Longest Balloon Voyage," *American Magazine of Aeronautics,* Vol. I, No. 4 (October 1907), p. 35.
95. *Daily Missouri Republican,* July 7, 1859, p. 2.
96. Wise, *Through the Air,* p. 519.
97. *Encyclopedia Britannica* (Chicago: Encyclopedia Britannica, Inc., 1954), II, p. 1009.
98. "Daring Feats of Acrobats & Aeronauts," p. 39.
99. Esther M. Douty, " 'Greatest Balloon Trip Ever Made.' " *The* (Cleveland) *Plain Dealer* July 5, 1959, p. 8B.
100. Rotch, p. 35.
101. *Appleton's Cyclopedia of American Biography* (New York: D. Appleton and Company, 1889), VI, p. 581. The map printed in the *St. Louis Globe-Democrat,* October 23, 1907, p. 2, seems to bear this out.
102. Josephy, p. 44.
103. Walter Wellman, "Long Distance Balloon Racing," *McClure's Magazine,* Vol. XVII, No. 3 (July 1901), p. 204.
104. Wise, *Through the Air,* p. 520.
105. *Ibid.,* p. 489.
106. *Daily Missouri Republican,* July 4, 1859, p. 2.
107. Wise, *Through the Air,* pp. 523-527.
108. *Ibid.,* p. 554.
109. Wise, *Through the Air,* p. 603.
110. *Ibid.,* p. 604.
111. Dumas Malone (editor), *Dictionary of American Biography* (New York: Charles Scribner's Sons, 1936), XX, p. 428.
112. Ward, p. 24.
113. *The Missouri Republican,* September 28, 1879, p. 3.
114. *The Missouri Republican,* October 1, 1879, p. 5.
115. *Ibid.,* September 29, 1879, p. 3.
116. *Ibid.,* October 2, 1879, p. 3.
117. *Ibid.,* October 1, 1879, p. 5.
118. *Idem.*
119. *Ibid.,* October 6, 1879, p. 1.
120. *The Missouri Republican,* October 2, 1879, p. 3.
121. Quoted in *Ibid.,* October 4, 1879, p. 3.
122. *Ibid.,* October 7, 1879, p. 3.
123. *The Missouri Republican,* October 8, 1879, p. 2.

124. *Ibid.,* October 25, 1879, p. 3.
125. *Ibid.,* October 26, 1879, p. 8.
126. Donovan, p. 29.
127. *The Missouri Republican,* October 6, 1879, p. 8.
128. "Ballooning in St. Louis Long Ago," *St. Louis Post-Dispatch,* July 16, 1949.
129. *St. Louis Republic,* September 18, 1900, p. 7. This account incorrectly attributes the demonstrations to a "Professor Kayser."
130. *St. Louis Globe-Democrat,* September 18, 1900, p. 7.
131. *St. Louis Republic,* September 18, 1900, p. 7.
132. *St. Louis Globe-Democrat,* September 18, 1900, p. 7.
133. *Idem.*
134. *Daily Missouri Republican,* July 4, 1859, p. 2.

CHAPTER III

1. Paul E. Garber, *The National Aeronautical Collections* (Washington: The Smithsonian Institution, 1956), p. 20.
2. David C. Cooke, *The Story of Aviation* (New York: Archer House, 1958), p. 25.
3. *Idem.*
4. Baldwin H. Ward, *et. al.* (editors), *Flight: A Pictorial History of Aviation* (New York: Simon and Schuster, 1953), p. 48.
5. Pearl I. Young, "Airships and Balloons at the St. Louis Fair, 1904 — Part I," *Wingfoot Lighter-Than-Air Society Bulletin,* Vol. 11, No. 4 (February 1964), p. 2. Cited hereafter as Young, "Airships — Part I."
6. "Santos Dumont Coming," *World's Fair Bulletin,* Vol. 3, No. 6 (April 1902), p. 31.
7. Ward, p. 27.
8. *Ibid.,* p. 25.
9. *St. Louis Republic,* October 26, 1904, p. 6.
10. Ward, p. 27.
11. *Idem.*
12. Howard L. Scamehorn, *Balloons to Jets: A Century of Aeronautics in Illinois, 1855-1955* (Chicago: Henry Regnery Company, 1957), p. 15. Cited hereafter as Scamehorn, *Balloons to Jets.*
13. Ward, p. 26.
14. *Ibid.,* p. 48.
15. Howard Lee Scamehorn, "Thomas Scott Baldwin: The Columbus of the Air," *Journal of the Illinois State Historical Society,* Vol. XLIX, No. 2 (Summer 1956), p. 164. Cited hereafter as Scamehorn, "Thomas Scott Baldwin,"
16. Ward, p. 26.

17. Lloyd Morris and Kendall Smith, *Ceiling Unlimited: The Story of American Aviation from Kitty Hawk to Super-Sonics* (New York: Macmillan, 1958), p. 79.
18. *Ibid.,* p. 80.
19. Scamehorn, "Thomas Scott Baldwin," p. 179.
20. *St. Louis Republic,* January 11, 1899, p. 4.
21. David R. Francis, *The Universal Exposition of 1904* (St. Louis: Louisiana Purchase Exposition Company, 1913), I, 41.
22. Francis, I, 42.
23. *Ibid.,* p. 41.
24. *Congressional Record,* 56 Congress, 2 Session, p. 2585.
25. *Ibid.,* 1 Session, p. 3129.
26. *Ibid.,* 2 Session, pp. 2588-2589.
27. *Ibid.,* p. 2875.
28. *Ibid.,* p. 3603.
29. *Ibid.,* pp. 2585-2586.
30. "A Brief Epitome," *World's Fair Bulletin,* Vol. 2, No. 9 (July 1901) p. 1.
31. *St. Louis Republic,* June 29, 1901, p. 1.
32. Francis, I, p. 47.
33. *Ibid.,* p. 46.
34. *Ibid.,* p. 50.
35. *Ibid.,* p. 53.
36. *Ibid.,* p. 62.
37. "Aerial Navigation," *World's Fair Bulletin,* Vol. 3, No. 4 (February 1902), p. 20.
38. Francis, I, p. 442.
39. *Ibid.,* p. 62.
40. Young, "Airships — Part I," p. 4.
41. *St. Louis Republic,* April 22, 1902, p. 1.
42. *Ibid.,* April 23, 1902, p. 1.
43. Telegram from Skiff to Francis, April 14, 1902, *David Francis Collection, 1902,* Missouri Historical Society Archives.
44. *St. Louis Republic,* April 22, 1902, p. 1.
45. Quoted in "Santos-Dumont in St. Louis," *World's Fair Bulletin,* Vol. 3, No. 7 (May 1902), p. 4.
46. The rules had been made available much earlier to those who had expressed their interest in participating in the contests.
47. *St. Louis Republic,* September 4, 1904, Part II, p. 3.
48. Willard A. Smith, "The Transportation Exhibits," *Harper's Weekly,* Vol. XLVIII, No. 2471 (April 30, 1904), p. 680.
49. "A Letter from Leo Stevens," *The Scientific American,* Vol. XC, No. 13 (March 16, 1904), p. 251.
50. "The World's Fair Postponed," *World's Fair Bulletin,* Vol. 3, No. 8 (June 1902), p. 3.
51. J.W. Buel, *Louisiana and the Fair* (St. Louis: World's Progress Publishing Company, 1905), pp. 4, 1370.
52. *St. Louis Republic,* May 1, 1904, p. 1.
53. Francis, I, p. 176.
54. Buel, pp. 4, 1438.
55. *St. Louis Post-Dispatch,* November 13, 1904, Sunday Magazine, p. 5.

56. *St. Louis Globe-Democrat,* February 11, 1940.

57. Francis, I, p. 442.

58. *St. Louis Republic,* June 12, 1904, p. 1.

59. Francis, I, p. 443.

60. "Aerial Navigation," *World's Fair Bulletin,* Vol. 3, No. 4 (February 1902), p. 21.

61. Advertising circular printed by the S.G. Adams Stamp and Seal Company of St. Louis, c. 1902, *Aeronautics Papers, 1830-1939,* Missouri Historical Society Archives.

62. *St. Louis Globe-Democrat,* May 24, 1904, p. 2.

63. Pearl I. Young, "Airships and Balloons at the St. Louis Fair, 1904 — Part III," *Wingfoot Lighter-Than-Air Society Bulletin,* Vol. 11, No. 6 (April 1964), p. 5.

64. Quoted in Francis, I, p. 443.

65. Quoted in *St. Louis Republic,* May 25, 1904, p. 1.

66. *Ibid.,* June 8, 1904, p. 3.

67. *St. Louis Republic,* June 22, 1904, Part II, p. 1.

68. *St. Louis Globe-Democrat,* June 18, 1904, p. 1.

69. *St. Louis Republic,* June 24, 1904, p. 1.

70. *St. Louis Globe-Democrat,* June 24, 1904, p. 1.

71. *St. Louis Republic,* June 25, 1904, Part I, p. 1.

72. *Idem.*

73. *St. Louis Globe-Democrat,* June 27, 1904, p. 2.

74. *St. Louis Republic,* June 28, 1904, p. 3.

75. Francis, I, p. 443.

76. *St. Louis Republic,* June 29, 1904, p. 1.

77. *Ibid.,* p. 3.

78. *Ibid.,* p. 1.

79. *Ibid.,* p. 3.

80. Francis, I, p. 443.

81. Quoted in *St. Louis Republic,* July 15, 1904, p. 1.

82. *Ibid.,* July 4, 1904, p. 7.

82. *Ibid.,* July 4, 1904, p. 7.

83. Wilfred de Fontvielle, "A Year's Progress in Flying," *Harper's Weekly,* Vol. XLVIII, No. 2495 (October 15, 1904), p. 1584.

84. *St. Louis Post-Dispatch,* October 22, 1907, p. 1.

85. *St. Louis Globe-Democrat,* June 11, 1904, p. 2.

86. "Independence Day Celebrated With Patriotic Ceremonies July 4th," *World's Fair Bulletin,* Vol. 5, No. 10 (August 1904), p. 6.

87. *St. Louis Republic,* July 5, 1904, p. 5.

88. "Report of Balloonists," *World's Fair Bulletin,* Vol. 5, No. 10 (August 1904), p. 40.

89. *St. Louis Globe-Democrat,* August 30, 1904, p. 2.

90. *Ibid.,* August 26, 1904, p. 3.

91. *Idem.*

92. Francis, I, p. 447.

93. *St. Louis Globe-Democrat,* August 28, 1904, p. 1.

94. Quoted in *St. Louis Republic,* August 28, 1904, p. 1.

95. *St. Louis Globe-Democrat,* August 29, 1904, p. 1.

96. Francis, I, p. 447.

97. *St. Louis Republic,* August 30, 1904, p. 1.
98. *St. Louis Republic,* August 31, 1904, Part II, p. 1.
99. *St. Louis Globe-Democrat,* August 30, 1904, p. 1.
100. *St. Louis Republic,* September 18, 1900, p. 7. See Chapter II, pp. 53-54.
101. Pearl I. Young, "Airships and Balloons at the St. Louis Fair, 1904 — Part II," *Wingfoot Lighter-Than-Air Society Bulletin,* Vol. 11, No. 5 (March 1964), p. 4. Cited hereafter as Young, "Airships — Part II."
102. Young, "Airships — Part II," p. 4.
103. *St. Louis Republic,* August 31, 1904, p. 1.
104. *Idem.*
105. Mark Bennitt, Frank Parker Stockbridge, *et. al., History of the Louisiana Purchase Exposition* (St. Louis: Universal Exposition Company, 1905), p. 609.
106. *Daily Official Program, World's Fair, Louisiana Purchase Exposition, St. Louis, U.S.A.,* Number 184, November 30, 1904, p. 11, Cited hereafter as *Daily Official Program,* November 30, 1904.
107. *St. Louis Globe-Democrat,* November 19, 1904, p. 3.
108. *Daily Official Program,* November 30, 1904, p. 11.
109. *St. Louis Republic,* September 7, 1904, p. 1.
110. Francis, I, p. 446.
111. *St. Louis Republic,* September 9, 1904, p. 2.
112. *St. Louis Republic,* September 18, 1904, Part III, p. 1.
113. *Idem.*
114. "Air Story of St. Louis," *St. Louis Globe-Democrat,* December 15, 1929, p. 4s.
115. *St. Louis Republic,* September 18, 1904, Part III, p. 1.
116. *Ibid.,* September 29, 1904, p. 4.
117. *St. Louis Globe-Democrat,* October 1, 1904, p. 3.
118. *St. Louis Republic,* October 1, 1904, p. 5.
119. *Daily Official Program,* November 30, 1904, p. 11.
120. *St. Louis Republic,* July 30, 1904, p. 9.
121. *Daily Official Program,* November 30, 1904, p. 11.
122. *St. Louis Globe-Democrat,* October 14, 1904, p. 3.
123. *Daily Official Program,* November 30, 1904, p. 11.
124. *St. Louis Republic,* October 6, 1904, p. 4.
125. Quoted in *Ibid.,* October 5, 1904, p. 2.
126. *St. Louis Globe-Democrat,* October 5, 1904, p. 2.
127. *St. Louis Republic,* October 6, 1904, p. 4.
128. *Ibid.,* October 8, 1904, p. 4.
129. Francis, I, p. 448.
130. *St. Louis Republic,* October 8, 1904, p. 4.
131. *Ibid.,* October 26, 1904, p. 6.
132. Francis, I, p. 448.
133. Scamehorn, *Balloons to Jets* p. 44.
134. *St. Louis Republic,* October 17, 1904, p. 5.
135. *St. Louis Republic,* September 10, 1904, p. 8, and October 17, 1904, p. 5.
136. *Ibid.,* October 17, 1904, p. 5.
137. *Idem.*
138. *Idem.*
139. *St. Louis Republic,* October 18, 1904, p. 7.

140. *Ibid.,* October 19, 1904, p. 2.
141. *St. Louis Globe-Democrat,* October 20, 1904, p. 4.
142. *St. Louis Republic,* October 22, 1904, p. 5.
143. *Ibid.,* October 23, 1904, Part III, p. 2.
144. *Ibid.,* October 26, 1904, p. 6.
145. *St. Louis Republic,* October 23, 1904, Part III, p. 2.
146. *Ibid.,* August 5, 1904, p. 2.
147. *Ibid.,* October 26, 1904, p. 6.
148. Francis, I, p. 627.
149. *St. Louis Post-Dispatch,* November 13, 1904, Sunday Magazine, p. 5.
150. Quoted in *St. Louis Post-Dispatch,* November 13, 1904, Sunday Magazine, p. 5.
151. *Idem.*
152. *St. Louis Republic,* November 1, 1904, p. 1.
153. *St. Louis Republic,* October 26, 1904, p. 6.
154. *St. Louis Globe-Democrat,* October 26, 1904, p. 1.
155. *St. Louis Republic,* October 26, 1904, pp. 1, 5.
156. *Ibid.,* p. 5.
157. Francis, I, p. 627.
158. *St. Louis Republic,* October 26, 1904, p. 6.
159. *Ibid.,* October 27, 1904, p. 6.
160. *Ibid.,* November 7, 1904, p. 3.
161. *Ibid.,* November 5, 1904, p. 1.
162. Francis, I., p. 445.
163. *St. Louis Republic,* November 5, 1904, p. 1.
164. *St. Louis Globe-Democrat,* October 30, 1904, p. 10.
165. *St. Louis Republic,* October 28, 1904, p. 1.
166. *St. Louis Globe-Democrat,* October 28, 1904, p. 5.
167. *St. Louis Republic,* October 30, 1904, Part III, p. 5.
168. *St. Louis Republic,* November 1, 1904, p. 3.
169. *Ibid.,* p. 1.
170. Quoted in *St. Louis Post-Dispatch,* November 1, 1904, p. 1.
171. Quoted in *St. Louis Globe-Democrat,* November 1, 1904, p. 1.
172. Quoted in *St. Louis Republic,* November 1, 1904, p. 1.
173. *St. Louis Republic,* November 1, 1904, p. 3.
174. *St. Louis Globe-Democrat,* November 2, 1904, p. 1.
175. *St. Louis Republic,* November 2, 1904, p. 1.
176. *Ibid.,* November 3, 1904, p. 1.
177. *St. Louis Post-Dispatch,* November 2, 1904, p. 1.
178. *St. Louis Republic,* November 3, 1904, p. 1.
179. *Ibid.,* p. 2.
180. *St. Louis Globe-Democrat,* November 4, 1904, p. 1.
181. *St. Louis Post-Dispatch,* November 12, 1904, p. 10.
182. Scamehorn, ''Thomas Scott Baldwin,'' p. 183.
183. *St. Louis Globe-Democrat,* November 7, 1904, p. 5.
184. *St. Louis Republic,* November 4, 1904, p. 1.
185. *St. Louis Globe-Democrat,* November 4, 1904, p. 1.
186. *Ibid.,* November 6, 1904, p. 1.
187. *St. Louis Post-Dispatch,* November 5, 1904, p. 1.
188. *St. Louis Globe-Democrat,* November 7, 1904, p. 5.

189. *St. Louis Republic,* November 12, 1904, p. 5.
190. Quoted in *St. Louis Globe-Democrat,* November 12, 1904, p. 1.
191. *St. Louis Republic,* November 12, 1904, p. 5.
192. *St. Louis Republic,* November 15, 1904, p. 1.
193. *St. Louis Post-Dispatch,* November 15, 1904, p. 1.
194. *St. Louis Republic,* November 15, 1904, p. 1.
195. *St. Louis Globe-Democrat,* November 15, 1904, p. 2.
196. *St. Louis Republic,* November 16, 1904, p. 1.
197. *St. Louis Post-Dispatch,* November 17, 1904, p. 1.
198. Francis, I, p. 446.
199. *St. Louis Republic,* November 17, 1904, p. 4.
200. *St. Louis Republic,* November 19, 1904, p. 1.
201. *St. Louis Globe-Democrat,* November 19, 1904, p. 3.
202. *St. Louis Republic,* November 19, 1904, p. 1.
203. *Ibid.,* p. 2.
204. *Ibid.,* November 23, 1904, p. 5.
205. *St. Louis Post-Dispatch,* November 22, 1904, p. 1.
206. *St. Louis Republic,* November 23, 1904, p. 5.
207. Francis, I, p. 445.
208. *St. Louis Republic,* November 20, 1904, Part III, p. 2.
209. Francis, I, p. 445.
210. *Idem.*
211. *St. Louis Republic,* November 30, 1904, p. 1.
212. Buel, pp. 9, 3259-3261.
213. *St. Louis Globe-Democrat,* December 2, 1904, p. 1.
214. Buel, pp. 10, 3846.
215. Bennitt, Stockbridge, *et. al.* p. 609. Francis, II, xxv, cites a total figure of $43,749.98 but does not go into detail with the specific expenses.
216. Francis, I, p. 448.

CHAPTER IV

1. Majors Albert Bond Lambert and William B. Robertson, "Early History of Aeronautics in St. Louis," *Missouri Historical Society Collections,* Vol. V, No. 3 (June 1928), p. 238.
2. *Official Program of the Second Competition for the Gordon Bennett Aeronautic Cup, Forest Park, St. Louis, U.S.A., October 1907* (St. Louis: Lesar-Gould Advertising and Publishing Company, 1907), p. 3. Cited hereafter as *Official Program, 1907.*
3. *Idem.*
4. *Ibid.,* p. 18.
5. *Ibid.,* p. 3.
6. *Ibid.,* pp. 18-19.
7. *Ibid.,* p. 3.
8. "Gordon Bennett Race," *American Magazine of Aeronautics,* Vol. I, No. 4 (October 1907), p. 4.
9. *Aero Club of America, 1911* (New York: Aero Club of America, 1911), p. 52.

10. *Official Program, 1907,* pp. 21-22.

11. *St. Louis Globe-Democrat,* October 19, 1907, p. 3.

12. See Chapter V, p. 129.

13. *Official Program, 1907,* p. 23.

14. *St. Louis Post-Dispatch,* October 27, 1907, p. 12.

15. *Idem.*

16. *Idem.*

17. *St. Louis Globe-Democrat,* September 21, 1907, editorial, p. 6.

18. *Aero Club of St. Louis: Purposes — Results, 1907-1910* (St. Louis, 1910), p. 3.

19. *Articles of Incorporation, Bylaws, Officers and Members: Aero Club of St. Louis, 1909* (St. Louis, 1909), pp. 7-8. Cited hereafter as *Aero Club Articles.*

20. *Ibid.,* p. 18.

21. *St. Louis Post-Dispatch,* October 27, 1907, p. 12.

22. *St. Louis Globe-Democrat,* October 25, 1907, p. 1.

23. Augustus Post, ''Aero Club of America,'' *Fly,* Vol. I, No. 1 (November 1908), p. 10.

24. *Idem.* The Aero Club of St. Louis died out during World War I, but was revived in 1931, with the famed Jimmy Doolittle as a member. Shortly thereafter, it again dissolved, but was resurrected in 1944 under the name ''Aviation Foundation of St. Louis,'' which was changed to ''Aero Club of St. Louis'' about 1954. David Brown, ''Air Race,'' *St. Louis Globe-Democrat.* October 13, 1963, Sunday Magazine, p. 7.

25. Samuel T. Larkin (editor), *Who's Who in Saint Louis, 1928-1929* (St. Louis: Civic Union of St. Louis, 1928), p. 63.

26. *Albert Bond Lambert Aeronautical Papers,* Missouri Historical Society Archives.

27. M.W. Childs, ''Interesting St. Louisans: Major Albert Bond Lambert,'' *St. Louis Post-Dispatch,* September 21, 1930, Sunday Magazine, p. 5.

28. *Aeronautics Papers, 1830-1939,* Missouri Historical Society Archives.

29. *Official Program, 1907,* p. 14.

30. Childs, p. 5.

31. *Official Program, 1907,* pp. 3-4.

32. ''Flying Machine and Airship Competitions at St. Louis,'' *American Magazine of Aeronautics,* Vol. I, No. 4 (October 1907), p. 8.

33. *Official Program, 1907,* p. 24.

34. *Idem.*

35. *Idem.*

36. ''Flying Machine and Airship Competitions at St. Louis,'' p. 8.

37. *Official Program, 1907,* p. 25.

38. ''Flying Machine and Airship Competitions at St. Louis,'' p. 8.

39. *Official Program, 1907,* p. 26.

40. *Ibid.,* pp. 27-28.

41. *St. Louis Republic,* September 29, 1907, p. 1.

42. *St. Louis Globe-Democrat,* October 10, 1907, p. 2.

43. *St. Louis Post-Dispatch,* October 9, 1907, p. 2.

44. *St. Louis Republic,* October 9, 1907, p. 3.

45. *St. Louis Globe-Democrat,* October 12, 1907, p. 1.

46. *Official Program, 1907,* p. 17.

47. Samuel W. Forder, ''Manufacture of Coal Gas for Balloons,'' *American Aeronaut,* Vol. I, No. 5 (May 1908), p. 182.

48. *Idem.*
49. *St. Louis Post-Dispatch,* October 21, 1907, p. 1.
50. *St. Louis Globe-Democrat,* October 12, 1907, p. 1.
51. *St. Louis Republic,* October 12, 1907, p. 3.
52. *St. Louis Globe-Democrat,* October 10, 1907, p. 1.
53. *St. Louis Republic,* October 9, 1907, p. 3.
54. *St. Louis Globe-Democrat,* October 17, 1907, p. 1.
55. *Ibid.,* October 22, 1907, p. 4.
56. *Idem.*
57. "Gordon Bennett Race," *American Magazine of Aeronautics,* Vol. I, No. 4 (October 1907), pp. 6-7.
58. *Official Program, 1907,* pp. 12-13.
59. "Gordon Bennett Race," p. 29.
60. *St. Louis Globe-Democrat,* October 21, 1907, p. 12.
61. *Idem.*
62. *Official Program, 1907,* p. 14.
63. *St. Louis Globe-Democrat,* October 21, 1907, p. 12.
64. *St. Louis Post-Dispatch,* September 30, 1907, p. 20
65. *St. Louis Globe-Democrat,* October 21, 1907, p. 12.
66. *St. Louis Post-Dispatch,* October 21, 1907, p. 2. See Chapter III, p. 90.
67. *Official Program, 1907,* p. 15.
68. *St. Louis Post-Dispatch,* October 21, 1907, p. 2.
69. *Official Program, 1907,* pp. 11, 16.
70. *St. Louis Globe-Democrat,* October 21, 1907, p. 12.
71. *Ibid.,* October 25, 1907, p. 1.
72. *Official Program, 1907,* p. 13.
73. *St. Louis Globe-Democrat,* October 21, 1907, p. 12.
74. *Official Program, 1907,* p. 13.
75. See Chapter III, pp. 78-81, 82-84.
76. Howard Lee Scamehorn, "Thomas Scott Baldwin: The Columbus of the Air," *Journal of the Illinois State Historical Society,* Vol. XLIX, No. 2 (Summer 1956), p. 183.
77. *St. Louis Post-Dispatch,* October 19, 1907, p. 1.
78. *Official Program, 1907,* p. 24.
79. *St. Louis Republic,* October 7, 1907, p. 5. The *St. Louis Globe-Democrat,* October 23, 1907, p. 1, cites his age as 14, but the *St. Louis Post-Dispatch,* October 17, 1907, p. 1, also lists him as 15. It is most probable that Dixon was 15 years old.
80. *Official Program, 1907,* p. 24.
81. See Chapter II, pp. 53-54, and Chapter III, pp. 70-71.
82. *St. Louis Globe-Democrat,* October 23, 1907, p. 1.
83. See Chapter III, pp. 81-82, 88, 89-90.
84. *Official Program, 1907,* p. 24.
85. *St. Louis Globe-Democrat,* October 23, 1907, p. 1.
86. *St. Louis Republic,* October 13, 1907, Part I, p. 4.
87. *Official Program, 1907,* p. 25.
88. *St. Louis Republic,* October 4, 1907, p. 3.
89. *St. Louis Globe-Democrat,* October 23, 1907, p. 1.
90. H.C. Gammeter, "The Gammeter Orthopter," *American Magazine of Aeronautics,* Vol. I, No. 4 (October 1907), p. 16.

91. See Chapter III, p. 73.
92. Welman A. Shrader, *Fifty Years of Powered Flight: A Chronicle of the Aviation Industry in America, 1903-1953* (Cleveland: Eaton Manufacturing Company, 1953), p. 8.
93. *St. Louis Republic,* October 13, 1907, Part I, p. 4.
94. *St. Louis Globe-Democrat,* September 21, 1907, editorial, p. 6.
95. *Ibid.,* October 13, 1907, p. 1.
96. *St. Louis Post-Dispatch,* October 17, 1907, p. 13.
97. "Aero Club of America Ascensions, 1907," *American Magazine of Aeronautics,* Vol. I, No. 4 (October 1907), p. 11.
98. *St. Louis Republic,* October 15, 1907, p. 1.
99. *St. Louis Post-Dispatch,* October 16, 1907, p. 2.
100. *St. Louis Globe-Democrat,* October 18, 1907, p. 1.
101. *St. Louis Republic,* October 18, 1907, p. 1.
102. *Ibid.,* October 19, 1907, p. 2.
103. Quoted in *St. Louis Globe-Democrat,* October 19, 1907, p. 2.
104. *Ibid.,* October 20, 1907, p. 1.
105. *Aero Club of America,* 1911, p. 52.
106. *St. Louis Globe-Democrat,* October 21, 1907, p. 12.
107. *Ibid.,* October 20, 1907, p. 1.
108. *St. Louis Post-Dispatch,* October 18, 1907, p. 1.
109. *St. Louis Globe-Democrat,* October 19, 1907, p. 2.
110. *St. Louis Post-Dispatch,* October 19, 1907, p. 1.
111. *St. Louis Globe-Democrat,* October 22, 1907, p. 2.
112. *St. Louis Post-Dispatch,* October 21, 1907, p. 1.
113. *St. Louis Globe-Democrat,* October 21, 1907, p. 1.
114. *Idem.*
115. *Idem.*
116. *St. Louis Republic,* October 19, 1907, p. 2.
117. *St. Louis Post-Dispatch,* October 20, 1907, p. 1.
118. *St. Louis Globe-Democrat,* October 21, 1907, p. 12.
119. *Ibid.,* October 22, 1907, p. 3.
120. *St. Louis Republic,* October 18, 1907, p. 2.
121. *St. Louis Globe-Democrat,* October 22, 1907, p. 1.
122. *Ibid.,* October 22, 1907, p. 2.
123. *Ibid.,* October 18, 1907, p. 1.
124. *Ibid.,* October 22, 1907, p. 2.
125. *Idem.*
126. *Ibid.,* pp. 1-2.
127. *Ibid.,* p. 4.
128. *St. Louis Republic,* October 22, 1907, p. 1.
129. *Ibid.,* October 23, 1907, p. 1.
130. *St. Louis Globe-Democrat,* October 23, 1907, p. 1. See Chapter III, pp. 82-83, 84.
131. See Chapter III, p. 89.
132. *St. Louis Republic,* October 23, 1907, p. 1.
133. *St. Louis Globe-Democrat,* October 23, 1907, p. 1.
134. *Aero Club Articles,* p. 53.
135. *St. Louis Post-Dispatch,* October 22, 1907, p. 1.
136. *St. Louis Republic,* October 25, 1907, p. 2.

137. *St. Louis Globe-Democrat,* October 24, 1907, p. 1.
138. *St. Louis Post-Dispatch,* October 23, 1907, p. 1.
139. *St. Louis Globe-Democrat,* October 24, 1907, p. 1.
140. *St. Louis Republic,* October 25, 1907, p. 1.
141. Scamehorn, "Thomas Scott Baldwin," p. 184.
142. *St. Louis Globe-Democrat,* October 24, 1907, p. 1.
143. Scamehorn, "Thomas Scott Baldwin," p. 184.
144. *St. Louis Globe-Democrat,* October 24, 1907, p. 1.
145. *St. Louis Republic,* October 25, 1907, p. 2.
146. *St. Louis Globe-Democrat,* October 24, 1907, p. 1.
147. *St. Louis Republic,* October 25, 1907, p. 2.
148. *Ibid.,* October 3, 1911, p. 1.
149. *Aero Club Articles,* p. 52.
150. *St. Louis Republic,* October 6, 1907, Part IV, p. 1.
151. Quoted in *St. Louis Globe-Democrat,* October 23, 1907, p. 2.
152. See Chapter II, p. 50.
153. *St. Louis Post-Dispatch,* October 24, 1907, p. 2.
154. Augustus Post, "Aero Club of America," p. 10.
155. *Aero Club Articles,* p. 51.
156. *St. Louis Post-Dispatch,* October 24, 1907, p. 2.
157. *Aero Club Articles,* p. 54.
158. Henry Helm Clayton, "The Use of Air Currents in Ballooning," *American Aeronaut,* Vol. I, No. 4 (February-March 1908), 115.
159. *St. Louis Globe-Democrat,* October 24, 1907, p. 2.
160. *St. Louis Republic,* October 24, 1907, p. 6.
161. *St. Louis Globe-Democrat,* October 25, 1907, p. 1.
162. *St. Louis Republic,* October 25, 1907, p. 1.
163. *St. Louis Post-Dispatch,* October 25, 1907, p. 1.
164. *Idem.*
165. Augustus Post, "Aero Club of America," p. 10.
166. Quoted in *St. Louis Globe-Democrat.* October 24, 1907, p. 3.

CHAPTER V

1. Walter B. Stevens (editor), *St. Louis: One Hundred Years in a Week* (St. Louis: St. Louis Centennial Association, 1910), p. 7. Cited hereafter as Stevens, *100 Years.*
2. Dena Lange, "A History of St. Louis — Volume I," *Public School Messenger,* Vol. 28, No. 9 (November 20, 1930), p. 98.
3. Walter B. Stevens, *Centennial of the Incorporation of St. Louis: Official Program of the Celebration, October 3-9, 1909* (St. Louis: Woodward and Tiernan Printing Company, 1909), p. 2. Cited hereafter as Stevens, *Official Program, 1909.*
4. Baldwin H. Ward, *et. al.* (editors), *Flight — A Pictorial History of Aviation* (New York: Simon and Schuster, 1953), p. 32.
5. David C. Cooke, *The Story of Aviation* (New York: Archer House, 1958), pp. 20-23.

6. Ward, p. 20.
7. *Ibid.,* p. 29.
8. Cooke, pp. 28-29.
9. Paul E. Garber, *The National Aeronautical Collections* (Washington: The Smithsonian Institution, 1956), pp. 28-32.
10. Ward, pp. 40-41.
11. *St. Louis Globe-Democrat,* September 9, 1908, p. 1.
12. *Ibid.,* October 3, 1908, p. 1.
13. See Chapter IV, p. 112.
14. *St. Louis Globe-Democrat,* October 4, 1908, p. 1.
15. *Ibid.,* October 13, 1908, p. 1.
16. See Chapter III, pp. 89-90, and Chapter IV, p. 109.
17. *St. Louis Globe-Democrat,* August 17, 1908, p. 1.
18. Majors Albert Bond Lambert and William B. Robertson, "Early History of Aeronautics in St. Louis," *Missouri Historical Society Collections,* Vol. V, No. 3 (June 1928), p. 238.
19. *Ibid.,* pp. 238-239.
20. *St. Louis Republic,* November 19, 1908, p. 1. See Chapter IV, pp. 103-104.
21. *St. Louis Globe-Democrat,* November 19, 1908, p. 1.
22. *St. Louis Republic,* November 20, 1908, p. 8.
23. *St. Louis Globe-Democrat,* November 20, 1908, p. 1.
24. Lambert and Robertson, p. 239.
25. *St. Louis Globe-Democrat,* November 20, 1908, p. 1.
26. Undated newspaper clipping in *Morris A. Heimann Collection,* Missouri Historical Society Library.
27. *Idem.*
28. *St. Louis Times,* July 20, 1909, p. 9.
29. Undated newspaper clipping in *Morris A. Heimann Collection,* Missouri Historical Society Library.
30. *St. Louis Times,* July 17, 1909, p. 1.
31. *St. Louis Post-Dispatch,* July 18, 1909, p. 1.
32. *St. Louis Republic,* July 25, 1909, p. 1.
33. *St. Louis Star,* July 17, 1909, p. 1.
34. *Daily Missouri Republican,* October 14, 1841, p. 2. See Chapter II, p.41.
35. *St. Louis Post-Dispatch,* September 8, 1909, p. 1.
36. Quoted in *St. Louis Republic,* September 1, 1909, p. 1.
37. Ward, pp. 46-47.
38. Alvin M. Josephy Jr., *et. al.* (editors), *The American Heritage History of Flight* (New York: Simon and Schuster, 1962), p. 122.
39. Quoted in *St. Louis Post-Dispatch,* September 8, 1909, p. 1.
40. Quoted in *idem.*
41. *St. Louis Republic,* September 9, 1909, p. 2.
42. *St. Louis Post-Dispatch,* September 10, 1909, p. 4.
43. *St. Louis Republic,* September 22, 1909, p. 1.
44. *Ibid.,* September 1, 1909, pp. 1-2.
45. *St. Louis Post-Dispatch,* September 13, 1909, p. 4.
46. Quoted in *St. Louis Republic,* September 25, 1909, p. 3.
47. *Ibid.,* September 26, 1909, Part I, p. 2.
48. *St. Louis Post-Dispatch,* October 8, 1909, p. 1.
49. *St. Louis Republic,* September 18, 1909, p. 3. See Chapter III, pp. 70-71, 73.

50. *St. Louis Republic,* October 5, 1909, p. 2.
51. *Ibid.,* September 16, 1909, p. 5.
52. *St. Louis Post-Dispatch,* September 30, 1909, p. 6.
53. *St. Louis Republic,* October 6, 1909, p. 2.
54. *St. Louis Republic,* September 1, 1909, p. 2.
55. *Ibid.,* September 23, 1909, p. 7.
56. See Chapter III, pp. 76-77.
57. Stevens, *Official Program, 1909,* p. 28.
58. *St. Louis Republic,* September 12, 1909, p. 1.
59. *Ibid.,* October 2, 1909, p. 4.
60. Stevens, *100 Years,* p. 59.
61. Stevens, *Official Program, 1909,* p. 11.
62. *St. Louis Post-Dispatch,* October 5, 1909, p. 2.
63. *St. Louis Republic,* September 28, 1909, p. 1.
64. Stevens, *Official Program, 1909,* p. 11.
65. Stevens, *100 Years,* p. 64.
66. *St. Louis Republic,* October 9, 1909, p. 1.
67. *Ibid.,* October 1, 1909, p. 4.
68. *Ibid.,* October 3, 1909, Part V, p. 14, and October 6, 1909, p. 2.
69. *St. Louis Republic,* October 7, 1909, p. 1.
70. *St. Louis Post-Dispatch,* October 1, 1909, p. 16.
71. *Idem.*
72. *St. Louis Republic,* September 25, 1909, p. 1.
73. *St. Louis Post-Dispatch,* September 6, 1909, p. 3.
74. *Ibid.,* September 30, 1909, p. 6.
75. *St. Louis Republic,* September 6, 1909, p. 4.
76. *St. Louis Post-Dispatch,* September 6, 1909, p. 3.
77. *St. Louis Republic,* September 6, 1909, p. 4.
78. *St. Louis Republic,* September 21, 1909, p. 4.
79. *Ibid.,* October 3, 1909, p. 1.
80. Stevens, *Official Program, 1909,* p. 11.
81. *St. Louis Republic,* October 3, 1909, Part V, p. 14.
82. *Ibid.,* September 23, 1909, p. 7.
83. *Aero Club Articles,* pp. 18-39, 43, 48.
84. *St. Louis Post-Dispatch,* October 5, 1909, p. 1.
85. *St. Louis Republic,* October 5, 1909, p. 1.
86. Stevens, *100 Years,* p. 60.
87. *St. Louis Post-Dispatch,* October 4, 1909, p. 2.
88. *St. Louis Republic,* October 5, 1909, p. 1.
89. Stevens, *100 Years,* p. 60.
90. *Ibid.,* p. 61.
91. "Balloon Championship," *Fly,* Vol. I, No. 9 (July 1909), p. 9.
92. *St. Louis Republic,* October 3, 1909, Part V, p. 14.
93. Stevens, *100 Years,* pp. 61-62.
94. *Ibid.,* p. 62.
95. *Idem.*
96. *St. Louis Republic,* October 2, 1909, p. 4.
97. *St. Louis Post-Dispatch,* October 5, 1909, p. 2.
98. *Ibid.,* September 29, 1909, p. 1.
99. *St. Louis Republic,* October 7, 1909, p. 6.

100. *Ibid.,* October 6, 1909, p. 2.
101. *Ibid.,* October 5, 1909, p. 2.
102. *Ibid.,* October 7, 1909, p. 6.
103. Quoted in *Idem.*
104. *Idem.*
105. *St. Louis Post-Dispatch,* October 6, 1909, p. 1.
106. *Aero Club Articles,* p. 50.
107. Stevens, *100 Years,* p. 63.
108. *Aero Club Articles,* p. 49.
109. Stevens, *100 Years,* p. 64.
110. *St. Louis Republic,* October 8, 1909, p. 2. See Chapter IV, p. 111.
111. "Official World and American Air Records," *Aviation,* Vol. XXIII, No. 16 (October 17, 1927), p. 947.
112. *St. Louis Republic,* October 8, 1909, p. 2.
113. Stevens, *100 Years,* p. 64.
114. *Aero Club Articles,* p. 50.
115. Stevens, *100 Years,* p. 63.
116. *St. Louis Republic,* October 9, 1909, p. 2.
117. Quoted in *St. Louis Republic,* October 7, 1909, p. 3.
118. *Aero Club Articles,* pp. 41-42.
119. Stevens, *100 Years,* p. 64.
120. *St. Louis Post-Dispatch,* October 9, 1909, p. 2.
121. *St. Louis Republic,* October 9, 1909, p. 2.
122. *Idem.*
123. *St. Louis Post-Dispatch,* October 7, 1909, p. 1.
124. *Idem.*
125. *St. Louis Republic,* October 8, 1909, p. 1.
126. Stevens, *Official Program, 1909,* p. 29.
127. *St. Louis Republic,* October 8, 1909, pp. 1-2.
128. *St. Louis Post-Dispatch,* October 8, 1909, p. 2.
129. *St. Louis Republic,* October 8, 1909, p. 2.
130. *St. Louis Post-Dispatch,* October 8, 1909, p. 1.
131. *St. Louis Republic,* October 9, 1909, pp. 1-2.
132. *Idem.*
133. Stevens, *100 Years,* p. 148.
134. Quoted in *St. Louis Republic,* October 10, 1909, p. 2.
135. *Idem.*
136. *St. Louis Post-Dispatch,* October 11, 1909, p. 2.
137. *St. Louis Republic,* October 12, 1909, p. 2.
138. *Ibid.,* October 7, 1909, p. 1.
139. *St. Louis Republic,* October 11, 1909, p. 1.
140. *St. Louis Post-Dispatch,* October 11, 1909, p. 2.
141. *St. Louis Republic,* October 12, 1909, p. 2.
142. *Ibid.,* October 11, 1909, p. 2.
143. *St. Louis Post-Dispatch,* October 8, 1909, p. 1.
144. *Aero Club Articles,* p. 45.
145. Quoted in *St. Louis Republic,* October 11, 1909, p. 2.
146. *St. Louis Post-Dispatch,* October 11, 1909, p. 2.
147. Quoted in *Ibid.,* October 13, 1909, p. 2.
148. *St. Louis Republic,* October 13, 1909, p. 9.

149. See Chapter IV, pp. 103-104.
150. *Aero Club of America, 1911,* p. 52.
151. *St. Louis Post-Dispatch,* October 16, 1909, p. 2.
152. *Ibid.,* October 17, 1909, p. 1.
153. *St. Louis Republic,* October 16, 1909, p. 2.
154. *St. Louis Post-Dispatch,* July 6, 1914, p. 7.

CHAPTER VI

1. E. Percy Noel, "First American Convention of Aero Clubs," *Aeronautics,* Vol. 6, No. 3 (March 1910), pp. 87-88.
2. "With the Balloonists," *Aeronautics,* Vol. 6, No. 3, (March 1910), p. 102.
3. "St. Louis Gets Balloon Race," *Aeronautics,* Vol. 6, No. 4 (April 1910), p. 138.
4. *Aero Club of St. Louis: Purposes — Results, 1907-1910* (St. Louis, 1910), p. 8.
5. "Club News," *Aeronautics,* Vol. 6, No. 4 (April 1910), p. 142.
6. "Aero Club of St. Louis," *Aero,* Vol. I, No. 1 (October 8, 1910), p. 16. This was the inaugural issue of a magazine published in St. Louis which was "the first weekly aeronautic publication in America." "A Portfolio of Early Aviation Pictures," *Bulletin of the Missouri Historical Society,* Vol. VIII, No. 4 (July 1952), p. 378.
7. *St. Louis Globe-Democrat,* October 15, 1910, p. 2.
8. *Aero Club of St. Louis: Purposes — Results, 1907-1910,* p. 5.
9. *St. Louis Republic,* September 2, 1910, p. 1.
10. "Many Machines Building at St. Louis," *Aeronautics,* Vol. 6, No. 5 (May 1910), p. 165. See Chapter V, p. 121.
11. *Idem.*
12. *Aeronautics,* Vol. 6, No. 3 (March 1910), footnote, p. 92.
13. *St. Louis Globe-Democrat,* September 2, 1910, p. 2.
14. *St. Louis Republic,* September 9, 1910, p. 5.
15. *Ibid.,* September 15, 1910, p. 4.
16. "Many Machines Building at St. Louis," p. 165.
17. See Chapter III, pp. 81-82.
18. *St. Louis Globe-Democrat,* September 19, 1910, p. 1.
19. *St. Louis Republic,* September 19, 1910, p. 2.
20. *St. Louis Globe-Democrat,* September 19, 1910, p. 1.
21. "Many Machines Building at St. Louis," p. 165.
27. *St. Louis Republic,* September 19, 1910, p. 2.
23. *Ibid.,* September 13, 1910, p. 4.
24. See Chapter V, pp. 132-133.
25. *St. Louis Globe-Democrat,* October 3, 1910, p. 3.
26. *St. Louis Republic,* September 2, 1910, p. 1.
27. Douglas J. Ingalls, "The Sport of Wings," *Pegasus,* August 1956, p. 1.
28. *St. Louis Globe-Democrat,* November 9, 1910, p. 1.
29. See Chapter V, p. 128.
30. *St. Louis Post-Dispatch,* September 11, 1910, p. 3.

31. Quoted in *ibid.,* September 8, 1910, p. 1.
32. *Ibid.,* September 4, 1910, p. 1.
33. *Ibid.,* September 7, 1910, p. 3.
34. *St. Louis Globe-Democrat,* September 7, 1910, p. 1.
35. *St. Louis Post-Dispatch,* September 7, 1910, p. 3.
36. *Ibid.,* September 8, 1910, p. 1.
37. *St. Louis Globe-Democrat,* September 12, 1910, p. 1.
38. *St. Louis Republic,* September 10, 1910, p. 5.
39. *St. Louis Globe-Democrat,* September 2, 1910, p. 1.
40. *Ibid.,* September 10, 1910, p. 2.
41. *Idem.*
42. Quoted in *St. Louis Post-Dispatch,* September 11, 1910, p. 2.
43. *St. Louis Republic,* September 11, 1910, p. 1.
44. *St. Louis Globe-Democrat,* September 11, 1910, p. 1.
45. *Idem.*
46. *St. Louis Republic,* September 12, 1910, p. 1.
47. *St. Louis Post-Dispatch,* September 14, 1910, p. 9.
48. *St. Louis Globe-Democrat,* September 12, 1910, p. 6.
49. *St. Louis Republic,* September 2, 1910, p. 1.
50. *St. Louis Globe-Democrat,* October 3, 1910, p. 3.
51. *St. Louis Post-Dispatch,* October 7, 1910, p. 8.
52. "St. Louis Meet Opens With a Rush to Lambert Field," *Aero,* Vol. I, No. 1 (October 8, 1910), p. 4.
53. *St. Louis Globe-Democrat,* October 8, 1910, p. 1.
54. "St. Louis Meet Opens With a Rush to Lambert Field," p. 4.
55. Henry Ladd Smith, *Airways: The History of Commercial Aviation in the United States* (New York: Alfred A. Knopf, 1942), p. 27.
56. *Idem.*
57. *St. Louis Globe-Democrat,* October 8, 1910, p. 2.
58. Lloyd Morris and Kendall Smith, *Ceiling Unlimited: The Story of American Aviation from Kitty Hawk to Supersonics* (New York: Macmillan, 1958), p. 116.
59. "St. Louis Meet Opens With a Rush to Lambert Field," p. 4.
60. *St. Louis Globe-Democrat,* October 2, 1910, p. 13. See Chapter IV, p. 111.
61. "St. Louis Meet Opens With a Rush to Lambert Field," p. 4.
62. *St. Louis Republic,* October 2, 1910, p. 1.
63. *St. Louis Globe-Democrat,* October 2, 1910, p. 13.
64. Quoted in *ibid.,* October 2, 1910, p. 1.
65. *St. Louis Post-Dispatch,* October 8, 1910, p. 2H.
66. *St. Louis Globe-Democrat,* October 9, 1910, pp. 1, 10.
67. *Ibid.,* October 7, 1910, p. 1.
68. "Hoxsey Leads Flying," *Aero,* Vol. I, No. 2 (October 15, 1910), p. 9.
69. *St. Louis Globe-Democrat,* October 9, 1910, p. 10.
70. *Ibid.,* October 10, 1910, p. 1.
71. "Hoxsey Leads Flying," p. 9.
72. *St. Louis Republic,* October 10, 1910, p. 1.
73. *St. Louis Globe-Democrat,* October 10, 1910, p. 1.
74. *St. Louis Republic,* October 11, 1910, p. 1.
75. *Idem.*
76. Majors Albert Bond Lambert and William B. Robertson, "Early History of

Aeronautics in St. Louis," *Missouri Historical Society Collections,* Vol. V, No. 3 (June 1928), p. 241.

77. *St. Louis Post-Dispatch,* October 10, 1910, p. 1.
78. Quoted in "Col. Roosevelt Rides With Arch Hoxsey," *Aero,* Vol. I, No. 2 (October 15, 1910), p. 7.
79. Quoted in *St. Louis Globe-Democrat,* October 12, 1910, p. 4.
80. National Committee to Observe the 50th Anniversary of Powered Flight, *Fifty Years of Powered Flight: 1903-1953 — A Reference Book of Signficant Air Achievements* (Toledo: Admaster Creations Company, 1952), p. 99.
81. *St. Louis Republic,* October 12, 1910, p. 1.
82. "Col. Roosevelt Rides With Arch Hoxsey," p. 8.
83. *St. Louis Globe-Democrat,* October 12, 1910, p. 1.
84. *St. Louis Republic,* October 13, 1910, p. 1.
85. *St. Louis Globe-Democrat,* October 13, 1910, pp. 1-2.
86. *St. Louis Republic,* October 13, 1910, p. 1.
87. *Idem.*
88. *St. Louis Globe-Democrat,* October 14, 1910, pp. 1-2.
89. *St. Louis Republic,* October 14, 1910, p. 1.
90. *St. Louis Globe-Democrat,* October 15, 1910, p. 1.
91. *St. Louis Post-Dispatch,* October 15, 1910, p. 1.
92. *St. Louis Republic,* October 15, 1910, p. 1.
93. *St. Louis Globe-Democrat,* October 15, 1910, p. 2.
94. Quoted in *idem.*
95. *Ibid.,* October 16, 1910, p. 1.
96. See Chapter V, pp. 124-125.
97. Quoted in Lambert and Robertson, p. 241. Major Lambert incorrectly cites Arch Hoxsey as the pilot of this flight.
98. *St. Louis Republic,* October 17, 1910, p. 1.
99. *St. Louis Globe-Democrat,* October 17, 1910, p. 1.
100. *Idem.*
101. *Idem.*
102. *St. Louis Republic,* October 17, 1910, p. 1.
103. *St. Louis Globe-Democrat,* November 18, 1910, p. 1.
104. Henry Ladd Smith, p. 32.
105. Morris and Smith, p. 108.
106. *St. Louis Post-Dispatch,* October 23, 1910, p. 1.
107. "Authorized Official Program of the Fifth International Balloon Race," *Aero,* Vol. I, Extra (October 17, 1910).
108. "Ten in International Spherical Race," *Aero,* Vol. I, No. 2 (October 15, 1910), p. 5.
109. "Elimination Race Results," *Aero,* Vol. I, No. 2 (October 15, 1910), p. 20.
110. *St. Louis Post-Dispatch,* October 17, 1910, p. 2.
111. "Ten in International Spherical Race," p. 5.
112. *St. Louis Globe-Democrat,* October 17, 1910, p. 4.
113. *Ibid.,* October 18, 1910, p. 2.
114. *St. Louis Republic,* October 18, 1910, p. 2.
115. *St. Louis Post-Dispatch,* October 17, 1910, p. 2.
116. *St. Louis Globe-Democrat,* October 29, 1910, p. 1.
117. "Authorized Official Program of the Fifth International Balloon Race."
118. *St. Louis Globe-Democrat,* October 14, 1910, p. 1.

119. *Ibid.,* October 17, 1910, p. 1.
120. *St. Louis Republic,* October 18, 1910, p. 1.
121. *St. Louis Globe-Democrat,* October 4, 1910, p. 1.
122. *Ibid.,* October 18, 1910, p. 2.
123. *Ibid.,* October 17, 1910, p. 4.
124. *St. Louis Post-Dispatch,* October 17, 1910, p. 2.
125. See Chapter V, p. 116.
126. *St. Louis Globe-Democrat,* October 18, 1910, p. 2.
127. *St. Louis Post-Dispatch,* October 17, 1910, p. 2.
128. *St. Louis Globe-Democrat,* October 17, 1910, p. 1.
129. *Ibid.,* October 19, 1910, p. 1.
130. *St. Louis Republic,* October 20, 1910, p. 1.
131. *Ibid.,* October 22, 1910, p. 1.
132. *St. Louis Globe-Democrat,* October 27, 1910, p. 1.
133. *St. Louis Republic,* October 27, 1910, p. 1.
134. See Chapter IV, p. 111.
135. See Chapter V, p. 133.
136. *Aero Club of America, 1911* (New York: Aero Club of America, 1911), p. 52. See Chapter IV, p. 104.
137. It was broken by Edward Yost in an unsuccessful transatlantic attempt in the *Silver Fox* from Milbridge, Maine, to 200 miles east of San Miguel Island, Azores, 2,475.03 miles in 107 hours and 37 minutes, October 5-10, 1976. (Letters to the author from Mitchell E. Giblo, executive director of the National Aeronautic Association, December 2, 1964; and from Wanda D. Odom, administrative assistant to the director of the National Aeronautic Association, August 2, 1984.)
138. The Atlantic Ocean was spanned for the first time August 12-17 (GMT), 1978, by Maxie Anderson, Ben Abruzzo, and Larry Newman, all of Albuquerque, New Mexico, in a 3,107.61-mile flight in 137 hours, 5 minutes, and 50 seconds from Sprague Farm, Presque Isle, Maine, to Conquerel Farm, Miserey, France, in the *Double Eagle II.* (Letter to the author from Wanda D. Odom, administrative assistant to the director of the National Aeronautic Association, August 2, 1984.)

Anderson and his son Kris made the first trans-North America voyage May 8-12, 1980, in the *Kitty Hawk,* 2,417 miles from Fort Baker, California, to Matane, Quebec, on the Gaspé Peninsula, Canada. (Tom D. Crouch, *The Eagle Aloft: Two Centuries of the Balloon in America,* Washington, D.C.: Smithsonian Institution Press, 1983, p. 662.) Maxie Anderson and his copilot, Don Ida, were killed in a crash near Bad Brueckenau, Federal Republic of Germany, June 27, 1983, while participating in the James Gordon Bennett International Balloon Race from Paris. *(St. Petersburg Times,* June 28, 1983).

The first trans-United States balloon crossing took place October 9-11, 1981, when John Shoecraft and Frederick Gorrell, both of Phoenix, Arizona, sailed the *Super Chicken III* 2,515 miles from Costa Mesa, California, to Blackbeard Island, near Savannah, Georgia. (Crouch, p. 662.)

The longest balloon flight ever made occurred with the first crossing of the Pacific Ocean, November 9-12, 1981, by Ben Abruzzo, Larry Newman, and Ron Clark, all of Albuquerque, New Mexico, and Rocky Aoki of Key Biscayne, Florida, in the *Double Eagle V,* 5,208.67 miles from Nagashima, Japan, to Covelo, California. (Letter to the author from Wanda D. Odom, August 2, 1984.)

139. *Aero Club of America, 1911*, p. 47.
140. *St. Louis Globe-Democrat,* October 29, 1910, p. 1.
141. *Aero Club of St. Louis: Purposes — Results, 1907-1910*, p. 27.
142. *St. Louis Globe-Democrat,* November 13, 1910, p. 10.
143. *Ibid.,* November 3, 1910, p. 1.
144. *St. Louis Republic,* November 11, 1910, p. 12.
145. *Ibid.,* November 16, 1910, p. 5.
146. *Ibid.,* November 22, 1910, p. 5.
147. *St. Louis Republic,* November 16, 1910, p. 5.
148. See Chapter XIV, p. 295.
149. *St. Louis Republic,* November 24, 1910, p. 9.
150. *Ibid.,* December 1, 1910, p. 1.
151. *Aero Club of St. Louis: Purposes — Results, 1907-1910*, p. 7.
152. *St. Louis Globe-Democrat,* October 27, 1910, p. 2.

CHAPTER VII

1. *St. Louis Republic,* October 5, 1911, p. 2.
2. "St. Louis Balloon Pilots Win First Three Places," *Aero,* Vol. II, No. 16 (July 22, 1911), p. 345.
3. *St. Louis Globe-Democrat,* October 27, 1911, p. 4.
4. *St. Louis Republic,* September 9, 1911, p. 3.
5. See Chapter VI, pp. 143-144, 148-149.
6. *Aero Club of America, 1911* (New York: Aero Club of America, 1911), p. 43.
7. *Aeronautics Papers, 1830-1939,* Missouri Historical Society Archives.
8. *Albert Bond Lambert Aeronautical Papers,* Missouri Historical Society Archives.
9. *St. Louis Republic,* September 9, 1911, p. 3.
10. *St. Louis Globe-Democrat,* October 23, 1911, p. 1.
11. *St. Louis Republic,* October 10, 1909, Part I, p. 7.
12. "St. Louis — The First Metropolis of the Sky," *Sterling Magazine,* Vol. 3 No. 3 (October 1911). No page numbers are given in this article from the files of the Missouri Historical Society Library.
13. *Idem,*
14. *St. Louis Republic,* October 1, 1911, p. 9.
15. *St. Louis Globe-Democrat,* October 1, 1911, p. 10.
16. See Chapter VI, p. 146.
17. "St. Louis — The First Metropolis of the Sky."
18. *St. Louis Republic,* October 29, 1911, p. 2.
19. *Ibid.,* September 24, 1911, p. 1.
20. *Ibid.,* September 23, 1911, p. 1.
21. *Official Souvenir Program, October 1st-8th, 1911* (St. Louis: Aero Club of St. Louis, 1911), p. 3. Cited hereafter as *Official Program, 1911.*
22. *St. Louis Globe-Democrat,* October 1, 1911, p. 1. See Chapter VI, p. 150.
23. Letter from Wilbur Wright to the Pioneer Aeroplane and Exhibition Company, *Aeronautics Papers, 1830-1939,* Missouri Historical Society Archives.
24. *St. Louis Republic,* October 12, 1911, p. 7.
25. *Aeronautics Papers, 1830-1939,* Missouri Historical Society Archives.
26. *Idem.*

27. *St. Louis Republic,* October 1, 1911, p. 9. See Chapter IV, p. 110, and Chapter V, pp. 128, 130, 132.
28. *Official Program, 1911,* p. 6.
29. *St. Louis Republic,* October 1, 1911, p. 9.
30. *Official Program, 1911,* p. 6.
31. See Chapter V, pp. 121, 127, 130, and Chapter VI, p. 136.
32. *Official Program, 1911,* p. 6.
33. *St. Louis Globe-Democrat,* October 2, 1911, p. 10.
34. "St. Louis — The First Metropolis of the Sky."
35. Quoted in *St. Louis Republic,* October 2, 1911, p. 6.
36. *St. Louis Globe-Democrat,* October 1, 1911, p. 10.
37. *St. Louis Republic,* October 2, 1911, p. 6.
38. *Ibid.,* October 5, 1911, p. 1.
39. *St. Louis Globe-Democrat,* October 3, 1911, p. 1.
40. *St. Louis Republic,* October 5, 1911, p. 2.
41. *St. Louis Globe-Democrat,* October 5, 1911, p. 6.
42. *St. Louis Republic,* October 5, 1911, p. 1.
43. *Official Program, 1911,* p. 6.
44. Henry Ladd Smith, *Airways: The History of Commercial Aviation in the United States* (New York: Alfred A. Knopf, 1942), pp. 52-53.
45. *St. Louis Globe-Democrat,* October 5, 1911, p. 6.
46. *St. Louis Republic,* October 5, 1911, p. 2.
47. *Idem.*
48. *St. Louis Republic,* October 5, 1911, p. 1.
49. *Ibid.,* October 6, 1911, p. 2.
50. Quoted in *St. Louis Globe-Democrat,* October 7, 1911, p. 6.
51. Quoted in *St. Louis Republic,* October 7, 1911, p. 3.
52. *St. Louis Globe-Democrat,* October 7, 1911, p. 1.
53. *St. Louis Republic,* October 7, 1911, p. 3.
54. *Ibid.,* October 8, 1911, p. 1.
55. Quoted in *St. Louis Globe-Democrat,* October 8, 1911, p. 6.
56. *Ibid.,* October 9, 1911, p. 2.
57. *St. Louis Republic,* October 9, 1911, p. 2.
58. *Idem.*
59. See Chapter VI, pp. 139-141.
60. *St. Louis Republic,* October 9, 1911, p. 1.
61. *St. Louis Globe-Democrat,* October 9, 1911, p. 1.
62. *St. Louis Republic,* October 22, 1911, p. 4.
63. Howard L. Scamehorn, *Balloons to Jets: A Century of Aeronautics in Illinois, 1855-1955* (Chicago: Henry Regnery Company, 1957), pp. 94-95.
64. Quoted in *St. Louis Globe-Democrat,* October 9, 1911, p. 2.
65. *St. Louis Republic,* October 13, 1911, p. 1.
66. *St. Louis Globe-Democrat,* October 12, 1911, p. 2.
67. *Aeronautics Papers, 1830-1939,* Missouri Historical Society Archives.
68. *St. Louis Globe-Democrat,* October 15, 1911, p. 8.
69. *Ibid.,* October 14, 1911, p. 1.
70. Quoted in *St. Louis Republic,* October 12, 1911, p. 7.
71. Quoted in *ibid.,* October 11, 1911, p. 4.
72. *St. Louis Republic,* October 15, 1911, p. 1.
73. *St. Louis Globe-Democrat,* October 12, 1911, p. 1.

74. *Ibid.,* September 7, 1910, p. 1.
75. *St. Louis Republic,* October 15, 1911, p. 1.
76. *St. Louis Globe-Democrat,* October 15, 1911, p. 8.
77. *St. Louis Republic,* October 15, 1911, p. 1.
78. *Ibid.,* October 16, 1911, p. 4.
79. *St. Louis Globe-Democrat,* October 16. 1911, p. 1.
80. Quoted in *St. Louis Republic,* October 17, 1911, p. 2.
81. *Idem.*
82. Quoted in *St. Louis Republic,* October 18, 1911, p. 1.
83. Quoted in *idem.*
84. *Idem.*
85. *St. Louis Globe-Democrat,* October 18, 1911, p. 1.
86. *St. Louis Republic,* October 18, 1911, p. 1.
87. *Idem.*
88. *St. Louis Republic,* October 19, 1911, p. 3.
89. *St. Louis Globe-Democrat,* October 19, 1911, p. 1.
90. See Chapter VI, p. 146.
91. *St. Louis Republic,* October 20, 1911, p. 2.
92. Quoted in *St. Louis Globe-Democrat,* October 20, 1911, p. 1.
93. *St. Louis Republic,* October 20, 1911, p. 2.
94. *St. Louis Globe-Democrat,* October 21, 1911, p. 10.
95. *Idem.*
96. *St. Louis Republic,* October 21, 1911, p. 1.
97. Quoted in *St. Louis Globe-Democrat,* October 22, 1911, p. 10.
98. Quoted in *St. Louis Republic,* October 22, 1911, p. 4.
99. Scamehorn, *Balloons to Jets,* p. 95.
100. Baldwin H. Ward, *et. al.* (editors), *Flight — A Pictorial History of Aviation* (New York: Simon and Schuster, 1953), p. 65.
101. *St. Louis Republic,* October 11, 1911, p. 3.
102. National Committee to Observe the 50th Anniversary of Powered Flight, *Fifty Years of Powered Flight: 1903-1953 — A Reference Book of Significant Air Achievements* (Toledo: Admaster Creations Company, 1952), p. 77.
103. *St. Louis Republic,* October 23, 1911, p. 4.
104. *Idem.*
105. *Ibid.,* October 29, 1911, p. 2.

CHAPTER VIII

1. National Committee to Observe the 50th Anniversary of Powered Flight, *Fifty Years of Powered Flight: 1903-1953 — A Reference Book of Significant Air Achievements* (Toledo: Admaster Creations Company, 1952), p. 24.
2. *St. Louis Globe-Democrat,* March 2, 1912, p. 1.
3. *St. Louis Republic,* March 2, 1912, p. 2.
4. *St. Louis Globe-Democrat,* March 2, 1912, p. 2.
5. National Committee to Observe the 50th Anniversary of Powered Flight, p. 39.

6. "First Parachute Landing from an Airplane," *American Aviation Historical Journal,* Vol. 9, No. 2 (Summer 1964). p. 143.

7. "U.S. Wins Balloon Race the Fourth Time," *Aero and Hydro,* Vol. VII, No. 4 (October 25, 1913), p. 37.

8. "United States Gets First and Second," *Aero and Hydro,* Vol. VII, No. 5 (November 1, 1913), p. 57.

9. "St. Louis May Ask for Race Next Year," *Aero and Hydro,* Vol. VII, No. 4 (October 25, 1913), p. 38.

10. *St. Louis Globe-Democrat,* July 12, 1914, p. 1.

11. "Summer's Balloon Races Grow More Important," *Aero and Hydro,* Vol. VII, No. 26 (March 28, 1914), p. 321.

12. *St. Louis Globe-Democrat,* July 5, 1914, p. 12.

13. *St. Louis Post-Dispatch,* July 12, 1914, p. 2.

14. *Ibid.,* July 6, 1914, p. 7.

15. *St. Louis Globe-Democrat,* July 5, 1914, p. 12.

16. *Idem.*

17. *St. Louis Post-Dispatch,* July 6, 1914, p. 7.

18. *Idem.*

19. See Chapter VI, p. 154.

20. See Chapter V, p. 128.

21. See Chapter V, pp. 133-134.

22. *St. Louis Globe-Democrat,* July 5, 1914, p. 12.

23. *Ibid.,* October 11, 1913.

24. *St. Louis Post-Dispatch,* July 11, 1914, p. 1.

25. *St. Louis Globe-Democrat,* July 5, 1914, p. 12.

26. *St. Louis Post-Dispatch,* July 6, 1914, p. 7.

27. *St. Louis Globe-Democrat,* July 5, 1914, p. 12.

28. *St. Louis Post-Dispatch,* July 6, 1914, p. 7.

29. *St. Louis Globe-Democrat,* July 11, 1914, p. 2.

30. *St. Louis Post-Dispatch,* July 11, 1914, p. 1.

31. *Idem.*

32. *St. Louis Globe-Democrat,* July 5, 1914, p. 12.

33. *St. Louis Post-Dispatch,* July 12, 1914, p. 1.

34. *St. Louis Globe-Democrat,* July 12, 1914, p. 1.

35. *Ibid.,* July 5, 1914, p. 12.

36. *Ibid.,* July 12, 1914, p. 1.

37. *St. Louis Post Dispatch,* July 12, 1914, p. 1.

38. Quoted in *St. Louis Globe-Democrat,* July 12, 1914, p. 1.

39. *St. Louis Post-Dispatch,* July 12, 1914, p. 1.

40. *Ibid.,* July 11, 1914, p. 1.

41. *Ibid.,* July 12,1914, pp. 1-2.

42. *Ibid.,* July 10, 1914, p. 5.

43. *St. Louis Globe-Democrat,* July 12, 1914, p. 2.

44. *Ibid.,* July 13, 1914, p. 1.

45. Quoted in *St. Louis Globe-Democrat,* July 13, 1914, p. 3.

46. *St. Louis Post-Dispatch,* July 13, 1914, p. 1.

47. "The Gordon Bennett Balloon Races," *Aviation,* Vol. XXIII, No. 9 (August 29, 1927), p. 479.

CHAPTER IX

1. *St. Louis Post-Dispatch,* September 27, 1919, p. 2.
2. Maj. Albert Bond Lambert, "St. Louis — On World's Air Map for 16 Years," *St. Louis Post-Dispatch,* September 30, 1923, Sunday Magazine, p.3.
3. *St. Louis Globe-Democrat,* September 21, 1919, p. 4.
4. *Ibid.,* September 26, 1919, p. 1.
5. Robert de la Croix, *They Flew the Atlantic,* translated by Edward Fitzgerald (New York: W.W. Norton, 1958), p. 39.
6. *St. Louis Post-Dispatch,* September 26, 1919, p. 1.
7. *St. Louis Globe-Democrat,* September 26, 1919, p. 1.
8. *St. Louis Post-Dispatch,* September 27, 1919, p. 2.
9. *Ibid.,* September 25, 1919, p. 1.
10. *Idem.*
11. *St. Louis Globe-Democrat,* September 26, 1919, p. 1.
12. *St. Louis Post-Dispatch,* September 26, 1919, p. 1.
13. Quoted in *ibid.,* September 25, 1919, p. 1.
14. *Ibid.,* September 26, 1919, p. 1.
15. *Ibid.,* September 25, 1919, p. 1.
16. *St. Louis Globe-Democrat,* September 23, 1919, p. 13. This account incorrectly attributes the demonstration to "Lieutenant J.H. Sykes."
17. See Chapter III, p. 90, and Chapter IV, p. 111.
18. *St. Louis Post-Dispatch,* September 27, 1919, p. 1.
19. *Ibid.,* September 26, 1919, p. 1.
20. *Ibid.,* September 25, 1919, p. 1.
21. *St. Louis Globe-Democrat,* September 27, 1919, p. 2.
22. *St. Louis Post-Dispatch,* September 27, 1919, p. 2.
23. *St. Louis Globe-Democrat,* September 27, 1919, p. 2.
24. *Ibid.,* September 28, 1919, p. 3.
25. *St. Louis Post-Dispatch,* September 27, 1919, p. 1.
26. *St. Louis Globe-Democrat,* September 28, 1919, p. 3.
27. *St. Louis Post-Dispatch,* September 28, 1919, p. 1.
28. *Ibid.,* October 2, 1919, p. 1.
29. Quoted in *St. Louis Post-Dispatch,* September 29, 1919, p. 1.
30. *St. Louis Globe-Democrat,* October 10, 1919, p. 3.
31. *Ibid.,* September 28, 1919, p. 3.
32. *St. Louis Post-Dispatch,* October 10, 1919, p. 3.
33. *St. Louis Globe-Democrat,* July 16, 1919, p. 1.
34. *St. Louis Post-Dispatch,* July 16, 1919, p. 3.
35. "St. Louis Balloon Pilots Win First Three Places," *Aero,* Vol. II, No. 16 (July 22, 1911), p. 346.
36. "The Gordon Bennett Balloon Races," *Aviation,* Vol. XXIII, No. 9 (August 29, 1927), p. 479.
37. *St. Louis Post-Dispatch,* October 1, 1919, p. 9.
38. *Idem.*
39. *Ibid.,* September 30, 1919, p. 8.
40. *Ibid.,* October 1, 1919, p. 9.

41. Quoted in *St. Louis Globe-Democrat,* October 2, 1919, p. 3.
42. *St. Louis Post-Dispatch,* October 2, 1919, p. 1.
43. *Ibid.,* September 30, 1919, p. 8.
44. *St. Louis Globe-Democrat,* October 2, 1919, p. 3.
45. *St. Louis Post-Dispatch,* October 1, 1919, p. 9.
46. *St. Louis Globe-Democrat,* October 4, 1919, p. 1.
47. *St. Louis Post-Dispatch,* October 2, 1919, p. 1.
48. Quoted in *St. Louis Globe-Democrat,* October 2, 1919, p. 3.
49. *Ibid.,* October 4, 1919, p. 5.
50. *Ibid.,* p. 1.
51. *St. Louis Post-Dispatch,* October 3, 1919, p. 1.
52. *St. Louis Globe-Democrat,* October 4, 1919, p. 1.
53. *Idem.*
54. *St. Louis Post-Dispatch,* October 6, 1919, p. 1.
55. *Ibid.,* October 7, 1919, p. 11. Neither available newspaper mentions the mileage of their flight.
56. *St. Louis Globe-Democrat,* October 9, 1919, p. 13. See Chapter VI, p. 54.
57. Quoted in *ibid,* October 11, 1919, p. 9.
58. *St. Louis Post-Dispatch,* October 22, 1919, p. 1.
59. *St. Louis Globe-Democrat,* October 17, 1919, p. 2.
60. *St. Louis Post-Dispatch,* October 22, 1919, p. 1.
61. See Chapter II, pp. 52-53.

CHAPTER X

1. "International Air Races, St. Louis Field, October 1-2-3, 1923," *Aviation,* Vol. XV, No. 12 (September 17, 1923), p. 340.
2. *St. Louis Post-Dispatch,* September 26, 1923, p. 1.
3. B. Russell Shaw, *International Air Races: Report of the Contest Committee, Lambert-St. Louis Field, St. Louis, Mo., October 3, 4, 5, 6, 1923* (St. Louis, 1923), pp. 5-19.
4. Arthur C. Hoskins, "St. Louis as a Dirigible Center to Rehabilitate Free Ballooning," *Aeronautical Digest,* Vol. 3, No. 4 (October 1923), p. 242.
5. *International Air Races, October 1, 2, 3: Official Program, Saint Louis, 1923* (St. Louis, 1923), p. 81. Cited hereafter as *Official Program, 1923.*
6. *Official Program, 1923,* p. 81.
7. "Pulitzer Trophy," *Aeronautical Digest,* Vol. 3, No. 4 (October 1923), p. 239.
8. "The N.A.A. Annual Convention," *Aviation,* Vol. XV, No. 17 (October 22, 1923), p. 513.
9. *St. Louis Post-Dispatch,* September 30, 1923, p. 32.
10. *Official Program, 1923,* p. 83.
11. *International Air Race Papers, 1923,* Missouri Historical Society Library.
12. "Stockholders' Report: St. Louis Aeronautic Corporation, February 28, 1924," *International Air Race Papers, 1923,* Missouri Historical Society Library. Cited hereafter as "SLAC Stockholders' Report, 1924."
13. *Idem.*
14. *International Air Race Papers, 1923,* Missouri Historical Society Library.
15. *Idem.*

16. *Official Program, 1923,* p. 9.
17. Shaw, p. 2.
18. *Official Program, 1923,* p. 9. See Chapter IV, pp. 93.
19. *International Air Race Papers, 1923,* Missouri Historical Society Library.
20. Arthur B. Birge, "Progress of Construction Work on St. Louis Field," *Aviation,* Vol. XV, No. 11 (September 10, 1923), p. 307.
21. "A Brief Summary Relative to the Early History of the Lambert-St. Louis Municipal Airport," *Albert Bond Lambert Aeronautical Papers,* Missouri Historical Society Archives.
22. *St. Louis Post-Dispatch,* June 18, 1920, p. 11.
23. St. Louis Aeronautic Corporation, *St. Louis: The Aerial Crossroads of America* (St. Louis, 1923), p. 5.
24. "SLAC Stockholders' Report, 1924."
25. *International Air Race Papers, 1923,* Missouri Historical Society Library.
26. W. Frank Carter, "What St. Louis Field Means to St. Louis," *The Cherry Diamond,* September 1923, p. 13.
27. "SLAC Stockholders' Report, 1924."
28. Birge, "Progress of Construction Work on St. Louis Field," p. 307.
29. Carter, p. 13.
30. "SLAC Stockholders' Report, 1924."
31. "St. Louis Ready for International Air Races," *Aviation,* Vol. XV, No. 14 (October 1, 1923), p. 392.
32. Carter, p. 13.
33. "St. Louis — the Aerial Magnet," *Aviation,* Vol. XV, No. 11 (September 10, 1923), p. 301.
34. *Rules and Entry Blank, International Air Races, St. Louis, U.S.A., October 1, 2, 3, 1923* (St. Louis, 1923), p. 5. Cited hereafter as *Rules and Entry Blank, 1923.*
35. "Program and Entries for the St. Louis Air Meet," *Aviation,* Vol. XV, No. 14 (October 1, 1923), pp. 393, 398.
36. *Ibid.,* pp. 7-8.
37. Randall Foster, "Program for the Saint Louis Meet," *Aeronautical Digest,* Vol. 3, No. 4 (October 1923), p. 241.
38. Shaw, p. 9.
39. "Program and Entries for the St. Louis Air Meet," p. 396.
40. Shaw, p. 13.
41. Foster, p. 241.
42. "Program and Entries for the St. Louis Air Meet," p. 397.
43. *Ibid.,* p. 399.
44. *St. Louis Post-Dispatch,* September 30, 1923, p. 29.
45. *Idem.*
46. Foster, p. 241.
47. "Program and Entries for the St. Louis Air Meet," pp. 393-403.
48. *Ibid.,* pp. 394, 396.
49. *Rules and Entry Blank, 1923,* p. 5.
50. "The Italian Entrants," *Aviation,* Vol. XV, No. 14 (October 1, 1923), p. 407.
51. "The Coming Contests," *America at Work,* Vol. VII, No. 7 (September 5, 1923), p. 22.
52. Arthur B. Birge, "Concerning the St. Louis Aeronautic Corporation," *America at Work,* Vol. VII, No. 7 (September 5, 1923), p. 32.

53. Birge, "Progress of Construction Work on St. Louis Field," p. 308.
54. "Distinguished Guests to Attend International Air Races," *Civic Review,* August 1923, p. 8.
55. "Prizes Presented to Contestants at Smoker," *Aviation,* Vol. XV, No. 17 (October 22, 1923), p. 520.
56. "St. Louis Races Postponed," *Aviation,* Vol. XV, No. 15 (October 8, 1923), p. 443.
57. "SLAC Stockholders' Report, 1924."
58. "The N.A.A. Annual Convention," p. 513.
59. "The N.A.A. Annual Convention," pp. 513-516.
60. *St. Louis Post-Dispatch,* September 27, 1923, p. 3.
61. "Program of the Second National Air Institute," *Aviation,* Vol. XV, No. 14 (October 1, 1923), p. 411.
62. *St. Louis Post-Dispatch,* September 26, 1923, p. 1.
63. "First Trial Flight of the U.S. Naval Airship *ZR1,"* *Aviation,* Vol. XV, No. 11, (September 10, 1923), p. 311.
64. *St. Louis Post-Dispatch,* October 3, 1923, p. 5.
65. "Flight of the *ZR-1,"* *Aeronautical Digest,* Vol. 3, No. 4 (October 1923) p. 236.
66. Shafto Dene, *Trail Blazing in the Skies* (Akron: Goodyear Tire and Rubber Company, 1943), p. 38.
67. "Flight of the *ZR-1,"* p. 236.
68. "First Trial Flight of the U.S. Naval Airship *ZR1,"* p. 311.
69. "*ZR1* Makes Successful 2200 Mile Flight," *Aviation,* Vol. XV, No. 16 (October 15, 1923), p. 490.
70. *Ibid.,* p. 491.
71. *St. Louis Post-Dispatch,* October 3, 1923, p. 5.
72. "*ZR1* Completes St. Louis Flight," *Aviation,* Vol. XV, No. 15 (October 8, 1923), p. 445.
73. "*ZR1* Completes St. Louis Flight," p. 445.
74. "An Outline of Aviation," *The Literary Digest,* Vol. XCIII, No. 13 (June 25, 1927), p. 10.
75. Lloyd Morris and Kendall Smith, *Ceiling Unlimited: The Story of American Aviation from Kitty Hawk to Supersonics* (New York: Macmillan, 1958), pp. 209-210.
76. *St. Louis Post-Dispatch,* September 30, 1923, p. 1.
77. "The Barling Bomber," *Aeronautical Digest,* Vol. 3, No. 4 (October 1923), p. 249.
78. Baldwin H. Ward, *et. al.* (editors), *Flight — A Pictorial History of Aviation* (New York: Simon and Schuster, 1953), p. 33.
79. "Side Lights on the St. Louis Meet," *Aviation,* Vol. XV, No. 16 (October 15, 1923), p. 489.
80. F.G. Swanborough and Peter M. Bowers, *United States Military Aircraft Since 1909* (London: Putnam, 1963), p. 504.
81. General H.H. Arnold, *Global Mission* (New York: Harper and Brothers, 1949), pp. 110, 128-129.
82. "On-to-St. Louis Race Won by C.S. Jones," *Aviation,* Vol. XV, No. 16 (October 15, 1923), p. 476.
83. Shaw, p. 5.
84. "On-to-St. Louis Race Won by C.S. Jones," p. 476.

85. Shaw, p. 5.
86. *Ibid.*, p. 15.
87. Quoted in "E.J. Lange Wins Mulvihill Model Trophy Contest," *Aviation,* Vol. XV, No. 16 (October 15, 1923), p. 484.
88. *St. Louis Globe-Democrat,* October 5, 1923, p. 1.
89. Quoted in "Side Lights of the St. Louis Meet," p. 487.
90. Shaw, p. 7.
91. "W.E. Lees Wins Flying Club of St. Louis Trophy," *Aviation,* Vol. XV, No. 16 (October 15, 1923), p. 477.
92. "Capt. Burt E. Skeel Wins Mitchell Trophy Race," *Aviation,* Vol. XV, No. 16, (October 15, 1923), p. 478.
93. "Lieut. C. McMullen Wins Liberty Engine Builders' Trophy," *Aviation,* Vol. XV, No. 16 (October 15, 1923), pp. 479-480.
94. *St. Louis Globe-Democrat,* October 6, 1923, p. 1.
95. "J. Atkinson Wins Country Club of Detroit Trophy Race," *Aviation,* Vol. XV, No. 16 (October 15, 1923), pp. 481-482.
96. "Lieut. H.L. George Wins Merchants' Exchange Trophy Race," *Aviation,* Vol. XV, No. 16 (October 15, 1923), p. 483.
97. *St. Louis Globe-Democrat,* October 7, 1923, p. 1.
98. "J.F. Moore Wins Air Mail Trophy Race," *Aviation,* Vol. XV, No. 16 (October 15, 1923), pp. 474-475.
99. "Army and Navy Entries in the Pulitzer Trophy Race," *Aviation,* Vol. XV, No. 14 (October 1, 1923), pp. 400-403.
100. "Lieutenant A.J. Williams Wins Pulitzer Trophy Race," *Aviation,* Vol. XV, No. 16 (October 15, 1923), p. 469.
101. *Ibid.,* p. 470.
102. Charles Guggenheim and Associates, Inc. (producers), "A Bicentennial Tribute: St. Louis, 1764-1964," KSD-TV, February 16, 1964, 9:00-10:30 p.m.
103. Lieutenant J. Parker Van Zandt, "The 1923 Pulitzer Air Classic," *U.S. Air Service,* Vol. 8, No. 11 (November 1923), p. 15.
104. "Lieutenant A.J. Williams Wins Pulitzer Trophy Race," p. 470. The prizes awarded were less than those originally announced for this event.
105. Shaw, p. 3.
106. Quoted in "St. Louis — 1923," *Aviation,* Vol. XV, No. 16 (October 15, 1923), p. 467.
107. Van Zandt, "The 1923 Pulitzer Air Classic," p. 15.
108. Quoted in "Lieutenant A.J. Williams Wins Pulitzer Trophy Race," p. 473.
109. Lieutenant J. Parker Van Zandt, "Greatest Air Meet in History of Aviation," *U.S. Air Service,* Vol. 8, No. 11 (November 1923), p. 28.
110. "Hundreds of Air Travelers Attend St. Louis Meet," *Aviation,* Vol. XV, No. 16 (October 15, 1923), p. 485.
111. Kenneth S. Davis, *The Hero: Charles A. Lindbergh and the American Dream* (Garden City: Doubleday, 1959), p. 105.
112. *Aircraft Year Book, 1924* (New York: Aeronautical Chamber of Commerce of America, 1924), p. 173.
113. "St. Louis — 1923," p. 467.
114. "SLAC Stockholders' Report, 1924."
115. "Side Lights on the St. Louis Meet," p. 488.
116. "Our Own Story of the St. Louis Meet," *Aviation,* Vol XV, No. 16 (October 15, 1923), p. 468.

CHAPTER XI

1. Charles A. Lindbergh, *"We"* (New York: Grosset and Dunlap, 1927), p. 20.
2. Kenneth S. Davis, *The Hero: Charles A. Lindbergh and the American Dream* (Garden City: Doubleday, 1959), p. 32.
3. *Idem.*
4. Lindbergh, *"We,"* p. 21.
5. Davis, p. 21.
6. *Ibid.,* pp. 66-67.
7. See Chapter IV, p. 95.
8. Lindbergh, *"We,"* p. 23.
9. Davis, pp. 77-78.
10. Lindbergh, *"We,"* pp. 24-25.
11. Davis, p. 80.
12. Lindbergh, *"We,"* pp. 27-28.
13. Davis, pp. 82-83.
14. Lindbergh, *"We,"* p. 28.
15. Davis, p. 80.
16. Lindbergh, *"We,"* p. 28.
17. Charles A. Lindbergh, *The Spirit of St. Louis* (New York: Charles Scribner's Sons, 1953), p. 256. Cited hereafter as Lindbergh, *Spirit.*
18. *Ibid.,* p. 267.
19. Lindbergh, *"We,"* p. 39.
20. *Ibid.,* p. 41.
21. See Chapter X, p. 214.
22. *St. Louis Post-Dispatch,* May 22, 1927, p. 3.
23. Davis, p. 108.
24. Lindbergh, *"We,"* pp. 104, 109.
25. Lindbergh, *Spirit,* p. 421.
26. Davis, p. 115.
27. George Buchanan Fife, *Lindbergh, The Lone Eagle: His Life and Achievements* (New York: A.L. Burt Company, 1927), p. 58.
28. Lindbergh, *"We,"* pp. 150-151.
29. Lindbergh, *Spirit,* p. 419.
30. Davis, p. 115.
31. *Ibid.,* p. 126.
32. *Ibid.,* p. 128.
33. Lindbergh, *"We,"* p. 169.
34. Davis, p. 126.
35. Lindbergh, *"We,"* p. 170.
36. *40th Anniversary of the 110th Tac. Ftr. Squadron, Missouri Air National Guard, and Progress of General Aviation in St. Louis* (St. Louis, 1963), p. 6.
37. Davis, p. 179.
38. *Aircraft Year Book, 1926.* (New York: Aeronautical Chamber of Commerce of America, 1926), p. 292.
39. Davis, p. 135.
40. Lindbergh, *"We,"* p. 175.

41. *Ibid.,* p. 172.
42. Lindbergh, *Spirit,* pp. 3-4.
43. Fife, p. 100.
44. Lindbergh, *"We,"* p. 176.
45. Fife, p. 100.
46. Davis, p. 131.
47. Fife, p. 74.
48. Davis, p. 132.
49. Stated to the author by Theodore Lorenz, a St. Louis aviator who knew Charles Lindbergh in 1926.
50. Lindbergh, *Spirit,* p. 50.
51. Quoted in *ibid,* p. 530.
52. Davis, pp. 141-142.
53. Lindbergh, *Spirit,* p. 530.
54. Baldwin H. Ward, *et. al.* (editors), *Flight — A Pictorial History of Aviation* (New York: Simon and Schuster, 1953), p. 94.
55. John D. Scott, *Vickers: A History* (London: Weidenfield and Nicolsen, 1962), pp. 175-176.
56. Robert de la Croix, *They Flew the Atlantic,* translated by Edward Fitzgerald (New York: W.W. Norton, 1958), p. 39.
57. Ward, p. 96.
58. *Aeronautics Papers, 1830-1939,* Missouri Historical Society Archives.
59. *Idem.*
60. Lindbergh, *"We,"* pp. 199-200.
61. Lindbergh, *Spirit,* p. 14.
62. *Ibid.,* p. 25.
63. *Ibid.,* p. 23.
64. *Ibid.,* pp. 22, 25-26.
65. *Ibid.,* pp. 30, 32.
66. *Ibid.,* p. 67.
67. *Ibid.,* p. viii.
68. Quoted in Alvin M. Josephy Jr., *et. al.* (editors), *The American Heritage History of Flight* (New York: Simon and Schuster, 1962), p. 239.
69. Lindbergh, *Spirit,* p. 75.
70. *Ibid.,* pp. 29, 68.
71. *Ibid.,* p. 85.
72. Lindbergh, *"We,"* pp. 200-201.
73. Lindbergh, *Spirit,* p. 74.
74. "Lindbergh's Spirit of St. Louis," *Air Progress,* Special Edition, 1952, p. 55.
75. Lindbergh, *Spirit,* pp. 538-539.
76. Fife, p. 155.
77. Robert A. Sheppler, *Aviation Instruments: A Brief History* (Davenport, Iowa: Bendix Corporation, 1962), p. 9.
78. Lindbergh, *Spirit,* p. 87.
79. *Ibid.,* pp. 93-94.
80. *Ibid.,* pp. 88, 90, 96, 154.
81. *Ibid.,* p. 101.
82. *Idem.*
83. "The New York-Paris Flight Projects," *Aviation,* Vol XXII, No. 17 (April 25, 1927), p. 823.

84. Lindbergh, *"We,"* p. 206.
85. Fife, p. 112.
86. Lindbergh, *Spirit,* p. 175.
87. Lindbergh, *"We,"* p. 206.
88. *St. Louis Post-Dispatch,* May 11, 1927, pp. 1, 3, and May 22, 1927, p. 5.
89. Lindbergh, *Spirit,* p. 93.
90. Quoted in *New York Times,* May 12, 1927, p. 2.
91. *St. Louis Post-Dispatch,* May 12, 1927, p. 1.
92. Ward, p. 96.
93. *New York Times,* May 13, 1927, p. 1.
94. Lindbergh, *Spirit,* p. 155.
95. *New York Times,* May 10, 1927, p. 1.
96. Quoted in *ibid,* May 11, 1927, p. 1.
97. Fife, p. 188.
98. Lloyd Morris and Kendall Smith, *Ceiling Unilimted: The Story of American Aviation from Kitty Hawk to Supersonics* (New York: Macmillan, 1958), p. 524.
99. Lindbergh, *Spirit,* p. 107.
100. Davis, p. 164.
101. *New York Times,* May 12, 1927, p. 2.
102. Lindbergh, *Spirit,* p. 131.
103. Davis, p. 162.
104. *New York Times,* May 13, 1927, p. 3.
105. *Ibid.,* May 21, 1927, p. 6.
106. Lindbergh, *Spirit,* pp. 166-167.
107. *New York Times,* May 14, 1927, p. 1.
108. Davis, p. 181.
109. Quoted in Lindbergh, *Spirit,* p. 169.
110. *Idem.*
111. *Ibid.,* pp. 173, 177.
112. Leon Schloss, "A Requiem for Roosevelt Field," *Pegasus,* May 1952, p. 4.
113. Lindbergh, *Spirit,* p. 155.
114. Lindbergh, *"We,"* pp. 204-205.
115. Davis, pp. 177-178.
116. Lindbergh, *Spirit,* p. 181.
117. *Ibid.,* p. 538.
118. Fife, p. 1.
119. Lindbergh, *Spirit,* p. 193.
120. *New York Times,* May 21, 1927, p. 1.
121. Fife, p. 14.
122. Lindbergh, *Spirit,* p. 187.
123. *Ibid.,* p. 189.
124. *Ibid.,* pp. 198-199.
125. *Ibid.,* p. 297.
126. *New York Times,* May 21, 1927, p. 1.
127. Lindbergh, *Spirit,* p. 235.
128. *Ibid.,* pp. 321-322.
129. *Ibid.,* p. 157.
130. *Ibid.,* p. 452.
131. Lindbergh, *"We,"* pp. 221-222.

132. Lindbergh, *Spirit*, p. 337.
133. *Ibid.,* p. 466.
134. *Idem.*
135. *Ibid.,* p. 484.
136. *Ibid.,* p. 486.
137. *Ibid.,* p. 487.
138. *New York Times,* May 22, 1927, p. 1.
139. Lindbergh, *"We,"* pp. 224-225.
140. Lindbergh, *Spirit,* p. 513.
141. *Ibid.,* p. 539.
142. *Ibid.,* p. 469.
143. Fife, p. 126.
144. Quoted in *New York Times,* May 22, 1927, p. 1.
145. Quoted in *St. Louis Post-Dispatch,* May 21, 1927, p. 1.
146. Fife, p. 32.
147. Lindbergh, *Spirit,* p. 491.
148. Davis, p. 209.
149. Lindbergh, *Spirit,* pp. 499-500.
150. Davis, p. 210.
151. Lindbergh, *Spirit,* p. 501.
152. Fife, p. 263.
153. "Rulers of Three Nations Confer Honors Upon Captain Charles A. Lindbergh," *Aviation,* Vol. XXII, No. 23 (June 6, 1927), p. 1216.
154. Lindbergh, *"We."* p. 263.
155. Quoted in Davis, p. 216.
156. Lindbergh, *"We,"* p. 229.
157. *Ibid.,* p. 265.
158. Lindbergh, *Spirit,* p. 517.
159. *Ibid.,* p. 530.
160. Charles Guggenheim and Associates, Inc. (producers), "City of Flight," KETC-TV, June 5, 1963, 9:30-10:30 p.m.
161. Lindbergh, *Spirit,* p. 526.
162. *Ibid.,* pp. 523, 526-527.
163. Nettie Beauregard (editor), *Lindbergh's Decorations and Trophies* (St. Louis: Missouri Historical Society, 1935), p. 5.
164. Lindbergh, *Spirit,* p. 530.
165. *Congressional Record,* 70 Congress, 1 Session, p. 412.
166. *Ibid.,* p. 488.
167. *Ibid.,* p. 834.
168. *Ibid.,* p. 412.
169. Frank Donovan, *The Early Eagles* (New York: Dodd, Mead, 1962), p. 280.
170. "Uncle Sam's Second Flying Hop Across the Pond," *The Literary Digest,* Vol. XCIII, No. 13 (June 25, 1927), p. 37.
171. De la Croix, p. 107.
172. Lindbergh, *Spirit,* p. 516.
173. Roy Cross, "Men and Ships," *Model Airplane News,* January 1959, p. 13.
174. Lindbergh, *Spirit,* p. 513.
175. Donovan, pp. 280-281.
176. Josephy, p. 243.
177. Davis, p. 265.

178. Charles J. Kelly Jr., *The Sky's the Limit: The History of the Airlines* (New York: Coward-McCann, 1963), pp. 132-133.
179. Davis, pp. 373-381.
180. General H.H. Arnold, *Global Mission* (New York: Harper and Brothers, 1949), pp. 188-189.
181. Davis, pp. 399-412.
182. Morris and Smith, p. 274.
183. Walter Ross, "What Became of Charles Lindbergh?" *Reader's Digest,* Vol. 84, No. 502 (February 1964), p. 92.
184. *New York Times,* August 27, 1974.

CHAPTER XII

1. "The Gordon Bennett Balloon Race," *Aviation,* Vol. XXIII, No. 9 (August 29, 1927), p. 479.
2. *St. Louis Globe-Democrat,* August 16, 1928.
3. *St. Louis Post-Dispatch,* September 29, 1929, p. 2.
4. *St. Louis Globe-Democrat,* September 28, 1929, p. 2.
5. *Ibid.,* December 19, 1928, p. 14.
6. *St. Louis Post-Dispatch,* September 27, 1929, p. 2.
7. *St. Louis Globe-Democrat,* December 19, 1928, p. 14.
8. *Ibid.,* September 25, 1929, p. 17.
9. *St. Louis Post-Dispatch,* September 27, 1929, p. 2.
10. *St. Louis Globe-Democrat,* September 25, 1929, p. 17. See Chapter VI, p. 154.
11. *St. Louis Post-Dispatch,* September 23, 1929, p. 4.
12. *St. Louis Globe-Democrat,* September 28, 1929, p. 6.
13. *St. Louis Post-Dispatch,* September 27, 1929, p. 2.
14. *St. Louis Globe-Democrat,* September 26, 1929, p. 9.
15. *Ibid.,* August 16, 1928.
16. *Ibid.,* September 25, 1929, p. 17.
17. *Ibid.,* September 28, 1929, p. 2.
18. *St. Louis Post-Dispatch,* September 24, 1929, p. 22.
19. *St. Louis Globe-Democrat,* September 28, 1929, p. 2.
20. *St. Louis Post-Dispatch,* September 23, 1929, p. 4.
21. *St. Louis Globe-Democrat,* September 28, 1929, p. 2.
22. *New York Times,* September 29, 1929, p. 18.
23. *St. Louis Post-Dispatch,* September 28, 1929, p. 2.
24. *Ibid.,* September 27, 1929, p. 2.
25. *St. Louis Globe-Democrat,* September 26, 1929, p. 9.
26. Quoted in *ibid.,* September 27, 1929, p. 10.
27. *Ibid.,* September 26, 1929, p. 9.
28. *St. Louis Post-Dispatch,* September 28, 1929, p. 2.
29. *St. Louis Globe-Democrat,* September 29, 1929, p. 7.
30. *Idem.*
31. *St. Louis Post-Dispatch,* September 29, 1929, p. 2.
32. *New York Times,* September 29, 1929, p. 18.
33. *St. Louis Post-Dispatch,* September 28, 1929, p. 1.

34. *St. Louis Globe-Democrat,* September 29, 1929, p. 7.
35. See Chapter II, pp. 52-53.
36. *St. Louis Post-Dispatch,* September 29, 1929, p. 2.
37. *St. Louis Globe-Democrat,* September 29, 1929, p. 7.
38. *St. Louis Post-Dispatch,* September 28, 1929, p. 2.
39. *St. Louis Globe-Democrat,* September 29, 1929, p. 7.
40. *St. Louis Post-Dispatch,* September 29, 1929, p. 1.
41. *Ibid.,* pp. 1-2.
42. Quoted in *ibid.,* p. 1.
43. *St. Louis Globe-Democrat,* September 30, 1929, p. 1.
44. Aeronautical Chamber of Commerce of America, *The Aircraft Year Book for 1930* (New York: D. Van Nostrand, 1930), p. 586.
45. See Chapter VIII, pp. 178-180.
46. *New York Times,* October 1, 1929, p. 4.
47. Letter to the author from Mitchell E. Giblo, executive director of the National Aeronautic Association, December 17, 1964.
48. *Ibid.,* December 2, 1964.
49. Crouch, p. 588.
50. Telephone conversation between the author and Nikki Caplan, historian of the Balloon Federation of America, August 24, 1984. In this race the celebrated American balloonist Maxie Anderson and his copilot Don Ida were killed when their gondola became detached as the result of a defective explosive squib over the Federal Republic of Germany on June 27, 1983.
51. Telephone conversation between the author and Debra Spaeth, operations chair of the Balloon Federation of America, August 31, 1984.
52. Jan Boesman, *Gordon Bennett Balloon Race,* The Hague: The Netherlands Aeronautical Museum, 1976, pp. 120-128.

CHAPTER XIII

1. *St. Louis Post-Dispatch,* June 1, 1937, p. 60.
2. "Transport: 'Stunt Flight,'" *Time,* Vol. XXIX, No. 22 (May 31, 1937), p. 45.
3. Alvin M. Josephy Jr., *et. al.* (editors), *The American Heritage History of Flight* (New York: Simon and Schuster, 1962), p. 242.
4. Quoted in "Transport: 'Stunt Flight,'" pp. 45-46.
5. *St. Louis Globe-Democrat,* May 29, 1937, p. 1.
6. *Ibid.,* May 8, 1937, p. 1.
7. *Ibid.,* May 23, 1937, p. 5B.
8. *Ibid.,* May 21, 1937, p. 13.
9. *St. Louis Post-Dispatch,* May 18, 1937, p. 5A.
10. *St. Louis Globe-Democrat,* May 27, 1937, p. 6A.
11. *Ibid.,* May 28, 1937, p. 14A.
12. *Ibid.,* May 30, 1937, p. 5A.
13. *Ibid.,* May 18, 1937, p. 6A.
14. *St. Louis Post-Dispatch,* May 30, 1937, p. 3.
15. *St. Louis Globe-Democrat,* May 27, 1937, p. 6A.
16. *St. Louis Post-Dispatch,* May 29, 1937, p. 3A.

17. *St. Louis Globe-Democrat,* May 29, 1937, p. 1.
18. *St. Louis Post-Dispatch,* June 1, 1937, p. 6C.
19. See Chapter X, p. 212.
20. See Chapter XI, p. 222.
21. *St. Louis Post-Dispatch,* May 18, 1937, p. 5A.
22. *St. Louis Globe-Democrat,* May 27, 1937, p. 6A.
23. *St. Louis Post-Dispatch,* May 29, 1937, p. 1.
24. *St. Louis Globe-Democrat,* May 30, 1937, p. 5A.
25. *St. Louis Post-Dispatch,* May 29, 1937, p. 1.
26. *St. Louis Globe-Democrat,* May 30, 1937, p. 5A.
27. Quoted in *idem.*
28. *St. Louis Post-Dispatch,* May 30, 1937, p. 1.
29. *St. Louis Globe-Democrat,* May 30, 1937, p. 5A.
30. *St. Louis Post-Dispatch,* May 30, 1937, p. 3.
31. *St. Louis Globe-Democrat,* May 30, 1937, p. 5A.
32. *Idem.*
33. Quoted in *idem.*
34. *St. Louis Post-Dispatch,* May 30, 1937, p. 1.
35. Howard Mingos (editor), *The Aircraft Year Book for 1938* (New York: Aeronautical Chamber of Commerce of America, 1938), p. 410.
36. *St. Louis Globe-Democrat,* May 31, 1937, pp. 1, 6A.
37. *Ibid.,* p. 1.
38. *Idem.*
39. *Ibid.,* p. 6A.
40. *Idem.*
41. Baldwin H. Ward, *et. al.* (editors), *Flight — A Pictorial History of Aviation* (New York: Simon and Schuster, 1953), p. 133.
42. *St. Louis Globe-Democrat,* May 31, 1937, p. 6A.
43. *Idem.*
44. *St. Louis Post-Dispatch,* May 27, 1937, p. 4C.
45. *St. Louis Globe-Democrat,* May 31, 1937, p. 6A.
46. *Ibid.,* June 1, 1937, pp. 1, 9A.
47. *St. Louis Post-Dispatch,* June 1, 1937, p. 6C.
48. *St. Louis Globe-Democrat,* June 1, 1937, p. 9A.
49. *Idem.*
50. *Idem.*
51. *Ibid.,* May 28, 1937, p. 14A.
52. *St. Louis Post-Dispatch,* June 1, 1937, p. 6C.
53. *Idem.*
54. *St. Louis Globe-Democrat,* June 1, 1937, p. 1.
55. *St. Louis Post-Dispatch,* June 1, 1937, p. 6C.
56. *St. Louis Globe-Democrat,* June 1, 1937, p. 9A.
57. *St. Louis Post-Dispatch,* June 1, 1937, p. 6C.
58. *Ibid.,* November 12, 1946, p. 6.
59. *Ibid.,* June 1, 1937, p. 6C.

CHAPTER XIV

1. Howard L. Scamehorn, *Balloons to Jets: A Century of Aeronautics in Illi-*

nois, 1855-1955 (Chicago: Henry Regnery Company, 1957), p. 8. See Chapter II, p. 42.

2. David R. Francis, *The Universal Exposition of 1904* (St. Louis: Louisiana Purchase Exposition Company, 1913), I, p. 445. See Chapter III, pp. 81-82, 89-90.

3. *Morris A. Heimann Collection,* Missouri Historical Society Library.

4. *St. Louis Globe-Democrat,* August 17, 1908, p. 1. See Chapter V, p. 115.

5. *St. Louis Republic,* September 15, 1910, p. 4. See Chapter VI, p. 137.

6. *M.A. Heimann Manufacturing Co.: Designers and Manufacturers of Balloons and Airships* (St. Louis: c. 1909), p. 2.

7. *Morris A. Heimann Collection.* See Chapter V, p. 117.

8. *St. Louis Republic,* October 5, 1911, p. 1. See Chapter VII, p. 163.

9. *St. Louis Globe-Democrat,* February 11, 1940. See Chapter III, p. 63.

10. *Ibid.,* October 3, 1908, p. 1. See Chapter V, p. 115.

11. *St. Louis Republic,* September 25, 1909, p. 3. See Chapter V, p. 123.

12. *St. Louis Republic,* October 14, 1909, p. 2.

13. "Authorized Official Program of the Fifth International Balloon Race," *Aero,* Vol. I, Special Edition (October 17, 1910). See Chapter VI, p. 153.

14. "St. Louis Meet Opens With a Rush to Lambert Field," *Aero,* Vol. I, No. 1 (October 8, 1910), p. 4. See Chapter VI, p. 142.

15. *Official Souvenir Program, October 1st-8th, 1911* (St. Louis: Aero Club of St. Louis, 1911), p. 5.

16. *St. Louis Globe-Democrat,* May 27, 1928.

17. *Ibid.,* February 11, 1940.

18. *St. Louis Globe-Democrat,* May 27, 1928.

19. Lee Brashear, "Early Birdman," *St. Louis Globe-Democrat,* June 15, 1952.

20. *St. Louis Republic,* November 5, 1904, p. 1. See Chapter III, pp. 81-82.

21. Brashear, *op. cit.* The date for the commencement of this operation is cited also as 1909 in "Air Story of St. Louis," *St. Louis Globe-Democrat,* February 9, 1930, p. 6S, and "News and Comment," *Bulletin of the Missouri Historical Society,* Vol. IX, No. 2 (January 1953), p. 205.

22. "News and Comment," *Bulletin of the Missouri Historical Society,* Vol. IX, No. 2 (January 1953), p. 205.

23. "Advertisement for the Aeronautical Supply Company," *Aero,* Vol. I, No. 2 (October 15, 1910), p. 24.

24. Brashear, *op. cit.*

25. *St. Louis Globe-Democrat,* August 28, 1910, p. 12.

26. *Ibid.,* September 23, 1928.

27. *Official Souvenir Program, October 1st-8th, 1911,* p. 5.

28. "Many Machines Building at St. Louis," *Aeronautics,* Vol. 6, No. 5 (May 1910), p. 165.

29. *St. Louis Republic,* September 19, 1910, p. 2. See Chapter VI, p. 137.

30. *Ibid.,* October 13, 1910, p. 1. See Chapter VI, p. 148.

31. "Advertisement for The Phoenix Auto Supply Company," *Aero,* Vol. I, No. 2 (October 15, 1910), p. 31.

32. "Advertisement for The Aeromotion Company of America," *Aero,* Vol. I, No. 2 (October 15, 1910), p. 32.

33. "Advertisement for The Carter Carburetor Company," *Aero,* Vol. I, No. 2 (October 15, 1910), p. 21.

34. "Advertisement for The Missouri Tent and Awning Company," *Aero,* Vol. I, No. 2 (October 15, 1910), p. 23.

35. Christy C. Magrath, "Wings of Old Kinloch," *The* (Berkeley, Missouri) *Public News,* June 25, 1953, p. 2.
36. *Idem.*
37. *Official Souvenir Program, October 1st-8th, 1911,* p. 6. See Chapter VII, pp. 161-167.
38. Scamehorn, *Balloons to Jets,* p. 62.
39. *Official Souvenir Program, October 1st-8th, 1911,* p. 6.
40. "Activities at the Flying Fields and Hydro Havens — Missouri: Kinloch," *Aero and Hydro,* Vol. V, No. 9 (February 8, 1913), p. 343.
41. "State of Missouri Certificate of Incorporation of the Pioneer Aeroplane and Exhibition Company," *Aeronautics Papers, 1830-1939,* Missouri Historical Society Archives.
42. See Chapter VII, pp. 160-161.
43. *Aeronautics Papers, 1830-1939,* Missouri Historical Society Archives.
44. *St. Louis Republic,* October 21, 1911, p. 1. See Chapter VII, p. 171.
45. *St. Louis Times,* May 21, 1914.
46. Magrath, p. 2.
47. *St. Louis Globe-Democrat,* March 2, 1912, p. 1. See Chapter VIII, pp. 174-175.
48. Magrath, p. 2.
49. *Idem.*
50. Quoted in "In the Slip Stream," *Aero and Hydro,* Vol. V, No. 19 (February 8, 1913), p. 345.
51. Harold E. Morehouse, "Flight from the Water," *American Aviation Historical Society Journal,* Vol. 9, No. 3 (Fall 1964), p. 172.
52. *Ibid.,* p. 175.
53. Walter T. Bonney, "The Heritage of Kitty Hawk: Part VII," *Pegasus,* August 1956, p. 14.
54. Morehouse, pp. 174-175.
55. Brashear, *op. cit.*
56. Morehouse, p. 175.
57. Charles Guggenheim and Associates, Inc. (producers), "City of Flight," KETC-TV, June 5, 1963, 9:30-10:30 p.m.
58. Morehouse, p. 175.
59. Brashear, *op. cit.*
60. Magrath, p. 2.
61. Baldwin H. Ward, *et. al.* (editors), *Flight — A Pictorial History of Aviation* (New York: Simon and Schuster, 1953), p. 94. See Chapter XI, p. 225.
62. Magrath, p. 2.
63. Civil Aeronautics Board, *Handbook of Airline Statistics* (Washington: United States Government Printing Office, 1963), p. 441. That was true for scheduled airlines, but Count Ferdinand von Zeppelin and Dr. Hugo Eckener started *Deutsche Luftschiffahrt Aktien Gesellschaft* (German Airship Travel Stock Company) — *DELAG* — in 1909. It operated five dirigibles *(Schwaben, Deutschland, Hansa, Sachen,* and *Viktoria-Luise),* on irregular schedules serving Frankfort, Stuttgart, Hamburg, Dresden, Berlin, and other German cities. A total of 1,600 flights was made between 1909 and 1913, logging 100,000 miles, with neither loss nor injury to passengers. Of all commercial passenger flights of all dirigibles, from 1909 until the last one in 1939, the only passenger fatalities were the 13 lost in the spectacular

fire and crash of the *Hindenburg* in Lakehurst, New Jersey, on May 6, 1937. *(Check List,* Midcoast Aviation Services, No. 1422, 1981).

64. "Weather Halts Benoist Flying Boat Testing," *St. Petersburg Times,* January 10, 1964, p. 1-B.

65. "Benoist 1914 Flying Boat Described," *Aero and Hydro,* Vol. VII, No. 2 (October 11, 1913), p. 17.

66. "Benoist's Aero-Boat Line Running Smoothly," *Aero and Hydro,* Vol. VII, No. 15 (January 10, 1914), pp. 177, 178.

67. "Air Line Travels 682 Miles First 10 Days," *Aero and Hydro,* Vol. VII, No. 17, (January 24, 1914), p. 213.

68. *Ibid.,* p. 214. According to Civil Aeronautics Board, p. 441, however, only one more plane, a three-place Benoist XIV, was added.

69. Magrath, p. 2.

70. Morehouse, p. 177.

71. *Idem.* Morehouse incorrectly cites the opening date as January 2, 1914.

72. Civil Aeronautics Board, p. 441.

73. Morehouse, p. 177.

74. Civil Aeronautics Board, p. 441.

75. "Benoist School Moves to Florida," *Aero and Hydro,* Vol. VII, No. 14 (January 3, 1914), p. 165.

76. *St. Louis Times,* May 21, 1914.

77. Brashear, *op. cit.*

78. Magrath, p. 2.

79. Brashear, *op. cit.*

80. "A History of the U.S. Army Air Corps," *Aviation,* Vol. XXI, No. 5 (August 2, 1926), p. 172.

81. Alvin M. Josephy Jr., *et. al.* (editors), *The American Heritage History of Flight* (New York: Simon and Schuster, 1962), p. 179.

82. Charles J. Kelly Jr., *The Sky's the Limit: The History of the Airlines* (New York: Coward-McCann, 1963), p. 23.

83. Henry Ladd Smith, *Airways: The History of Commercial Aviation in the United States* (New York: Alfred A. Knopf, 1942), p. 4.

84. *Ibid.,* p. 38.

85. *Aircraft Year Book, 1919* (New York: Manufacturers' Aircraft Association, 1919), p. 225.

86. *Idem.*

87. James C. Fahey, *U.S. Army Aircraft, 1908-1946* (Falls Church, Virginia: Ships and Aircraft, 1964), p. 8.

88. "A History of the U.S. Army Air Corps," p. 172.

89. William Glenn Cunningham, *The Aircraft Industry: A Study in Industrial Location* (Los Angeles: Lorris A. Morrison, 1951), p. 37.

90. *Aircraft Year Book,* 1919, p. 227.

91. Majors Albert Bond Lambert and William B. Robertson, "Early History of Aeronautics in St. Louis," *Missouri Historical Society Collections,* Vol. V, No. 3 (June 1928), p. 244.

92. *Morris A. Heimann Collection.*

93. *St. Louis Republic,* June 7, 1917, p. 1.

94. *Ibid.,* May 5, 1917.

95. *Ibid.,* June 7, 1917, p. 1.

96. *St. Louis Republic,* May 5, 1917.

97. *St. Louis Globe-Democrat,* April 21, 1914, p. 1.

98. *Ibid.,* April 28, 1914, p. 1.

99. *Ibid.,* May 16, 1917.

100. *Ibid.,* June 6, 1917.

101. *St. Louis Republic,* June 7, 1917.

102. "Do You Know or Don't You?" *Missouri Historical Review,* Vol. XXXI, No. 1 (October 1936), p. 72.

103. *St. Louis Star-Times,* August 9, 1935.

104. *Albert Bond Lambert Aeronautical Papers,* Missouri Historical Society Archives.

105. Maj. Albert Bond Lambert, "St. Louis — on World's Air Map for 16 Years," *St. Louis Post-Dispatch,* September 30, 1923, Sunday Magazine, p. 3. The number of students graduated is variously cited as 340 in Lambert and Robertson, p. 244, and as 352 in *St. Louis Star-Times,* August 9, 1935.

106. See Chapter XV, pp. 305-307.

107. *Aircraft Year Book for 1926* (New York: Aeronautical Chamber of Commerce of America, 1926), p. 60.

108. "Airports and Airways: St. Louis, Mo.," *Aviation,* Vol. XXIII, No. 18 (October 31, 1927), p. 1068.

109. "Von Hoffmann Aircraft Co. to Distribute B.F. Mahoney Planes," *Aviation,* Vol. XXIII, No. 16 (October 17, 1927), p. 954.

110. *St. Louis Globe-Democrat,* January 5, 1930, p. 4R.

111. Welman A. Shrader, *Fifty Years of Flight: A Chronicle of the Aviation Industry in America, 1903-1953* (Cleveland: Eaton Manufacturing Company, 1953), p. 46.

112. *St. Louis Globe-Democrat,* February 16, 1930, p. 13S.

113. "Distribution of American Eagle Granted to St. Louis Aircraft Co.," *Aviation,* Vol. XXIV, No. 9 (February 27, 1928), p. 517.

114. "Manufacturer's Specifications on American Commercial Airplanes and Seaplanes as Compiled by *Aviation,*" *Aviation,* Vol. XXIV, No. 6 (February 6, 1928), p. 326.

115. Aeronautical Chamber of Commerce of America, *The Aircraft Year Book for 1933* (New York: D. Van Nostrand, 1933), p. 255.

116. See Chapter XI, pp. 230-231.

117. "Manufacturer's Specifications on American Commercial Airplanes and Seaplanes as Compiled by *Aviation,*" pp. 326-327.

118. *St. Louis Globe-Democrat,* May 18, 1928.

119. "B.F. Mahoney Aircraft Corp. to Move its Factory to St. Louis," *Aviation,* Vol. XXIV, No. 3 (January 16, 1928), p. 158.

120. Lambert and Robertson, p. 255.

121. "B.F. Mahoney Aircraft Corp. to Move its Factory to St. Louis," p. 158.

122. *St. Louis Globe-Democrat,* May 18, 1928.

123. "B.F. Mahoney Aircraft Corp. to Move its Factory to St. Louis," p. 158.

124. *Chilton Aero Directory and Catalogue, 1929* (Philadelphia: Chilton Class Journal Company, 1929), p. 280.

125. "Lindbergh Backers Will Finance New Mahoney Factory at St. Louis," *Aviation,* Vol. XXIV, No. 4 (January 23, 1928), p. 210. See Chapter XI, p. 228.

126. Aeronautical Chamber of Commerce of America, *The Aircraft Year Book for 1930* (New York: D. Van Nostrand, 1930), p. 89.

127. *St. Louis Globe-Democrat,* February 9, 1930, p. 6S.

128. Aeronautical Chamber of Commerce of America, *The Aircraft Year Book for 1931* (New York: D. Van Nostrand, 1931), p. 132.

129. *Aeronautics Papers, 1830-1939,* Missouri Historical Society Archives.

130. *St. Louis Globe-Democrat,* February 9, 1930, p. 6S.

131. *Ibid.,* February 17, 1930, p. 6S.

132. See Chapter XI, p. 222.

133. *St. Louis Globe-Democrat,* February 19, 1930, p. 1.

134. *Ibid.,* February 23, 1930, p. 1.

135. See Chapter VI, pp. 155-156.

156. Aeronautical Chamber of Commerce of America, *The Aircraft Year Book for 1932* (New York: D. Van Nostrand, 1932), p. 316. See Chapter XV, p. 309.

137. "Yesterday's Wings: The Monocoupe," *The AOPA Pilot,* February 1953, p. 76.

138. *Idem.*

139. Shrader, p. 46.

140. Aeronautical Chamber of Commerce of America, *The Aircraft Year Book for 1932,* p. 316.

141. "Yesterday's Wings: The Monocoupe," p. 76.

142. Aeronautical Chamber of Commerce of America, *The Aircraft Year Book for 1932,* p. 316.

143. Shrader, p. 57. See Chapter VI, p. 156.

144. "Col. Lindbergh's 'Lambert 145 Monocoupe' — 1934," *Flying,* August 1963, p. 67.

145. "Monocoupe Club," *Antique Airplane Association News,* March 1963. Unpaginated article in the files of the Missouri Historical Society.

146. Howard Mingos (editor), *The Aircraft Year Book for 1936* (New York: Aeronautical Chamber of Commerce of America, 1936), p. 271.

147. *St. Louis Globe-Democrat,* October 13, 1935.

148. Peter M. Bowers, "The Sixty Best Commercial Airplanes, 1927-1936," *Air Progress,* August/September 1963, p. 34.

149. Howard Mingos (editor), *The Aircraft Year Book for 1941* (New York: Aeronautical Chamber of Commerce of America, 1941), p. 244.

150. Aeronautical Chamber of Commerce of America, *The Aircraft Year Book for 1935.* (New York: D. Van Nostrand, 1935), p. 261.

151. Shrader, p. 59.

152. Howard Mingos (editor), *The Aircraft Year Book for 1936* (New York: Aeronautical Chamber of Commerce of America, 1936), p. 277.

153. F.G. Swanborough and Peter M. Bowers, *United States Military Aircraft Since 1909* (London: Putnam, 1963), p. 581.

154. *Ibid.,* p. 526.

155. Howard Mingos (editor), *The Aircraft Year Book for 1941,* p. 267.

156. *Idem.*

157. Howard Mingos (editor), *The Aircraft Year Books for 1942, 1943, 1944* (New York: Aeronautical Chamber of Commerce of America, 1942, 1943, 1944), p. 338, 276, 300.

158. Fahey, p. 37.

159. Irving Brinton Holley Jr., *United States Army in World War II, Special Studies — Buying Aircraft: Materiel Procurement for the Army Air Forces* (Washington: Office of the Chief of Military History, Department of the Army, 1964), p. 578.

160. *St. Louis Globe-Democrat,* February 11, 1945, p. 6E.
161. *Ibid.,* August 2, 1943, p. 2A.
162. Fahey, p. 37.
163. Swanborough and Bowers, p. 515.
164. Fahey, p. 37.
165. *St. Louis Globe-Democrat,* August 2, 1943, p. 2A.
166. Swanborough and Bowers, pp. 462-465.
167. *St. Louis Globe-Democrat,* February 11, 1945, p. 6E.
168. *Idem.*
169. Fahey, p. 37.
170. Swanborough and Bowers, p. 572.
171. *St. Louis Globe-Democrat,* February 11, 1945, p. 6E. The headline for the story cites 97 companies as engaging in air industry in the city, but the accompanying list numbers 98 firms.
172. *Idem.*
173. Howard Mingos (editor), *The Aircraft Year Book for 1946* (New York: Lanciar Publishers, Inc., 1946), p. 291.
174. Shrader, p. 93.

CHAPTER XV

1. *St. Louis Globe-Democrat,* July 8, 1928, Sunday Magazine, pp. 8-9.
2. Samuel T. Larkin (editor), *Who's Who in Saint Louis, 1928-1929* (St. Louis: Civic Union of St. Louis, 1928), p. 91.
3. *St. Louis Globe-Democrat,* July 8, 1928, Sunday Magazine, p. 9.
4. *St. Louis Post-Dispatch,* August 23, 1920, p. 13.
5. *St. Louis Globe-Democrat,* July 8, 1928, Sunday Magazine, p. 9.
6. Kenneth S. Davis, *The Hero: Charles A. Lindbergh and the American Dream* (Garden City: Doubleday, 1959), p. 124.
7. *Aircraft Year Book, 1927* (New York: Aeronautical Chamber of Commerce of America, 1927), p. 25. According to this source, the firm was originally capitalized at $50,000.
8. See Chapter I, pp. 8-10.
9. Larkin, p. 91.
10. *Aircraft Year Book, 1922* (New York: Aeronautical Chamber of Commerce of America, 1922), p. 27.
11. *110th Bombardment Squadron, 131st Bombardment Wing, Missouri Air National Guard: 30th Anniversary Year, 1923-1953* (St. Louis, 1953), p. 1.
12. *The Robertson Air National Guard Base, Saint Louis* (St. Louis, 1959), pp. 11-15.
13. *40th Anniversary of the 110th Tac. Ftr. Squadron, Missouri Air National Guard, and Progress of General Aviation in St. Louis* (St. Louis, 1963), p. 11.
14. *The Robertson Air National Guard Base, Saint Louis,* p. 2.
15. Earl D. Osborn, "St. Louis — Wichita and Denver Air Centers," *Aviation,* Vol. XXII, No. 25 (June 20, 1927), p. 1386.
16. "Advertisement for the Robertson Aircraft Corporation," *Aviation,* Vol. XIX, No. 3 (July 20, 1925), p. 79.

17. "Robertson Aircraft Co. Prospers," *Aviation,* Vol. XIX, No. 26 (December 28, 1925), p. 920.

18. *Aircraft Year Book 1924* (New York: Aeronautical Chamber of Commerce of America, 1924), pp. 28-29.

19. *The Robertson Air National Guard Base, Saint Louis,* p. 2.

20. *Aircraft Year Book, 1924,* p. 28.

21. See Chapter XIV, p. 280.

22. *St. Louis Globe-Democrat,* July 8, 1928, Sunday Magazine, p. 14.

23. "Robertson Gets Chicago-St. Louis Mail Contract," *Aviation,* Vol. XIX, No. 17 (October 26, 1925), p. 596.

24. "Advertisement for Robertson Aircraft Corporation," p. 79.

25. "Robertson Aircraft Co. Prospers," p. 919.

26. Earl D. Osborn, p. 1386.

27. "Robertson Aircraft Co. Prospers," p. 919.

28. "Robertson Gets Chicago-St. Louis Mail Contract," p. 596.

29. "Robertson Aircraft Co. Prospers," p. 920.

30. *Aircraft Year Book, 1926,* (New York: Aeronautical Chamber of Commerce of America, 1926), p. 35.

31. "Advertisement for the Robertson Aircraft Corporation," *Chilton Aero Directory and Catalogue, 1929* (Philadelphia: Chilton Class Journal Company, 1929), p. 86.

32. *Congressional Record,* 68 Congress, 2 Session, p. 742.

33. See Chapter I, pp. 6-7.

34. *Congressional Record,* 68 Congress, 2 Session, p. 751.

35. *Ibid.,* p. 787.

36. *Ibid.,* p. 2523.

37. *Ibid.,* p. 3747.

38. Captain Benjamin B. Lipsner, *The Airmail: Jennies to Jets* (Chicago: Wilcox and Follett, 1951), p. 212.

39. Henry Ladd Smith, *Airways: The History of Commercial Aviation in the United States* (New York: Alfred A. Knopf, 1942), p. 104.

40. "The New Air Mail Contracts," *Aviation,* Vol. XIX, No. 16 (October 19, 1925), p. 552.

41. Quoted in *idem.*

42. "The Chicago-St. Louis Air Mail Line," *Aviation,* Vol. XX, No. 14 (April 5, 1926), p. 449.

43. "Robertson Gets Chicago-St. Louis Mail Contract," p. 596.

44. *Aircraft Year Book, 1926,* p. 292. "The Chicago-St. Louis Air Mail Line," p. 499, cites the same figure, but both Henry Ladd Smith, p. 107, and Davis, p. 130, hold that the company started operations with fourteen DH-4s and two "Orioles," while Earl D. Osborn, p. 1386, records that the corporation began with fourteen DH-4s which it had purchased from the government.

45. Charles A. Lindbergh, *"We,"* (New York: Grosset and Dunlap, 1927), p. 175. See Chapter XI, p. 222.

46. "The Chicago-St. Louis Air Mail Line," p. 499.

47. Majors Albert Bond Lambert and William B. Robertson, "Early History of Aeronautics in St. Louis," *Missouri Historical Society Collections,* Vol. V, No. 3 (June 1928), p. 250.

48. See Chapter I, p. 7.

49. Lindbergh, *"We,"* p. 176.
50. *Idem.*
51. Henry Ladd Smith, p. 117.
52. "Air Mail Contract Payments," *Aviation,* Vol. XXII, No. 21 (May 23, 1927), p. 1078.
53. Henry Ladd Smith, p. 151.
54. See Chapter XIV, p. 293.
55. *St. Louis Globe-Democrat,* October 6, 1927.
56. *Ibid.,* November 10, 1927.
57. Stated to the author by Lloyd F. Engelhardt, an aeronautical engineer who came to St. Louis for the Curtiss-Wright Corporation in 1932.
58. *St. Louis Globe-Democrat,* October 6, 1927.
59. "Maj. Robertson Resigns to Head Curtiss-Robertson Airplane Mfg. Co.," *Aviation,* Vol. XXIV, No. 7 (February 13, 1928), p. 398.
60. Henry Ladd Smith, p. 206.
61. *St. Louis Globe-Democrat,* January 29, 1928.
62. *Idem.*
63. "Airports and Airways: St. Louis, Mo.," *Aviation,* Vol. XXIV, No. 9 (February 27, 1928), p. 541.
64. *Aircraft Year Book, 1928* (New York: Aeronautical Chamber of Commerce of America, 1928), p. 72.
65. *St. Louis Globe-Democrat,* April 7, 1928.
66. *Idem.*
67. Henry Ladd Smith, p. 206.
68. *St. Louis Globe-Democrat,* June 16, 1928.
69. Untitled newspaper clipping, 1928, *Aviation Scrapbook,* Missouri Historical Society Library.
70. *St. Louis Globe-Democrat,* June 16, 1928.
71. *Ibid.,* August 19, 1928.
72. *Ibid.,* July 27, 1928.
73. *Ibid.,* August 2, 1928.
74. *Ibid.,* July 10, 1928.
75. *Ibid.,* October 26, 1928, p. 6S.
76. *Ibid.,* October 7, 1928.
77. *Ibid.,* October 29, 1928.
78. *Ibid.,* October 7, 1928.
79. *Ibid.,* October 24, 1928.
80. *Aircraft Year Book, 1929* (New York: Aeronautical Chamber of Commerce of America, 1929), p. 33. According to the *St. Louis Globe-Democrat,* March 28, 1929, Robertson carried 63,807 pounds of mail over CAM-2 in 1928.
81. *Aviation: What It Means To You* (St. Louis: Universal Aviation Schools, c. 1929), p. 47.
82. *Ibid.,* pp. 10-26.
83. *St. Louis Globe-Democrat,* February 7, 1929.
84. *Ibid.,* March 28, 1929.
85. *Ibid.,* May 1, 1929.
86. *Ibid.,* October 2, 1929.
87. *Ibid.,* May 18, 1929.
88. *Ibid.,* February 9, 1930.

89. Howard L. Scamehorn, *Balloons to Jets: A Century of Aeronautics in Illinois, 1855-1955* (Chicago: Henry Regnery Company, 1957), p. 151.

90. "Maj. Robertson Resigns to Head Curtiss-Robertson Airplane Mfg. Co.," p. 398.

91. *St. Louis Globe-Democrat,* November 10, 1927.

92. Joseph P. Juptner, *U.S. Civil Aircraft,* Vol. 1: *ATC 1-ATC 100* (Los Angeles: Aero Publishers, 1962), p. 174.

95. *St. Louis Post-Dispatch,* August 7, 1928, p. 3. See Chapter I, p. 12.

94. Juptner, I, p. 111.

95. *The Curtiss-Robertson Airplane Mfg. Co., Division of Curtiss-Wright* (New York: Curtiss-Wright Sales Corporation, 1930), pp. 9-10.

96. *St. Louis Globe-Democrat,* November 10, 1927.

97. Lesley N. Forden, "Whatever Became of . . . the Curtiss Robin," undated magazine clipping from the files of L.J. Sutorius of St. Louis, p. 54.

98. Peter M. Bowers, "The Sixty Best Commercial Airplanes, 1927-1936," p. 24.

99. Juptner, I, p. 177.

100. Joseph P. Juptner, *U.S. Civil Aircraft,* Vol. 2: *ATC 101-ATC 200* (Los Angeles: Aero Publishers, 1964), p. 130.

101. *The Curtiss-Robertson Airplane Mfg. Co., Division of Curtiss-Wright,* p. 8.

102. Forden, p. 54.

103. "History of the Saint Louis Airplane Division of Curtiss-Wright Corporation," Missouri Historical Society Library.

104. *St. Louis Globe-Democrat,* December 18, 1928.

105. Forden, pp. 54, 84.

106. Russell Plehinger, "Endurance Flying: The Pilots and Planes," *American Aviation Historical Society Journal,* Vol. 9, No. 4 (Winter 1964), p. 283.

107. Juptner, I, p. 79.

108. Plehinger, p. 285.

109. *St. Louis Globe-Democrat,* July 13, 1929, p. 1.

110. *Idem.*

111. *The Curtiss-Robertson Airplane Mfg. Co., Division of Curtiss-Wright,* pp. 11-12.

112. Theodore P. Wagner, "Pioneer St. Louis Pilot Looks Back," *St. Louis Post-Dispatch,* December 10, 1958.

113. *St. Louis Globe-Democrat,* July 31, 1929, p. 1.

114. *Ibid.,* July 31, 1929, p. 3.

115. *Idem.*

116. Quoted in Aeronautical Chamber of Commerce of America, *The Aircraft Year Book for 1930* (New York: D. Van Nostrand, 1930), p. 152.

117. *St. Louis Globe-Democrat,* July 31, 1929, p. 1.

118. *St. Louis Republic,* October 12, 1910, p. 1. See Chapter VI, p. 100.

119. *Ibid.,* October 20, 1911, p. 2. See Chapter VII, p. 170.

120. *St. Louis Globe-Democrat,* July 31, 1929, p. 3.

121. *Ibid.,* July 31, 1929, pp. 1-2.

122. Scamehorn, *Balloons to Jets,* p. 225.

123. *St. Louis Globe-Democrat,* August 18, 1930, p. 1.

124. *Ibid.,* July 31, 1929, p. 1.

125. *Ibid.,* August 18, 1930, pp. 1-2.

126. Paul E. Garber, *The National Aeronautical Collections* (Washington: The Smithsonian Institution, 1956), p. 149.

127. *St. Louis Globe-Democrat,* June 20, 1944.

128. Juptner, I, p. 175.

129. Forden, p. 84.

130. Aeronautical Chamber of Commerce of America, *The Aircraft Year Book for 1930,* p. 83.

131. Juptner, II, p. 172.

132. *Ibid.,* p. 169.

133. Aeronautical Chamber of Commerce of America, *The Aircraft Year Book for 1930,* p. 83.

134. "History of the Saint Louis Airplane Division of Curtiss-Wright Corporation."

135. Juptner, II, p. 172.

136. *St. Louis Globe-Democrat,* June 27, 1929.

137. Letter to the author from George A. Page Jr., January 31, 1965. Mr. Page was an engineer with Curtiss and Curtiss-Wright from 1917 to 1951 (rising to the position of chief design engineer for the entire Airplane Division). He bases his information on a commemorative medallion issued at the time of the merger.

138. Welman A. Shrader, *Fifty Years of Flight: A Chronicle of the Aviation Industry in America, 1903-1953* (Cleveland: Eaton Manufacturing Company, 1953), p. 48.

139. Henry Ladd Smith, p. 206.

140. *St. Louis Post-Dispatch,* October 12, 1929.

141. Henry Ladd Smith, pp. 206-209.

142. Henry Ladd Smith, p. 209. According to Shrader, p. 65, Frank Robertson died on March 25, 1938.

143. *Ibid.,* p. 210.

144. John J. Foy, "Curtiss-St. Louis: The Milestone Builder," *Curtiss Fly Leaf,* Vol. XXV, No. 1 (January-February 1942), p. 5.

145. Juptner, II, pp. 282-284.

146. *St. Louis Globe-Democrat,* May 4, 1930.

147. Bowers, "The Sixty Best Commercial Airplanes, 1927-1936," p. 24.

148. Foy, p. 5.

149. "History of the Saint Louis Airplane Division of Curtiss-Wright Corporation."

150. Aeronautical Chamber of Commerce of America, *The Aircraft Year Book for 1932.* (New York: D. Van Nostrand, 1932), p. 311.

151. Foy, p. 5.

152. "History of the Saint Louis Airplane Division of Curtiss-Wright Corporation."

153. *The Robertson Air National Guard Base,* Saint Louis, p. 4.

154. "History of the Saint Louis Airplane Division of Curtiss-Wright Corporation."

155. Bowers, "The Sixty Best Commercial Airplanes, 1927-1936," p. 25.

156. Quoted in Foy, pp. 6-8.

157. "History of the Saint Louis Airplane Division of Curtiss-Wright Corporation." George A. Page Jr., in his letter to the author of January 31, 1965, believes that the number was 48.

158. "Curtiss Condors Never Grow Too Old To Fly," *Curtiss Fly Leaf,* Vol. XXVIII, No. 3 (May-June 1945), p. 12.

159. "History of the Saint Louis Airplane Division of Curtiss Wright Corporation."

160. Foy, p. 6.

161. Letter to the author from George A. Page Jr., January 31, 1965.

162. Aeronautical Chamber of Commerce of America, *The Aircraft Year Book for 1933* (New York: D. Van Nostrand, 1933), p. 251. According to George A. Page Jr., in his letter to the author of January 31, 1965, these were all leftovers from the Beech-Travel Air line which Curtiss-Wright acquired at its 1929 merger.

163. Aeronautical Chamber of Commerce of America, *The Aircraft Year Book for 1933,* pp. 251-252.

164. Foy, p. 8.

165. *Idem.*

166. Howard Mingos (editor), *The Aircraft Year Book for 1938* (New York: Aeronautical Chamber of Commerce of America, 1938), p. 278.

167. William Green, *War Planes of the Second World War: Fighters* (New York: Hanover House, 1961), pp. 76-77.

168. "History of the Saint Louis Airplane Division of Curtiss-Wright Corporation."

169. Howard Mingos (editor), *The Aircraft Year Book for 1936* (New York: Aeronautical Chamber of Commerce of America, 1936), p. 262.

170. Aeronautical Chamber of Commerce of America, *The Aircraft Year Book for 1935* (New York: D. Van Nostrand, 1935), p. 250. According to "St. Louis-Built Curtiss Planes and Year in Which First of Model Was Completed," *The Curtiss Wright-er,* Vol. 5, No. 29 (July 20, 1945), p. 2, the "Courtney Amphibian" came out in 1936.

171. Foy, p. 11.

172. Letter to the author from George A. Page Jr., January 31, 1965.

173. "History of the Saint Louis Airplane Division of Curtiss-Wright Corporation."

174. John Foster Jr., "Design Analysis of the Curtiss Commando," *Aviation,* August 1943, p. 131.

175. F.G. Swanborough and Peter M. Bowers, *United States Military Aircraft Since 1909* (London: Putnam, 1963), p. 193.

176. Ibid., p. 195.

177. Foy, p. 10.

178. Foy, pp. 9-10.

179. Swanborough and Bowers, p. 193.

180. "History of the Saint Louis Airplane Division of Curtiss-Wright Corporation."

181. "The Saga of the 'St. Louis,'" *The Curtiss Wright-er,* Vol. 3, No. 53 (December 17, 1943), p. 3.

182. "History of the Saint Louis Airplane Division of Curtiss-Wright Corporation."

183. Letter to the author from George A. Page Jr., January 31, 1965.

184. Swanborough and Bowers, p. 193.

185. "Last St. Louis-Built Curtiss Commando," *The Curtiss Wright-er,* Vol. 5, No. 30 (July 27, 1945), p. 1. According to George A. Page Jr., Curtiss-Wright built a total of 3,181 "Commandos" of all types: 2,684 at Buffalo, 438 at Louisville, 57 at St. Louis, and 2 at Higgins-New Orleans. According

to both Swanborough and Bowers, pp. 193-194, and James C. Fahey, *U.S. Army Aircraft, 1908-1946* (Falls Church, Virginia: Ships and Aircraft, 1964) p. 25, only 29 "Commandos" were built at St. Louis.

186. Swanborough and Bowers, p. 194.
187. *St. Louis Globe-Democrat,* February 11, 1945, p. 6E.
188. See Chapter XIV, pp. 297-299.
189. Howard Mingos (editor), *The Aircraft Year Book for 1945* (New York: Lanciar Publishers, Inc., 1945), p. 290.
190. *St. Louis Globe-Democrat,* February 11, 1945, p. 6E.
191. Fahey, p. 37.
192. Mingos, *The Aircraft Year Book for 1945,* p. 290.
193. *St. Louis Globe-Democrat,* August 2, 1943, p. 1.
194. "U.S. At War," *Time,* Vol. XLII, No. 6 (August 9, 1943), p. 20.
195. *St. Louis Globe-Democrat,* August 2, 1943, p. 1.
196. *Idem.*
197. *Ibid.,* August 5, 1943, p. 1.
198. *Ibid.,* August 4, 1943, p. 1.
199. See Chapter XIV, p. 300.
200. "History of the Saint Louis Airplane Division of Curtiss-Wright Corporation."
201. "Quick Facts on the Curtiss Plant in Strategic St. Louis," *Curtiss Fly Leaf,* Vol. XXV, No. 1 (January-February 1942), p. 29.
202. Foy, pp. 12-13.
203. "Quick Facts on the Curtiss Plant in Strategic St. Louis," p. 24.
204. "The Curtiss Jeep (AT-9)," *The Curtiss Wright-er,* Vol. 3, No. 53 (December 17, 1943), p. 5.
205. Shrader, p. 78.
206. Shrader, p. 80. According to George A. Page Jr., in his letter to the author of January 31, 1965, the A-25 was used primarily as a glider "tug."
207. *St. Louis Globe-Democrat,* February 11, 1945, p. 6E.
208. *Ibid.,* February 4, 1945, p. 6E.
209. *Ibid.,* February 11, 1945, p. 6E.
210. Letter to the author from George A. Page Jr., January 31, 1965.
211. "History of the Saint Louis Airplane Division of Curtiss-Wright Corporation."
212. Letter to the author from George A. Page Jr., January 31, 1965.
213. Fahey, p. 27.
214. Letter to the author from George A. Page Jr., January 31, 1965.
215. "The Ascender," *Curtiss Fly Leaf,* Vol. XXVIII, No. 1 (January-February 1945), p. 14.
216. Green, pp. 63-65.
217. Letter to the author from George A. Page Jr., January 31, 1965.
218. *First in Flight* (New York: Curtiss-Wright Corporation, c. 1949), p. 26. According to Howard Mingos (editor), *The Aircraft Year Book for 1946* (New York: Lanciar Publishers, Inc., 1946), p. 321, the Curtiss-Wright Corporation built 22,977 planes during the war.
219. Mingos, *The Aircraft Year Book for 1946,* p. 321.
220. Irving Brinton Holley Jr., *United States Army in World War II, Special Studies — Buying Aircraft: Materiel Procurement fot he Army Air Forces* (Washington: Office of the Chief of Military History, Department of the

Army, 1964), p. 577. Holley cites 29 "Commandos," but George A. Page Jr. holds that 57 were built at St. Louis.

221. Stated to the author by Lloyd F. Engelhardt, an engineer with the company at that time.

CHAPTER XVI

1. "McDonnell Banshee," *Aero Digest,* Vol. 65, No. 3 (September 1952), p. 23.
2. Richard J. Whalen, "Banshee, Demon, Voodoo, Phantom — and Bingo! *Fortune,* Vol. LXX, No. 5 (November 1964), p. 258.
3. "McDonnell Banshee," p. 23.
4. See Chapter XI, p. 218.
5. "McDonnell Banshee," p. 23.
6. *Ibid.,* pp. 23-24.
7. "Modest Wizard," *Newsweek,* January 26, 1959, p. 79.
8. Douglas Rolfe, "Air Progress: The McDonnell Story," *Air Trails,* Vol. XXXIV, No. 6 (September 1950), p. 28.
9. Alexander Klemin, "Notes on the Guggenheim Safety Competition," *Aviation,* Vol. XXIV, No. 5 (January 30, 1928), p. 246.
10. "McDonnell Banshee," p. 25.
11. "Personalities," *Forbes,* March 1, 1962, p. 17.
12. "McDonnell Banshee," pp. 25-26.
13. *Ibid.,* p. 27.
14. Dickson Terry, "McDonnell Aims for the Moon," *St. Louis Post-Dispatch,* June 24, 1962, p. 1I.
15. *St. Louis Globe-Democrat,* January 26, 1930, p. 5S.
16. "McDonnell Banshee," p. 27.
17. Whalen, p. 258.
18. Quoted in *St. Louis Post-Dispatch,* March 1, 1949.
19. "Mercury's Father," *Time,* March 9, 1962, p. 86.
20. Whalen, p. 258. According to the *St. Louis Post-Dispatch,* March 1, 1949, Rockefeller invested $10,000.
21. "McDonnell Celebrates Its 25th Birthday," *McDonnell Airscoop,* Vol. XXIII, No. 6 (July 1964), p. 1.
22. "Personalities," p. 17.
23. *McDonnell Aircraft Corporation: Achievements, 1939-1956* (St. Louis: McDonnell Aircraft Corporation, 1956), p. 4.
24. "McDonnell Celebrates Its 25th Birthday," p. 1.
25. Whalen, p. 258.
26. "McDonnell Banshee," p. 27.
27. *St. Louis Post-Dispatch,* March 1, 1949.
28. *McDonnell: The First 25 Years, 1939-1964* (St. Louis: McDonnell Aircraft Corporation, 1964), p. 1.
29. Whalen, p. 258.
30. "McDonnell Celebrates Its 25th Birthday," p. 1.
31. *McDonnell Aircraft Corporation: Achievements, 1939-1956,* p. 5.
32. F.G. Swanborough and Peter M. Bowers, *United States Military Aircraft Since 1909* (London: Putnam, 1963), p. 256. James C. Fahey, *U.S. Army*

Aircraft, 1908-1946 (Falls Church, Virginia: Ships and Aircraft, 1964), p. 22, corroborates this figure, while "McDonnell Banshee," p. 30, erroneously reports that the Memphis factory delivered 192 AT-21 "Gunners."

33. "McDonnell Banshee," p. 30.
34. *McDonnell Aircraft Corporation: Achievements, 1939-1956,* p. 6.
35. *St. Louis Globe-Democrat,* February 4, 1945, p. 6E.
36. Howard Mingos (editor), *The Aircraft Year Book for 1946* (New York: Lanciar Publishers, Inc., 1946), pp. 342-343.
37. *McDonnell Aircraft Corporation: Achievements, 1939-1956,* p. 6.
38. William Green, *War Planes of the Second World War: Fighters* (Garden City: Hanover House, 1961), p. 129.
39. *The Future is at McDonnell* (St. Louis: McDonnell Aircraft Corporation, 1961), p. 4.
40. Green, pp. 130-131.
41. Whalen, p. 258.
42. Green, p. 133.
43. "McDonnell Banshee," p. 31.
44. Green, p. 132.
45. *Ibid.,* p. 133.
46. Leslie E. Neville and Nathaniel F. Silsbee, *Jet Propulsion Progress* (New York: McGraw-Hill, 1948), pp. 149-150. The authors incorrectly cite January 1, 1945, as the date of the "Phantom's" first flight.
47. "McDonnell Banshee," pp. 31-32.
48. *McDonnell: The First 25 Years, 1939-1964,* p. 2. The Army Air Force's Lockheed P-80 "Shooting Star" was the first operational American jet to attain that speed: it accomplished the feat in January 1944, one year before the "Phantom." Green, p. 127.
49. *St. Louis Post-Dispatch,* July 22, 1946.
50. Vice Admiral Thomas S. Combs and Rear Admiral James S. Russell, *United States Naval Aviation, 1910-1960* (Washington: Department of the Navy, 1960), p. 135.
51. "McDonnell Banshee," p. 32.
52. "McDonnell Celebrates Its 25th Birthday," p. 2. A total of 62 "Phantoms" were delivered to the Navy — 60 FH-1s and two of the XFD-1 prototypes. "25th Anniversary Plant Tour Fact Sheets," p. 3. The third prototype was destroyed in a crash which killed chief test pilot Woodward Burke in northern St. Louis County on November 1, 1945. *St. Louis Post-Dispatch,* July 22, 1946.
53. *St. Louis Post-Dispatch,* July 22, 1946.
54. Mingos, *The Aircraft Year Book for 1946,* p. 344.
55. Combs and Russell, p. 107.
56. *Ibid.,* p. 130.
57. Mingos, *The Aircraft Year Book for 1946,* p. 346.
58. *McDonnell Aircraft Corporation: Achievements, 1939-1956,* p. 5.
59. *St. Louis Globe-Democrat,* October 27, 1946.
60. *McDonnell 1946 Annual Report,* 30 June 1946 (St. Louis: McDonnell Aircraft Corporation, 1946), pp. 2-3.
61. *St. Louis Post-Dispatch,* March 1, 1949.
62. "McDonnell — A Fabulous Saga of Men and Jets," *St. Louis Commerce,* June 1956, p. 70.

63. "McDonnell Banshee," pp. 26-27.
64. Whalen, p. 260.
65. "McDonnell Banshee," p. 34.
66. *McDonnell Aircraft Corporation: Achievements, 1939-1956,* p. 7.
67. Combs and Russell, p. 137.
68. *McDonnell Aircraft Corporation: Achievements, 1939-1956,* p. 8.
69. *You and McDonnell: A Handbook for Employees* (St. Louis: McDonnell Aircraft Corporation, 1963), p. 5.
70. "McDonnell — A Fabulous Saga of Men and Jets," p. 72.
71. *McDonnell: The First 25 Years, 1939-1964,* p. 4.
72. *The Future is at McDonnell,* p. 5.
73. "McDonnell Celebrates Its 25th Birthday," p. 3.
74. Whalen, p. 260.
75. "McDonnell Banshee," p. 34.
76. *McDonnell Aircraft Corporation: Achievements, 1939-1956,* p. 6.
77. "McDonnell Banshee," pp. 26-27.
78. *You and McDonnell: A Handbook for Employees,* p. 4.
79. "McDonnell Banshee," p. 27.
80. Welman A. Shrader, *Fifty Years of Flight: A Chronicle of the Aviation Industry in America, 1903-1953* (Cleveland: Eaton Manufacturing Company, 1953), p. 117.
81. Swanborough and Bowers, p. 573.
82. *McDonnell Aircraft Corporation: Achievements, 1939-1956,* p. 7.
83. "McDonnell — A Fabulous Saga of Men and Jets," p. 72.
84. "McDonnell Banshee," pp. 26-27.
85. Swanborough and Bowers, p. 575.
86. *McDonnell Aircraft Corporation: Achievements, 1939-1956,* p. 6.
87. "McDonnell Banshee," pp. 26-27.
88. Swanborough and Bowers, p. 323.
89. Whalen, p. 260.
90. Combs and Russell, p. 152.
91. *St. Louis Globe-Democrat,* September 25, 1955, p. 11A.
92. "Aviation: Demon on the Ground," *Time,* Vol. LXVI, No. 19 (November 7, 1955), p. 101.
93. *Idem.*
94. *St. Louis Globe-Democrat,* September 15, 1955, pp. 1, 11A. Not surprisingly, the various McDonnell publications previously cited make no mention at all of any problems ever encountered with the "Demon."
95. *Ibid.,* September 28, 1955, p. 8A.
96. *Ibid.,* September 27, 1955, p. 1.
97. *Ibid.,* September 30, 1955, p. 1.
98. Quoted in "Aviation: Demon on the Ground," p. 101.
99. "Corporations: The Problems of Westinghouse," *Time,* Vol. LXVI, No. 17 (October 24, 1955), p. 99.
100. *St. Louis Globe-Democrat,* September 25, 1955, p. 11A.
101. Whalen, p. 260.
102. *You and McDonnell: A Handbook for Employees,* p. 5.
103. *McDonnell: The First 25 Years, 1939-1964,* p. 9.
104. "McDonnell's 3000th Plane, an F-4C Phantom, Delivered November 14," *McDonnell Airscoop,* Vol. XXIII, No. 11 (December 1964), p. 2.
105. "McDonnell Celebrates Its 25th Birthday," p. 3.

106. "Last Two Demons Retired From Fleet With Ceremonies," *McDonnell Airscoop,* Vol. XXIII, No. 11 (December 1964), p. 8.

107. *McDonnell Aircraft Corporation: Achievements, 1939-1956,* p. 9.

108. *McDonnell: The First 25 Years, 1939-1964,* p. 9.

109. *McDonnell Aircraft Corporation: Achievements, 1939-1956,* pp. 10-11.

110. *Ibid.,* p. 12.

111. *You and McDonnell: A Handbook for Employees,* p. 4.

112. Shrader, p. 159.

113. *McDonnell: The First 25 Years, 1939-1964,* p. 9.

114. Shrader, p. 165.

115. *McDonnell Aircraft Corporation: Achievements, 1939-1956,* p. 10.

116. *Ibid.,* p. 11.

117. *McDonnell: The First 25 Years, 1939-1964,* p. 6.

118. "Voodoo World Records," *McDonnell Airscoop,* Vol. XXIII, No. 6 (July 1964), p. 7.

119. *The Future is at McDonnell,* p. 6.

120. *McDonnell Aircraft Corporation Achievements, 1939-1956,* p. 12.

121. "McDonnell Celebrates Its 25th Birthday," p. 3.

122. *You and McDonnell: A Handbook for Employees,* p. 6.

123. *The Future is at McDonnell,* p. 6.

124. Ted Schafers, "McDonnell Aircraft Marks 25th Year," *St. Louis Globe-Democrat,* July 4-5, 1964, p. 1F.

125. *McDonnell: The First 25 Years, 1939-1964,* p. 10.

126. Combs and Russell, p. 175.

127. Whalen, p. 262.

128. *McDonnell 1963 Annual Report, 30 June 1963* (St. Louis: McDonnell Aircraft Corporation, 1963), p. 7

129. *McDonnell 1962 Annual Report, 30 June 1962* (St. Louis: McDonnell Aircraft Corporation, 1962), p. 7.

130. "Phantom World Records," *McDonnell Airscoop,* Vol. XXIII, No. 6 (July 1964), p. 7.

131. Whalen, p. 262.

132. "McDonnell Celebrates Its 25th Birthday," p. 3.

133. *You and McDonnell: A Handbook for Employees,* p. 6.

134. *McDonnell: The First 25 Years, 1939-1964,* p. 10.

135. *McDonnell 1964 Annual Report, 30 June 1964* (St. Louis: McDonnell Aircraft Corporation, 1964), p. 2.

136. Clarence E. Olson, "Phantoms on the Assembly Line," *St. Louis Post-Dispatch,* March 22, 1964, Sunday Magazine, p. 16.

137. "McDonnell's 3000th Plane, an F-4C Phantom, Delivered November 14," p. 2.

138. Whalen, pp. 137-139.

139. *St. Louis Post-Dispatch,* February 10, 1965, pp. 1, 10.

140 Whalen, p. 139.

141. *McDonnell 1963 Annual Report, 30 June 1963,* p. 10.

142. *St. Louis Globe-Democrat,* September 26-27, 1964, p. 4A.

143. *Facilities . . . McDonnell Aircraft* (St. Louis: McDonnell Aircraft Corporation, c. 1959), p. 8.

144. Whalen, p. 262.

145. *McDonnell 1962 Annual Report, 30 June 1962,* p. 8.

146. Notes taken by the author at a demonstration of the "McDonnell 188E" at the company's twenty-fifth anniversary open house on July 4, 1964.
147. *St. Louis Globe-Democrat,* July 6, 1964, p. 6A.
148. *Facilities . . . McDonnell Aircraft,* p. 13.
149. *McDonnell: The First 25 Years, 1939-1964,* p. 14.
150. *McDonnell 1962 Annual Report, 30 June 1962,* p. 9.
151. *The Future is at McDonnell,* p. 7.
152. *McDonnell 1963 Annual Report, 30 June 1963,* p. 10.
153. *McDonnell: The First 25 Years, 1939-1964,* p. 17.
154. The actual number is classified.
155. *McDonnell 1962 Annual Report, 30 June 1962,* p. 9.
156. *McDonnell: The First 25 Years, 1939-1964,* p. 17.
157. *The Future is at McDonnell,* p. 7.
158. United States Senate, Committee on Aeronautical and Space Sciences, *Report on Project Mercury: Man-in-Space Program of the National Aeronautics and Space Administration,* Report No. 1014, 80 Congress, 1 Session, December 1, 1959, p. 4. Cited hereafter as *Senate Mercury Report.*
159. *Ibid.,* p. 1.
160. James W. Grimwood, *Project Mercury: A Chronology* (Washington: National Aeronautics and Space Administration, 1963), p. 31.
161. *Senate Mercury Report,* p. 5.
162. Grimwood, p. 34.
163. Whalen, p. 262.
164. "McDonnell Celebrates Its 25th Birthday," p. 4.
165. "McDonnell Mercury Spacecraft," detailed drawing distributed at the McDonnell twenty-fifth anniversary open house on July 4, 1964.
166. Grimwood, p. 97.
167. *Ibid.,* p. 207.
168. *McDonnell 1963 Annual Report, 30 June 1963,* p. 2.
169. Grimwood, p. 145.
170. *Ibid.,* p. 207.
171. *McDonnell 1963 Annual Report, 30 June 1963,* p. 2.
172. "Mercury's Father," p. 86.
173. *McDonnell 1963 Annual Report, 30 June 1963,* p. 3.
174. Whalen, p. 262.
174. *St. Louis Globe-Democrat,* January 2-3, 1965, p. 10E.
176. *McDonnell 1962 Annual Report, 30 June 1962,* p. 2.
177. "McDonnell Celebrates Its 25th Birthday," p. 4.
178. *Ibid.,* p. 5.
179. Whalen, p. 262.
180. George Alexander, "First Successful Gemini Mission Points to Manned Flight in 1964," *Aviation Week & Space Technology,* Vol. 80, No. 15 (April 13, 1964), p. 29.
181. *St. Louis Globe-Democrat,* December 10, 1964, p. 1B.
182. George Alexander, "GT-2 Success Brings Go-Ahead Order for First Manned Gemini," *Aviation Week & Space Technology,* Vol. 82, No. 4 (January 25, 1965), pp. 30-31.
183. *St. Louis Post-Dispatch,* January 19, 1965, p. 1.
184. *St. Louis Globe-Democrat,* January 20, 1965, p. 1.
185. *McDonnell: The First 25 Years, 1939-1964,* p. 17.

186. "ASSET No. 2 Being Readied for Launch," *McDonnell Airscoop*, Vol. XXIII, No. 2 (March 1964), pp. 1, 8.
187. *McDonnell 1962 Annual Report, 30 June 1962*, p. 7.
188. *St. Louis Globe-Democrat*, January 4, 1965, p. 3A.
189. "ASSET No. 3," *McDonnell Airscoop*, Vol. XXIII, No. 7 (August 1964), p. 4.
190. *McDonnell 1963 Annual Report, 30 June 1963*, p. 6.
191. "McDonnell Celebrates Its 25th Birthday," p. 5.
192. "ASSET No. 5 Flight Resounding Success," *McDonnell Airscoop*, Vol. XXIII, No. 11, (December 1964), pp. 1-2.
193. *St. Louis Post-Dispatch*, February 25, 1965, p. 17D.
194. *Ibid*, November 13, 1964, p. 14A.
195. *McDonnell 1963 Annual Report, 30 June, 1963*, p. 10.
196. *McDonnell 1964 Annual Report, 30 June 1964*, p. 20.
197. "McDonnell Celebrates Its 25th Birthday," p. 1.
198. *McDonnell 1964 Annual Report, 30 June 1964*, inside front cover.
199. Schafers, p. 1F.
200. *McDonnell 1964 Annual Report, 30 June 1964*, inside front cover.
201. "Modest Wizard," p. 79.
202. Whalen, p. 258.
203. Quoted in "Personalities," p. 17.
204. Schafers, p. 1F.
205. "Mr. Mac Receives Guggenheim Medal," *McDonnell Airscoop*, Vol. XXIII, No. 1 (February 1964), p. 1.
206. *McDonnell 1962 Annual Report, 30 June 1962*, p. 15.
207. *St. Petersburg Times*, August 23, 1980.

Index

* — illustration

Marshall, William D., 76
(Glenn L.) Martin Co., 341-42, 360
Mason, Monck, 50
Matthews, T.K., 208
Maughan, Russell L., 211, 214
Mechel, Paul, 99, 102, 104, 111
Meissner, Edwin B., 12, 251, 281, 282*, 288, 289*
Mendall, Loran W., 315
Meramec Park, 5, 181, 186, 187*, 290, 291
Merchants Exchange of St. Louis Trophy Race, 197, 198, 210
Messner, E., 152, 155
Meyer, Carl F.G., 192, 251
Meyer, George M., 186
Meyer, W.W., 205
Meyers, George Francis, 101
Midcoast Aviation, 388*, 389, 401-05
Mid-Continent Airlines, 23
Middleton, Carl, 265
Mile High Contest, 76-77
Miller, Ada, 117
Miller, Victor, 11, 215, 245*, 312*
Miller, Walter, 212, 213
Million Population Club of St. Louis, 117, 152, 177
Missouri Aeronautical Reserve Corps, 181, 290, 291
Missouri Aeronautical Society, 5-8, 181-83, 185-86, 190, 191, 193, 290-91, 374
Missouri Historical Society, 246, 295
Missouri National Guard, 10, 16-17, 123-24, 139, 172, 221, 224, 246, 263, 268, 275, 303, 303*, 372
Missouri *Republican,* 41, 46, 48, 51, 54 (Called *Daily Republican,* p. 48)
Missouri Tent and Awning Co., 279
Mitchell, Roy L. 315
Mitchell, William ("Billy"), 198-99, 203
Mix, E.W., 95, 98, 102, 104; 111, 132, 135, 372
Moffett, William A., 199, 203
Monocoupe Corporation, 17, 294, 295, 300
Montgolfier, Etienne, 37-40
Montgolfier, Joseph, 37-40
Montgolfier (balloon), 38*, 39, 42, 55
Montgomery, John J., 115

Moore, J.F., 211
Morgan, A.H., 125, 128, 151, 159
Morganford Road Airfield, 24
Morrow, Anne, 248
Morrow, Dwight, 248
Moth Aircraft, 321, 323
Mueller, Henry L., 331
Mulvihill Model Trophy Contest (1923) 197-198, 206
Murphy, Francis, 251, 373
Murphy, Mike, 261, 265, 269
Myers, Bessie E., 54, 69, 70
Myers, Carl E., 53-54, 60, 69, 70, 73, 76, 100, 121, 383

National Advisory Committe for Aeronautics (NACA), 359
National Aero Congress, 191
National Aeronautic Association, 191-93, 201, 225, 231, 250, 251, 261, 263
National Aeronautics and Space Administration (NASA), 360-61, 364
Neely, James T., 187-88
Nelson, Thomas, 222, 224, 226*, 306
New, Harry S., 199, 242, 305, 306
Newcomb, Byron K., 315
Nicholas-Beazly Airplane Co., 294, 305
Niphur, F.E., 74, 76
Noel, E. Percy, 137, 145, 372
Nolker, Robert, 176, 178
Noonan, Fred, 267
Norvell-Shapleigh Co., 124
Nugent, Charles, 117, 119, 120
Nugent, Daniel C., 93-94
Nungesser, Charles, 233-35
O'Brine, Forrest, 315-19, 316*, 319*, 374, 375
Ogilvie, Alexander, 142, 144, 151
O'Neal, J.M., 81
"On to St. Louis Race," (1923), 196, 198
O'Reilly, Joseph M., 125, 127-28, 152-53, 155, 177, 186, 188, 290, 372
Orteig, Raymond, 224
Orteig Prize, 227, 231, 235, 242
Osborne, J.F., 81
Osmont, Francois, 120, 121, 127, 130, 133
Ovington, Earl, 163